# National Party Platforms

This compilation is based on Kirk H. Porter's **National Party Platforms,** first published in 1924.

Revised Edition

# National Party Platforms

## Volume II 1960-1976

### Compiled by Donald Bruce Johnson

UNIVERSITY OF ILLINOIS PRESS  Urbana  Chicago  London

**Library of Congress Cataloging in Publication Data**

Johnson, Donald Bruce, 1921-        comp.
  National party platforms.

  Edition for 1973 by D. B. Johnson and K. H. Porter
published under title: National party platforms, 1840-1972.
  Includes indexes.
  CONTENTS: v. 1. 1840-1956.—v. 2. 1960-1976.
  1. Political parties—United States—History.
I. Porter, Kirk Harold, 1891-        II. Title.
JK2255.J64 1978        329′.0213′0973        78-17373
ISBN 0-252-00692-5 (set)
ISBN 0-252-00687-9 (vol. 1)
ISBN 0-252-00688-7 (vol. 2)

# Contents

**VOLUME II    1960–1976**

# CAMPAIGN OF 1960

In 1960 the Republican delegates met in Chicago and nominated Vice-President Richard M. Nixon for the presidency and United Nations Ambassador (and former Massachusetts senator) Henry Cabot Lodge, Jr., for vice-president. The Democrats met in Los Angeles for the first time and nominated John F. Kennedy, senator from Massachusetts, for the presidency over eight other aspirants. The Senate majority leader, Lyndon B. Johnson of Texas, who was the second choice among the delegates, was chosen as his running mate. The platform written in this Democratic convention was the longest written by the party up to that time.

Among the comparatively permanent minor parties, the Prohibitionists nominated Rutherford L. Dicker of Missouri for president and E. Harold Munn of Michigan for vice-president; the Socialist Labor Party selected Eric Hass of New York and Georgia Cozzini of Wisconsin for its ticket; and the Socialist Workers again nominated Farrell Dobbs and Myra Tanner Weiss, both of New York. The Socialist Party adopted a platform but did not nominate a presidential candidate.

The campaign, which featured nationally televised debates between the two major party candidates, also produced the closest presidential election of the twentieth century. Of the nearly 68,800,000 ballots counted, the Democrats obtained 34,221,344 popular votes—49.72 percent—to 34,106,671—49.55 percent—for the Republicans. The Socialist Labor Party polled 47,522 votes, the Socialist Workers Party, 40,166 votes, and the Prohibition Party, 44,087 votes. An unpledged slate of electors in Mississippi received 116,248 votes. Local parties and scattered ballots throughout the nation accounted for an additional 382,313 votes, of which more than 200,000 were cast for Arkansas Governor Orval Faubus in several southern states.

In the electoral vote, John Kennedy received 303 votes to 219 votes for Richard Nixon and 15 (6 from Alabama, 8 from Mississippi, and 1 from Oklahoma) for Senator Harry F. Byrd of Virginia.

---

## Democratic Platform 1960

In 1796, in America's first contested national election, our Party, under the leadership of Thomas Jefferson, campaigned on the principles of "The Rights of Man."

Ever since, these four words have underscored our identity with the plain people of America and the world.

In periods of national crisis, we Democrats have returned to these words for renewed strength. We return to them today.

In 1960, "The Rights of Man" are still the issue.

It is our continuing responsibility to provide an effective instrument of political action for every American who seeks to strengthen these rights — everywhere here in America, and everywhere in our 20th Century world.

The common danger of mankind is war and the threat of war. Today, three billion human beings live in fear that some rash act or blunder may plunge us all into a nuclear holocaust which will leave only ruined cities, blasted homes, and a poisoned earth and sky.

Our objective, however, is not the right to co-exist in armed camps on the same planet with totalitarian ideologies; it is the creation of an enduring peace in which the universal values of human dignity, truth, and justice under law are finally secured for all men everywhere on earth.

If America is to work effectively for such a peace, we must first restore our national strength—military, political, economic, and moral.

NATIONAL DEFENSE

The new Democratic Administration will recast our military capacity in order to provide forces and weapons of a diversity, balance, and mobility sufficient in quantity and quality to deter both limited and general aggressions.

When the Democratic Administration left office in 1953, the United States was the pre-eminent power in the world. Most free nations had confidence in our will and our ability to carry out our commitments to the common defense.

Even those who wished us ill respected our power and influence.

The Republican Administration has lost that position of pre-eminence. Over the past 7½ years, our military power has steadily declined relative to that of the Russians and the Chinese and their satellites.

This is not a partisan election-year charge. It has been persistently made by high officials of the Republican Administration itself. Before Congressional committees they have testified that the Communists will have a dangerous lead in intercontinental missiles through 1963 — and that the Republican Administration has no plans to catch up.

They have admitted that the Soviet Union leads in the space race — and that they have no plans to catch up.

They have also admitted that our conventional military forces, on which we depend for defense in any non-nuclear war, have been dangerously slashed for reasons of "economy" — and that they have no plans to reverse this trend.

As a result, our military position today is measured in terms of gaps — missile gap, space gap, limited-war gap.

To recover from the errors of the past 7½ years will not be easy.

This is the strength that must be erected:

1. Deterrent military power such that the Soviet and Chinese leaders will have no doubt that an attack on the United States would surely be followed by their own destruction.

2. Balanced conventional military forces which will permit a response graded to the intensity of any threats of aggressive force.

3. Continuous modernization of these forces through intensified research and development, including essential programs now slowed down, terminated, suspended, or neglected for lack of budgetary support.

A first order of business of a Democratic Administration will be a complete re-examination of the organization of our armed forces.

A military organization structure, conceived before the revolution in weapons technology, cannot be suitable for the strategic deterrent, continental defense, limited war, and military alliance requirements of the 1960s.

We believe that our armed forces should be organized more nearly on the basis of function, not only to produce greater military strength, but also to eliminate duplication and save substantial sums.

We pledge our will, energies, and resources to oppose Communist aggression.

Since World War II, it has been clear that our own security must be pursued in concert with that of many other nations.

The Democratic Administrations which, in World War II, led in forging a mighty and victorious alliance, took the initiative after the war in creating the North Atlantic Treaty Organization, the greatest peacetime alliance in history.

This alliance has made it possible to keep Western Europe and the Atlantic Community secure against Communist pressures.

Our present system of alliances was begun in a time of an earlier weapons technology when our ability to retaliate against Communist attack required bases all around the periphery of the Soviet Union. Today, because of our continuing weakness in mobile weapons systems and intercontinental missiles, our defenses still depend in part on bases beyond our borders for planes and shorter-range missiles.

If an alliance is to be maintained in vigor, its unity must be reflected in shared purposes. Some of our allies have contributed neither devotion to the cause of freedom nor any real military strength.

The new Democratic Administration will review our system of pacts and alliances. We shall continue to adhere to our treaty obligations, including the commitment of the UN Charter to resist aggression. But we shall also seek to shift the emphasis of our cooperation from military aid to economic development, wherever this is possible.

### Civil Defense

We commend the work of the civil defense groups throughout the nation. A strong and effective civil defense is an essential element in our nation's defense.

The new Democratic Administration will undertake a full review and analysis of the programs that should be adopted if the protection possible is to be provided to the civilian population of our nation.

## ARMS CONTROL

A fragile power balance sustained by mutual nuclear terror does not, however, constitute peace. We must regain the initiative on the entire international front with effective new policies to create the conditions for peace.

There are no simple solutions to the infinitely complex challenges which face us. Mankind's eternal dream, a world of peace, can only be built slowly and patiently.

A primary task is to develop responsible proposals that will help break the deadlock on arms control.

Such proposals should include means for ending nuclear tests under workable safeguards, cutting back nuclear weapons, reducing conventional forces, preserving outer space for peaceful purposes, preventing surprise attack, and limiting the risk of accidental war.

This requires a national peace agency for disarmament planning and research to muster the scientific ingenuity, coordination, continuity, and seriousness of purpose which are now lacking in our arms control efforts.

The national peace agency would develop the technical and scientific data necessary for serious disarmament negotiations, would conduct research in cooperation with the Defense Department and Atomic Energy Commission on methods of inspection and monitoring arms control agreements, particularly agreements to control nuclear testing, and would provide continuous technical advice to our disarmament negotiators.

As with armaments, so with disarmament, the Republican Administration has provided us with much talk but little constructive action. Representatives of the United States have gone to conferences without plans or preparation. The Administration has played opportunistic politics, both at home and abroad.

Even during the recent important negotiations at Geneva and Paris, only a handful of people were devoting full time to work on the highly complex problem of disarmament.

More than $100 billion of the world's production now goes each year into armaments. To the extent that we can secure the adoption of effective arms control agreements, vast resources will be freed for peaceful use.

The new Democratic Administration will plan for an orderly shift of our expenditures. Long-delayed reductions in excise, corporation, and individual income taxes will then be possible. We can also step up the pace in meeting our backlog of public needs and in pursuing the promise of atomic and space science in a peaceful age.

As world-wide disarmament proceeds, it will free vast resources for a new international attack on the problem of world poverty.

## THE INSTRUMENTS OF FOREIGN POLICY

American foreign policy in all its aspects must be attuned to our world of change.

We will recruit officials whose experience, humanity, and dedication fit them for the task of effectively representing America abroad.

We will provide a more sensitive and creative direction to our overseas information program. And we will overhaul our administrative machinery so that America may avoid diplomatic embarrassments and at long last speak with a single confident voice in world affairs.

### The "Image" of America

First, those men and women selected to represent us abroad must be chosen for their sensitive understanding of the peoples with whom they will live. We can no longer afford representatives who are ignorant of the language and culture and politics of the nations in which they represent us.

Our information programs must be more than news broadcasts and boastful recitals of *our* accomplishments and *our* material riches. We must find ways to show the people of the world that we share the same goals — dignity, health, freedom, schools for children, a place in the sun — and that we will work together to achieve them.

Our program of visits between Americans and people of other nations will be expanded, with special emphasis upon students and younger leaders. We will encourage study of foreign languages. We favor continued support and extension of such programs as the East-West cultural center established at the University of Hawaii. We shall study a similar center for Latin America, with due consideration of the existing facilities now available in the Canal Zone.

## National Policy Machinery

In the present Administration, the National Security Council has been used not to focus issues for decision by the responsible leaders of Government, but to paper over problems of policy with "agreed solutions" which avoid decisions.

The mishandling of the U-2 espionage flights — the sorry spectacle of official denial, retraction, and contradiction — and the admitted misjudging of Japanese public opinion are only two recent examples of the breakdown of the Administration's machinery for assembling facts, making decisions, and coordinating action.

The Democratic Party welcomes the study now being made by the Senate Subcommittee on National Policy Machinery. The new Democratic Administration will revamp and simplify this cumbersome machinery.

## WORLD TRADE

World trade is more than ever essential to world peace. In the tradition of Cordell Hull, we shall expand world trade in every responsible way.

Since all Americans share the benefits of this policy, its costs should not be the burden of a few. We shall support practical measures to ease the necessary adjustments of industries and communities which may be unavoidably hurt by increases in imports.

World trade raises living standards, widens markets, reduces costs, increases profits, and builds political stability and international economic cooperation.

However, the increase in foreign imports involves costly adjustment and damage to some domestic industries and communities. The burden has been heavier recently because of the Republican failure to maintain an adequate rate of economic growth, and the refusal to use public programs to ease necessary adjustments.

The Democratic Administration will help industries affected by foreign trade with measures favorable to economic growth, orderly transition, fair competition, and the long-run economic strength of all parts of our nation.

Industries and communities affected by foreign trade need and deserve appropriate help through trade adjustment measures such as direct loans, tax incentives, defense contracts priority, and retraining assistance.

Our Government should press for reduction of foreign barriers to the sale of the products of American industry and agriculture. These are particularly severe in the case of fruit products. The present balance-of-payments situation provides a favorable opportunity for such action.

The new Democratic Administration will seek international agreements to assure fair competition and fair labor standards to protect our own workers and to improve the lot of workers elsewhere.

Our domestic economic policies and our essential foreign policies must be harmonious.

To sell, we must buy. We therefore must resist the temptation to accept remedies that deny American producers and consumers access to world markets and destroy the prosperity of our friends in the non-Communist world.

## IMMIGRATION

We shall adjust our immigration, nationality and refugee policies to eliminate discrimination and to enable members of scattered families abroad to be united with relatives already in our midst.

The national-origins quota system of limiting immigration contradicts the founding principles of this nation. It is inconsistent with our belief in the rights of man. This system was instituted after World War I as a policy of deliberate discrimination by a Republican Administration and Congress.

The revision of immigration and nationality laws we seek will implement our belief that enlightened immigration, naturalization and refugee policies and humane administration of them are important aspects of our foreign policy.

These laws will bring greater skills to our land, reunite families, permit the United States to meet its fair share of world programs of rescue and rehabilitation, and take advantage of immigration as an important factor in the growth of the American economy.

In this World Refugee Year it is our hope to achieve admission of our fair share of refugees. We will institute policies to alleviate suffering among the homeless wherever we are able to extend our aid.

We must remove the distinctions between native-born and naturalized citizens to assure full protection of our laws to all. There is no place in the United States for "second-class citizenship."

The protections provided by due process, right of appeal, and statutes of limitation, can be extended to non-citizens without hampering the security of our nation.

We commend the Democratic Congress for the initial steps that have recently been taken toward liberalizing changes in immigration law. However, this should not be a piecemeal project and we are confident that a Democratic President in cooperation with Democratic Congresses will again implant a humanitarian and liberal spirit in our nation's immigration and citizenship policies.

To the peoples and governments beyond our shores we offer the following pledges:

### THE UNDERDEVELOPED WORLD

*To the non-Communist nations of Asia, Africa, and Latin America:* We shall create with you working partnerships, based on mutual respect and understanding.

In the Jeffersonian tradition, we recognize and welcome the irresistible momentum of the world revolution of rising expectations for a better life. We shall identify American policy with the values and objectives of this revolution.

To this end the new Democratic Administration will revamp and refocus the objectives, emphasis and allocation of our foreign assistance programs.

The proper purpose of these programs is not to buy gratitude or to recruit mercenaries, but to enable the peoples of these awakening, developing nations to make their own free choices.

As they achieve a sense of belonging, of dignity, and of justice, freedom will become meaningful for them, and therefore worth defending.

Where military assistance remains essential for the common defense, we shall see that the requirements are fully met. But as rapidly as security considerations permit, we will replace tanks with tractors, bombers with bulldozers, and tacticians with technicians.

We shall place our programs of international cooperation on a long-term basis to permit more effective planning. We shall seek to associate other capital-exporting countries with us in promoting the orderly economic growth of the underdeveloped world.

We recognize India and Pakistan as major tests of the capacity of free men in a difficult environment to master the age-old problems of illiteracy, poverty, and disease. We will support their efforts in every practical way.

We welcome the emerging new nations of Africa to the world community. Here again we shall strive to write a new chapter of fruitful cooperation.

In Latin America we shall restore the Good Neighbor Policy based on far closer economic cooperation and increased respect and understanding.

In the Middle East we will work for guarantees to insure independence for all states. We will encourage direct Arab-Israeli peace negotiations, the resettlement of Arab refugees in lands where there is room and opportunity for them, an end to boycotts and blockades, and unrestricted use of the Suez Canal by all nations.

A billion and a half people in Asia, Africa and Latin America are engaged in an unprecedented attempt to propel themselves into the 20th Century. They are striving to create or reaffirm their national identity.

But they want much more than independence. They want an end to grinding poverty. They want more food, health for themselves and their children, and other benefits that a modern industrial civilization can provide.

Communist strategy has sought to divert these aspirations into narrowly nationalistic channels, or external troublemaking, or authoritarianism. The Republican Administration has played into the hands of this strategy by concerning itself almost exclusively with the military problem of Communist invasion.

The Democratic programs of economic cooperation will be aimed at making it as easy as possible for the political leadership in these countries to turn the energy, talent and resources of their peoples to orderly economic growth.

History and current experience show that an annual per capita growth rate of at least 2% is feasible in these countries. The Democratic Administration's assistance program, in concert with the aid forthcoming from our partners in Western Europe, Japan, and the British Commonwealth, will be geared to facilitating this objective.

The Democratic Administration will recognize that assistance to these countries is not an emergency or short-term matter. Through the Development Loan Fund and otherwise, we shall seek to assure continuity in our aid programs for periods of at least five years, in order to permit more effective allocation on our part and better planning by the governments of the countries receiving aid.

More effective use of aid and a greater confidence in us and our motives will be the result.

We shall establish priorities for foreign aid which will channel it to those countries abroad which, by their own willingness to help themselves, show themselves most capable of using it effectively.

We shall use our own agricultural productivity as an effective tool of foreign aid, and also as a vital form of working capital for economic development. We shall seek new approaches which will provide assistance without disrupting normal world markets for food and fiber.

We shall give attention to the problem of stabilizing world prices of agricultural commodities and basic raw materials on which many underdeveloped countries depend for needed foreign exchange.

We shall explore the feasibility of shipping and storing a substantial part of our food abundance in a system of "food banks" located at distribution centers in the underdeveloped world.

Such a system would be an effective means of alleviating famine and suffering in times of natural disaster, and of cushioning the effect of bad harvests. It would also have a helpful anti-inflationary influence as economic development gets under way.

Although basic development requirements like transport, housing, schools, and river development may be financed by Government, these projects are usually built and sometimes managed by private enterprise. Moreover, outside this public sector a large and increasing role remains for private investment.

The Republican Administration has done little to summon American business to play its part in this, one of the most creative tasks of our generation. The Democratic Administration will take steps to recruit and organize effectively the best business talent in America for foreign economic development.

We urge continued economic assistance to Israel and the Arab peoples to help them raise their living standards. We pledge our best efforts for peace in the Middle East by seeking to prevent an arms race while guarding against the dangers of a military imbalance resulting from Soviet arms shipments.

## THE ATLANTIC COMMUNITY

*To our friends and associates in the Atlantic Community:* We propose a broader partnership that goes beyond our common fears to recognize the depth and sweep of our common political, economic, and cultural interests.

We welcome the recent heartening advances toward European unity. In every appropriate way, we shall encourage their further growth within the broader framework of the Atlantic Community.

After World War II, Democratic statesmen saw that an orderly, peaceful world was impossible with Europe shattered and exhausted.

They fashioned the great programs which bear their names — the Truman Doctrine and the Marshall Plan — by which the economies of Europe were revived. Then in NATO they renewed for the common defense the ties of alliance forged in war.

In these endeavors, the Democratic Administrations invited leading Republicans to full participation as equal partners. But the Republican Administration has rejected this principle of bipartisanship.

We have already seen how the mutual trust and confidence created abroad under Democratic leadership have been eroded by arrogance, clumsiness, and lack of understanding in the Republican Administration.

The new Democratic Administration will restore the former high levels of cooperation within the Atlantic Community envisaged from the beginning by the NATO treaty in political and economic spheres as well as military affairs.

We welcome the progress towards European unity expressed in the Coal and Steel Community, Euratom, the European Economic Community, the European Free Trade Association, and the European Assembly.

We shall conduct our relations with the nations of the Common Market so as to encourage the opportunities for freer and more expanded trade, and to avert the possibilities of discrimination that are inherent in it.

We shall encourage adjustment with the so-called "Outer Seven" nations so as to enlarge further the area of freer trade.

### THE COMMUNIST WORLD

*To the rulers of the Communist World:* We confidently accept your challenge to competition in every field of human effort.

We recognize this contest as one between two radically different approaches to the meaning of life — our open society which places its highest value upon individual dignity, and your closed society in which the rights of men are sacrificed to the state.

We believe your Communist ideology to be sterile, unsound, and doomed to failure. We believe that your children will reject the intellectual prison in which you seek to confine them, and that ultimately they will choose the eternal principles of freedom.

In the meantime, we are prepared to negotiate with you whenever and wherever there is a realistic possibility of progress without sacrifice of principle.

If negotiations through diplomatic channels provide opportunities, we will negotiate.

If debate before the United Nations holds promise, we will debate.

If meetings at high level offer prospects of success, we will be there.

But we will use all the power, resources, and energy at our command to resist the further encroachment of Communism on freedom — whether at Berlin, Formosa, or new points of pressure as yet undisclosed.

We will keep open the lines of communication with our opponents. Despite difficulties in the way of peaceful agreement, every useful avenue will be energetically explored and pursued.

However, we will never surrender positions which are essential to the defense of freedom, nor will we abandon peoples who are now behind the Iron Curtain through any formal approval of the status quo.

Everyone proclaims "firmness" in support of Berlin. The issue is not the desire to be firm, but the capability to be firm. This the Democratic Party will provide as it has done before.

The ultimate solution of the situation in Berlin must be approached in the broader context of settlement of the tensions and divisions of Europe.

The good faith of the United States is pledged likewise to defending Formosa. We will carry out that pledge.

The new Democratic Administration will also reaffirm our historic policy of opposition to the establishment anywhere in the Americas of governments dominated by foreign powers, a policy now being undermined by Soviet threats to the freedom and independence of Cuba. The Government of the United States under a Democratic Administration will not be deterred from fulfilling its obligations and solemn responsibilities under its treaties and agreements with the nations of the Western Hemisphere. Nor will the United States, in conformity with its treaty obligations, permit the establishment of a regime dominated by international, atheistic Communism in the Western Hemisphere.

*To the people who live in the Communist World and its captive nations:* We proclaim an enduring friendship which goes beyond governments and ideologies to our common human interest in a better world.

Through exchanges of persons, cultural contacts, trade in non-strategic areas, and other non-governmental activities, we will endeavor to preserve and improve opportunities for human relationships which no Iron Curtain can permanently sever.

No political platform promise in history was more cruelly cynical than the Republican effort to buy votes in 1952 with false promises of painless liberation for the captive nations.

The blood of heroic freedom fighters in Hungary tragically proved this promise a fraud. We Democrats will never be party to such cruel cultivation of false hopes.

We look forward to the day when the men and women of Albania, Bulgaria, Czechoslovakia, East Germany, Estonia, Hungary, Latvia, Lithuania, Poland, Rumania, and the other captive nations will stand again in freedom and justice. We will hasten, by every honorable and responsible means, the arrival of the day.

We shall never accept any deal or arrangement which acquiesces in the present subjugation of these peoples.

We deeply regret that the policies and actions of the Government of Communist China have interrupted the generations of friendship between the Chinese and American peoples.

We reaffirm our pledge of determined opposition to the present admission of Communist China to the United Nations.

Although normal diplomatic relations between our Governments are impossible under present conditions, we shall welcome any evidence that the Chinese Communist Government is genuinely prepared to create a new relationship based on respect for international obligations, including the release of American prisoners.

We will continue to make every effort to effect the release of American citizens and servicemen now unjustly imprisoned in Communist China and elsewhere in the Communist empire.

THE UNITED NATIONS

*To all our fellow members of the United Nations:* We shall strengthen our commitments in this, our great continuing institution for conciliation and the growth of a world community.

Through the machinery of the United Nations, we shall work for disarmament, the establishment of an international police force, the strengthening of the World Court, and the establishment of world law.

We shall propose the bolder and more effective use of the specialized agencies to promote the world's economic and social development.

Great Democratic Presidents have taken the lead in the effort to unite the nations of the world in an international organization to assure world peace with justice under law.

The League of Nations, conceived by Woodrow Wilson, was doomed by Republican defeat of United States participation.

The United Nations, sponsored by Franklin Roosevelt, has become the one place where representatives of the rival systems and interests which divide the world can and do maintain continuous contact.

The United States' adherence to the World Court contains a so-called "self-judging reservation" which, in effect, permits us to prevent a Court decision in any particular case in which we are involved. The Democratic Party proposes its repeal.

To all these endeavors so essential to world peace, we, the members of the Democratic Party, will bring a new urgency, persistence, and determination, born of the conviction that in our thermonuclear century all of the other Rights of Man hinge on our ability to assure man's right to peace.

The pursuit of peace, our contribution to the stability of the new nations of the world, our hopes for progress and well-being at home, all these depend in large measure on our ability to release the full potential of our American economy for employment, production, and growth.

Our generation of Americans has achieved a historic technological breakthrough. Today we are capable of creating an abundance in goods and services beyond the dreams of our parents. Yet on the threshold of plenty the Republican Administration hesitates, confused and afraid.

As a result, massive human needs now exist side by side with idle workers, idle capital, and idle machines.

The Republican failure in the economic field has been virtually complete.

Their years of power have consisted of two recessions, in 1953-54 and 1957-60, separated by the most severe peacetime inflation in history.

They have shown themselves incapable of checking inflation. In their efforts to do so, they have brought on recessions that have thrown millions of Americans out of work. Yet even in these slumps, the cost of living has continued to climb, and it is now at an all-time high.

They have slowed down the rate of growth of the economy to about one-third the rate of the Soviet Union.

Over the past 7½-year period, the Republicans have failed to balance the budget or reduce the national debt. Responsible fiscal policy requires surpluses in good times to more than offset the deficits which may occur in recessions, in order to reduce the national debt over the long run. The Republican Administration has produced the deficits — in fact, the greatest deficit in any peacetime year in history, in 1958-59 — but only occasional and meager surpluses. Their first seven years produced a total deficit of nearly $19 billion.

While reducing outlays for essential public services which directly benefit our people, they have raised the annual interest charge on the national debt to a level $3 billion higher than when they took office. In the eight fiscal years of the Republican Administration, these useless higher interest payments will have cost the taxpayers $9 billion.

They have mismanaged the public debt not only by increasing interest rates, but also by failing to lengthen the average maturity of Government obligations when they had a clear opportunity to do so.

ECONOMIC GROWTH

The new Democratic Administration will confidently proceed to unshackle American enterprise and to free American labor, industrial leadership, and capital, to create an abundance that will outstrip any other system.

Free competitive enterprise is the most creative and productive form of economic order that the world has seen. The recent slow pace of American growth is due not to the failure of our free economy but to the failure of our national leadership.

We Democrats believe that our economy can and must grow at an average rate of 5% annually, almost twice as fast as our average annual rate since 1953. We pledge ourselves to policies that will achieve this goal without inflation.

Economic growth is the means whereby we improve the American standard of living and produce added tax resources for national security and essential public services.

Our economy must grow more swiftly in order to absorb two groups of workers: the much larger number of young people who will be reaching working age in the 1960s, and the workers displaced by the rapid pace of technological advances, including automation. Republican policies which have stifled growth could only mean increasingly severe unemployment, particularly of youth and older workers.

AN END TO TIGHT MONEY

As the first step in speeding economic growth, a

Democratic President will put an end to the present high-interest, tight-money policy.

This policy has failed in its stated purpose — to keep prices down. It has given us two recessions within five years, bankrupted many of our farmers, produced a record number of business failures, and added billions of dollars in unnecessary higher interest charges to Government budgets and the cost of living.

A new Democratic Administration will reject this philosophy of economic slowdown. We are committed to maximum employment, at decent wages and with fair profits, in a far more productive, expanding economy.

The Republican high-interest policy has extracted a costly toll from every American who has financed a home, an automobile, a refrigerator, or a television set.

It has foisted added burdens on taxpayers of state and local governments which must borrow for schools and other public services.

It has added to the cost of many goods and services, and hence has been itself a factor in inflation.

It has created windfalls for many financial institutions.

The $9 billion of added interest charges on the national debt would have been even higher but for the prudent insistence of the Democratic Congress that the ceiling on interest rates for long-term Government bonds be maintained.

CONTROL OF INFLATION

The American consumer has a right to fair prices. We are determined to secure that right.

Inflation has its roots in a variety of causes; its cure lies in a variety of remedies. Among those remedies are monetary and credit policies properly applied, budget surpluses in times of full employment, and action to restrain "administered price" increases in industries where economic power rests in the hands of a few.

A fair share of the gains from increasing productivity in many industries should be passed on to the consumer through price reductions.

The agenda which a new Democratic Administration will face next January is crowded with urgent needs on which action has been delayed, deferred, or denied by the present Administration.

A new Democratic Administration will undertake to meet those needs.

It will reaffirm the Economic Bill of Rights which Franklin Roosevelt wrote into our national conscience sixteen years ago. It will reaffirm these rights for all Americans of whatever race, place of residence, or station in life:

1. *"The right to a useful and remunerative job in the industries or shops or farms or mines of the nation."*

## FULL EMPLOYMENT

The Democratic Party reaffirms its support of full employment as a paramount objective of national policy.

For nearly 30 months the rate of unemployment has been between 5 and 7.5% of the labor force. A pool of three to four million citizens, able and willing to work but unable to find jobs, has been written off by the Republican Administration as a "normal" readjustment of the economic system.

The policies of a Democratic Administration to restore economic growth will reduce current unemployment to a minimum.

Thereafter, if recessionary trends appear, we will act promptly with counter-measures, such as public works or temporary tax cuts. We will not stand idly by and permit recessions to run their course as the Republican Administration has done.

## AID TO DEPRESSED AREAS

The right to a job requires action to create new industry in America's depressed areas of chronic unemployment.

General economic measures will not alone solve the problems of localities which suffer some special disadvantage. To bring prosperity to these depressed areas and to enable them to make their full contribution to the national welfare, specially directed action is needed.

Areas of heavy and persistent unemployment result from depletion of natural resources, technological change, shifting defense requirements, or trade imbalances which have caused the decline of major industries. Whole communities, urban and rural, have been left stranded in distress and despair, through no fault of their own.

These communities have undertaken valiant efforts of self-help. But mutual aid, as well as self-help, is part of the American tradition. Stricken communities deserve the help of the whole nation.

The Democratic Congress twice passed bills to provide this help. The Republican President twice vetoed them.

These bills proposed low-interest loans to private enterprise to create new industry and new jobs in depressed communities, assistance to the communities to provide public facilities necessary to encourage the new industry, and retraining of workers for the new jobs.

The Democratic Congress will again pass, and the Democratic President will sign, such a bill.

## DISCRIMINATION IN EMPLOYMENT

The right to a job requires action to break down artificial and arbitrary barriers to employment based on age, race, sex, religion, or national origin.

Unemployment strikes hardest at workers over 40, minority groups, young people, and women. We will not achieve full employment until prejudice against these workers is wiped out.

## COLLECTIVE BARGAINING

The right to a job requires the restoration of full support for collective bargaining and the repeal of the anti-labor excesses which have been written into our labor laws.

Under Democratic leadership a sound national policy was developed, expressed particularly by the Wagner National Labor Relations Act, which guaranteed the rights of workers to organize and to bargain collectively. But the Republican Administration has replaced this sound policy with a national anti-labor policy.

The Republican Taft-Hartley Act seriously weakened unions in their efforts to bring economic justice to the millions of American workers who remain unorganized.

By administrative action, anti-labor personnel appointed by the Republicans to the National Labor Relations Board have made the Taft-Hartley Act even more restrictive in its application than in its language.

Thus the traditional goal of the Democratic Party — to give all workers the right to organize and bargain collectively — has still not been achieved.

We pledge the enactment of an affirmative labor policy which will encourage free collective bargaining through the growth and development of free and responsible unions.

Millions of workers just now seeking to organize are blocked by Federally authorized "right-to-work" laws, unreasonable limitations on the right to picket, and other hampering legislative and administrative provisions.

Again, in the new Labor-Management Reporting and Disclosure Act, the Republican Administration perverted the constructive effort of the Democratic Congress to deal with improper activities of a few in labor and management by turning that Act into a means of restricting the legitimate rights of the vast majority of working men and women in honest labor unions. This law likewise strikes hardest at the weak or poorly organized, and it fails to deal with abuses of management as vigorously as with those of labor.

We will repeal the authorization for "right-to-work" laws, limitations on the rights to strike, to picket peacefully and to tell the public the facts of a labor dispute, and other anti-labor features of the Taft-Hartley Act and the 1959 Act. This unequivocal pledge for the repeal of the anti-labor and restrictive provisions of those laws will encourage collective bargaining and strengthen and support the free and honest labor movement.

The Railroad Retirement Act and the Railroad Unemployment Insurance Act are in need of improvement. We strongly oppose Republican attempts to weaken the Railway Labor Act.

We shall strengthen and modernize the Walsh-Healey and Davis-Bacon Acts, which protect the wage standards of workers employed by Government contractors.

Basic to the achievement of stable labor-management relations is leadership from the White House. The Republican Administration has failed to provide such leadership.

It failed to foresee the deterioration of labor-management relations in the steel industry last year. When a national emergency was obviously developing, it failed to forestall it. When the emergency came, the Administration's only solution was government-by-injunction.

A Democratic President, through his leadership and concern, will produce a better climate for continuing constructive relationships between labor and management. He will have periodic White House conferences between labor and management to consider their mutual problems before they reach the critical stage.

A Democratic President will use the vast fact-finding facilities that are available to inform himself, and the public, in exercising his leadership in labor disputes for the benefit of the nation as a whole.

If he needs more such facilities, or authority, we will provide them.

We further pledge that in the administration of all labor legislation we will restore the level of integrity, competence and sympathetic understanding required to carry out the intent of such legislation.

### PLANNING FOR AUTOMATION

The right to a job requires planning for automation, so that men and women will be trained and available to meet shifting employment needs.

We will conduct a continuing analysis of the nation's manpower resources and of measures which may be required to assure their fullest development and use.

We will provide the Government leadership necessary to insure that the blessings of automation do not become burdens of widespread unemployment. For the young and the technologically displaced workers, we will provide the opportunity for training and retraining that equips them for jobs to be filled.

### MINIMUM WAGES

2. *"The right to earn enough to provide adequate food and clothing and recreation."*

At the bottom of the income scale are some eight million families whose earnings are too low to provide even basic necessities of food, shelter, and clothing.

We pledge to raise the minimum wage to $1.25 an hour and to extend coverage to several million workers not now protected.

We pledge further improvements in the wage, hour and coverage standards of the Fair Labor Standards Act so as to extend its benefits to all workers employed in industries engaged in or affecting interstate commerce and to raise its standards to keep up with our general economic progress and needs.

We shall seek to bring the two million men, women and children who work for wages on the farms of the United States under the protection of existing labor and social legislation; and to assure migrant labor, perhaps the most underprivileged of all, of a comprehensive program to bring them not only decent wages but also adequate standards of health, housing, Social Security protection, education and welfare services.

AGRICULTURE

3. *"The right of every farmer to raise and sell his products at a return which will give him and his family a decent living."*

We shall take positive action to raise farm income to full parity levels and to preserve family farming as a way of life.

We shall put behind us once and for all the timidity with which our Government has viewed our abundance of food and fiber.

We will set new high levels of food consumption both at home and abroad.

As long as many Americans and hundreds of millions of people in other countries remain underfed, we shall regard these agricultural riches, and the family farmers who produce them, not as a liability but as a national asset.

*Using Our Abundance*

The Democratic Administration will inaugurate a national food and fiber policy for expanded use of our agricultural abundance. We will no longer view food stockpiles with alarm but will use them as powerful instruments for peace and plenty.

We will increase consumption at home. A vigorous, expanding economy will enable many American families to eat more and better food.

We will use the food stamp programs authorized to feed needy children, the aged and the unemployed. We will expand and improve the school lunch and milk programs.

We will establish and maintain food reserves for national defense purposes near important population centers in order to preserve lives in event of national disaster, and will operate them so as not to depress farm prices. We will expand research into new industrial uses of agricultural products.

We will increase consumption abroad. The Democratic Party believes our nation's capacity to produce food and fiber is one of the great weapons for waging war against hunger and want throughout the world. With wise management of our food abundance we will expand trade between nations, support economic and human development programs, and combat famine.

Unimaginative, outmoded Republican policies which fail to use these productive capacities of our farms have been immensely costly to our nation. They can and will be changed.

*Achieving Income Parity*

While farmers have raised their productive efficiency to record levels, Republican farm policies have forced their income to drop by 30%.

Tens of thousands of farm families have been bankrupted and forced off the land. This has happened despite the fact that the Secretary of Agriculture has spent more on farm programs than all previous Secretaries in history combined.

Farmers acting individually or in small groups are helpless to protect their incomes from sharp declines. Their only recourse is to produce more, throwing production still further out of balance with demand and driving prices down further.

This disastrous downward cycle can be stopped only by effective farm programs sympathetically administered with the assistance of democratically elected farmer committees.

The Democratic Administration will work to bring about full parity income for farmers in all segments of agriculture by helping them to balance farm production with the expanding needs of the nation and the world.

Measures to this end include production and marketing quotas measured in terms of barrels, bushels and bales, loans on basic commodities at not less than 90% of parity, production payments, commodity purchases, and marketing orders and agreements.

We repudiate the Republican administration of the Soil Bank Program, which has emphasized the retirement of whole farm units, and we pledge an orderly land retirement and conservation program.

We are convinced that a successful combination of these approaches will cost considerably less than present Republican programs which have failed.

We will encourage agricultural cooperatives by expanding and liberalizing existing credit facilities and developing new facilities if necessary to assist them in extending their marketing and purchasing activities, and we will protect cooperatives from punitive taxation.

The Democratic Administration will improve the marketing practices of the family-type dairy farm to reduce risk of loss.

To protect farmers' incomes in times of natural disaster, the Federal Crop Insurance Program, created and developed experimentally under Democratic Administrations, should be invigorated and expanded nationwide.

### Improving Working and Living on Farms

Farm families have been among those victimized most severely by Republican tight-money policies.

Young people have been barred from entering agriculture. Giant corporations and other non-farmers, with readier access to credit and through vertical integration methods, have supplanted hundreds of farm families and caused the bankruptcy of many others.

The Democratic Party is committed by tradition and conviction to preservation of family agriculture.

To this end, we will expand and liberalize farm credit facilities, especially to meet the needs of family-farm agriculture and to assist beginning farmers.

Many families in America's rural counties are still living in poverty because of inadequate resources and opportunity. This blight and personal desperation should have received national priority attention long ago.

The new Democratic Administration will begin at once to eradicate long-neglected rural blight. We will help people help themselves with extended and supervised credit for farm improvement, local industrial development, improved vocational training and other assistance to those wishing to change to non-farm employment, and with the fullest development of commercial and recreational possibilities. This is one of the major objectives of the area redevelopment program, twice vetoed by the Republican President.

The rural electric cooperatives celebrate this year the twenty-fifth anniversary of the creation of the Rural Electrification Administration under President Franklin D. Roosevelt.

The Democratic Congress has successfully fought the efforts of the Republican Administration to cut off REA loans and force high-interest-rate policies on this great rural enterprise.

We will maintain interest rates for REA co-ops and public power districts at the levels provided in present law.

We deplore the Administration's failure to provide the dynamic leadership necessary for encouraging loans to rural users for generation of power where necessary.

We promise the co-ops active support in meeting the ever-growing demand for electric power and telephone service, to be filled on a complete area-coverage basis without requiring benefits for special-interest power groups.

In every way we will seek to help the men, women, and children whose livelihood comes from the soil to achieve better housing, education, health, and decent earnings and working conditions.

All these goals demand the leadership of a Secretary of Agriculture who is conversant with the technological and economic aspects of farm problems, and who is sympathetic with the objectives of effective farm legislation not only for farmers but for the best interest of the nation as a whole.

### SMALL BUSINESS

*4. "The right of every businessman, large and small, to trade in an atmosphere of freedom from unfair competition and domination by monopolies at home and abroad."*

The new Democratic Administration will act to make our free economy really free — free from the oppression of monopolistic power, and free from the suffocating impact of high interest rates. We will help create an economy in which small businesses can take root, grow, and flourish.

We Democrats pledge:

1. Action to aid small business in obtaining credit and equity capital at reasonable rates. Small business which must borrow to stay alive has been a particular victim of the high-interest policies of the Republican administration.

The loan program of the Small Business Administration should be accelerated, and the independence of that agency preserved. The Small Business

Investment Act of 1958 must be administered with a greater sense of its importance and possibilities.

2. Protection of the public against the growth of monopoly.

The last 7½ years of Republican government has been the greatest period of merger and amalgamation in industry and banking in American history. Democratic Congresses have enacted numerous important measures to strengthen our anti-trust laws. Since 1950 the four Democratic Congresses have enacted laws like the Celler-Kefauver Anti-Merger Act, and improved the laws against price discriminations and tie-in sales.

When the Republicans were in control of the 80th and 83rd Congresses they failed to enact a single measure to strengthen or improve the anti-trust laws.

The Democratic Party opposes this trend to monopoly.

We pledge vigorous enforcement of the anti-trust laws.

We favor requiring corporations to file advance notice of mergers with the anti-trust enforcement agencies.

We favor permitting all firms to have access at reasonable rates to patented inventions resulting from Government-financed research and development contracts.

We favor strengthening the Robinson-Patman Act to protect small business against price discrimination.

We favor authorizing the Federal Trade Commission to obtain temporary injunctions during the pendency of administrative proceedings.

3. A more equitable share of Government contracts to small and independent business.

We will move from almost complete reliance on negotiation in the award of Government contracts toward open, competitive bidding.

HOUSING

5. "The right of every family to a decent home."

Today our rate of home building is less than that of ten years ago. A healthy, expanding economy will enable us to build two million homes a year, in wholesome neighborhoods, for people of all incomes.

At this rate, within a single decade we can clear away our slums and assure every American family a decent place to live.

Republican policies have led to a decline of the home building industry and the production of fewer homes. Republican high-interest policies have forced the cost of decent housing beyond the range of many families. Republican indifference has perpetuated slums.

We record the unpleasant fact that in 1960 at least 40 million Americans live in substandard housing.

One million new families are formed each year and need housing, and 300,000 existing homes are lost through demolition or other causes and need to be replaced. At present, construction does not even meet these requirements, much less permit reduction of the backlog of slum units.

We support a housing construction goal of more than two million homes a year. Most of the increased construction will be priced to meet the housing needs of middle- and low-income families who now live in substandard housing and are priced out of the market for decent homes.

Our housing programs will provide for rental as well as sales housing. They will permit expanded cooperative housing programs and sharply stepped-up rehabilitation of existing homes.

To make possible the building of two million homes a year in wholesome neighborhoods, the home building industry should be aided by special mortgage assistance, with low interest rates, long-term mortgage periods and reduced down payments. Where necessary, direct Government loans should be provided.

Even with this new and flexible approach, there will still be need for a substantial low-rent public housing program authorizing as many units as local communities require and are prepared to build.

HEALTH

6. "The right to adequate medical care and the opportunity to achieve and enjoy good health."

Illness is expensive. Many Americans have neither incomes nor insurance protection to enable them to pay for modern health care. The problem is particularly acute with our older citizens, among whom serious illness strikes most often.

We shall provide medical care benefits for the aged as part of the time-tested Social Security insurance system. We reject any proposal which would require such citizens to submit to the indignity of a means test — a "pauper's oath."

For young and old alike, we need more medical schools, more hospitals, more research laboratories to speed the final conquest of major killers.

### Medical Care for Older Persons

Fifty million Americans — more than a fourth of our people — have no insurance protection against the high cost of illness. For the rest, private health insurance pays, on the average, only about one-third of the cost of medical care.

The problem is particularly acute among the 16 million Americans over 65 years old, and among disabled workers, widows and orphans.

Most of these have low incomes and the elderly among them suffer two to three times as much illness as the rest of the population.

The Republican Administration refused to acknowledge any national responsibility for health care for elder citizens until forced to do so by an increasingly outraged demand. Then, its belated proposal was a cynical sham built around a degrading test based on means or income — a "pauper's oath."

The most practicable way to provide health protection for older people is to use the contributory machinery of the Social Security system for insurance covering hospital bills and other high-cost medical services. For those relatively few of our older people who have never been eligible for Social Security coverage, we shall provide corresponding benefits by appropriations from the general revenue.

### Research

We will step up medical research on the major killers and crippling diseases — cancer, heart disease, arthritis, mental illness. Expenditures for these purposes should be limited only by the availability of personnel and promising lines of research. Today such illness costs us $35 billion annually, much of which could be avoided. Federal appropriations for medical research are barely 1% of this amount.

Heart disease and cancer together account for two out of every three deaths in this country. The Democratic President will summon to a White House conference the nation's most distinguished scientists in these fields to map a coordinated long-run program for the prevention and control of these diseases.

We will also support a cooperative program with other nations on international health research.

### Hospitals

We will expand and improve the Hill-Burton hospital construction program.

### Health Manpower

To ease the growing shortage of doctors and other medical personnel we propose Federal aid for constructing, expanding and modernizing schools of medicine, dentistry, nursing and public health.

We are deeply concerned that the high cost of medical education is putting this profession beyond the means of most American families. We will provide scholarships and other assistance to break through the financial barriers to medical education.

### Mental Health

Mental patients fill more than half the hospital beds in the country today. We will provide greatly increased Federal support for psychiatric research and training, and community mental health programs, to help bring back thousands of our hospitalized mentally ill to full and useful lives in the community.

7. *"The right to adequate protection from the economic fears of old age, sickness, accidents, and unemployment."*

### A Program for the Aging

The Democratic Administration will end the neglect of our older citizens. They deserve lives of usefulness, dignity, independence, and participation. We shall assure them not only health care but employment for those who want work, decent housing, and recreation.

Already 16 million Americans — about one in ten — are over 65, with the prospect of 26 million by 1980.

### Health

As stated, we will provide an effective system for paid-up medical insurance upon retirement, financed during working years through the Social Security mechanism and available to all retired persons without a means test. This has first priority.

## Income

Half of the people over 65 have incomes inadequate for basic nutrition, decent housing, minimum recreation and medical care. Older people who do not want to retire need employment opportunity and those of retirement age who no longer wish to or cannot work need better retirement benefits.

We pledge a campaign to eliminate discrimination in employment due to age. As a first step we will prohibit such discrimination by Government contractors and subcontractors.

We will amend the Social Security Act to increase the retirement benefit for each additional year of work after 65, thus encouraging workers to continue on the job full time.

To encourage part-time work by others, we favor raising the $1200-a-year ceiling on what a worker may earn while still drawing Social Security benefits.

Retirement benefits must be increased generally, and minimum benefits raised from $33 a month to $50.

## Housing

We shall provide decent and suitable housing which older persons can afford. Specifically we shall move ahead with the program of direct Government loans for housing for older people initiated in the Housing Act of 1959, a program which the Republican Administration has sought to kill.

## Special Services

We shall take Federal action in support of state efforts to bring standards of care in nursing homes and other institutions for the aged up to desirable minimums.

We shall support demonstration and training programs to translate proven research into action in such fields as health, nutritional guidance, home care, counseling, recreational activity.

Taken together, these measures will affirm a new charter of rights for the older citizens among us — the right to a life of usefulness, health, dignity, independence and participation.

## WELFARE

### Disability Insurance

We shall permit workers who are totally and permanently disabled to retire at any age, removing the arbitrary requirement that the worker be 50 years of age.

We shall also amend the law so that after six months of total disability, a worker will be eligible for disability benefits, with restorative services to enable him to return to work.

### Physically Handicapped

We pledge continued support of legislation for the rehabilitation of physically handicapped persons and improvement of employment opportunities for them.

### Public Assistance

Persons in need who are inadequately protected by social insurance are cared for by the states and local communities under public assistance programs.

The Federal Government, which now shares the cost of aid to some of these, should share in all, and benefits should be made available without regard to residence.

### Unemployment Benefits

We will establish uniform minimum standards throughout the nation for coverage, duration, and amount of unemployment insurance benefits.

### Equality for Women

We support legislation which will guarantee to women equality of rights under the law, including equal pay for equal work.

### Child Welfare

The Child Welfare Program and other services already established under the Social Security Act should be expanded. Federal leadership is required in the nationwide campaign to prevent and control juvenile delinquency.

### Intergroup Relations

We propose a Federal bureau of intergroup relations to help solve problems of discrimination in housing, education, employment, and community opportunities in general. The bureau would assist in the solution of problems arising from the resettlement of immigrants and migrants within our own country, and in resolving religious, social and other tensions where they arise.

## EDUCATION

### 8. *"The right to a good education."*

America's young people are our greatest resource for the future. Each of them deserves the education which will best develop his potentialities.

We shall act at once to help in building the classrooms and employing the teachers that are essential if the right to a good education is to have genuine meaning for all the youth of America in the decade ahead.

As a national investment in our future we propose a program of loans and scholarship grants to assure that qualified young Americans will have full opportunity for higher education, at the institutions of their choice, regardless of the income of their parents.

The new Democratic Administration will end eight years of official neglect of our educational system.

America's education faces a financial crisis. The tremendous increase in the number of children of school and college age has far outrun the available supply of educational facilities and qualified teachers. The classroom shortage alone is interfering with the education of 10 million students.

America's teachers, parents and school administrators have striven courageously to keep up with the increased challenge of education.

So have states and local communities. Education absorbs two-fifths of all their revenue. With limited resources, private educational institutions have shouldered their share of the burden.

Only the Federal Government is not doing its part. For eight years, measures for the relief of the educational crisis have been held up by the cynical maneuvers of the Republican Party in Congress and the White House.

We believe that America can meet its educational obligations only with generous Federal financial support, within the traditional framework of local control. The assistance will take the form of Federal grants to states for educational purposes they deem most pressing, including classroom construction and teachers' salaries. It will include aid

for the construction of academic facilities as well as dormitories at colleges and universities.

We pledge further Federal support for all phases of vocational education for youth and adults; for libraries and adult education; for realizing the potential of educational television; and for exchange of students and teachers with other nations.

As part of a broader concern for young people we recommend establishment of a Youth Conservation Corps, to give underprivileged young people a rewarding experience in a healthful environment.

The pledges contained in this Economic Bill of Rights point the way to a better life for every family in America.

They are the means to a goal that is now within our reach — the final eradication in America of the age-old evil of poverty.

Yet there are other pressing needs on our national agenda.

## NATURAL RESOURCES

A thin layer of earth, a few inches of rain, and a blanket of air make human life possible on our planet.

Sound public policy must assure that these essential resources will be available to provide the good life for our children and future generations.

Water, timber and grazing lands, recreational areas in our parks, shores, forests and wildernesses, energy, minerals, even pure air — all are feeling the press of enormously increased demands of a rapidly growing population.

Natural resources are the birthright of all the people.

The new Democratic Administration, with the vision that built a TVA and a Grand Coulee, will develop and conserve that heritage for the use of this and future generations. We will reverse Republican policies under which America's resources have been wasted, depleted, underdeveloped, and recklessly given away.

We favor the best use of our natural resources, which generally means adoption of the multiple-purpose principle to achieve full development for all the many functions they can serve.

### Water and Soil

An abundant supply of pure water is essential to our economy. This is a national problem.

Water must serve domestic, industrial and irrigation needs and inland navigation. It must provide habitat for fish and wildlife, supply the base for much outdoor recreation, and generate electricity. Water must also be controlled to prevent floods, pollution, salinity and silt.

The new Democratic Administration will develop a comprehensive national water resource policy. In cooperation with state and local governments, and interested private groups, the Democratic Administration will develop a balanced, multiple-purpose plan for each major river basin, to be revised periodically to meet changing needs. We will erase the Republican slogan of "no new starts" and will begin again to build multiple-purpose dams, hydroelectric facilities, flood-control works, navigation facilities, and reclamation projects to meet mounting and urgent needs.

We will renew the drive to protect every acre of farm land under a soil and water conservation plan, and we will speed up the small-watershed program.

We will support and intensify the research effort to find an economical way to convert salt and brackish water. The Republicans discouraged this research, which holds untold possibilities for the whole world.

### Water and Air Pollution

America can no longer take pure water and air for granted. Polluted rivers carry their dangers to everyone living along their courses; impure air does not respect boundaries.

Federal action is needed in planning, coordinating and helping to finance pollution control. The states and local communities cannot go it alone. Yet President Eisenhower vetoed a Democratic bill to give them more financial help in building sewage treatment plants.

A Democratic President will sign such a bill.

Democrats will step up research on pollution control, giving special attention to:

1. the rapidly growing problem of air pollution from industrial plants, automobile exhausts, and other sources, and

2. disposal of chemical and radioactive wastes, some of which are now being dumped off our coasts without adequate knowledge of the potential consequences.

### Outdoor Recreation

As population grows and the work week shortens and transportation becomes easier and speedier, the need for outdoor recreation facilities mounts.

We must act quickly to retain public access to the oceans, gulfs, rivers, streams, lakes and reservoirs, and their shorelines, and to reserve adequate camping and recreational areas while there is yet time. Areas near major population centers are particularly needed.

The new Democratic Administration will work to improve and extend recreation opportunities in national parks and monuments, forests, and river development projects, and near metropolitan areas. Emphasis will be on attractive, low-cost facilities for all the people and on preventing undue commercialization.

The National Park System is still incomplete; in particular, the few remaining suitable shorelines must be included in it. A national wilderness system should be created for areas already set aside as wildernesses. The system should be extended but only after careful consideration by the Congress of the value of areas for competing uses.

Recreational needs of the surrounding area should be given important consideration in disposing of Federally owned lands.

We will protect fish and game habitats from commercial exploitation and require military installations to conform to sound conservation practices.

### Energy

The Republican Administration would turn the clock back to the days before the New Deal, in an effort to divert the benefits of the great natural energy resources from all the people to a favored few. It has followed for many years a "no new starts" policy.

It has stalled atomic energy development; it has sought to cripple rural electrification.

It has closed the pilot plant on getting oil from shale.

It has harrassed and hampered the TVA.

We reject this philosophy and these policies. The people are entitled to use profitably what they already own.

The Democratic Administration instead will foster the development of efficient regional giant power systems from all sources, including water, tidal, and nuclear power, to supply low-cost electricity to all retail electric systems, public, private, and cooperative.

The Democratic Administration will continue to develop "yardsticks" for measuring the rates of private utility systems. This means meeting the needs of rural electric cooperatives for low-interest loans for distribution, transmission and generation facilities; Federal transmission facilities, where appropriate, to provide efficient low-cost power supply; and strict enforcement of the public-preference clause in power marketing.

The Democratic Administration will support continued study and research on energy fuel resources, including new sources in wind and sun. It will push forward with the Passamaquoddy tidal power project with its great promise of cheaper power and expanded prosperity for the people of New England.

We support the establishment of a national fuels policy.

The $15 billion national investment in atomic energy should be protected as a part of the public domain.

### Federal Lands and Forests

The record of the Republican Administration in handling the public domain is one of complete lethargy. It has failed to secure existing assets. In some cases, it has given away priceless resources for plunder by private corporations, as in the Al Sarena mining incident and the secret leasing of game refuges to favored oil interests.

The new Democratic Administration will develop balanced land and forest policies suited to the needs of a growing America.

This means intensive forest management on a multiple-use and sustained-yield basis, reforestation of burnt-over lands, building public access roads, range reseeding and improvement, intensive work in watershed management, concern for small business operations, and insuring free public access to public lands for recreational uses.

### Minerals

America uses half the minerals produced in the entire Free World. Yet our mining industry is in what may be the initial phase of a serious long-term depression. Sound policy requires that we strengthen the domestic mining industry without interfering with adequate supplies of needed materials at reasonable costs.

We pledge immediate efforts toward the establishment of a realistic long-range minerals policy.

The new Democratic Administration will begin intensive research on scientific prospecting for mineral deposits.

We will speed up the geologic mapping of the country, with emphasis on Alaska.

We will resume research and development work on use of low-grade mineral reserves, especially oil shale, lignites, iron ore taconite, and radioactive minerals. These efforts have been halted or cut back by the Republican Administration.

The Democratic Party favors a study of the problem of non-uniform seaward boundaries of the coastal states.

### Government Machinery for Managing Resources

Long-range programming of the nation's resource development is essential. We favor creation of a council of advisers on resources and conservation, which will evaluate and report annually upon our resource needs and progress.

We shall put budgeting for resources on a businesslike basis, distinguishing between operating expense and capital investment, so that the country can have an accurate picture of the costs and returns. We propose the incremental method in determining the economic justification of our river basin programs. Charges for commercial use of public lands will be brought into line with benefits received.

### CITIES AND THEIR SUBURBS

A new Democratic Administration will expand Federal programs to help urban communities clear their slums, dispose of their sewage, educate their children, transport suburban commuters to and from their jobs, and combat juvenile delinquency.

We will give the city dweller a voice at the Cabinet table by bringing together within a single department programs concerned with urban and metropolitan problems.

The United States is now predominantly an urban nation.

The efficiency, comfort, and beauty of our cities and suburbs influence the lives of all Americans.

Local governments have found increasing difficulty in coping with such fundamental public problems as urban renewal, slum clearance, water supply, mass transportation, recreation, health, welfare, education and metropolitan planning. These problems are, in many cases, interstate and regional in scope.

Yet the Republican Administration has turned its back on urban and suburban America. The list of Republican vetoes includes housing, urban renewal and slum clearance, area redevelopment, public works, airports and stream pollution control. It has proposed severe cutbacks in aid for hospital construction, public assistance, vocational education, community facilities and sewage disposal.

The result has been to force communities to thrust an ever-greater tax load upon the already overburdened property taxpayer and to forgo needed public services.

The Democratic Party believes that state and local governments are strengthened — not weakened — by financial assistance from the Federal Government. We will extend such aid without impairing local administration through unnecessary Federal interference or red tape.

We propose a ten-year action program to restore our cities and provide for balanced suburban development, including the following:

1. The elimination of slums and blight and the restoration of cities and depressed areas within the next ten years.

2. Federal aid for metropolitan area planning and community facility programs.

3. Federal aid for comprehensive metropolitan transportation programs, including bus and rail mass transit, commuter railroads as well as highway programs, and construction of civil airports.

4. Federal aid in combating air and water pollution.

5. Expansion of park systems to meet the recreation needs of our growing population.

The Federal Government must recognize the financial burdens placed on local governments, urban and rural alike, by Federal installations and land holdings.

TRANSPORTATION

Over the past seven years, we have watched the steady weakening of the nation's transportation system. Railroads are in distress. Highways are congested. Airports and airways lag far behind the needs of the jet age.

To meet this challenge we will establish a national transportation policy, designed to coordinate and modernize our facilities for transportation by road, rail, water, and air.

Air

The jet age has made rapid improvement in air safety imperative. Rather than "an orderly withdrawal" from the airport grant programs as proposed by the Republican Administration, we pledge to expand the program to accommodate growing air traffic.

Water

Development of our inland waterways, our harbors, and Great Lakes commerce has been held back by the Republican President.

We pledge the improvement of our rivers and harbors by new starts and adequate maintenance.

A strong and efficient American-flag merchant marine is essential to peacetime commerce and defense emergencies. Continued aid for ship construction and operation to offset cost differentials favoring foreign shipping is essential to these goals.

Roads

The Republican Administration has slowed down, stretched out and greatly increased the costs of the interstate highway program.

The Democratic Party supports the highway program embodied in the Acts of 1956 and 1958 and the principle of Federal-state partnership in highway construction.

We commend the Democratic Congress for establishing a special committee which has launched an extensive investigation of this highway program. Continued scrutiny of this multi-billion-dollar highway program can prevent waste, inefficiency and graft and maintain the public's confidence.

Rail

The nation's railroads are in particular need of freedom from burdensome regulation to enable them to compete effectively with other forms of transportation. We also support Federal assistance in meeting certain capital needs, particularly for urban mass transportation.

SCIENCE

We will recognize the special role of our Federal Government in support of basic and applied research.

*Space*

The Republican Administration has remained incredibly blind to the prospects of space exploration. It has failed to pursue space programs with a sense of urgency at all close to their importance to the future of the world.

It has allowed the Communists to hit the moon first, and to launch substantially greater payloads. The Republican program is a catchall of assorted projects with no clearly defined, long-range plan of research.

The new Democratic Administration will press forward with our national space program in full realization of the importance of space accomplishments to our national security and our international prestige. We shall reorganize the program to achieve both efficiency and speedy execution. We shall bring top scientists into positions of responsibility. We shall undertake long-term basic research in space science and propulsion.

We shall initiate negotiations leading toward the international regulation of space.

*Atomic Energy*

The United States became pre-eminent in the development of atomic energy under Democratic Administrations.

The Republican Administration, despite its glowing promises of "Atoms for Peace," has permitted the gradual deterioration of United States leadership in atomic development both at home and abroad.

In order to restore United States leadership in atomic development, the new Democratic Administration will:

1. Restore truly nonpartisan and vigorous administration of the vital atomic energy program.

2. Continue the development of the various promising experimental and prototype atomic power plants which show promise, and provide increasing support for longer-range projects at the frontiers of atomic energy application.

3. Continue to preserve and support national laboratories and other Federal atomic installations as the foundation of technical progress and a bulwark of national defense.

4. Accelerate the Rover nuclear rocket project and auxiliary power facilities so as to achieve world leadership in peaceful outer space exploration. tion.

5. Give reality to the United States international atoms-for-peace programs, and continue and expand technological assistance to underdeveloped countries.

6. Consider measures for improved organization and procedure for radiation protection and reactor safety, including a strengthening of the role of the Federal Radiation Council, and the separation of quasi-judicial functions in reactor safety regulations.

7. Provide a balanced and flexible nuclear defense capability, including the augmentation of the nuclear submarine fleet.

*Oceanography*

Oceanographic research is needed to advance such important programs as food and minerals from our Great Lakes and the sea. The present Administration has neglected this new scientific frontier.

GOVERNMENT OPERATIONS

We shall reform the processes of Government in all branches — Executive, Legislative, and Judicial. We will clean out corruption and conflicts of interest, and improve Government services.

*The Federal Service*

Two weeks before this Platform was adopted, the difference between the Democratic and Republican attitudes toward Government employees was dramatically illustrated. The Democratic Congress passed a fully justified pay increase to bring Government pay scales more nearly into line with those of private industry.

The Republican President vetoed the pay raise.

The Democratic Congress decisively overrode the veto.

The heavy responsibilities of modern government require a Federal service characterized by devotion to duty, honesty of purpose and highest competence. We pledge the modernization and strengthening of our Civil Service system.

We shall extend and improve the employees' appeals system and improve programs for recognizing the outstanding merits of individual employees.

### Ethics in Government

We reject totally the concept of dual or triple loyalty on the part of Federal officials in high places.

The conflict-of-interest statutes should be revised and strengthened to assure the Federal service of maximum security against unethical practices on the part of public officials.

The Democratic Administration will establish and enforce a Code of Ethics to maintain the full dignity and integrity of the Federal service and to make it more attractive to the ablest men and women.

### Regulatory Agencies

The Democratic Party promises to clean up the Federal regulatory agencies. The acceptance by Republican appointees to these agencies of gifts, hospitality, and bribes from interests under their jurisdiction has been a particularly flagrant abuse of public trust.

We shall bring all contacts with commissioners into the open, and will protect them from any form of improper pressure.

We shall appoint to these agencies men of ability and independent judgment who understand that their function is to regulate these industries in the public interest.

We promise a thorough review of existing agency practices, with an eye toward speedier decisions, and a clearer definition of what constitutes the public interest.

The Democratic Party condemns the usurpation by the Executive of the powers and functions of any of the independent agencies and pledges the restoration of the independence of such agencies and the protection of their integrity of action.

### The Postal Service

The Republican policy has been to treat the United States postal service as a liability instead of a great investment in national enlightenment, social efficiency and economic betterment.

Constant curtailment of service has inconvenienced every citizen.

A program must be undertaken to establish the Post Office Department as a model of efficiency and service. We pledge ourselves to:

1. Restore the principle that the postal service is a public service.

2. Separate the public service costs from those to be borne by the users of the mails.

3. Continue steady improvement in working conditions and wage scales, reflecting increasing productivity.

4. Establish a long-range program for research and capital improvements compatible with the highest standards of business efficiency.

### Law Enforcement

In recent years, we have been faced with a shocking increase in crimes of all kinds. Organized criminals have even infiltrated into legitimate business enterprises and labor unions.

The Republican Administration, particularly the Attorney General's office, has failed lamentably to deal with this problem despite the growing power of the underworld. The new Democratic Administration will take vigorous corrective action.

### Freedom of Information

We reject the Republican contention that the workings of Government are the special private preserve of the Executive.

The massive wall of secrecy erected between the Executive branch and the Congress as well as the citizen must be torn down. Information must flow freely, save in those areas in which the national security is involved.

### Clean Elections

The Democratic Party favors realistic and effective limitations on contributions and expenditures, and full disclosure of campaign financing in Federal elections.

We further propose a tax credit to encourage small contributions to political parties. The Democratic Party affirms that every candidate for public office has a moral obligation to observe and uphold traditional American principles of decency, honesty and fair play in his campaign for election.

We deplore efforts to divide the United States into regional, religious and ethnic groups.

We denounce and repudiate campaign tactics that substitute smear and slander, bigotry and false accusations of bigotry, for truth and reasoned argument.

*District of Columbia*

The capital city of our nation should be a symbol of democracy to people throughout the world. The Democratic Party reaffirms its long-standing support of home rule for the District of Columbia, and pledges to enact legislation permitting voters of the District to elect their own local government.

We urge the legislatures of the 50 states to ratify the 23rd Amendment, passed by the Democratic Congress, to give District citizens the right to participate in Presidential elections.

We also support a Constitutional amendment giving the District voting representation in Congress.

*Virgin Islands*

We believe that the voters of the Virgin Islands should have the right to elect their own Governor, to have a delegate in the Congress of the United States and to have the right to vote in national elections for a President and Vice President of the United States.

*Puerto Rico*

The social, economic, and political progress of the Commonwealth of Puerto Rico is a testimonial to the sound enabling legislation, and to the sincerity and understanding with which the people of the 50 states and Puerto Rico are meeting their joint problems.

The Democratic Party, under whose administration the Commonwealth status was established, is entitled to great credit for providing the opportunity which the people of Puerto Rico have used so successfully.

Puerto Rico has become a show place of worldwide interest, a tribute to the benefits of the principles of self-determination. Further benefits for Puerto Rico under these principles are certain to follow.

## Congressional Procedures

In order that the will of the American people may be expressed upon all legislative proposals, we urge that action be taken at the beginning of the 87th Congress to improve Congressional procedures so that majority rule prevails and decisions can be made after reasonable debate without being blocked by a minority in either House.

The rules of the House of Representatives should be so amended as to make sure that bills reported by legislative committees reach the floor for consideration without undue delay.

## Consumers

In an age of mass production, distribution, and advertising, consumers require effective Government representation and protection.

The Republican Administration has allowed the Food and Drug Administration to be weakened. Recent Senate hearings on the drug industry have revealed how flagrant profiteering can be when essential facts on costs, prices, and profits are hidden from scrutiny. The new Democratic Administration will provide the money and the authority to strengthen this agency for its task.

We propose a consumer counsel, backed by a suitable staff, to speak for consumers in the formulation of Government policies and represent consumers in administrative proceedings.

The consumer also has a right to know the cost of credit when he borrows money. We shall enact Federal legislation requiring the vendors of credit to provide a statement of specific credit charges and what these charges cost in terms of true annual interest.

## Veterans Affairs

We adhere to the American tradition dating from the Plymouth Colony in New England in 1636:

"... any soldier injured in defense of the colony shall be maintained competently by the colony for the remainder of his life."

We pledge adequate compensation for those with service-connected disabilities and for the survivors of those who died in service or from service-connected disabilities. We pledge pensions adequate for a full and dignified life for disabled and distressed veterans and for needy survivors of deceased veterans.

Veterans of World War I, whose Federal benefits have not matched those of veterans of subsequent service, will receive the special attention of the Democratic Party looking toward equitable adjustments.

We endorse expanded programs of vocational rehabilitation for disabled veterans, and education for orphans of servicemen.

The quality of medical care furnished to the disabled veterans has deteriorated under the Republican Administration. We shall work for an increased availability of facilities for all veterans in need and we shall move with particular urgency to fulfill the need for expanded domiciliary and nursing-home facilities.

We shall continue the veterans home loan guarantee and direct loan programs and educational benefits patterned after the G.I. Bill of Rights.

## American Indians

We recognize the unique legal and moral responsibility of the Federal Government for Indians in restitution for the injustice that has sometimes been done them. We therefore pledge prompt adoption of a program to assist Indian tribes in the full development of their human and natural resources and to advance the health, education, and economic well-being of Indian citizens while preserving their cultural heritage.

Free consent of the Indian tribes concerned shall be required before the Federal Government makes any change in any Federal-Indian treaty or other contractual relationship.

The new Democratic Administration will bring competent, sympathetic, and dedicated leadership to the administration of Indian affairs which will end practices that have eroded Indian rights and resources, reduced the Indians' land base and repudiated Federal responsibility. Indian claims against the United States can and will be settled promptly, whether by negotiation or other means, in the best interests of both parties.

## The Arts

The arts flourish where there is freedom and where individual initiative and imagination are encouraged. We enjoy the blessings of such an atmosphere.

The nation should begin to evaluate the possibilities for encouraging and expanding participation in and appreciation of our cultural life.

We propose a Federal advisory agency to assist in the evaluation, development, and expansion of cultural resources of the United States. We shall support legislation needed to provide incentives for those endowed with extraordinary talent, as a worthy supplement to existing scholarship programs.

## Civil Liberties

With democratic values threatened today by Communist tyranny, we reaffirm our dedication to the Bill of Rights. Freedom and civil liberties, far from being incompatible with security, are vital to our national strength. Unfortunately, those high in the Republican Administration have all too often sullied the name and honor of loyal and faithful American citizens in and out of Government.

The Democratic Party will strive to improve Congressional investigating and hearing procedures. We shall abolish useless disclaimer affidavits such as those for student educational loans. We shall provide a full and fair hearing, including confrontation of the accuser, to any person whose public or private employment or reputation is jeopardized by a loyalty or security proceeding.

Protection of rights of American citizens to travel, to pursue lawful trade and to engage in other lawful activities abroad without distinction as to race or religion is a cardinal function of the national sovereignty.

We will oppose any international agreement or treaty which by its terms or practices differentiates among American citizens on grounds of race or religion.

The list of unfinished business for America is long. The accumulated neglect of nearly a decade cannot be wiped out overnight. Many of the objectives which we seek will require our best efforts over a period of years.

Although the task is far-reaching, we will tackle it with vigor and confidence. We will substitute planning for confusion, purpose for indifference, direction for drift and apathy.

We will organize the policymaking machinery of the Executive branch to provide vigor and leadership in establishing our national goals and achieving them.

The new Democratic President will sign, not veto, the efforts of a Democratic Congress to create more jobs, to build more homes, to save family farms, to clean up polluted streams and rivers, to help depressed areas, and to provide full employment for our people.

## Fiscal Responsibility

We vigorously reject the notion that America, with a half-trillion-dollar gross national product, and nearly half of the world's industrial resources, cannot afford to meet our needs at home and in our world relationships.

We believe, moreover, that except in periods of recession or national emergency, these needs can be met with a balanced budget, with no increase in present tax rates, and with some surplus for the gradual reduction of our national debt.

To assure such a balance we shall pursue a four-point program of fiscal responsibility.

First, we shall end the gross waste in Federal expenditures which needlessly raises the budgets of many Government agencies.

The most conspicuous unnecessary item is, of course, the excessive cost of interest on the national debt. Courageous action to end duplication and competition among the armed services will achieve large savings. The cost of the agricultural program can be reduced while at the same time prosperity is being restored to the nation's farmers.

Second, we shall collect the billions in taxes which are owed to the Federal Government but not now collected.

The Internal Revenue Service is still suffering from the cuts inflicted upon its enforcement staff by the Republican Administration and the Republican Congress in 1953.

The Administration's own Commissioner of Internal Revenue has testified that billions of dollars in revenue are lost each year because the Service does not have sufficient agents to follow up on tax evasion.

We will add enforcement personnel, and develop new techniques of enforcement, to collect tax revenue which is now being lost through evasion.

Third, we shall close the loopholes in the tax laws by which certain privileged groups legally escape their fair share of taxation.

Among the more conspicuous loopholes are depletion allowances which are inequitable, special consideration for recipients of dividend income, and deductions for extravagant "business expenses" which have reached scandalous proportions.

Tax reform can raise additional revenue and at the same time increase legitimate incentives for growth, and make it possible to ease the burden on the general taxpayer who now pays an unfair share of taxes because of special favors to the few.

Fourth, we shall bring in added Federal tax revenues by expanding the economy itself. Each dollar of additional production puts an additional 18 cents in tax revenue in the national treasury. A 5% growth rate, therefore, will mean that at the end of four years the Federal Government will have had a total of nearly $50 billion in additional tax revenues above those presently received.

By these four methods we can sharply increase the Government funds available for needed services, for correction of tax inequities, and for debt or tax reduction.

Much of the challenge of the 1960s, however, remains unforeseen and unforeseeable.

If, therefore, the unfolding demands of the new decade at home or abroad should impose clear national responsibilities that cannot be fulfilled without higher taxes, we will not allow political disadvantage to deter us from doing what is required.

As we proceed with the urgent task of restoring America's productivity, confidence, and power, we will never forget that our national interest is more than the sum total of all the group interests in America.

When group interests conflict with the national interest, it will be the national interest which we serve.


On its values and goals the quality of American life depends. Here above all our national interest and our devotion to the Rights of Man coincide.

Democratic Administrations under Wilson, Roosevelt, and Truman led the way in pressing for economic justice for all Americans.

But man does not live by bread alone. A new Democratic Administration, like its predecessors, will once again look beyond material goals to the spiritual meaning of American society.

We have drifted into a national mood that accepts payola and quiz scandals, tax evasion and false expense accounts, soaring crime rates, influence peddling in high Government circles, and the exploitation of sadistic violence as popular entertainment.

For eight long critical years our present national leadership has made no effective effort to reverse this mood.

The new Democratic Administration will help create a sense of national purpose and higher standards of public behavior.

## CIVIL RIGHTS

We shall also seek to create an affirmative new atmosphere in which to deal with racial divisions and inequalities which threaten both the integrity of our democratic faith and the proposition on which our nation was founded — that all men are created equal. It is our faith in human dignity that distinguishes our open free society from the closed totalitarian society of the Communists.

The Constitution of the United States rejects the notion that the Rights of Man means the rights of some men only. We reject it too.

The right to vote is the first principle of self-government. The Constitution also guarantees to all Americans the equal protection of the laws.

It is the duty of the Congress to enact the laws necessary and proper to protect and promote these constitutional rights. The Supreme Court has the power to interpret these rights and the laws thus enacted.

It is the duty of the President to see that these rights are respected and that the Constitution and laws as interpreted by the Supreme Court are faithfully executed.

What is now required is effective moral and political leadership by the whole Executive branch of our Government to make equal opportunity a living reality for all Americans.

As the party of Jefferson, we shall provide that leadership.

In every city and state in greater or lesser degree there is discrimination based on color, race, religion, or national origin.

If discrimination in voting, education, the administration of justice or segregated lunch counters are the issues in one area, discrimination in housing and employment may be pressing questions elsewhere.

The peaceful demonstrations for first-class citizenship which have recently taken place in many parts of this country are a signal to all of us to make good at long last the guarantees of our Constitution.

The time has come to assure equal access for all Americans to all areas of community life, including voting booths, schoolrooms, jobs, housing, and public facilities.

The Democratic Administration which takes office next January will therefore use the full powers provided in the Civil Rights Acts of 1957 and 1960 to secure for all Americans the right to vote.

If these powers, vigorously invoked by a new Attorney General and backed by a strong and imaginative Democratic President, prove inadequate, further powers will be sought.

We will support whatever action is necessary to eliminate literacy tests and the payment of poll taxes as requirements for voting.

A new Democratic Administration will also use its full powers — legal and moral — to ensure the beginning of good-faith compliance with the Constitutional requirement that racial discrimination be ended in public education.

We believe that every school district affected by the Supreme Court's school desegregation decision should submit a plan providing for at least first-step compliance by 1963, the 100th anniversary of the Emancipation Proclamation.

To facilitate compliance, technical and financial assistance should be given to school districts facing special problems of transition.

For this and for the protection of all other Constitutional rights of Americans, the Attorney General should be empowered and directed to file civil injunction suits in Federal courts to prevent the denial of any civil right on grounds of race, creed, or color.

The new Democratic Administration will support Federal legislation establishing a Fair Employment Practices Commission to secure effectively for everyone the right to equal opportunity for employment.

In 1949 the President's Committee on Civil Rights recommended a permanent Commission on Civil Rights. The new Democratic Administration will broaden the scope and strengthen the powers of the present commission and make it permanent.

Its functions will be to provide assistance to communities, industries, or individuals in the implementation of Constitutional rights in education, housing, employment, transportation, and the administration of justice.

In addition, the Democratic Administration will use its full executive powers to assure equal employment opportunities and to terminate racial segregation throughout Federal services and institutions, and on all Government contracts. The successful desegregation of the armed services took place through such decisive executive action under President Truman.

Similarly the new Democratic Administration will take action to end discrimination in Federal housing programs, including Federally assisted housing.

To accomplish these goals will require executive orders, legal actions brought by the Attorney General, legislation, and improved Congressional procedures to safeguard majority rule.

Above all, it will require the strong, active, persuasive, and inventive leadership of the President of the United States.

The Democratic President who takes office next January will face unprecedented challenges. His Administration will present a new face to the world.

It will be a bold, confident, affirmative face. We will draw new strength from the universal truths which the founder of our Party asserted in the Declaration of Independence to be "self-evident."

Emerson once spoke of an unending contest in human affairs, a contest between the Party of Hope and the Party of Memory.

For 7½ years America, governed by the Party of Memory, has taken a holiday from history.

As the Party of Hope it is our responsibility and opportunity to call forth the greatness of the American people.

In this spirit, we hereby rededicate ourselves to the continuing service of the Rights of Man — everywhere in America and everywhere else on God's earth.

## Prohibition Platform 1960

PREAMBLE

We, the representatives of the Prohibition Party, assembled in the National Convention at Winona Lake, Indiana, September 1, 2, and 3, 1959, recognizing Almighty God as the source of all just government, and with faith in the teachings of the Lord Jesus Christ, do solemnly promise that, if our party is chosen to administer the affairs of the

nation, we will, with earnest dedication to the principles of righteousness, seek to serve the needs and to preserve the rights, the prerogatives and the basic freedoms, of the people of the United States. For the realization of these ends we propose the following programs of government:

CONSTITUTIONAL GOVERNMENT

First of all, we affirm our sincere loyalty to the Constitution of the United States, and express our deep confidence in that document as the basic law of our land. We deplore all attempts to violate it, whether by legislation, by means of evasion, or through judicial interpretation. We believe in the principles of liberty and justice enunciated in the Declaration of Independence and in the Preamble and Bill of Rights of our Constitution. We declare ourselves in hearty support of our system of representative government, with its plan of checks and balances, and express our firm intent to serve the people of our nation with a constructive, forward-looking program of good government, dedicated to the welfare of our citizenry.

COMMUNISM-TOTALITARIANISM

We are positively, aggressively and unalterably, opposed to Communism as a way of life or as a governmental system. We believe that the program of Communism, with its intent to infiltrate and to overthrow our present form of government, must be pitilessly exposed. We challenge all loyal citizens to become fully aware of this menace to civilization, to exert every effort to defeat these "masters of deceit," and to help preserve our American way of life.

We also declare ourselves opposed to any other form of totalitarian philosophy or form of government. We endorse the efforts of those agencies which have been honestly and earnestly exposing subversive activities and groups.

GOVERNMENTAL ECONOMY AND TAXATION

We live in an era of extravagance and wasteful spending. This spirit has invaded government at all levels, demanding an ever-increasing tax load upon our people. The constant increase in taxation, requiring nearly one-third of the total income of our citizens to pay the expenses of government, is approaching the point of confiscation, leading to economic bankruptcy. We believe that good government ought not to attempt to do for people what they can do for themselves. With proper economy, governmental costs can be lowered, the tax load can be lightened, and the public debt can be reduced. We promise to devote ourselves to such an end, even though it involves the reorganization and/or abolition of certain departments, bureaus and vested interests.

## Money and Finance

A sound financial program and a dependable monetary policy are fundamental to a stable economy. Our Constitution gives to Congress the power to "coin money" and to "regulate the value thereof." We believe that Congress, working with the executive department of our government, should take immediate steps to establish a financial program that will block inflationary trends, insure a sound currency, stabilize price levels and provide for systematic retirement of the national debt. We urge that careful consideration be given to a return to the gold standard, suggesting that such a step would help stabilize our economy, would promote confidence in our monetary system and would underwrite a continuing program of sound finance and expanding industrial progress.

## The Federal Budget

Good government and a sound economy demand a balanced federal budget. The inflationary effects and the disturbing influences of unbalanced budgets must be eliminated. We cannot, with impunity, continue to increase the mortgage on our future and the interest load of the present. As the level of taxation is already excessive, there must be either a decided reduction in governmental services and federal spending or a substantial improvement in efficiency, with consequent elimination of waste in both personnel and materials. Actually, both areas need careful exploration with a view not only to maintaining a balanced budget, but also to reduction of the national debt.

## Foreign Aid

Many billions of dollars of our taxpayers' money have been and are still being given to foreign countries. Unfortunately, substantial portions have been used to support governments and programs considerably at variance with American ideals and concepts. It is frankly recognized that complex and baffling problems are involved in this area of international relations, but it is likewise believed that the practice needs most careful scrutiny and review.

## Free Enterprise

We deplore the current trend toward development of a socialistic state. We are strongly opposed to governmental restraints on our free enterprise system, to detailed regulation of our economic life and to federal interference with individual initiative. We declare ourselves for freedom of opportunity, for private industry financed within the structure of our present anti-trust laws and for a sound economic system based upon recognized business practice. To this end, we propose that our government withdraw, with reasonable promptness, from the field of business activity and sell to private industry those business enterprises now owned and operated by the federal government.

## Labor and Industry

In the area of labor and industrial relations we believe that the public welfare must be given paramount consideration. Both management and labor must be held responsible for their economic and their social behavior. Neither should be permitted to dominate at the expense of the other or of the common good. Rather, the anti-trust laws must be applied equally to all monopolies, whether of business or labor. Whenever the public welfare is seriously endangered because of disputes affecting quasi-public businesses and utilities we favor the compulsory arbitration of labor-management disputes.

## Employee-Employer Rights

Every individual has certain basic and fundamental rights. A person's right to join or not to join a labor union without affecting his employment and his right to work for an employer willing to hire him must be protected. Likewise, employees and employers must be free to bargain and to contract as they wish. Mass picketing, rioting, terrorism, and all other forms of violence and coercion, secondary boycotts and industry-wide bargaining should be prohibited.

## Individual and States' Rights

Our founding fathers recognized the importance of both individual and states' rights, and determined to preserve them by making the Bill of Rights an integral part of our Constitution. During recent years there has been an increasing tendency toward an undesirable concentration of power and authority in the federal government. We pledge ourselves to action that will preserve all legitimate individual rights and will maintain among the several states their constitutional place in our system of government. We maintain that all American citizens, regardless of race, religion or national origin, are equal before the law and are entitled to equality of treatment under the laws of our land. We deplore the use of violence, from whatever source, as a means of trying to resolve tensions and divergencies of opinion among our citizenry.

## Public Morality and Law Enforcement

Moral and spiritual considerations must be primary factors in determining both state and national policies. We deplore the gross neglect of such matters by the dominant political parties, culminating in the shocking revelations of crime and of political and economic corruption which have characterized recent years. We charge these parties with basic responsibility for the rapid decline in moral standards which followed repeal of the Eighteenth Amendment. We believe that the program of nullification of law through non-enforcement which led to repeal contributed greatly to the disintegration of public morals, to a general deterioration of standards and to a lowering of values among our people.

We pledge ourselves to break the unholy alliance which has made these things possible. We propose to strengthen and to enforce laws against gambling, narcotics, and commercialized vice, to emphasize the basic importance of spiritual and moral values to the development and growth of an enduring nation, and to maintain the integrity of our democracy by careful enforcement of law and loyal support of our Constitution.

## World Peace

We live in an age of atomic and hydrogen bombs, in an era of missiles and jet propulsion, in a world filled with animosities and cruel hatreds. Instruments for the destruction of civilization have been developed. Under these conditions, we pledge ourselves to search for peaceful solutions to international conflict, by seeking to deal creatively and constructively with the underlying causes of international tension, and, to strive for world peace and order based upon the teachings and practices of the Prince of Peace.

## Universal Military Training

Although we seek for world peace and order, we declare our firm belief, under existing world conditions, in a sound program of national preparedness. At the same time, we seriously question the desirability of the existing program of peacetime compulsory military training. We doubt that it represents a genuine safeguard to world peace. Rather, we believe it to be contrary, in principle, to our American way of life, to place an unnecessary burden upon our peacetime economy, to threaten us with possible military dictatorship, and, as currently conducted, to permit and very often to promote the moral and spiritual deterioration of our Youth. Therefore, we declare our opposition to any program of peacetime compulsory military training and urge a complete evaluation and re-orientation of our entire program of national preparedness.

## Nuclear Bomb Tests

Many scientists throughout the world have warned us that radioactive fallout, resulting from the testing of nuclear weapons, endangers the health of human beings throughout the world, and will increase the number of seriously defective children who will be born to future generations. It is unjust that the people of the world, and especially those of nations not engaged in nuclear testing, should be exposed to this peril without their consent. The danger and the injustice will become progressively greater with each additional test. In addition, there is the added danger that continuation of the armaments race will lead to an atomic war of annihilation.

We, therefore, urge that, as a step toward world disarmament, all testing of nuclear weapons be indefinitely suspended on a multilateral basis and that our government seek with renewed vigor and persistence an agreement among all nuclear powers for the permanent and complete cessation of nuclear tests for military purposes.

## Religious Liberty

We believe in religious liberty. Freedom of the individual to worship, to fellowship with others of similar faith, to evangelize, to educate and to establish religious institutions, must be preserved. When religious liberty is lost political liberty will perish with it. We believe, also, that our government should take a firm, positive position against religious intolerance and persecution anywhere in the world.

## Marriage and Divorce

Ordained of God, the home is a sacred institution. Its sanctity must be protected and preserved. We favor the enactment of uniform marriage and divorce laws in the various states as an aid to building strong and enduring homes throughout our nation.

## Old Age Insurance

We endorse the general principle of an actuarially sound social security program which includes all employed groups. We question the soundness of the existing program. We deplore the widespread current abuse of the privileges involved; we condemn the maladministration of its provisions for political ends; we pledge ourselves to correct these evils.

## Ballot Law Reform

True democracy requires that the needs and interests of minority groups be given fair, honest and appropriate consideration. Instead, in many of our states, ballot laws have been enacted which are designed to make a two-party system into a bipartisan political monopoly, keeping minor parties off the ballot. We demand the repeal of all laws which deny to independent voters and to loyal minority groups the fundamental right of free political expression.

## Separation of Church and State

We affirm our continuing loyalty to the constitutional principle of separation of Church and State. We will expose, and resist vigorously, any attempt from whatever source to weaken or subvert this fundamental principle. In the area of government, we endorse encouragement of non-profit educational and religious institutions on a tax-exempt basis, but we declare strong opposition to all efforts, direct or indirect, to secure appropriations of public money for private religious or sectarian purposes.

## Education

It is altogether appropriate that our federal government should be interested in and concerned about matters pertaining to all areas of educational growth and development. However, under the Tenth Amendment, public education is clearly a matter of state concern. We approve of the work of the Office of Education in collecting and disseminating essential educational information, but we are opposed to any sort of direct federal aid to education, believing that each state should both support and control its own educational program.

## Agriculture

The production and distribution of agricultural products is of vital importance to the economy of any people. We believe that those engaged in agricultural pursuits, like other American citizens, should be free from authoritarian control and coercion. Hence we declare ourselves opposed to regimentation of farms and farmers and urge a sensible and orderly return to a free market program.

## Public Health

The health of our people is a matter of high importance. We are deeply concerned with this problem in its numerous aspects. In particular, we insist that genuine caution be taken when dealing with mental health cases lest there be unjust and prejudiced incarcerations. Also we deplore those programs of mass medication which many maintain are in violation of the rights of individuals under our Constitution.

## Service, Not Spoils

In spite of our "civil service" system, first sponsored by the Prohibition Party, the dominant political parties are positively committed to the "spoils" system and, when in office, have prostituted governmental power to serve their own selfish party interests instead of the whole people. This has led to excessive expenditures, higher taxes and, in some situations, to an unfortunate alliance of crime with politics. We pledge ourselves to an honest, efficient and economical administration.

## THE ALCOHOL PROBLEM

The widespread and increasing use of alcoholic beverages has now become a national tragedy and must be recognized as a major cause of poverty, broken homes, juvenile delinquency, vice, crime, political corruption, wasted manpower and highway accidents. Of all the unfortunate mistakes of our government and people, none has been worse than the legalization of the liquor traffic. It can be legitimately said that no political issue confronting the citizens of our land compares in magnitude with the need for suppressing the beverage alcohol industry.

The sponsors of this national curse are not only highly capitalized and strongly organized, but are also socially irresponsible. Out of enormous profits the liquor industry spends huge sums to promote sales, to create habitual use of its products by both youth and adults and to encourage a weakening of moral resistance to its program of social and economic exploitation. It is linked with and supports a nationwide network of organized gambling, vice and crime. Through its advertising it has corrupted large segments of the nation's press, and it is endeavoring to extend its control increasingly to both radio and television.

Unfortunately, the liquor traffic has been able to extend its power until, in all too many instances, it dominates our political life and controls our governmental officials. Both of our major political parties are dominated by it, and neither dares to take a stand against it. And so long as they continue to be yoked by party membership with the liquor traffic and the underworld, just so long will they be unable to make moral principles prevail.

The beverage alcohol problem is a matter of national concern. It has reached proportions which demand immediate action looking to a solution. First of all, scientific facts about beverage alcohol must be widely publicized. People must come to know and to understand the demon which we harbor. Secondly, a program of publicity, education, legislation and administration, leading to the elimination of the beverage alcohol industry, must be developed. People must come to know that there is no satisfactory solution to the problem except through political action which supresses it and a political administration which destroys it.

Accordingly the Prohibition Party demands the repeal of all laws which legalize the liquor traffic and the enactment and rigorous enforcement of new laws which prohibit the manufacture, distribution and sale of alcoholic beverages. You are urged to elect an administration pledged to the above program. Such is essential to the permanent solution of this devastating problem.

## CONCLUSION

The need today in the United States of America is a re-alignment of voters and the union of all good citizens in a political party that is dedicated to a constructive program of clean, honest, and humane government. The Prohibition Party is that kind of political organization. Therefore, we challenge the citizens of our land to elect the candidates of the Prohibition Party; to put into office persons of unquestioned integrity, who will set an example of public and private morality, and who will marshal the resources of government — executive, legislative and judicial — to right the wrong and to preserve for our nation a government "of the people, by the people and for the people," under God.

## Republican Platform 1960

### PREAMBLE

The United States is living in an age of profoundest revolution. The lives of men and of nations are undergoing such transformations as history has rarely recorded. The birth of new nations, the impact of new machines, the threat of new weapons, the stirring of new ideas, the ascent into a new dimension of the universe — everywhere the accent falls on the new.

At such a time of world upheaval, great perils match great opportunities — and hopes, as well as fears, rise in all areas of human life. Such a force as nuclear power symbolizes the greatness of the choice before the United States and mankind. The energy of the atom could bring devastation to humanity. Or it could be made to serve men's hopes for peace and progress — to make for all peoples a more healthy and secure and prosperous life than man has ever known.

One fact darkens the reasonable hopes of free men: the growing vigor and thrust of Communist imperialism. Everywhere across the earth, this force challenges us to prove our strength and wisdom, our capacity for sacrifice, our faith in ourselves and in our institutions.

Free men look to us for leadership and support, which we dedicate ourselves to give out of the abundance of our national strength.

The fate of the world will be deeply affected, perhaps determined, by the quality of American leadership. American leadership means both how we govern ourselves and how we help to influence others. We deliberate the choice of national leadership and policy, mindful that in some measure our proposals involve the fate of mankind.

The leadership of the United States must be responsible and mature; its promises must be rational and practical, soberly pledged and faithfully undertaken. Its purposes and its aspirations must ascend to that high ground of right and freedom upon which mankind may dwell and progress in decent security.

We are impressed, but not dismayed, by the revolutionary turbulence that is wracking the world. In the midst of violence and change, we draw strength and confidence from the changeless principles of our free Constitution. Free men are invincible when the power and courage, the patience and the fortitude latent in them are drawn forth by reasonable appeal.

In this Republican Platform we offer to the United States our program — our call to service, our pledge of leadership, our proposal of measures in the public interest. We call upon God, in whose hand is every blessing, to favor our deliberations with wisdom, our nation with endurance, and troubled mankind everywhere with a righteous peace.

FOREIGN POLICY

The Republican Party asserts that the sovereign purpose of our foreign policy is to secure the free institutions of our nation against every peril, to hearten and fortify the love of freedom everywhere in the world, and to achieve a just peace for all of anxious humanity.

The pre-eminence of this Republic requires of us a vigorous, resolute foreign policy — inflexible against every tyrannical encroachment, and mighty in its advance toward our own affirmative goals.

The Government of the United States, under the administration of President Eisenhower and Vice President Nixon, has demonstrated that firmness in the face of threatened aggression is the most dependable safeguard of peace. We now reaffirm our determination to defend the security and the freedom of our country, to honor our commitments to our allies at whatever cost or sacrifice, and never to submit to force or threats. Our determination to stand fast has forestalled aggression before Berlin, in the Formosa Straits, and in Lebanon. Since 1954 no free nation has fallen victim behind the Iron Curtain. We mean to adhere to the policy of firmness that has served us so well.

We are unalterably committed to maintaining the security, freedom and solidarity of the Western Hemisphere. We support President Eisenhower's reaffirmation of the Monroe Doctrine in all its vitality. Faithful to our treaty commitments, we shall join the Republics of the Americas against any intervention in our hemisphere, and in refusing to tolerate the establishment in this hemisphere of any government dominated by the foreign rule of communism.

In the Middle East, we shall continue to support the integrity and independence of all the states of that area including Israel and the Arab States.

With specific reference to Israel and the Arab Nations we urge them to undertake negotiations for a mutually acceptable settlement of the causes of tension between them. We pledge continued efforts:

To eliminate the obstacles to a lasting peace in the area, including the human problem of the Arab refugees.

To seek an end to transit and trade restrictions, blockades and boycotts.

To secure freedom of navigation in international waterways, the cessation of discrimination against Americans on the basis of religious beliefs, and an end to the wasteful and dangerous arms race and to the threat of an arms imbalance in the area.

Recognition of Communist China and its admission to the United Nations have been firmly opposed by the Republican Administration. We will continue in this opposition because of compelling evidence that to do otherwise would weaken the cause of freedom and endanger the future of the free peoples of Asia and the world. The brutal suppression of the human rights and the religious traditions of the Tibetan people is an unhappy evidence of the need to persist in our policy.

The countries of the free world have been benefited, reinforced and drawn closer together by the vigor of American support of the United Nations, and by our participation in such regional organizations as NATO, SEATO, CENTO, the Organization of American States and other collective security alliances. We assert our intention steadfastly to uphold the action and principles of these bodies.

We believe military assistance to our allies under the mutual security program should be continued with all the vigor and funds needed to maintain the strength of our alliances at levels essential to our common safety.

The firm diplomacy of the Eisenhower-Nixon Administration has been supported by a military power superior to any in the history of our nation or in the world. As long as world tensions menace us with war, we are resolved to maintain an armed power exceeded by no other.

Under Republican administration, the Government has developed original and constructive programs in many fields — open skies, atoms for peace, cultural and technical exchanges, the peaceful uses of outer space and Antarctica — to make known to men everywhere our desire to advance the cause of peace. We mean, as a Party, to continue in the same course.

We recognize and freely acknowledge the support given to these principles and policies by all Americans, irrespective of party. Standing as they do above partisan challenge, such principles and policies will, we earnestly hope, continue to have bipartisan support.

We established a new independent agency, the United States Information Agency, fully recognizing the tremendous importance of the struggle for men's minds. Today, our information program throughout the world is a greatly improved medium for explaining our policies and actions to audiences overseas, answering Communist propaganda, and projecting a true image of American life.

This is the Republican record. We rededicate ourselves to the principles that have animated it; and we pledge ourselves to persist in those principles, and to apply them to the problems, the occasions, and the opportunities to be faced by the new Administration.

We confront today the global offensive of Communism, increasingly aggressive and violent in its enterprises. The agency of that offensive is Soviet policy, aimed at the subversion of the world.

Recently we have noted Soviet Union pretexts to intervene in the affairs of newly independent countries, accompanied by threats of the use of nuclear weapons. Such interventions constitute a form of subversion against the sovereignty of these new nations and a direct challenge to the United Nations.

The immediate strategy of the Soviet imperialists is to destroy the world's confidence in America's desire for peace, to threaten with violence our mutual security arrangements, and to sever the bonds of amity and respect among the free nations. To nullify the Soviet conspiracy is our greatest task. The United States faces this challenge and resolves to meet it with courage and confidence.

To this end we will continue to support and strengthen the United Nations as an instrument for peace, for international cooperation, and for the advancement of the fundamental freedoms and humane interests of mankind.

Under the United Nations we will work for the peaceful settlement of international disputes and the extension of the rule of law in the world.

And, in furtherance of President Eisenhower's proposals for the peaceful use of space, we suggest that the United Nations take the initiative to develop a body of law applicable thereto.

Through all the calculated shifts of Soviet tactics and mood, the Eisenhower-Nixon Administration has demonstrated its willingness to negotiate in earnest with the Soviet Union to arrive at just settlements for the reduction of world tensions. We pledge the new Administration to continue in the same course.

We are similarly ready to negotiate and to institute realistic methods and safeguards for disarmament, and for the suspension of nuclear tests. We advocate an early agreement by all nations to forego nuclear tests in the atmosphere, and the suspension of other tests as verification techniques permit. We support the President in any decision he may make to re-evaluate the question of re-sumption of underground nuclear explosions test-ing, if the Geneva Conference fails to produce a satisfactory agreement. We have deep concern about the mounting nuclear arms race. This con-cern leads us to seek disarmament and nuclear agreements. And an equal concern to protect all peoples from nuclear danger, leads us to insist that such agreements have adequate safeguards.

We recognize that firm political and military policies, while imperative for our security, cannot in themselves build peace in the world.

In Latin America, Asia, Africa and the Middle East, peoples of ancient and recent independence, have shown their determination to improve their standards of living, and to enjoy an equality with the rest of mankind in the enjoyment of the fruits of civilization. This determination has become a primary fact of their political life. We declare our-selves to be in sympathy with their aspirations.

We have already created unprecedented dimen-sions of diplomacy for these purposes. We recog-nize that upon our support of well-conceived pro-grams of economic cooperation among nations rest the best hopes of hundreds of millions of friendly people for a decent future for themselves and their children. Our mutual security program of economic help and technical assistance; the De-velopment Loan Fund, the Inter-American Bank, the International Development Association and the Food for Peace Program, which create the condi-tions for progress in less-developed countries; our leadership in international efforts to help children, eliminate pestilence and disease and aid refugees — these are programs wise in concept and gener-ous in purpose. We mean to continue in support of them.

Now we propose to further evolution of our pro-grams for assistance to and cooperation with other nations, suitable to the emerging needs of the future.

We will encourage the countries of Latin Amer-ica, Africa, the Middle East and Asia, to initiate appropriate regional groupings to work out plans for economic and educational development. We anticipate that the United Nations Special Fund would be of assistance in developing such plans. The United States would offer its cooperation in planning, and the provision of technical personnel for this purpose. Agreeable to the developing na-tions, we would join with them in inviting countries with advanced economies to share with us a pro-portionate part of the capital and technical aid required. We would emphasize the increasing use of private capital and government loans, rather than outright grants, as a means of fostering inde-pendence and mutual respect. The President's recent initiative of a joint partnership program for Latin America opens the way to this approach.

We would propose that such groupings adopt means to attain viable economies following such examples as the European Common Market. And if from these institutions, there should follow stronger economic and political unions, we would welcome them with our support.

Despite the counterdrive of international Com-munism, relentless against individual freedom and subversive of the sovereignty of nations, a power-ful drive for freedom has swept the world since World War II and many heroic episodes in the Communist countries have demonstrated anew that freedom will not die.

The Republican Party reaffirms its determina-tion to use every peaceful means to help the cap-tive nations toward their independence, and thus their freedom to live and worship according to conscience. We do not condone the subjugation of the peoples of Hungary, Poland, East Germany, Czechoslovakia, Rumania, Albania, Bulgaria, Lat-via, Lithuania, Estonia, and other once-free na-tions. We are not shaken in our hope and belief that once again they will rule themselves.

Our time surges with change and challenge, peril and great opportunities. It calls us to great tasks and efforts — for free men can hope to guard freedom only if they prove capable of historic acts of wisdom and courage.

Dwight David Eisenhower stands today through-out the world as the greatest champion of peace and justice and good.

The Republican Party brings to the days ahead trained, experienced, mature and courageous lead-ership.

Our Party was born for freedom's sake. It is still the Party of full freedom in our country. As in Lincoln's time, our Party and its leaders will meet the challenges and opportunities of our time and keep our country the best and enduring hope of freedom for the world.

NATIONAL DEFENSE

The future of freedom depends heavily upon America's military might and that of her allies. Under the Eisenhower-Nixon Administration, our military might has been forged into a power second to none. This strength, tailored to serve the needs of national policy, has deterred and must continue to deter aggression and encourage the growth of freedom in the world. This is the only sure way to a world at peace.

We have checked aggression. We ended the war in Korea. We have joined with free nations in creating strong defenses. Swift technological change and the warning signs of Soviet aggressiveness make clear that intensified and courageous efforts are necessary, for the new problems of the 1960's will of course demand new efforts on the part of our entire nation. The Republican Party is pledged to making certain that our arms, and our will to use them, remain superior to all threats. We have, and will continue to have, the defenses we need to protect our freedom.

*The strategic imperatives of our national defense policy are these:*

A second-strike capability, that is, a nuclear retaliatory power that can survive surprise attack, strike back, and destroy any possible enemy.

Highly mobile and versatile forces, including forces deployed, to deter or check local aggressions and "brush fire wars" which might bring on all-out nuclear war.

National determination to employ all necessary military capabilities so as to render any level of aggression unprofitable. Deterrence of war since Korea, specifically, has been the result of our firm statement that we will never again permit a potential aggressor to set the ground rules for his aggression; that we will respond to aggression with the full means and weapons best suited to the situation.

*Maintenance of these imperatives requires these actions:*

Unremitting modernization of our retaliatory forces, continued development of the manned bomber well into the missile age, with necessary numbers of these bombers protected through dispersal and airborne alert.

Development and production of new strategic weapons, such as the Polaris submarine and ballistic missile. Never again will they be neglected, as intercontinental missile development was neglected between the end of World War II and 1953.

Accelerate as necessary, development of hardening, mobility, dispersal, and production programs for long-range missiles and the speedy perfection of new and advanced generations of missiles and anti-missile missiles.

Intensified development of active civil defense to enable our people to protect themselves against the deadly hazards of atomic attack, particularly fallout; and to develop a new program to build a reserve of storable food, adequate to the needs of the population after an atomic attack.

Constant intelligence operations regarding Communist military preparations to prevent another Pearl Harbor.

A military establishment organized in accord with a national strategy which enables the unified commands in Europe, the Pacific, and this continent to continue to respond promptly to any kind of aggression.

Strengthening of the military might of the free-world nations in such ways as to encourage them to assume increasing responsibility for regional security.

Continuation of the "long pull" preparedness policies which, as inaugurated under the Eisenhower-Nixon Administration, have avoided the perilous peaks and slumps of defense spending and planning which marked earlier administrations.

There is no price ceiling on America's security. The United States can and must provide whatever is necessary to insure its own security and that of the free world and to provide any necessary increased expenditures to meet new situations, to guarantee the opportunity to fulfill the hopes of men of good will everywhere. To provide more would be wasteful. To provide less would be catastrophic. Our defense posture must remain steadfast, confident, and superior to all potential foes.

ECONOMIC GROWTH AND BUSINESS

To provide the means to a better life for individual Americans and to strengthen the forces of freedom in the world, we count on the proved productivity of our free economy.

Despite the lamentations of the opposition in viewing the economic scene today, the plain fact is that our 500 billion dollar economy finds more

Americans at work, earning more, spending more, saving more, investing more, building more than ever before in history. The well-being of our people, by virtually every yardstick, has greatly advanced under this Republican Administration.

But we can and must do better. We must raise employment to even higher levels and utilize even more fully our expanding, overall capacity to produce. We must quicken the pace of our economic growth to prove the power of American free enterprise to meet growing and urgent demands: to sustain our military posture, to provide jobs for a growing labor force in a time of rapid technological change, to improve living standards, to serve all the needs of an expanding population.

We therefore accord high priority to vigorous economic growth and recognize that its mainspring lies in the private sector of the economy. We must continue to foster a healthy climate in that sector. We reject the concept of artificial growth forced by massive new federal spending and loose money policies. The only effective way to accelerate economic growth is to increase the traditional strengths of our free economy — initiative and investment, productivity and efficiency. To that end we favor:

Broadly-based tax reform to foster job-making and growth-making investment for modernization and expansion, including realistic incentive depreciation schedules.

Use of the full powers of government to prevent the scourges of depression and inflation.

Elimination of featherbedding practices by labor and business.

Maintenance of a stable dollar as an indispensable means to progress.

Relating wage and other payments in production to productivity — except when necessary to correct inequities — in order to help us stay competitive at home and abroad.

Spurring the economy by advancing the successful Eisenhower-Nixon program fostering new and small business, by continued active enforcement of the anti-trust laws, by protecting consumers and investors against the hazard and economic waste of fraudulent and criminal practices in the market place, and by keeping the federal government from unjustly competing with private enterprise upon which Americans mainly depend for their livelihood.

Continued improvement of our vital transportation network, carrying forward rapidly the vast Eisenhower-Nixon national highway program and promoting safe, efficient, competitive and integrated transport by air, road, rail and water under equitable, impartial and minimal regulation directed to those ends.

Carrying forward, under the Trade Agreements Act, the policy of gradual selective — and truly reciprocal — reduction of unjustifiable barriers to trade among free nations. We advocate effective administration of the Act's escape clause and peril point provisions to safeguard American jobs and domestic industries against serious injury. In support of our national trade policy we should continue the Eisenhower-Nixon program of using this government's negotiating powers to open markets abroad and to eliminate remaining discrimination against our goods. We should also encourage the development of fair labor standards in exporting countries in the interest of fair competition in international trade. We should, too, expand the Administration's export drive, encourage tourists to come from abroad, and protect U.S. investors against arbitrary confiscations and expropriations by foreign governments. Through these and other constructive policies, we will better our international balance of payments.

Discharge by government of responsibility for those activities which the private sector cannot do or cannot so well do, such as constructive federal-local action to aid areas of chronic high unemployment, a sensible farm policy, development and wise use of natural resources, suitable support of education and research, and equality of job opportunity for all Americans.

Action on these fronts, designed to release the strongest productive force in human affairs — the spirit of individual enterprise — can contribute greatly to our goal of a steady, strongly growing economy.

## LABOR

America's growth cannot be compartmentalized. Labor and management cannot prosper without each other. They cannot ignore their mutual public obligation.

Industrial harmony, expressing these mutual interests, can best be achieved in a climate of free collective bargaining, with minimal government intervention except by mediation and conciliation.

Even in dealing with emergency situations imperiling the national safety, ways of solution must be found to enhance and not impede the processes of free collective bargaining — carefully considered ways that are in keeping with the policies of national labor relations legislation and with the need to strengthen the hand of the President in dealing with such emergencies.

In the same spirit, Republican leadership will continue to encourage discussions, away from the bargaining table, between labor and management to consider the mutual interest of all Americans in maintaining industrial peace.

Republican policy firmly supports the right of employers and unions freely to enter into agreements providing for the union shop and other forms of union security as authorized by the Labor-Management Relations Act of 1947 (the Taft-Hartley Act).

Republican-sponsored legislation has supported the right of union members to full participation in the affairs of their union and their right to freedom from racketeering and gangster interference whether by labor or management in labor-management relations.

Republican action has given to millions of American working men and women new or expanded protection and benefits, such as:

Increased federal minimum wage;

Extended coverage of unemployment insurance and the payment of additional temporary benefits provided in 1958-59;

Improvement of veterans' re-employment rights;

Extension of federal workman's compensation coverage and increase of benefits;

Legislative assurance of safety standards for longshore and harbor workers and for the transportation of migratory workers;

An increase of railroad workers' retirement and disability benefits.

Seven past years of accomplishments, however, are but a base to build upon in fostering, promoting and improving the welfare of America's working men and women, both organized and unorganized. We pledge, therefore, action on these constructive lines:

Diligent administration of the amended Labor-Management Relations Act of 1947 (Taft-Hartley Act) and the Labor-Management Reporting and Disclosure Act of 1959 (Landrum-Griffin Act) with recommendations for improvements which experience shows are needed to make them more effective or remove any inequities.

Correction of defects in the Welfare and Pension Plans Disclosure Act to protect employees' and beneficiaries' interests.

Upward revision in amount and extended coverage of the minimum wage to several million more workers.

Strengthening the unemployment insurance system and extension of its benefits.

Improvement of the eight-hour laws relating to hours and overtime compensation on federal and federally-assisted construction, and continued vigorous enforcement and improvement of minimum wage laws for federal supply and construction contracts.

Continued improvement of manpower skills and training to meet a new era of challenges, including action programs to aid older workers, women, youth, and the physically handicapped.

Encouragement of training programs by labor, industry and government to aid in finding new jobs for persons dislocated by automation or other economic changes.

Improvement of job opportunities and working conditions of migratory farm workers.

Assurance of equal pay for equal work regardless of sex; encouragement of programs to insure on-the-job safety, and encouragement of the States to improve their labor standards legislation, and to improve veterans' employment rights and benefits.

Encouragement abroad of free democratic institutions, higher living standards and higher wages through such agencies as the International Labor Organization, and cooperation with the free trade union movement in strengthening free labor throughout the world.

### AGRICULTURE

Americans are the best-fed and the best-clothed people in the world. Our challenge fortunately is one of dealing with abundance, not overcoming shortage. The fullness of our fields, forests and grazing lands is an important advantage in our struggle against worldwide tyranny and our crusade against poverty. Our farmers have provided us with a powerful weapon in the ideological and economic struggle in which we are now engaged.

Yet, far too many of our farm families, the source of this strength, have not received a fair return for their labors. For too long, Democratic-controlled Congresses have stalemated progress by clinging to obsolete programs conceived for different times and different problems.

Promises of specific levels of price support or a single type of program for all agriculture are cruel deceptions based upon the pessimistic pretense that only with rigid controls can farm familes be aided. The Republican Party will provide within the framework of individual freedom a greater bargaining power to assure an equitable return for the work and capital supplied by farmers.

The Republican Party pledges itself to develop new programs to improve and stabilize farm family income. It recognizes two main challenges: the immediate one of utilizing income-depressing surpluses, and the long-range one of steady balanced growth and development with a minimum of federal interference and control.

*To utilize immediately surpluses in an orderly manner, with a minimum impact on domestic and foreign markets, we pledge:*

Intensification of the Food for Peace program, including new cooperative efforts among food-surplus nations to assist the hungry peoples in less favored areas of the world.

Payment-in-kind, out of existing surpluses, as part of our land retirement program.

Creation of a Strategic Food Reserve properly dispersed in forms which can be preserved for long periods against the contingency of grave national emergency.

Strengthened efforts to distribute surpluses to schools and low-income and needy citizens of our own country.

A reorganization of Commodity Credit Corporation's inventory management operations to reduce competition with the marketings of farmers.

*To assure steady balanced growth and agricultural progress, we pledge:*

A crash research program to develop industrial and other uses of farm products.

Use of price supports at levels best fitted to specific commodities, in order to widen markets, ease production controls, and help achieve increased farm family income.

Acceleration of production adjustments, including a large scale land conservation reserve program on a voluntary and equitable rental basis, with full consideration of the impact on local communities.

Continued progress in the wise use and conservation of water and soil resources.

Use of marketing agreements and orders, and other marketing devices, when approved by producers, to assist in the orderly marketing of crops, thus enabling farmers to strengthen their bargaining power.

Stepped-up research to reduce production costs and to cut distribution costs.

Strengthening of the educational programs of the U.S. Department of Agriculture and the Land-Grant institutions.

Improvement of credit facilities for financing the capital needs of modern farming.

Encouragement of farmer owned and operated cooperatives including rural electric and telephone facilities.

Expansion of the Rural Development Program to help low-income farm families not only through better farming methods, but also through opportunities for vocational training, more effective employment services, and creation of job opportunities through encouragement of local industrialization.

Continuation and further improvement of the Great Plains Program.

Legislative action for programs now scheduled to expire for the school milk program, wool, and sugar, including increased sugar acreage to domestic areas.

Free movement in interstate commerce of agricultural commodities meeting federal health standards.

To prevent dumping of agricultural imports upon domestic markets.

*To assure the American farmer a more direct voice in his own destiny, we pledge:*

To select an official committee of farmers and ranchers, on a regional basis, broadly representative of American agriculture, whose function will be to recommend to the President guidelines for improving the operation of government farm programs.

NATURAL RESOURCES

A strong and growing economy requires vigorous and persistent attention to wise conservation and sound development of all our resources. Teamwork between federal, state and private entities is essential and should be continued. It has resulted in sustained conservation and resource development programs on a scale unmatched in our history.

The past seven years of Republican leadership have seen the development of more power capacity, flood control, irrigation, fish and wildlife projects, recreational facilities, and associated multipurpose benefits than during any previous administration in history. The proof is visible in the forests and waters of the land and in Republican initiation of and support for the Upper Watershed Program and the Small Reclamation Projects Act. It is clear, also, in the results of continuing administration-encouraged forest management practices which have brought, for the first time, a favorable balance between the growth and cutting of America's trees.

Our objective is for further growth, greater strength, and increased utilization in each great area of resource use and development.

*We pledge:*

Use of the community watershed as the basic natural unit through which water resource, soil, and forest management programs may best be developed, with interstate compacts encouraged to handle regional aspects without federal domination.

Development of new water resource projects throughout the nation.

Support of the historic policy of Congress in preserving the integrity of the several States to govern water rights.

Continued federal support for Republican-initiated research and demonstration projects which will supply fresh water from salt and brackish water sources.

Necessary measures for preservation of our domestic fisheries.

Continued forestry conservation with appropriate sustained yield harvesting, thus increasing jobs for people and increasing revenue.

To observe the "preference clause" in marketing federal power.

Support of the basic principles of reclamation.

Recognition of urban and industrial demands by making available to states and local governments, federal lands not needed for national programs.

*Full use and preservation of our great outdoors are pledged in:*

Completion of the "Mission 66" for the improvement of National Park areas as well as sponsorship of a new "Mission 76" program to encourage establishment and rehabilitation of local, state, and regional parks, to provide adequate recreational facilities for our expanding population.

Continued support of the effort to keep our great out-of-doors beautiful, green, and clean.

Establishment of a citizens board of conservation, resource and land management experts to inventory those federal lands now set aside for a particular purpose; to study the future needs of the nation for parks, seashores, and wildlife and other recreational areas; and to study the possibility of restoring lands not needed for a federal program.

*Minerals, metals, fuels, also call for carefully considered actions in view of the repeated failure of Democratic-controlled Congresses to enact any long-range minerals legislation. Republicans, therefore, pledge:*

Long-range minerals and fuels planning and programming, including increased coal research.

Assistance to mining industries in bridging the gap between peak defense demands and anticipated peacetime demands.

Continued support for federal financial assistance and incentives under our tax laws to encourage exploration for domestic sources of minerals and metals, with reasonable depletion allowances.

*To preserve our fish and wildlife heritage, we pledge:*

Legislation to authorize exchange of lands between state and federal governments to adapt programs to changing uses and habits.

Vigorous implementation of long-range programs for fish and wildlife.

GOVERNMENT FINANCE

To build a better America with broad national purposes such as high employment, vigorous and steady economic growth, and a dependable currency, responsible management of our federal finances is essential. Even more important, a sound economy is vital to national security. While leading Democrats charge us with a "budget balancing" mentality, their taunts really reflect their frustration over the people's recognition that as a nation we must live within our means. Government that is careless with the money of its citizens is careless with their future.

Because we are concerned about the well-being of people, we are concerned about protecting the value of their money. To this end, we Republicans believe that:

Every government expenditure must be tested by its contribution to the general welfare, not to any narrow interest group.

Except in times of war or economic adversity, expenditures should be covered by revenues.

We must work persistently to reduce, not to increase, the national debt, which imposes a heavy economic burden on every citizen.

Our tax structure should be improved to provide greater incentives to economic progress, to make it fair and equitable, and to maintain and deserve public acceptance.

We must resist assaults upon the independence of the Federal Reserve System; we must strengthen, not weaken, the ability of the Federal Reserve System and the Treasury Department to exercise effective control over money and credit in order better to combat both deflation and inflation that retard economic growth and shrink people's savings and earnings.

In order of priority, federal revenues should be used: first, to meet the needs of national security; second, to fulfill the legitimate and urgent needs of the nation that cannot be met by the States, local governments or private action; third, to pay down on the national debt in good times; finally, to improve our tax structure.

National security and other essential needs will continue to make enormous demands upon public revenues. It is therefore imperative that we weigh carefully each demand for a new federal expenditure. The federal government should undertake not the most things nor the least things, but the right things.

Achieving this vital purpose demands:

That Congress, in acting on new spending bills, have figures before it showing the cumulative effect of its actions on the total budget.

That spending commitments for future years be clearly listed in each budget, so that the effect of built-in expenditure programs may be recognized and evaluated.

That the President be empowered to veto individual items in authorization and appropriation bills.

That increasing efforts be made to extend business-like methods to government operations, particularly in purchasing and supply activities, and in personnel.

GOVERNMENT ADMINISTRATION

The challenges of our time test the very organization of democracy. They put on trial the capacity of free government to act quickly, wisely, resolutely. To meet these challenges:

The President must continue to be able to reorganize and streamline executive operations to keep the executive branch capable of responding effectively to rapidly changing conditions in both foreign and domestic fields. The Eisenhower-Nixon Administration did so by creating a new Department of Health, Education and Welfare, by establishing the National Aeronautics and Space Agency and the Federal Aviation Agency, and by reorganizations of the Defense Department.

Two top positions should be established to assist the President in, (1) the entire field of National Security and International Affairs, and, (2) Governmental Planning and Management, particularly in domestic affairs.

We must undertake further reorganization of the Defense Department to achieve the most effective unification of defense planning and command.

Improved conflict-of-interest laws should be enacted for vigilant protection of the public interest and to remove deterrents to governmental service by our most able citizens.

The federal government must constantly strengthen its career service and must be truly progressive as an employer. Government employment must be a vocation deserving of high public respect. Common sense demands continued improvements in employment, training and promotion practices based on merit, effective procedures for dealing with employment grievances, and salaries which are comparable to those offered by private employers.

As already practiced by the Republican membership, responsible Policy Committees should be elected by each party in each house of Congress. This would provide a mechanism for meetings of party Congressional leaders with the President when circumstances demand.

Needed federal judgeships, appointed on the basis of the highest qualifications and without limitation to a single political party, should be created to expedite administration of justice in federal courts.

The remarkable growth of the Post Office since 1952 to serve an additional 9 million urban and 1½ million farm families must be continued. The Post Office must be continually improved and placed on a self-sustaining basis. Progressive Republican policies of the past seven years have resulted in reduced costs, decentralization of postal operations, liberal pay, fringe benefits, improved working conditions, streamlined management, and improved service.

Vigorous state and local governments are a vital part of our federal union. The federal government should leave to state and local governments those programs and problems which they can best handle and tax sources adequate to finance them. We must continue to improve liaison between federal, state and local governments. We believe that the federal government, when appropriate, should render significant assistance in dealing with our urgent problems of urban growth and change. No vast new bureaucracy is needed to achieve this objective.

We favor a change in the Electoral College system to give every voter a fair voice in presidential elections.

We condemn bigotry, smear and other unfair tactics in political campaigns. We favor realistic and effective safeguards against diverting non-political funds to partisan political purposes.

Republicans will continue to work for Congressional representation and self-government for the District of Columbia and also support the constitutional amendment granting suffrage in national elections.

We support the right of the Puerto Rican people to achieve statehood, whenever they freely so determine. We support the right of the people of the Virgin Islands to an elected Governor, national representation and suffrage, looking toward eventual statehood, when qualified. We also support the right of the people of Guam to an elected Governor and national representation. These pledges

are meaningful from the Republican leadership under which Alaska and Hawaii have newly entered the Union.

Congress should submit a constitutional amendment providing equal rights for women.

EDUCATION

The rapid pace of international developments serves to re-emphasize dramatically the challenge which generations of Americans will face in the years ahead. We are reminded daily of the crucial importance of strengthening our system of education to prepare our youth for understanding and shaping the powerful emerging forces of the modern world and to permit the fullest possible development of individual capacities and potentialities.

We express our gratefulness and we praise the countless thousands of teachers who have devoted themselves in an inspired way towards the development of our greatest heritage — our own children — the youth of the country.

Education is not a luxury, nor a gift to be bestowed upon ourselves and our children. Education is an investment; our schools cannot become second best. Each person possesses the right to education — it is his birthright in a free Republic.

Primary responsibility for education must remain with the local community and state. The federal government should assist selectively in strengthening education without interfering with full local control of schools. One objective of such federal assistance should be to help equalize educational opportunities. Under the Eisenhower-Nixon Administration, the federal government will spend more than a billion dollars in 1960 to strengthen American education.

We commend the objective of the Republican Administration in sponsoring the National Defense Education Act to stimulate improvement of study and teaching in selected fields at the local level.

Toward the goal of fullest possible educational opportunity for every American, we pledge these actions:

Federal support to the primary and secondary schools by a program of federal aid for school construction — pacing it to the real needs of individual school districts in states and territories, and requiring state approval and participation.

Stimulation of actions designed to update and strengthen vocational education for both youth and adults.

Support of efforts to make adequate library facilities available to all our citizens.

Continued support of programs to strengthen basic research in education; to discover the best methods for helping handicapped, retarded, and gifted children to realize their highest potential.

The federal government can also play a part in stimulating higher education. Constructive action would include:

The federal program to assist in construction of college housing.

Extension of the federal student loan program and graduate fellowship program.

Consideration of means through tax laws to help offset tuition costs.

Continued support of the East-West Center for cultural and technical interchange in Hawaii for the purpose of strengthening our relationship with the peoples of the Pacific world.

Federal matching grants to help states finance the cost of state surveys and inventories of the status and needs of their school systems.

Provision should be made for continuous attention to education at all levels by the creation of a permanent, top-level commission to advise the President and the Secretary of Health, Education and Welfare, constantly striving to focus the interest of each citizen on the quality of our education at every level, from primary through postgraduate, and for every age group from children to adults.

We are aware of the fact that there is a temporary shortage of classrooms for our elementary and secondary schools in a limited number of states. But this shortage, due to the vigilant action of state legislatures and local school boards, is not increasing, but is decreasing.

We shall use our full efforts in all the states of the Union to have these legislatures and school boards augment their present efforts to the end that this temporary shortage may be eliminated and that every child in this country shall have the opportunity to obtain a good education. The respective states as a permanent program can shoulder this long-standing and cherished responsibility easier than can the federal government with its heavy indebtedness.

We believe moreover that any large plan of federal aid to education, such as direct contributions to or grants for teachers salaries can only lead ultimately to federal domination and control of our schools to which we are unalterably opposed.

In the words of President Eisenhower, "Education best fulfills its high purpose when responsibility for education is kept close to the people it serves — when it is rooted in the homes, nurtured in the community and sustained by a rich variety of public, private and individual resources. The bond linking home and school and community — the responsiveness of each to the needs of the others—is a precious asset of American education."

SCIENCE AND TECHNOLOGY

Much of America's future depends upon the inquisitive mind, freely searching nature for ways to conquer disease, poverty and grinding physical demands, and for knowledge of space and the atom.

We Republicans express our profound gratitude to the great scientists and engineers of our country, both in and out of government, for the remarkable progress they have made. Reliable evidence indicates, all areas of scientific knowledge considered, that our country has been, is, and under our system of free inquiry, will continue to be the greatest arsenal and reservoir of effective scientific knowledge in the world.

We pledge our continued leadership in every field of science and technology, earthbound as well as spacial, to assure a citadel of liberty from which the fruits of freedom may be carried to all people.

Our continuing and great national need is for basic research — a wellspring of knowledge and progress. Government must continue to take a responsible role in science to assure that worthwhile endeavors of national significance are not retarded by practical limitations of private and local support. This demands from all Americans the intellectual leadership and understanding so necessary for these creative endeavors and an equal understanding by our scientists and technicians of the needs and hopes of mankind.

We believe the federal roles in research to be in the area of (1) basic research which industry cannot be reasonably expected to pursue, and (2) applied research in fields of prime national concern such as national defense, exploration and use of space, public health, and better common use of all natural resources, both human and physical. We endorse the contracting by government agencies for research and urge allowance for reasonable charges for overhead and management in connection therewith.

The vigor of American science and technology may best be inspired by:

An environment of freedom and public understanding in which intellectual achievement and scientific research may flourish.

A decentralization of research into as many centers of creativity as possible.

The encouragement of colleges and universities, private enterprise, and foundations as a growing source of new ideas and new applications.

Opportunity for scientists and engineers, in and out of government, to pursue their search with utmost aggressiveness.

Continuation of the advisory committee to represent the views of the scientific community to the President and of the Federal Council for Science and Technology to foster coordination in planning and execution.

Continued expansion of the Eisenhower-Nixon Atoms-for-Peace program and a constant striving, backed by scientific advice, for international agreement for peaceful and cooperative exploration and use of space.

## HUMAN NEEDS

The ultimate objective of our free society and of an ever-growing economy is to enable the individual to pursue a life of dignity and to develop his own capacities to his maximum potential.

Government's primary role is to help provide the environment within which the individual can seek his own goals. In some areas this requires federal action to supplement individual, local and state initiative. The Republican Party has acted and will act decisively, compassionately, and with deep human understanding in approaching such problems as those of the aged, the infirm, the mentally ill, and the needy.

This is demonstrated by the significant increase in social security coverage and benefits as a result of recommendations made by the Eisenhower-Nixon Administration. As a result of these recommendations and normal growth, 14 million persons

are receiving benefits today compared to five million in 1952, and benefit payments total $10.3 billion as compared to $2.5 billion in 1952. In addition, there have been increases in payments to those on public assistance, both for their basic needs and for their health and medical care; and a broad expansion in our federal-state program for restoring disabled persons to useful lives — an expansion which has accomplished the rehabilitation of over half a million persons during this Administration.

New needs, however, are constantly arising in our highly complex, interdependent, and urbanized society.

### Older Citizens

To meet the needs of the aging, we pledge:

Expansion of coverage, and liberalization of selected social security benefits on a basis which would maintain the fiscal integrity of the system.

Support of federal-state grant programs to improve health, welfare and rehabilitation services for the handicapped older persons and to improve standards of nursing home care and care and treatment facilities for the chronically and mentally ill.

Federal leadership to encourage policies that will make retirement at a fixed age voluntary and not compulsory.

Support of programs that will persuade and encourage the nation to utilize fully the skills, wisdom and experience of older citizens.

Prompt consideration of recommendations by the White House Conference on Aging called by the President for January, 1961.

### Health Aid

Development of a health program that will provide the aged needing it, on a sound fiscal basis and through a contributory system, protection against burdensome costs of health care. Such a program should:

Provide the beneficiaries with the option of purchasing private health insurance — a vital distinction between our approach and Democratic proposals in that it would encourage commercial carriers and voluntary insurance organizations to continue their efforts to develop sound coverage plans for the senior population.

Protect the personal relationship of patient and physician.

Include state participation.

For the needs which individuals of all age groups cannot meet by themselves, we propose:

Removing the arbitrary 50-year age requirement under the disability insurance program while amending the law also to provide incentives for rehabilitated persons to return to useful work.

A single, federal assistance grant to each state for aid to needy persons rather than dividing such grants into specific categories.

A strengthened federal-state program to rehabilitate the estimated 200,000 persons who annually could become independent after proper medical services and occupational training.

A new federal-state program, for handicapped persons completely dependent on others, to help them meet their needs for personal care.

## Juvenile Delinquency

The Federal Government can and should help state and local communities combat juvenile delinquency by inaugurating a grant program for research, demonstration, and training projects and by placing greater emphasis on strengthening family life in all welfare programs for which it shares responsibility.

## Veterans

We believe that military service in the defense of our Republic against aggressors who have sought to destroy the freedom and dignity of man imposes upon the nation a special responsibility to those who have served. To meet this responsibility, we pledge:

Continuance of the Veterans Administration as an independent agency.

The highest possible standard of medical care with increasing emphasis on rehabilitation.

## Indian Affairs

As recently as 1953, thirty per cent of Indian school-age children were unable to obtain an education. Through Republican efforts, this fall, for the first time in history, every eligible Indian child will be able to attend an elementary school. Having accomplished this, we will now accelerate our efforts to open up both secondary and higher education opportunities for every qualified Indian youth.

As a result of a stepped-up health program there has been a marked decrease in death rates from tuberculosis and in the infant mortality rate. Also substantial progress has been made in the modernization of health facilities. We pledge continued progress in this area.

We are opposed to precipitous termination of the federal Indian trusteeship responsibility, and pledge not to support any termination plan for any tribe which has not approved such action.

## Housing

Despite noteworthy accomplishments, stubborn and deep-seated problems stand in the way of achieving the national objective of a decent home in a suitable environment for every American. Recognizing that the federal government must help provide the economic climate and incentives which make this objective obtainable, the Republican Party will vigorously support the following steps, all designed to supplement and not supplant private initiative.

Continued effort to clear slums, and promote rebuilding, rehabilitation, and conservation of our cities.

New programs to stimulate development of specialized types of housing, such as those for the elderly and for nursing homes.

A program of research and demonstration aimed at finding ways to reduce housing costs, including support of efforts to modernize and improve local building codes.

Adequate authority for the federal housing agencies to assist the flow of mortgage credit into private housing, with emphasis on homes for middle- and lower-income families and including assistance in urban residential areas.

A stepped-up program to assist in urban planning, designed to assure far-sighted and wise use of land and to coordinate mass transportation and other vital facilities in our metropolitan areas.

## Health

There has been a five-fold increase in government-assisted medical research during the last six years. We pledge:

Continued federal support for a sound research program aimed at both the prevention and cure of diseases, and intensified efforts to secure prompt and effective application of the results of research. This will include emphasis on mental illness.

Support of international health research programs.

We face serious personnel shortages in the health and medical fields. We pledge:

Federal help in new programs to build schools of medicine, dentistry, and public health and nursing, and financial aid to students in those fields.

We are confronted with major problems in the field of environmental health. We pledge:

Strengthened federal enforcement powers in combatting water pollution and additional resources for research and demonstration projects. Federal grants for the construction of waste disposal plants should be made only when they make an identifiable contribution to clearing up polluted streams.

Federal authority to identify, after appropriate hearings, air pollution problems and to recommend proposed solutions.

Additional resources for research and training in the field of radiological medicine.

### Protection of Consumers

In safeguarding the health of the nation the Eisenhower-Nixon Administration's initiative has resulted in doubling the resources of the Food and Drug Administration and in giving it new legal weapons. More progress has been made during this period in protecting consumers against harmful food, drugs, and cosmetics than in any other time in our history. We will continue to give strong support to this consumer-protection program.

### Civil Rights

This nation was created to give expression, validity and purpose to our spiritual heritage — the supreme worth of the individual. In such a nation — a nation dedicated to the proposition that all men are created equal — racial discrimination has no place. It can hardly be reconciled with a Constitution that guarantees equal protection under law to all persons. In a deeper sense, too, it is immoral and unjust. As to those matters within reach of political action and leadership, we pledge ourselves unreservedly to its eradication.

Equality under law promises more than the equal right to vote and transcends mere relief from discrimination by government. It becomes a reality only when all persons have equal opportunity, without distinction of race, religion, color or national origin, to acquire the essentials of life — housing, education and employment. The Republican Party — the party of Abraham Lincoln — from its very beginning has striven to make this promise a reality. It is today, as it was then, unequivocally dedicated to making the greatest amount of progress toward the objective.

We recognize that discrimination is not a problem localized in one area of the country, but rather a problem that must be faced by North and South alike. Nor is discrimination confined to the discrimination against Negroes. Discrimination in many, if not all, areas of the country on the basis of creed or national origin is equally insidious. Further we recognize that in many communities in which a century of custom and tradition must be overcome heartening and commendable progress has been made.

The Republican Party is proud of the civil rights record of the Eisenhower Administration. More progress has been made during the past eight years than in the preceding 80 years. We acted promptly to end discrimination in our nation's capital. Vigorous executive action was taken to complete swiftly the desegregation of the armed forces, veterans' hospitals, navy yards, and other federal establishments.

We supported the position of the Negro school children before the Supreme Court. We believe the Supreme Court school decision should be carried out in accordance with the mandate of the Court.

Although the Democratic-controlled Congress watered them down, the Republican Administration's recommendations resulted in significant and effective civil rights legislation in both 1957 and 1960 — the first civil rights statutes to be passed in more than 80 years.

Hundreds of Negroes have already been registered to vote as a result of Department of Justice action, some in counties where Negroes did not vote before. The new law will soon make it possible for thousands and thousands of Negroes previously disenfranchised to vote.

By executive order, a committee for the elimination of discrimination in government employment has been reestablished with broadened authority. Today, nearly one-fourth of all federal employees are Negro.

The President's Committee on Government Contracts, under the chairmanship of Vice President Nixon, has become an impressive force for the elimination of discriminatory employment practices of private companies that do business with the government.

Other important achievements include initial steps toward the elimination of segregation in federally-aided housing; the establishment of the Civil Rights Division of the Department of Justice, which enforces federal civil rights laws; and the appointment of the bi-partisan Civil Rights Commission, which has prepared a significant report that lays the groundwork for further legislative action and progress.

The Republican record is a record of progress — not merely promises. Nevertheless, we recognize that much remains to be done.

Each of the following pledges is practical and within realistic reach of accomplishment. They are serious — not cynical — pledges made to result in maximum progress.

1. *Voting.* We pledge:

Continued vigorous enforcement of the civil rights laws to guarantee the right to vote to all citizens in all areas of the country.

Legislation to provide that the completion of six primary grades in a state accredited school is conclusive evidence of literacy for voting purposes.

2. *Public Schools.* We pledge:

The Department of Justice will continue its vigorous support of court orders for school desegregation. Desegregation suits now pending involve at least 39 school districts. Those suits and others already concluded will affect most major cities in which school segregation is being practiced.

It will use the new authority provided by the Civil Rights Act of 1960 to prevent obstruction of court orders.

We will propose legislation to authorize the Attorney General to bring actions for school desegregation in the name of the United States in appropriate cases, as when economic coercion or threat of physical harm is used to deter persons from going to court to establish their rights.

Our continuing support of the President's proposal, to extend federal aid and technical assistance to schools which in good faith attempted to desegregate.

We oppose the pretense of fixing a target date 3 years from now for the mere submission of plans for school desegregation. Slow-moving school districts would construe it as a three-year moratorium during which progress would cease, postponing until 1963 the legal process to enforce compliance. We believe that each of the pending court actions should proceed as the Supreme Court has directed and that in no district should there be any such delay.

3. *Employment.* We pledge:

Continued support for legislation to establish a Commission on Equal Job Opportunity to make permanent and to expand with legislative backing the excellent work being performed by the President's Committee on Government Contracts.

Appropriate legislation to end the discriminatory membership practices of some labor union locals, unless such practices are eradicated promptly by the labor unions themselves.

Use of the full-scale review of existing state laws, and of prior proposals for federal legislation, to eliminate discrimination in employment now being conducted by the Civil Rights Commission, for guidance in our objective of developing a Federal-State program in the employment area.

Special consideration of training programs aimed at developing the skills of those now working in marginal agricultural employment so that they can obtain employment in industry, notably in the new industries moving into the South.

4. *Housing.* We pledge:

Action to prohibit discrimination in housing constructed with the aid of federal subsidies.

5. *Public Facilities and Services.* We pledge:

Removal of any vestige of discrimination in the operation of federal facilities or procedures which may at any time be found.

Opposition to the use of federal funds for the construction of segregated community facilities.

Action to ensure that public transportation and other government authorized services shall be free from segregation.

6. *Legislative Procedure.* We pledge:

Our best efforts to change present Rule 22 of the Senate and other appropriate Congressional procedures that often make unattainable proper legislative implementation of constitutional guarantees.

We reaffirm the constitutional right to peaceable assembly to protest discrimination in private business establishments. We applaud the action of the businessmen who have abandoned discriminatory practices in retail establishments, and we urge others to follow their example.

Finally we recognize that civil rights is a responsibility not only of states and localities; it is a national problem and a national responsibility. The federal government should take the initiative in promoting inter-group conferences among those who, in their communities, are earnestly seeking solutions of the complex problems of desegregation — to the end that closed channels of communication may be opened, tensions eased, and a cooperative solution of local problems may be sought.

In summary, we pledge the full use of the power, resources and leadership of the federal government to eliminate discrimination based on race, color, religion or national origin and to encourage understanding and good will among all races and creeds.

## IMMIGRATION

Immigration has historically been a great factor in the growth of the United States, not only in numbers but in the enrichment of ideas that immigrants have brought with them. This Republican Administration has given refuge to over 32,000 victims of Communist tyranny from Hungary, ended needless delay in processing applications for naturalization, and has urged other enlightened legislation to liberalize existing restrictions.

Immigration has been reduced to the point where it does not provide the stimulus to growth that it should, nor are we fulfilling our obligation as a haven for the oppressed. Republican conscience and Republican policy require that:

The annual number of immigrants we accept be at least doubled.

Obsolete immigration laws be amended by abandoning the outdated 1920 census data as a base and substituting the 1960 census.

The guidelines of our immigration policy be based upon judgment of the individual merit of each applicant for admission and citizenship.

## CONCLUSION

We have set forth the program of the Republican Party for the government of the United States. We have written a Party document, as is our duty, but we have tried to refrain from writing a merely partisan document. We have no wish to exaggerate differences between ourselves and the Democratic Party; nor can we, in conscience, obscure the differences that do exist. We believe that the Republican program is based upon a sounder understanding of the action and scope of government. There are many things a free government cannot do for its people as well as they can do them for themselves. There are some things no government should promise or attempt to do. The functions of government are so great as to bear no needless enlargement. We limit our proposals and our pledges to those areas for which the government of a great republic can reasonably be made responsible. To the best of our ability we have avoided advocating measures that would go against the grain of a free people.

The history and composition of the Republican Party make it the natural instrument for eradicating the injustice and discrimination in this country. We Republicans are fortunate in being able to contend against these evils, without having to contend against each other for the principle.

We believe that we see, so far as men can see through the obscurity of time and trouble, the prudent course for the nation in its hour of trial. The Soviet Union has created another of the new situations of peril which has been the Communist record from the beginning and will continue to be until our strategy for victory has succeeded. The speed of technological change makes it imperative that we measure the new situations by their special requirements and accelerate as appropriate our efforts in every direction, economic and military and political to deal with them.

As rapidly as we perfect the new generations of weapons we must arm ourselves effectively and without delay. In this respect the nation stands now at one of the new points of departure. We must never allow our technology, particularly in nuclear and propulsion fields, to lag for any reason until such time as we have dependable and honest safeguards of inspection and control. We must take steps at once to secure our position in this regard and at the same time we must intensify our efforts to develop better safeguards in the field of disarmament.

The free nations of the world must ever be rallied to the cause and be encouraged to join together in more effective alliances and unions strong enough to meet all challenges and sustain the common effort. It is urgent that we innovate to keep the initiative for our free cause.

We offer toil and sweat, to ward off blood and tears. We advocate an immovable resistance against every Communist aggression. We argue for a military might commensurate with our universal tasks. We end by declaring our faith in the Republic and in its people, and in the deathless principles of right from which it draws its moral force.

## Socialist Platform 1960

INTRODUCTION

### The Dilemma of Modern Man

Never have Americans talked more about the importance of the private citizen; never has he felt more powerless in the face of events.

We possess the tools to build a world of peace and prosperity, and use them instead to engage in a deadly arms race. We possess the power to abolish poverty, yet unemployment continues. We possess the time to devote ourselves to great causes, but can find nothing to believe in.

From earliest schooldays to the age of retirement, on the job and at home and in our use of leisure time, when we buy and when we vote, we are subjected to a barrage of commercial, political, and social hucksterism. Our lives are shaped by public and private bureaucracies, self-perpetuating and outside our immediate control. Leaders in every field, who should be our servants, see us not as people but as *things* to be lied to, prodded, and manipulated into acquiescence. We live in a rigged society, in that the whole economy depends upon the manufacture of consent, *our* consent — to planned obsolescence, to tailfins instead of schools, to cold war and the armaments race. We live frustrated lives, because we are allowed to express our yearnings only through commercially-successful channels. We live trammelled lives, because dissent is stifled. We live cheap lives, because we are taught to value ourselves cheaply.

If we are to be free, we must discover new patterns for our lives. And then we must live according to those patterns, in the midst of a hostile society, until we have created nothing less than a new social order, a society in which the commanding value is the infinite preciousness of the human spirit and of every single man, woman, and child.

For man must master society instead of being mastered by it. This is the most fundamental statement of the socialist goal.

### The Role of the Socialist Party

There are many ways in which free men can live free lives within a rigged society; but if their lives are to have social meaning beyond an immediate circle of friends, they need to join together and work for change in a way that is politically meaningful. It is this need which the Socialist Party is designed to meet. For the SP-SDF seeks to bring together, and give political expression to, the entire spectrum of democratic dissent in America. It gives unity, coherence, and practical purpose to what would otherwise be inchoate strivings.

Since the 1930's the two old parties have produced virtually no progressive social legislation. As productivity has grown, so have slums; as medical research has advanced, the ability of ordinary people to pay for medical care has regressed; as our standard of living has risen, fifty million Americans have continued to dwell in poverty. The weapons of a new warfare threaten our very lives, and we are offered only the insane satisfaction of knowing that two minutes after we die, so will our enemies. We stand condemned before the world and in our own hearts for our inability to achieve the racial justice that most of us so much desire. Our society is deadlocked and frustration is our predominant feeling in every area of life; and the primary source of our political frustration is a party alignment that cannot reflect the will of the people. A coalition of Northern Republicans and Southern Democrats thwarts the wishes of the majority, and will continue to do so until there is a political realignment in this country.

The potential for political change exists. It is found in the millions of trade unionists, farmers, Negroes, liberals, lovers of peace, who together form the bulk of the populace. And the prospect for change moves closer, for there are stirrings in the land: the reunited labor movement, the civil rights movement, the growing protest against nuclear weapons. It is to our fellow-citizens engaged with us in these activities that we especially direct this platform, for we share their aspirations and believe that they share ours. We offer them a vision of a new society, a vision that gives depth and meaning to the things that we and they are doing now.

### The Socialist Vision

Our goal is a new and truly democratic society in the United States, a society in which human rights come before property rights. We are pledged to building and maintaining this new society by democratic means: For just as there can be no meaningful and enduring freedom without socialism, so there can be no true socialism without freedom.

Socialists call for social ownership and democratic control of the commanding heights of industry, not as an end in itself, but as a step in the creation of a truly human society in which all economic and class barriers to individual freedom have been removed. For the enduring ethical values which now are falteringly applied to our political institutions are absent most conspicuously in our economic institutions, and this absence affects the whole quality of our lives. If we are to lead full lives a prerequisite is that production be democratically planned for the benefit of all.

We do *not* propose totalitarian nationalization as under Communism. We oppose it because in theory it is oriented toward the welfare of posterity, at the expense of the welfare and even the human dignity of the present generation; and because in practice it means that the economy is run for the benefit of the bureaucratic class that controls the state. Neither do we propose simply nationalization with political democracy; for under such a system the people participate only at election time in the decisions that control their lives. We propose rather a society of free, continuing, and democratic *participation* — through political parties in the determination of basic economic and social and political policy for the nation; through shop councils, consumer cooperatives, neighborhood associations, and all the other organs of community in the decisions of daily life; through decentralized agencies for the management of each industry by those most affected by it; through encouragement of the maximum expression of individual creativity.

We propose a society in which democratic participation in economic and political life will set us free to attack and conquer war, racial antagonism, hunger, disease, poverty, and oppression. We propose a nation which can take its place in a World Federation of Cooperative Commonwealths, to the end that all men may lead lives that are rich and free. We propose a world in which man is the measure of all things.

### FOREIGN POLICY

The end of the old colonialisms, the rise of new nations, the explosion of populations without birth control, the drive of dictatorial Communism — these are taking place in our anarchic world of absolute national states grossly unequal in wealth and power. In this situation men by their own scientific and technological genius have made war, immemorially the grim arbiter of their disputes, unusable for any purpose but annihilation of their civilization if not of their race. If there are to be survivors of a war inevitably to be fought with chemical, bacteriological, and nuclear weapons, liberty will not be among them. The supreme task of our time is the avoidance of war in the settlement of national conflict.

This would be our supreme task even if there had not been a Communist imperialist drive for power. All the more so, then, when this drive against the politically democratic but capitalist nations of the West has resulted in the Cold War and the arms race — clearly the outstanding fact affecting American foreign policy.

The present conflict has often been presented as ideological. To the Western nations, it is the struggle of democracy against totalitarianism; to the Communists, it is a contest between "socialism" and "capitalism." Yet beneath these descriptions exists a more sordid reality of two rival alliances each seeking economic, social, and political power. In the Soviet Union, the military bureaucracy and, doubtless, other elements, have acquired a stake in the continuation of a cold war which brings them prestige and power. Likewise in the United States the military, the great corporations, and many scientists have acquired a vital material interest in the arms race. For this reason the economics of disarmament must be a major concern of socialist planning.

No political solution can be achieved by opposing Communist imperialism with free-enterprise capitalism. Democracy is debased when Soviet satellites are called "People's Democracies"; freedom is debased when the word "free" is applied to any despot allied to the West, when it is used to cover up the search for areas of exploitation. Saudi Arabia and Spain are cases in point. As this platform is written, Cuba is going through a social revolution which the Communists are trying to exploit, though they were not part of the revolutionary movement itself; South Korea and Turkey have overthrown native dictators, only yesterday supported by the United States, and the movements which accomplished this were hardly Communist.

The situation cries out for political, economic, and moral support by the United States of *all* struggles for self-determination, of *all* efforts of people everywhere to free themselves from exploitation. If we wish the friendship of those who seek freedom, we must cease making alliances of expediency with tyrannous regimes; we must cease our dogmatic espousal of a "capitalism" which other nations cannot understand, could not use, and do not want. We must learn to support the demand of underdeveloped countries for independence, and we must support them *on their terms*. We must make their new independence meaningful by underwriting democratic paths to industrialization. Our answer to Mao's dictatorship cannot be Chiang's dictatorship; rather, it must be a commitment to aid in the creation of democratic, modern societies throughout the ex-colonial world.

A socialist foreign policy is wholly inconsistent with indefinite continuation of the Cold War and the arms race. In that race neither national security nor human freedom can be achieved. At most balance of terror can give only a little time for precarious peace behind the so-called shield of deterrence. Sooner or later this poor protection will be shattered by accident, by the mistakes of fallible men, or by the passions of men and nations mad for power. And while the arms race goes on the nations waging it will inevitably be caught in the toils of a garrison state, whose assumed needs will increasingly dictate their economy and override their supposedly inalienable rights as private citizens.

Prevention of war obviously requires the nations to dispossess themselves of the terrible weapons which they now frantically seek to make more terrible. We can no more trust ourselves with H-bombs, missiles, chemical and bacteriological weapons, than we can trust kindergarten children with rifles and bayonets. Disarmament is a necessity. But not mere disarmament without a conscious provision of law as an alternative to war and conscious dedication to the universal conquest of bitter poverty, a dedication which in our generation must be the moral equivalent of war. Recognition of these facts not only in words but in action must lie — as it does not today — at the basis of our foreign policy.

The life-line to peace must then be braided of four strands —

*Disarmament*

Universal disarmament down to a police level for maintaining order within nations and between nations. Such disarmament may be achieved by stages; but to be genuine and enduring, it must rapidly become universal and total. It must be begun by a treaty for ending tests of atomic weapons above or below ground. The fact that as yet all conceivable underground tests cannot be detected does not justify failure to reach an agreement now nearly arrived at. No risk is as great as a continuance of tests adding inevitably to the hazards of atomic fallout and inviting nation after nation to join the nuclear club, thereby tremendously increasing the danger of war by accident or design.

If no agreement should be reached at Geneva, the Socialist Party will call for the immediate unilateral cessation of nuclear weapons production and testing by this government. We will propose that U.N. teams be invited to establish monitoring stations on our territory for the purpose of proving to the world the reality of our action. We would then be in a sound position to call upon the Soviet Union to take similar action. Present U.S. nuclear power is such that the unilateral action we outline would not impair our security but would, on the contrary, break the present stalemate and create a new possibility — of turning the arms race into a disarmament race.

Successful progress in disarmament requires supranational authority not only for verification and inspection but for progressively assuring peace by substituting law for war. Hence our second essential:

### Strengthening the United Nations

The strengthening of the United Nations and the creation or strengthening of regional federations. Such regional federations are peculiarly necessary to the healthy economy of the emerging nations of Africa. Our present imperfect U.N. has proved its value, but cannot adequately serve the great cause of peace without some revision of its charter and some provision for an international police force subject only to it, adequate to deal with brushfire wars before they kindle the great conflagration. The appeal to law instead of war must be strengthened by repeal of the Connolly reservations under which the United States is the judge of the cases involving it that it will allow to go to the World Court.

### Disengagement

Progressive disengagement from imperfectly understood but probably binding commitments which cannot be fulfilled without war. But with this must go friendly cooperation for peace. This means, among other things, the progressive but rapid termination of agreements providing for American military bases on foreign soil; a principle which should be urged on every nation.

Progress toward either disarmament or disengagement requires them to go hand in hand. Disarmament is not possible without disengagement, nor disengagement without disarmament. This principle requires special and immediate application —

In pressing our ally, France, for negotiated peace fully recognizing the principle of self-determination in Algeria.

In giving moral and economic support to peoples emerging from colonialism or domestic tyranny and in giving moral and political support to struggles of still-subject peoples for liberty and self-determination in the "free world" as well as in the Communist world. This means an end of all aid to Franco, Trujillo, or any other despot. It means opposing racism and apartheid in South Africa, in particular by ending any possible subsidy to that government through unrestricted purchase of its gold. It means that our proposals for European disengagement must have as one of their objectives the self-determination of the Russian-dominated countries in Eastern Europe.

In beginning at once negotiation looking to recognition of the effective government of China, the most populous nation on earth. It is admitted by our nation's leaders that the absolutely essential ending of tests of nuclear weapons must require Communist China's adherence to any agreement. Yet we contemplate a situation in which we will say, "We don't recognize you, but sign on the dotted line." Sooner or later, we shall either get the real China into the U.N. or fight her. We Americans, under both Democratic and Republican governments, compounded our folly in dealing with China by insisting that Chiang, ingloriously driven out of China to an island in which he has not dared commit his rule to popular election, represents the whole nation. He represents only the American Seventh Fleet. We are obligated not to throw Chiang and the people of Taiwan into the arms of the vengeful Communist government. But they must be protected under an agreement which provides self-determination for the people of Taiwan.

In extending the Austrian principle of demilitarization into Central Europe by phased withdrawal of military forces on both sides. In a disarmed Central Europe, West Berlin can be guaranteed against imposed Communist rule and the Germans left to work out their own reunification. The SP-SDF is unalterably opposed to the rearmament of a united or divided Germany.

In seeking to get Soviet agreement to support U.N. action looking toward disarmament in the Middle East and a guarantee of any and all nations in it against military aggression or any attempt to change boundaries by force. The U.S. should be a party to a solution of the Arab refugee problem with the cooperation of the U.N., Israel, and the Arab nations.

### War Against Poverty

Cooperative struggle against the bitter poverty in which 70 per cent of the world's people live — this at a time when all the nations, poor and rich, spend together $100 billion annually on the arms race. Less than one-third that amount, properly spent, might conquer world poverty in one or two generations.

Loans and grants to industrial and agricultural projects should be administered by the U.N. or its agencies. The SP-SDF heartily support the suggestion of the Socialist International, to which it belongs, that each nation pay at least 1 per cent of its national income into a general fund out of which grants be made according to need. So long as any such aid must be given on a bilateral basis the Socialist Party insists that it be genuinely economic, not military.

Implementation of the principles we have set forth, in a world where the United States has neither the power nor the wisdom to play Almighty God, will necessarily depend somewhat on the stream of events and the opinions and actions of other nations. But the purpose and the general direction outlined in this statement must be the fixed policy of the United States in its leadership for peace with freedom and justice.

DOMESTIC AFFAIRS

THE ECONOMY

American capitalism today is far different from what it was even a generation ago. It has moved in the direction of a welfare state. It has acquired a subsidized sector, mainly devoted to war spending, which affects a major portion of the gross national product. It is characterized by a growing concentration of corporate wealth, by intervention of the state in many areas of economic life, by private, public, and military bureaucracies which are increasingly powerful and all-pervasive.

Some of these changes are the result of popular demands for reforms which Socialists pioneered: social security, minimum wage laws, unemployment insurance, child labor laws, and so on.

Some of these changes are part of the drift toward a bureaucratized, centralized capitalism, more impersonal and powerful than ever before.

Some of these changes have been brought about by the Cold War. They point toward a garrison state, in which personal liberties are increasingly stifled and the nation is increasingly mobilized around one overriding purpose, the need to be prepared at all times for total war.

Contrary to popular myth, Socialists do not favor "big government." However, where the Federal government is the only institution capable of fairly and efficiently administering a social pro-

gram, we do not dogmatically shy away from using it. But we oppose all unnecessary government bureaucracy, and seek always to find alternative ways of doing things, ways based on direct participation by the citizenry. We believe bureaucracy is the result less of carefully-considered planning, than of hasty and improvised methods of meeting emergencies which arise precisely because of lack of planning. Wherever possible we advocate a maximum of decentralized control under national standards.

It is undeniable that American capitalism has proved resourceful beyond the expectation of Socialists in the past. But the theory that this society has conquered all the fundamental problems of the old capitalism is patently false.

Thus, the enormous growth of American productivity has meant more money to go around and has concealed glaring inequality in the *division* of wealth. Yet it is a fact that the lower half of our population receives a smaller percentage of the total money income now than it did in 1910.

Thus, we are seriously told that America has banished economic want and insecurity — when one family in ten receives an annual income of less than $1,000 a year, and more than two families in ten have less than $2,000. According to the most recent statistics of the Joint Economic Committee of Congress, well over twenty million Americans live below the most minimal standard of life; if the definition of adequacy is the one proposed by the AFL-CIO, this figure rises to over fifty million, and includes semi-skilled workers, the aged, residents of economically-depressed areas, members of minority groups, poor farmers and farm workers.

The American economy in the post-war period has been periodically wracked by crises of "overproduction" — that is, in a nation and a world that desperately needs goods, there is a glut of those items which are most profitable. In 1949, 1954, and 1958, millions of American workers were thrown out of work. Each "recovery" has seen the definition of "normal" unemployment increase, until now America accepts four million jobless as consonant with prosperity.

These glaring inequities can be corrected only by a society which allocates its resources on the basis of need rather than of profit. That is basic to the socialist program.

In the absence of such a society, here and now socialists join with trade unionists and liberals in demanding immediate action —

For a higher minimum wage, from which farm labor must not be excluded;

For an integrated national campaign against poverty, with massive Federal aid to housing, community services, and education;

For a program of public investment as an anti-recession measure;

For an Area Redevelopment Bill to provide aid for distressed sections of the nation — a Point Four for our own underdeveloped regions;

For a national resources policy which will extend the program which proved itself in the Tennessee Valley Authority to other areas of the country, such as the Columbia River Valley and the Missouri River Valley;

For socialization of the oil industry on terms that give due regard to the needs and interests of a world peculiarly dependent upon oil. Today this industry is a power unto itself influencing domestic and foreign policy. Socialization of the oil industry must include social ownership of the oil fields.

For socialization of basic means of transportation. We deplore and oppose the tendency to subsidize railroad passenger traffic while allowing private operators to reap the profits from freight traffic.

For overhauling our confused system of taxation, imposing withholding taxes on dividends, ending favoritism to the oil industry, regulating exemptions on expense accounts, and imposing a tax for the recovery of socially-created rental values of land. We oppose general sales taxes, which hit low-income families the hardest.

In making these demands, we note that the one piece of important social legislation passed since World War II, the Employment Act of 1946, is hardly more than a general statement of good intentions. In the post-war recessions, that Act failed to commit the Executive to any specific action, and the battle for meaningful remedies had to be fought anew each time in Congress. Therefore, we stand for a new law which will automatically require Executive action whenever unemployment rises: Federal spending for worthwhile social purposes, progressive tax relief for the broad mass of consumers, a government banking and finance policy to stimulate maximum investment, and so on.

We note further that these are no more than the things which need to be done *first* and that their effect will be nullified unless they are followed by further legislation in the same direction, a direction which we believe must lead to a democratic socialist society. In the following sections, therefore, we spell out in detail some of the further changes we feel are most necessary in the immediate future.

SOCIAL WELFARE

The ranks of the chronically poor are swelled constantly by those who are rendered penniless by sickness, sudden unemployment, and other forms of personal disaster. Whether poverty is individual or general, in a country as wealthy as ours it is unnecessary, and therefore a reproach to all of us. We propose Federal action to guarantee to every family (1) a decent minimum standard of living and (2) maximum protection against economic mischance. As immediate steps toward this goal, we offer the following proposals:

*Unemployment*

Unemployment compensation must be made available to all citizens who cannot find work, for as long as they remain unemployed. It should amount to two-thirds of normal income. The Federal government must supplement compensation payments (1) by creating jobs, where unemployment is general; (2) by introducing new industry into depressed areas, or relocating the unemployed where this cannot be done; (3) by retraining those displaced by technological change.

*Disability*

Disabled persons must be trained so far as possible to perform useful work, with benefits ranging up to two-thirds of normal income for the totally disabled. A special no-interest loan fund must be made available to disabled persons who wish to build new lives as small businessmen. Persons handicapped from childhood must be given scholarships or job training so far as it can benfit them, and should receive pensions on the basis of need to whatever degree is necessary for a decent standard of living. All payments must be pegged to the cost-of-living index.

*Social Security*

Social Security should not be, as it is today, merely a palliative measure designed to supplement the savings of retired citizens. It must be extended to become a true national pension plan, designed to supply the full economic security necessary for a dignified and fruitful old age. Payments must be much higher than they are now, must be pegged to the cost-of-living index, and must be available to all persons of appropriate age regardless of their prior contributions in taxes. Women should receive benefits at age 60; maternal and child services must be greatly expanded; family allowances must be made for children of low-income families. Orphan beneficiaries, for whom payments now lapse when they reach age 18, must have access to a special fund for college scholarships or for training for a trade.

## Medical Care

We support, as a step in the right direction, current efforts to give medical benefits to old people, although we deplore the inadequacy of this approach to a proper program of socialized medicine. At very least, the programs now being considered should provide coverage for medical, dental, psychiatric, and out-of-hospital care, as well as surgical fees and hospitalization; coverage should not be limited as to time.

We propose a National Health Service for the United States which will provide every man, woman, and child in this country with the best available medical care. We regard it as a scandal that health care in America is still run on the antiquated, nineteenth-century basis of cash and carry. Nations whose resources are much less than those of America have proved that socialized medicine is the way to safeguard national health while retaining a maximum of individual freedom in the doctor-patient relationship. The American people should not be denied the benefits which the citizens of Britain, Scandinavia, and other countries enjoy.

Under a program of socialized medicine, the individual is free to choose the doctor and the type of medical care he desires. Medical cooperatives should be encouraged through tax incentives and other measures; these are the plans in which a group of consumers build a clinic and hire physicians on a salary basis to give them complete medical care. Fee-for-service medicine would continue so long as the people in a given community wanted it, with the health service paying the cost.

Administration of the medical program would be local and democratically responsible to the public, with the Federal government's role limited to maintaining standards and underwriting costs.

We have socialized the protection of the citizenry from crime and fire. Now we must socialize the protection of life itself.

We favor drastic government action in support of the costs of medical education. It must be made possible for any qualified person to become a doctor so long as there is a shortage of doctors, and to live a decent life during the many years of medical and specialist training. We favor subsidy of the costs of training nurses and medical technologists. We favor a decent wage scale for lower-echelon hospital employees, and endorse their right to form unions. We support, and favor extension of, present government hospital-building programs; every community should possess a medical center with emergency-ward and nursing-home facilities.

Prescribed drugs should be available to all citizens without cost. Pharmaceutical companies should have their profits held down to a reasonable level, and an independent government corporation should enter and become a major competitive entity in the pharmaceutical industry. At the same time the drug companies should continue to receive financial incentives for genuine pharmaceutical research. The government itself should engage much more heavily in pharmaceutical and medical research.

## Other Reforms

Our social services must be expanded and strengthened to provide for more adequate treatment and rehabilitation of the victims of alcoholism and narcotic addiction. They should be strengthened to deal more adequately with mental illness and the ravages of community and family deterioration.

It cannot be expected that our competitive and segregated society will effectively prevent juvenile delinquency. However, we urge the immediate provision of ample Federal financial aid for carefully-prepared projects for preventing and treating juvenile delinquency.

We urge the institution of a full-scale program for rehabilitation of criminals as well as for eradication of the societal and environmental causes of criminal behavior. We are opposed to the punitive rather than the rehabilitative approach to criminal jurisprudence, and consequently we regard capital punishment as a grim and uncivilized vestige of the past. We pledge ourselves to work for its eradication.

## Administration of Social Services

Social services are not charity, but a right of all members of the human family. They must be administered with courtesy and dignity, and in a manner that permits recipients to retain their self-respect.

### LABOR

As Socialists, we support the labor movement and view it as the greatest single mass basis for democratic change in America. Its efforts to raise the living standards of working people, and enlarge their role in society, are a basic contribution to our freedom.

In recent years sectors of the American labor movement have become bureaucratic and have lost much of the social idealism that sparked labor's great advances in the past. We believe the solution to this problem must come from within the labor movement itself. Therefore we join with all those unionists who fight corruption and undemocratic bureaucracy within their unions. The fundamental solution to the problems of the labor movement will come only with a revival of social and political consciousness on all levels within the trade unions.

We opposed the Taft-Hartley law in the past; we oppose the Landrum-Griffin law today. The latter is a hastily-assembled jumble of reform measures and reactionary attacks upon America's organized workers. Both were aimed at weakening the power of organized labor; whereas Socialists seek to strengthen and extend unionism in America.

We believe that legislation has a positive role to play in helping the democratic forces within the American labor movement. The impact of the law should be in the direction of encouraging voluntary union creation of democratic structures, with government intervention confined to the minority of crooked and undemocratic unions. Therefore we propose a "reserved powers" approach. Where an international union is found to have voluntarily established adequate guarantees for rights designated in a national labor policy, it should be free

of any legal obligations which might be applied to unions refusing to take such steps on their own. In the absence of appropriate action by the union, the law should require dsclosure of union funds (and of labor relations expenditures by management); it should set limits upon trusteeship; it should provide for the right of appeal to the courts where the union appeals process is inordinately prolonged; it should guarantee free elections within the unions.

We particularly hail the United Automobile Workers for its institution of a Public Review Board providing an impartial system of appeal for union members. We believe that the review-board principle, if adopted by the rest of the labor movement, can be a major aid in strengthening democratic unionism and an unanswerable argument to those reactionaries who use union abuses as a cover for labor-wrecking laws.

We advocate the repeal of "right-to-work" laws.

We uphold the right of government employees to organize into unions and to strike.

Unionists have long opposed speed-up, stretchout, and other inhuman techniques which management uses to increase its profits. Socialists support, of course, all union measures taken to *defend* the worker against the inhumanity of the machine and management. But we also propose that the labor movement consider a positive program on this issue. We suggest that unionists begin to raise questions of machine design in collective bargaining, and that the power of organized workers be turned toward fostering the human factor in industrial engineering. Other useful proposals include the rotation of work, the "self-pacing" of the work process in the shop, and so on; and we consider it vital that the union movement make the character of the work process an important factor in its thinking and actions.

### CIVIL RIGHTS AND CIVIL LIBERTIES

## Negro Struggle for Freedom

The most dynamic single social struggle in the United States today is the magnificent movement of America's Negroes and their white allies for civil rights. Socialists have always been wholeheartedly part of this struggle.

The Negro in America is doubly the victim of oppression. As a member of a racial minority, he suffers the special indignity of segregation. And as a worker, he is hired last and fired first, given the dirtiest and lowest-paid jobs, is herded into the most miserable of slums. Yet in this fact of double oppression lies a great hope: the natural alliance of the Negroes, in their struggle for civil rights, and the labor movement in its battle against exploitation.

In May 1954 the great legal struggle of the National Association for the Advancement of Colored People brought about the historic decision on school desegregation. Since then the racists have responded with a variety of tactics: token integration, the threat of a "century of litigation," outright refusal to comply with the Court's decision, economic pressure, and direct violence.

The legal battle remains important, but now the civil rights movement has entered a new stage. The generalties of the May 1954 decision can only be made meaningful through a mobilization of millions of Negroes and whites for political and direct, nonviolent action.

The very necessities of this political struggle point toward political realignment. It was a coalition of Northern Republicans and reactionary Southern Democrats who made the Civil Rights Acts of 1957 and 1960 into pitiful documents. This same coalition united to fight against medical care for the aged, against a program to relieve distressed areas, and for anti-labor legislation. Its power rests, to a considerable extent, upon the fact that the racist Democrats of the South gain important committe chairmanships in Congress because of their alliance with the Northern labor and liberal forces and through the workings of the seniority system. A vote for a Northern liberal Democrat *is* a vote to make Eastland chairman of the Senate Judiciary Committee under our present party alignment. If there is to be civil rights — if there is to be any real social progress on any major issue — the power of this coalition must be shattered. In practical terms, this means that the progressive forces, the Negroes, the labor movement, the farmers, the liberals, must take the road of independent political action. To achieve civil rights, there must be a real second party in the United States.

The immediate political fight focuses upon the attainment of a meaningful Civil Rights Act. It must include —

Adequate guarantees of the right of Negroes to vote, with the power of action, once a pattern of discrimination is found, vested in the Executive;

Legislation requiring the Federal government to initiate legal action on behalf of school integration, voting rights, or any other civil right;

Adoption of the principle that only integrated institutions shall qualify for Federal funds;

Implementation of Section 2 of the Fourteenth Amendment, depriving states of representation in Congress in proportion to the number of citizens they deprive of the right to vote on account of race, color, or previous servitude.

Another vital aspect of the struggle for civil rights is the fight against discrimination in housing, education, and employment, particularly in the North. Much attention, and rightfully so, has been given to the fight against separate public-school facilities for Negroes in the South. However, the *de facto* segregation that exists in Northern schools must be opposed also, for the damage it does is just as great in terms of inferior education resulting from overcrowding, inadequate facilities, and inequitable distribution of teaching personnel.

We support legislation and board-of-education policies designed to foster integration in school districting, in the building of schools, in the assignment of teachers.

Ghetto patterns buttress *de facto* segregation in Northern public schools. We oppose the use of government funds, whether Federal or local, in the financing of segregated housing. We support all efforts directed toward ending housing discrimination, public and private, such as open-occupancy legislation and the dispersal of public housing in such a manner as to foster integration.

Discrimination in employment has been and continues to be of major concern to Negroes and other minority groups. The average annual wage today for the white worker is almost twice as much as that of the Negro worker. Employment barriers, particularly in the white-collar and technical fields, still exist for Negroes. We urge the enactment of FEPC legislation with adequate enforcement provisions on a Federal level, and in cities and states where nonexistent.

Finally, there must be a gigantic, nonviolent mobilization of Negroes and whites for a direct challenge to Jim Crow wherever it exists. The

Montgomery Bus Boycott and the Sit-In Campaign of the Negro students point the path of this development. We gladly pledge our energies and resources to the support of nonviolent mass action for civil rights. We believe that this, along with legal action and the fight for political realignment, is the essence of the battle for civil rights today.

### Other Minorities

Mexican-Americans, Puerto Ricans, and other minority groups are also the victims of discrimination. We support the democratic movement of all these minorities as part of the united struggle for the principle of equality for all.

We are opposed to the current effort to deprive American Indians of their remaining community lands and resources. Premature and enforced assimilation of Indians into the dominant culture is no answer to their special problems. No major programs affecting Indians should be launched without the free consent of the tribes or bands involved. As a first step to alleviate sufferings and amend ancient wrongs, we endorse the proposal of the National Congress of American Indians, for a "Point Four" program for Indians.

### McCarthyism

We urge a campaign to root the institutions of McCarthyism out of our life: repeal of the Smith Act and pardon for all its victims; abolition of the Attorney General's "subversive" list; repeal of the loyalty-oath provision of the National Defense Education Act; abolition of the House Un-American Activities Committee and the Senate Internal Security Committee.

### Ballot Access

We advocate a Constitutional amendment guaranteeing the right of ready ballot access in all states to minority political parties.

### Conscription

Hostility to peacetime conscription in the Old World was one of the great forces motivating immigration to this country, and Americans have traditionally regarded it as alien and a threat to freedom. Under the conditions of modern military technology it cannot even be justified on grounds of need. It serves only to maintain the power of military bureaucracy and to subject a portion of the populace each year to military conditioning.

We demand its immediate abolition. We also condemn compulsory ROTC as military conditioning which has no place in our educational system.

### AGRICULTURE

In the post-war period mechanization has rapidly increased productivity per worker in agriculture as in other fields. Our government has so far utterly failed to cope with the problems this has created. It has failed to assume responsibility for helping displaced farmers and farm workers find productive employment; and has, indeed, adopted farm policies which have made their problems much more acute. Corporate farms with absentee ownership have more and more tended to dominate American agriculture; these huge managerial units are the prime beneficiaries of the Federal subsidy program. The family farm, long regarded as an important institution of our democracy, is almost completely forgotten in our agricultural policy. Hundreds of thousands of people are forced to flee the land and start from scratch in the unfamiliar, frustrating environment of the big city.

The farm worker, and particularly the migratory laborer, is victimized by the most cruel exploitation. Unorganized, unprotected by the laws which cover industrial workers, the men and women who toil in the factories of the field live under the miserable conditions which predated the rise of the mass union movement and the emergence of the welfare state.

Our basic principle in confronting this situation is that occupancy and use should be the only rightful title to farmland. Where conditions favor family farming, the security of such farmers should be strengthened through cooperative credit purchasing and marketing, aided by government financing. Where modern techniques and specialization require large-scale farm ownership, we call for social ownership and cooperative operation to replace the corporation farm.

More immediately, we strongly oppose all those programs which seek to foster scarcity as a means to agricultural equity. Our nation contains millions of families who desperately need assistance to maintain a decent diet. Consequently, we seek the enlargement of the school lunch program and other public-welfare food programs. We also favor a domestic food-allotment program for low-income families.

Internationally, food "surpluses" can play an important role in the fight against world poverty. Specifically, we favor the international administration of a U.N. food program to alleviate starvation, to promote economic development, and to encourage price stability.

We wholeheartedly support the labor movement in its effort to bring the benefits of trade unionism to America's farm workers. We believe that the American labor movement must give top priority to this effort, with more financial assistance than is now provided for. Jurisdictional disputes should in no way be allowed to block development of the organization of farm workers.

We favor extension to farm workers of all the safeguards now protecting industrial workers: minimum wage, safety and sanitary legislation, and so on.

We see an immediate need for Federal aid to farmers' cooperatives and a strengthening of the rural electrification program.

We demand a major attack on rural slums.

In short, the family farmer and the farm worker cannot be our forgotten citizens. A vigorous, immediate program to protect them, and to limit the power of the corporate farm, must be a basic goal of all those who favor social change in the United States today.

URBAN PROBLEMS

*Planning for People*

The old-party politicians have concocted plans without vision and projects without plans. Proposals for urban renewal are not arrived at through democratic participation of the people involved; they are not designed as part of a comprehensive and rational scheme to rebuild cities around the human needs of the people who live in them.

Highways are given priority over communities; largesse is distributed to real-estate speculators in the name of slum-clearance. Neighborhoods and communities are destroyed; neighborliness is made more difficult; ordinary natural contact between people is frustrated. "Old" slums are spreading as the nation falls well behind the rate of housing obsolescence; "new" slums are created by our haphazard and inadequate public housing. Too much

public housing is built in the form of high-rise human rabbit-warrens, income ghettoes. Our government has not created housing for human beings; it has not planned communities.

One conspicuous example of bad planning is the half-billion dollar Federal highway program, which puts a misplaced emphasis on private modes of vehicular transport at a time when our congested cities urgently require a revamping of the means of mass transportation. The new highways continue the process of disrupting communities in the interests of automobiles. Moreover, they must meet design requirements for the moving of military equipment through, as well as between, cities. The Socialist Party believes that cities are for people, not for cars — and most emphatically, not for atomic missiles.

We advocate reestablishment of the National Resources Planning Board for properly coordinating the use of resources and their distribution from area to area. We urge the creation by the Federal government of regional planning agencies in cooperation with state and local governments, to supervise overall planning for all Federal expenditures in public improvement. These agencies should help each region to help itself. They should play a major role in handling such problems as massive population displacement.

In the long run what is needed is democratic planning to make possible a tremendous decentralization of living, a nation of home-owners and communities. This clearly cannot be accomplished by private industry, nor even by the Federal government acting as it now does. It requires a human concept of the economy and of the problem of the city; a determination to build on the basis of need rather than of profit.

*The City*

As immediate steps to meet the problems of our cities, we advocate —

A Department of Urban Development, with a cabinet-rank Secretary in the Federal government;

National sponsorship of satellite cities to reduce urban congestion and to provide a decent environment for the rearing of children and the enjoyment of life;

Permanent and automatic reapportionment of all state legislatures subject to review by the courts, so as to end minority domination of state governments, and so that city governments will no longer find it necessary to bypass the state and look for aid solely to the Federal government;

Federal matching funds for metropolitan planning, sewer control, water-works expansion, and mass transportation;

Public ownership and nonprofit operation of power and transportation utilities.

### Housing

The Socialist Party calls for planning a human housing environment in a vastly-expanded program of public housing. There should be as much decentralization and local autonomy as possible in the handling of Federal housing funds. Public housing must be planned as part of a community — with architecture related to the needs of people; with integration of races, income groups, and types of housing in genuine neighborhoods. Above all, public housing must avoid the tendency to create huge impersonal ghettoes. We do not need modern poor-farms; we need new communities.

Here and now, we call for a housing program that incorporates —

Arrangements for the relocation of persons displaced by renewal projects protecting not only their right to sanitary housing, but also their investment in their community. Relocation must be designed to prevent the disruption of societal ties as is now so brutally prevalent.

Application of the principle that the rental value of land is a social creation and should be appropriated by taxation for social purposes. All housing projects should insure a continuous return to the local government of increases in values created by public investment.

Sanctions against the creation of income or racial ghettoes. Grants-in-aid should be withheld where discrimination of any kind exists.

Approaches that will foster the idea of community, and encourage democratic participation of citizens in community decisions. Rochdale-type cooperatives should receive high priority.

Aid for lower and middle income home-owners who are able to refurbish existing homes as part of the program of community renewal.

Special programs for the housing of the aged, the economically-displaced, and the socially backward.

### EDUCATION

A democratic society requires an educational system which gives to each child opportunity for maximum development of all his potentialities. We reject the demand, made popular by Russia's launching of the Sputniks, for gearing our educational system to the needs of a war machine, or for imitating the narrow objectives of education in the Soviet Union and other totalitarian states. We believe in education for the whole man, education geared to the aptitude of each student and designed to produce well-informed citizens capable of thinking for themselves and participating responsibly in the rights and duties of citizenship.

We favor Federal aid for school construction, for higher teacher salaries, and for guidance services. We favor a Federal college scholarship plan. We oppose giving Federal aid to communities which refuse to integrate their school system as required by the May 1954 decision of the Supreme Court. We favor the extension of unionism among teachers. We oppose loyalty oaths in schools and colleges, for either teachers or students, because their only effect is to create a climate of suspicion incongruous to education in a free society.

### RESOLUTIONS

*This platform was adopted at a national convention of the SP-SDF held May 28-30, 1960, in Washington, D.C. The same convention also adopted a number of resolutions; of which it directed that the following three be printed with the platform because they serve to expand on special topics of outstanding importance, which could not appropriately be treated within the editorial confines of the platform itself.*

#### RESOLUTION ON FOREIGN AID

It is imperative that the United States, with nearly 50 per cent of the total world income and only 7 per cent of its population, do its utmost to aid the rapidest possible development of the underdeveloped two-thirds of the world. For the peoples of the underdeveloped countries, economic aid is essential not only for their standard of living, but also for the future of their democracy.

So far United States aid has been insufficient, and has too often been unacceptable because of the political and military considerations which have largely inspired it. We therefore urge that the U.S. foreign aid program be given a general re-orientation —

The United States should propose, and push in the United Nations for, a world-wide crusade against low productivity, poverty, and misery. As a first step, we should give full backing to the suggested Special United Nations Fund for Economic Development (SUNFED). We should also move to expand greatly the facilities of such U.N. subsidiaries as the International Finance Corporation and the International Development Association.

Pending establishment of a world-wide U.N. program, the United States should greatly increase its own program of aid to the underdeveloped nations. Special attention should be given to the pressing needs of the Republic of India.

All United States aid should be extended in a spirit of cooperation, with the intention of bringing mutual advantages to the underdeveloped nations and to this country. Our present attitude must be abandoned; for now we offer aid in the spirit of the charity of a profit-hungry banker. The SP-SDF especially opposes those policies which force underdeveloped nations to turn their petroleum industries over to exploitation by U.S. firms, and which force recipient nations to accept stringent austerity programs as the price of getting even inadequate help from this country.

Finally, the United States must take the lead in working out arrangements for stabilizing at equitable levels the prices of the raw material and food-stuff exports on which underdeveloped nations depend for their foreign-exchange income. Without such stabilization, even very large intergovernmental grant and loan programs may be completely negated by sudden declines in world prices.

RESOLUTION ON LATIN AMERICA

At no time in the past thirty years has U.S. prestige in Latin America been at a lower ebb. Our government has only itself to blame for this situation. It results from the U.S. policy of supporting dictatorial regimes, and from U.S. failure to give adequate support to the economic development efforts of the peoples of Latin America.

The bankruptcy and harm that this policy has done to U.S.-Latin American relations is being dramatically demonstrated by the anti-U.S. attitude of the revolutionary government of Cuba, and the response this attitude has evoked elsewhere in Latin America. The Socialist Party salutes the Cuban people and expresses its full support of the revolutionary overthrow of the criminal Batista regime. We are in full sympathy with the objectives of the Cuban revolution, and are emphatically opposed to any attempt on the part of the U.S. government to intervene either directly or indirectly against the Castro regime.

We believe that the U.S. must show by deeds, not words, that it does not support dictatorial regimes. It should make clear its disgust with the Trujillo dictatorship in the Dominican Republic and protest the frequent meddling of that regime in the internal affairs of the United States and other American republics. It should name as ambassadors to the Dominican Republic — and to Nicaragua, Paraguay, and Haiti — men who will clearly act as representatives of a democracy and not as apologists for the dictatorship to which they are accredited. The U.S. should also strongly support the new Inter American Commission on Human Rights established in 1959 by the Foreign Ministers Conference in Santiago, Chile.

The United States must abandon forthwith all programs of military aid to regimes that use the equipment thus acquired to oppress their own people. It should encourage and promote the idea advocated by the government of Chile for general disarmament by the Latin American nations, and for application of the funds so saved to education, health, and other social purposes. It should itself contribute technical and financial assistance to these and similar projects.

The slow pace of economic growth in Latin America is leading many to conclude that development is only possible if political democracy is sacrificed. The U.S. has ignored this tendency, and indeed has stimulated it by giving aid that is insufficient and bound by too-orthodox banking conditions. U.S. aid must be enormously expanded; our country must seek to assist materially toward raising the standard of living of the Latin American peoples by helping to lay the foundations for industrialization and future economic growth. To this end —

The U.S. must cooperate in programs for stabilizing the prices of the principal exports on which the Latin American countries depend for their foreign-exchange income; and

The U.S., through the Organization of American States, must propose to the other republics of this hemisphere a general cooperative program for economic development. In such a program, each of the Latin American countries should draw up a plan for overcoming all the principal bottlenecks hampering its development, and should estimate what portion of the cost of that plan can be met from its own resources, by cooperative endeavor with other Latin American countries, and from extrahemispheric resources. The United States should then be prepared to supply however much additional aid may be required.

### RESOLUTION ON MEXICAN FARM LABORERS

During the domestic farm labor shortage of World War II, the emergency program of importing Mexican workers reached a peak of 63,000 in 1944. Today there is no longer a domestic farm labor shortage — yet nearly 450,000 Mexican workers are being imported annually.

For hungry workers from the poor rural regions of northern Mexico, this program means the relative wealth of wages ranging from 50 cents an hour in Texas to nearly 90 cents in northern California. But it also means working under conditions which, in the words of Father Vizzard of the National Catholic Rural Life Association, are "an ill-disguised substitute for slavery." For some two million American farm workers, and the 500,000 among them who migrate with their families in search of work, the Mexican program means continued poverty and oppression, since these workers are displaced by the Mexicans and are forced to work for 30 cents an hour in Texas and 40 cents an hour in Arkansas.

For the big factory farms and growers associations of California and the Southwest, the Mexicans provide an abundance of cheap labor. It was these growers who fostered the mass ingress of illegal workers or "wetbacks," an influx which reached an estimated one million a year at its height. It was these growers whose persistent pressure brought about enactment of Public Law 78 in 1951, which legalized and made "moral" an illegal and immoral system. It is these growers who dominate the employment and farm placement

services and have made a dead letter of the law giving preference to domestic workers. It is these growers who have nurtured corruption throughout the Mexican placement system, corruption evidenced last year by the limited removal of public officials in California. It is the selfishness and arrogance of these growers, and their great influence within the Eisenhower administration, which has made impossible any real solution to the general problem of migratory labor.

Therefore, in addition to our other proposals concerning migratory labor (see under "Agriculture," page 630), the SP-SDF urges —

That Public Law 78 be allowed to terminate on its expiration date of June, 1961; and

That Congress prepare for its termination by authorizing a program of economic and technical aid designed to provide a stable means of livelihood in those areas of Mexico from which the Mexican workforce of 450,000 is drawn.

## Socialist Labor Platform 1960

The overriding issue of the 1960 campaign is SOCIALISM and SURVIVAL V. CAPITALISM and CATASTROPHE.

This conclusion is based on a sober and realistic appraisal of a situation that actually exists and from which no one can hide. The whole human race is poised on the razor edge of nuclear catastrophe. As each day ends with the missiles resting on their launching pads, the danger is so much greater that the next will witness the outbreak, by accident or design, of a suicidal nuclear war.

The political heads of the great Powers solemnly declare that all-out thermonuclear war is unthinkable. We are told that there is an atomic stalemate — a balance of terror that deters both sides from starting World War III. But, for two reasons, this confidence is unjustified.

The first reason is that behind the fateful arms race there is a fierce international struggle between capitalist imperialism and Soviet imperialism for the markets and raw materials of the world. For the capitalist masters of the Western bloc and the bureaucratic masters of the Soviet bloc — the ones who really determine their nations' policies regardless of which politicians or bureaucrats hold office — the markets of the world are indispensable. In the case of U.S. capitalism, lack of these overseas outlets for the surplus products that result from the exploitation of American labor causes commodities to pile up and threatens the economy with mass unemployment, stagnation and final collapse.

Reason and experience tell us that ruling classes faced with the breakdown of their system, and blinded by the threatened loss of their property and privileges, become desperate. Desperate men do desperate things. It is cause for the most sober reflection that today a few hundred top capitalists and their military and political pawns – or their Soviet imperialist adversaries – can, when they feel compelled by their material interests, set in motion fateful forces that could destroy the world.

The second reason our fears are not allayed by the assurances of statesmen is the danger that an unauthorized or accidental nuclear explosion may trigger an all-out nuclear war. The grim but simple facts are these: First, each side now has ready for instant use nuclear weapons of unimaginable power. Second, these weapons are in charge of militarists who, being human, are prone to err. As one deeply perturbed Congressman described our peril:

"If you place six champanzees in a small room with a couple of baskets of live hand grenades, a minor catastrophe is inevitable. If you place error-prone human beings in proximity to thousands of nuclear weapons, a major catastrophe is inevitable and the triggering of an all-out massive exchange is probable."

The Socialist Labor Party urges every person to face this grim truth: We survive from day to day as hostages of a criminal, outmoded social system careening to its doom.

Nor does the danger to our survival stem from war alone. As a result of the capitalists' insatiable profit hunger we are all exposed to a host of mortal dangers – unsuspected chemical poisons in our food, chemical and radioactive pollutants in our water, noxious gases in the air we breathe. Capitalism's irresponsible hunger to exploit for private profit the advances of science is illustrated by the fact that there are now 65 million gallons of high-level, boiling-hot, radioactive waste stored in tanks that are estimated to last from 10 to 50 years. This is enough radioactive material to pollute all the land and water area of the United States, and it

will remain deadly to man for centuries. By 1980 there will be another 65 million gallons. Neither the Atomic Energy Commission nor anyone else knows how to dispose of this poisonous atomic waste.

The Socialist Labor Party declares that the alternative to capitalist catastrophe is Socialism. Socialism, which will eliminate competitive production for the profit of a handful of capitalist parasites, and which will create the economic conditions for peace and cooperation, is the only hope of humanity. Socialism has nothing in common with the bureaucratic despotism that masquerades as "Socialism" in Soviet Russia. Socialism, as its founder, Karl Marx, conceived it, as Daniel De-Leon, the great American Marxist and social scientist, developed it, and as advocated by the Socialist Labor Party, is a society of industrial democracy –

in which the factories, mills, mines, railroads, land, etc., are owned collectively by all the people;

in which production is carried on for use and not for the profit of a handful of capitalists;

and in which the industries are administered democratically by the workers themselves through an integrated industrial union.

In the United States the capitalist class is master. In Soviet Russia the master is a bureaucratic hierarchy. But the Socialist Industrial Union government proposed by the Socialist Labor Party eliminates both capitalist masters and bureaucratic masters. It is the only conceivable form of social and industrial administration that gives the workers collectively a democratic mastery of their tools and products.

Socialism is the answer to all our grave and pressing social problems.

It is the cure for recurring war because it replaces the international struggle for markets and other forms of economic competition with economic cooperation, thus creating a foundation for durable peace.

It is the cure for recurring economic depression because it replaces capitalist production for private profit with production for human needs, thus freeing social production from the anarchy, waste and restrictions of private ownership and an unpredictable market.

It is the answer to the problem of poverty in the midst of plenty, for it ends the exploitation of class by class and assures that every worker will receive the full social value of his labor.

It is the answer to the threat of unemployment — a threat underscored by the rapid spread of automation — because democratic control of industry empowers the workers to utilize new machinery to reduce working hours rather than to eliminate jobs.

It is the cure for race prejudice because it cleanses society of the sordid material interests that foment racism and because it creates the economic foundation and cooperative climate for universal human brotherhood.

Socialism is also the answer to crime and juvenile delinquency, to the alarming spread of mental illness, alcoholism, dope addiction, and other manifestations of capitalist decadence, for it will replace irrational, inhuman relationships with rational, human ones.

To bring to birth this same society of peace, abundance and freedom, the Socialist Labor Party appeals to the working class of America, and to all social-minded citizens, to support its principles at the polls by voting for the candidates of the Socialist Labor Party. It appeals to all voters to repudiate the Republican and Democratic parties, the political Siamese twins of capitalism. It appeals to them also to reject the self-styled "radicals" and "liberals" whose platforms consist of reform demands, every one of which is a concealed measure of reaction.

Finally, the Socialist Labor Party appeals to the working class to repudiate the present procapitalist unions. All of them accept capitalism as a finality, and they are under the domination and control of leaders who are in effect "labor lieutenants" of the capitalist class. The Socialist Labor Party calls on the workers to build a new union, one which denies the false claim that there is a brotherhood between exploiting capital and exploited labor — a union which has Socialism as its goal. It calls on them to build the all-embracing integral Socialist Industrial Union as the only power capable of enforcing a majority vote for Socialism and of taking over the administration of social production.

Supported at the polls by the working-class majority, the elected candidates of the Socialist Labor Party will take over the political State, not to administer it, but to disband it. The reins of government will simultaneously be passed to the integrally organized Socialist Industrial Union.

This is the peaceful and civilized way to accomplish the Socialist revolution in America so imperatively demanded in this greatest crisis in human history.

We repeat: The issue in this campaign is *Socialism and survival versus capitalism and catastrophe.*

Unite with us to save humanity from destruction — and to set an example in free industrial self-government for all mankind! Unite with us to establish the Socialist Commonwealth of Peace, Plenty and International Brotherhood!

## Socialist Workers Platform 1960

Humanity today faces three key problems: (1) How can the world be freed from the threat of nuclear destruction? (2) How can hunger and poverty be wiped out? (3) How can equality and democracy be won and maintained?

These are also the three key issues in the 1960 elections. What can America contribute toward a world of enduring peace, abundance and freedom?

THE STRUGGLE FOR PEACE

At one time America was regarded as the hope of the oppressed everywhere. This is no longer true. The majority of the human race have turned toward the Soviet Union and China as representing the road of progress. Whether we like it or not, this happens to be today's outstanding fact. It is high time to ask ourselves, why has America become so feared and hated?

One of the main reasons is that people in other countries have become convinced that America bears chief responsibility for the frightening drift toward a third world war. They note that our military experts have repeatedly admitted that the Soviet Union does not need war, does not want war, and is not planning an attack. Yet the Pentagon continues to spend approximately $40 billion a year for armaments; continues to stockpile nuclear weapons; continues to tighten a vast ring of military bases around the Soviet bloc countries; and continues such aggressive actions as spy-plane invasions deep into Soviet territory. The public abroad noted the State Department insistence on the "need" to renew nuclear tests and the Soviet initiative in giving them up. The contrast in attitudes is explainable only if America is actively preparing for nuclear war while the Soviet bloc seeks to avoid such a catastrophe.

It is common knowledge in other lands that the basic causes of war are economic. America's drive toward nuclear disaster is therefore seen as the end result of the need of its capitalist economy for cheap labor, cheap raw materials and lucrative markets, not to mention the profits in armament and a war boom. The Soviet avoidance of war, on the other hand, is seen to follow from the antagonism of planned economy to private profits and its need for peace to run in a smooth, co-ordinated way.

This is the basic explanation for the fact that more and more people in the world today feel that they must oppose America's belligerent foreign aims and support the Soviet bloc. They see it as an elemental question of survival.

## The Struggle for Economic Security

Out of every eleven persons on this earth, it has been estimated that seven go to bed hungry every night. Few of these unfortunates believe any longer that this fate is beyond remedy. The sputniks orbiting overhead are daily reminders of what a daring, energetic and forward-looking people can accomplish through revolution and a planned economy.

Two roads offer economic security — the American and the Soviet. During World War II and for a few years after, the American road appeared more attractive to the colonial peoples. But they ran into bitter experiences. They found in practice that America blocked them from achieving freedom and independence.

The U.S. poured some $2 billion in arms and economic aid into the effort to keep dictator Chiang Kai-shek in power. The U.S. plunged into full-scale war in Korea to prevent the country from uniting and ousting dictator Syngman Rhee. In Indochina, the U.S. backed emperor Bao Dai and the French invaders; in Indonesia, the Dutch imperialists; in Japan, the Mikado; in Cuba, the bloody Batista. The State Department still backs butcher Franco and the unspeakable Trujillo. When a civil war broke out in Iraq, the U.S. landed marines in Lebanon. This year the State Department shoved a war pact down the throats

of the Japanese people despite protest demonstrations involving hundreds of thousands of student youth and millions of organized workers. Ten years after the Chinese Revolution, both Democrats and Republicans still refuse to recognize the new government.

To the underprivileged of the earth, America appears as a frighteningly malevolent country. With $9 billion worth of grain in storage, prominent Americans answer pleas for bread with stony advice to cut down the colored birth rate; and to emphasize the advice, Democrats and Republicans have withdrawn millions of acres of the most fertile American soil from production. A spectacular instance of this inhuman foreign policy was the refusal to help Egypt build the Aswan dam. Today the bipartisan Republican and Democratic coalition is bringing increasing pressure against tiny Cuba's efforts to win a decent standard of living.

Hungry people, scorned by America, are inclined to turn in the Soviet direction. Sympathetic help from this source becomes quite dramatic, for the Soviet people are not yet well to do. More important, the Soviet Union appears as a living example of how to achieve industrialization without waiting for aid that may never arrive from the cruel North American power.

As a result, hundreds of millions of the poverty-stricken, from China to Africa, from the Middle East to the Caribbean, have felt forced, however reluctantly, to take the road of revolution in defiance to advice, threats and reprisals from Wall Street, Congress, the White House and the Pentagon. The starved and the ragged see planned economy as the shortest way from feudal stagnation to the benefits of modern civilization.

Two big lessons can be learned from this: (1) We cannot afford to leave our fate in the hands of self-seeking corporations and money-mad monopolists bent on blocking world progress for the sake of private profit. Instead, we should listen to the agonized cries to help make this globe a livable place. (2) The demonstrated successes of planned economy in underdeveloped countries show what tremendous benefits it could bring to America. In less than forty years planned economy brought Russia from one of the weakest of powers to one of the mightiest; and that despite gross bureaucracy, bad government, mismanagement, dire poverty, a heritage of backwardness and the most terrible war in history. There is not the least doubt that a planned economy in the United States, with our skilled labor, our rich resources, tremendous industrial plant and highly developed science, could quickly end poverty on this continent and assure everyone a life of abundance, opportunity and deeply satisfying achievement.

## THE STRUGGLE FOR DEMOCRACY AND FULL EQUALITY

Both Republicans and Democrats proclaim that America stands for a "free" world of democracy and equality whereas the Soviet Union and the countries allied with it stand for totalitarianism. It is obvious that these lands suffer from bureaucratic police regimes that stifle freedom of thought and expression not only in politics but in many other spheres. We have the right and the duty to express our opinions about such evils but we have neither the right nor the duty to meddle in the internal affairs of other countries. The Russian people, the Chinese, the East Europeans will most certainly rectify matters themselves in due time by installing democratic workers and farmers governments. Their tendency to do this has already been amply demonstrated in the uprisings in East Germany, Poland and Hungary.

Our first concern must be with the shape of things at home. Here we confront a sorry spectacle. Forty-three years after entering the first global conflict to "Make the World Safe for Democracy," America has yet to make its lunch counters safe for Negroes in the South. Negro children are still barred from equal educational facilities. Job opportunities are still restricted by skin color, sex, age and religious belief. In the fields of government, industry, education and even entertainment, political inquisitors decide according to secret blacklist who shall work and who shall not.

In the South a totalitarian one-party system prevails, while in the country as a whole a bipartisan coalition of agents of big business monopolize politics. Labor does not have a single spokesman of its own in Congress. Minority parties are systematically excluded from the ballot and denied equal access to TV, radio and the public press.

The ranks of the armed forces of the country have no democratic rights whatever and a monstrous military caste, built on the notorious Prussian model, is spreading like a cancer throughout all our institutions.

How far America has slipped toward dictatorial rule is demonstrated by a single outstanding fact — the people have lost the right to decide the most fateful of all questions, war or peace. Congress has abdicated its war powers, leaving these to whatever figure big business puts in the White House. And the White House, in turn, has placed an obscure general in charge of the row of nuclear push buttons.

The erosion of democracy in America is evident in every sector, including the unions where a reactionary bureaucracy, hostile to the least manifestations of militancy or assertion of democratic rights by the rank and file, guards its special privileges by any means.

This land of Jim Crow and antilabor laws, of political witch-hunting and lying commercials, of multitudinous mechanical gadgets and crushing conformity of spirit, is boasted as a model of freedom and morality. The fact is that falsehood, cynicism and worship of the dollar have become entrenched from the White House down to the TV quiz.

## FOR A SOCIALIST AMERICA

We urge every thinking American to consider the socialist alternative. We mean the socialist alternative first brought to nationwide attention by Albert Parsons, Daniel DeLeon, William D. Haywood and Eugene V. Debs. We mean the international economic order, based on scientific planning, advocated by Karl Marx and Frederick Engels. We mean a democracy, such as V. I. Lenin and Leon Trotsky fought for, that will give the working people control over their economy and government, free the arts and sciences, and eventually reduce government to scientific management of industry.

The Socialist Workers party urges an immediate end to the insane preparations for nuclear suicide. The Socialist Workers party urges that we turn our industrial plant away from war and toward an economy of abundance. The Socialist Workers party urges that we revive the democratic outlook and the democratic practices that were once the pride of America. Instead of resisting the course taken by the majority of mankind, the United States, we think, should help lead in winning the benefits of socialism for the entire world.

We realize that the road to a rational economy is not an easy one and that many partial steps must be taken before success is finally achieved. As a beginning, we propose the following planks for your consideration in 1960:

*(1) For a peaceful foreign policy.*

Let Congress and the White House pledge to the world that America will never resort to war under any circumstances. As proof of our desire for peace, let us withdraw all troops from foreign soil, give up all foreign military bases, put a permanent halt to nuclear-weapon tests, and dismantle the stockpile of A-bombs and H-bombs.

Support all colonial struggles against imperialism and the right of all peoples to a government of their own choice.

Recognize the government of the People's Republic of China. Support the Cuban revolution.

*(2) Against capitalist militarism.*

Turn the armaments budget into a peace budget for homes, schools, hospitals, medical research, nurseries, playgrounds, highways, transportation and public parks. End capitalist conscription and the Prussian-type military training practiced in the armed forces and ROTC which poison the minds of the youth against the labor movement at home, struggles for freedom and independence abroad and the movement for international socialism. Grant full democratic rights to the ranks of the armed forces, including free speech, free assembly, election of officers and collective bargaining.

*(3) End economic insecurity.*

For the 30-hour week at 40 hours pay. Extend unemployment insurance to every worker, and at the full union scale for the full period of waiting for a job. Let the government take over all facilities made idle by cutbacks, automation, mergers, decentralization, run-aways, or depression and operate them under charge of committees elected by the workers. Place control of production rates and speeds in the hands of the unions.

Equal pay for equal work regardless of sex or age. Full job and seniority rights and maternity care for women.

A government-guaranteed college education for all youth. Federally financed nurseries and summer camps for children.

For America's "Forgotten Generation," our thirteen million aged people, let's provide full disability benefits, free medical care and hospitalization, and adequate pensions. As an immediate measure, pass the Forand bill.

*(4) Restore and expand democratic rights.*

End restrictions on the right to organize, strike and picket. No government interference in internal union affairs. Repeal the oppressive Kennedy-Landrum-Griffin, Taft-Hartley, and Humphrey-Butler Acts, the misnamed "right to work" laws and other federal, state and city antilabor laws and ordinances.

Abolish the "subversive" list. Repeal the McCarran Internal Security and Immigration laws. Halt all deportations. Repeal the Smith Act and grant amnesty to all remaining victims of this thought-control law. Abolish "loyalty" oaths and "loyalty" purges. Repeal the law abridging the Fifth Amendment. Uphold the First Amendment. Abolish the House Un-American Activities Committee and the Senate Internal Security Subcommittee. Halt all political prosecutions for "contempt" and "perjury" based on the testimony of stool pigeons.

Liberalize the election laws. Lower the voting age to 18. Give minority parties equal time on TV and radio and in the columns of the public press.

*(5) Guarantee minority rights.*

Full economic, social and political equality to the Negro people and to all other minority groups. Solidarity with mass actions aimed at securing these rights as exemplified in the sit-in movement of the Negro students and their allies.

For immediate enforcement of the Supreme Court decision to desegregate the schools.

Enact and enforce federal legislation against lynch murder and police brutality. Abolish the poll tax.

For a federal agency fully empowered to combat all forms of racist discrimination and segregation in employment, politics and public and private services.

End the barbaric death penalty. Reform our antiquated prison system.

*(6) For adequate government aid to the farmers.*

Under a federal program set up and administered by elected representatives of the working farmers, let the government underwrite the full cost of production on all farm commodities. No limitation on crops so long as people suffer from hunger anywhere in the world. Government food subsidies for families in America living on a substandard diet.

Moratoriums on repayment of distress loans as long as debtors need them.

Abolish sharecropping and landlordism — crops to those who grow them; land to those who work it.

*(7) For an emergency government housing and public works program.*

As a starter on ending the scandalous national housing crisis, let the government build twenty million low-rent housing units on an emergency schedule. Put rigid rent controls on all private housing; elect tenants committees to supervise enforcement.

For a full-scale federal program on flood control, water supply, irrigation, cheap electricity and conservation of natural resources.

*(8) Repeal taxes on low incomes.*

Abolish all payroll and sales taxes and hidden forms of taxes passed on to the consumer. No taxes on incomes under $7,500 a year. A 100% tax on incomes above $25,000 a year. Confiscate all profits on war goods. Open the tax returns of the rich to public scrutiny.

*(9) For government ownership of industry.*

Nationalize the banks, basic industries, food trusts, medical monopolies and all natural resources, including nuclear power. Elect committees of workers and technicians to manage these facilities in the interests of the producers and consumers. Institute a planned system of economy.

*(10) For independent political action.*

End the Democratic-Republican monopoly of politics. Break all ties with the capitalist political machines. Organize an independent labor party, basing it on the unions and including the Negro people and working farmers. Put a Workers and Farmers government in office to reorganize America on a socialist basis.

# CAMPAIGN OF 1964

In 1964, united and optimistic Democrats met in Atlantic City, New Jersey, and nominated President Lyndon B. Johnson by acclamation. He then selected Minnesota Senator Hubert H. Humphrey as his vice-presidential running mate. Both candidates and the lengthy platform were adopted without a roll-call vote. The Republicans, in contrast, were divided into liberal and conservative factions after a bitter primary election battle between Senator Barry Goldwater of Arizona and Governor Nelson Rockefeller of New York. When they met in San Francisco, Goldwater was clearly the choice of the delegates and he defeated six other candidates on the first ballot. He then chose Representative William E. Miller of New York as his vice-presidential candidate.

The Prohibition Party nominated E. Harold Munn for president and Mark Shaw of Massachusetts for vice-president. The Socialist Labor Party again nominated Eric Hass, running this year with Henning A. Blomen, also of Massachusetts. Clifton deBerry and Edward Shaw, both of New York, constituted the Socialist Workers Party ticket. A half dozen other temporary parties also offered presidential candidates, but minor parties received fewer than 150,000 votes in 1964.

The 1964 election was a relatively clear contest of issues and ideologies, and the Democratic Party polled 43,126,584 popular votes—61 percent of the more than 70 million ballots cast—and amassed the largest popular vote plurality in American history. The Republican Party, with 27,177,838 votes, was victorious in six southern states and Arizona. The Socialist Labor Party received 45,187 votes, the Socialist Workers garnered 32,701, and the Prohibitionists polled 23,266 votes.

President Johnson received 486 electoral votes to 52 for Senator Goldwater.

---

## Democratic Platform 1964

### ONE NATION, ONE PEOPLE

America is *One Nation, One People.* The welfare, progress, security and survival of each of us reside in the common good—the sharing of responsibilities as well as benefits by all our people.

Democracy in America rests on the confidence that people can be trusted with freedom. It comes from the conviction that we will find in freedom a unity of purpose stronger than all our differences.

We have drawn upon that unity when the forces of ignorance, hate, and fear fired an assassin's bullet at the nation's heart, incited violence in our land, and attacked the outposts of freedom around the world.

Because of this unity, those who traffic in fear, hate, falsehood, and violence have failed to undermine our people's deep love of truth and quiet faith in freedom.

Our program for the future is to make the national purpose—the human purpose of us all—fulfill our individual needs.

Accordingly, we offer this platform as a covenant of unity.

We invite all to join us who believe that narrow partisanship takes too small account of the size of our task, the penalties for failure and the boundless rewards to all our people for success.

We offer as the goal of this covenant peace for all nations and freedom for all peoples.

## PEACE

Peace should be the first concern of all governments as it is the prayer of all men.

At the start of the third decade of the nuclear age, the preservation of peace requires the strength to wage war and the wisdom to avoid it. The search for peace requires the utmost intelligence, the clearest vision, and a strong sense of reality.

Because for four years our nation has patiently demonstrated these qualities and persistently used them, the world is closer to peace today than it was in 1960.

In 1960, freedom was on the defensive. The Communists—doubting both our strength and our will to use it—pressed forward in Southeast Asia, Latin America, Central Africa and Berlin.

President Kennedy and Vice President Johnson set out to remove any question of our power or our will. In the Cuban crisis of 1962 the Communist offensive shattered on the rock of President Kennedy's determination—and our ability—to defend the peace.

Two years later, President Johnson responded to another Communist challenge, this time in the Gulf of Tonkin. Once again power exercised with restraint repulsed Communist aggression and strengthened the cause of freedom.

Responsible leadership, unafraid but refusing to take needless risk, has turned the tide in freedom's favor. No nation, old or new, has joined the Communist bloc since Cuba during the preceding Republican Administration. Battered by economic failures, challenged by recent American achievements in space, torn by the Chinese-Russian rift, and faced with American strength and courage—international Communism has lost its unity and momentum.

## NATIONAL DEFENSE

By the end of 1960, military strategy was being shaped by the dictates of arbitrary budget ceilings instead of the real needs of national security. There were, for example, too few ground and air forces to fight limited war, although such wars were a means to continued Communist expansion.

Since then, and at the lowest possible cost, we have created a balanced, versatile, powerful defense establishment, capable of countering agression across the entire spectrum of conflict, from nuclear confrontation to guerrilla subversion.

We have increased our intercontinental ballistic missiles and Polaris missiles from fewer than 100 to more than 1,000, more than four times the force of the Soviet Union. We have increased the number of combat ready divisions from 11 to 16.

Until such time as there can be an enforceable treaty providing for inspected and verified disarmament, we must, and we will, maintain our military strength, as the sword and shield of freedom and the guarantor of peace.

Specifically, we must and we will:

Continue the overwhelming supremacy of our Strategic Nuclear Forces.

Strengthen further our forces for discouraging limited wars and fighting subversion.

Maintain the world's largest research and development effort, which has initiated more than 200 new programs since 1961, to ensure continued American leadership in weapons systems and equipment.

Continue the nationwide Civil Defense program as an important part of our national security.

Pursue our examination of the Selective Service program to make certain that it is continued only as long as it is necessary and that we meet our military manpower needs without social or economic injustice.

Attract to the military services the highest caliber of career men and women and make certain they are adequately paid and adequately housed.

Maintain our Cost Reduction Program, to ensure a dollar's worth of defense for every dollar spent, and minimize the disruptive effects of changes in defense spending.

## BUILDING THE PEACE

As citizens of the United States, we are determined that it be the most powerful nation on earth.

As citizens of the world, we insist that this power be exercised with the utmost responsibility.

Control of the use of nuclear weapons must remain solely with the highest elected official in the country—the President of the United States.

Through our policy of never negotiating from

fear but never fearing to negotiate, we are slowly but surely approaching the point where effective international agreements providing for inspection and control can begin to lift the crushing burden of armaments off the backs of the people of the world.

In the Nuclear Test Ban Treaty, signed now by over 100 nations, we have written our commitment to limitations on the arms race, consistent with our security. Reduced production of nuclear materials for weapons purposes has been announced and nuclear weapons have been barred from outer space.

Already the air we and our children breathe is freer of nuclear contamination.

We are determined to continue all-out efforts through fully-enforceable measures to halt and reverse the arms race and bring to an end the era of nuclear terror.

We will maintain our solemn commitment to the United Nations, with its constituent agencies, working to strengthen it as a more effective instrument for peace, for preventing or resolving international disputes, and for building free nations through economic, technical, and cultural development. We continue to oppose the admission of Red China to the United Nations.

We believe in increased partnership with our friends and associates in the community which spans the North Atlantic. In every possible way we will work to strengthen our ties and increase our cooperation, building always more firmly on the sure foundation of the NATO treaty.

We pledge unflagging devotion to our commitments to freedom from Berlin to South Vietnam.

We will:

Help the people of developing nations in Asia, Africa and Latin America raise their standards of living and create conditions in which freedom and independence can flourish.

Place increased priority on private enterprise and development loans as we continue to improve our mutual assistance programs.

Work for the attainment of peace in the Near East as an urgent goal, using our best efforts to prevent a military unbalance, to encourage arms reductions and the use of national resources for internal development and to encourage the resettlement of Arab refugees in lands where there is room and opportunity. The problems of political adjustment between Israel and the Arab countries can and must be peacefully resolved and the territorial integrity of every nation respected.

Support the partnership of free American Republics in the Alliance for Progress.

Move actively to carry out the Resolution of the Organization of American States to further isolate Castroism and speed the restoration of freedom and responsibility in Cuba.

Support our friends in and around the rim of the Pacific, and encourage a growing understanding among peoples, expansion of cultural exchanges, and strengthening of ties.

Oppose aggression and the use of force or the threat of force against any nation.

Encourage by all peaceful means the growing independence of the captive peoples living under Communism and hasten the day that Albania, Bulgaria, Czechoslovakia, East Germany, Estonia, Hungary, Latavia, Lithuania, Poland, Rumania and the other captive nations will achieve full freedom and self-determination. We deplore Communist oppression of Jews and other minorities.

Encourage expansion of our economic ties with other nations of the world and eliminate unjustifiable tariff and non-tariff barriers, under authority of the Trade Expansion Act of 1962.

Expand the Peace Corps.

Use even more of our Food for Peace.

THE CONQUEST OF SPACE

In four vigorous years we have moved to the forefront of space exploration. The United States must never again settle for second place in the race for tomorrow's frontiers.

We will continue the rapid development of space technology for peaceful uses.

We will encourage private industry to increase its efforts in space research.

We will continue to ensure that any race in space is won for freedom and for peace.

THE LEADERSHIP WE OFFER

The complications and dangers in our restless, constantly changing world require of us consummate understanding and experience. One rash act, one thoughtless decision, one unchecked reaction —and cities could become smouldering ruins and farms parched wasteland.

The leadership we offer has already been tested

in the crucible of crisis and challenge. To this Nation and to all the world we reaffirm President Johnson's resolve to ". . . use every resource at the command of the Government . . . and the people . . . to find the road to peace."

We offer this platform as a guide for that journey.

FREEDOM AND WELL BEING

There can be full freedom only when all of our people have opportunity for education to the full extent of their ability to learn, followed by the opportunity to employ their learning in the creation of something of value to themselves and to the nation.

*The Individual*

Our task is to make the national purpose serve the human purpose: that every person shall have the opportunity to become all that he or she is capable of becoming.

We believe that knowledge is essential to individual freedom and to the conduct of a free society. We believe that education is the surest and most profitable investment a nation can make.

Regardless of family financial status, therefore, education should be open to every boy or girl in America up to the highest level which he or she is able to master.

In an economy which will offer fewer and fewer places for the unskilled, there must be a wide variety of educational opportunities so that every young American, on leaving school, will have acquired the training to take a useful and rewarding place in our society.

It is increasingly clear that more of our educational resources must be directed to pre-school training as well as to junior college, college and post-graduate study.

The demands on the already inadequate sources of state and local revenues place a serious limitation on education. New methods of financial aid must be explored, including the channeling of federally collected revenues to all levels of education, and, to the extent permitted by the Constitution, to all schools. Only in this way can our educational programs achieve excellence throughout the nation, a goal that must be achieved without interfering with local control and direction of education.

In order to insure that all students who can meet the requirements for college entrance can continue their education, we propose an expanded program of public scholarships, guaranteed loans, and work-study grants.

We shall develop the potential of the Armed Forces for training young men who might otherwise be rejected for military service because their work skills are underdeveloped.

The health of the people is important to the strength and purpose of our country and is a proper part of our common concern.

In a nation that lacks neither compassion nor resources, the needless suffering of people who cannot afford adequate medical care is intolerable:

We will continue to fight until we have succeeded in including hospital care for older Americans in the Social Security program, and have insured adequate assistance to those elderly people suffering from mental illness and mental retardation.

We will go forward with research into the causes and cures of disease, accidents, mental illness and mental retardation.

We will further expand our health facilities, especially medical schools, hospitals, and research laboratories.

America's veterans who served their Nation so well must, in turn, be served fairly by a grateful Nation. First-rate hospitals and medical care must be provided veterans with service-connected injuries and disabilities, and their compensation rates must insure an adequate standard of living. The National Service Life Insurance program should be reopened for those who have lost their insurance coverage, and an equitable and just pension system must help meet the need of those disabled veterans and their survivors who require financial assistance.

*Democracy of Opportunity*

The variety of our people is the source of our strength and ought not to be a cause of disunity or discord. The rights of all our citizens must be protected and all the laws of our land obeyed if America is to be safe for democracy.

The Civil Rights Act of 1964 deserves and requires full observance by every American and fair, effective enforcement if there is any default.

Resting upon a national consensus expressed by the overwhelming support of both parties, this new law impairs the rights of no American; it affirms the rights of all Americans. Its purpose is not to divide, but to end division; not to curtail the opportunities of any, but to increase opportunities for all; not to punish, but to promote further our commitment to freedom, the pursuit of justice, and a deeper respect for human dignity.

We reaffirm our belief that lawless disregard for the rights of others is wrong—whether used to deny equal rights or to obtain equal rights.

We cannot and will not tolerate lawlessness. We can and will seek to eliminate its economic and social causes.

True democracy of opportunity will not be served by establishing quotas based on the same false distinctions we seek to erase, nor can the effects of prejudice be neutralized by the expedient of preferential practices.

The immigration laws must be revised to permit families to be reunited, to welcome the persecuted and oppressed, and to eliminate the discriminatory provisions which base admission upon national origins.

We will support legislation to carry forward the progress already made toward full equality of opportunity for women as well as men.

We will strive to eliminate discrimination against older Americans, especially in their employment.

Ending discrimination based on race, age, sex, or national origin demands not only equal opportunity but the opportunity to be equal. We are concerned not only with people's right to be free, but also with their ability to use their freedom.

We will:

Carry the War on Poverty forward as a total war against the causes of human want.

Move forward with programs to restore those areas, such as Appalachia, which the Nation's progress has by-passed.

Help the physically handicapped and mentally disadvantaged develop to the full limit of their capabilities.

Enhance the security of older Americans by encouraging private retirement and welfare programs, offering opportunities like those provided for the young under the Economic Opportunities Act of 1964, and expanding decent housing which older citizens can afford.

Assist our Indian people to improve their standard of living and attain self-sufficiency, the privileges of equal citizenship, and full participation in American life.

The Social Security program, initiated and developed under the National leadership of the Democratic Party and in the face of ceaseless partisan opposition, contributes greatly to the strength of the Nation. We must insure that those who have contributed to the system shall share in the steady increase in our standard of living by adjusting benefit levels.

We hold firmly to the conviction, long embraced by Democratic Administrations, that the advancing years of life should bring not fear and loneliness, but security, meaning, and satisfaction.

We will encourage further support for the arts, giving people a better chance to use increased leisure and recognizing that the achievements of art are an index of the greatness of a civilization.

We will encourage the advance of science and technology—for its material rewards, and for its contribution to an understanding of the universe and ourselves.

### The Economy

The American free enterprise system is one of the great achievements of the human mind and spirit. It has developed by a combination of the energetic efforts of working men and women, bold private initiative, the profit motive and wise public policy, until it is now the productive marvel of mankind.

In spite of this, at the outset of 1961, America was in the depths of the fourth postwar recession.

Since then, in 42 months of uninterrupted expansion under Presidents Kennedy and Johnson, we have achieved the longest and strongest peacetime prosperity in modern history:

Almost four million jobs have been added to the economy—almost 1½ million since last December.

Workers' earnings and corporate profits are at the highest level in history.

Prices have been more stable than in any other industrial nation in the free world.

This did not just happen. It has come about because we have wisely and prudently used our increasing understanding of how the economy works.

It is the national purpose, and our commitment, to continue this expansion of the American economy toward its potential, without a recession, with continued stability, and with an extension of the benefits of this growth and prosperity to those who have not fully shared in them.

This will require continuation of flexible and innovative fiscal, monetary, and debt management policies, recognizing the importance of low interest rates.

We will seek further tax reduction—and in the process we need to remove inequities in our present tax laws. In particular we should carefully review all our excise taxes and eliminate those that are obsolete. Consideration should be given to the development of fiscal policies which would provide revenue sources to hard-pressed state and local governments to assist them with their responsibilities.

Every penny of Federal spending must be accounted for in terms of the strictest economy, efficiency and integrity. We pledge to continue a frugal government, getting a dollar's value for a dollar spent, and a government worthy of the citizen's confidence.

Our goal is a balanced budget in a balanced economy.

Our enviable record of price stability must be maintained—through sound fiscal and monetary policies and the encouragement of responsible private wage and price policies. Stability is essential to protect our citizens—particularly the retired and handicapped—from the ravages of inflation. It is also essential to maintain confidence in the American dollar; this confidence has been restored in the past four years through sound policies.

Radical changes in technology and automation contribute to increased productivity and a higher standard of living. They must not penalize the few while benefiting the many. We maintain that any man or woman displaced by a machine or by technological change should have the opportunity, without penalty, to another job. Our common responsibility is to see that this right is fulfilled.

Full employment is an end in itself and must be insisted upon as a priority objective.

It is the national purpose, and our commitment, that every man or woman who is willing and able to work is entitled to a job and to a fair wage for doing it.

The coverage of the Fair Labor Standards Act must be extended to all workers employed in industries affecting interstate commerce, and the minimum wage level and coverage increased to assure those at the bottom of the economic scale a fairer share in the benefits of an ever-rising standard of American living.

Overtime payment requirements must be increased to assure maximum employment consistent with business efficiency. The matter of the length of work periods should be given continuing consideration.

The unemployment insurance program must be basically revised to meet the needs of the unemployed and of the economy, and to assure that this program meets the standards the nation's experience dictates.

Agricultural and migratory workers must be given legal protection and economic encouragement.

We must develop fully our most precious resource—our manpower. Training and retraining programs must be expanded. A broad-gauge manpower program must be developed which will not only satisfy the needs of the economy but will also give work its maximum meaning in the pattern of human life.

We will stimulate as well as protect small business, the seedbed of free enterprise and a major source of employment in our economy.

The antitrust laws must be vigorously enforced.

Our population, which is growing rapidly and becoming increasingly mobile, and our expanding economy are placing greater demands upon our transportation system than ever before. We must have fast, safe, and economic modes of transportation. Each mode should be encouraged to develop in accordance with its maximum utility, available at the lowest cost under the principles of fair competition. A strong and efficient American Flag merchant marine is essential to peacetime commerce and defense emergencies.

The industrial democracy of free, private collective bargaining and the security of American trade unions must be strengthened by repealing Section 14(b) of the Taft-Hartley Act. The present inequitable restrictions on the right to organize and to strike and picket peaceably must also be eliminated.

In order to protect the hard earned dollars of American consumers, as well as promote their basic consumer rights, we will make full use of existing authority, and continue to promote efforts on behalf of consumers by industry, voluntary organizations, and state and local governments. Where protection is essential, we will enact legislation to protect the safety of consumers and to provide them with essential information. We will continue to insist that our drugs and medicines are safe and effective, that our food and cosmetics are free from harm, that merchandise is labeled and packaged honestly and that the true cost of credit is disclosed.

It is the national purpose, and our commitment to increase the freedom and effectiveness of the essential private forces and processes in the economy.

## RURAL AMERICA

The roots of our economy and our life as a people lie deep in the soil of America's farm land.

Our policies and programs must continue to recognize the significant role of agricultural and rural life.

To achieve the goals of higher incomes to the farm and ranch, particularly the family-sized farm, lower prices for the consumer, and lower costs to the government, we will continue to carry forward this three-dimensional program.

1. Commodity Programs to strengthen the farm income structure and reach the goal of parity of income in every aspect of American agriculture. We will continue to explore and develop new domestic and foreign markets for the products of our farms and ranches.

2. Consumer Programs including expansion of the Food Stamp Program and the school lunch and other surplus food programs, and acceleration of research into new industrial uses of farm products, in order to assure maximum use of and abundance of wholesome foods at fair prices here and abroad. We will also study new low-cost methods and techniques of food distribution for the benefit of our housewives to better feed their families.

3. Community Programs and agricultural cooperatives to assure rural America decent housing, economic security and full partnership in the building of the great society. We pledge our continued support of the rural telephone program and the Rural Electrification Administration, which are among the great contributions of the Democratic Party to the well-being and comfort of rural America.

## THE NATION'S NATURAL RESOURCES

America's bountiful supply of natural resources has been one of the major factors in achieving our position of world leadership, in developing the greatest industrial machine in the world's history, and in providing a richer and more complete life for every American. But these resources are not inexhaustible. With our vastly expanding population—an estimated 325 million people by the end of the century—there is an ever-increasing responsibility to use and conserve our resources wisely and prudently if we are to fulfill our obligation to the trust we hold for future generations. Building on the unsurpassed conservation record of the past four years, we shall:

Continue the quickened pace of comprehensive development of river basins in every section of the country, employing multi-purpose projects such as flood control, irrigation and reclamation, power generation, navigation, municipal water supply, fish and wildlife enhancement and recreation, where appropriate to realize the fullest possible benefits.

Provide the people of this nation a balanced outdoor recreation program to add to their health and well-being, including the addition or improved management of national parks, forests, lake shores, seashores and recreation areas.

Preserve for us and our posterity through the means provided by the Wilderness Act of 1964 millions of acres of primitive and wilderness areas, including countless beautiful lakes and streams.

Increase our stock of wildlife and fish.

Continue and strengthen the dynamic program inaugurated to assure fair treatment for American fishermen and the preservation of fishing rights.

Continue to support balanced land and forest development through intensive forest management on a multiple-use and sustained yield basis, reforestation of burned land, providing public access roads, range improvement, watershed management, concern for small business operations and recreational uses.

Unlock the resources of the sea through a strong oceanography program.

Continue the attack we have launched on the polluted air that envelops our cities and on eliminating the pollution of our rivers and streams.

Intensify our efforts to solve the critical water

problems of many sections of this country by de-salinization.

Sustain and promote strong, vigorous domestic minerals, metals, petroleum and fuels industries.

Increase the efficient use of electrical power through regional inter-ties and more extensive use of high voltage transmission.

Continue to promote the development of new and improved methods of generating electric power, such as the recent important gains in the field of atomic energy and the Passamaquoddy tidal power project.

Preserve the T.V.A., which has played such an instrumental role in the revitalization of the area it serves and which has been the inspiration for regional development programs throughout the world.

## THE CITY

The vitality of our cities is essential to the healthy growth of American civilization. In the next 40 years urban populations will double, the area of city land will double and we will have to construct houses, highways and facilities equal to all those built since this country was first settled.

Now is the time to redouble our efforts, with full cooperation among local, state and federal governments, for these objectives:

The goal of our housing program must be a decent home for every American family.

Special effort must be made in our cities to provide wholesome living for our young people. We must press the fight against narcotics and, through the war against poverty, increase educational and employment opportunities, turning juvenile delinquents into good citizens and tax-users into tax payers.

We will continue to assist broad community and regional development, urban renewal, mass transit, open space and other programs for our metropolitan areas. We will offer such aid without impairing local Administration through unnecessary Federal interference.

Because our cities and suburbs are so important to the welfare of all our people, we believe a department devoted to urban affairs should be added to the President's cabinet.

## THE GOVERNMENT

We, the people, are the government.

The Democratic Party believes, as Thomas Jefferson first stated that "the care of human life and happiness is the first and only legitimate object of good government:"

The government's business is the people's business. Information about public affairs must continue to be freely available to the Congress and to the public.

Every person who participates in the government must be held to a standard of ethics which permits no compromise with the principles of absolute honesty and the maintenance of undivided loyalty to the public interest.

The Congress of the United States should revise its rules and procedures to assure majority rule after reasonable debate and to guarantee that major legislative proposals of the President can be brought to a vote after reasonable consideration in committee.

We support home rule for the District of Columbia. The seat of our government shall be a workshop for democracy, a pilot-plant for freedom, and a place of incomparable beauty.

We also support a constitutional amendment giving the District voting representation in Congress and, pending such action, the enactment of legislation providing for a non-voting delegate from District of Columbia to the House of Representatives.

We support the right of the people of the Virgin Islands to the fullest measure of self-government, including the right to elect their Governor.

The people of Puerto Rico and the people of the United States enjoy a unique relationship that has contributed greatly to the remarkable economic and political development of Puerto Rico. We look forward to the report on that relationship by a commission composed of members from Puerto Rico and the United States, and we are confident that it will contribute to the further enhancement of Puerto Rico and the benefit that flows from the principles of self-determination.

The Democratic Party holds to the belief that government in the United States—local, state and federal—was created in order to serve the people. Each level of government has appropriate powers and each has specific responsibilities. The first responsibility of government at every level is to protect the basic freedoms of the people. No government at any level can properly complain of violation of its power, if it fails to meet its responsibilities.

The federal government exists not to grow larger, but to enlarge the individual potential and achievement of the people.

The federal government exists not to subordinate the states, but to support them.

All of us are Americans. All of us are free men. Ultimately there can be no effective restraint on the powers of government at any level save as Americans exercising their duties as citizens insist upon and maintain free, democratic processes of our constitutional system.

ONE NATION, ONE PEOPLE

On November 22, 1963, John Fitzgerald Kennedy was shot down in our land.

We honor his memory best—and as he would wish—by devoting ourselves anew to the larger purposes for which he lived.

Of first priority is our renewed commitments to the values and ideals of democracy.

We are firmly pledged to continue the Nation's march towards the goals of equal opportunity and equal treatment for all Americans regardless of race, creed, color or national origin.

We cannot tolerate violence anywhere in our land—north, south, east or west. Resort to lawlessness is anarchy and must be opposed by the Government and all thoughtful citizens.

We must expose, wherever it exists, the advocacy of hatred which creates the clear and present danger of violence.

We condemn extremism, whether from the Right or Left, including the extreme tactics of such organizations as the Communist Party, the Ku Klux Klan and the John Birch Society.

We know what violence and hate can do. We have seen the tragic consequences of misguided zeal and twisted logic.

The time has come now for all of us to understand and respect one another, and to seek the unity of spirit and purpose from which our future greatness will grow—for only as we work together with the object of liberty and justice for all will the peace and freedom of each of us be secured.

These are the principles which command our cause and strengthen our effort as we cross the new frontier and enter upon the great society.

## AN ACCOUNTING OF STEWARDSHIP, 1961—1964

One hundred and twenty-four years ago, in 1840, the Democratic National Convention meeting in Baltimore adopted the first platform in the history of a national political party. The principles stated in that platform are as valid as ever:

"Resolved, That the liberal principles embodied by Jefferson in the Declaration of Independence, and sanctioned in the Constitution, which makes ours the land of liberty, and the asylum of the oppressed of every nation, have ever been cardinal principles in the democratic faith."

One hundred and twenty years later, in 1960, our nation had grown from 26 to 50 states, our people from 17 million to 179 million.

That year, in Los Angeles, the Democratic National Convention adopted a platform which reflected, in its attention to 38 specific subjects, the volume of unfinished business of the American people which had piled up to the point of national crisis.

The platform declared that as a Party we would put the people's business first, and stated in plain terms how we proposed to get on with it.

Four year have passed, and the time has come for the people to measure our performance against our pledges.

We welcome the comparison; we seek it.

*For the record is one of four years of unrelenting effort, and unprecedented achievement—not by a political party, but by a people.*

## THE RECORD

NATIONAL DEFENSE

In 1960, we proposed to—

"Recast our military capacity in order to provide forces and weapons of a diversity, balance, and mobility sufficient in quantity and quality to deter both limited and general aggression."

Since January 1961, we have achieved:

A 150% increase in the number of nuclear warheads and a 200% increase in total megatonnage available in the Strategic Alert Forces.

A 60% increase in the tactical nuclear strength in Western Europe.

A 45% increase in the number of combat-ready Army divisions.

A 15,000 man increase in the strength of the Marine Corps.

A 75% increase in airlift capability.

A 100% increase in ship construction to modernize our fleet.

A 44% increase in the number of tactical fighter squadrons.

An 800% increase in the special forces trained to deal with counter-insurgency threats.

In 1960, we proposed to create—

"Deterrent military power such that the Soviet and Chinese leaders will have no doubt that an attack on the United States would surely be followed by their own destruction."

Since 1961, we have increased the intercontinental ballistic missiles and Polaris missiles in our arsenal from fewer than 100 to more than 1,000.

Our Strategic Alert Forces now have about 1,100 bombers, including 550 on 15-minute alert, many of which are equipped with decoy missiles and other penetration aids to assure that they will reach their targets.

In 1960, we proposed—

"Continuous modernization of our forces through intensified research and development, including essential programs slowed down, terminated, suspended, or neglected for lack of budgetary support."

Since 1961, we have—

Increased funds for research and development by 50% over the 1957-60 level.

Added 208 major new research and development projects including 77 weapons programs with costs exceeding $10 million each, among which are the SR-71 long-range, manned, supersonic strategic military reconnaissance aircraft, the NIKE-X anti-ballistic missile system, the A7A navy attack aircraft, and the F-111 fighter-bomber and a new main battle tank.

Increased, by more than 1,000%, the funds for the development of counter-insurgency weapons and equipment, from less than $10 million to over $103 million per year.

In 1960, we proposed—

"Balanced conventional military forces which will permit a response graded to the intensity of any threats of aggressive force."

Since 1961, we have—

Increased the regular strength of the Army by 100,000 men, and the numbers of combat-ready Army divisions from 11 to 16.

Increased the number of tactical fighter squadrons from 55 to 79 and have substantially increased the procurement of tactical fighters.

Trained over 100,000 officers in counter-insurgency skills necessary to fight guerilla and anti-guerilla warfare, and increased our special forces trained to deal with counter-insurgency by 800%.

Acquired balanced stocks of combat consumables for all our forces so that they can engage in combat for sustained periods of time.

In reconstructing the nation's defense establishment, the Administration has insisted that the services be guided by these three precepts:

Buy only what we need.

Buy only at the lowest sound price.

Reduce operating costs through standardization, consolidation, and termination of unnecessary operations.

As a result, our expanded and reconstituted defense force has cost billions of dollars less than it would have cost under previous inefficient and unbusinesslike methods of procurement and operation. These savings amounted to more than $1 billion in the fiscal year 1963, and to $2.5 billion in the fiscal year just completed. Furthermore, under the cost reduction program we have established, we will be saving $4.6 billion each year, every year, by Fiscal Year 1968.

We have successfully met the challenges of Berlin and Cuba, and attacks upon our Naval forces on the high seas, thus decreasing the prospect of further such challenges and brightening the outlook for peace.

ARMS CONTROL

In 1960, we proposed—

"A national peace agency for disarmament planning and research to muster the scientific ingenuity, coordination, continuity, and seriousness of purpose which are now lacking in our arms control efforts."

In 1961, the United States became the first nation in the world to establish an "agency for peace"—the Arms Control and Disarmament Agency.

This agency is charged by law with the development of a realistic arms control and disarmament policy to promote national security and provide an impetus towards a world free from the threat of war. Working closely with the senior military leaders of the Department of Defense, the Arms Control and Disarmament Agency has enabled the United States to lead the world in a new, continuous, hard-headed and purposeful discussion, negotiation and planning of disarmament.

In 1960, we proposed—

"To develop responsible proposals that will help break the deadlock on arms control."

In the aftermath of the Cuban crisis the United States pressed its advantage to seek a new breakthrough for peace. On June 10, 1963, at American University, President Kennedy called on the Soviet leadership to join in concrete steps to abate the nuclear arms race. After careful negotiations experienced American negotiators reached agreement with the Russians on a Nuclear Test Ban Treaty—an event that will be marked forever in the history of mankind as a first step on the difficult road of arms control.

One hundred and six nations signed or acceded to the treaty.

In the United States it was supported by the Joint Chiefs of Staff, and ratified in the Senate by an 80-20 vote.

To insure the effectiveness of our nuclear development program in accord with the momentous Test Ban Treaty, the Joint Chiefs of Staff recommended, and the Administration has undertaken:

A comprehensive program of underground testing of nuclear explosives.

Maintenance of modern nuclear laboratory facilities.

Preparations to test in the atmosphere if essential to national security, or if the treaty is violated by the Soviet Union.

Continuous improvement of our means for detecting violations and other nuclear activities elsewhere in the world.

In 1960, we proposed—

"To the extent we can secure the adoption of effective arms control agreeemnts, vast resources will be freed for peaceful use."

In January and April 1964, President Johnson announced cutbacks in the production of nuclear materials: twenty percent in plutonium production and forty percent in enriched uranium. When the USSR followed this United States initiative with a similar announcement, the President welcomed the response as giving hope "that the world may yet, one day, live without the fear of war."

INSTRUMENTS OF FOREIGN POLICY

In 1960, we proposed that—

"American foreign policy in all its aspects must be attuned to our world of change.

"We will recruit officials whose experience, humanity and dedication fit them for the task of effectively representing America abroad.

"We will provide a more sensitive and creative direction to our overseas information program."

Since 1961, the Department of State has had its self-respect restored, and has been vitalized by more vigorous recruitment and more intensive training of foreign service officers representing all elements of the American people.

Forty days after taking office President Kennedy established the Peace Corps. The world did not change overnight. Neither will it ever be quite the same again. The foreign minister of one large Asian nation has called the Peace Corps "the most powerful idea in recent times."

One hundred thousand Americans have volunteered for the Peace Corps. Nine thousand have served in a total of 45 countries.

Nearly every country to which volunteers have been sent has asked for more. Two dozen new countries are on the waiting list.

Volunteer organizations on the Peace Corps model are already operating in 12 countries and there has been a great expansion of volunteer service in many others.

An International Secretariat for Volunteer Service is working in 32 economically advanced and developing nations.

The United States Information Agency has been transformed into a powerful, effective and respected weapon of the free world. The new nations of the world have come to know an America that is not afraid to tell the truth about itself— and so can be believed when it tells the truth about Communist imperialism.

WORLD TRADE

In 1960, we said—

". . . We shall expand world trade in every responsible way.

"Since all Americans share the benefits of this policy, its costs should not be the burden of a few. We shall support practical measures to ease the necessary adjustments of industries and communities which may be unavoidably hurt by increases in imports.

"Our government should press for reduction of foreign barriers on the sale of the products of American industry and agriculture."

This pledge was fulfilled in the Trade Expansion Act of 1962.

The Trade Expansion Act of 1962, gives the President power to negotiate a 50 percent across-the-board cut in tariff barriers to take place over a five-year period.

Exports have expanded over 10 percent—by over $2 billion—since 1961.

Foreign trade now provides jobs for more than 4 million workers.

Negotiations now underway will permit American businessmen and farmers to take advantage of the greatest trading opportunity in history—the rapidly expanding European market.

The Trade Expansion Act provides for worker training and moving allowances, and for loans, tax rebates and technical assistance for businesses if increased imports resulting from concessions granted in trade agreements result in unemployment or loss of business.

Where American agriculture or industrial products have been unfairly treated in order to favor domestic products, prompt and forceful action has been taken to break down such barriers. These efforts have opened new United States export opportunities for fruits and vegetables, and numerous other agricultural and manufactured products to Europe and Japan.

The Long Term Cotton Textile Agreement of 1962 protects the textile and garment industry against disruptive competition from imports of cotton textiles. The Cotton Act of 1964 enables American manufacturers to buy cotton at the world market price, so they can compete in selling their products at home and abroad.

## IMMIGRATION

In 1960, we proposed to—

"Adjust our immigration, nationality and refugee policies to eliminate discrimination and to enable members of scattered families abroad to be united with relatives already in our midst.

"The national-origins quota system of limiting immigration contradicts the founding principles of this nation. It is inconsistent with our belief in the rights of men."

The immigration law amendments proposed by the Administration, and now before Congress, by abolishing the national-origin quota system, will eliminate discrimination based upon race and place of birth and will facilitate the reunion of families.

The Cuban Refugee Program begun in 1961 has resettled over 81,000 refugees, who are now self-supporting members of 1,800 American communities. The Chinese Refugee Program, begun in 1962, provides for the admission to the United States of 12,000 Hong Kong refugees from Red China.

## THE UNDERDEVELOPED WORLD

In 1960, we pledged—

"To the non-Communist nations of Asia, Africa, and Latin America: We shall create with you working partnerships based on mutual respect and understanding" and "will revamp and refocus the objectives, emphasis and allocation of our foreign assistance programs."

In 1961, the administration created the Agency for International Development, combining the three separate agencies that had handled foreign assistance activities into an orderly and efficient instrument of national policy.

Since 1961, foreign aid has been conducted on a spartan, cost conscious basis, with emphasis on self-help, reform and performance as conditions of American help.

These new policies are showing significant returns.

Since the beginning of the Marshall Plan in 1948, U. S. economic assistance has been begun and ended in 17 countries. In 14 other countries in Asia, Africa and Latin America, the transition to economic self-support is well under way, and U. S. assistance is now phasing out. In the 1965 AID program, 90 percent of economic assistance will go to just 25 countries.

In 1960, only 41 percent of aid-financed commodities were purchased in America. In 1964, under AID, 85 percent of all aid-financed commodities were U. S. supplied.

The foreign aid appropriation of $3.5 billion for fiscal year 1965 represents the smallest burden on U. S. resources that has been proposed since foreign aid began after World War II.

Since 1961, the United States has insisted that our allies in Europe and Japan must share responsibility in the field of foreign assistance, particularly to their former colonies. They have responded with major programs. Several nations now contribute a larger share of their gross national production to foreign assistance than does the United States.

The Alliance for Progress, launched at the Conference of Punta del Este in Uruguay in 1961, has emerged as the greatest undertaking of social reform and international cooperation in the history of the Western Hemisphere.

The American republics agreed to work together "To make the benefits of economic progress available to all citizens of all economic and social groups through a more equitable distribution of national income, raising more rapidly the income and standard of living of the needier sectors of the population, at the same time that a higher proportion of the national product is devoted to investment."

The results so far:

Major tax reform legislation has been adopted in eight countries.

Agrarian reform legislation has been introduced in twelve countries, and agricultural credit, technical assistance and resettlement projects are going forward in sixteen countries.

Fifteen countries have self-help housing programs, and savings and loan legislation has been adopted by nine countries.

Private or public development banks have been established or are being established in eight countries, providing new sources of capital for the small businessman.

Education budgets have risen by almost 13 percent a year, and five million more children are going to school. U. S. aid has helped build 23,000 schoolrooms.

A Latin American school lunch program is feeding 10 million children at least one good meal every day, and the program will reach 12 million by the end of the year.

The Alliance for Progress has immeasurably strengthened the collective will of the nations of the Western Hemisphere to resist the massive efforts of Communist subversion that conquered Cuba in 1959 and then headed for the mainland.

In 1960, we urged—

". . . Continued economic assistance to Israel and the Arab peoples to help them raise their living standards.

"We pledge our best efforts for peace in the Middle East by seeking to prevent an arms race while guarding against the dangers of a military imbalance resulting from Soviet arms shipments."

In the period since that pledge was made the New East has come closer to peace and stability than at any time since World War II.

Economic and technical assistance to Israel and Arab nations continues at a high level, although with more and more emphasis on loans as against grants. The United States 's determined to help bring the revolution in the technology of desalinization to the aid of the desert regions of this area.

## THE ATLANTIC COMMUNITY

In 1960, we said—

"To our friends and associates in the Atlantic Community: We propose a broader partnership that goes beyond our common fears to recognize the depth and sweep of our common political, economic, and cultural interests."

In 1961, the United States ratified the conventions creating the Organization for Economic Cooperation and Development, a body made up of ourselves, Canada and 18 European States which carries forward on a permanent basis the detailed cooperation and mutual assistance that began with the Marshall Plan.

Since 1961, we have progressed in the building of mutual confidence, unity, and strength. NATO has frequently been used for consultation on foreign policy issues. Strong Atlantic unity emerged in response to Soviet threats in Berlin and in Cuba. Current trade negotiations reflect the value of the Trade Expansion Act and the utility of arrangements for economic cooperation. NATO military forces are stronger in both nuclear and conventional weapons.

The United States has actively supported the proposal to create a multilateral, mix-manned, seaborne nuclear missile force which could give all NATO countries a direct share in NATO's nuclear deterrent without proliferating the number of independent, national nuclear forces.

## THE COMMUNIST WORLD

In 1960, we said—

"To the rulers of the Communist World: We confidently accept your challenge to competition in every field of human effort.

"We believe your Communist ideology to be sterile, unsound, and doomed to failure . . .

". . . We are prepared to negotiate with you whenever and wherever there is a realistic possibility of progress without sacrifice of principle.

"But we will use all the will, power, resources, and energy at our command to resist the further encroachment of Communism on freedom—whether at Berlin, Formosa or new points of pressure as yet undisclosed."

Following the launching of Sputnik in 1957, the Soviet Union began a world-wide offensive. Russian achievements in space were hailed as the forerunners of triumph on earth.

Now, seven years later, the Communist influence has failed in its efforts to win Africa. Of the 31 African nations formed since World War II, not one has chosen Communism.

Khrushchev had to back down on his threat to sign a peace treaty with East Germany. Access to West Berlin remains free.

In Latin America, the Alliance for Progress has begun to reduce the poverty and distress on which Communism breeds.

In Japan, where anti-American riots in 1960 prevented a visit from the President, relations with the United States have been markedly improved.

In the United Nations the integrity of the office of Secretary General was preserved despite the Soviet attack on it through the Troika proposal.

When Red China attacked India, the U. S. promptly came to India's aid with modern infantry supplies and equipment.

On the battlefield of the Cold War one engagement after another has been fought and won.

Frustrated in its plans to nibble away at country after country, the Soviet Union conceived a bold stroke designed to reverse the trend against it. With extreme stealth Soviet intermediate range and medium range offensive missiles were brought into Cuba in 1962.

Shortly after the missiles arrived in Cuba, and before any of them became operational, they were discovered and photographed by U. S. reconnaissance flights.

The U. S. response was carefully planned and prepared, and calmly, deliberately, but effectively executed. On October 22, President Kennedy called on the Soviet Union to dismantle and remove the weapons from Cuba. He ordered a strict quarantine on Cuba enforced by the U. S. Navy.

The Organization of American States acted swiftly and decisively by a unanimous vote of 20 to 0 to authorize strong measures, including the use of force, to ensure that the missiles were withdrawn from Cuba and not re-introduced.

At the end of a tense week Khrushchev caved in before this demonstration of Western power and determination. Soviet ships, closely observed by U. S. pilots, loaded all the missiles and headed back to Russia. U. S. firmness also compelled withdrawal of the IL-28 bombers.

A turning point of the Cold War had been reached.

The record of world events in the past year reflects the vigor and successes of U. S. policy:

*Berlin, October-November 1963.* Communist efforts to interfere with free Western access to Berlin were successfully rebuffed.

*Venezuela, March 1964.* Despite the threats and terror tactics of Castro-inspired agitators, over 90 percent of the people voted in the election that chose President Leoni to succeed Romulo Betancourt—the first democratic succession in that office in Venezuela in Venezuela's history.

*Panama, 1964.* Patient negotiation achieved a resumption of diplomatic relations, which had been severed after the riots in January; President Johnson achieved a dignified and an honorable solution of the crisis.

*Vietnam, August 1964.* Faced with sudden unprovoked attacks by Communist PT boats on American destroyers on the high sea, President Johnson ordered a sharp immediate retaliation on the hostile vessels and their supporting facilities.

Speaking on that occasion, the President said:

"Aggression—deliberate, willful and systematic aggression has unmasked its face to the world. The world remembers—the world must never forget—that aggression unchallenged is aggression unleashed.

"We of the United States have not forgotten.

"That is why we have answered this aggression with action."

*Cuba, 1961-1964.* Cuba and Castro have been virtually isolated in the Hemisphere.

Only 2 out of 20 OAS countries maintain diplomatic relations with Cuba.

Cuban trade with the Free World has dropped sharply from the 1958 level.

Free world shipping to Cuba has fallen sharply. Isolation of Cuba by air has tightened greatly.

Hundreds of thousands of Cubans have left the island or have indicated their desire to come to the United States.

The Castro regime has been suspended from participation in the OAS.

The Cuban economy is deteriorating: the standard of living is 20 percent below pre-Castro levels, with many items rationed; industrial output is stagnant; sugar production is at the lowest level since the 1940's.

## THE UNITED NATIONS

In 1960, we pledged—

"To our fellow members of the United Nations: we shall strengthen our commitments in this, our great continuing institution for conciliation and the growth of a world community."

Over the past four years the Administration has fulfilled this pledge as one of the central purposes of foreign policy.

During that time the United States has supported—and frequently led—efforts within the United Nations.

—to strengthen its capacity as peacekeeper and peacemaker—with the result that the UN remained on guard on armistice lines in Korea, Kashmir and the Middle East; preserved peace in the Congo, West New Guinea and Cyprus; provided a forum for the U. S. during crises in the Caribbean and the Gulf of Tonkin; began to develop a flexible call-up system for emergency peace-keeping forces; and moved toward a revival of the Security Council as the primary organ for peace and security without loss of the residual powers of the General Assembly.

—to discover and exploit areas of common interest for the reduction of world dangers and world tensions—with the result that the orbiting of weapons of mass destruction has been banned and legal principles adopted for the use of outer space; projects of scientific cooperation in meteorology, oceanography, Antarctic exploration and peaceful uses of atomic energy, have been promoted; and the search for further moves toward arms control have been pursued to supplement the limited test ban treaty.

—to further the work of the United Nations in improving the lot of mankind—with the result that the Decade of Development has been launched; the World Food Program undertaken; aid to children extended; projects to promote economic and social progress in the developing world have been expanded; and the impact of technology and world trade upon development has been explored.

—to maintain the integrity of the organization —its Charter and its Secretariat—with the result that the Troika proposal was defeated; the functions of the Secretary-General have been kept intact; the authority of the General Assembly to levy assessments for peacekeeping has been sustained despite attempted financial vetoes by Communist and other members.

In fulfilling its pledge to the United Nations, the Administration has helped to strengthen peace, to promote progress, and to find areas of international agreement and cooperation.

## ECONOMIC GROWTH

In 1960, we said—

"The new Democratic Administration will confidently proceed to unshackle American enterprise and to free American labor, industrial leadership, and capital, to create an abundance that will outstrip any other system.

"We Democrats believe that our economy can and must grow at an average rate of 5 percent annually, almost twice as fast as our average annual rate since 1953. We pledge ourselves to policies that will achieve this goal without inflation."

In January 1961, the nation was at the bottom of the fourth recession of the postwar period—the third in the eight-year period, 1953-60. More men and women were out of work than at any time since the Great Depression of the 1930's. In February 1961, the unemployment rate was 6.8 percent, with a total of 5,705,000 unemployed.

Today we are in the midst of the longest peacetime expansion in our history, during the past 42 months of unbroken economic expansion:

Our economic growth rate has risen now to over 5 percent—twice the average rate for the 1953-60 period.

3,900,000 jobs have been added to the economy, and the unemployment rate was down in July 1964 to 4.9 percent.

The Gross National Product has risen by $120 billion in less than four years! No nation in peacetime history has ever added so much to its wealth in so short a time.

The average manufacturing worker's weekly earnings rose from $89 in January 1961, to $103 in July 1964—an increase of over 15 percent.

Industrial production has increased 28 percent; average operating rates in manufacturing have risen from 78 percent of capacity to 87 percent.

Profits after taxes have increased 62 percent—from an annual rate of $19.2 billion in early 1961 to an estimated $31.2 billion in early 1964.

Total private investment has increased by 43 percent—from an annual rate of $61 billion in early 1961 to $87 billion in the spring of 1964.

There are a million and a half more Americans at work today than there were a year ago.

Our present prosperity was brought about by the enterprise of American business, the skills of the American work force, and by wise public policies.

The provision in the Revenue Act of 1962 for a credit for new investment in machinery and equipment, and the liberalization of depreciation allowance by administrative ruling, resulted in a reduction of $2.5 billion in business taxes.

The Revenue Act of 1964 cut individual income taxes by more than $9 billion, increasing consumer purchasing power by that amount; and corporate taxes were cut another $2.5 billion, with the effect of increasing investment incentives. Overall individual Federal income taxes were cut an average of 19 percent; taxpayers earning $3,000 or less received an average 40 percent cut.

The Temporary Extended Unemployment Compensation Act of 1961 provided $800 million to 2.8 million jobless workers who had exhausted their benefits.

The Area Redevelopment Act of 1961 has meant a $227 million Federal investment in economically hard-hit areas, creating 110,000 new jobs in private enterprise.

The Accelerated Public Works Act of 1962 added $900 million for urgently needed State and local government construction projects.

## AN END TO TIGHT MONEY

In 1960, we proposed—

"As the first step in speeding economic growth, a Democratic president will put an end to the present high interest, tight money policy.

"This policy has failed in its stated purpose—to keep prices down. It has given us two recessions within five years, bankrupted many of our farmers, produced a record number of business failures, and added billions of dollars in unnecessary higher interest charges to government budgets and the cost of living."

Since 1961, we have maintained the free flow of credit so vital to industry, home buyers, and State and local governments.

Immediately, in February 1961, the Federal Housing Agency interest rate was cut from 5¾ percent to 5½ percent. It is now down to 5¼ percent.

Today's home buyer will pay about $1,700 less for FHA-insured financing of a 30-year $15,000 home mortgage than he would have had he taken the mortgage in 1960.

Today after 42 months of expansion, conventional home mortgage rates are lower than they were in January 1961, in the midst of a recession. So are borrowing costs for our States and municipalities, and for long-term corporate issues.

Short-term interest rates have been brought into reasonable balance with interest rates abroad, reducing or eliminating incentives to place short-term funds abroad and thus reducing gold outflow.

We have prudently lengthened the average maturity of the Federal debt, in contrast to the steady shortening that characterized the 1950's.

## CONTROL OF INFLATION

In 1960, we asserted—

"The American consumer has a right to fair prices. We are determined to secure that right.

"A fair share of the gains from increasing productivity in many industries should be passed on to the consumer through price reductions."

Today, after 42 months of economic expansion, wholesale prices are lower than they were in January 1961, in the midst of a recession! The Wholesale Price Index was 101.0 in January 1961; in July 1964, it is 100.4.

The Consumer Price Index, which measures the price of goods and services families purchase, has been brought back to stability, averaging now less than 1.3% increase per year—as compared, for example, with an increase rate about three times this large in the European common market countries.

Since January 1961, the increase in average after-tax family income has been twice the increase in prices.

The Administration has established guideposts

for price and wage movements alike, based primarily on productivity developments, and designed to protect the economy against inflation.

In the single year, 1960, the overall balance of payments deficit reached $3.9 billion, and we lost $1.7 billion in gold. Now for 1964, the prospective balance of payments deficit has been cut to $2 billion, and the gold outflow has ceased.

## FULL EMPLOYMENT

In 1960, we reaffirmed our—

"support of full employment as a paramount objective of national policy."

In July 1964, total employment in the United States rose to the historic peak of 72,400,000 jobs. This represents an increase of 3,900,000 jobs in 42 months.

In the past twelve months, total civilian employment has increased by 1,600,000 jobs, and nonfarm employment by 1,700,000. Most of this job expansion has occurred in the past eight months.

In July 1964, the jobless total was one-half million below a year ago, and was at its lowest July level since 1959.

In July, 1964, the overall unemployment rate was 4.9%—compared with 6.5% in January 1961; and the jobless rate for men who are heads of families was down to 2.7%.

There have been more than a million full-time jobs added to the private profit sector of the economy in the past 12 months. This is the largest increase in any one-year period in the past decade.

We have brought ourselves now within reach of the full employment objective.

## AID TO DEPRESSED AREAS

In 1960, we recognized that—

"General economic measures will not alone solve the problems of localities which suffer some special disadvantage. To bring prosperity to these depressed areas and to enable them to make their full contribution to the national welfare, specially directed action is needed."

The Area Redevelopment Administration was created in 1961 to help depressed areas organize their human and material resources for economic growth. Since its establishment, the ARA has:

Approved 512 financial assistance projects involving a Federal investment of $243.5 million.

Created, in partnership with local govern-

ment, private workers and other investors, 118,-000 new jobs in private enterprise.

Provided retraining programs, with tuition and subsistence, for 37,327 jobless workers, equipping them with new skills to fill available jobs in their areas.

In 1961, Congress authorized $900 million for the Accelerated Public Works Program to speed construction of urgently needed public facilities and increase employment in areas which had failed to recover from previous recessions.

Between October 1962, when the first appropriations were made available, and April 1, 1964, 7,762 projects, involving an estimated 2,500,000 man-months of employment, were approved.

In early 1961, there were 101 major areas in the United States in which unemployment was 6 percent or more, discounting seasonal or temporary factors. By July 1964, this number had been cut two-thirds, to a total of 35.

The concept of "depressed areas" has been broadened in these 3½ years to include clear recognition of the inequity and waste of poverty wherever it exists, and in the Economic Opportunity Act of 1964 the nation has declared, in historic terms, a War on Poverty.

Title I of the Economic Opportunity Act creates the Job Corps, Work-Training programs, and Work-Study programs to provide useful work for about 400,000 young men and women. Job Corps volunteers will receive work and vocational training, part of which will involve conservation work in rural areas. The Work-Training, or Neighborhood Youth Corps program, is open to young persons living at home, including those who need jobs in order to remain in school. The Work-Study programs will enable youth from poor families to earn enough income to enable them to attend college.

Title II of the Act authorized $340 million for the Community Action programs to stimulate urban and rural communities to mobilize their resources to combat poverty through programs designed especially to meet local needs.

Title III provides for special programs to combat poverty in rural areas, including loans up to $1,500 for low income farmers, and loans up to $2,500 for families, to finance non-agricultural enterprises which will enable such families to supplement their incomes. This section of the law provides funds for housing, sanitation education, and day care of children of migrant farm workers.

Title IV of the Act provides for loans up to $25,000 for small businesses to create jobs for the long-term unemployed.

Title V of the Act provides constructive work experience and other needed training to persons who are unable to support or care for themselves or their families.

The Report of the President's Appalachian Regional Commission, submitted to President Johnson in April 1964, proposed a wide-ranging development program. The Appalachian Redevelopment Act, now before Congress, provides for more than $1.1 billion investment in needed basic facilities in the area, together with a regional organization to help generate the full development potential of the human and material resources of this mountain area.

Registration and regulation of migrant labor crew chiefs has been provided to require that crew chiefs or labor brokers, who act on behalf of domestic migrant labor and operate across state lines, shall be registered, show financial responsibility, and meet certain requirements as to moral character and honest dealing with their clients.

### DISCRIMINATION IN EMPLOYMENT

In 1960, we insisted that—

"The right to a job requires action to break down artificial and arbitrary barriers to employment based on age, race, sex, religion, or national origin."

The great Civil Rights Act of 1964 is the strongest and most important law against discrimination in employment in the history of the United States.

It states unequivocally that "It shall be an unlawful employment practice for an employer . . . an employment agency . . . or a labor organization" to discriminate against any person because of his or her "race, color, religion, sex, or national origin."

On March 6, 1961, President Kennedy issued an Executive Order establishing the President's Committee on Equal Employment Opportunity to combat racial discrimination in the employment policies of Government agencies and private firms holding Government contracts. Then–Vice President Johnson, in his capacity as Chairman of the new Committee, assumed personal direction of this program.

As a consequence of the enforcement of the Executive Order, not only has discrimination been eliminated in the Federal Government, but strong affirmative measures have been taken to extend meaningful equality of opportunity to compete for Federal employment to all citizens.

The private employers of 8,076,422 men and women, and trade unions with 12,500,000 members, have signed public agreements establishing non-discriminatory practices.

The Equal Pay Act of 1963 guarantees equal pay to women doing the same work as men, by requiring employers who are covered by the Fair Labor Standards Act to pay equal wages for equal work, regardless of the sex of their workers.

Executive Order 11141, issued by President Johnson on February 12, 1964, establishes for the first time in history a public policy that "contractors and subcontractors engaged in the performance of Federal contracts shall not, in connection with the employment, advancement, or discharge of their employees, or in connection with the terms, conditions, or privileges of their employment, discriminate against persons because of their age . . ."

### COLLECTIVE BARGAINING

In 1960, we pledged—

"an affirmative labor policy which will encourage free collective bargaining through the growth and development of free and responsible unions."

These have been good years for labor-management relations. Time lost from strikes is at the lowest point in history.

The President's Advisory Committee on Labor-Management Policy, made up of distinguished leaders of business and trade unions, has spoken out consistently in favor of creative and constructive solutions to common problems.

Executive Order 10988, issued by President Kennedy on January 17, 1962, extended the rights of union recognition to Federal employees—a goal which some employee organizations had been trying to reach for three quarters of a century.

In the spring of 1964, under President Johnson's personal leadership, the five-year-old railroad dispute that would have resulted in a critical nationwide strike, was at last ended—by free collective bargaining. A cause many thought lost was won; industrial self-government was saved from a disastrous setback.

## PLANNING FOR AUTOMATION

In 1960, we proposed to—

"provide the government leadership necessary to insure that the blessings of automation do not become burdens of widespread unemployment. For the young and the technologically displaced workers, we will provide the opportunity for training and retraining that equips them for jobs to be filled."

The Manpower Development and Training Act of 1962 provides for the training or retraining of unemployed or underemployed people, particularly those threatened or displaced by technological advances. The 1963 amendments to the Act emphasize the problem of youth employment.

In the two years of the administration of this program, training projects for 240,471 persons have been approved, and more than 54,000 persons have completed their training.

Under the Manpower Development and Training Act an active manpower policy is being developed to keep the nation ahead of the problems of automation.

Congress has now enacted, in August 1964, legislation creating a National Commission on Technology, Automation and Economic Progress to undertake a searching inquiry into the problems created by automation, and means by which they can be prevented or solved.

In its own activities, the Federal Government has taken full account of human considerations in instituting technological developments.

## MINIMUM WAGES

In 1960, we pledged—

"To raise the minimum wage to $1.25 an hour and to extend coverage to several million workers not now covered."

The Fair Labor Standards Act Amendments of 1961 raised the minimum wage to $1.25 over a three-year period, and extended the coverage of the Act to 3.6 million additional workers.

The Administration has proposed further amendments to the Fair Labor Standards Act, which are now before the Congress, and which would extend minimum wage coverage to near three quarters of a million workers in laundry, and dry cleaning establishments. Overtime coverage would be extended to an additional 2.6 million workers.

It has proposed a Fringe Benefit amendment to the Bacon-Davis law to provide that the cost of fringe benefits should be included in the definition of "prevailing wage" under the Bacon-Davis law, so that wage rates required in government construction contracts will be in accord with prevailing practice.

## AGRICULTURE

In 1960, we said—

"In every way we will seek to help the men, women, and children whose livelihood comes from the soil to achieve better housing, education, and decent earnings and working conditions."

This is the record:

Total net farm income in 1961-63 averaged nearly a billion dollars a year higher than in 1960.

Total net income per farm was 18 percent higher in 1963 than in 1960.

Farm purchasing power, or gross farm income, rose from $37.9 billion in 1960 to nearly $42 billion in 1963.

Percent of family income spent for food today has declined. In 1960, 20 percent of disposable family income was spent for food. This has now been reduced to less than 19 percent.

Grain surpluses have been brought down to manageable levels; wheat surpluses this year will be the lowest since 1958, and feed grains have been reduced from 80 to 70 million tons.

Reduction of wheat and feed grain surpluses from their 1960 levels to present levels has resulted in an accumulated savings of about a quarter of a billion dollars in storage, transportation, interest and other costs.

Total farm exports have increased 35 percent in 4 years, and have reached a record high in fiscal 1964 of $6.1 billion.

Credit resources administered by the Farmers Home Administration are up 141 percent over 1960, and are averaging now $687 million a year.

Commodity programs to strengthen the farm income structure and reach the goal of parity of income in every aspect of American agriculture. We also cite the parity program providing American cotton to American factories and processes at the same price at which they are exported.

The Rural Areas Development program has

helped create an estimated 125,000 new jobs, and more than 12,000 projects in the process of approval will provide new employment for as many as 200,000 persons.

Participation in the Agricultural Conservation Program has increased 20 percent since 1960.

More than 20,000 farmers have received technical help to develop recreation as an income-making "crop" on land which had been producing surpluses.

Over 600 rural Communities have been aided in providing modern water services.

During the winter of 1964, a special lunch program was instituted for 315 schools and 12,000 children in rural areas where families have extremely low incomes.

Since January 1, 1961, $1.1 billion in electric loans has been made by the Rural Electrification Administration, to rural electric cooperatives, or some $350 million more than in the previous 3½ years. Improved service, as a result, has meant customer savings of $7.5 million a year.

American farmers, in 1964, have protected crop investments totaling $500.5 million with Federal All-Risk Crop Insurance—more than double the amount of insurance in force three years ago, and an all-time record.

Soil and water conservation activities in the past 3½ years have shown a constant upward trend in their contributions to the physical, social and economic welfare of rural areas.

289 new small upstream watershed projects were authorized.

3,000 local soil and water conservation districts have updated their long-range programs to reflect the broadened concepts of economic development.

The Great Plains Conservation Program has been extended for 10 years and 36 counties have been added to the program.

In June 1964, Congress authorized the creation of a National Commission on Food Marketing to investigate the operation of the food industry from producer to consumer.

On January 24, 1961, President Kennedy established by executive order, the Food for Peace program to utilize America's agricultural abundance "to promote the interests of peace . . . and to play an important role in helping to provide a more adequate diet for peoples all around the world."

In the last 3½ years, over $5 billion worth of surplus farm commodities went overseas under Public Law 480 programs. This is one and one-half billion dollars more than during the previous 3½ years.

## SMALL BUSINESS

In 1960, we pledged—

"Action to aid small business in obtaining credit and equity capital at reasonable rates.

"Protection of the public against the growth of monopoly.

"A more equitable share of government contracts to small and independent business."

Through liberalizing amendments to the Small Business Investment Act in 1961 and 1964, and special tax considerations, the investment of equity capital and long term loan funds in small businesses has been greatly accelerated by privately owned and operated small business investment companies licensed under that Act. Moreover, since January 1961, over 21,000 small businesses have obtained SBA business loans, totalling over $1.14 billion, as a result of liberalized and simplified procedures.

The Federal Trade Commission has stepped up its activities to promote free and fair competition in business, and to safeguard the consuming public against both monopolistic and deceptive practices.

The reorganized Antitrust Division of the Department of Justice has directed special emphasis to price fixing, particularly on consumer products, by large companies who distribute through small companies. These include eye glasses, salad oil, flour, cosmetics, swimsuits, bread, milk, and even sneakers.

Since January 1961, some 166,000 government contracts, worth $6.2 billion have been set aside for small business. In the preceding 3½ years there were 77,838 contracts set aside, with a worth of $2.9 billion.

## HOUSING

In 1960 we proposed—

"To make possible the building of 2,000,000 homes a year in wholesome neighborhoods, the home building industry should be aided by special mortgage assistance, with low interest rates, long-term mortgage periods and reduced down payments.

"There will still be need for a substantial low-rent public housing program authorizing as many units as local communities require and are prepared to build."

The Housing Act of 1961 provides many of the necessary new and improved tools for providing housing for low and moderate income families, and for housing for the elderly.

For the 3½ year period ending June 30, 1964, some 5.3 million new units of public and private housing have been built at a cost of approximately $65 billion. The construction rate has risen above 1.5 million units a year, with an annual output of over $20 billion, and we are moving close now to the goal of 2 million a year.

Since January 1961, nearly 400 local housing authorities have been formed to provide housing for low income families. More than 100,000 new units have been approved for construction, at an annual rate about three times that of 1960.

The annual rate of grant assistance for Urban Renewal has risen from $262 million per year (1956 through 1961) to a rate of better than $630 million during the past 12 months.

In the past 3½ years, more than 750 new urban renewal transactions have been approved, equal to nearly 90 percent of the number approved for the entire period from 1949 to 1960.

Cities with community urban renewal programs jumped from a cumulative total of seven in December 1960 to 118 by mid-1964.

To house families whose income is not quite low enough to qualify for public housing, a new rental housing program providing a "below market" interest rate (currently 3⅞%) insured by FHA, has been made available. Mortgage purchase funds have been allocated for about 78,000 such rental units.

Reflecting the fuller recognition of the special equities and needs of older people:

FHA mortgage insurance written on housing projects for the elderly since 1961 has provided more than 3 times as many units as were being provided prior to that time.

Low rent public housing under Federal assistance is being provided senior citizens at an annual rate more than twice that for 1960.

Direct loan authorizations for housing for the elderly increased from $50 million in 1961 to $275 million in 1963.

Maximum loan amounts have been increased to 100% of development cost.

The Housing Act of 1961 expanded and strengthened the Federal program in this area.

The Senior Citizens Housing Act of 1962 moved us another long step forward.

Applications for the provision of nursing homes increased from 30 in January 1961 to more than 580 by the middle of 1964, involving more than 50,000 beds for community nursing homes.

Assistance has been given for more than 1,000 college housing projects including housing for more than 290,000 students and faculty, plus dining halls and other school facilities.

The 1963 Executive Order on Equal Opportunity in Housing assures that the benefits of Federal housing programs and assistance are available without discrimination as to race, color, creed or national origin.

HEALTH

In 1960, we proposed to—

"Provide medical care benefits for the aged as part of the time-tested social security system.

"Step up medical research on the major killers and crippling diseases.

"Expand and improve the Hill-Burton hospital construction program.

"Federal aid for construction, expanding and modernizing schools of medicine, dentistry, nursing and public health.

"Greatly increased federal support for psychiatric research and training and community mental health programs."

More health legislation has been enacted during the past 3½ years than during any other period in American history.

The Community Health Services and Facilities Act of 1961 has made possible 149 projects for testing and demonstrating new or improved services in nursing homes, home care services, central information and referral centers; and providing additional personnel to serve the chronically ill and aged. It has also provided additional federal funds for the construction of nursing homes.

The Hill-Burton Amendments of 1964, extend the program of Federal grants for construction of hospitals, public health centers, long-term facilities, rehabilitation facilities and diagnostic or treatment centers for five additional years. For the first time provision is made for the modernization and renovation of hospitals and health facilities. Funds for the construction of nursing homes and other long-term care facilities are substantially increased.

The Mental Retardation Facilities and Community Mental Health Construction Act of 1963, authorized grants of $150,000,000 to States for constructing community Mental Health Centers, which emphasize the new approach to the care of the mentally ill, centered on care and treatment in the patients' home communities. Thirty-six States have already budgeted more than 75% of their share of Federal funds for planning these new systems.

The Maternal and Child Health and Mental Retardation Planning Amendments of 1963, along with the Mental Retardation Facilities and Community Mental Health Construction Act of 1963, authorized a broad program to prevent, treat, and ameliorate mental retardation. The program provides States and communities needed research, manpower developments, and facilities for health, education rehabilitation, and vocational services to the retarded.

As part of the Federal Government's program to employ the mentally retarded in suitable Federal jobs, the State rehabilitation agencies are certifying persons as qualified for specific suitable Federal jobs. A rising number of placements already made in Federal installations over the country constitutes an encouraging start.

The current need for another 200,000 qualified teachers for the estimated 6 million handicapped children of school age, has been recognized in legislation authorizing grants in aid for the training of professional personnel.

Other legislation provides funds for training teachers of the deaf.

A 1962 amendment to the Public Health Act authorizes a new program of project grants to help meet critical health needs of domestic migratory workers and their families through establishment of family health service clinics.

Forty-nine projects in 24 States have received grants to assist an estimated 300,000 migrant workers.

One out of every ten migrant laborers is estimated to have received some health services through these projects.

The National Institute of Child Health and Human Development, authorized in 1962, is now supporting research and training in eight major areas.

The National Institute of General Medical Sciences, also authorized in 1962, gives recognition to the significance of research training in the sciences basic to medicine. Two thousand research projects are currently being supported.

A $2 million Radiological Health Grant Program was established in 1962 to provide matching grants to assist States in assuming responsibility for adequate radiation control and protection. During Fiscal Year 1964, forty-nine States and Puerto Rico and the Virgin Islands participated.

After two years of scientific evaluation of research and findings, the Report of the Surgeon General's Advisory Committee on Smoking and Health was released in January 1964, calling attention to the health hazards of smoking. An information clearinghouse and a public education program directed toward preventing young people from acquiring the smoking habit are being developed.

A PROGRAM FOR THE AGING

In 1960, we proposed to—

"End the neglect of our older citizens. They deserve lives of usefulness, dignity, independence, and participation. We shall assure them not only health care, but employment for those who want to work, decent housing, and recreation."

The Social Security Act Amendments of 1961 broadened benefits to 5.3 million persons, increased minimum benefits for retired workers from $33 to $40 per month, permitted men as well as women to begin collecting reduced benefits at age 62.

The Social Security program now provides $1.3 billion in benefits each month to 19.5 million persons. One out of every ten Americans receives a Social Security check every month.

The Welfare and Pension Plans Disclosure Act Amendments of 1962 put "enforcement teeth" into this measure, protecting workers' assets in pension programs.

The Housing Act of 1961 increased the scope of Federal housing aids for the elderly by raising from $50 million to $125 million the authorization for low-interest-rate direct loans. In 1962, this was raised further to $225 million and in 1963 to $275 million.

Insurance written by the Federal Housing Administration for mortgage insurance for the elderly since 1961 provides three times as many units as during the preceding Administration.

Low rent public housing under Federal assistance has been provided senior citizens at an annual rate more than twice that for 1960.

The Community Health Services and Facilities Act of 1961 raised the ceiling on appropriations for the construction of nursing homes under the Hill-Burton legislation from $10 million to $20 million; and authorized $10 million per year for a 5-year program of special project grants for the development of new or improved methods of providing health services outside the hospital for the chronically ill or aged.

Executive Order 11114, issued by President Johnson on February 12, 1964, establishes for the first time the policy of non-discrimination in employment based on age by Federal contractors.

WELFARE

In 1960, we proposed to—

"Permit workers who are totally and permanently disabled to retire at any age, removing the arbitrary requirement that the worker be 50 years of age.

"Amend the law so that after six months of total disability, a worker will be eligible for disability benefits, with restorative services to enable the worker to return to work.

"Continued support of legislation for the rehabilitation of physically handicapped persons and improvement of employment opportunities for them.

"Persons in need who are inadequately protected by social insurance are cared for by the states and local communities under public assistance programs. The Federal Government, which now shares the cost of aid to some of these, should share in all, and benefits should be made available without regard to residence.

"Uniform minimum standards throughout the nation for coverage, duration, and amount of unemployment insurance benefits.

"Legislation which will guarantee to women equality of rights under the law, including equal pay for equal work.

"The Child Welfare Program and other services already established under the Social Security Act should be expanded. Federal leadership is required in the nationwide campaign to prevent and control juvenile delinquency.

"A federal bureau of inter-group relations to help solve problems of discrimination in housing, education, employment and community opportunities in general. The bureau would assist in the solution of problems arising from the resettlement of immigrants and migrants within our own country, and in resolving religious, social and other tensions where they arise."

The 1961 Public Assistance Amendments, extended aid for the first time to families with dependent children in which the parent is unemployed. Currently, 18 States have adopted this program. Aid is being provided to about 75,000 families with nearly 280,000 children.

The food stamp program is providing improved purchasing powers and a better diet for families and persons receiving general assistance.

The 1962 Public Welfare amendments provide the authority and financial resources for a new approach to the problems of prolonged dependency and some of the special needs of children.

Under these enactments and related provisions:

49 States have now qualified for increased Federal financial aid to provide help to families with economic and social problems, and to assist families dependent on public assistance back to economic independence.

9 pilot projects have been initiated to help children stay in school.

41 demonstration projects have been designed to improve public assistance operations and to find ways of helping low-income families and individuals to become independent.

18,000 unemployed fathers in needy families are currently on community work and training projects.

Three million children are now covered by the program of aid to families with dependent children; and under the 1962 amendments these children receive, in addition to financial assistance, other needed help toward normal growth and development.

46 States now have approved plans for day care services.

Grants for research and demonstrations in child welfare were first awarded in 1962, and 62 projects have since been approved.

Starting for the first time in 1963, grants for training child welfare workers have been made to 58 institutions of higher learning.

Approximately 453,000 older persons received medical assistance under the Kerr-Mills program in fiscal year 1964.

The Temporary Extended Unemployment Compensation Act of 1961 provided 13 additional weeks of benefits to the long-term unemployed. 2.8 million jobless workers received $800 million in assistance.

The Juvenile Delinquency and Youth Offenses Control Act of 1961 made possible the establishment of training centers at 12 universities. By the end of fiscal year 1964, the program will have reached 12,500 trainees for work in delinquency prevention and control.

The Equal Pay Act of 1963 and the work of the President's Commission on the Status of Women, which reported to the President that same year, were events of historic importance in the struggle for equal opportunity and full partnership for women. The inclusion of women in the employment provisions of the Civil Rights Act of 1964 makes equality in employment at long last the law of the land.

Title X of the Civil Rights Act of 1964 establishes a Community Relations Service "to provide assistance to communities and persons therein in resolving disputes, disagreements, or difficulties relating to discriminatory practices based on race, color, or national origin. . ."

## Education

In 1960, we pledged—

"We believe that America can meet its educational obligations only with generous federal financial support, within the trad tional framework of local control. The assistance will take the form of federal grants to States for educational purposes they deem most pressing, including classroom construction and teachers' salaries. It will include aid for the construction of academic facilities as well as dormitories at colleges and universities.

"We pledge further federal support for all phases of vocational education for youth and adults; for libraries and adult education; for realizing the potential of educational television; and for exchange of students and teachers with other nations.

"As part of a broader concern for young people we recommend establishment of a Youth Conservation Corps, to give underprivileged young people a rewarding experience in a healthful environment."

The Higher Education Facilities Act of 1963 provides $1.2 billion for college construction over a three-year period. Over 2,000 institutions are eligible to benefit from its provisions in helping them meet current enrollment increases of 350,000 students each year.

The Health Professions Educational Assistance Act of 1963 will increase the number of professional health personnel through construction grants for health teaching facilities, and through low-interest student loans to assist up to 10,000 students of medicine, dentistry, or osteopathy to pay for their high-cost education.

The Vocational Education Act of 1963 authorizes a $956 million increase in Federal support for vocational education over the next five fiscal years —1964 through 1968. It is estimated that 7,000,-000 students will be enrolled in vocational education in 1968, an increase of about 3,000,000 over present annual enrollment.

Legislation approved in 1963, which increased authorization for loans to needy students for college education, will mean that in the coming school year approximately 280,000 students will be borrowing about $142 million from the loan funds to help pay for their higher education, as compared with 115,450 students borrowing $50,-152,000 in 1960.

In the last three fiscal years, there have been grants of $153.1 million in Federal funds to the States for purchases of equipment and materials, and remodeling classrooms to strengthen instruction in science, mathematics, and modern foreign languages.

A $32 million program of grants to help establish non-commercial educational television stations was approved in 1962. Thirty-seven grants have been approved, totaling $6.1 million—18 for new stations and 19 for expansion.

The Library Services and Construction Act of 1964 broadened Federal aid to cover urban as well as rural areas, and to provide construction grants in addition to other library services. The new legislation increased the authorization for Federal aid to develop libraries from $7.5 million to the present level of $25 million and included a new program of assistance for public library construction, with an appropriation for Fiscal Year 1965 of $30 million.

The Youth Conservation Corps envisioned by the 1960 proposal is provided for under Title I of the Economic Opportunity Act of 1964.

NATURAL RESOURCES

In 1960, we said—

"A thin layer of earth, a few inches of rain, and a blanket of air makes human life possible on our planet."

"Sound public policy must assure that these essential resources will be available to provide the good life for our children and future generations."

After the 1960 election President Kennedy and President Johnson implemented this platform by a whole series of new conservation policies and programs, some of which emanated from the first White House Conference on Conservation called by any President since the 1908 conference called by President Theodore Roosevelt.

During this Administration two historic conservation measures were enacted. These were:

The Wilderness Bill and the Land and Water Conservation Fund Bill which will together do more to help conserve outdoor America than any legislation passed in a generation.

In addition to this landmark legislation new emphasis has been placed on science as the modern midwife of conservation, and new impetus has been given across the board in the conservation of natural resources.

*In the field of water conservation*

Twenty-one new major water resources projects have been authorized or started in the West;

A highwater mark has been achieved in the annual level of national investment in water resource projects;

The saline water conversion effort has been quadrupled, and should achieve a dramatic cost-breakthrough during the next Administration.

*In electric power*

Ending 16 years of argument, a bold plan was developed under President Johnson's personal leadership to interconnect the electric power systems of the Pacific Northwest and the Southwest, thus providing benefits for power users in 11 Western States; under this plan, construction will soon begin on the first direct current long-distance lines in the United States, stretching all the way from the Columbia River to Los Angeles—and a new era of public and private power cooperation will commence.

Federal hydroelectric generating capacity has been increased by 2,600,000 kilowatts, and 5,150,000 kilowatts of non-Federal capacity has been licensed by the Federal Power Commission.

3,350 miles of vital transmission lines have been added to Federal systems and about 25,000 miles of new transmission lines have also been built by non-Federal power systems.

The FPC has conducted a National Power Survey to encourage both public and private power companies to join in power pools which are bringing lower cost electricity to consumers throughout the nation.

The world's largest atomic electric power plant (at Hanford, Washington) was funded and will soon be generating as much power as two Bonneville dams.

Federal REA loans have made it possible to open up the lignite coal fields of the Dakotas, and to exploit the coal fields of Western Colorado.

In addition, the Congress authorized the Delaware Basin Compact to permit the multi-purpose development of that river, and the Senate ratified the Columbia River Treaty which enables the joint U.S.-Canadian development of the full potential of that great river to begin later this year.

*In outdoor recreation*

The Congress created three superb new national seashores at Cape Cod (Massachusetts), Padre Island (Texas) and Point Reyes (California).

Pioneering a new park concept, Ozark Rivers National Riverway (Missouri) was established as the first river preservation national park in the Nation, and 12 other major new additions to the Park System were recommended for action by future Congresses.

A Bureau of Outdoor Recreation was created. As a vital part of the war on poverty, during the next year, 20 thousand young Americans will set to work in conservation camps across the land tackling the big backlog of work in the land and water areas owned by all of the people.

*In the conservation and development of mineral resources*

Research helped coal production surge upward, and there were initiated a series of action steps (including activation of the huge Rifle, Colorado, research center) which will lead to the orderly development of the vast oil shale resources of the Colorado plateau.

*For wildlife*

Enactment of the Wetlands Bill of 1961 made it possible to create more new Waterfowl Refuges (27) than during any previous four-year period in our history.

The Clean Air Act of 1963 is already providing the first full-scale attack on the air pollution problems that blight living conditions in so many of our cities.

Enactment of the Federal Water Pollution Control Act of 1961 launched the first massive attack on this conservation problem which has already resulted in 1,300 municipal waste treatment plans and the approval of projects that have improved the water quality in 18,000 miles of streams that provide water for 22 million people.

CITIES AND THEIR SUBURBS

In 1960, we declared—

"A new Democratic administration will expand Federal programs to aid urban communities to clear their slums, dispose of their sewage, educate their children, transport suburban commuters to and from their jobs, and combat juvenile delinquency."

The Housing Act of 1961 marked the beginning of a new era of Federal commitment to the problems of a nation in which three-fourths of the population has come to live in urban areas.

Under that Act, funds available for urban planning grants were increased by $55 million and a new $50 million Federal grant program to assist localities in the acquisition of permanent open space land to be used as parks and playgrounds was established.

The Housing Act of 1961 and the Area Redevelopment Act of 1961 authorized public facilities loans of $600 million.

The Juvenile Delinquency and Youth Offenses Control Act of 1961 launched a broad attack on youth problems by financing demonstration projects, training personnel in delinquency work, and providing technical assistance for community youth programs.

In 1960, we pledged—

"Federal aid for comprehensive metropolitan

transportation programs, including bus and rail mass transit, commuter railroads as well as highway programs and construction of civil airports."

The Housing Act of 1961 launched the first efforts to help metropolitan and other urban areas solve their mass transportation problems; 75 million in loans and demonstration grants were provided to States and localities to construct and improve mass transportation systems.

The Urban Mass Transportation Act of 1964 establishes a new long-range program for this purpose and authorizes $375 million in Federal grants, over 3 years, for capital construction and improvement which local transit systems cannot otherwise finance.

TRANSPORTATION

In 1960, we observed—

"Over the past seven years we have watched the steady weakening of the Nation's transportation system, and we noted the need for 'a national transportation policy.'"

The National Transportation policy was enunciated in the first Presidential message ever to be sent to the Congress dealing solely with transportation.

The Highway Act of 1961 resolved the lagging problem of financing the 41,000 mile interstate highway program, and the finished construction rate has almost doubled.

The Federal Maritime Commission has been established as an independent agency to guard against prejudice or discrimination harmful to the growth of U. S. World Trade.

The Maritime Administration, U. S. Department of Commerce, was set up to give its full attention to promoting a vigorous policy of strengthening and modernizing our merchant fleet. Seventy big modern cargo and cargo-passenger ships have been added to the U. S. merchant fleet. The Savannah, the world's first nuclear-powered merchant ship, is now on her first foreign voyage.

The far-reaching decision has been made that the United States will design and build a supersonic air transport plane—and thereby maintain our leadership position in international aviation. Congress has provided $60 million for the development of detailed designs. Twenty airlines already have placed orders.

On August 13, President Johnson signed a new highway bill to provide better primary and secondary highways on a 50/50 basis with the states. In addition, it will support needed efforts to improve forest highways, public land roads and national park roads.

SCIENCE

In 1960, we declared—
"We will recognize the special role of our Federal Government in support of basic and applied research," mentioning in particular Space, Atomic Energy, and Oceanography.

*Space*

Since 1961, the United States has pressed vigorously forward with a 10-year, $35-billion national space program for clear leadership in space exploration, space use, and all important aspects of space science and technology.

Already this program has enabled the United States to challenge the early Soviet challenge in space booster power and to effectively counter the Soviet bid for recognition as the world's leading nation in science and technology.

In the years 1961-1964, the United States has

Successfully flown the Saturn I rocket, putting into orbit the heaviest payloads of the space age to date.

Moved rapidly forward with much more powerful launch vehicles, the Saturn IB and the Saturn V. The Saturn IB, scheduled to fly in 1966, will be able to orbit a payload of 16 tons; and Saturn V, scheduled to fly in 1967 or 1968, will be able to orbit 120 tons or send 45 tons to the moon or 35 tons to Mars or Venus.

Mastered the difficult technology of using liquid hydrogen as a space rocket fuel in the Centaur upper stage rocket and the Saturn I second stage —assuring American leadership in space science and manned space flight in this decade.

Successfully completed six manned space flights in Project Mercury, acquiring 54 hours of space flight experience.

Successfully flight-tested the two-man Gemini spacecraft and Titan II space rocket so that manned Gemini flights can begin late in 1964 or early in 1965.

Developed the three-man Apollo spacecraft which will be able to spend up to two months in earth orbit, operate out to a quarter of a million miles from earth, and land our first astronaut-explorers on the moon.

Taken all actions to conduct a series of manned space flights in the Gemini and Apollo programs which will give the United States some 5,000 man-hours of flight experience in earth orbit, develop U. S. capabilities for rendezvous and joining of spacecraft in orbit, and prove out man's ability to perform valuable missions during long stays in space.

Made man's first close-up observations of another planet during the highly successful Mariner II fly-by of Venus.

Obtained the first close-up pictures of the moon, taken and relayed to earth by Ranger VII.

Initiated an ambitious long-range program for scientific investigations in space utilizing large, versatile spacecraft called Orbiting Observatories for geophysical, solar and stellar studies.

Operated the world's first weather satellites (Tiros).

Set up, under the Communications Satellite Act of 1962, the Communications Satellite Corporation, which is well on the way to establishing a global satellite communications system to provide reliable, low-cost telephone, telegraph, and television services to all parts of the world.

In short, the United States has matched rapid progress in manned space flight with a balanced program for scientific investigations in space, practical uses of space, and advanced research and technological pioneering to assure that the new challenges of space in the next decade can also be met, and U. S. leadership maintained.

*Atomic Energy*

The number of civilian nuclear power plants has increased from 3 to 14 since January 1961; and now the advent of economic nuclear power provides utilities a wider choice of competitive power sources in many sections of the country.

The world's largest nuclear power reactor, the Atomic Energy Commission's Production Reactor near Richland, Washington, achieved a controlled, self-sustained nuclear reaction on December 31, 1963.

The first deep-sea anchored, automatic weather station powered by nuclear energy has gone into unattended operation in the Gulf of Mexico, and the first lighthouse powered by nuclear energy flashes now in Chesapeake Bay.

Nuclear energy was extended to space for the first time in 1961. Compact nuclear generators supplied part of the power for instruments in two satellites, and in 1963 provided all of the power needs of two other satellites.

Vigorous support has been given to basic research in atomic energy. The world's highest energy accelerator, the AGS, has come into productive operation.

### Oceanography

For the first time in history the United States is building a fleet expressly designed for oceanographic research. Since 1961, 29 ships have been completed or are currently under construction. Shoreside facilities and training programs have been established as part of a major government-wide effort, begun in 1961, to capture the enormous potential rewards of research in this area which until now have been almost as remote and inaccessible as space itself.

### Government Operations

"We shall reform the processes of government in all branches—executive, legislative, and judicial. We will clean out corruption and conflicts of interest, and improve government services."

This Administration has brought the personnel, morale, ethics, and performance of the Federal service to a point of high excellence. To accomplish this transformation it made improvements in a broad range of activities affecting the operation of the government.

The conflict of interest laws were strengthened by the first major revision in a century. The comprehensive new law eliminates ambiguities and inconsistencies in existing laws, and increases the range of government matters in which conflict of interest is prohibited. In addition, President Kennedy issued an Executive Order which established more rigid standards of conduct for Federal officials and employees.

The regulatory agencies were made more effective by reorganization programs and by the appointment of highly-qualified officials, dedicated to protecting the public interest.

The Department of Justice has cracked down effectively on organized crime under new anti-racketeering statutes, has uncovered and prosecuted important foreign spies, and has made progress toward more effective procedures for protecting the rights of poor defendants to bail and counsel.

Federal Employee Organizations, many of which have existed for over half a century, were at last extended formal recognition under Executive Order 10988, issued by President Kennedy.

The Federal Pay Raise Act of 1964 updated the pay structure for Federal employees on a basis of equal salary rates for comparable levels of work in private industry. Completing the reforms initiated in the Act of 1962, it provided for long-needed increases in salary for top level Government administrators upon whom major responsibility for program results must rest. In President Johnson's words, this law established a basis for a standard of "brilliance" and "excellence" in the Federal Government.

### Congressional Procedures

In 1960, we urged action—

"To improve Congressional procedures so that majority rule prevails."

In 1961, the House Rules Committee was enlarged from 12 to 15 members, making it more representative of the views of the majority, and thereby enabling much important legislation to be reported to the floor for a vote by the entire House membership.

In 1964, for the first time in history, the Senate voted to limit debate on a civil rights measure, thus permitting the Civil Rights Act to come to a vote, and thereby to be enacted.

### Consumers

In 1960, we proposed—

"Effective Government representation and protection" for consumers.

In 1962, President Kennedy became the first Chief Executive to send a message to Congress on consumer matters.

This Executive action was closely followed by the creation of a Consumer Advisory Council.

In 1964, President Johnson appointed the first Special Assistant to the President for Consumer Affairs, and created a new President's Committee on Consumer Interests.

The Kefauver-Harris Drug Amendments of 1962 were the most far-reaching improvements in the Food, Drug and Cosmetics Act since 1938. Under these amendments:

Effective legal tools were provided to insure greater safety in connection with the manufacture, distribution and use of drugs.

Vital safeguards were added for drug research and manufacture.

Interstate distribution of new drugs for testing was barred until an adequate plan of investigation was made available to the Food and Drug Administration.

Domestic drug manufacturing establishments will now be required to register annually and be inspected by the FDA at least once a year.

The Administration has vigorously supported Truth-in-Lending, Truth-in-Packaging, and Truth-in-Securities bills.

The titles of these bills explain their objectives. Together, they form a triple armor of protection: for buyers of packaged goods, from prevailing deceptive practices; for borrowers of money, from hidden and unscrupulous interest and carrying charges; and for investors in securities from unfair practices threatening to vital savings. The first two bills are still awaiting Congressional action; the third is now a law.

The upward spiral in the price of natural gas which took place in the decade of the 1950's has been halted by vigorous regulatory action of the Federal Power Commission and the nation's 36 million consumers of natural gas have benefited from rate reductions and refunds in excess of $600 million. Natural gas moving largely in interstate pipelines now supplies almost a third of the nation's energy requirements. Regulation to insure its availability in ample supply and at reasonable prices is an important consumer protection function which is now being effectively discharged.

VETERANS AFFAIRS

In 1960, we proposed—

"Adequate compensation for those with service-connected disabilities," and "pensions adequate for a full and dignified life for disabled and distressed veterans and for needy survivors of deceased veterans."

Since 1961, we have achieved:

Increased disability payments for veterans with service-connected disabilities. In the first year alone, this increase provided veterans with additional payments of about $98 million.

An increase of about 10 percent a month in the compensation for widows, children, and parents of veterans who died of service-connected disabilities.

An increase from $112 to $150 a month in the dependency and indemnity compensation payable to widows of veterans who died of service-connected disabilities.

Increased compensation benefits to veterans disabled by blindness, deafness, and kidney disorders, and increased benefits to widows and orphans of veterans whose deaths were service-connected.

In 1960, we endorsed—

"Expanded programs of vocational rehabilitation for disabled veterans, and education for orphans of servicemen."

Since 1961, vocational rehabilitation and training has enabled thousands of GI's to choose occupations and acquire valuable training. For the first time, veterans with peacetime service-connected disabilities have been afforded vocational rehabilitation training. In addition, vocational rehabilitation was extended to blinded World War II and Korean conflict veterans, and war orphans' educational assistance was extended in behalf of certain reservists called to active duty.

In 1960, we stated—

"The quality of medical care furnished to the disabled veterans has deteriorated. . . . We shall work for an increased availability of facilities for all veterans in need and we shall move with particular urgency to fulfill the need for expanded domiciliary and nursing-home facilities."

Since 1961, we have—

Approved the construction of new, modern hospitals, a number of which are being built near medical schools to improve veterans' care and research.

Added more full-time doctors to the VA staff, bringing it to an all-time high of nearly 5,000.

Provided hospital and medical care, including out-patient treatment, to peacetime ex-servicemen for service-connected disabilities on the same basis furnished war veterans.

Stepped up medical research programs, which have made outstanding contributions to American medicine.

In 1960, we pledged—

"We shall continue the veterans home loan guarantee and direct loan programs and education benefits patterned after the GI Bill of Rights."

Since 1961, legislation has extended veterans home loans for both World War II and Korean conflict veterans. The GI Bill of Rights for Korean veterans was also extended for the benefit of certain reservists called to active duty.

Despite this considerably increased activity, the Veterans Administration has reduced its operating costs.

## AMERICAN INDIANS

In 1960, we pledged—

"Prompt adoption of a program to assist Indian tribes in the full development of their human and natural resources and to advance the health, education and economic well-being of Indian citizens while preserving their cultural heritage."

In these 3½ years:

New classrooms have been provided for more than 7,000 Indian children; summer educational programs have been expanded tenfold so they now serve more than 20,000 students; and a special institute to train artistically gifted Indian youth has been established.

Indian enrollment in vocational training programs has been doubled.

For the first time in history, Federal low-rent housing programs have been launched on Indian reservations, and more than 3,100 new housing units have now been authorized.

Industrial plants offering employment opportunities for thousands of Indians are being opened on Indian reservations.

Accelerated Public Works projects on 89 reservations in 21 States have provided nearly 30,000 man-months of employment.

The Vocational Education Act and the Adult Indian Vocational Training Act have been amended to provide improved training for Indians.

## THE ARTS

In 1960, we observed—

"The arts flourish where there is freedom and where individual initiative and imagination are encouraged."

No single quality of the new Administration was more immediately evident to the Nation and the world than the recognition it gave to American artists.

President Kennedy early created an advisory commission to assist in the growth and development of the arts, and the Administration secured amendments to the Educational and Cultural Ex-

change Act to improve the quality and effectiveness of the international educational and cultural exchange programs. This past year, the John F. Kennedy Center for the Performing Arts was established to stimulate widespread interest in the arts.

On Washington's Birthday 1963, President Kennedy, by Executive Order, created a new Presidential Medal of Freedom as the highest civil honor conferred by the President in peace time upon persons who have made distinctive contributions to the security and national interest of the United States, to world peace, or to cultural activities. Henceforth, those men and women selected by the President for the Medal will be announced annually on the Fourth of July and will be presented with medals at an appropriate White House ceremony.

In his address to the University of Michigan in May 1964, President Johnson proposed that we begin to build the Great Society first of all in the cities of America, restoring the beauty and dignity which urban centers have lost.

That same month the President's Council on Pennsylvania Avenue presented to him a sweeping proposal for the reconstruction of the center of the City of Washington. The proposal has been hailed as "a blueprint for glory . . . a realistic and far-seeing redevelopment scheme that may be Washington's last chance to save its 'Avenue of Presidents.'"

## CIVIL LIBERTIES

In 1960, we reaffirmed—

"Our dedication to the Bill of Rights. Freedom and civil liberties, far from being incompatible with security, are vital to our national strength."

The era of fear and suspicion brought on by accusations, true and false, of subversive activities and security risks has passed. The good sense of the American people, and the overwhelming loyalty of our citizenry have combined to restore balance and calm to security activities, without in any way diminishing the scope or effectiveness of those activities.

The Administration has jealously guarded the right of each American to protect his good name. Except in those instances where the national security is overriding, confrontation of the accuser is now required in all loyalty hearings. Individuals whose loyalty is being questioned must also be notified of the charges in sufficient time for them to prepare their defense.

The Criminal Justice Act of 1964, now before the President for signature, will for the first time in history ensure that poor defendants in criminal cases will have competent legal counsel in defending themselves in Federal courts.

## FISCAL RESPONSIBILITY

In 1960, we promised—

"We shall end the gross waste in Federal expenditures which needlessly raises the budgets of many Government agencies."

Since 1961, we have moved boldly and directly to eliminate waste and duplication wherever it occurs.

For example, the Department of Defense has embarked on a far-reaching program to realize savings through improvements in its efficiency and management. This program has already produced savings of more than $1 billion in Fiscal Year 1963 and $2.5 billion in the Fiscal Year just completed. By 1964, it is expected that the program will produce yearly savings of over $4 billion.

At the close of the past Fiscal Year Federal employment had been reduced by 22,000 over the total one year earlier. The 1965 budget calls for lower expenditures than in the preceding year— only the second time such a feat has been accomplished in the past 10 years.

In 1960, we pledged—

"We shall collect the billions in taxes which are owed to the Federal Government but are not now collected."

To handle additional work in income tax collection, 3,971 new employees were added to the Internal Revenue Service by the Congress in fiscal 1961; 2,817 new positions were added in fiscal 1963; and about 1,000 more in fiscal 1964. The additional revenue which these employees will produce will far exceed the cost of their employment.

In 1960, we pledged—

"We shall close the loopholes in the tax laws by which certain privileged groups legally escape their fair share of taxation."

The Revenue Acts of 1962 and 1964 eliminated more loopholes than all the revenue legislation

from 1941 to 1962 combined. They raised $1.7 billion annually in new revenue, nine times the sum raised in this manner during the 1953-60 period. These bills sharply limited expense account abuses, special preferences to U. S. firms and individuals operating abroad, escapes from taxation through personal holding companies and many other unjustified advantages.

## CIVIL RIGHTS

In 1960, we pledged—

"We shall . . . seek to create an affirmative new atmosphere in which to deal with racial divisions and inequalities which threaten both the integrity of our democratic faith and the proposition on which our Nation was founded—that all men are created equal."

That pledge was made from the deepest moral conviction.

It was carried out on the same basis.

From the establishment of the President's Committee on Equal Employment Opportunity, under the chairmanship of the then Vice President Lyndon B. Johnson, on March 6, 1961 to this moment, the efforts of the Administration to provide full and equal civil rights for all Americans have never relaxed.

The high point of achievement in this effort was reached with the passage of the Civil Rights Act of 1964, the greatest civil rights measure in the history of the American people.

This landmark of our Democracy bars discrimination in the use of public accommodations, in employment, and in the administering of Federally-assisted programs. It makes available effective procedures for assuring the right to vote in Federal elections, directs Federal technical and financial assistance to local public school systems in desegregation, and strengthens the Civil Rights Commission. This comprehensive legislation resolves many of the festering conflicts which had been a source of irritating uncertainty, and smooths the way for favorable resolution of these problems.

We have also insisted upon non-discrimination in apprenticeship, and have made free, unsegregated access a condition for Federal financial assistance to public libraries, programs for training of teachers of the handicapped, counseling, guidance and foreign language institutes, adult civil defense classes, and manpower development and training programs.

In supporting construction of Hill-Burton hospitals, mental retardation and community health facilities, we have required non-discrimination in admission and provision of services and granting of staff privileges.

We have been equally firm in opposing any policy of quotas or "discrimination in reverse," and all other arbitrary or irrelevant distinctions in American life.

This, then, is the accounting of our stewardship.

The 1960 platform was not directed to any one sector or group of Americans with particular interests.

It proclaimed, rather, the Rights of Man.

The platform asserted the essential fact of that moment in our history—that the next administration to take office would face as never before the "responsibility and opportunity to call forth the greatness of the American people."

That responsibility was met; that opportunity was seized. The years since have been times of towering achievement.

We are proud to have been a part of this history. The task of leadership is to lead, and that has been our purpose. But the achievements of the nation over this period outreach the contribution of any party: they are the work of the American people.

In the 1,000 days of John F. Kennedy, in the eventful and culminating months of Lyndon B. Johnson, there has been born a new American greatness.

Let us continue.

## Prohibition Platform 1964

### PREAMBLE

We, the representatives of the Prohibition Party, assembled in the National Convention at St. Louis, Mo., August 29-30, 1963, recognizing Almighty God as the source of all just government, and with faith in the teachings of the Lord Jesus Christ, do solemnly promise that, if our party is chosen to administer the affairs of the nation, we will, with earnest dedication to the principles of righteousness, seek to serve the needs and to preserve the rights, the prerogatives and

the basic freedoms, of the people of the United States. For the realization of these ends we propose the following program of government:

### CONSTITUTIONAL GOVERNMENT

We affirm our sincere loyalty to the Constitution of the United States, and express our deep confidence in that document as the basic law of our land. We deplore all attempts to violate it, whether by legislation, by means of evasion, or through judicial interpretation. We believe in the principles of liberty and justice enunciated in the Declaration of Independence and in the Preamble and Bill of Rights of our Constitution. We declare ourselves in hearty support of our system of representative government, with its plan of checks and balances, and express our firm intent to serve the people of our nation with a constructive, forward-looking program of good government, dedicated to the general welfare.

### COMMUNISM-TOTALITARIANISM

We are positively, aggressively and unalterably, opposed to Communism as a way of life or as a governmental system. We believe that the program of Communism, with its intent to infiltrate and to overthrow our present form of government, must be pitilessly exposed. We challenge all loyal citizens to become fully aware of this menace to civilization, to exert every effort to defeat these "masters of deceit," and to help preserve our American way of life.

We also declare ourselves opposed to any other form of totalitarian philosophy or form of government. We endorse the efforts of those agencies which have been honestly and earnestly exposing subversive activities and groups.

### GOVERNMENTAL ECONOMY AND TAXATION

We live in an era of extravagance and wasteful spending. This spirit has invaded government at all levels, demanding an ever-increasing tax load upon our people. The constant increase in taxation, requiring nearly one-third of the total income of our citizens to pay the expenses of government, is approaching the point of confiscation, leading to economic bankruptcy. We believe that good government ought not to attempt to do for people what they can do for themselves. With proper economy, governmental costs can be lowered, the tax load can be lightened, and the public debt can be reduced. We promise to devote ourselves to such an end, even though it involves the reorganization and/or abolition of certain departments, bureaus and vested interests.

## Money and Finance

A sound financial program and a dependable monetary policy are fundamental to a stable economy. Our Constitution gives to Congress the power to "coin money" and to "regulate the value thereof." We believe that Congress, working with the executive department of our government, should take immediate steps to establish a financial program that will block inflationary trends, insure a sound currency, stabilize price levels and provide for systematic retirement of the national debt. We urge that careful consideration be given to a return to the gold standard, suggesting that such a step would help stabilize our economy, would promote confidence in our monetary system and would underwrite a continuing program of sound finance and expanding industrial progress.

## The Federal Budget

Good government and a sound economy demand a balanced federal budget. The inflationary effects and the disturbing influences of unbalanced budgets must be eliminated. We cannot, with impunity, continue to increase the mortgage on our future and the interest load of the present. As the level of taxation is already excessive, there must be either a decided reduction in governmental services and federal spending or a substantial improvement in efficiency, with consequent elimination of waste in both personnel and materials. Actually, both areas need careful exploration with a view not only to maintaining a balanced budget, but also to reduction of the national debt.

## Foreign Aid

Many billions of dollars of our taxpayers' money have been and are still being given to foreign countries. Unfortunately, substantial portions have been used to support governments and programs considerably at variance with American ideals and concepts. It is frankly recognized that complex and baffling problems are involved in this area of international relations, but it is likewise believed that the practice needs most careful scrutiny and review.

## Free Enterprise

We are strongly opposed to governmental restraints on our free enterprise system, to detailed regulation of our economic life and to federal interference with individual initiative. We believe that free enterprise is threatened in three ways: (1) by excessive governmental regulation, (2) by growth of public and/or private monopoly, and (3) by unethical practices of unscrupulous groups.

It will be the policy of our administration to encourage independent, non-monopolistic business enterprises which serve genuine consumer needs and are operated with a sense of responsibility to the public. We will take necessary steps to prevent the evils both of monopoly, and of excessive regulation by government and to protect adequately the consuming public from irresponsible or deceptive practices contrary to public welfare.

We propose that our government withdraw, with reasonable promptness, from the field of business activity and sell to private industry, at proper investment prices, those business enterprises now owned and operated by the federal government.

## Labor and Industry

In the area of labor and industrial relations we believe that the public welfare must be given paramount consideration. Both management and labor must be held responsible for their economic and their social behavior. Neither should be permitted to dominate at the expense of the other or of the common good. Rather, the anti-trust laws must be applied equally to all monopolies, whether of business or labor. Whenever the public welfare is seriously endangered because of disputes affecting quasi-public businesses and utilities we favor the compulsory arbitration of labor-management disputes.

## Employee-Employer Rights

Every individual has certain basic and fundamental rights. A person's right to join or not to join a labor union without affecting his employment and his right to work for an employer willing to hire him must be protected. Likewise, employees and employers must be free to bargain and to contract as they wish. Mass picketing, rioting, terrorism, and all other forms of violence and coercion, secondary boycotts and industry-wide bargaining should be prohibited.

## INDIVIDUALS AND STATES' RIGHTS

Our founding fathers recognized the importance of both individual and states' rights, and determined to preserve them by making the Bill of Rights an integral part of our Constitution. During recent years there has been an increasing tendency toward an undesirable concentration of power and authority in the federal government.

This tendency has two principal causes: (1) the ever-growing power and influence of the "military-industrial complex," and (2) a widespread tendency of groups of citizens to look to the federal government for the protection of rights and the satisfaction of needs which they feel are not adequately cared for by state and local governments or by private enterprise.

To deal with the first of these causes, we pledge the utmost vigilance in resisting the growth of militarism and to maintain the constitutional principle of civilian supremacy over the military.

To deal with over-centralization we urge more vigorous action by state and local governments for the protection of the rights and the promotion of the welfare of their people, greater resort to the solution of local community problems through the voluntary action of existing or new civic and other non-governmental associations, where this is feasible, and the increasing pursuit by private business concerns of policies which promote the public interest.

We pledge ourselves to action that will preserve all legitimate individual rights and will maintain among the several states their constitutional place in our system of government.

## CIVIL RIGHTS

We maintain that all American citizens, regardless of race, religion, or National origin, are entitled to equality of treatment under the provisions of our Constitution and under the laws of our land. No person or group of persons shall be subjected to ostracism, humiliation, or embarrassment because of color or national background. At the same time we must deplore the use of violence and/or arbitrary pressure tactics, from whatever source, as a means of seeking to resolve tensions and divergencies of opinion among our citizens.

We are opposed to those proposals which would destroy our neighborhood school systems through a program of artificial integration or convey special privileges to any minority group.

## PUBLIC MORALITY AND LAW ENFORCEMENT

Moral and spiritual considerations must be primary factors in determining both state and national policies. We deplore the gross neglect of such matters by the dominant political parties, culminating in the shocking revelations of crime and of political and economic corruption which have characterized recent years. We charge these parties with basic responsibility for the rapid decline in moral standards which followed repeal of the Eighteenth Amendment. We believe that the program of nullification of law through non-enforcement which led to repeal contributed greatly to the disintegration of public morals, to a general deterioration of standards and to a lowering of values among our people.

We pledge ourselves to break the unholy alliance which has made these things possible. We propose to strengthen and to enforce laws against gambling, narcotics, and commercialized vice, to emphasize the basic importance of spiritual and moral values to the development and growth of an enduring nation, and to maintain the integrity of our democracy by careful enforcement of law and loyal support of our Constitution.

## WORLD PEACE

We live in an age of atomic and hydrogen bombs, in an era of missiles and jet propulsion, in a world filled with animosities and cruel hatreds. Instruments for the destruction of civilization have been developed. Under these conditions, we pledge ourselves to search for peaceful solutions to international conflict, by seeking to deal creatively and constructively with the underlying causes of international tension, and to strive for world peace and order based upon the teachings and practices of the Prince of Peace.

## NATIONAL SOVEREIGNTY

We declare our belief in national sovereignty and oppose surrender of this sovereignty to any international group.

## MILITARY TRAINING

Although we seek for world peace and order, we declare our firm belief, under existing world conditions, in a sound program of national preparedness. At the same time, we seriously question the desirability of the existing program of peacetime compulsory military training. We doubt that it represents a genuine safeguard to world peace. Rather, we believe it to be contrary, in principle, to our American way of life, to place an unnecessary burden upon our peacetime economy, to threaten us with possible military dictatorship, and, as currently conducted, to permit and very often to promote the moral and spiritual deterioration of our Youth. Therefore, we declare our opposition to any program of peacetime compulsory military training and urge a complete evaluation and re-orientation of our entire program of national preparedness.

## Nuclear Weapons Testing

Many of the leading scientists of our day have warned that radioactive fallout, resulting from testing of nuclear weapons, endangers the health of human beings throughout the world, and, if continued, will increase the number of seriously defective children who will be born to future generations. It is unjust that the people of the world, and especially those of nations not engaged in the development of nuclear weapons, should be exposed to such peril. The danger and the injustice will become progressively greater with any additional testing. In addition, there is the danger that continuation of the armaments race will lead to an atomic war of annihilation.

In our 1960 platform we urged that, "as a step toward world disarmament, all testing of nuclear weapons be indefinitely suspended on a multilateral basis and that our government seek with renewed vigor and persistence an agreement among all nuclear power for the permanent and complete cessation of nuclear tests for military purposes." It appears that some progress has been made toward realization of this goal. We insist that continual attention must be given to this problem.

## Religious Liberty

We believe in religious liberty. Freedom of the individual to worship, to fellowship with others of similar faith, to evangelize, to educate and to establish religious institutions, must be preserved. When religious liberty is lost political liberty will perish with it. We believe, also, that our government should take a firm, positive position against religious intolerance and persecution anywhere in the world.

## Marriage and Divorce

Ordained of God, the home is a sacred institution. Its sanctity must be protected and preserved. We favor the enactment of uniform marriage and divorce laws in the various states as an aid to building strong and enduring homes throughout our nation.

## Old Age Insurance

We endorse the general principle of an actuarially sound voluntary social security program which includes all employed groups. We question the soundness of the existing program. We deplore the wide-spread current abuse of the privileges involved; we condemn the maladministration of its provisions for political ends; we pledge ourselves to correct these evils.

## Ballot Law Reform

True democracy requires that the needs and interests of minority groups be given fair, honest and appropriate consideration. Instead, in many of our states, ballot laws have been enacted which are designed to make a two-party system into a bipartisan political monopoly, keeping minor parties off the ballot. We demand the repeal of all laws which deny to independent voters and to loyal minority groups the fundamental right of free political expression.

## Separation of Church and State

We affirm our continuing loyalty to the constitutional principle of separation of Church and State. We will expose, and resist vigorously, any attempt from whatever source to weaken or subvert this fundamental principle.

We declare our belief that the Bible is not a sectarian book, but is a volume of universal appeal and application which is woven into our history, our laws, and our culture. We deplore any interpretation which would limit its use in any area of our national life.

In the area of government, we endorse encouragement of non-profit educational and religious institutions on a tax-exempt basis, but we declare strong opposition to all efforts, direct or indirect, to secure appropriations of public money for private religious or sectarian purposes.

## Education

It is altogether appropriate that our federal

government should be interested in and concerned about matters pertaining to all areas of educational growth and development. However, under the Tenth Amendment, public education is clearly a matter of state concern. We approve of the work of the Office of Education in collecting and disseminating essential educational information, but we are opposed to any sort of direct federal aid to education, believing that each state should both support and control its own educational program.

## AGRICULTURE

The production and distribution of agricultural products is of vital importance to the economy of any people. We believe that those engaged in agricultural pursuits, like other American citizens, should be free from authoritarian control and coercion. Hence we declare ourselves opposed to regimentation of farms and farmers and urge a sensible and orderly return to a free market program.

## PUBLIC HEALTH

The health of our people is a matter of high importance. We are deeply concerned with this problem in its numerous aspects. In particular, we insist that genuine caution be taken when dealing with mental health cases lest there be unjust and prejudiced incarcerations. Also we deplore those programs of mass medication which many maintain are in violation of the rights of individuals under our Constitution.

## SERVICE, NOT SPOILS

In spite of our "civil service" system, first sponsored by the Prohibition Party, the dominant political parties are positively committed to the "spoils" system and, when in office, have prostituted governmental power to serve their own selfish party interests instead of the whole people. This has led to excessive expenditures, higher taxes and, in some situations, to an unfortunate alliance of crime with politics. We pledge ourselves to an honest, efficient and economical administration.

## THE ALCOHOL PROBLEM

The widespread and increasing use of alcoholic beverages has now become a national tragedy and must be recognized as a major cause of poverty,

broken homes, juvenile delinquency, vice, crime, political corruption, wasted manpower, and highway accidents. Of all the unfortunate mistakes of our government and people, none has been worse than the legalization of the liquor traffic. It can be legitimately said that no political issue confronting the citizens of our land compares in magnitude with the need for suppressing the beverage alcohol industry.

The sponsors of this national curse are not only highly capitalized and strongly organized, but are also socially irresponsible. Out of enormous profits the liquor industry spends huge sums to promote sales, to create habitual use of its products by both youth and adults and to encourage a weakening of moral resistance to its program of social and economic exploitation. It is linked with and supports a nationwide network of organized gambling, vice and crime. Through its advertising it has corrupted large segments of the nation's press, and it is endeavoring to extend its control increasingly to both radio and television.

Unfortunately, the liquor traffic has been able to extend its power until, in all too many instances, it dominates our political life and controls our governmental officials. Both of our major political parties are dominated by it, and neither dares to take a stand against it. And so long as they continue to be yoked by party membership with the liquor traffic and the underworld, just so long will they be unable to make moral principles prevail.

The beverage alcohol problem is a matter of national concern. It has reached proportions which demand immediate action looking to a solution. First of all, scientific facts about beverage alcohol must be widely publicized. People must come to know and to understand the demon which we harbor. Secondly, a program of publicity, education, legislation and administration, leading to the elimination of the beverage alcohol industry, must be developed. People must come to know that there is no satisfactory solution to the problem except through political action which suppresses it and a political administration which destroys it.

Accordingly the Prohibition Party demands the repeal of all laws which legalize the liquor traffic and the enactment and rigorous enforcement of new laws which prohibit the manufacture, distribution and sale of alcoholic beverages. You are urged to elect an administration pledged to the above program. Such is essential to the permanent solution of this devastating problem.

## Republican Platform 1964

"FOR THE PEOPLE"

Section One

*For a Free People*

Humanity is tormented once again by an age-old issue—is man to live in dignity and freedom under God or be enslaved—are men in government to serve, or are they to master, their fellow men?

It befalls us now to resolve this issue anew—perhaps this time for centuries to come. Nor can we evade the issue here at home. Even in this Constitutional Republic, for two centuries the beacon of liberty the world over, individual freedom retreats under the mounting assault of expanding centralized power. Fiscal and economic excesses, too long indulged, already have eroded and threatened the greatest experiment in self-government mankind has known.

We Republicans claim no monopoly of love of freedom. But we challenge as unwise the course the Democrats have charted; we challenge as dangerous the steps they plan along the way; and we deplore as self-defeating and harmful many of the moves already taken.

Dominant in their council are leaders whose words extol human liberty, but whose deeds have persistently delimited the scope of liberty and sapped its vitality. Year after year, in the name of benevolence, these leaders have sought the enlargement of Federal power. Year after year, in the guise of concern for others, they have lavishly expended the resources of their fellow citizens. And year after year freedom, diversity and individual, local and state responsibility have given way to regimentation, conformity and subservience to central power.

We Republicans hold that a leadership so misguided weakens liberty in America and the world. We hold that the glittering enticements so invitingly proffered the people, at their own expense, will inevitably bring disillusionment and crue disappointment in place of promised happiness.

Such leaders are Federal extremists—impulsive in the use of national power, improvident in the management of public funds, thoughtless as to the long-term effects of their acts on individual freedom and creative, competitive enterprise. Men so recklessly disposed cannot be safely entrusted with authority over their fellow citizens.

To Republicans, liberty is still today man's most precious possession. For every citizen, and for the generations to come, we Republicans vow that it shall be preserved.

In substantiation of this belief the Republican Party submits this platform. To the American people it is our solemn bond.

*To Stay Free*

The shape of the future is our paramount concern. Much of today's moral decline and drift—much of the prevailing preoccupation with physical and material comforts of life—much of today's crass political appeals to the appetites of the citizenry—can be traced to a leadership grown demagogic and materialistic through indifference to national ideals founded in devoutly held religious faith. The Republican Party seeks not to renounce this heritage of faith and high purpose; rather, we are determined to reaffirm and reapply it. So doing, these will be our guides:

1. Every person has the right to govern himself, to fix his own goals, and to make his own way with a minimum of governmental interference.

2. It is for government to foster and maintain an environment of freedom encouraging every individual to develop to the fullest his God-given powers of mind, heart and body; and, beyond this, government should undertake only needful things, rightly of public concern, which the citizen cannot himself accomplish.

We Republicans hold that these two principles must regain their primacy in our government's relations, not only with the American people, but also with nations and peoples everywhere in the world.

3. Within our Republic the Federal Government should act only in areas where it has Constitutional authority to act, and then only in respect to proven needs where individuals and local or state governments will not or cannot adequately perform. Great power, whether governmental or private, political or economic, must be so checked, balanced and restrained and, where necessary, so

dispersed as to prevent it from becoming a threat to freedom any place in the land.

4. It is a high mission of government to help assure equal opportunity for all, affording every citizen an equal chance at the starting line but never determining who is to win or lose. But government must also reflect the nation's compassionate concern for those who are unable, through no fault of their own, to provide adequately for themselves.

5. Government must be restrained in its demands upon and its use of the resources of the people, remembering that it is not the creator but the steward of the wealth it uses; that its goals must ever discipline its means; and that service to all the people, never to selfish or partisan ends, must be the abiding purpose of men entrusted with public power.

## Deeds Not Words

The future we pledge, then, for freedom, by faithful adherence to these guides. Let the people compare these guides with those of the Democratic Party, then test, not the words of the two Parties, but their performance during the past four years of Democratic control.

Let the people ask:

Is the Republic stronger today or wiser than when the present Administration took office four years ago?

Is its guardianship of freedom more respected at home and throughout the world?

For these four years the leaders of the Democratic Party have been entrusted with the nation's executive power and overwhelmingly in control of the Congress. The question must be asked: Have these leaders successfully advanced the purposes of this mightiest nation mankind has known?

Tragically, in each instance, the answer must be "no."

Let the Democratic Party stand accused.

## SECTION TWO

## Failures of Foreign Policy

This Democratic Administration has been, from its beginning, not the master but the prisoner of major events. The will and dependability of its leadership, even for the defense of the free world, have come to be questioned in every area of the globe.

### DISREGARD OF ALLIES

This Administration has neglected to consult with America's allies on critical matters at critical times, leading to lack of confidence, lack of respect and disintegrating alliances.

It has permitted an erosion of NATO force and unity, alienating most of its member nations by negotiating with the common foe behind their backs. It has offered concessions to the Communists while according our allies little understanding, patience, or cooperation.

This Administration has created discord and distrust by failing to develop a nuclear policy for NATO.

It has provoked crises of confidence with our oldest friends, including England and France, by bungling such major projects as Skybolt and NATO's nuclear needs.

It has allowed other great alliances—SEATO and CENTO—also to deteriorate, by failing to provide the leadership required for their revitalization and by neglecting their cooperation in keeping the peace.

### WEAKNESS BEFORE COMMUNISM

This Administration has sought accommodations with Communism without adequate safeguards and compensating gains for freedom. It has alienated proven allies by opening a "hot line" first with a sworn enemy rather than with a proven friend, and in general pursued a risky path such as began at Munich a quarter century ago.

It has misled the American people and forfeited a priceless opportunity to win concessions for freedom by mishandling sales of farm commodities to Communists. At first it disavowed any intent to subsidize prices or use credit; later it demanded such authority and forced the Democrats in Congress to acquiesce. At first it hinted at concessions for freedom in return for wheat sold to Russia; later it obtained no concessions at all. At first it pledged not to breach restraints on trade with Communist countries in other parts of the world; later it stimulated such trade itself, and thus it encouraged trade with Cuba by America's oldest friends.

This Administration has collaborated with Indonesian imperialism by helping it to acquire territory belonging to the Netherlands and control over the Papuan people.

It has abetted further Communist takeover in

Laos, weakly accepted Communist violations of the Geneva Agreement, which the present Administration perpetrated, and increased Soviet influence in Southeast Asia.

It has encouraged an increase of aggression in South Vietnam by appearing to set limits on America's willingness to act—and then, in the deepening struggle, it has sacrificed the lives of American and allied fighting men by denial of modern equipment.

This Administration has permitted the shooting down of American pilots, the mistreatment of American citizens, and the destruction of American property to become hallmarks of Communist arrogance.

It has stood by as a wire barricade in Berlin became a wall of shame, defacing that great city, humiliating every American, and disgracing free men everywhere.

It has turned its back on the captive peoples of Eastern Europe, abandoning their cause in the United Nations and in the official utterances of our government.

This Administration has forever blackened our nation's honor at the Bay of Pigs, bungling the invasion plan and leaving brave men on Cuban beaches to be shot down. Later the forsaken survivors were ransomed, and Communism was allowed to march deeper into Latin America.

It has turned a deaf ear to pleas from throughout the Western Hemisphere for decisive American leadership to seal off subversion from the Soviet base just off our shore.

It has increased the long-term troubles for America by retreating from its pledge to obtain on-the-spot proof of the withdrawal of Soviet offensive weapons from Cuba.

It left vacant for many critical months the high posts of ambassador in Panama and with the Organization of American States, and thus it failed to anticipate and forestall the anti-American violence that burst forth in Panama.

UNDERMINING THE UNITED NATIONS

This Administration has failed to provide forceful, effective leadership in the United Nations.

It has weakened the power and influence of this world organization by failing to demand basic improvements in its procedures to guard against its becoming merely a forum of anti-Western insult and abuse.

It has refused to insist upon enforcement of the United Nations' rules governing financial support though such enforcement is supported by an advisory opinion of the International Court of Justice.

It has shouldered virtually the full costs of the United Nations' occupation of the Congo, only to have the ousted leadership asked back when United Nations forces had withdrawn.

FORSAKING AMERICA'S INTERESTS

This Administration has subsidized various forms of socialism throughout the world, to the jeopardy of individual freedom and private enterprise.

It has proved itself inept and weak in international trade negotiations, allowing the loss of opportunities historically open to American enterprise and bargaining away markets indispensable to prosperity of American farms.

*Failure of National Security Planning*

LOSING A CRITICAL LEAD

This Administration has delayed research and development in advanced weapons systems and thus confronted the American people with a fearsome possibility that Soviet advances, in the decade of the 1970's, may surpass America's present lead. Its misuse of "cost effectiveness" has stifled the creativity of the nation's military, scientific and industrial communities.

It has failed to originate a single new major strategic weapons system after inheriting from a Republican Administration the most powerful military force of all time. It has concealed a lack of qualitative advance for the 1970's by speaking of a quantitative strength which by then will be obsolete. It has not demonstrated the foresight necessary to prepare a strategic strength which in future years will deter war.

It has endangered security by downgrading efforts to prepare defenses against enemy ballistic missiles. It has retarded our own military development for near and outer space, while the enemy's development moves on.

INVITATIONS TO DISASTER

This Administration has adopted policies which will lead to a potentially fatal parity of power with Communism instead of continued military superiority for the United States.

It has permitted disarmament negotiations to

proceed without adequate consideration of military judgment—a procedure which tends to bring about, in effect, a unilateral curtailment of American arms rendered the more dangerous by the Administration's discounting known Soviet advances in nuclear weaponry.

It has failed to take minimum safeguards against possible consequences of the limited nuclear test ban treaty, including advanced underground tests where permissible and full readiness to test elsewhere should the need arise.

### DISTORTIONS AND BLACKOUTS

This Administration has adopted the policies of news management and unjustifiable secrecy, in the guise of guarding the nation's security; it has shown a contempt of the right of the people to know the truth.

This Administration, while claiming major defense savings, has in fact raised defense spending by billions of dollars a year, and yet has shortchanged critical areas.

### UNDERMINING MORALE

This Administration has weakened the bonds of confidence and understanding between civilian leaders and the nation's top military professionals. It has bypassed seasoned military judgment in vital national security policy decisions.

It has permitted non-military considerations, political as well as spurious economic arguments, to reverse professional judgment on major weapons and equipment such as the controversial TFX, the X-22, and the nuclear carrier.

In sum, both in military and foreign affairs, the Democratic record all the world around is one of disappointment and reverses for freedom.

And this record is no better at home.

### Failures at Home

#### INABILITY TO CREATE JOBS

This Administration has failed to honor its pledges to assure good jobs, full prosperity and a rapidly growing economy for all the American people:

—failing to reduce unemployment to four percent, falling far short of its announced goal every single month of its tenure in office; and

—despite glowing promises, allowing a disheartening increase in long-term and youth unemployment.

This Administration has failed to apply Republican-initiated retraining programs where most needed particularly where they could afford new economic opportunities to Negro citizens. It has preferred, instead, divisive political proposals.

It has demonstrated its inability to measure up to the challenge of automation which, wisely guided, will enrich the lives of all people. Administration approaches have been negative and unproductive, as for example the proposed penalties upon the use of overtime. Such penalties would serve only to spread existing unemployment and injure those who create jobs.

It has failed to perform its responsibility under Republican amendments to the Manpower Training Act. It has neglected, for example, the basic requirement of developing a dictionary of labor skills which are locally, regionally and nationally in short supply, even though many thousands of jobs are unfilled today for lack of qualified applicants.

### FAILING THE POOR

This Administration has refused to take practical free enterprise measures to help the poor. Under the last Republican Administration, the percentage of poor in the country dropped encouragingly from 28% to 21%. By contrast, the present Administration, despite a massive increase in the Federal bureaucracy, has managed a mere two percentage point reduction.

This Administration has proposed a so-called war on poverty which characteristically overlaps, and often contradicts, the 42 existing Federal poverty programs. It would dangerously centralize Federal controls and bypass effective state, local and private programs.

It has demonstrated little concern for the acute problems created for the poor by inflation. Consumer prices have increased in the past three and a half years by almost 5%, amounting in effect to a 5% national sales tax on the purchases of a family living on fixed income.

Under housing and urban renewal programs, notably in the Nation's Capital, it has created new slums by forcing the poor from their homes to make room for luxury apartments, while neglecting the vital need for adequate relocation assistance.

RETARDING ENTERPRISES

This Administration has violently thrust Federal power into the free market in such areas as steel prices, thus establishing precedents which in future years could critically wound free enterprise in the United States.

It has so discouraged private enterprise that the annual increase in the number of businesses has plummeted from the Republican level of 70,000 a year to 47,000 a year.

It has allowed the rate of business failures to rise higher under its leadership than in any period since depression days.

It has aggravated the problems of small business by multiplying Federal record-keeping requirements and has hurt thousands of small businessmen by forcing up their costs.

This Administration has curtailed, through such agencies as the National Labor Relations Board, the simple, basic right of Americans voluntarily to go into or to go out of business.

It has failed to stimulate new housing and attract more private capital into the field. In the past three years it has fallen short by 1,500,000 units of meeting its pledge of 2,000,000 new homes each year.

It has sought to weaken the patent system which is so largely responsible for America's progress in technology, medicine and science.

It has required private electric power companies to submit to unreasonable Federal controls as a condition to the utilization of rights-of-way over public lands. It has sought to advance, without Congressional authorization, a vastly expensive nationwide electrical transmission grid.

BETRAYAL OF THE FARMER

This Administration has refused, incredibly, to honor the clear mandate of American wheat farmers, in the largest farm referendum ever held, to free them of rigid Federal controls and to restore their birthright to make their own management decisions.

It has strangled the Republican rural development program with red tape and neglected its most essential ingredient, local initiative.

It has broken its major promises to farm people, dropping the parity ratio to its lowest level since 1939. It has dumped surplus stocks so as to lower farm income and increase the vicious cost-price squeeze on the farmer.

It has evidenced hostility toward American livestock producers by proposals to establish mandatory marketing quotas on all livestock, to fine and imprison dairy farmers failing to maintain Federally-acceptable records, and to establish a subsidized grazing cropland conversion program. It has allowed imports of beef and other meat products to rise to an all-time high during a slump in cattle prices which was aggravated by government grain sales.

NEGLECT OF NATURAL RESOURCES

This Administration has delayed the expeditious handling of oil shale patent applications and the early development of a domestic oil shale industry.

It has allowed the deterioration of the domestic mining and petroleum industries including displacement of domestic markets by foreign imports.

It has failed to protect the American fishing industry and has retreated from policies providing equitable sharing of international fishing grounds.

FISCAL IRRESPONSIBILITY

This Administration has misled the American people by such budget manipulations as crowding spending into the previous fiscal year, presenting a proposal to sell off $2.3 billion in government assets as a cut in spending, and using bookkeeping devices to make expenditures seem smaller than they actually are.

It has, despite pledges of economy, burdened this nation with four unbalanced budgets in a row, creating deficits totaling $26 billion, with still more debt to come, reflecting a rate of sustained deficit spending unmatched in peacetime.

It has failed to establish sensible priorities for Federal funds. In consequence, it has undertaken needlessly expensive crash programs, as for example accelerating a trip to the moon, to the neglect of other critical needs such as research into health and the increasingly serious problems of air and water pollution and urban crowding.

This Administration has continued to endanger retirement under Social Security for millions of citizens; it has attempted to overload the System with costly, unrelated programs which ignore the dangers of overly regressive taxation and the unfairness of forcing the poor to finance such programs for the rich.

It has demanded the elimination of a substantial portion of personal income tax deductions for charitable and church contributions, for real property taxes paid by home owners, and for interest payments. The elimination of these deductions would impose great hardship upon millions of our citizens and discourage the growth of some of the finest organizations in America.

This Administration has impeded investigations of suspected wrongdoing which might implicate public officials in the highest offices in the land. It has thus aroused justifiable resentment against those who use the high road of public service as the low road to illicitly acquired wealth.

It has permitted the quality and morale of the postal system to deteriorate and drastically restricted its services. It has made the Post Office almost inaccessible to millions of working people, reduced the once admired Parcel Post System to a national laughing stock—and yet it is intimated that Americans may soon have to pay 8¢ for a first-class postage stamp.

It has resisted personal income tax credits for education, always preferring the route leading to Federal control over our schools. Some leading Democrats have even campaigned politically in favor of such tax credits while voting against them in Congress.

Contrary to the intent of the Manpower Training Act, it has sought to extend Department of Labor influence over vocational education.

### DISCORD AND DISCONTENT

This Administration has exploited interracial tensions by extravagant campaign promises, without fulfillment, playing on the just aspirations of the minority groups, encouraging disorderly and lawless elements, and ineffectually administering the laws.

It has subjected career civil servants and part-time Federal employees, including employees of the Agriculture Department, to political pressures harmful to the integrity of the entire Federal service. It has weakened veterans' preference in Federal jobs.

It has made Federal intervention, even on the Presidential level, a standard operating practice in labor disputes, thus menacing the entire system of free collective bargaining.

It has resorted to police state tactics, using the great power of Federal Departments and agencies, to compel compliance with Administration desires, notably in the steel price dispute. The Department

of Justice, in particular, has been used improperly to achieve partisan political, economic, and legislative goals. This abuse of power should be the subject of a Congressional investigation.

### WEAKENING RESPONSIBILITY

This Administration has moved, through such undertakings as its so-called war on poverty, accelerated public works and the New Communities Program in the 1964 housing proposal, to establish new Federal offices duplicating existing agencies, bypassing the state capitals, thrusting aside local government, and siphoning off to Washington the administration of private citizen and community affairs.

It has undermined the Federally-assisted, State-operated medical and hospital assistance program, while using—and abusing—Federal authority to force a compulsory hospital program upon the people and the Congress.

This enumeration is necessarily incomplete. It does not exhaust the catalog of misdeeds and failures of the present Administration. And let the nation realize that the full impact of these many ill-conceived and ill-fated activities of the Democratic Administration is yet to come.

### SECTION THREE

*The Republican Alternative*

We Republicans are not content to record Democratic misdeeds and failures. We now offer policies and programs new in conception and dynamic in operation. These we urge to recapture initiative for freedom at home and abroad and to rebuild our strength at home.

Nor is this a new role. Republican Presidents from Abraham Lincoln to Dwight D. Eisenhower stand as witness that Republican leadership is steadfast in principle, clear in purpose and committed to progress. The many achievements of the Eisenhower Administration in strengthening peace abroad and the well-being of all at home have been unmatched in recent times. A new Republican Administration will stand proudly on this record.

We do not submit, in this platform, extravagant promises to be cynically cast aside after election day. Rather, we offer examples of Republican initiatives in areas of overriding concern to the whole nation—North, South, East and West—which befit a truly national party. In the interest of brevity, we do not repeat the commitments of the 1960 Republican Platform, "Building a Better America," and the 1962 "Declaration of Republican Principle and Policy." We incorporate into this Platform as pledges renewed those commitments which are relevant to the problems of 1964.

These, then, will be our guides, and these our additional pledges, in meeting the nation's needs.

*Faith in the Individual*

1. We Republicans shall first rely on the individual's right and capacity to advance his own economic well-being, to control the fruits of his efforts and to plan his own and his family's future; and, where government is rightly involved, we shall assist the individual in surmounting urgent problems beyond his own power and responsibility to control. For instance, we pledge:

—enlargement of employment opportunities for urban and rural citizens, with emphasis on training programs to equip them with needed skills; improved job information and placement services; and research and extension services channeled toward helping rural people improve their opportunities;

—tax credits and other methods of assistance to help needy senior citizens meet the costs of medical and hospital insurance;

—a strong, sound system of Social Security, with improved benefits to our people;

—continued Federal support for a sound research program aimed at both the prevention and cure of diseases, and intensified efforts to secure prompt and effective application of the results of research. This will include emphasis on mental illness, drug addiction, alcoholism, cancer, heart disease and other diseases of increasing incidence;

—revision of the Social Security laws to allow higher earnings, without loss of benefits, by our elderly people;

—full coverage of all medical and hospital costs for the needy elderly people, financed by general revenues through broader implementation of Federal-State plans, rather than the compulsory Democratic scheme covering only a small percentage of such costs, for everyone regardless of need;

—adoption and implementation of a fair and adequate program for providing necessary supplemental farm labor for producing and harvesting agricultural commodities;

—tax credits for those burdened by the expenses of college education;

—vocational rehabilitation, through cooperation between government—Federal and State—and industry, for the mentally and physically handicapped, the chronically unemployed and the poverty-stricken;

—incentives for employers to hire teenagers, including broadening of temporary exemptions under the minimum wage law;

—to repeal the Administration's wheat certificate "bread-tax" on consumers, so burdensome to low-income families and overwhelmingly rejected by farmers;

—revision of present non-service-connected pension programs to provide increased benefits for low income pensioners, with emphasis on rehabilitation, nursing homes and World War I veterans;

—re-evaluation of the armed forces' manpower procurement programs with the goal of replacing involuntary inductions as soon as possible by an efficient voluntary system, offering real career incentives;

—enactment of legislation, despite Democratic opposition, to curb the flow through the mails of obscene materials which has flourished into a multimillion dollar obscenity racket;

—support of a Constitutional amendment permitting those individuals and groups who choose to do so to exercise their religion freely in public places, provided religious exercises are not prepared or prescribed by the state or political subdivision thereof and no person's participation therein is coerced, thus preserving the traditional separation of church and state;

—full implementation and faithful execution of the Civil Rights Act of 1964, and all other civil rights statutes, to assure equal rights and opportunities guaranteed by the Constitution to every citizen;

—improvements of civil rights statutes adequate to changing needs of our times;

—such additional administrative or legislative actions as may be required to end the denial, for whatever unlawful reason, of the right to vote;

—immigration legislation seeking to re-unite families and continuation of the "Fair Share" Refugee Program;

—continued opposition to discrimination based on race, creed, national origin or sex. We recognize that the elimination of any such discrimination is a matter of heart, conscience, and education, as well as of equal rights under law.

In all such programs, where Federal initiative is properly involved to relieve or prevent misfortune or meet overpowering need, it will be the Republican way to move promptly and energetically, and wherever possible to provide assistance of a kind enabling the individual to gain or regain the capability to make his own way and to have a fair chance to achieve his own goals. In all matters relating to human rights it will be the Republican way fully to implement all applicable laws and never to lose sight of the intense need for advancing peaceful progress in human relations in our land. The Party of Abraham Lincoln will proudly and faithfully live up to its heritage of equal rights and equal opportunities for all.

In furtherance of our faith in the individual, we also pledge prudent, responsible management of the government's fiscal affairs to protect the individual against the evils of spendthrift government —protecting most of all the needy and fixed-income families against the cruelest tax, inflation —and protecting every citizen against the high taxes forced by excessive spending, in order that each individual may keep more of his earnings for his own and his family's use. For instance, we pledge:

—a reduction of not less than five billion dollars in the present level of Federal spending;

—an end to chronic deficit financing, proudly reaffirming our belief in a balanced budget;

—further reduction in individual and corporate tax rates as fiscal discipline is restored;

—repayments on the public debt;

—maintenance of an administrative, legislative and regulatory climate encouraging job-building enterprise to help assure every individual a real chance for a good job;

—wise, firm and responsible conduct of the nation's foreign affairs, backed by military forces kept modern, strong and ready, thereby assuring every individual of a future promising peace.

In all such matters it will be the Republican way so to conduct the affairs of government as to give the individual citizen the maximum assurance of a peaceful and prosperous future, freed of the discouragement and hardship produced by wasteful and ineffectual government.

In furtherance of our faith in the individual, we also pledge the maximum restraint of Federal intrusions into matters more productively left to the individual. For instance, we pledge:

—to continue Republican sponsorship of practical Federal-State-local programs which will effectively treat the needs of the poor, while resisting direct Federal handouts that erode away individual self-reliance and self-respect and perpetuate dependency;

—to continue the advancement of education on all levels, through such programs as selective aid to higher education, strengthened State and local tax resources, including tax credits for college education, while resisting the Democratic efforts which endanger local control of schools;

—to help assure equal opportunity and a good education for all, while opposing Federally-sponsored "inverse discrimination," whether by the shifting of jobs, or the abandonment of neighborhood schools, for reasons of race;

—to provide our farmers, who have contributed so much to the strength of our nation, with the maximum opportunity to exercise their own management decisions on their own farms, while resisting all efforts to impose upon them further Federal controls;

—to establish realistic priorities for the concentration of Federal spending in the most productive and creative areas, such as education, job training, vocational rehabilitation, educational research, oceanography, and the wise development and use of natural resources in the water as well as on land, while resisting Democratic efforts to spend wastefully and indiscriminately;

—to open avenues of peaceful progress in solving racial controversies while discouraging lawlessness and violence.

In all such matters, it will be the Republican way to assure the individual of maximum freedom as government meets its proper responsibilities, while resisting the Democratic obsession to impose from above, uniform and rigid schemes for meeting varied and complex human problems.

*Faith in the Competitive System*

2. We Republicans shall vigorously protect the dynamo of economic growth—free, competitive enterprise—that has made America the envy of the world. For instance, we pledge:

—removal of the wartime Federal excise taxes, favored by the Democratic Administration, on pens, pencils, jewelry, cosmetics, luggage, handbags, wallets and toiletries;

—assistance to small business by simplifying

Federal and State tax and regulatory requirements, fostering the availability of longer term credit at fair terms and equity capital for small firms, encouraging strong State programs to foster small business, establishing more effective measures to assure a sharing by small business in Federal procurement, and promoting wider export opportunities;

—an end to power-grabbing regulatory actions, such as the reach by the Federal Trade Commission for injunctive powers and the ceaseless pressing by the White House, the Food and Drug Administration and Federal Trade Commission to dominate consumer decisions in the market place;

—returning the consumer to the driver's seat as the chief regulator and chief beneficiary of a free economy, by resisting excessive concentration of power, whether public or private;

—a drastic reduction in burdensome Federal paperwork and overlapping regulations, which weigh heavily on small businessmen struggling to compete and to provide jobs;

—a determined drive, through tough, realistic negotiations, to remove the many discriminatory and restrictive trade practices of foreign nations;

—greater emphasis on overseas sales of surplus farm commodities to friendly countries through long-term credits repayable in dollars under the Republican Food for Peace program;

—dedication to freedom of expression for all news media, to the right of access by such media to public proceedings, and to the independence of radio, television and other news-gathering media from excessive government control;

—improvement, and full and fair enforcement, of the anti-trust statutes, coupled with long-overdue clarification of Federal policies and interpretations relating thereto in order to strengthen competition and protect the consumer and small business;

—constant opposition to any form of unregulated monopoly, whether business or labor;

—meaningful safeguards against irreparable injuries to any domestic industries by disruptive surges of imports, such as in the case of beef and other meat products, textiles, oil, glass, coal, lumber and steel;

—enactment of law, such as the Democratic Administration vetoed in the 88th Congress, requiring that labels of imported items clearly disclose their foreign origin;

—completely reorganize the National Labor Relations Board to assure impartial protection of the rights of the public, employees and employers, ending the defiance of Congress by the present Board;

—the redevelopment of an atmosphere of confidence throughout the government and across the nation, in which vigorous competition can flourish.

In all such matters it will be the Republican way to support, not harass—to encourage, not restrain—to build confidence, not threaten—to provide stability, not unrest—to speed genuine growth, not conjure up statistical fantasies and to assure that all actions of government apply fairly to every element of the nation's economy.

In furtherance of our faith in the competitive system, we also pledge:

—a continual re-examination and reduction of government competition with private business, consistent with the recommendations of the second Hoover Commission;

—elimination of excessive bureaucracy;

—full protection of the integrity of the career governmental services, military and civilian, coupled with adequate pay scales;

—maximum reliance upon subordinate levels of government and individual citizens to meet the nation's needs, in place of establishing even more Federal agencies to burden the people.

In all such matters relating to Federal administration it will be the Republican way to provide maximum service for each tax dollar expended, watchfully superintend the size and scope of Federal activities, and assure an administration always fair, efficient and cooperatively disposed toward every element of our competitive system.

*Faith in Limited Government*

3. We Republicans shall insist that the Federal Government have effective but limited powers, that it be frugal and efficient, and that it fully meet its Constitutional responsibilities to all the American people. For instance, we pledge:

—restoration of collective bargaining responsibility to labor and management, minimizing third-party intervention and preventing any agency of government from becoming an advocate for any private economic interest;

—development of truly voluntary commodity programs for commercial agriculture, including payments in kind out of government-owned surpluses, diversion of unneeded land to conservation uses, price supports free of political manipulation in order to stimulate and attain fair market prices, together with adequate credit facilities and continued support of farm-owned and operated co-operatives including rural electric and telephone facilities, while resisting all efforts to make the farmer dependent, for his economic survival, upon either compensatory payments by the Federal Government or upon the whim of the Secretary of Agriculture;

—full cooperation of all governmental levels and private enterprise in advancing the balanced use of the nation's natural resources to provide for man's multiple needs;

—continuing review of public-land laws and policies to assure maximum opportunity for all beneficial uses of the public lands; including the development of mineral resources;

—comprehensive water-resource planning and development, including projects for our growing cities, expanded research in desalinization of water, and continued support of multi-purpose reclamation projects;

—support of sustained yield management of our forests and expanded research for control of forest insects, disease, and forest fires;

—protection of traditional domestic fishing grounds and other actions, including tax incentives, to encourage modernization of fishing vessels, and improve processing and marketing practices;

—continued tax support to encourage exploration and development of domestic sources of minerals and metals, with reasonable depletion allowances;

—stabilization of present oil programs, private development of atomic power, increased coal research and expansion of coal exports;

—a replanning of the present space program to provide for a more orderly, yet aggressively pursued, step-by-step development, remaining alert to the danger of overdiversion of skilled personnel in critical shortage from other vital areas such as health, industry, education and science.

In furtherance of our faith in limited, frugal and efficient government we also pledge:

—credit against Federal taxes for specified State and local taxes paid, and a transfer to the States of excise and other Federal tax sources, to reinforce the fiscal strength of State and local govern-

ments so that they may better meet rising school costs and other pressing urban and suburban problems such as transportation, housing, water systems and juvenile delinquency;

—emphasis upon channeling more private capital into sound urban development projects and private housing;

—critical re-examination and major overhaul of all Federal grant-in-aid programs with a view to channeling such programs through the States, discontinuing those no longer required and adjusting others in a determined effort to restore the unique balance and creative energy of the traditional American system of government;

—revitalization of municipal and county governments throughout America by encouraging them, and private citizens as well, to develop new solutions of their major concerns through a streamlining and modernizing of state and local processes of government, and by a renewed consciousness of their ability to reach these solutions, not through Federal action, but through their own capabilities;

—support of a Constitutional amendment, as well as legislation, enabling States having bicameral legislatures to apportion one House on bases of their choosing, including factors other than population;

—complete reform of the tax structure, to include simplification as well as lower rates to strengthen individual and business incentives;

—effective budgetary reform, improved Congressional appropriation procedures, and full implementation of the anti-deficiency statute;

—a wide-ranging reform of other Congressional procedures, including the provision of adequate professional staff assistance for the minority membership on Congressional Committees, to insure that the power and prestige of Congress remain adequate to the needs of the times;

—high priority for the solution of the nation's balance of payment difficulties to assure unquestioned confidence in the dollar, maintenance of the competitiveness of American products in domestic and foreign markets, expansion of exports, stimulation of foreign tourism in the United States, greater foreign sharing of mutual security burdens abroad, a drastic reorganization and redirection of the entire foreign aid effort, gradual reductions in overseas U. S. forces as manpower can be replaced by increased firepower; and strengthening of the international monetary system without sacrifice of our freedom of policy making.

In all such matters it will be the Republican way to achieve not feigned but genuine savings, allowing a reduction of the public debt and additional tax reductions while meeting the proper responsibilities of government. We pledge an especially determined effort to help strengthen the ability of State and local governments to meet the broad range of needs facing the nation's urban and suburban communities.

SECTION FOUR

*Freedom Abroad*

The Republican commitment to individual freedom applies no less abroad.

America must advance freedom throughout the world as a vital condition of orderly human progress, universal justice, and the security of the American people.

The supreme challenge to this policy is an atheistic imperialism-Communism.

Our nation's leadership must be judged by—indeed, American independence and even survival are dependent upon—the stand it takes toward Communism.

That stand must be: victory for freedom. There can be no peace, there can be no security, until this goal is won.

As long as Communist leaders remain ideologically fixed upon ruling the world, there can be no lesser goal. This is the supreme test of America's foreign policy. It must not be defaulted. In the balance is human liberty everyplace on earth.

*Reducing the Risks of War*

A dynamic strategy aimed at victory pressing always for initiatives for freedom, rejecting always appeasement and withdrawal—reduces the risk of nuclear war. It is a nation's vacillation, not firmness, that tempts an aggressor into war. It is accommodation, not opposition, that encourages a hostile nation to remain hostile and to remain aggressive.

The road to peace is a road not of fawning amiability but of strength and respect. Republicans judge foreign policy by its success in advancing freedom and justice, not by its effect on international prestige polls.

In making foreign policy, these will be our guidelines:

*Trusting Ourselves and Our Friends*

1. Secrecy in foreign policy must be at a minimum, public understanding at a maximum. Our own citizens, rather than those of other nations, should be accorded primary trust.

2. Consultation with our allies should take precedence over direct negotiations with Communist powers. The bypassing of our allies has contributed greatly to the shattering of free world unity and to the loss of free world continuity in opposing Communism.

*Communism's Course*

3. We reject the notion that Communism has abandoned its goal of world domination, or that fat and well-fed Communists are less dangerous than lean and hungry ones. We also reject the notion that the United States should take sides in the Sino-Soviet rift.

Republican foreign policy starts with the assumption that Communism is the enemy of this nation in every sense until it can prove that its enmity has been abandoned.

4. We hold that trade with Communist countries should not be directed toward the enhancement of their power and influence but could only be justified if it would serve to diminish their power.

5. We are opposed to the recognition of Red China. We oppose its admission into the United Nations. We steadfastly support free China.

6. In negotiations with Communists, Republicans will probe tirelessly for reasonable, practicable and trustworthy agreements. However, we will never abandon insistence on advantages for the free world.

7. Republicans will continue to work for the realization of the Open Skies policy proposed in 1955 by President Eisenhower. Only open societies offer real hope of confidence among nations.

*Communism's Captives*

8. Republicans reaffirm their long-standing commitment to a course leading to eventual liberation of the Communist-dominated nations of Eastern Europe, Asia and Latin America, including the peoples of Hungary, Poland, East Germany, Czechoslovakia, Rumania, Albania, Bulgaria, Latvia, Lithuania, Estonia, Armenia, Ukraine, Yugoslavia, and its Serbian, Croatian and Slovene peoples, Cuba, mainland China, and many others.

We condemn the persecution of minorities, such as the Jews, within Communist borders.

### The United Nations

9. Republicans support the United Nations. However, we will never rest in our efforts to revitalize its original purpose.

We will press for a change in the method of voting in the General Assembly and in the specialized agencies that will reflect population disparities among the member states and recognize differing abilities and willingness to meet the obligations of the Charter. We will insist upon General Assembly acceptance of the International Court of Justice advisory opinion, upholding denial of the votes of member nations which refuse to meet properly levied assessments, so that the United Nations will more accurately reflect the power realities of the world. Further to assure the carrying out of these recommendations and to correct the above abuses, we urge the calling of an amending convention of the United Nations by the year 1967.

Republicans will never surrender to any international group the responsibility of the United States for its sovereignty, its own security, and the leadership of the free world.

### NATO: The Great Shield

10. Republicans regard NATO as indispensable for the prevention of war and the protection of freedom. NATO's unity and vitality have alarmingly deteriorated under the present Administration. It is a keystone of Republican foreign policy to revitalize the Alliance.

To hasten its restoration, Republican leadership will move immediately to establish an international commission, comprised of individuals of high competence in NATO affairs, whether in or out of government, to explore and recommend effective new ways to strengthen alliance participation and fulfillment.

### Freedom's Further Demands

11. To our nation's associates in SEATO and CENTO, Republicans pledge reciprocal dedication of purpose and revitalized interest. These great alliances, with NATO, must be returned to the forefront of foreign policy planning. A strengthened alliance system is equally necessary in the Western Hemisphere.

This will remain our constant purpose: Republicans will labor tirelessly with free men everywhere and in every circumstance toward the defeat of Communism and victory for freedom.

### The Geography of Freedom

12. In diverse regions of the world, Republicans will make clear to any hostile nation that the United States will increase the costs and risks of aggression to make them outweigh hopes for gain. It was just such a communication and determination by the Eisenhower Republican Administration that produced the 1953 Korean Armistice. The same strategy can win victory for freedom and stop further aggression in Southeast Asia.

We will move decisively to assure victory in South Vietnam. While confining the conflict as closely as possible, America must move to end the fighting in a reasonable time and provide guarantees against further aggression. We must make it clear to the Communist world that, when conflict is forced with America, it will end only in victory for freedom.

We will demand that the Berlin Wall be taken down prior to the resumption of any negotiations with the Soviet Union on the status of forces in, or treaties affecting, Germany.

We will reassure our German friends that the United States will not accept any plan for the future of Germany which lacks firm assurance of a free election on reunification.

We will urge the immediate implementation of the Caracas Declaration of Solidarity against international Communist intervention endorsed in 1954 by the Organization of American States during the Eisenhower Administration, which Declaration, in accordance with the historic Monroe Doctrine, our nation's official policy since 1823, opposes domination of any of our neighbor-nations by any power outside this Hemisphere.

We will vigorously press our OAS partners to join the United States in restoring a free and independent government in Cuba, stopping the spread of Sino-Soviet subversion, forcing the withdrawal of the foreign military presence now in Latin America, and preventing future intrusions. We Republicans will recognize a Cuban government in exile; we will support its efforts to regain the independence of its homeland; we will assist Cuban freedom fighters in carrying on guerrilla warfare against the Communist regime; we will work for an economic boycott by all nations of the free world in trade with Cuba; and we will encourage free elections in Cuba after liberty and stability are restored.

We will consider raising the economic participation of the Republic of Panama in the operation of the Panama Canal and assure the safety of Americans in the area. We will reaffirm this nation's treaty rights and study the feasibility of a substitute, sea-level canal at an appropriate location including the feasibility of nuclear excavation.

Republicans will make clear to all Communists now supporting or planning to support guerrilla and subversive activities, that henceforth there will be no privileged sanctuaries to protect those who disrupt the peace of the world. We will make clear that blockade, interception of logistical support, and diplomatic and economic pressure are appropriate United States counters to deliberate breaches of the peace.

We will make clear to all Communist leaders everywhere that aggressive actions, including those in the German air corridors, will be grounds for re-evaluation of any and all trade or diplomatic relations currently to Communism's advantage.

We will take the cold war offensive on all fronts, including, for example, a reinvigorated USIA. It will broadcast not our weaknesses but our strengths. It will mount a psychological warfare attack on behalf of freedom and against Communist doctrine and imperialism.

Republicans will recast foreign aid programs. We will see that all will serve the cause of freedom. We will see that none bolster and sustain anti-American regimes; we will increase the use of private capital on a partnership basis with foreign nationals, as a means of fostering independence and mutual respect but we assert that property of American Nationals must not be expropriated by any foreign government without prompt and adequate compensation as contemplated by international law.

Respecting the Middle East, and in addition to our reaffirmed pledges of 1960 concerning this area, we will so direct our economic and military assistance as to help maintain stability in this region and prevent an imbalance of arms.

Finally, we will improve the efficiency and coordination of the foreign service, and provide adequate allowance for foreign service personnel.

### The Development of Freedom

13. Freedom's wealth must never support freedom's decline, always its growth. America's tax revenues derived from free enterprise sources must never be employed in support of socialism. America must assist young and underdeveloped nations. In the process, however, we must not sacrifice the trust of old friends.

Our assistance, also, must be conditional upon self-help and progress toward the development of free institutions. We favor the establishment in underdeveloped nations of an economic and political climate that will encourage the investment of local capital and attract the investment of foreign capital.

### Freedom's Shield—and Sword

Finally, Republicans pledge to keep the nation's sword sharp, ready, and dependable.

We will maintain a superior, not merely equal, military capability as long as the Communist drive for world domination continues. It will be a capability of balanced force, superior in all its arms, maintaining flexibility for effective performance in the rapidly changing science of war.

Republicans will never unilaterally disarm America.

We will demand that any arms reduction plan worthy of consideration guarantee reliable inspection. We will demand that any such plan assure this nation of sufficient strength, step by step, to forestall and defend against possible violations.

We will take every step necessary to carry forward the vital military research and development programs. We will pursue these programs as absolutely necessary to assure our nation of superior strength in the 1970's.

We will revitalize research and development programs needed to enable the nation to develop advanced new weapons systems, strategic as well as tactical.

We will include the fields of anti-submarine warfare, astronautics and aeronautics, special guerrilla forces, and such other defense systems required to keep America ready for any threat.

We will fully implement such safeguards as our security requires under the limited nuclear test ban treaty. We will conduct advanced tests in permissible areas, maintain facilities to test elsewhere in case of violations, and develop to the fullest our ability to detect Communist transgressions. Additionally, we will regularly review the status of nuclear weaponry under the limited nuclear test ban to assure this nation's protection. We shall also provide sensible, continuing reviews of the treaty itself.

We will end "second-best" weapons policies. We will end the false economies which place price ahead of the performance upon which American lives may depend. Republicans will bring an end once again to the "peak and valley" defense planning, so costly in morale and strength as well as in dollars. We will prepare a practical civil defense program.

We will restore the morale of our armed forces by upgrading military professionalism, and we will allow professional dissent while insuring that strong and sound civilian authority controls objective decision-making.

We will return the Joint Chiefs of Staff to their lawful status as the President's principal military advisors. We will insure that an effective planning and operations staff is restored to the National Security Council.

We will reconsecrate this nation to human liberty, assuring the freedom of our people, and rallying mankind to a new crusade for freedom all around the world.

We Republicans, with the help of Almighty God, will keep those who would bury America aware that this nation has the strength and also the will to defend its every interest. Those interests, we shall make clear, include the preservation and expansion of freedom—and ultimately its victory—everyplace on earth.

We do not offer the easy way. We offer dedication and perseverance, leading to victory. This is our Platform. This is the Republican way.

## Socialist Labor Platform 1964

The Socialist Labor Party of America, in National Convention assembled on the 3rd day of May, 1964, reaffirms its previous platform pronouncements and declares:

Humanity stands today on the threshold of a new social order. The old order—capitalism—is doomed; it is an outmoded system charged with fatal contradictions.

On the one hand, since World War II, there have come into being productive industrial and scientific forces which no former epoch in human history ever experienced. On the other hand, there exist unmistakable symptoms of social anarchy, dissolution and decay. "Everything seems pregnant with its contrary." Automated machinery, gifted with the wonderful power of freeing mankind from want and arduous toil, becomes a menace, intensifying the insecurity of the workers.

It is a grim and portentous fact that for the mass of mankind, that is, for the wage workers who perform the mental and manual labors of society, the future never loomed more threateningly. At the very time when, because of the great upsurge in population, youths are pouring into the labor market in unprecedented numbers, automation is wiping out jobs at the rate of more than 2,000,000 a year. And there is every evidence that this rate will rise as new automation techniques and systems, already completed and tested, spread through America's offices and factories.

President Johnson has attested that by 1970 "this country, because of increased productivity, will be able to match the output of the 1960s with 20 million fewer workers."

### Phony Antipoverty Wars

Against this bleak background, the antipoverty "wars" recently declared by the politicians of both major parties—to the accompaniment of much self-glorification—are exposed as hypocritical exercises in utter futility.

The forces under capitalism that breed poverty and that make the lives of workers more insecure, are in the ascendant. Therefore, reform attempts at lessening poverty must inevitably fail.

In opposition to the capitalist politicians with their phony antipoverty "wars", the Socialist Labor Party proposes a plan, not for lessening poverty, but for its total abolition. We present a summary of the plan here and earnestly urge the serious consideration of it by all thoughtful voters.

In all previous epochs of human history poverty for the mass of the people was inescapable. There was simply not enough to go around. It was unavoidable that some should suffer deprivation in order that others might have the freedom from want and the leisure in which to develop science and culture.

## CAPITALISM'S BEST-KEPT SECRET

Not so today. The most luminous fact of our age is this: *There is no longer any excuse whatever for the involuntary poverty of a single member of society.* Material conditions have changed so radically that, far from insufficiency, there is today the material possibility of abundance for everyone, and the promise of leisure in which to enjoy it.

Accordingly, today—right now—the material foundations exist for a world of general affluence, cooperation and social harmony, which is to say, for a Socialist world. In this world, all the means of production, distribution and social services will be socially owned and democratically controlled and administered in the interest of all society. The insane contradiction of poverty in the midst of plenty will be completely eliminated. Private profit, as the objective of human endeavor, will be abolished. Instead, every decision will be determined by human needs and human desires. The ugly, unsanitary workshops of capitalism will be turned into pleasant, sanitary production laboratories. Factories will be designed and constructed to insure the greatest possible measure of safety, health and efficiency.

Work itself will cease to be an ordeal in tedium, a spiritless repetition of motions for someone else's profits. Wherever possible tasks that are hazardous or strenuous will be mechanized. Where this is not possible, special dispensations will be made, such as shorter hours of work for those performing these tasks. Meanwhile, in this Socialist world, the working day, week and year for everyone will be cut to a fraction of what it is today.

The whole concept of work will undergo drastic change. Education, emancipated from the anti-intellectual conditions and restrictions of capitalism, will be greatly expanded and revolutionized. Every youth will have the widest possible opportunity to develop all his potentialities for living fully, cooperatively and constructively.

In this Socialist world all who perform useful work will receive, directly and indirectly, all that they produce. And this will be the equivalent of several times the average income of workers today.

In our Socialist world, democracy will be a vibrant, meaningful reality, not the mask for economic despotism that it is today. There will be no such ridiculous thing as a political government based, as today, on wholly arbitrary and artificial demarcations. (Some of our state boundaries were determined by a king's grant two and a half centuries ago; they are meaningless in the industrial age!) To administer social production in the interests of the people we need an *industrial democracy*, a government based on industrial constituencies.

In this society there will be no capitalist masters and no political or bureaucratic masters either. We will vote where we work, electing our representatives to administrative and planning bodies on an ascending scale. But note this: The people whom we elect to administrative posts will have the privilege to serve, never the power to rule. For the same rank and file that elects them will have the power to recall and replace them at will.

## GOVERNMENT'S DUTIES UNDER SOCIALISM

Unlike the politicians of capitalism, who spend their time pulling the wool over the eyes of the workers, the democratically elected administrators and planners of Socialism will be concerned with such practical things as what and how much to produce to insure an uninterrupted flow of the good things of life in abundance; the number of working hours required in the various industries; the erection of plants of production and of educational, health and recreational facilities; the development of new technology; the disposition of machinery; the erection of new housing in the proper places; the de-pollution of streams and lakes; the conservation of resources and the restoration of the natural environment and its preservation in perpetuity.

All that stands in the way of this heaven on earth, a world in which all may enjoy good housing, abundant and nourishing food, the finest clothing, and the best of cultural, educational and recreational advantages, is the outmoded capitalist system.

This is no exaggeration. Nor merely a beautiful dream. It is based on the solid foundation of present facts. Automation, the supreme triumph of technology, has brought this heaven on earth within our reach. Yet, privately owned, as are all productive instruments under capitalism, automation is a blessing only to the capitalist owner; for workers—white collar and blue collar alike—it is a curse, a job-killer, which adds terrifying dimensions to their insecurity and suffering.

THE NUMBER ONE QUESTION

Thus the question we face comes down to this: In the words of Supreme Court Justice William O. Douglas: *"When the machine displaces man and does most of the work, who will own the machines and receive the rich dividends?"*

The American Constitution, in effect, legalizes revolution. The right to alter or abolish the social system and form of government is implicit in Article V, the Constitution's amendment clause. The Socialist Labor Party proposes to the American workers that we use our huge majorities at the polls to outlaw capitalist ownership and to make the means of social production the property of all the people collectively.

The Socialist Labor Party proposes further that we workers consolidate our economic forces on the industrial field in one integral Socialist Industrial Union to back up the peaceful Socialist ballot with an irresistible and invincible might capable of taking and holding the industries, locking out the outvoted capitalist class, if it defies the victory at the ballot box, and continuing social production without interruption.

The Scottish essayist and historian, Thomas Carlyle, is credited with the following statement: "We must some day, at last and forever, cross the line between Nonsense and Common Sense. And on that day we shall pass from Class Paternalism . . . to Human Brotherhood . . . ; from Political Government to Industrial Administration; from Competition in Individualism to Individuality in Cooperation; from War and Despotism, in any form, to Peace and Liberty."

We must cross that line some day—why not now? Repudiate the Republican and Democratic parties, the political Siamese twins of capitalism—and reject also the self-styled "radicals" and "liberals" whose platforms consist of measures to reform and patch up the poverty-breeding capitalist system, which is past reforming and patching. Study the Socialist Labor Party's Socialist Industrial Union program. Support the Socialist Labor Party's entire ticket at the polls. Unite with us to save humanity from catastrophe—and to set an example in free industrial self-government for all mankind, in affluence and enduring peace!

## Socialist Workers Platform 1964

In his State of the Union message President Johnson spoke of "one-fifth of all American families with income too small to even meet their basic needs." It is to these underprivileged millions, and to all whose lives are blighted under capitalism, that the Socialist Workers Party addresses itself. We advance a socialist program for a real and lasting solution of the grave problems afflicting our society today, and they are many.

Technological change and speed-up, designed to cut labor costs and hike corporation profits, displace workers from their jobs at an increasing rate. Meanwhile, the rate at which new jobs are created is slowing down, causing a built-in rise in chronic unemployment. Hardest hit are the unskilled and older workers, youth, Negroes and other minorities; and to an increasing degree whole local areas are becoming depression pockets of hunger and poverty.

At the best, jobless benefits fall short of take-home pay and force a cut in living standards, and in no case is compensation guaranteed for the full period of unemployment. Some categories of workers get no jobless benefits at all. Older people retired from their jobs get pitifully small pensions, sometimes none whatever. People forced to ask for public relief get a stingy dole; they are subjected to a humiliating "poverty" test; children are pressured to take financial responsibility for their parents; and those on relief are slandered as "shiftless and immoral" by venal politicians anxious to curry favor with the wealthy tax dodgers.

People able to earn their own income are gouged by stiff taxes in open and concealed forms. Employed and unemployed alike face steadily rising prices. To try to get ahead, and often even to get by, families must resort more and more to installment buying, mortgaging tomorrow's earnings to meet today's needs.

Decent housing becomes ever scarcer and rents more outrageous. Public transportation systems break down almost as fast as fares go up. Classrooms in decaying school buildings are overcrowded with students and understaffed by underpaid teachers. There are not enough hospitals, not enough nurses or doctors, and the cost of medical care under the profit system is a crime against humanity.

BLEAK FUTURE

Millions of the nation's youth face a bleak future. Those lucky enough to get a fairly good education have no assurance they will find a decent, permanent job with good prospects for advancement, on which they could begin to build a secure and rewarding life. Young men have far greater assurance of being drafted into military service, maybe to die in some far away land, made to fight for something they don't really understand. When jobless in civilian life, youth generally are treated more as a police problem of "juvenile delinquency" than as economically-displaced humans who deserve a better break from society.

For Negroes, Mexicans, Puerto Ricans and other minorities the problems are the most severe. Those employed usually draw the dirtiest, hardest, lowest-paid jobs. They are largely restricted to ghetto life in slum areas where they must pay high rent for squalid quarters. Their neighborhood schools are the poorest, most overcrowded, least well staffed. Such social services as are extended to them are at the lowest level. Police brutality is an unending part of their everyday existence, and most everywhere they go they face open or thinly-veiled discrimination that violates their human dignity and blights their lives.

Under capitalism today only one thing is shared by all. Men and women, old and young, the well-off and the poverty stricken, white and colored—all face the danger of nuclear war. Fear of a nuclear cataclysm haunts the lives of every adult, every child of knowing age, and there is no place to hide. The pretense of setting up bomb shelters is simply a cruel hoax.

The Socialist Workers Party contends that these social evils stem directly from the capitalist system under which the country is ruled by big banks and giant corporations. The few who control the monopolies put their private interests ahead of the needs of the many who do the work. These privileged few enjoy lavish and growing prosperity, but their greed remains insatiable. Not content with today's peak profits, they clamor and scheme to get more.

In their quest for greater wealth the monopolists resort to the imperialist practice of exploiting peoples in other lands for private profit. But in country after country, right up to Cuba, 90 miles off our shores, the working people are revolting against such exploitation. They demand use of the national wealth, not to fatten profiteers, but to meet the needs of those who produce the wealth. Dire necessity steadily pushes them away from

capitalism and impels them toward nationalized production and a planned economy, as they take the first steps to reorganize society on a socialist basis.

## USE PRETEXT

The American banks and corporations plot to crush these revolts abroad. Using as a pretext the violations of workers' democracy in the Soviet-bloc, they even hope to restore capitalism in countries where it has been abolished, including China and the Soviet Union. Cloaking their aims with hate propaganda against a so-called "communist conspiracy," they resort to increasingly brutal and unscrupulous methods. The revolutionary Cuban workers and farmers are branded enemies, while the fascist dictator Franco is embraced as an ally. Military interventions in other people's affairs become harsher and more brazen, even going to the brink of all-out nuclear war. No wonder America is feared and hated throughout the world.

Bluntly stating the monopolist creed in a recent speech at the University of Chicago, Henry Ford II said, "The target of private business is private profit." He argued for bigger profits on the ground that business could then invest more to create new jobs, implying that all social problems could thus be solved. His kind want the tax money to be used for military measures to maintain a "free world" open to their exploitation for private profit. They will brook no nonsense about government spending to correct the social evils inflicted by "free-enterprise" profiteering here at home; and the monopolists of Ford's class carry more weight in Washington than all the working people in the country.

Apologists for the Democrats claim it is only the Republicans who act as political flunkies for the monopolists, but the facts don't bear them out. In basic foreign policy, Democratic and Republican outlook is consistently bipartisan; so much so that one party can take over the White House from the other without a moment's pause in military interventions abroad. On the bread-and-butter issues in domestic policy the two parties act as one in the services of the banks and corporations. The Democrats, masquerading as a "people's" party, are simply a shade more hypocritical about it than the Republicans, and they are notorious for the accommodations to the Dixiecrats.

Through bipartisan endeavor, military alliances

have been forged with other capitalist governments. A far-flung network of American military bases rings the world. Deadly nuclear weapons, able to "over-kill" all humanity, stand ready for use in missile silos and U.S. submarines. Since 1948 universal military service has been imposed to conscript American youth into the armed forces, in which there is no democracy, and send them overseas as occupation troops to prop up puppet regimes. And the government has repeatedly been caught lying here at home about what it is doing abroad.

Our tax money is used to arm and train counter-revolutionary gangs who try to suppress revolts against poverty and overturn anti-capitalist governments in other lands. The bipartisans refuse to recognize the chosen government of 700 million Chinese, but they back to the hilt military overlords in South Vietnam. Eisenhower's administration first sent U.S. troops into Vietnam as "advisers," and the Kennedy and Johnson administrations continued and intensified the policy at the cost of mounting American casualties.

Troops commanded by a Democratic President shoot down unarmed Panamanians demonstrating against U.S. exploitation of their country and the Republicans back him up. The bipartisans maintain an economic blockade against Cuba and try to discipline allied countries who disagree with their policy. The criminal Bay of Pigs invasion in 1961 was planned under the Republicans and set into motion under the Democrats. Washington's anti-Cuba policy was carried to the very brink of general nuclear war in the 1962 missile crisis. The brutal tensions of that crisis made clear that under today's capitalist rule the question of war or peace can hinge on the decision of one man, the President. America's millions have no voice whatever.

Washington claims to know all about everything going on in Cuba, but its CIA-FBI gang can't find the bombers who murdered four little Negro girls in a Birmingham, Alabama, church. The bipartisans are too busy sabotaging and trying to overthrow the Castro regime that established genuine equality for racial minorities in Cuba.

TOKEN RIGHTS BILL

With great fanfare a token civil-rights bill is introduced into Congress where capitalist politicians will cynically play preelection politics with it. Negro freedom fighters peacefully demonstrating for their civil rights are subjected to brutal police attacks. Freedom fighters who defend themselves against white supremacist violence are framed up, as were four people recently convicted on fake "kidnap" charges in Monroe, North Carolina, and sentenced to long prison terms.

Those who would maintain racial oppression have, as a current NAACP report correctly states, "resisted the Constitution and court rulings by force, by deceit, by tokenism, by stalling litigation and by such legislative maneuvers as the filibuster."

As in the case of civil rights, tokenism and repression typify bipartisan policy on all questions of general social need. What little they do under mass pressure follows the "trickle-down" theory of the banks and corporations. The new tax cut does far more for the tax-dodging monopolies than it does for the tax-gouged working people. For economically-depressed areas like Appalachia plans are afoot to make low-interest federal loans to local capitalists who would use the money to turn a handsome profit for themselves. As a sop to the unemployed a vague promise is made of future government pressure to cut down on overtime hours and spread the work a little.

President Johnson was quick to reaffirm the long-standing White House opposition to union demands for a reduction in hours with no cut in take-home pay and to warn labor against "inflationary" wage demands. On these matters the bipartisans mean business. They demonstrated as much last year by rushing a bill through Congress which legalized compulsory arbitration and in effect outlawed a railroad strike.

On the minimum wage, jobless benefits, public relief, housing, health, education and other social problems, the Democratic administration makes token promises of slow improvement. For his much-publicized "war on poverty" which President Johnson calls "unconditional," about $1 billion, only one-third of it new money, is promised for the next fiscal year. In the same budget 54 times as much is allocated to the Pentagon for its military crackdown on poverty-stricken people in other countries who are in revolt against capitalist exploitation.

To conceal the truth about events elsewhere in the world the Democrats and Republicans join in imposing unconstitutional restrictions on the right to travel. Inside the country they resort to thought-control measures designed to suppress criticism and enforce conformity. Advocates of social change are branded "subversive." Critics of Washington's policies are harassed by the FBI on their jobs and in their neighborhoods. The despised stoolpigeon is glorified as a patriot. Mail is tampered with. Electronic eavesdropping devices are used to invade people's privacy. And the military brass is penetrating all civilian institutions.

## CONGRESSIONAL INQUISITIONS

Congressional committees hold public inquisitions over TV in which people are cruelly pilloried before the whole nation. The victims are bombarded with loaded questions that violate their democratic rights and invade their personal lives. Those who invoke their constitutional right not to answer the inquisitors are publicly smeared as suspicious characters who "have something to hide." Victims of the Congressional inquisitors have been framed up on "contempt" or "perjury" charges.

Abuse of youth's inherent right to challenge the status quo is vividly illustrated in the case of three University of Indiana students. They had criticized Washington's Cuba policy; they had invited a Negro youth to address a student meeting on the right of self-defense against white-supremacist violence; and they had expressed the view that the American people would fare better in a socialist society. For that, and nothing more, a politically-ambitious prosecutor secured indictments against them under an Indiana thought-control law on the ridiculous charge of conspiring to advocate the overthrow of the government. The trial judge held the law unconstitutional and quashed the indictments. In an effort to overturn the ruling the prosecutor has appealed to a higher court where the case is now pending.

Minority political parties trying to exercise their democratic right to contend for votes run up against repressive election laws rigged to maintain a two-party monopoly of the ballot. Bipartisan schemes are hatched to deny minority parties equal free time with the Democrats and Republicans over TV and radio. Manipulating the two major parties like a pair of loaded dice, the banks and corporations use them against all non-capitalist organizations.

Legislative enactments, executive orders and court rulings steadily encroach on labor's freedom. The right to strike becomes more restricted; whether openly or through trickery, public officials side with the bosses in collective bargaining; and the bosses' government intrudes more and more into internal union affairs. The capitalists are equally quick to use police measures against the civil-rights movement. Whenever pious promises and token concessions fail to keep dissatisfied people in line, repression is the inevitable weapon to which the political custodians of capitalism resort. At all hazards they uphold the sacred capitalist principle that sets private profit above human need.

Fed up with a century of tokenism, the Negro people are demanding *freedom now,* and they are fighting for it. Their mood was symbolized by the big Southern demonstrations last year, called to protest discrimination and segregation and to demand the right to vote. Wave after wave of Negro freedom fighters went up against police dogs and fire hoses; undaunted by mass arrests, they came out of jail determined to continue the battle for human dignity and elementary rights.

In the giant March on Washington, sparked by the Southern demonstrations, Negroes came from all over the land to voice their demands for jobs and freedom. The big turnout reflected a rise in Northern militancy under the impetus of the Southern struggle. Rent strikes soon began in Northern cities where minorities are segregated in rat-infested slums. School boycotts followed in opposition to segregation of Negro and Puerto Rican children in the educational system. Negroes, and Puerto Ricans inspired by the Negro example, are demanding their democratic rights in the unions and pressing for union support of their right to full equality in employment.

Confronted with a lack of response from conservative union officials, they are taking action on their own. Construction sites, hotels and other places are picketed to protest discrimination in hiring and to demand equal rights on the job. Demands are pressed for higher minimum-wage laws covering all workers and for a shorter workweek to provide more jobs. Protest demonstrations are conducted against police brutality and there is growing sentiment to exercise the constitutional right of self-defense against extra-legal hooligan attacks on civil-rights demonstrators.

NEGRO AND WHITE YOUTH

Stimulated by the heroism of the Negro freedom fighters and sensing a basic kinship with them, white student youth are coming to their support in increasing numbers. A goodly number participated in the Freedom Rides and there has since been a widening involvement of white students in the overall struggle. Negro and white youth face a common plight in many aspects of modern life under capitalism. Together they are confronted with militarism, economic insecurity, witch hunting and other problems. As a result, to quote uneasy liberals on the subject, "They are asking deep and complicated questions."

Slower to respond to the fighting example set by Negroes are the unions which suffer paralysis under a conservative and dictatorial leadership. Strikes are made official only under extreme provocation from the bosses. No real support is given the civil-rights movement, even though most Negroes are workers. Little effort is made to fuse Negro and white labor in united efforts to defend their common interests as wage earners. Instead, the general run of union officials resist Negro demands for union equality.

The union officialdom calls for reliance on the Democrats to solve labor's problems. Most Negro leaders take a similar view of Democrats outside the South as allies in the civil-rights fight. But in neither case have these capitalist politicians fulfilled the hopes placed in them. What to do then? "Elect more liberals," the Negro freedom fighters and union members are told. Rejuvenate the government with "true friends" of labor and civil rights.

The record shows, however, that liberals, Democrats and Republicans alike, are simply masters of the pious promise and token concession. In the name of peace they consistently support a warlike foreign policy. In dealing with the nation's grave social problems they prove to be nothing more than glib bipartisans who talk a lot but do nothing that would cut across the sanctity of private profit. As do all capitalist politicians, they take reprisals against people who refuse to accept gradualism in social reform.

Consider the example of the newly-enacted "Stop-and-Frisk" and "No-Knock" laws in New York. Governor Rockefeller, a liberal Republican, rammed them through the state legislature over strong protests from civil-rights groups. Negroes and Puerto Ricans are concerned because the laws empower the police to search people on the streets and to barge into private quarters without even knocking. Harlem residents know very well that Rockefeller's new laws will be freely invoked against them by New York City cops under the command of Mayor Wagner, a liberal Democrat, who urged swift passage of these repressive measures.

John Lewis, chairman of the Student Nonviolent Coordinating Committee, stated a truth which describes all capitalist politicians, Democratic or Republican, liberal or conservative. In the prepared text of a speech he was prevented from delivering at the March on Washington, he said, "This nation is still a place of cheap political leaders who build their careers on immoral compromises and ally themselves with open forms of political, economic and social exploitation." Then he put the question, "Where is *our* party?"

Echoing John Lewis' question, a group of prominent Negroes distributed a manifesto at the March on Washington calling for independent Negro political action. "One hundred years of waiting for Democratic and Republican politicians to correct our grievances is too long," they said. "We have to *take* our freedom; no one will hand it to us. That is why . . . we call upon all who believe in true emancipation to join us in forming the Freedom Now Party."

Although addressed directly to Negroes, this summons to independent political action describes an even larger need. It points the way for the whole working class, for all victims of capitalist misrule. Their problems can't be solved through the twin parties of war, racism, unemployment and witch hunts. Progress can be made only by breaking completely with both the Democrats and Republicans.

A FREEDOM NOW PARTY

For these reasons the Socialist Workers Party supports independent Negro political action of the type manifested in the call for a Freedom Now Party. We urge the formation of an independent labor party based on the unions. We advocate an anti-capitalist political alliance of all who suffer discrimination and exploitation, black and white, in industry and on the land, in blue collars and white. As a means to register a desire for such political change, we ask those whose thinking runs along similar lines to support the SWP candidates in the November elections.

To solve the nation's many problems fully, we contend that capitalism must be abolished and a socialist society created. A society with jobs for all. One in which those who produce would democratically organize and plan production to serve everybody's needs on a fair basis. A society free from discrimination and segregation wherein all would have equal opportunity to prosper. A society in which all individuals could freely develop their creative powers, artistic talents and human potentialities. An America that would lend a helping hand to people in other lands instead of mobilizing and arming to make war on them.

As concrete steps toward the creation of a society of peace, prosperity, freedom and equality, the Socialist Workers Party submits the following planks:

### 1) *For a peaceful foreign policy*

Stop the "dirty war" in Vietnam. Pull out of Guantanamo. Lift the economic blockade and restore friendly relations with Cuba. Recognize Panamanian sovereignty over the Panama Canal. Give up all military alliances and foreign military bases. Withdraw all troops from foreign soil. Halt all nuclear-weapon tests and scrap the stockpile of A and H-bombs.

Recognize the Peking government and establish trade relations with China. Support the right of all peoples to a government of their own choice.

No secret diplomacy or propaganda lies. Tell the whole truth. Let the people vote on all issues of war and peace.

### 2) *Against capitalist militarism*

Turn the arms budget into a peace budget devoted to the nation's social needs. End capitalist conscription, ROTC and Prussian-type rule over the military establishment. Grant full democratic rights to the ranks of the armed forces, including free speech and assembly, election of officers and collective bargaining.

### 3) *FREEDOM NOW for all minorities*

Full economic, social and political equality for the Negro people and for all other minority groups. Solidarity with mass actions aimed at securing these rights as exemplified in the rent strikes, school boycotts, picketing of construction sites, public demonstrations and sit-ins. Uphold the right of self-defense against white-supremacist violence.

Full use of the federal power to enforce all laws and court orders against discrimination and segregation. Enforce existing laws against lynch murder and police brutality and enact new ones. End the barbaric death penalty and reform the antiquated prison system.

Establish an FEPC with teeth and compensate minorities for the disadvantages they have suffered. Create a federal agency fully empowered and equipped to enforce minority rights in all spheres of national life. Federal action to guarantee and protect the right to vote in all national, state, county and city elections. Abolish all existing poll taxes.

Teach Negro and African history in the nation's schools. Combat all forms of anti-Semitism.

### 4) *Restore and expand democratic rights*

Repeal all federal, state and local laws restricting labor's right to organize, strike and picket. No government interference in internal union affairs.

Abolish the "subversive" list, "loyalty" oaths and "loyalty" purges. No political tampering with social-security benefits. End FBI harassment of political dissidents. Abolish the House Un-American Activities Committee, the Senate Internal Security Sub-committee and their counterparts in state legislatures.

Repeal all legislative enactments, executive decrees and court orders violating the Bill of Rights. Stop the thought-control frame-ups and political prosecutions for "contempt" and "perjury." Rescind all deportation orders and lift all restrictions on the right to travel. Amnesty all victims of the witch hunt.

Liberalize the election laws. Lower the voting age to 18. Give minority parties equal time on TV and radio and in all public media.

### 5) *End economic insecurity*

For the 30-hour week at 40 hours' pay and further reductions in hours without cuts in pay when needed to secure full employment. Jobless benefits to every worker at the full union scale for the entire period of unemployment. Let the government take over all idle production facilities and operate them under charge of committees elected by the workers. Union control of production speeds by majority vote of the workers involved.

Equal pay for equal work regardless of race, sex

or age. Full job and seniority rights and maternity care for women. Federally financed nurseries and summer camps for children. A government guaranteed college education for all youth.

Provide the millions of aged people with full disability benefits, free medical care and hospitalization, and adequate pensions. Nationalize the entire medical system. As an immediate measure pass the King-Anderson Medicare Bill now bottled up in Congress.

### 6) *For adequate government aid to the farmers*

A federal program, set up and administered by elected representatives of working farmers, to guarantee them the full cost of production on all farm commodities. No limitation on crops so long as people suffer from hunger anywhere in the world. Government food subsidies for families in America living on a substandard diet.

Moratoriums on repayment of distress loans made to working farmers as long as debtors need them. Abolish share-cropping and landlordism—crops to those who grow them; land to those who work it.

### 7) *For an emergency housing and public works program*

Immediate government construction of 20 million low-rent housing units. Rigid rent controls on all private housing, enforced by elected representatives of the tenants. A large-scale federal program to build schools, hospitals and other public facilities. Government action on flood control, improved water supply, irrigation, cheap electricity and conservation of natural resources. All programs to be financed with funds now spent for armaments.

### 8) *Repeal taxes on low incomes*

Abolish all payroll and sales taxes, all hidden taxes passed on to the consumer. No taxes on incomes under $7,500 a year. A 100 per cent tax on incomes above $25,000 a year. Confiscate all profits on war goods. Open the tax returns of the rich to public scrutiny.

### 9) *For government ownership of industry*

Nationalize the banks, basic industries, food trusts and all natural resources, including nuclear power. Elect committees of workers and technicians to manage these facilities in the interests of the producers and consumers. Institute a planned system of economy.

### 10) *For independent political action*

End the Democratic-Republican monopoly of politics. Break all ties with the capitalist political machines. For an independent labor party based on the unions. For an independent Negro party running its own candidates. For an anti-capitalist political alliance of all who suffer discrimination and exploitation.

Bring to power a Workers' and Farmers' government, with full representation for minorities, to reorganize America on a socialist basis.

# CAMPAIGN OF 1968

The 1968 election, which took place during the controversy over the war in Vietnam, was distinctive because the Republican candidate won by a margin of less than 1 percent of the votes and a former Alabama governor received the largest percentage of the popular vote cast for a third-party candidate since 1924.

Early in the year, the incumbent president, Lyndon B. Johnson, declared that he would not seek reelection. This announcement sparked a series of spirited presidential primary elections, including the final contest in California won by Senator Robert Kennedy the day before he was assassinated. The primaries revealed some support for the antiwar stands of Senators Eugene McCarthy and George McGovern, much ambivalence among the public concerning the war, and regional approval of the policies of Governor George Wallace of Alabama.

However, when the delegates met in a tumultuous convention in Chicago in August, party loyalists nominated the incumbent vice-president, Hubert H. Humphrey, who had not participated in the primaries, on the first ballot. Senator Edmund Muskie of Maine was nominated by acclamation for the vice-presidency. The platform plank on the Vietnam issue simulated a bitter debate but the administration's position was eventually endorsed.

The Republicans, meeting in Miami Beach, selected Richard M. Nixon, the former vice-president, on the first ballot. He defeated eleven other candidates, including Governors Nelson Rockefeller of New York and Ronald Reagan of California. Governor Spiro T. Agnew of Maryland was chosen as his running mate.

The strong third-party contender, George C. Wallace, was the nominee of the American Independent Party, which he created to place his candidacy before the public. General Curtis LeMay of Ohio was announced in October, 1968, as his vice-presidential choice. Other minor-party candidates included E. Harold Munn and Rolland E. Fisher, of Kansas, on the Prohibition Party ticket; Henning A. Blomen of Massachusetts and George Sam Taylor of Pennsylvania representing the Socialist Labor Party; and Fred Halstead of New York and Paul Boutelle of New Jersey for the Socialist Workers.

As in the previous editions of this collection, the platforms of the permanent, organized, minor parties have been included; those of the many parties that appeared for the first time in 1968 or those that received only a few scattered votes, together with those that named candidates ineligible for the presidency, have been omitted. Thus, for 1968 statements of principles from the New Party, the Best Party, the Peace and Freedom Party, the Universal Party, the Constitution Party, the Freedom and Peace Party, and the revived Communist Party have not been included. The Socialist Party published a platform that is not included here because the party nominated no candidate for president.

In the November election, the contest was exceedingly close. The Republicans received 31,785,148 popular votes—43.42 percent of the more than 73 million votes cast. The Democrats polled 31,274,503 votes—42.72 percent of the total. The American Independent Party was supported by 9,901,151 persons, 13.53 percent of the total. The Socialist Labor Party polled 52,591 votes, the Socialist Workers received 41,390, and the Prohibition Party, 14,915 votes. These minor parties and the others mentioned above, with the exception of the American Independent Party, received less than one-third of one percent of the votes.

When the electoral votes were cast, Richard Nixon received 301, Hubert Humphrey 191, and George Wallace 46, from five southern states.

## American Independent Platform 1968

PREAMBLE

A sense of destiny pervades the creation and adoption of this first Platform of the American Independent Party, a Platform personifying the ideals, hopes, aspirations and proposals for action of the Party and its candidates for the Presidency and Vice Presidency of the United States, George C. Wallace and Curtis E. LeMay.

As this great nation searched vainly for leadership while beset by riots, minority group rebellions, domestic disorders, student protests, spiraling living costs, soaring interest rates, a frightening increase in the crime rate, war abroad and loss of personal liberty at home; while our national political parties and their leaders paid homage to the legions of dissent and disorder and worshipped at the shrine of political expediency, only this Party, the American Independent Party, and its candidates, George C. Wallace and Curtis E. LeMay, possessed the courage and fortitude to openly propose and advocate to the nation those actions which are necessary to return this country to its accustomed and deserved position of leadership among the community of nations and to offer hope to our people of some relief from the continued turmoil, frustration and confusion brought about through the fearful and inept leadership of our national political parties.

It is to this end and for this purpose that this Platform is designed. Herein will be set forth the policies, attitude, proposals and position of this Party and its candidates, with matters of deepest concern to the average American, his home, his family, his property, his employment, his right to safety and security in the pursuit of the activities of his daily life, his right to freedom from interference and harassment from and by the government at all levels and, lastly, his pride in himself and this nation and all that it has stood for.

We feel that this American has an intense devotion to his country, glorifies in its accomplishments and is saddened by its failures and shortcomings; that he is tolerant of the mistakes of political leaders if he senses their actions to be in good faith and directed to the best interest of the country, but he is confused and dismayed when these leaders desert the principle of government for the people and dedicate themselves to minority appeasement as the country burns and decays.

This document treats both foreign and domestic policy and is basically designed to present the proposals and action programs of this Party and its candidates in the area of:

1. Peace abroad and domestic tranquility at home.

2. An enlightened and advancing educational program, assisted but not controlled by the federal government.

3. Job training and opportunity for all Americans willing and able to seek and hold gainful employment.

4. An alliance and partnership with the private sector of our economy seeking an end to poverty among our people.

5. Efficiency and prudence in governmental spending leading to a helpful and stable economy free from the need for ever continuing taxation.

6. Inclusion of the farmer in our program of prosperity through his own efforts rather than total reliance on government subsidy.

7. Reestablishment of the authority and responsibility of local government by returning to the states, counties and cities those matters properly falling within their jurisdiction and responsibility.

8. Ending the inflationary spiral of the past decade through fiscal responsibility and efficiency in all echelons of government.

9. The orderly and economical utilization of the natural resources of this nation coupled with a sensible program of conservation of these resources.

10. An insistence that the laboring man and woman be given his fair share of responsibility and reward for the development of the mighty potential of this nation.

11. A re-dedication of this country to the love of God and country and the creation of a judiciary mindful of the attitudes of the people in this regard.

With these cardinal principles in mind, we herein set forth the precepts of our Party and Candidates in the following areas of concern:

DOMESTIC POLICY

Clearly, our citizens are deeply concerned over the domestic plight of this nation. Its cities are in decay and turmoil; its local schools and other institutions stand stripped of their rightful authority; law enforcement agencies and officers are hampered by arbitrary and unreasonable restrictions imposed by a beguiled judiciary; crime runs rampant through the nation; our farmers exist only through unrealistic government subsidies; welfare rolls and costs soar to astronomical heights; our great American institutions of learning are in chaos; living costs rise ever higher as do taxes; interest rates are reaching new heights; disciples of dissent and disorder are rewarded for their disruptive actions at the expense of our law-abiding, God fearing, hard working citizenry. America is alarmed that these conditions have come to exist and that our national leadership takes no corrective action. We feel that the programs and policies of our Party offer this leadership and provide constructive proposals of action for the elimination of the conditions now existing. This we would do in the following manner:

## Local Government

The Founding Fathers of our country, when they had won their freedom from King George III in the American Revolution, and were engaged in setting up our Federal Government, in their infinite wisdom, visualized the tyranny and despotism which would inevitably result from an omnipotent central government; and, they sought to avoid that peril by delegating to that central or federal government only those powers which could best be administered by a central or federal government, such as the laying and collecting of taxes to pay the national debt, providing for the common defense, regulating commerce between the states, declaring and waging war, coining money and establishing and maintaining a postal system. And then they provided, in Article X of the Bill of Rights, the Tenth Amendment to the Constitution of the United States, that:

"The powers, not delegated to the United States by the Constitution, nor prohibited by it to the states, are reserved to the states respectively, or to the people."

The Federal Government, in derogation and flagrant violation of this Article of the Bill of Rights, has in the past three decades seized and usurped many powers not delegated to it, such as, among others: the operation and control of

the public school system of the several states; the power to prescribe the eligibility and qualifications of those who would vote in our state and local elections; the power to intrude upon and control the farmer in the operation of his farm; the power to tell the property owner to whom he can and cannot sell or rent his property; and, many other rights and privileges of the individual citizen, which are properly subject to state or local control, as distinguished from federal control. The Federal Government has forced the states to reapportion their legislatures, a prerogative of the states alone. The Federal Government has attempted to take over and control the seniority and apprenticeship lists of the labor unions; the Federal Government has adopted so-called "Civil Rights Acts," particularly the one adopted in 1964, which have set race against race and class against class, all of which we condemn.

It shall be our purpose to take such steps and pursue such courses as may be necessary and required to restore to the states the powers and authority which rightfully belong to the state and local governments, so that each state shall govern and control its internal affairs without interference or domination of the Federal Government. We feel that the people of a given state are in better position to operate its internal affairs, such as its public schools, than is the Federal Government in Washington; and, we pledge our best efforts to restore to state governments those powers which rightfully belong to the respective states, and which have been illegally and unlawfully seized by the Federal Government, in direct violation of Article X of the Bill of Rights.

## The Federal Judiciary

Our forebears, in building our government, wisely provided and established, in the Constitution of the United States, that the Federal Government should consist of three branches, the Legislative, represented by the Congress, whose duty and responsibility it is to enact the laws; the Executive, represented by the President, whose duty it is to enforce the laws enacted by the Congress; and, the Judicial, whose duty and responsibility it is to interpret and construe those laws, not to enact them.

The Constitution of the United States provides that the judicial power of the United States shall be vested in a Supreme Court and in such inferior courts as the Congress shall from time to time ordain and establish; and, further, that the judges of the Federal courts shall hold their offices for life, during good behavior.

In the period of the past three decades, we have seen the Federal judiciary, primarily the Supreme Court, transgress repeatedly upon the prerogatives of the Congress and exceed its authority by enacting judicial legislation, in the form of decisions based upon political and sociological considerations, which would never have been enacted by the Congress. We have seen them, in their solicitude for the criminal and lawless element of our society, shackle the police and other law enforcement agencies; and, as a result, they have made it increasingly difficult to protect the law-abiding citizen from crime and criminals. This is one of the principal reasons for the turmoil and the near revolutionary conditions which prevail in our country today, and particularly in our national capitol. The members of the Federal judiciary, feeling secure in their knowledge that their appointment is for life, have far exceeded their constitutional authority, which is limited to interpreting or construing the law.

It shall be our policy and our purpose, at the earliest possible time, to propose and advocate and urge the adoption of an amendment to the United States Constitution whereby members of the Federal judiciary at District level be required to face the electorate on his record at periodical intervals; and, in the event he receives a negative vote upon such election, his office shall thereupon become vacant, and a successor shall be appointed to succeed him.

With respect to the Supreme Court and the Courts of Appeals I would propose that this amendment require re-confirmations of the office holder by the United States Senate at reasonable intervals.

### PRIVATE PROPERTY

We hold that the ownership of private property is the right and privilege of every American citizen and is one of the foundation stones upon which this nation and its free enterprise system has been built and has prospered. We feel that private property rights and human rights are inseparable and indivisible. Only in those nations that guarantee the right of ownership of private property as basic and sacred under their law is there any recognition of human rights.

We feel that the American system of private property ownership, coupled with its system of free enterprise, upon the basis of which our country has grown and prospered for more than two hundred years, is sacred; and, we repudiate and condemn those who propose to transform our nation into a socialist state; and, we propose to furnish and provide a national leadership that is dedicated to the preservation and perpetuation of the great American system of private enterprise and private ownership of property.

We repudiate and condemn any federal action regulating or controlling the sale or rental of private property as a socialistic assault upon not only the system of private ownership of property, but upon the right of each American citizen to manage his private affairs without regulation from an all-powerful central government.

There is no provision in the Federal Constitution which gives Congress the power to regulate the sale or rental of private property. Such legislation strikes at the very heart of the American system and if followed to its logical conclusion will inevitably lead to a system alien to our concept of free government, where citizens are no longer able to make decisions for themselves or manage their personal affairs. We pledge to take the Federal Government out of the business of controlling private property and return to the people the right to manage their lives and property in a democratic manner.

### CRIME AND DISORDER

Lawlessness has become commonplace in our present society. The permissive attitude of the executive and judiciary at national level sets the tone for this moral decay. The criminal and anarchist who preys on the decent law-abiding citizen is rewarded for his misconduct through never ending justification and platitudes from those in high places who seem to have lost their concern for that vast segment of America that so strongly believes in law and order.

We hear much of the "root causes" for the depredations committed in our streets and in our towns and cities. We hold that these are to be found in the apparent absence of respect for the law on the part of the perpetrators of these offenses, and the unexplainable compassion for the criminal evidenced by our executive and judicial officers and officials. We advocate and seek a society and a government in which there is an attitude of respect for the law and for those who seek its enforcement and an insistence on the part of our citizens that the judiciary be ever mindful of their primary duty and function of punishing the guilty and protecting the innocent.

We urge full support for law enforcement agencies and officers at every level of government and a situation in which their actions will not be unreasonably fettered by arbitrary judicial decrees.

We will insist on fair and equal treatment for all persons before the bar of justice.

We will provide every assistance to the continued training and improvement of our law enforcement facilities at federal and local level, providing and encouraging mutual cooperation between each in his own sphere of responsibility.

We will support needed legislation and action to seek out and bring to justice the criminal organizations of national scope operating in our country.

We will appoint as Attorney General a person interested in the enforcement rather than the disruption of legal processes and restore that office to the dignity and stature it deserves and requires.

We will provide leadership and action in a national effort against the usage of drugs and drug addiction, attacking this problem at every level and every source in a full-scale campaign to drive this evil from our society.

We will provide increased emphasis in the area of juvenile delinquency and juvenile offenses in order to deter and rehabilitate young offenders.

We will not accept violence as the answer to any problem be it social, economic, or self-developed. Anarchists and law violators will be treated as such and subjected to prompt arrest and prosecution.

We will oppose federal legislation to enforce the registration of guns by our citizens, feeling that this measure would do little or nothing to deter criminal activity, but, rather, would prove restrictive to our decent, law-abiding citizens, and could well encourage further activity by the criminal. We will preserve to the states their rights to take such reasonable measures as they deem appropriate in this area.

CITIES AND SUBURBS

The urban areas of our nation are in a state of social and economic unrest, largely brought about through unfilled promises hastily and carelessly made and the failure of ill-conceived programs enacted under duress and compulsion. For this, we must hold responsible the national leadership of the other two parties, for they were joint partners in this disastrous course of action resulting in the situation now existing in our cities.

We object to a federal policy which has poured billions of dollars into our cities over the past decades but which has not been able to prevent their stagnation and decay and has resulted in the flight of millions to the suburbs. We reject the notion that the solution is untold additional billions to be poured into the cities in the same manner, whether such huge sums are to be raised from taxes on the middle class in general, or by unwelcome taxes on those who live in the suburbs of the individual cities. We submit that no government can buy contentment for those living in the cities, suburbs, or rural areas. We advocate the formulation of a mutually arrived at, joint federal, state and local policy which will make it economically and socially attractive and physically safe for people to live again in all sections of all of our cities. We submit that the science and technology, which made possible the development and growth of these cities, is the instrument whereby this can be brought about.

Specifically, there must be a restoration and maintenance of law and order before any program, no matter how well conceived, will succeed. We pledge ourselves to this accomplishment and will exert forceful leadership at local level to such effort.

Those totally unfitted by training, background and environment for urban living who have been lured to the metropolitan areas by the wholly false promises and commitments of self-seeking political leaders must be afforded an opportunity for training or, in the alternative, an opportunity to return to gainful employment in the less urbanized area from whence they came. This we propose to accomplish in conjunction with private industry through a program of diversification and decentralization of expanding industry into areas away from metropolitan centers, thereby providing relief for many of the problems of the area while providing productive life for those afforded the opportunity to depart these overcrowded areas.

We advocate assistance, but not control, to

local governmental units from the federal level to enable them to cope with their multiplicity of problems, feeling they are better prepared to offer solution than those more removed therefrom.

We advocate and will sponsor a partnership with the private sector of our economy in the restoration of job opportunity and a healthy living environment to our cities through programs made economically attractive to industry.

We will support programs designed to provide means by which home-ownership can become a reality to our city dwellers, thereby instilling a greater feeling of dignity, stability and responsibility in those benefiting from such a program.

Above all, there must be a restoration of order in our cities as a prelude to any program of assistance, for without order neither government nor private industry will meet with success. Herein lies the cause of much failure in the past.

### Job Opportunity and the Poor

We feel that the matter of our citizens in need and the existence of job opportunies are so closely related as to warrant concurrent consideration.

We are convinced that the average American believes in the inherent dignity of gainful employment, preferring this method of attaining a livelihood to any welfare grant or benefit not earned through his own efforts. For this reason we consider the solution to the problem of our needy citizens, capable of gainful employment to be the provision of job opportunity. This will be the goal of our Party and our administration.

Our first consideration will be the inclusion of private industry in this program and effort. We believe that the private sector of our economy has the will and capability of providing a solution to the problem of poverty much more promptly and efficiently than any or all governmental programs of indiscriminate welfare contributions. Based on this premise, we will work in partnership with private industry in a program mutually beneficial to each to provide these job opportunities. We propose to make this program economically attractive to industry through tax incentives and other means of economic benefit, believing fully that the answer to this problem lies in the vigor and capability of our tremendous free enterprise system.

We would propose that the federal government aid and assist in a well-designed program of job training or retraining for those in need thereof. This will be at the vocational school and lower level, depending on the needs of the trainees. We will encourage and assist the states in programs of job training or retraining through realistic productive efforts in this respect, including assistance to the establishment and maintenance of vocational trade schools and other like institutions designed to provide skilled and semi-skilled personnel for industrial employment, as well as means whereby 'in-training" programs can be carried out by private industry in cooperation with government.

In the event a public works program becomes necessary to provide employment for all employable Americans, we will provide such a program assuring, however, that these programs be needful and productive and that the participants engage in labor beneficial to the nation and its economy rather than becoming wards of the government and the recipients of gratuitous handouts.

For those unemployable by reason of age, infirmity, disability or otherwise, provision will be made for their adequate care through programs of social services based on the requirements and needs of these persons. We hold that all Americans are deserving of and will have the care, compassion and benefits of the fullness of life.

### Health and Welfare: Our Senior Citizens

Social Security is basically an old age, survivors and disability Insurance Plan. It provides for citizens to pay into the Trust Fund during their working years and is designed to replace part of the earning capacity of the participant, or his family, lost due to retirement, death or disability. During past administrations, the Social Security Trust Fund has been depleted and current payments are being made from current revenues. Social Security cannot be financed from current revenues or from the Federal Treasury without raising taxes or jeopardizing other essential programs of government. Such a policy is irresponsible.

We pledge to restore the Social Security Trust Fund to a sound financial basis and by responsible fiscal policies to insure the following:

1. An immediate increase in Social Security payments with a goal of a 60% increase in benefits.

2. An increase in the minimum payment to $100, with annual cost of living increases.

3. Restoration of the 100% income tax deduction for drugs and medical expenses paid out by people 65 and over.

4. Removal of the earnings limitation of people 65 and over in order that they may earn any amount of additional income.

Our goal is to make every senior citizen a first-class citizen; to restore their dignity, prestige, self-respect, independence and their security, without intrusion into their private lives by federal bureaucrats and guideline writers.

HEALTH CARE

It is the obligation of a responsible government to help people who are unable to help themselves. There should be adequate medical assistance available to the aged and those unable to afford treatment. This can best be achieved through a partnership between federal and state governments and private enterprise. Medicare should be improved. It should be strengthened in conjunction with medical care provided at state and local governmental levels and by private insurance. Through sound fiscal management we set as a goal the following improvements in Medicare:

1. Relief to persons unable to pay deductible charges under Medicare.

2. Relief to persons unable to have deducted from their Social Security checks the monthly fee for physician service coverage under Medicare.

3. Providing for uninterrupted nursing home care for those with chronic illness who require such care.

4. We will encourage low-cost insurance programs for the elderly and will assist the states and local communities in building hospitals, nursing homes, clinics as well as medical and nursing schools.

In this land of plenty, no one should be denied adequate medical care because of his financial condition.

We are particularly disturbed about the doctor-patient, and the hospital-patient relationship. We stand solidly for freedom of choice in this rela-tionship. It is our intent that medical care programs be carried out without subjecting our professional people and our hospital administrators and personnel to the harassment which has been their lot since the implementation of the Medicare program. We believe that those assisted by the Medicare program should have some degree of selection in the medical and hospital services furnished to them, and that simplification in the administration of this program would prove of benefit to government, patient and the professional practitioner alike.

American medical and dental practice is the admitted marvel of the world. Its traditional freedom is one of the chief reasons why this is so. The American Independent Party pledges continuous study and effort to maintain that freedom both for doctor and for patient.

OTHER SOCIAL SERVICES

The people of this land are the fiber of our nation. Their well-being is essential to a strong America. Unfortunately, many of our citizens are unable to earn an adequate living, due to no fault of their own. Our aged, our blind, and our disabled who are unemployed are the concern of us all.

In every area of social welfare, rehabilitation should be of paramount concern. This includes physical restoration where possible, training to develop new skills, adult education in many instances, and broad cooperative endeavors between government and private industry to develop jobs that the less skilled can fill. We believe that every American prefers independence and a wage earned. For those whose infirmities, age, or other problems prevent such independence, welfare services should be adequate to provide a living with dignity and honor.

Dependent children become the responsibility of government when they lack the care and support of parents or guardians. Every effort should be made to provide support by responsible persons rather than the government, where possible. However, when children are separated permanently, by death or other cause from their families, all facilities of government should safeguard, protect, serve and care for them.

In every area possible, federal grants should be administered through existing state and local governmental agencies, thus eliminating additional federal offices and agencies which merely duplicate efforts of existing state and local agencies.

We will review and examine the administration of these programs with a view to the elimination of waste and duplication and thereby better serve the purposes and people designed to be assisted. We subscribe to the principle of block grants, administered by state agencies as a possible solution to these problems.

NATIONAL ECONOMY

The national economy must be restored to and maintained in a healthy, viable posture under conditions assuring to each individual American the opportunity to participate in and enjoy the benefits arising from a real prosperity, as distinguished from the false, inflationary conditions presently existing. As a first step the nation's business, industry and other agencies and organizations of production must be freed from the ever-increasing intrusions of government into the affairs of these institutions and organizations. This nation achieved its economic greatness under a system of free enterprise, coupled with human effort and ingenuity, and thus it must remain. This will be the attitude and objective of this Party.

There must be an end to inflation and the ever-increasing cost of living. This is of vital concern to the laborer, the housewife, the farmer and the small business man, as well as the millions of Americans dependent upon their weekly or monthly income for sustenance. It wrecks the planned lives and retirement of our elderly who must survive on pensions or savings gauged by the standards of another day.

We will take immediate, affirmative steps to bring these conditions to an end through selective decreases in the lavish expenditures of our federal government and through the institution of efficiency into the operation of the machinery of government, so badly plagued with duplication, overlapping and excesses in employment and programs. Bureaucracy will cease to exist solely for bureaucracy's own sake, and the institutions and functions of government will be judged by their efficiency of operation and their contribution to the lives and welfare of our citizens.

We will support and assist business and industry in those areas needful and desirable, such as in the area of small business.

We will enforce those laws designed to protect the consumer and wage earner, but will eliminate those programs and agencies serving only to harass and intimidate our business community.

We will review and propose revisions to our present tax structure so as to ease the load of the small income citizen and to place upon all their rightful share of the tax burden.

We will work toward a reduction in the tax burden for all our citizens, using as our tools efficiency and economy in the operation of government, the elimination of unnecessary and wasteful programs and reduction in government expenditures at home and abroad.

We will eliminate the favorable treatment now accorded the giant, non-tax-paying foundations and institutions and require these organizations to assume their rightful responsibility as to the operation of our government.

To achieve these goals and objectives, we would use government for the strengthening of the free enterprise system rather than the replacement of the free enterprise system by government. We believe that strength and confidence in the American political and economic system will tend to encourage domestic private investment and prosperity in our economy.

We would propose that effective use be made during our administration of economic advisors dedicated to the preservation and strengthening of our economic freedoms in the areas of enterprise, labor and marketing that have contributed so much to the strength of the American system.

Our administration will be dedicated to the maintenance of prosperity and price stability in our economy. We will institute a strong anti-inflationary fiscal, monetary and debt management policy in our nation as the first requirement to solving international problems.

We propose to rely heavily upon a competitive market structure rather than upon prices administered or fixed by bureaucratic procedures.

We do not propose to use periodic, intermittent tax adjustments or surcharges as a tool of economic policy under the guise of stabilizing the inflationary spiral we are experiencing.

We feel little is done to curb inflationary trends in the nation's economy merely by taking from the taxpayer in order to enrich the spending programs of big government. We propose, rather, a stabilized and equitable tax base affording fair treatment to those of small income and designed to cause all persons, organizations and foundations to assume their rightful financial responsibility for government coupled with selective and prudent reductions in the wasteful expenditures of government.

AGRICULTURE

America's agriculture, and especially the small farmer, is on the brink of disaster. Under both Democratic and Republican administrations, the income of our farmers has steadily declined. Farm prices have been ranging at a parity level the lowest since the dark days of the great depression. Individual producers are unable to regulate the output or price of their products and stringent government controls have been forced upon farmers. Revolutionary methods of production have resulted in increased yield from less acreage and requiring less manpower. The farmer is hampered by a faulty system of distribution, and his costs have continued to increase at an astronomical rate. Yet, all America's farmers have received from either of the other two parties have been broken promises.

The following is the pledge of the American Independent Party to our nation's farmers:

1. We pledge ourselves to the protection and preservation of the family farm, which is the backbone of American Agriculture.

2. We pledge that the new Secretary of Agriculture will immediately begin to support prices at 90% of parity which is the highest level provided under present law.

3. Congress will be urged to increase the maximum support to 100% of parity.

4. Legislation will be sought to permit farmers to exercise their freedom of choice to vote whether or not to come under self-imposed controls.

5. We propose the creation of a National Feed Grain Authority, authorized to make long-term loans for development of farmer-owned and controlled warehouses, to be strategically located, permitting farmers to store large quantities of grain and to sell direct to the trade through their own local organizations.

6. We propose that no portion of the nation's emergency reserves of food, feed or fiber be sold for less than 115% of the prevailing farm price support of that commodity.

7. A limit to subsidy payments should be set in order to prevent an unfair advantage being built up by giant corporate farm structures over our small farmer or family farms.

8. We propose to impose reasonable limitations on the import of foreign farm and meat products into this country.

9. It is our belief that continued support of the REA and other cooperative programs designed to improve marketing methods and conditions throughout the nation is vital to our farming interests.

10. It is our belief that federal support for farm research is important, and that Agriculture Colleges and Extension Services should be more effectively utilized.

11. Governmental agencies similar to the Farm Home Administration have been beneficial to farmers and should be improved and continued.

12. We propose that the State Department and the Agriculture Department work together in a joint effort to develop new foreign markets for our farm products and develop a vigorous export program.

13. We support a good soil conservation program and pledge the continuation and improvement of such program.

14. It is our policy to assist in improving farm production reporting in order that farmers obtain more accurate production forecasts for planning purposes.

15. It is our intention to simplify the administration of all farm programs, and to eliminate wasteful duplication and red tape within the Department of Agriculture.

16. We will work toward gradual relaxation and elimination of farm regulation and control with a concurrent reduction in required subsidization as farm income increases, the eventual goal being the elimination of both controls and the need for subsidy, such program being contingent upon the increase in farm income to a level making subsidy unnecessary.

17. We will require that programs for disease and insect control be continued and expanded where needed if it is indicated that state and local bodies need and desire assistance from the federal level. Such program would, among other things, provide for necessary steps to eradicate the imported fire ants. This pest is now prevalent

throughout a major portion of the southern region but will eventually affect three-fourths of the land area of the United States if eradication is not accomplished promptly.

The farmers of this nation are entitled to a fair, just and equitable profit on their investment, just as citizens in other fields of endeavor. It is our belief that a major step toward solving our problems in agriculture would be to insure a substantial increase in farm income. It is time for a new Secretary of Agriculture who represents the views and interests of the farmer and the rancher, and who will work ceaselessly and tirelessly to improve the income and the lives of America's farm families. We pledge to you such a Secretary and such a program.

## LABOR

America achieved its greatness through the combined energy and efforts of the working men and women of this country. Retention of its greatness rests in their hands.

Through the means of their great trade organizations, these men and women have exerted tremendous influence on the economic and social life of the nation and have attained a standard of living known to no other nation. In the meantime, American labor has become a bulwark against the intrusion of foreign ideology into our free society. America must be eternally grateful to its working men and women.

The concern of this Party is that the gains which labor struggled so long to obtain not be lost to them either through inaction or subservience to illogical domestic policies of our other national parties.

We propose and pledge:

To guarantee and protect labor in its right of collective bargaining;

To assert leadership at the federal level toward assuring labor its rightful reward for its contribution to the productivity of America;

To propose and support programs designed to improve living and employment conditions of our working men and women;

To prohibit intrusion by the federal government into the internal affairs of labor organizations, seeking to direct and control actions as to seniority and apprentice lists and other prerogatives;

To provide for and protect the working men

and women in the exercise of democratic processes and principles in the conduct of the affairs of their organizations, free from threats, coercion, or reprisals from within or without such organization;

To support programs and legislation designed to afford an equitable minimum wage, desirable working hours and conditions of employment, and protection in the event of adversity or unemployment;

To add efficiency and dispatch to the actions and activities of the National Labor Relations Board, resulting in more prompt decisions by this agency;

To pledge and assure that labor will be adequately represented in all deliberations of this Party and its administration of the affairs of government;

To cause all agents of government to refrain from any coercive action in strike settlements, serving in the role of counselor and advisor only, believing that good faith bargaining between the parties concerned is the best solution to any settlement.

## EDUCATION

Without question education offers the answer to many of the nation's social and economic problems. It is tragic that during the past two decades, while governed alternately by the Republican and Democratic parties, we have witnessed the deterioration of our public school systems into a state of disruption wherein the maintenance of order is the major problem and quality education is a forgotten objective. Our educational leaders and administrators are discouraged and dismayed by the continuing attacks upon, and erosion of, their duties and authority by agents of the federal bureaucracy and members of the federal judiciary.

Local educational officials have been stripped of their authority to administer the affairs of their school systems. Harassing directives and requirements of an unreasonable and unrealistic nature are constantly being imposed upon them. Parents, students and educators alike are dismayed, confused and at a loss as to where to turn for relief. Many of our institutions of higher learning have been completely disrupted by a small band of revolutionaries, encouraged by the permissive attitude of executive and judicial officials of government and the activities of other anarchists throughout the nation.

Many of our primary and secondary school systems have become centers for social experimentation rather than centers of learning, serving merely as pawns for the whims and caprices of some member of the federal judiciary or some agent of the federal bureaucracy.

These conditions must come to an end. Our educational systems and institutions must once again be given the opportunity to resume their rightful duty of preparing the youth of America for entry into our highly competitive society.

As a first and immediate step we must absolutely prohibit the agencies and agents of the federal government from intruding into and seeking to control the affairs of the local school systems of the states, counties and cities of the nation. Control of these schools must be returned to the local officials, representatives of the people, who have the rightful duty and authority to administer such school.

Once returned to proper control, order must be restored and education of our children again become the primary matter of concern in these schools. Sociological experiments must cease. The people of the several states, counties, cities and communities must be given the right to administer the affairs of their schools as they see fit without fear or threat or reprisal, economic or punitive, from the federal government.

We must cooperate with the administrators of our institutions of higher learning now in the hands of revolutionaries. We must support these officials in the restoration of order on their campuses and we must assure that no assistance, financial or otherwise, from the federal level be given to those seeking to disrupt and destroy these great institutions.

America is a nation "Under God" and we must see that it remain such a nation. We will support with all the power of the Executive action to restore to our educational institutions and the children they serve the right and freedom of prayer and devotions to God.

We must assure that the federal government assist in all phases of the educational processes of the nation without attempting to control these processes.

With these thoughts in mind:

We advocate a greater role of the states in administering federal aid and in determining national policy;

We advocate the return of our school systems to the states and to local, county and city officials;

We advocate support for administrators of our educational institutions in their efforts to restore order to these institutions;

We advocate fewer federal guidelines, regulations, and administrative procedures and greater simplification and consolidation of programs and procedures;

We advocate less categorical aid and more general aid to states with funding provided for well in advance;

We advocate educational opportunity for all people regardless of race, creed, color, economic or social status.

The complexities of education are many. State and local officials are faced with tremendous pressures to provide early childhood education, increased teacher salaries, provide vocational technical education, improved elementary and secondary education, provide adult education, continuing education, and urban and rural education, provide for higher education, graduate and professional education.

The goals of the American Independent Party are to improve the educational opportunity for all our citizens from early childhood through the graduate level. We believe that the improvement of educational opportunity can best be accomplished at the state and local level with adequate support from the federal level.

### SCIENCE AND TECHNOLOGY

The scientific and technological skills and accomplishments of America are the marvel of modern civilization. Our potential in this area is unlimited. Our development of this potential must be commensurate with our capability. We live in a fiercely competitive world in the area of science and technology. For social, economic and security reasons we must not lag behind.

We would propose, encourage and provide from the federal level assistance to those of our youth showing demonstrated capacity in these areas of endeavor. Federal grants based on ability and aptitude will be provided to assure development of skills in this field.

Federal assistance will be made available for research in various fields of science for in research lies the key to tomorrow. Such assistance will be directed both to individuals and to institutions.

We propose that this research, development and scientific knowledge so acquired be directed to human problems as well as national security. In the fields of housing, transportation, education, industry and related activities, these skills and the knowledge so acquired can make for a better life for all Americans.

Emphasis on the further exploration and utilization of space must be renewed. This, again, is a highly competitive area between nations, but not for this reason alone, but for the welfare and security of this nation, we must not be lacking in our effort in this field.

We fully support renewed and expanded efforts in our space program with the objective of acquiring knowledge and experience of benefit to the peaceful pursuits of mankind as well as that essential to the military security of this nation.

TRANSPORTATION

The expansion of America's industry, commerce and its economy depends upon its transportation system. America cannot maintain its position as world leader in industry and commerce unless all modes of transportation are able to meet the demanding challenges of the future. To solve America's transportation problems requires ingenuity and planning.

Airport congestion around most major cities is not only a growing problem, but an ever-increasing danger. We face a major railroad crisis and citizens in many urban areas are unable to travel short distances without delays due to congested highway traffic. Our merchant marine fleet has dwindled and our shipbuilding industry suffers today. This not only affects our economy, but is a serious handicap to America's military might.

We therefore favor:

1. The development of a modern, low-cost domestic mass transportation system within our congested urban areas;

2. Development of high-speed passenger trains between urban areas;

3. An emergency program carried out co-operatively by the federal government and the airline industry to develop adequate methods of controlling air congestion, and for financing and improving airport facilities;

4. Developing a program of assistance to modernize and stimulate our merchant marine fleet and our shipbuilding industry.

The Interstate Highway System is one of America's wisest investments. Every effort must be made to speed up construction on existing plans, and farsighted planning of additional facilities must be accomplished. The Interstate Highway System must be expanded, adding new routes between population centers, and extra attention should be given to constructing additional freeways in and around congested urban areas. Not only is this necessary for the expansion of commerce and the economy, but highway safety demands it.

Thousands of Americans lose their lives each year on the nation's highways. Most of these deaths are unnecessary. With proper highway planning, stricter enforcement of highway laws, and intensified driver education, along with proper safety devices provided on automobiles, we will be able to cut these needless and tragic fatalities to a small fraction.

Public safety and convenience demand that we engage in a vast program to improve and four-lane many of the local road and highway networks. Highway construction is financed by those persons using the highways and is one of the few federal programs that is self-financed which amounts to a capital investment of public funds, and this we greatly favor.

We will encourage the development within the transportation industry of organizations who are specialists in the movement of passenger and cargo from point to point, using all modes and means of transportation, and we will encourage healthy competition between such agencies and organizations.

NATURAL RESOURCES AND CONSERVATION

The preservation of our natural resources and the quality of our natural environment has greatly been ignored during the past decade. We are vitally concerned about the future well-being of our citizens and fully realize that positive action programs must be undertaken, in a cooperative effort between the federal government and the states, to assure adequate outdoor recreational facilities and to assure necessary health safeguards for generations to come. To these ends we make the following pledge to the American people:

1. We will promote an aggressive campaign at all levels of government to combat the serious air and water pollution problem.

2. Full support will be given to the establishment of adequate water quality standards to protect the present high quality waters, to abate pollution, and to improve the status of waters not now considered of high quality.

3. We will work in close cooperation with private industry and governmental agencies toward engineering designs to abate the mounting air pollution problems.

4. We will actively support research to control pests through biological means and chemical means which are more selective and less persistent than those now used.

5. Legislation and an active program are necessary to protect our endangered wildlife species. This problem is of serious concern and will receive our immediate attention and action.

6. We will work for protection of our waterfowl wetlands and nesting areas.

7. Our estuarine areas must be protected as vital to the production of fish, shellfish, furbearers, waterfowl and other aquatic creatures.

8. All federal assistance programs to the states in the areas of game and fish and for outdoor recreation will be streamlined to gain the maximum benefit from each dollar invested.

9. Our increasing population demands improved and additional outdoor recreational areas. To this end we will support active programs at all levels of government for the development of existing parks and proper outdoor recreational programs. Public lands must be utilized for multiple uses to benefit all of our people.

10. The preservation of our forest and timber resources is of utmost concern to the nation. We pledge federal cooperation with efforts of state and local governments and with private industry for a sound and economically regulated basis to avoid depletion of this vital natural resource. Government and industry will be encouraged to participate in planned reforestation programs, and programs for protection of our forests from the ravages of fire and other destructive causes.

America is blessed with an abundance of natural resources, with beautiful scenery and bountiful waters. This land of ours should not be marred and its resources wasted. We recognize that progress invites construction and industrial development and we recognize its necessity, but we must assure that the intangible values of our parks, forests and estuarine areas will be protected, promoted and developed and that America shall retain its scenic beauty for centuries to come.

We will place particular emphasis on the problems of air and water pollution and will initiate joint cooperative programs with private industry to attack and solve these problems, as their correction is in the interest of all segments of our national life, the people, the government and the nation's industry.

VETERANS

America owes no other group of citizens so much as it does our veterans. To that group of self-sacrificing and patriotic individuals who have risked their lives for our nation and its principles in past wars and conflicts, and to our brave men and women returning from service in Vietnam, we pledge the support of the American Independent Party. We pledge to you and your dependents our assurance of active and vigorous assistance in seeking out job opportunities, job training, further educational opportunities and business opportunities. We likewise support a program to provide educational benefits to children of deceased veterans in order that they may receive a quality education and participate in America's competitive society of the future.

We pledge to our veterans, their families and dependents the cooperation and active assistance of their government in providing adequate medical treatment and hospital care. Veterans' benefits and disability benefits will be updated and revised periodically in order to meet the increased cost of living. The Veterans Administration and its hospitals will remain as an independent agency of the government, and its one objective will be to serve our veterans and their families.

INDIAN AFFAIRS

For over 100 years the other two parties have been making promises to our fellow citizens, the American Indians and Eskimos. For over 100 years the promises of those parties have not been kept. Our Party offers to these independent and hard-working people a new hope. We promise that all of the programs of the federal government which have so lavishly bestowed benefits upon minority groups of this country will be made equally applicable to the American Indians and Eskimos. There will be no discrimination with respect to these two ancient and noble races.

We also promise that the federal government will cooperate fully to insure that job opportunity, job training, full educational opportunity, and equal application of all health and housing programs are afforded to these, our native citizens, in order that they may enjoy the same benefits and privileges enjoyed by every American. We will foster and support measures through which the beauties and accomplishments of their native culture will be preserved and enhanced.

FOREIGN POLICY

One of the greatest needs of our country at this moment in history is a strong, realistic, well-defined policy to guide our relationship with the other nations of the world. The policy developed to govern our actions in foreign affairs must be one well stated and well understood, first by our own people and, equally as important, by friends and foes alike throughout the world. The absence of any such well-defined and consistent policy throughout the past two decades has contributed immeasurably to the chaotic world conditions now existing.

Our foreign policy will be one designed to secure a just and lasting peace. We feel that such a situation can best come to exist when nations deal with one another on a basis of mutual trust and understanding. If this be lacking, as is so often the case in today's world, the only alternative is complete frankness and determination to adhere to stated objectives and courses of action. If a nation, as is the case with an individual, will only say what it means and mean what it says, it will gain the respect, if not always the admiration, of its sister nations. It is in this regard that we have failed, so often equivocating in such a manner as to cause friendly, as well as unfriendly, nations to have grave doubt as to our stability, determination and reliability of purpose.

We feel that the road to peace lies through international cooperation and understanding. We will pursue this goal to the limits consistent with our own national interest. We will become participants in international programs of aid and development from which all member nations, including our own, derive benefit.

We will not abandon the United Nations Organization unless it first abandons us. It should be given fair opportunity at resolving international disputes; however, we will not subordinate the interest of our nation to the interest of any international organization. We feel that in this organization, as in any other, participating members should bear proportionate shares of the cost of operation and we will insist on financial responsibility on the part of the member nations. We also feel that the officers and officials of such organization must conduct themselves with an abstract air of objectivity and impartiality, and we will so insist. We will give this organization every opportunity to succeed in its purpose but should it fail, we will reappraise our relationship with it.

*Foreign Aid*

Foreign aid and assistance, both of an economic and military nature, will be granted on a basis of what is in the best interest of our own nation as well as the receiving nation.

We will deny aid and assistance to those nations who oppose us militarily in Vietnam and elsewhere, as well as those who seek our economic and military destruction by giving aid and comfort to our avowed enemies. This must be so in order to protect the economic welfare and national security of this country.

We will continue aid to those countries who need, deserve and have earned the right to our help. This will be done freely and willingly with every effort directed to elimination of waste and dishonesty from such programs.

Foreign aid must become an instrument of foreign policy and be used in such manner as to further the interest of this nation.

*Export-Import*

We believe strongly in the free enterprise system for America, internally as well as in its trade relations with other nations. However, should the increasing inflow of imports from low-wage nations endanger employment or marketing by American industry, we will approve reasonable quantitative limits on these imports. We feel that our home industry is entitled to a fair share of the present market and of future growth. Before seeking additional legislation in the import field all efforts will be exerted toward securing negotiated agreements that would fully protect American industry.

We will insist on equitable tax treatment for any industry adversely affected by foreign imports, in the area of depreciation allowances for plants and equipment and in like measure.

We will cause the Department of State and other interested agencies of government to work toward the lowering of trade barriers against American goods in a manner consistent with the policy of our administration on controlling imports into the American market.

In the event certain segments of our industrial economy are adversely affected by foreign imports to such an extent as to cause economic harm, we will sponsor and develop programs of re-training and re-employment for those so affected.

*Balance of Payments*

A serious situation now exists in our balance of payments and this must be ended.

We feel that the adoption of the programs and proposals set out in this Platform will result in a more favorable balance of payments situation. Specifically, we feel that the relief we so badly need in this respect may be achieved through reductions in spending for foreign aid, more efficiency in the use of funds for international programs, and more reliance on our allies in meeting heavy military expenditures abroad.

We have earlier proposed that foreign aid be granted on a basis of need and in a manner consistent with the best interest of this country and that it be denied those who aggressively seek our destruction. We strongly advocate efficiency in operation and the elimination of waste and corruption from expenditures under international programs and we will insist that our allies assume their proportionate and rightful share of the burden of defenses in those areas in which we have mutual interest.

Our export-import situation remains in reasonable balance but our disastrous situation as to balance of payments is caused by excesses in our foreign aid program and other international gratuitous expenditures.

We will work to reduce our military expenditures overseas, not by lessening our military strength and preparedness, but by causing our allies to assume and bear their proportionate share of the burden.

*Middle East*

The Middle East remains a source of high potential danger to world peace. In the interest of securing a stable peace in this part of the world, we will take the initiative in seeking mutual cooperation between the adversaries in this area in reaching agreement in their age-old dispute. We will encourage the initiation of multilateral discussions to arrive at the best possible terms of settlement. This will mean resolving and stabilizing boundaries and the free use of water and land routes throughout this area. Binding non-aggression agreements must be developed and we must seek the mutual respect of both Israel and the Arab nations.

First and foremost is the need for sincere negotiations between these two parties. Until this is accomplished we must assure that no imbalance of force comes to exist in this area. Nothing could more endanger the peace.

Should arms continue to be introduced into this area by foreign powers to such an extent as to endanger the peace in this part of the world, we must take steps to assure that a balance of force is brought to exist. We will join with other nations of the free world in providing the means whereby this balance of force will continue and the threat of aggression of one nation against another is made less likely. More importantly, this nation will strive in every way to merit and receive the friendship of all parties to this dispute and to earn the respect and good will of Israel and the Arab nations alike. The road to peace in the Middle East lies in this direction rather than in the continued use of military might.

*Europe*

We continue to regard Western Europe as an area of vital importance to America. In our concern with the interminable conflict in Southeast Asia we must not lose sight of the strategic importance of our relationship with our European allies. We must retain a posture of strength in this area and must work with and for our allies to assure that they remain economically and militarily strong.

We will continue to support the North Atlantic Treaty Organization and seek to strengthen it through the cooperative efforts of all member nations. We will retain the necessary troop strength in this vital area and will insist that our allies and member nations do likewise.

We will deal patiently but firmly with the present French Government feeling that in due time its actions will, of necessity, be directed toward increased cooperation with its Western allies of long standing.

We will remain concerned for the captive satellite nations of Eastern Europe and share with them their hopes and aspirations for their eventual and inevitable return to the family of free nations.

### Latin America

The interests of the nations of Latin America are closely related to those of this country, economically, geographically, security-wise, socially and politically.

We must and will provide aid and assistance to these nations to enable them to achieve political and economic stability and to better prepare them to resist the threat of communist infiltration and subversion from the Red satellite, Cuba.

We will develop a program of assistance to these countries designed to relieve the conditions of economic and social poverty existing in some segments of these nations and to provide for their less fortunate citizens a better condition of life.

We will assist in the development of the agricultural and industrial potential of these nations and the development and proper utilization of their tremendous natural resources rather than the exploitation thereof, to the end that the nations of this hemisphere may live in peace, prosperity and harmony with one another and that the principles of the Monroe Doctrine may once again become a cornerstone of our national policy.

We will work with and support the Organization of American States.

### Cuba

As for Cuba, we will continue and strengthen the economic pressures on the Castro tyranny. In order to do this, we must secure a greater degree of cooperation from nations of the free world than we have had in the past. Trade with Cuba by our allies must be effectively minimized, if not completely curtailed.

To frustrate Castro's attempt to export subversion, we must increase the quality and effectiveness of our military aid and assistance to Latin American allies with a primary objective of developing realistic indigenous counterinsurgency capabilities within those countries. Economic aid, more carefully planned and scrupulously administered, will be continued through the Alliance for Progress Program, or an improved version thereof.

### Africa and Asia

The emerging nations of Africa and Asia desiring assistance and demonstrating a capability of reasonably assimilating such help and assistance will be aided. We will not aid in the replacing of one form of despotism with another, nor will we become concerned with the internal quarrelings of dissident groups and factions.

We disagree with present economic sanctions and pressures applied to Rhodesia and the Union of South Africa and will seek to have these removed and eliminated. We consider these to be nations friendly to this country and they will be respected and treated as such.

### General

We will conduct the foreign affairs of this country on a basis of aiding, assisting and cooperating with our friends and recognizing and treating our enemies and adversaries as such. We feel that foreign affairs can be conducted effectively only when there is respect for our nation and this respect is best engendered by attaining a position of strength and adopting an attitude of firmness and fairness. This we will do.

We feel that when this nation again becomes a strong and determined nation, dedicated to a fixed national and international policy, many of our existing difficulties throughout the world will become resolved and new difficulties are less likely to arise.

We will oppose aggression and subversion, Communist or otherwise, whenever it infringes upon the national interest of this country or its friendly allies through means appropriate to the situation.

We do not propose, nor does this or any other nation have the capability, to police the entire world. We will avoid unilateral entanglement in situations not vital to our national interest and will seek the cooperation of our allies at every opportunity.

VIETNAM

The current situation in Southeast Asia, and particularly in Vietnam, is one of the most critical which has ever faced this nation. The American people are angry, frustrated and bewildered as they seek for leadership which apparently fails to exist. There is no parallel in American history of such a situation as now exists, not even our engagement in Korea, where there were at least vaguely defined objectives.

It is too late to engage in debate as to why we are so deeply involved and committed in Vietnam. The fact is that we are so involved. No one can retrace the steps of the last ten years and correct and adjust all that has gone wrong. We presently have more than one-half million Americans committed to this conflict and they must be supported with the full resources of this nation. The question now is what does America do to maintain its honor, its respect and its position in this most strategic part of the world, Southeast Asia?

The prime consideration at this time is the honorable conclusion of hostilities in Vietnam. This must be accomplished at the earliest possible moment.

We earnestly desire that the conflict be terminated through peaceful negotiations and we will lend all aid, support, effort, sincerity and prayer to the efforts of our negotiators. Negotiation will be given every reasonable and logical chance for success and we will be patient to an extreme in seeking an end to the war through this means. If it becomes evident that the enemy does not desire to negotiate in good faith, that our hopes of termination of hostilities are not being realized and that the lives and safety of our committed troops are being further endangered, we must seek a military conclusion.

Hopefully such a situation will never arise, but should it come to pass, I would then seek the advice and good judgment of my joint Chiefs of Staff as to ways and means of reaching a military conclusion to this conflict with the least loss of life to our American servicemen and our South Vietnamese allies, stressing the fact that this is to be accomplished through the use of conventional weapons.

Military force has always been recognized as an instrument of national policy and its use to obtain national objectives has always been ac-cepted. However, once national policy is established by the civilian government and military force has been selected as one of the means of attaining national objectives, the tactical employment of this force should be left to the military so long as this employment is consistent with national policy, and the mission of the military should be to attain these national objectives—nothing less.

I would retain full control, as a civilian Commander-in-Chief, of final decision, but I would pay heed to and consider to the fullest extent the advice and judgment of my military advisors.

Unfortunately, there is no clearly defined national policy with respect to the conflict in Vietnam. If there were, much of the doubt, debate and despair of the American people would be eased. There is a total absence of clearly announced and understood national objectives with respect to Vietnam. We are told that it is not victory over the enemy we seek but something else—what we do not know. In battle, and certainly this is battle, there can be but one objective—that is victory. Anything worth dying for is worth winning.

As a first step we must develop a clearly defined national policy as to Vietnam. This policy will be made known to the people of this country and will be based on our own national interest. The essence of this policy will be a timely and successful termination of the conflict, either through negotiation or by victory over the enemy. We will not allow this conflict to drag on indefinitely with its great drain on our national resources and manpower.

As President, we will designate a Secretary of Defense who holds the confidence and trust of the people, the Congress and the military establishments and one with the capability and desire of working in harmony with each. He will be required to reduce the excessive manpower of the Pentagon and rid the Department of Defense of those who have fostered the "no-win" policy.

We will then require the establishment of firm objectives in Vietnam. Should negotiations fail, and we pray that they will not fail, these objectives must provide for a military conclusion to the war. This would require the military defeat of the Vietcong in the South and the destruction of the will to fight or resist on the part of the government of North Vietnam, which is equipping and supporting the enemy troops in the South. We feel that the prompt and effective application of military force could achieve this objective with minimized loss of life, and the tactical employment of this force will be left in the hands of the military commanders, so long as they act pursuant to defined national policy.

We will require the military to plan and conduct military operations once policies and objectives are established and we will not, nor will we permit civilian subordinates, to usurp these functions and assume the role of "commander" or "tactician." This must be a team effort with officials and leaders of civil government performing their required functions and the military establishment being allowed to perform in the manner and for the purpose for which it is trained.

Once hostilities have ceased, efforts must be undertaken to stabilize the government and economy of Vietnam. This must be through programs of self-help and not through completely meaningless "give away" programs. We are dealing with a proud people of ancient culture. They are not, and never will be, adapted to all the facets of western civilization, nor should they be. We must help them to become secure in their government, their lands, their economy and in their homes, as their friends and allies and not as sanctimonious intruders. In this manner, we will gain a lasting ally.

NATIONAL DEFENSE

Nothing is of greater importance to the American people at this time than the state of our National Defense, and, sadly, there is no area of our national structure so fraught with misrepresentations and inconsistencies. As we near the end of the era of "computerized defense" and "cost effectiveness" rather than military reliability, it is difficult, if not impossible, for the nation to ascertain the true state of its defenses.

We are aware of basic fallacies in the doctrines and logic of those who have been charged with the responsibility of our national security.

We have been told that strength is weakness and weakness is strength—This is not true.

We have been told that parity rather than superiority in weapons and munitions is sufficient to assure the keeping of the peace and the protection of this country—This is not true.

We have been told a "deterrent" capability is preferable to an offensive capability in maintaining peace and assuring freedom from attack— This is not true.

We have been told that commitment of our military forces need not always be followed by a quest for victory—This is not true.

We have been led to believe in the proven invulnerability of our "second strike" capability —This is not true.

We have been told that the complete disruption of the structure of our Reserve Components resulted in a more readily responsive Reserve— This is not true.

We have been told that our research and development program, especially in the area of space research and development, is not lagging —This is not true,—And so on.

We propose an intensive and immediate review of the policies, practices and capabilities of the Department of Defense with a view to reestablishing sound principles of logic and reasoning to the decisions and directives of that agency and to eliminating from its ranks all of those who have been party to the dissemination and promulgation of the false doctrines of security and the coercion, intimidation and punishment of all who would oppose or disagree with them.

We are in accord with civilian control of our defense establishment but will insist that the civilian authorities work in partnership and harmony with the splendid military force with which this country is blessed. We propose to restore to their proper duties, functions and authority the leaders of our military services so that the nation may once again profit from their wisdom and experience.

We will require our civilian and military leaders of defense to establish a reasonable relationship between defensive and offensive capabilities and provide our services with the proper arms, munitions and equipment to afford a proper mix of both type weapons and munitions.

We will place increased emphasis on research and development in the area of space, weaponry and mobility, as well as other areas vital to our national security.

We support the installation of an anti-ballistic missile defense for the protection of our nation and its citizens. We will expedite this program.

We will assure to our services the best attainable weapons, equipment, machines and munitions without resort to devious distinctions of cost effectiveness and the substitution of arbitrary, unsound judgment for that of the professional military.

We will guarantee to the services and to the nation that American troops will never be committed with less than full support of available resources.

We will seek efficiency in the collection and evaluation of vital intelligence throughout the services.

We will never permit a static situation to develop wherein America stands still while her potential enemies continue to advance in all areas of development.

We will hasten the reconstitution of an adequate and efficiently organized reserve force throughout the several states of the nation. We will accept these reserve component forces into full partnership with the regular military establishment and will assure stability to their organizational structure and operation.

We will take all steps necessary to return our Merchant Marine fleet to its rightful place among the maritime nations of the world. This is not only vital to our national security but to the economic progress and viability of the nation. Maritime shipping has been, and will once again become, a vital part of the nation's economy and trade activity.

We will take steps to make military service more attractive to the enlistee, the inductee and the career personnel at all levels. We will support programs for better pay; better housing and living conditions, both on and off post; more realistic programs of promotion potential so that merit and performance may be rewarded; equitable sharing of hardship assignments; an increase and more uniform retirement benefit to correct serious inequities now existing; a pay scale commensurate with that of private employment, with provisions for periodic increases measured by the cost of living index; improved and expanded medical and hospital benefits for dependents, and a restoration of the dignity and prestige rightfully due those engaged in the defense of our nation.

With military services becoming more attrac-

tive the requirement for involuntary inductions through the Selective Service System is reduced. However, we favor retention of such system for so long as there is a need for manpower being acquired by this means. We would approve any changes to such system designed to eliminate inequities in the selection of inductees, and quite likely some do exist.

We would feel that eventually manpower requirements may be met on a voluntary basis. In such event, a fair and equitable system of civilian induction will be kept in existence, on standby basis, for use in the event of national emergency.

Conclusion

This Platform represents the attitude, policy, position, judgment and determination of this Party with respect to the major problems confronting America.

We believe that our analysis of the nature of these problems is in keeping with the feelings of the great majority of our people. We further feel that our approach to solution of these matters is sound, logical, practical and attainable and in keeping with the basic, inherent good judgment of the American people.

Among other proposals:

We offer opportunity for early peace to a nation at war.

We offer order and domestic tranquility to a nation sorely beset by disorder.

We offer a program of job opportunity for the jobless.

We offer a return to respect for the law and an opportunity for every citizen to pursue his daily activities in safety and security.

We offer to relieve our citizens, their businesses and institutions, from harassment and intimidation by agents of the federal bureaucracy.

We offer to return to the officials of local government those matters rightly and properly falling within their scope of responsibility.

We offer the laboring man and woman an opportunity to provide for himself and his family a better and fuller life and a greater democratic freedom in the management of the affairs of his organizations, free from intrusion by the federal government.

We offer to the farmer an opportunity to regain a place of prominence in the economy of this nation, a fair price for the products of his labor and less dependence on federal subsidation.

We offer to restore the dignity, strength and prestige of this nation to a level commensurate with its position as acknowledged leader of the nations of the free world.

We offer a national defense designed to assure the security of this nation and its citizens.

And, above all, we offer to each individual citizen a system of government recognizing his inherent dignity and importance as an individual and affording him an opportunity to take a direct hand in the shaping of his own destiny and the destiny of this nation. Under such a system, we are convinced, America will reach new heights of greatness.

## Democratic Platform 1968

### THE TERMS OF OUR DUTY

America belongs to the people who inhabit it. The source of the nation's strength is the people's freedom to be the source of the laws governing them. To uphold this truth, when Thomas Jefferson and James Madison brought the Democratic Party to birth 175 years ago, they bound it to serve the people and their government as a united whole.

Today, in our 175th anniversary year, the Democratic Party in national convention assembled, again renews the covenant of our birth. We affirm the binding force of our inherited duty to serve the people and their government. We here, therefore, account for what we have done in the Democratic years since 1961. We here state what we will do when our party is again called to lead the nation.

In America and in the world over, strong forces for change are on the move. Systems of thought have been jarred, ways of life have been uprooted, institutions are under siege. The governed challenge those who govern.

We are summoned, therefore, to a fateful task —to ensure that the turmoil of change will prove to be the turmoil of birth instead of decay. We cannot stand still until we are overtaken by events. We dare not entrust our lives to the blind play of accident and force. By reflection and choice, we must make the impulse for change the agent of orderly progress.

There is no alternative.

In the world around us, people have patiently lived with hopes long deferred, with grievances long endured. They are now impatient with patience. Their demands for change must not only be heard, they must be answered.

This is the reality the world as a whole faces.

In America itself, now, and not later, is the right time to strengthen the fabric of our society by making justice and equity the cornerstones of order. Now, and not later, is the right time to uphold the rule of law by securing to all the people the natural rights that belong to them by virtue of their being human. Now, and not later, is the right time to unfurl again the flag of human patriotism and rededicate ourselves under it, to the cause of peace among nations. Now, and not later, is the right time to reclaim the strength spent in quarrels over the past and to apply that strength to America's future. Now is the right time to proceed with the work of orderly progress that will make the future become what we want it to be.

It has always been the object of the Democratic Party to march at the head of events instead of waiting for them to happen. It is our resolve to do that in the years ahead—just as we did in the Democratic years since 1961 when the nation was led by two Democratic Presidents and four Democratic Congresses.

### THIS WE HAVE DONE

Our pride in the achievements of these Democratic years in no way blinds us to the large and unfinished tasks which still lie ahead. Just as we know where we have succeeded, we know where our efforts still fall short of our own and the nation's hopes. And we candidly recognize that the cost of trying the untried, of ploughing new ground, is bound to be occasional error. In the future, as in the past, we will confront and correct such errors as we carry our program forward.

In this, we are persuaded that the Almighty judges in a different scale those who err in warmly striving to promote the common good, and those who are free from error because they risked nothing at all and were icily indifferent to good and evil alike. We are also persuaded of something else. What we have achieved with the means at hand—the social inventions we have made since 1961 in all areas of our internal life, and the initiatives we have pressed along a broad front in the world arena—gives us a clear title of right to claim that we know how to move the nation forward toward the attainment of its highest goals in a world of change.

## THE ECONOMY

In presenting first the record of what we have achieved in the economic life of the American people, we do not view the economy as being just dollar signs divorced from the flesh and blood concerns of the people. Economics, like politics, involves people and it means people. It means for them the difference between what they don't want and what they do want. It means the difference between justice or injustice, health or sickness, better education or ignorance, a good place to live or a rat infested hovel, a good job or corrosive worry.

In the Democratic years since 1961, under the leadership of Presidents Kennedy and Johnson, we managed the national economy in ways that kept the best aspirations of people in clear view, and brought them closer to fulfillment.

The case was different in the 1950's, when the Republicans held the trust of national leadership. In those years, the American economy creaked and groaned from recurrent recessions. One wasteful recession came in 1954, another in 1958, and a third in 1960. The loss in national production from all three recessions and from a sluggish rate of growth—a loss that can fairly be called the GOP-gap—was a staggering $175 billion, computed in today's prices.

The Democratic Party, seeing the Republican inertia and the dangers it led to, promised to get America moving again. President Kennedy first made that promise for us, and we kept it. We brought an end to recurring recessions, each one of which had followed closer on the heels of the last. Full cooperation between our government officials and all sectors of American life led to new public policies which unlocked the creative power of America's free enterprise system. The magnificent response of all the people comprising that system made the world stand in awe of the results.

Since 1961, we have seen:

A 90-month period of recession-free prosperity, the longest and strongest period of sustained eco-

nomic growth in American history;

A slash in the unemployment rate from 7 to under 4 percent;

An increase of nearly 40 percent in real wages and salaries and nearly one-third in the average person's real income;

And, on the eight year average, a reduction in the rate levels of the individual income tax.

America's private enterprise system flourished as never before in these years of Democratic leadership. Compared with the preceding eight Republican years, private enterprise in the Democratic 1960's grew twice as fast, profits increased twice as rapidly, four times as many jobs were created, and thirteen million Americans—or one-third of those in poverty in 1960—have today escaped its bondage.

Democrats, however, were not satisfied. We saw—and were the first to see—that even sustained prosperity does not eliminate hardcore unemployment. We were the first to see that millions of Americans would never share in America's abundance unless the people as a whole, through their government, acted to supplement what the free enterprise could do.

So, under the leadership of President Johnson, this nation declared war on poverty—a war in which the government is again working in close cooperation with leaders of the free enterprise system.

It would compromise the integrity of words to claim that the war on poverty and for equal opportunity has been won. Democrats are the first to insist that it has only begun—while 82 percent of the House Republicans and 69 percent of the Senate Republicans voted against even beginning it at all. Democrats know that much more remains to be done. What we have done thus far is to test a series of pilot projects before making them bigger, and we have found that they DO work.

Thus:

The new pre-school program known as Head Start has proven its effectiveness in widening the horizons of over two million poor children and their parents.

The new programs known as the Job Corps and the Neighborhood Youth Corps, entailing close cooperation between the government and private enterprise, have helped nearly two million unskilled boys and girls—most of them dropouts from school—get work in the community and in industry.

The new program known as Upward Bound has helped thousands of poor but talented young men and women prepare themselves for college.

The new structure of neighborhood centers brings modern community services directly to the people who need them most.

THE PEOPLE

We emphasize that the coldly stated statistics of gains made in the war on poverty must be translated to mean people, in all their yearnings for personal fulfillment. That is true as well of all other things in the great outpouring of constructive legislation that surpassed even the landmark years of the early New Deal.

Education is one example. From the beginning of our Party history, Democrats argued that liberty and learning must find in each other the surest ground for mutual support. The inherited conviction provided the motive force behind the educational legislation of the 1960's that we enacted:

Because of the Elementary and Secondary Education Act of 1965, local education has been enriched to the benefit of over 13 million young Americans;

Because of the Higher Education Act of 1965, new college classrooms, laboratories and libraries have been built to assure that higher education will not be the monopoly of the few but the right of the many;

Because of federal assistance to students, the doors to college have been opened for over a million young men and women coming from families with modest means—so that about one out of every five college students is now pursuing his higher education with some kind of federal help;

Because Democrats are convinced that the best of all investments is in the human resources represented by the youth of America, we brought about a four-fold increase in the federal investment in education since 1960. The level now approaches $12 billion annually.

As it promoted better education, so did Democratic leadership promote better health for all.

The program of mercy and justice known as health care for the aged, which President Truman originally proposed and Presidents Kennedy and Johnson fought for, finally became law in the summer of 1965. Because of it, more than seven million older citizens each year are now receiving modern medical care in dignity—no longer forced to depend on charity, no longer a burden on relatives, no longer in physical pain because they cannot afford to pay for the healing power of modern medicine. Virtually all older Americans, the well and the sick alike, are now protected, their lives more secure, their afflictions eased.

To deal with other aspects of the nation's health needs, measures were enacted in the Democratic years representing an almost four-fold increase in the government's investment in health. Programs were enacted to cope with the killing diseases of heart, cancer and stroke; to combat mental retardation and mental illness; to increase the manpower supply of trained medical technicians; to speed the construction of new hospitals.

Democrats in the Presidency and in the Congress have led the fight to erase the stain of racial discrimination that tarnished America's proudly announced proposition that all men are created equal.

We knew that racial discrimination was present in every section of the country. We knew that the enforcement of civil rights and general laws is indivisible. In this conviction, Democrats took the initiative to guarantee the right to safety and security of the person, the right to all the privileges of citizenship, the right to equality of opportunity in employment, and the right to public services and accommodations and housing. For example:

Because of the Civil Rights Act of 1964, all men born equal in the eyes of their Creator are by law declared to be equal when they apply for a job, or seek a night's lodging or a good meal;

Because of the Voting Rights Act of 1965, the right to the ballot box—the right on which all other rights depend—has been reinforced by law;

Because of the Civil Rights Act of 1968, all families will have an equal right to live where they wish.

THE NATION

The frontier on which most Americans live is the vertical frontier of the city. It is a frontier whose urgent needs hold a place of very high priority on the national agenda—and on the agenda of the Democratic Party.

Democrats recognize that the race to save our cities is a race against the absolute of time itself. The blight that threatens their future takes many forms. It is the physical decay of homes and neighborhoods. It is poverty and unemployment. It is broken homes and social disintegration. It is crime. It is congestion and pollution. The Democratic program attacked all of these forms of blight—and all at once.

Since we know that the cities can be saved only by the people who live there, Democrats have invigorated local effort through federal leadership and assistance. In almost every city, a community action agency has mounted a many-sided assault on poverty. Through varied neighborhood organizations, the poor themselves are tackling their own problems and devising their own programs of self-help. Under Model Cities legislation, enacted in 1966, seventy-five cities are now launching the most comprehensive programs of economic, physical, and social development ever undertaken—and the number of participating cities will be doubled soon. In this effort, the residents of the areas selected to become the model neighborhoods are participating fully in planning their future and deciding what it will be.

In a series of housing acts beginning in 1961, Democrats have found ways to encourage private enterprise to provide modern, decent housing for low-income and moderate-income families. The Housing and Urban Development Act of 1968 is the most far-reaching housing legislation in America's history. Under its terms, the genius of American business will combine with the productivity of American labor to meet a 10-year goal of 26 million new housing units—6 million of them for the poor. The objective is to enable the poor to own their own homes, to rebuild entire neighborhoods, to spur the pace of urban renewal, and to deal more humanely with the problems of displaced people.

To give our cities a spokesman of Cabinet rank, Democrats in 1965 took the lead in creating a Department of Housing and Urban Development.

Democratic Presidents and Congresses have moved with equal vigor to help the people of America's vast hinterland outside the metropolitan centers to join the march of economic progress. Of the 101 major areas classified as "depressed areas" when the Democrats assumed office in 1961, 90 have now solved their problems of excessive unemployment and the others are on their way. The Area Redevelopment Act, the expansion of resource development programs, and the massive effort to restore Appalachia and other lagging regions to economic health assisted the people of these areas in their remarkable progress.

In these legislative undertakings of primary concern to people—American people—it is to the credit of some Republicans that they joined the Democratic majority in a common effort. Unfortunately, however, most Republicans sat passively by while Democrats wrote the legislation the nation's needs demanded. Worse, and more often, Republicans did what they could to obstruct and defeat the measures that were approved by Democrats in defiance of hostile Republican votes. Thus:

In the case of the Elementary and Secondary Education Act, 73 percent of the Republicans in the House voted to kill it.

In the case of medical care for the aged, 93 percent of the Republicans in the House and 64 percent in the Senate voted to kill it.

In the case of the Model Cities program, 88 percent of the Republicans in the House voted to kill it.

In the case of the program to help Appalachia, 81 percent of House Republicans and 58 percent of Senate Republicans voted to kill it, and 75 percent of House Republicans voted to kill corresponding programs of aid for other depressed regions of the country.

The same negative attitude was present among Republicans in the 1950's, and one of the results was a crisis in the farm sector of the economy—which the Democrats inherited in the 1960's. In the late Republican 1950's, the glut of farm surpluses amounted to over $8 billion, and the taxpayers were forced to pay $1 billion every year in interest and storage charges alone. Democrats, however, set out resolutely to reverse the picture. Democratic farm programs supported farm income, expanded farm exports and domestic consumption, helped farmers adjust their production to the size of the expanded markets, and reduced farm surpluses and storage costs to the lowest level since 1952.

Democrats have also acted vigorously to assure that American science and technology shall continue to lead the world.

In atomic energy, in space exploration, in communications, in medicine, in oceanology, in fundamental and applied research in many fields, we have provided leadership and financial aid to the nation's scientists and engineers. Their genius has, in turn, powered our national economic growth.

Other measures affected all Americans everywhere.

Under our constitutional system of federalism, the primary responsibility for law enforcement rests with selected local officials and with governors, but the federal government can and should play a constructive role in support of state and local authorities.

In this conviction, Democratic leadership secured the enactment of a law which extended financial assistance to modernize local police departments, to train law enforcement personnel, and to develop modern police technology. The effect of these provisions is already visible in an improved quality of law enforcement throughout the land.

Under Democratic leadership, furthermore, the Juvenile Delinquence Prevention and Control Act was passed to aid states and communities to plan and carry out comprehensive programs to prevent and combat youth crime. We have added more personnel to strengthen the Federal Bureau of Investigation and the enforcement of narcotics laws, and have intensified the campaign against organized crime. The federal government has come swiftly to the aid of cities needing help to bring major disturbances under control, and Democratic leadership secured the enactment of a new gun control law as a step toward putting the weapons of wanton violence beyond the reach of criminal and irresponsible hands.

To purify the air we breathe and the water we drink, Democrats led the way to the enactment of landmark anti-pollution legislation.

To bring order into the administration of transportation programs and to coordinate transportation policy, Democrats in 1966 established a new Cabinet-level Department of Transportation.

For the consumer, new standards of protection were enacted—truth-in-lending and truth-in-packaging, the Child Safety Act, the Pipeline Safety Act, the Wholesome Meat and Wholesome Poultry Acts.

For America's 100 million automobile drivers, auto and highway safety legislation provided protection not previously known.

For every American family, unparalleled achievements in conservation meant the development of balanced outdoor recreation programs—involving magnificent new national parks, seashores, and lakeshores—all within an afternoon's drive of 110 million Americans. For the first time, we are beating the bulldozer to the nation's remaining open spaces.

For the sake of all living Americans and for their posterity, the Wilderness Preservation Act of 1964 placed in perpetual trust millions of acres of primitive and wilderness areas.

For America's sons who manned the nation's defenses, a new G.I. bill with greatly enlarged equitable benefits was enacted gratefully and proudly.

America's senior citizens enjoyed the large t increase in social security since the system was inaugurated during the Democratic Presidency of Franklin D. Roosevelt.

For the hungry, our food distribution programs were expanded to provide more than $1 billion worth of food a year for domestic use, giving millions of children, for the first time, enough to eat.

A new minimum wage law raised paychecks and standards of living for millions, while a new network of training programs enabled more than a million Americans to learn new skills and become productive workers in the labor force.

A new Immigration Act removed the harsh injustice of the national origins quota system and opened our shores without discrimination to those who can contribute to the growth and strength of America.

Many more measures enacted under Democratic leadership could be added to this recital of achievements in our internal life since 1961. But what we could list shares the character of what we have listed. All the measures alike are a witness to our desire to serve the people as a united whole, to chart the way for their orderly progress, to possess their confidence—by striving through our conduct to deserve to possess it.

THE WORLD

The conscience of the entire world has been shocked by the brutal and unprovoked Soviet aggression against Czechoslovakia. By this act, Moscow has confessed that it is still the prisoner of its fear of freedom. And the Czechoslovakian people have shown that the love of freedom, in their land and throughout Eastern Europe, can never be crushed.

This severe blow to freedom and self-determination reinforces our commitment to the unending quest for peace and security in the world. These dark days should not obscure the solid achievements of the past eight years. Nuclear war has been avoided. West Berlin and Western Europe are still free.

The blend of American power and restraint, so dramatically demonstrated in the Cuban missile crisis, earned the respect of the world and prepared the way for a series of arms control agreements with the Soviet Union. Long and patient negotiation by Presidents Kennedy and Johnson resulted in the Nuclear Test Ban, Nuclear Non-Proliferation, and Space treaties and the "hot line." These hard-won agreements provide the base for pursuing other measures to reduce the risk of nuclear war.

The unprecedented expansion of the American economy has invigorated the whole free world. Many once skeptical nations, including some communist states, now regard American economic techniques and institutions as a model.

In Asia the tragic Vietnam war has often blinded us to the quiet and constructive developments which affect directly the lives of over a billion people and the prospects for peace everywhere.

An economically strong and democratic Japan has assumed a more active role in the development of the region. Indonesia has a nationalist, non-communist government seeking to live at peace with its neighbors. Thailand, Taiwan, Singapore, Malaysia, and the Republic of Korea have more stable governments and steadily growing economies. They have been aided by American economic assistance and by the American military presence in the Pacific. They have also been encouraged by a confidence reflecting successive Presidential decisions to assist nations to live in peace and freedom.

Elsewhere in the developing world, there has been hopeful political and economic progress. Though Castro's Cuba is still a source of subversion, the other Latin American states are moving ahead under the Alliance for Progress. In Africa, many of the new states have chosen moderate leaders committed to peaceful nation-building. They are beginning to cooperate with their neighbors in regional agencies of their own design. And like developing countries on other continents, they are for the first time giving serious attention to agricultural development. This new emphasis on food will buy time to launch effective programs of population control.

* * *

In all these constructive changes America, under Democratic leadership, has played a significant role. But we Democrats do not believe in resting on past achievements. We view any success as a down payment on the hard tasks that lie ahead. There is still much to be done at home and abroad and we accept with confidence the challenge of the future.

THIS WE WILL DO

TOWARD A PEACEFUL WORLD

In the pursuit of our national objectives and in the exercise of American power in the world, we assert that the United States should:

Continue to accept its world responsibilities— not turn inward and isolate ourselves from the cares and aspirations of mankind;

Seek a world of diversity and peaceful change, where men can choose their own governments and where each nation can determine its own destiny without external interference;

Resist the temptation to try to mold the world, or any part of it, in our own image, or to become the self-appointed policeman of the world;

Call on other nations, great and small, to contribute a fair share of effort and resources to world peace and development;

Honor our treaty obligations to our allies;

Seek always to strengthen and improve the United Nations and other international peace-keeping arrangements and meet breaches or threatened breaches of the peace according to our carefully assessed interests and resources;

In pursuing these objectives, we will insure that our policies will be subject to constant review so they reflect our true national interests in a changing world.

## National Defense

The tragic events in Czechoslovakia are a shocking reminder that we live in a dangerous and unpredictable world. The Soviet attack on and invasion of a small country that only yesterday was Moscow's peaceful ally, is an ominous reversal of the slow trend toward greater freedom and independence in Eastern Europe. The reimposition of Soviet tyranny raises the spectre of the darkest days of the Stalin era and increases the risk of war in Central Europe, a war that could become a nuclear holocaust.

Against this somber backdrop, whose full portent cannot now be seen, other recent Soviet military moves take on even greater significance. Though we have a significant lead in military strength and in all vital areas of military technology, Moscow has steadily increased its strategic nuclear arsenal, its missile-firing nuclear submarine fleet, and its anti-missile defenses. Communist China is providing political and military support for so-called wars of national liberation. A growing nuclear power, Peking has disdained all arms control efforts.

We must and will maintain a strong and balanced defense establishment adequate to the task of security and peace. There must be no doubt about our strategic nuclear capability, our capacity to meet limited challenges, and our willingness to act when our vital interests are threatened.

To this end, we pledge a vigorous research and development effort. We will also continue to pursue the highly successful efforts initiated by Democratic administrations to save tax dollars by eliminating waste and duplication.

We face difficult and trying times in Asia and in Europe. We have responsibilities and commitments we cannot escape with honor. But we are not alone. We have friends and allies around the world. We will consult with them and ask them to accept a fair share of the burdens of peace and security.

## North Atlantic Community

The North Atlantic Community is strong and free. We must further strengthen our ties and be constantly alert to new challenges and opportunities. We support a substantially larger European contribution to NATO.

Soviet troops have never stepped across the border of a NATO country. By harassment and threat the Kremlin has repeatedly attempted to push the West out of Berlin. But West Berlin is still free. Western Europe is still free. This is a living tribute to the strength and validity of the NATO alliance.

The political differences we have had with some of our allies from time to time should not divert us from our common task of building a secure and prosperous Atlantic community based on the principles of mutual respect and mutual dependence. The NATO alliance has demonstrated that free nations can build a common shield without sacrificing their identity and independence.

## Arms Control

We must recognize that vigilance calls for the twin disciplines of defense and arms control. Defense measures and arms control measures must go hand in hand, each serving national security and the larger interests of peace.

We must also recognize that the Soviet Union and the United States still have a common interest in avoiding nuclear war and preventing the spread of nuclear weapons. We also share a common interest in reducing the cost of national defense. We must continue to work together. We will press for further arms control agreements, insisting on effective safeguards against violations.

For almost a quarter of a century America's pre-eminent military strength, combined with our political restraint, has deterred nuclear war. This great accomplishment has confounded the prophets of doom.

Eight years ago the Democratic Party pledged new efforts to control nuclear weapons. We have fulfilled that pledge. The new Arms Control and Disarmament Agency has undertaken and coordinated important research. The sustained initiatives of President Kennedy and President Johnson have resulted in the "hot line" between the White House and the Kremlin, the limited Nuclear Test Ban Treaty, the Non-Proliferation Treaty, and the treaty barring the orbiting of weapons of mass destruction.

Even in the present tense atmosphere, we

strongly support President Johnson's effort to secure an agreement with the Soviet Union under which both states would refrain from deploying anti-missile systems. Such a treaty would result in the saving of billions of dollars and would create a climate for further arms control measures. We support concurrent efforts to freeze the present level of strategic weapons and delivery systems, and to achieve a balanced and verified reduction of all nuclear and conventional arms.

*The Middle East*

The Middle East remains a powder keg. We must do all in our power to prevent a recurrence of war in this area. A large Soviet fleet has been deployed to the Mediterranean. Preferring short-term political advantage to long-range stability and peace, the Soviet Union has rushed arms to certain Arab states to replace those lost in the Arab-Israeli War of 1967. As long as Israel is threatened by hostile and well-armed neighbors, we will assist her with essential military equipment needed for her defense, including the most advanced types of combat aircraft.

Lasting peace in the Middle East depends upon agreed and secured frontiers, respect for the territorial integrity of all states, the guaranteed right of innocent passage through all international waterways, a humane resettlement of the Arab refugees, and the establishment of a non-provocative military balance. To achieve these objectives, we support negotiations among the concerned parties. We strongly support efforts to achieve an agreement among states in the area and those states supplying arms to limit the flow of military equipment to the Middle East.

We support efforts to raise the living standards throughout the area, including desalinization and regional irrigation projects which cut across state frontiers.

*Vietnam and Asia*

Our most urgent task in Southeast Asia is to end the war in Vietnam by an honorable and lasting settlement which respects the rights of all the people of Vietnam. In our pursuit of peace and stability in the vital area of Southeast Asia we have borne a heavy burden in helping South Vietnam to counter aggression and subversion from the North.

We reject as unacceptable a unilateral withdrawal of our forces which would allow that aggression and subversion to succeed. We have never demanded, and do not now demand, unconditional surrender by the communists.

We strongly support the Paris talks and applaud the initiative of President Johnson which brought North Vietnam to the peace table. We hope that Hanoi will respond positively to this act of statesmanship.

In the quest for peace no solutions are free of risk. But calculated risks are consistent with the responsibility of a great nation to seek a peace of reconciliation.

Recognizing that events in Vietnam and the negotiations in Paris may affect the timing and the actions we recommend, we would support our Government in the following steps:

Bombing: Stop all bombing of North Vietnam when this action would not endanger the lives of our troops in the field; this action should take into account the response from Hanoi.

Troop Withdrawal: Negotiate with Hanoi an immediate end or limitation of hostilities and the withdrawal from South Vietnam of all foreign forces—both United States and allied forces, and forces infiltrated from North Vietnam.

Election of Postwar Government: Encourage all parties and interests to agree that the choice of the postwar government of South Vietnam should be determined by fair and safeguarded elections, open to all major political factions and parties prepared to accept peaceful political processes. We would favor an effective international presence to facilitate the transition from war to peace and to assure the protection of minorities against reprisal.

Interim Defense and Development Measures: Until the fighting stops, accelerate our efforts to train and equip the South Vietnamese army so that it can defend its own country and carry out cutbacks of U.S. military involvement as the South Vietnamese forces are able to take over their larger responsibilities. We should simultaneously do all in our power to support and encourage further economic, political and social development and reform in South Vietnam, including an extensive land reform program. We support President Johnson's repeated offer to provide a substantial U.S. contribution to the postwar reconstruction of South Vietnam as well as to the economic development of the entire region, including North Vietnam. Japan and the European industrial states should be urged to join in this postwar effort.

For the future, we will make it clear that U.S. military and economic assistance in Asia will be selective. In addition to considerations of our vital interests and our resources, we will take into account the determination of the nations that request our help to help themselves and their willingness to help each other through regional and multilateral cooperation.

We want no bases in South Vietnam; no continued military presence and no political role in Vietnamese affairs. If and when the communists understand our basic commitment and limited goals and are willing to take their chances, as we are, on letting the choice of the post-war government of South Vietnam be determined freely and peacefully by all of the South Vietnamese people, then the bloodshed and the tragedy can stop.

Japan, India, Indonesia, and most of the smaller Asian nations are understandably apprehensive about Red China because of its nuclear weapons, its support of subversive efforts abroad, and its militant rhetoric. They have been appalled by the barbaric behavior of the Red Guards toward the Chinese people, their callous disregard for human life and their mistreatment of foreign diplomats.

The immediate prospect that China will emerge from its self-imposed isolation is dim. But both Asians and Americans will have to coexist with the 750 million Chinese on the mainland. We shall continue to make it clear that we are prepared to cooperate with China whenever it is ready to become a responsible member of the international community. We would actively encourage economic, social and cultural exchange with mainland China as a means of freeing that nation and her people from their narrow isolation.

We support continued assistance to help maintain the independence and peaceful development of India and Pakistan.

Recognizing the growing importance of Asia and the Pacific, we will encourage increased cultural and educational efforts, such as those undertaken in multi-racial Hawaii, to facilitate a better understanding of the problems and opportunities of this vast area.

*The Developing World*

The American people share the aspirations for a better life in the developing world. But we are committed to peaceful change. We believe basic political rights in most states can be more effectively achieved and maintained by peaceful action than by violence.

In their struggle for political and economic development, most Asian, African, and Latin American states are confronted by grinding poverty, illiteracy and a stubborn resistance to constructive change. The aspirations and frustrations of the people are frequently exploited by self-serving revolutionaries who employ illegal and violent means.

Since World War II, America's unprecedented program of foreign economic assistance for reconstruction and development has made a profound contribution to peace, security, and a better life for millions of people everywhere. Many nations formerly dependent upon American aid are now viable and stable as a result of this aid.

We support strengthened U.S. and U.N. development aid programs that are responsive to changing circumstances and based on the recognition, as President Johnson put it, that "self-help is the lifeblood of economic development." Grant aid and government loans for long-term projects are part of a larger transfer of resources between the developed and underdeveloped states, which includes international trade and private capital investment as important components.

Like the burden of keeping the peace, the responsibility for assisting the developing world must be shared by Japan and the Western European states, once recipients of U.S. aid and now donor states.

Development aid should be coordinated among both donors and recipients. The World Bank and other international and regional agencies for investment and development should be fully utilized. We should encourage regional cooperation by the recipients for the most efficient use of resources and markets.

We should press for additional international agreements that will stimulate mutually beneficial trade and encourage a growing volume of private investment in the developing states. World-wide commodity agreements that stabilize prices for particular products and other devices to stabilize export earnings will also spur development.

We believe priority attention should be given to agricultural production and population control. Technical assistance which emphasizes manpower training is also of paramount importance. We support the Peace Corps which has sent thousands of ambassadors of good will to three continents.

Cultural and historic ties and a common quest for peace with freedom and justice have made Latin America an area of special concern and interest to the United States. We support a vigorous Alliance for Progress program based upon the Charter of Punta del Este which affirms that "free men working through the institutions for representative democracy can best satisfy man's aspirations."

We support the objective of Latin American economic integration endorsed by the presidents of the American Republics in April 1967 and urge further efforts in the areas of tax reform, land reform, educational reform, and economic development to fulfill the promise of Punta del Este.

### United Nations

Since the birth of the United Nations, the United States has pursued the quest for peace, security and human dignity through United Nations channels more vigorously than any other member state. Our dedication to its purpose and its work remains undiminished.

The United Nations contributed to dampening the fires of conflict in Kashmir, the Middle East, Cyprus and the Congo. The agencies of the United Nations have made a significant contribution to health, education and economic well-being in Asia, Africa and Latin America. These efforts deserve continued and expanded support. We pledge that support.

Since we recognize that the United Nations can be only as effective as the support of its members, we call upon other states to join with us in a renewed commitment to use its facilities in the great tasks of economic development, the non-military use of atomic energy, arms control and peace-keeping. It is only with member nations working together that the organization can make its full contribution to the growth of a world community of peace under law, rather than by threat or use of military force.

We are profoundly concerned about the continued repression of Jews and other minorities in the Soviet Union and elsewhere, and look forward to the day when the full light of liberty and freedom shall be extended to all countries and all peoples.

### Foreign Trade and Financial Policy

World trade is essential to economic stability. The growing interdependence of nations, particularly in economic affairs, is an established fact of contemporary life. It also spells an opportunity for constructive international cooperation that will bring greater well-being for all and improve the prospects for international peace and security.

We shall build upon the Trade Expansion Act of 1962 and the Kennedy round of trade negotiations, in order to achieve greater trade cooperation and progress toward freer international trade. In future negotiations, which will require careful preparation, we shall: 1) seek continued reciprocal reduction and elimination of tariff barriers, based on the most favored nation principle; 2) negotiate the reciprocal removal of non-tariff barriers to international trade on all products, including agriculture; 3) give special attention to the needs of the developing countries for increased export earnings; and 4) develop and improve the rules governing fair international competition affecting both foreign commerce and investment.

To lessen the hardships suffered by industries and workers as the result of trade liberalization, we support improvements in the adjustment assistance provisions of present law. Provision of law to remedy unfair and destructive import competition should be reviewed and strengthened, and negotiated international agreements to achieve this purpose should be employed where appropriate.

The United States has experienced balance-of-payments deficits for over a decade, mainly because of our security obligations in the free world. Faced with these deficits, we have behaved responsibly by avoiding both economic deflation at home and severe unilateral restrictive measures on international transactions, which would have weakened the international economy and international cooperation.

We shall continue to take the path of constructive measures by relying on steps to increase our exports and by the development of further cooperative arrangements with the other countries. We intend, as soon as possible, to dismantle the restrictions placed on foreign investment and finance, so that American free enterprise can play its full part as the agent of economic development. We will continue to encourage persons from other lands to visit America.

Steps of historical importance have already been taken to improve the functioning of the international monetary system, most notably the new special drawing rights under the international monetary fund. We shall continue to work for the further improvement of the international monetary system so as to reduce its vulnerability to monetary crises.

ECONOMIC GROWTH AND STABILITY

The Democratic policies that more than doubled the nation's rate of economic expansion in the past eight years can double and redouble our national income by the end of this century. Such a rate of economic growth will enable us to win total victory in our wars on ignorance, poverty, and the misery of the ghettos.

But victory will not come automatically. To realize our full economic potential will require effective, businesslike planning and cooperation between government and all elements of private economy. The Democratic Party pledges itself to achieve that purpose in many ways.

*Fiscal and Monetary Policy*

Taxes were lowered in 1962, 1964, and 1965 to encourage more private spending and reach full employment; they were raised in 1966 and 1968 to help prevent inflation, but with a net reduction in the eight Democratic years. We will continue to use tax policy to maintain steady economic growth by helping through tax reduction to stimulate the economy when it is sluggish and through temporary tax increases to restrain inflation. To promote this objective, methods must be devised to permit prompt, temporary changes in tax rates within prescribed limits with full participation of the Congress in the decisions.

The goals of our national tax policy must be to distribute the burden of government equitably among our citizens and to promote economic efficiency and stability. We have placed major reliance on progressive taxes, which are based on the democratic principle of ability to pay. We pledge ourselves to continue to rely on such taxes, and to continue to improve the way they are levied and collected so that every American contributes to government in proportion to his ability to pay.

A thorough revamping of our federal taxes has been long overdue to make them more equitable as between rich and poor and as among people with the same income and family responsibilities. All corporation and individual preferences that do not serve the national interest should be removed. Tax preferences, like expenditures, must be rigorously evaluated to assure that the benefit to the nation is worth the cost.

We support a proposal for a minimum income tax for persons of high income based on an individual's total income regardless of source in order that wealthy persons will be required to make some kind of income tax contribution, no matter how many tax shelters they use to protect their incomes. We also support a reduction of the tax burden on the poor by lowering the income tax rates at the bottom of the tax scale and increasing the minimum standard deduction. No person or family below the poverty level should be required to pay federal income taxes.

Our goal is a balanced budget in a balanced economy. We favor distinguishing current operating expenditures from long term capital outlays and repayable loans, which should be amortized consistent with sound accounting principles. All government expenditures should be subject to firm tests of efficiency and essentiality.

An effective policy for growth and stability requires careful coordination of fiscal and monetary policies. Changes in taxes, budgets, interest rates, and money supply must be carefully blended and flexibly adjusted to assure:

Adaptation to changing economic conditions;

Adequate supplies of money and credit for the expansion of industry, commerce, and housing;

Maintenance of the lowest possible interest rates;

Avoidance of needless hardships on groups that depend heavily on credit.

Cooperation between fiscal and monetary authorities was greatly strengthened in the past eight years, and we pledge ourselves to continue to perfect this cooperation.

### Price Stability with Growth

Price stability continues to be an essential goal of expansive economic policy. Price inflation hurts most of the weak among us and could interfere with the continued social gains we are determined to achieve in the immediate years ahead.

The answer to rising prices will never be sought, under Democratic administrations, in unemployment and idle plant facilities. We are firmly committed to the twin objectives of full employment and price stability.

To promote price stability in a dynamic and growing economy, we will:

Pursue flexible fiscal and monetary policies designed to keep total private and public demand in line with the economy's rising productive capacity.

Work effectively with business, labor, and the public in formulating principles for price and wage policies that are equitable and sound for consumers as well as for workers and investors.

Strictly enforce antitrust and trade practice laws to combat administered pricing, supply limitations and other restrictive practices.

Strengthen competition by keeping the doors of world trade open and resisting the protectionism of captive markets.

Stimulate plant modernization, upgrade labor skills, and speed technological advance to step up productivity.

### Agriculture

Twice in this century the Republican Party has brought disaster to the American farmer—in the thirties and in the fifties. Each time, the American farmer was rescued by the Democratic Party, but his prosperity has not yet been fully restored.

Farmers must continue to be heard in the councils of government where decisions affecting agriculture are taken. The productivity of our farmers—already the world's most productive—must continue to rise, making American agricul-

ture more competitive abroad and more prosperous at home.

A strong agriculture requires fair income to farmers for an expanding output. Family farmers must be protected from the squeeze between rising production costs and low prices for their products. Farm income should grow with productivity just as industrial wages rise with productivity. At the same time, market prices should continue to reflect supply and demand conditions and American farm products must continue to compete effectively in world markets. In this way, markets at home and abroad will continue to expand beyond the record high levels of recent years.

To these ends, we shall:

Take positive action to raise farm income to full parity level in order to preserve the efficient, full-time family farm. This can be done through present farm programs when these programs are properly funded, but these programs will be constantly scrutinized with a view to improvement.

Actively seek out and develop foreign commercial markets, since international trade in agricultural products is a major favorable factor in the nation's balance of payments. In expanding our trade, we shall strive to ensure that farmers get adequate compensation for their production going into export.

Expand our food assistance programs to America's poor and our Food for Peace program to help feed the world's hungry.

Establish a Strategic Food and Feed Reserve Plan whereby essential commodities such as wheat, corn and other feed grains, soybeans, storable meat and other products will be stockpiled as a safeguard against crop failures, to assist our nation and other nations in time of famine or disaster, and to ensure adequate supplies for export markets, as well as to protect our own farm industry. This reserve should be insulated from the market.

Support the right of farmers to bargain collectively in the market place on a commodity by commodity basis. Labor and industry have long enjoyed this right to bargain collectively under existing legislation. Protective legislation for bargaining should be extended to agriculture.

Continue to support and encourage agricultural co-operatives by expanded and liberal credit, and to protect them from punitive taxation.

Support private or public credit on reasonable terms to young farmers to enable them to purchase farms on long term, low interest loans.

Support the federal crop insurance program.

Reaffirm our support of the rural electrification program, recognizing that rural America cannot be revitalized without adequate low-cost electric power. We pledge continued support of programs to assure supplemental financing to meet the growing generating and distributing power needs of rural areas. We support the rural telephone program.

Support a thorough study of the effect of unlimited payments to farmers. If necessary, we suggest graduated open-end limitations of payments to extremely large corporate farms that participate in government programs.

Take a positive approach to the public interest in the issue of health and tobacco at all levels of the tobacco economy. We recommend a co-operative effort in health and tobacco research by government, industry and qualified scientific bodies, to ascertain relationships between human health and tobacco growth, curing, storage and manufacturing techniques, as well as specific medical aspects of tobacco smoke constituents.

### Small Business

Small business plays a vital role in a dynamic, competitive economy; it helps maintain a strong social fabric in communities across the land; it builds concerned community leadership deriving from ownership of small enterprises; and it maintains the challenge and competition essential to a free enterprise system.

To assure a continuing healthy environment for small business, the Democratic Party pledges to:

Assure adequate credit at reasonable costs;

Assure small business a fair share of government contracts and procurement;

Encourage investment in research and development of special benefit to small enterprise;

Assist small business in taking advantage of technological innovations;

Provide centers of information on government procurement needs and foreign sales opportunities.

The Democratic Party is pledged to develop programs that will enable members of minority groups to obtain the financing and technical management assistance needed to succeed in launching and operating new enterprises.

### Labor-Management Relations

Private collective bargaining and a strong and independent labor movement are essential to our system of free enterprise and economic democracy. Their development has been fostered under each Democratic administration in this century.

We will thoroughly review and update the National Labor Relations Act to assure an effective opportunity to all workers to exercise the right to organize and to bargain collectively, including such amendments as:

Repeal of the provision permitting states to enact compulsory open shop laws;

Extension of the Act's protection to farm workers, employees of private non-profit organizations, and other employees not now covered;

Removal of unreasonable restrictions upon the right of peaceful picketing, including situs picketing;

Speedier decisions in unfair labor practice cases and representation proceedings;

Greater equality between the remedies available under the Act to labor and those available to management;

Effective opportunities for unions as well as employers to communicate with employees, without coercion by either side or by anyone acting in their behalf.

The Federal Government will continue to set an example as an employer to private business and to state and local governments. The Government will not do business with firms that repeatedly violate Federal statutes prohibiting discrimination against employees who are union members or refuse to bargain with duly authorized union representatives.

By all these means, we will sustain the right of workers to organize in unions of their own choosing and will foster truly effective collective bargaining to provide the maximum opportunity for just and fair agreements between management and labor.

### Consumer Protection

Rising incomes have brought new vigor to the market place. But the march of technology which has brought unparalleled abundance and opportunity to the consumer has also exposed him to new hazards and new complexities. In providing economic justice for consumers, we shall strengthen business and industry and improve the quality of life for all 200 million Americans.

We commend the Democratic Congress for passing the landmark legislation of the past several years which has ushered in a new era of consumer protection—truth-in-lending, truth-in-packaging, wholesome meat and poultry, auto and highway safety, child safety, and protection against interstate land swindles.

We shall take steps, including necessary legislation, to minimize the likelihood of massive electric power failures, to improve the safety of medical devices and drugs, to penalize deceptive sales practices, and to provide consumer access to product information now being compiled in the Federal Government.

We will help the states to establish consumer fraud and information bureaus, and to update consumer credit laws.

A major objective of all consumer programs, at all levels, must be the education of the buying public, particularly the poor who are the special targets of unscrupulous and high-pressure salesmanship.

We will make the consumer's voice increasingly heard in the councils of government. We will strengthen consumer education and enforcement programs by consolidation of functions now dispersed among various agencies, through the establishment of an Office of Consumer Affairs to represent consumer interests within the government and before courts and regulatory agencies.

## Housing

For the first time in history, a nation is able to rebuild or replace all of its substandard housing, even while providing housing for millions of new families.

This means rebuilding or replacing 4.5 million dwelling units in our urban areas and 3.9 million in rural areas, most in conditions of such dilapidation that they are too often dens of despair for millions of Americans.

Yet this performance is possible in the next decade because of goals and programs fashioned by Democratic Presidents and Democratic Congresses in close partnership with private business.

The goal is clear and pressing—"a decent home and a suitable living environment for every American family," as set forth in the 1949 Housing Act by a Democratic Congress and Administration.

To achieve this goal in the next ten years:

We will assist private enterprise to double its volume of homebuilding, to an annual rate of 2.6 million units a year—a ten year total of 26 million units. This is the specific target of the history-making Housing and Urban Development Act of 1968.

We will give the highest priority to Federally-assisted home-building for low income families, with special attention given to ghetto dwellers, the elderly, the physically handicapped, and families in neglected areas of rural America, Indian reservations, territories of the United States, and migratory worker camps. All federal subsidy programs—whether in the form of public housing, interest rates at 1%, rent supplements, or direct loans—will be administered to favor these disadvantaged families, with full participation by the neighborhood residents themselves.

We will cooperate with private home builders to experiment boldly with new production technology, with financial institutions to marshal capital for housing where it is most needed, and with unions to expand the labor force needed for a doubling of production.

Above all, we will work toward the greatest possible freedom of choice—the opportunity for every family, regardless of race, color, religion, or income, to choose home ownership or rental, high-rise or low-rise, cooperatives or condominiums, detached or town house, and city, suburban or country living.

We urge local governments to shape their own zoning laws and building codes to favor consumers and hold down costs.

Rigid enforcement of State and local health and building codes is imperative to alleviate conditions of squalor and despair in deteriorating neighborhoods.

Democrats are proud of their housing record. But we are also painfully aware of how much more needs to be done to reach the final goal of decent shelter for all Americans and we pledge a steadfast pursuit of that goal.

*Transportation*

America is a nation on the move. To meet the challenge of transportation, we propose a dynamic partnership between industry and government at all levels.

Of utmost urgency is the need to solve congestion in air traffic, especially in airports and between major metropolitan centers. We pledge intensified efforts to devise equitable methods of financing new and improved airport and airway facilities.

Urban and inter-urban transportation facilities are heavily overburdened. We support expanded programs of assistance to mass transit in order to avoid unnecessary congestion in air traffic, especially at air-link residential and work areas.

Despite the tremendous progress of our interstate highway program, still more super-highways are needed for safe and rapid motor transport. We need to establish local road networks to meet regional requirements.

The efficiency of our railroads has improved greatly but there is need for further strengthening of the nation's railroads so that they can contribute more fully to the nation's transport requirements. In particular, we will press forward with the effort to develop high-speed passenger trains to serve major urban areas.

To assume our proper place as a leading maritime nation, we must launch an aggressive and balanced program to replace and augment our obsolete merchant ships with modern vessels built in American shipyards. We will assist U.S. flag operators to overcome the competitive disparity between American and foreign costs.

We will continue to foster development of harbors, ports, and inland waterways, particularly regional waterways systems, and the St. Lawrence Seaway, to accommodate our expanded water-borne commerce. We support modernization of the Panama Canal.

We pledge a greater investment in transportation research and development to enhance safety and increase speed and economy; to implement the acts that have been passed to control noxious vehicle exhausts; and to reduce aircraft noise.

The expansion of our transportation must not be carried out at the expense of the environment through which it moves. We applaud the leadership provided by the First Lady to enhance the highway environment and initiate a national beautification program.

*Communications*

America has the most efficient and comprehensive communications system in the world. But a healthy society depends more on the quality of what is communicated than on either the volume or form of communication.

Public broadcasting has already proven that it can be a valuable supplement to formal education and a direct medium for non-formal education. We pledge our continuing support for the prompt enactment of a long-range financing plan that will help ensure the vigor and independence of this potentially vital but still underdeveloped new force in American life.

We deplore the all too frequent exploitation of violence as entertainment in all media.

In 1962 the Democratic Party sensed the great potential of space communication and quickly translated this awareness into the Communications Satellite Act. In a creative partnership between government and business, this revolutionary idea soon became a reality. Six years later we helped establish a consortium of 61 nations devoted to the development of a global satellite network.

We will continue to develop new technology and utilize communications to promote worldwide understanding as an essential pre-condition of world peace. But, in view of rapidly changing technology, the entire federal regulatory system dealing with telecommunication should be thoroughly reappraised.

*Science and Technology*

We lead the world in science and technology. This has produced a dramatic effect on the daily lives of all of us. To maintain our undisputed national leadership in science and further its manifold applications for the betterment of mankind, the Federal Government has a clear obligation to foster and support creative men and women in the research community, both public and private.

Our pioneering space program has helped mankind on earth in countless ways. The benefits from improved weather forecasting which can soon be available thanks to satellite observations and communications will by themselves make the space efforts worthwhile.

Observation by satellite of crops and other major earth resources will for the first time enable man to see all that is available to him on earth, and therefore to take maximum advantage of it. High endurance metals developed for spacecraft help make commercial planes safer; similarly, micro-electronics are now found in consumer appliances. Novel space food-preservation techniques are employed in the tropical climates of underdeveloped countries. We will move ahead in aerospace research and development for their unimagined promise for man on earth as well as their vital importance to national defense.

We shall continue to work for our goal of leadership in space. To this end we will maximize the effectiveness and efficiency of our space programs through utilization of the best program, planning and budgeting systems.

To maintain our leadership in the application of energy, we will push forward with research and development to assure a balanced program for the supply of energy for electric power, both public and private. This effort should go hand in hand with development of "breeder" reactors and large-scale nuclear desalting plants that can provide pure water economically from the sea for domestic use and agricultural and industrial development in arid regions, and with broadened medical and biological applications of atomic energy.

In addition to the physical sciences, the social sciences will be encouraged and assisted to identify and deal with the problem areas of society.

## Opportunity For All

We of the Democratic Party believe that a nation wealthy beyond the dreams of most of mankind—a nation with a twentieth of the world's population, possessing half the world's manufactured goods—has the capacity and the duty to assure to all its citizens the opportunity to enjoy the full measure of the blessings of American life.

For the first time in the history of the world, it is within the power of a nation to eradicate from within its borders the age-old curse of poverty.

Our generation of Americans has now made those commitments. It remains to implement and adequately fund the host of practical measures

that demonstrate their effectiveness and to continue to devise new approaches.

We are guided by the recommendations of the National Advisory Commission on Civil Disorders concerning jobs, housing, urban renewal, and education on a scale commensurate with the needs of the urban ghettos. We are guided by the report of the Commission on Rural Poverty in tackling the equally compelling problems of the rural slums.

Economic growth is our first antipoverty program. The best avenue to an independent, confident citizenry is a dynamic, full-employment economy. Beyond that lie the measures necessary to assure that every American, of every race, in every region, truly shares in the benefits of economic progress.

Those measures include rehabilitation of the victims of poverty, elimination of the urban and rural slums where poverty is bred, and changes throughout the system of institutions that affect the lives of the poor.

In this endeavor, the resources of private enterprise—not only its economic power but its leadership and ingenuity—must be mobilized. We must marshal the power that comes from people working together in communities—the neighborhood communities of the poor and the larger communities of the city, the town, the village, the region.

We support community action agencies and their programs, such as Head Start, that will prevent the children of the poor from becoming the poor of the next generation. We support the extension of neighborhood centers. We are committed to the principle of meaningful participation of the poor in policy-making and administration of community action and related programs.

Since organizations of many kinds are joined in the war on poverty, problems of coordination inevitably arise. We pledge ourselves to review current antipoverty efforts to assess how responsibility should be distributed among levels of government, among private and public agencies, and between the permanent agencies of the federal government and an independent antipoverty agency.

### Toward a Single Society

We acknowledge with concern the findings of the report of the bi-partisan National Advisory

Commission on Civil Disorders and we commit ourselves to implement its recommendations and to wipe out, once and for all, the stain of racial and other discrimination from our national life.

"The major goal," the Commission wrote, "is the creation of a true union—a single society and a single American identity." A single society, however, does not mean social or cultural uniformity. We are a nation of many social, ethnic and national groups. Each has brought richness and strength to America.

The Civil Rights Act of 1964 and 1968 and the Voting Rights Act of 1965, all adopted under the vigorous leadership of President Johnson, are basic to America's long march toward full equality under the law.

We will not permit these great gains to be chipped away by opponents or eroded by administrative neglect. We pledge effective and impartial enforcement of these laws. If they prove inadequate, or if their compliance provisions fail to serve their purposes, we will propose new laws. In particular, the enforcement provisions of the legislation prohibiting discrimination in employment should be strengthened. This will be done as a matter of first priority.

We have also come to recognize that freedom and equality require more than the ending of repression and prejudice. The victims of past discrimination must be encouraged and assisted to take full advantage of opportunities that are now opening to them.

We must recognize that for too long we have neglected the abilities and aspirations of Spanish speaking Americans to participate fully in American life. We promise to fund and implement the Bilingual Education Act and expand recruitment and training of bilingual federal and state employees.

The American Indian has the oldest claim on our national conscience. We must continue and increase federal help in the Indian's battle against poverty, unemployment, illiteracy, ill health and poor housing. To this end, we pledge a new and equal federal-Indian partnership that will enable Indian communities to provide for themselves many services now furnished by the federal government and federal sponsorship of industrial development programs owned, managed, and run by Indians. We support a quick and fair settlement of land claims of Indians, Eskimo and Aleut citizens of Alaska.

### The Inner City

In the decaying slums of our larger cities, where so many of our poor are concentrated, the attack on poverty must embrace many interrelated aspects of development—economic development, the rehabilitation or replacement of dilapidated and unsafe housing, job training and placement, and the improvement of education, health, recreation, crime control, welfare, and other public services.

As the framework of such an effort, we will continue to support the Model Cities program under which communities themselves are planning and carrying out the most comprehensive plans ever put together for converting their worst slum areas into model neighborhoods—with full participation and leadership by the neighborhood residents themselves. The Model Cities program will be steadily extended to more cities and more neighborhoods and adequately financed.

The resources and leadership of private enterprise must be marshaled in the attack on slums and poverty, and such incentives as may be essential for that purpose we will develop and enact.

Some of the most urgent jobs in the revival of the inner city remain undone because the hazards are too great and the rewards too limited to attract sufficient private capital. To meet this problem, we will charter a new federal banking structure to provide capital and investment guaranties for urban projects planned and implemented through local initiative—neighborhood development corporations, minority programs for self-employment, housing development corporations, and other urban construction and planning operations. We will also enact legislation providing tax incentives for new business and industrial enterprises in the inner city. Our experience with aid to small business demonstrates the importance of increased local ownership of business enterprises in the inner city.

We shall aid the universities to concentrate their resources more fully upon the problems of the cities and facilitate their cooperation with municipal agencies and local organizations in finding solutions to urban problems.

## Rural Development

Balanced growth is essential for America. To achieve that balanced growth, we must greatly increase the growth of the rural non-farm economy. One-third of our people live in rural areas, but only one rural family in ten derives its principal income from farming. Almost thirty percent of the nation's poor are non-farm people in rural areas.

The problem of rural poverty and the problem of migration of poor people from rural areas to urban ghettos are mainly non-farm problems. The creation of productive jobs in small cities and towns can be the best and least costly solution of these problems.

To revitalize rural and small-town America and assure equal opportunity for all Americans wherever they live, we pledge to:

Create jobs by offering inducements to new enterprises—using tax and other incentives—to locate in small towns and rural areas;

Administer existing federal programs and design new programs where necessary to overcome the disparity between rural and urban areas in opportunities for education, for health services, for low income housing, for employment and job training, and for public services of all kinds;

Encourage the development of new towns and new growth centers;

Encourage the creation of comprehensive planning and development agencies to provide additional leadership in non-metropolitan areas, and assist them financially.

The experience of the Appalachian and other regional commissions indicates that municipalities, counties, and state and federal agencies can work together in a common development effort.

## Jobs and Training

Every American in need of work should have opportunity not only for meaningful employment, but also for the education, training, counselling, and other services that enable him to take advantage of available jobs.

To the maximum possible extent, our national goal of full employment should be realized through creation of jobs in the private economy, where six of every seven Americans now work. We will continue the Job Opportunities in the Business Sector (JOBS) program, which for the first time has mobilized the energies of business and industry on a nationwide scale to provide training and employment to the hardcore unemployed. We will develop whatever additional incentives may be necessary to maximize the opportunities in the private sector for hardcore unemployed.

We will continue also to finance the operation by local communities of a wide range of training programs for youth and retraining for older workers whose skills have become obsolete, coupled with related services necessary to enable people to undertake training and accept jobs—including improved recruitment and placement services, day-care centers, and transportation between work and home.

For those who can work but cannot find jobs, we pledge to expand public job and job-training programs, including the Neighborhood Youth Corps, to provide meaningful employment by state and local government and nonprofit institutions.

For those who cannot obtain other employment, the federal government will be the employer of last resort, either through federal assistance to state and local projects or through federally sponsored projects.

## Employment Standards

American workers are entitled to more than the right to a job. They have the right to fair and safe working conditions and to adequate protection in periods of unemployment or disability.

In the last thirty years Democratic administrations and Congresses have enacted, extended and improved a series of measures to provide safeguards against exploitation and distress. We pledge to continue these efforts.

The minimum standards covering terms and conditions of employment must be improved:

By increasing the minimum wage guarantee to assure those at the bottom of the economic scale a fairer share in rising living standards;

By extending the minimum wage and overtime provision of the Fair Labor Standards Act to all workers;

By enacting occupational health and safety legislation to assure the material reduction of the present occupational death rate of 14,500 men and women each year, and the disabling accident rate of over 2 million per year;

By assuring that the "green card" worker does not depress wages and conditions of employment for American workers;

By updating of the benefit provisions of the Longshoremen and Harbor Workers Act.

The unemployment compensation program should be modernized by national minimum standards for level and duration of benefits, eligibility, and universal coverage.

### Older Citizens

A lifetime of work and effort deserves a secure and satisfying retirement.

Benefits, especially minimum benefits, under Old Age, Survivors, and Disability Insurance should be raised to overcome present inadequacies and thereafter should be adjusted automatically to reflect increases in living costs.

Medical care for the aged should be expanded to include the costs of prescription drugs.

The minimum age for public assistance should be lowered to correspond to the requirements for social security.

America's self-employed citizens should be encouraged by tax incentive legislation to supplement social security benefits for themselves and their employees to the same extent that employees of corporations are encouraged.

In addition to improving social security, we must develop in each community a wide variety of activities to enrich the lives of our older citizens, to enable them to continue to contribute to our society, and to permit them to live in dignity. The aged must have access to better housing, opportunites for regular or part-time employment and community volunteer services, and cultural and recreational activities.

### People in Need

Every American family whose income is not sufficient to enable its members to live in decency should receive assistance free of the indignities and uncertainties that still too often mar our present programs. To support family incomes of the working poor a number of new program proposals have recently been developed. A thorough evaluation of the relative advantages of such proposals deserves the highest priority attention

by the next Administration. This we pledge to do.

Income payments and eligibility standards for the aged, the blind, the disabled and dependent children should be determined and financed on a federal basis—in place of the present inequitable, under-financed hodge podge state plans. This would, among other things, assure the eligibility in all states of needy children of unemployed parents who are now denied assistance in more than half the states as long as the father remains in the home.

Assistance payments should not only be brought to adequate levels but they should be kept adequate by providing for automatic adjustment to reflect increases in living costs.

Congress has temporarily suspended the restrictive amendment of 1967 that placed an arbitary limit on the number of dependent children who can be aided in each state. We favor permanent repeal of that restriction and of the provision requiring mothers of young children to work.

The new federal-state program we propose should provide for financial incentives and needed services to enable and encourage adults on welfare to seek employment to the extent they are able to do so.

The time has come when we should make a national commitment that no American should have to go hungry or undernourished. The Democratic Party here and now does make that commitment. We will move rapidly to implement it through continued improvement and expansion of our food programs.

The Democratic Congress this year has already enacted legislation to expand and improve the school lunch and commodity distribution programs, and shortly will complete action on legislation now pending to expand the food stamp program. We will enact further legislation and appropriations to assure on a permanent basis that the school lunch program provides free and reduced price meals to all needy school children.

### Health

The best of modern medical care should be made available to every American. We support efforts to overcome the remaining barriers of distance, poverty, ignorance, and discrimination that separate persons from adequate medical services.

During the last eight years of Democratic administrations, this nation has taken giant steps forward in assuring life and health for its citizens. In the years ahead, we Democrats are determined to take those final steps that are necessary to make certain that every American, regardless of economic status, shall live out his years without fear of the high costs of sickness.

Through a partnership of government and private enterprise we must develop new co-ordinated approaches to stem the rise in medical and drug costs without lowering the quality or availability of medical care. Out-of-hospital care, comprehensive group practice arrangements, increased availability of neighborhood health centers, and the greater use of sub-professional aides can all contribute to the lowering of medical costs.

We will raise the level of research in all fields of health, with special programs for development of the artificial heart and the heart transplant technique, development of drugs to treat and prevent the recurrence of heart diseases, expansion of current task forces in cancer research and the creation of new ones including cancer of the lung, determination of the factors in mental retardation and reduction of infant mortality, development of drugs to reduce the incidence of suicide, and construction of health research facilities and hospitals.

We must build new medical, dental and medical service schools, and increase the capacity of existing ones, to train more doctors, dentists, nurses, and medical technicians.

Medical care should be extended to disabled beneficiaries under the Old Age, Survivors and Disability Insurance Act to the same extent and under the same system that such care is available to the aged.

Thousands of children die, or are handicapped for life, because their mothers did not receive proper pre-natal medical attention or because the infants were unattended in the critical first days of life. Maternal and child health centers, located and designed to serve the needs of the poor, and voluntary family planning information centers should be established throughout the country. Medicaid programs administered by the states should have uniform standards so that no mother or child is denied necessary health services. Finally, we urge consideration of a program comparable to Medicare to finance pre-natal care for mothers and post-natal care for children during the first year of life.

## Veterans

American veterans deserve our enduring gratitude for their distinguished service to the nation.

In 1968 some 750,000 returning servicemen will continue their education with increased benefits under the new G.I. Bill passed by an education-minded Democratic Congress. Two million disabled veterans and survivors of those killed in action are receiving larger pensions and higher disability payments.

Guided by the report of the Veterans Advisory Commission, established by the Democratic administration, we will:

Continue a strong one-stop agency vested with sole responsibility for all veterans programs;

Sustain and upgrade veteran medical services and expand medical training in VA hospitals;

Maintain compensation for disabled veterans and for widows and dependents of veterans who die of service-connected causes, in line with the rise in earnings and living standards;

Assure every veteran the right of burial in a national cemetery;

Provide incentives for veterans to aid their communities by serving in police, fire departments, educational systems and other public endeavors;

Make veterans and their widows eligible for pension benefits at the same age at which Social Security beneficiaries may receive old age benefits.

We recommend the establishment of a standing Committee on Veterans Affairs in the Senate.

## Education

Education is the chief instrument for making good the American promise. It is indispensable to every man's chance to achieve his full potential. We will seek to open education to all Americans.

We will assure equal opportunity to education and equal access to high-quality education. Our aim is to maintain state-local control over the nation's educational system, with federal financial assistance and help in stimulating changes through demonstration and technical assistance. New concepts of education and training employing new communications technology must be developed to educate children and adults.

Every citizen has a basic right to as much education and training as he desires and can master—from preschool through graduate studies —even if his family cannot pay for this education.

We will marshal our national resources to help develop and finance new and effective methods of dealing with the educationally disadvantaged —including expanded preschool programs to prepare all young children for full participation in formal education, improved teacher recruitment and training programs for inner city and rural schools, the Teacher Corps, assistance to community controlled schools to encourage pursuit of innovative practices, university participation in research and operation of school programs, a vocational education system that will provide imaginative new ties between school and the world of work, and improved and more widespread adult education programs.

We will fully fund Title I of the Elementary and Secondary Education Act of 1965, which provides federal funds for improving education in schools serving large numbers of students from low income families.

The financial burden of education continues to grow as enrollments spiral and costs increase. The home owner's property tax burden must be eased by increased levels of financial aid by both the states and the Federal government.

Our rapidly expanding educational frontiers require a redoubling of efforts to insure the vitality of a diverse higher education system— public and private, large and small, community and junior colleges, vocational and technical schools, and great universities. We also pledge support for high quality graduate and medical education.

We will enlarge the federal scholarship program to remove the remaining financial barriers to post-secondary education for low income youths, and increase assistance to students in the form of repayable loans out of future income.

We will encourage support for the arts and the humanities, through the national foundations established by a Democratic Congress, to provide incentives for those endowed with extraordinary talent, enhance the quality of our life, and make productive leisure available to all our people.

We recommend greater stress on the arts and humanities in elementary and secondary curricula to ensure a proper educational balance.

## Youth

For generations, the Democratic Party has renewed its vitality with young people and new ideas. Today, young people are bringing new vigor and a deep concern for social justice into the political process, yet many feel excluded from full participation.

We of the Democratic Party welcome the bold thinking and exciting ideas of youth. We recognize, with deep satisfaction, that their healthy desire for participation in the democratic system must lead to a series of reforms in the direction of a greater democracy and a more open America.

The Democratic Party takes pride in the fact that so many of today's youth have channeled their interests and energies into our Party. To them, and to all young Americans we pledge the fullest opportunity to participate in the affairs of our Party at the local, state, and national levels. We call for special efforts to recruit young people as candidates for public office.

We will support a Constitutional amendment lowering the voting age to 18.

We favor an increase in youth representation on state delegations in future Democratic conventions.

Steps should be taken to include youth advisers on all government studies, commissions, and hearings which are relevant to their lives.

We will establish a youth commission involving young people between the ages of 18 and 26.

Every young person should have an opportunity to contribute to the social health of his community or to humanitarian service abroad. The extraordinary experience of the Teacher Corps, VISTA, and the Peace Corps points the way for broadening the opportunities for such voluntary service. Hundreds of thousands of America's youth have sought to enlist in these programs, but only tens of thousands have been able to serve. We will expand these opportunities.

The lives of millions of young men are deeply affected by the requirement for military service. The present system leaves them in uncertainty through much of their early manhood. Until our manpower needs can be fully met by voluntary enlistment, the Democratic Party will insist upon the most equitable and just selection system that can be devised. We support a random system of selection which will reduce the period of eligibility to one year, guarantee fair selection, and remove uncertainty.

We urge review of draft board memberships to make them more representative of the communities they serve.

ENVIRONMENT, CONSERVATION AND NATURAL RESOURCES

These United States have undergone 200 years of continuous change and dramatic development resulting in the most technologically advanced nation in the world. But with rapid industrialization, the nation's air and water resources have been degraded, the public health and welfare endangered, the landscape scarred and littered, and the very quality of our national life jeopardized.

We must assure the availability of a decent environment for living, working and relaxation.

To this end, we pledge our efforts:

To accelerate programs for the enhancement of the quality of the nation's waters for the protection of all legitimate water uses, with special emphasis on public water supplies, recreation, fish and wildlife;

To extend the national emission control program to all moving sources of air pollution;

To work for programs for the effective disposal of wastes of our modern industrial society;

To support the efforts on national, state, and local levels to preserve the historic monuments and sites of our heritage;

To assist in planning energy production and transportation to fit into the landscape, to assure safety, and to avoid interference with more desirable uses of land for recreation and other public purposes;

To continue to work toward abating the visual pollution that plagues our land;

To focus on the outdoor recreation needs of those who live in congested metropolitan areas;

To continue to work toward strong measures for the reclamation of mined and depleted lands and the conservation of soil.

*Public Domain*

We pledge continued support of the Public Land Law Review Commission, which is reviewing public land laws and policies to assure maximum opportunity for all beneficial uses of the public lands, including lands under the sea, and to develop a comprehensive land use policy.

We support sustained yield management of our forests, and expanded research for control of forest insects, disease, and fires.

We plan to examine the productivity of the public lands in goods, services, and local community prosperity, with a view to increasing such productivity.

We shall enforce existing federal statutes governing federal timber.

We support the orderly use and development of mineral resources on federal lands.

*Recreation*

We will continue the vigorous expansion of the public recreational domain to meet tomorrow's increasing needs. We will add national parks, recreation areas and seashores, and create national systems of scenic and wild rivers and of trails and scenic roads. We will support a growing wilderness preservation system, preservation of our redwood forests, and conservation of marshland and estuarine areas.

Recognizing that the bulk of the task of acquisition and development must be accomplished at the state and local levels we shall foster federal assistance to encourage such action, as well as recreational expansion by the private sector. To this end, we shall build upon the landmark Land and Water Conservation Fund Act, which has assured a foundation of a recreational heritage for future generations. We will assist communities to rehabilitate and expand inadequate and deteriorating urban park systems, and develop open space, waterways, and waterfront renovation facilities.

*Resources of the Oceans*

In and beneath the seas are resources of untold dimension for the benefit of mankind. Recognizing and protecting the paramount public interest in the seas, Congress under Democratic leadership enacted the Sea Grant College Act of 1965 and the Marine Resources and Engineering

Development Act of 1966, which established for
the first time a comprehensive long-range policy
and program for the marine sciences. We pledge
to pursue vigorously the goals of that Act. Specifically, we will:

Foster marine application of new technology
—spacecraft, buoys, data networks, and advanced
navigation systems—and develop an engineering
capability to work on and under the sea at any
depth;

Encourage development of underseas resources
by intensified research and better weather forecasting, with recognition to the coastal, insular
and other littoral states of their unique interest
and responsibility;

Foster an extensive program of oceanologic research and development, financed by a portion
of the mineral-royalty receipts from the outer
continental shelf;

Accelerate public and private programs for
the development of food and other marine resources to meet world-wide malnutrition, to create new industries, and to utilize under-employed
manpower living near the waterfront;

Promote our fisheries by providing incentives
for private investment, enforcing our 12-mile
fishing zone, and discouraging other nations from
excessive territorial and fishery claims;

Conclude an appropriate Ocean Space treaty
to secure rules and agreements that will facilitate
public and private investment, guarantee security
of investment and encourage efficient and orderly
development of the sea's resources.

THE GOVERNMENT

In the coming four years, the Democratic
President and Democratic Congress will give priority to simplifying and streamlining the processes of government, particularly in the management of the great innovative programs enacted
in the 1960's.

The Executive branch of the federal government is the largest and most complicated enterprise in the world, with programs distributed
among 150 separate departments, agencies, bureaus, and boards. This massive operation contributes to and often results in duplication, administrative confusion, and delay.

We will seek to streamline this machinery by
improving coordination and management of federal programs.

We realize that government must develop the
capacity to anticipate problems. We support a
thorough study of agency operations to determine priorities for governmental action and spending, for examination of the structure of these
agencies, and for establishing more systematic
means of attacking our nation's problems.

We recognize that citizen participation in
government is most meaningful at the levels of
government closest to the people. For that reason, we recognize the necessity of developing a
true partnership between state, local, and Federal
governments, with each carrying its share of the
financial and administrative load. We acknowledge the tremendous strides made by President
Johnson in strengthening federal-state relations
through open communication with the governors
and local officials, and we pledge to continue
and expand on this significant effort.

The complexities of federal-state local relationships must be simplified, so that states and local
communities receiving federal aid will have maximum freedom to initiate and carry out programs
suited to their own particular needs. To give states
and communities greater flexibility in their programs, we will combine individual grant programs
into broader categories.

As the economy grows, it is the federal revenue
system that responds most quickly, yet it may be
the states and local governments whose responsibilities mount most rapidly. To help states and
cities meet their fiscal challenges, we must seek
new methods for states and local governments to
share in federal revenues while retaining responsibility for establishing their own priorities and for
operating their own programs. To this end, we
will seek out new and innovative approaches to
government to assure that our Federal system
does, in fact, deliver to the people the services
for which they are paying.

*Public Employees*

The Democratic administration has moved vigorously in the past eight years—particularly with
regard to pay scales—to improve the conditions
of public service.

We support:

A federal service that rewards new ideas and
leadership;

Continued emphasis on education and training

programs for public employees, before and during their service;

Parity of government salaries with private industry;

A proper respect for the privacy and independence of federal employees;

Equal opportunities for career advancement;

Continued application of the principles of collective bargaining to federal employment;

Encouragement to state and local governments to continue to upgrade their personnel systems in terms of pay scales and training;

Interchange of employees between federal and state government.

## Elections

We are alarmed at the growing costs of political participation in our country and the consequent reliance of political parties and candidates on large contributors, and we want to assure full public information on campaign expenditures. To encourage citizen participation we urge that limited campaign contributions be made deductible as a credit from the federal income tax.

We fully recognize the principle of one man, one vote in all elections. We urge that due consideration be given to the question of presidential primaries throughout the nation. We urge reform of the electoral college and election procedures to assure that the votes of the people are fully reflected.

We urge all levels of our Party to assume leadership in removing all remaining barriers to voter registration.

We will also seek to eliminate disenfranchisement of voters who change residence during an election year.

## The District of Columbia

With the reorganization of the government of the District of Columbia, the nation's capital has for the first time in nearly a century the strong leadership provided by a mayor-council form of government. This, however, is no substitute for an independent and fiscally autonomous District government. We support a federally funded charter commission—controlled by District residents—to determine the most appropriate form of government for the District, and the prompt implementation of the Commission's recommendations.

The Democratic Party supports full citizenship for residents of the District of Columbia and a Constitutional amendment to grant such citizenship through voting representation in Congress. Until this can be done, we propose non-voting representation.

## Puerto Rico

In accordance with the democratic principle of self-determination the people of Puerto Rico have expressed their will to continue in permanent union with the United States through commonwealth status. We pledge our continued support to the growth of the commonwealth status which the people of Puerto Rico overwhelmingly approved last year.

## Virgin Islands and Guam

We favor an elected governor and a non-voting delegate in the House of Representatives for the Virgin Islands and Guam, and will consider methods by which American citizens residing in American territories can participate in presidential elections.

## JUSTICE AND LAW

We are firm in our commitment that equal justice under law shall be denied to no one. The duty of government at every level is the safety and security of its people. Yet the fact and fear of crime are uppermost in the minds of Americans today. The entire nation is united in its concern over crime, in all forms and wherever it occurs. America must move aggressively to reduce crime and its causes.

Democratic Presidents, governors and local officials are dedicated to the principle that equal justice under law shall remain the American creed. Those who take the law into their own hands undermine that creed. Anyone who breaks the law must be held accountable. Organized crime cannot be accepted as a way of life, nor can individual crime or acts of violence be permitted.

As stated in the report of the National Advisory Commission on Civil Disorders, the two fundamental questions confronting the American people are:

"How can we as a people end the resort to violence while we build a better society?

"How can the nation realize the promise of

a single society—one nation indivisible—which yet remains unfulfilled?"

This platform commits the Democratic Party to seek resolution of these questions.

We pledge a vigorous and sustained campaign against lawlessness in all its forms—organized crime, white collar crime, rioting, and other violations of the rights and liberties of others. We will further this campaign by attack on the root causes of crime and disorder.

Under the recent enactments of a Democratic Congress we will continue and increase federal financial support and technical assistance to the states and their local governments to:

Increase the numbers, raise the pay, and improve the training of local police officers;

Reduce delays and congestion in our criminal courts;

Rehabilitate and supervise convicted offenders, to return offenders to useful, decent lives, and to protect the public against habitual criminals;

Develop and deploy the most advanced and effective techniques and equipment for the public safety;

Assure the availability in every metropolitan area of quick, balanced, coordinated control forces, with ample manpower, thoroughly trained and properly equipped, to suppress rioting;

Encourage responsible and competent civic associations and business and labor groups to cooperate with the law enforcement agencies in new efforts to combat organized crime, build community support for police work, and assist in rehabilitating convicted offenders—and for the attainment of these ends, encourage our police to cooperate with any such groups and to establish links of communication with every element of the public they serve, building confidence and respect;

Establish and maintain open and responsive channels of communication between the public and the police through creative police-community relations programs;

Develop innovative programs to reduce the incidence of juvenile delinquency;

Promote the passage and enforcement of effective federal, state and local gun control legislation.

In all these efforts, our aim is to strengthen state and local law enforcement agencies so that they can do their jobs. In addition, the federal government has a clear responsibility for national action. We have accepted that responsibility and will continue to accept it with these specific objectives:

Prompt and effective federal support, upon request of appropriate authorities, to suppress rioting: improvement of the capabilities of all agencies of law enforcement and justice—the police, the military, the courts—to handle more effectively problems attending riots;

A concentrated campaign by the Federal government to wipe out organized crime: by employment of additional Federal investigators and prosecutors; by computerizing the present system of collecting information; by enlarging the program of technical assistance teams to work with the states and local governments that request assistance in this fight; by launching a nationwide program for the country's business and labor leaders to alert them to the problems of organized crime;

Intensified enforcement, research, and education to protect the public from narcotics and other damaging drugs: by review of federal narcotics laws for loopholes and difficulties of enforcement; by increased surveillance of the entire drug traffic; through negotiations with those foreign nations which grow and manufacture the bulk of drug derivatives;

Vigorous federal leadership to assist and coordinate state and local enforcement efforts, and to ensure that all communities benefit from the resources and knowledge essential to the fight on crime;

Further implementation of the recommendations of the President's crime commission;

Creation in the District of Columbia of a model system of criminal justice;

Federal research and development to bring to the problems of law enforcement and the administration of justice the full potential of the scientific revolution.

In fighting crime we must not foster injustice. Lawlessness cannot be ended by curtailing the hard-won liberties of all Americans. The right of privacy must be safeguarded. Court procedures must be expedited. Justice delayed is justice denied.

A respect for civil peace requires also a proper respect for the legitimate means of expressing dissent. A democratic society welcomes criticism within the limits of the law. Freedom of speech, press, assembly and association, together with free exercise of the franchise, are among the legitimate means to achieve change in a democratic society. But when the dissenter resorts to violence he erodes the institutions and values which are the underpinnings of our democratic society. We must not and will not tolerate violence.

As President Johnson has stated, "Our test is to rise above the debate between the rights of the individual and the rights of society by securing the rights of both."

. . .

We freely admit that the years we live in are years of turbulence. But the wisdom of history has something hopeful to say about times like these. It tells us that the giant American nation, on the move with giant strides, has never moved —and can never move—in silence.

We are an acting, doing, feeling people. We are a people whose deepest emotions are the source of the creative noise we make—precisely because of our ardent desire for unity, our wish for peace, our longing for concord, our demand for justice, our hope for material well being, our impulse to move always toward a more perfect union.

In that never-ending quest, we are all partners together—the industrialist and the banker, the workman and the storekeeper, the farmer and the scientist, the clerk and the engineer, the teacher and the student, the clergyman and the writer, the men of all colors and of all the different generations.

The American dream is not the exclusive property of any political party. But we submit that the Democratic Party has been the chief instrument of orderly progress in our time. As heirs to the longest tradition of any political party on earth, we Democrats have been trained over the generations to be a party of builders. And that experience has taught us that America builds best when it is called upon to build greatly.

We sound that call anew. With the active consent of the American people, we will prove anew that freedom is best secured by a government that is responsive and compassionate and committed to justice and the rule of law.

## Prohibition Platform 1968

### PREAMBLE

We, the representatives of the Prohibition Party, assembled in National Convention at Detroit, Michigan, June 28 and 29, 1967, recognizing Almighty God as the source of all just government, and with faith in the teachings of the Lord Jesus Christ, do solemnly promise that, if our party is chosen to administer the affairs of the nation, we will, with earnest dedication to the principles of righteousness, seek to serve the needs and to preserve the rights, the prerogatives and the basic freedoms, of the people of the United States of America. For the realization of these ends we propose the following program of government.

### CONSTITUTIONAL GOVERNMENT

We affirm our sincere loyalty to the Constitution of the United States, and express our deep confidence in that document as the basic law of the land. We will resist all attempts to violate it, whether by legislation, by means of evasion, or through judicial interpretation. We believe in the principles of liberty and justice enunciated in the Declaration of Independence and in the Preamble and Bill of Rights of our Constitution. We declare ourselves in hearty support of our system of representative government, with its plan of checks and balances, and express our firm intent to serve the people of our nation with a constructive, forward-looking program of good government, dedicated to the general welfare.

### COMMUNISM-TOTALITARIANISM

Recognizing that Communism is aggressively and unalterably opposed to our Constitutional government, we declare our opposition to it both as a way of life and as a governmental system. We believe that the program of Communism, with its intent to infiltrate and to overthrow our present form of government, must be pitilessly exposed. We challenge all loyal citizens to become fully aware of this menace to civilization, to exert every effort to defeat these "masters of deceit," and to help preserve our American way of life.

We also declare ourselves opposed to any other form of totalitarian philosophy or form of government. We endorse the efforts of those agencies which have been honestly and earnestly exposing subversive activities and groups.

## GOVERNMENTAL ECONOMY AND TAXATION

We view with alarm the extravagance and wasteful spending which have invaded government at all levels, demanding an ever-increasing tax load upon our people. The constant increase in taxation, requiring approximately one third of the total income of our citizens to pay the expenses of government, is approaching the point of confiscation, leading to economic chaos. We believe that good government does not attempt to do for people what they can do for themselves. With proper economy, governmental costs can be lowered, the tax load lightened, and the public debt can be reduced. We promise to devote ourselves to such an end, even though it involves either the reorganization or abolition of certain departments, bureaus and vested interests.

## MONEY AND FINANCE

A sound financial program and dependable monetary policy are fundamental to a stable economy. Our Constitution gives to Congress the power to "coin money" and "to regulate the value thereof." We believe that Congress, working with the executive branch of government, should take immediate steps to establish a financial program that will block inflationary trends, insure a sound currency, stabilize price levels and provide for systematic retirement of the national debt. We urge that careful consideration be given to a return to the gold standard, believing that such a step would help stabilize our economy, would promote confidence in our monetary system and would underwrite a continuing program of sound finance and expanding industrial progress.

## TAX SHARING

Recognizing that local and state governments are having real difficulty in meeting their basic financial needs, we advocate a division of the revenue received from the federal income tax, with appropriate amounts of the tax collected in each state being distributed to each of the state governments before becoming the property of the federal government.

## THE FEDERAL BUDGET

Good government and a sound economy re-

quire a balanced budget. The inflationary effects and the disturbing influences of unbalanced budgets must be eliminated. We cannot, with impunity, continue to increase the mortgage on our future and the interest load of the present. As the level of taxation is already excessive, there must be either a decided reduction in governmental services and federal spending or a substantial improvement in efficiency, with consequent elimination of waste in both personnel and materials. Actually, both areas need careful exploration with a view not only to maintaining a balanced budget, but also to reduction of the national debt.

## THE INCOME TAX

A federal income tax was first proposed by the Prohibition Party in 1896. However, the graduated tax and confiscatory rates of the present day were not contemplated. We seriously question the appropriateness of the present system and demand a thorough review of the basic fiscal policies of our government.

## FOREIGN AID

Many billions of dollars of our taxpayers' money have been and are still being given to foreign countries. Unfortunately, substantial portions have been used to support governments and programs considerably at variance with American ideals and concepts. It is frankly recognized that complex and baffling problems are involved in this area of international relations, but we insist that foreign governments have no inherent right to financial gifts at the expense of American taxpayers. Such aid does not purchase friendship, so should usually be in the form of repayable loans which will enable the beneficiaries to maintain their dignity and self-respect.

## A FREE ECONOMY

We are strongly opposed to burdensome restraints on our free enterprise system, to detailed regulation of our economic life and to federal interference with individual initiative. We believe that free enterprise is threatened in three ways: (1) by excessive governmental regulation, (2) by growth of public or private monopoly, and (3) by unethical practices of unscrupulous groups.

It will be the policy of our administration

to encourage independent, non-monopolistic business enterprises which serve genuine consumer needs and are operated with a sense of responsibility to the public. We will take necessary steps to prevent the evils both of monopoly and of excessive regulation by government, and to protect adequately the consuming public from irresponsible or deceptive practices contrary to the general welfare.

We propose that our government withdraw, with reasonable promptness, from the fields of business activity and sell to private industry, at proper investment prices, those business enterprises now owned and operated by the federal government.

## Labor and Industry

In the area of labor and industrial relations we believe that the public welfare must be given paramount consideration. Both management and labor must be held responsible for their economic and their social behavior. Neither should be permitted to dominate at the expense of the other or of the common good. Rather, the anti-trust laws must be applied equally to all monopolies, whether of business or labor. Whenever the public welfare is seriously endangered because of disputes affecting quasi-public businesses and utilities we favor the compulsory arbitration of labor-management disputes.

## Employee-Employer Rights

Every individual has certain basic and fundamental rights. A person's right to join or not to join a labor union without affecting his employment and his right to work for an employer willing to hire him must be protected. Likewise, employees and employers must be free to bargain and to contract as they wish. Violence or coercion, whether on the part of management or labor, should be prohibited.

## States Rights

Our founding fathers recognized the importance of both individual and states rights, and determined to preserve them by making the Bill of Rights an integral part of our Constitution. During recent years there has been an increasing tendency toward an undesirable concentration of power and authority in the federal government. This tendency has two principal causes:

(1) the ever-growing power and influence of the "military-industrial complex," and (2) a widespread tendency of groups of citizens to look to the federal government for the protection of rights and the satisfaction of needs which they feel are not adequately cared for by state and local governments or by private enterprise.

To deal with the first of these causes, we pledge the utmost vigilance in resisting the growth of militarism and in maintaining the constitutional principle of civilian supremacy over the military. To deal with overcentralization we urge more vigorous action by the state and local governments for the protection of the rights and the promotion of the welfare of their people, greater resort to the solution of local community problems through the voluntary action of existing or new civic and other non-governmental associations, where this is feasible, and the increasing pursuit by private business concerns of policies which promote the public interest.

We pledge ourselves to action that will preserve all legitimate rights and will maintain among the several states their constitutional place in our system of government.

## Human Rights

All American citizens, regardless of race, religion, or national origin are entitled to equality of treatment under the provisions of our constitution and under the laws of our land. No person or group of persons should be subjected to ostracism, humiliation, or embarrassment because of color or national background. At the same time, we must deplore the use of either violence or arbitrary pressure tactics, from whatever source, as a means of seeking to resolve tensions and divergencies of opinion among our citizens.

We are opposed to those proposals which would destroy our neighborhood school systems through a program of artificial integration or convey special privileges to any minority group.

## Public Morality

Moral and spiritual considerations must be primary factors in determining both state and national policies. We deplore the gross neglect of such matters by the dominant political parties, culminating in the shocking revelations of crime and of political and economic corruption which have characterized recent years. We charge these parties with basic responsibility for the rapid decline in moral standards which followed repeal of the Eighteenth Amendment. We believe that the program of nullification of law through non-enforcement which led to repeal contributed greatly to the disintegration of public morals, to a general deterioration of standards and to a lowering of values among our people.

We pledge ourselves to break the unholy alliance which has made these things possible. We propose to strengthen and to enforce laws against gambling, narcotics, and commercialized vice, to emphasize the basic importance of spiritual and moral values to the development and growth of an enduring nation, and to maintain the integrity of our democracy by careful enforcement of law and loyal support of our Constitution.

### WORLD PEACE

We pledge ourselves to search for peaceful solutions to international conflict by seeking to deal creatively and constructively with the underlying causes of international tension before they explode into hostilities, and to strive for world peace and order based upon the teachings and practices of the Prince of Peace.

### NATIONAL SOVEREIGNTY

We declare our belief in national sovereignty and oppose surrender of this sovereignty to any international group.

### NATIONAL PREPAREDNESS

Believing that "eternal vigilance is the price of liberty," we declare for a sound program of national military preparedness. While praying for peace we cannot place our freedom in peril by ignoring the potential threat to our nation.

However, we believe that the present program of compulsory peacetime military training does not represent a genuine safeguard to world peace. We rather believe it to be contrary, in principle, to our American way of life. This system places an unnecessary burden upon our peacetime economy, threatens us with possible military dictatorship, and often permits and promotes the moral and spiritual deterioration of our youth.

We urge that our peacetime defense be entrusted to professionally trained volunteers.

### NUCLEAR WEAPONS TESTING

Radioactive fallout, resulting from testing of nuclear weapons, endangers the health of human beings throughout the world, and if testing is engaged in, will increase the number of seriously defective children who will be born to future generations. The danger may become progressively greater with any additional testing. Also, there is the danger that continuation of the armaments race will lead to an atomic war of annihilation. We urge that all testing of nuclear weapons be indefinitely suspended on a multilateral basis with proper inspection safeguards, and that our government seek with renewed vigor and persistence an agreement among all nuclear powers for the permanent and complete cessation of nuclear tests for military purposes.

### RELIGIOUS LIBERTY

We believe in religious liberty. Freedom of the individual to worship, to fellowship with others of similar faith, to evangelize, to educate and to establish religious institutions, must be preserved. When religious liberty is lost political liberty will perish with it. We deplore ever increasing efforts to restrict freedom of religious broadcasting and the establishment of new churches. We caution the Internal Revenue Service against using the power to control tax exemptions to discriminate against evangelical Christianity.

We believe, also, that our government should take a firm, positive position against religious intolerance and persecution anywhere in the world.

### MARRIAGE AND DIVORCE

Ordained of God, the home is a sacred institution. Its sanctity must be protected and preserved. We favor the enactment of uniform marriage and divorce laws in the various states as an aid to building strong and enduring homes throughout our nation.

### SOCIAL SECURITY

We endorse the general principle of an actuarially sound social security insurance program which includes all employed groups. We question the soundness of the existing program, and the recent trend toward a welfare emphasis. We deplore the widespread current abuse of the privileges involved; we condemn the maladministration of its provisions for political ends; we pledge ourselves to correct these evils.

## Ballot Law Reform

True democracy requires that the needs and interests of minority groups be given fair, honest and appropriate consideration. Instead, in many of our states, ballot laws have been enacted which are designed to make a two party system into a bipartisan political monopoly, keeping minor parties off the ballot. We demand the repeal of all laws which deny to independent voters and all loyal minority groups the fundamental right of free political expression.

## Church and State

We affirm our continuing loyalty to the constitutional principle of separation of Church and State. We will expose, and resist vigorously, any attempt from whatever source to weaken or subvert this fundamental principle.

We declare our belief that the Bible is not a sectarian book, but is a volume of universal appeal and application which is woven into our history, our laws, and our culture. We deplore any interpretation which would limit its use in any area of our national life.

In the area of government, we endorse encouragement of non-profit educational and religious institutions on a tax-exempt basis, but we declare strong opposition to all efforts, direct or indirect, to secure appropriations of public money for private religious or sectarian purposes.

## Education

It is altogether appropriate that our federal government should be interested in and concerned about matters pertaining to all areas of educational growth and development. However, under the Tenth Amendment, public education is clearly to be under the control of the states. We are opposed to direct federal aid to education, believing that each state should both support and control its own educational program.

## Agriculture

The production and distribution of agricultural products is of vital importance to the economy of any people. We believe that those engaged in agricultural pursuits, like other American citizens, should be free from authoritarian control

and coercion. Hence we declare ourselves opposed to regimentation of farms and farmers and urge a sensible and orderly return to a free market program.

## Public Health

The health of our people is a matter of fundamental importance. We are deeply concerned with this matter in its many aspects. We are disturbed by the increasing use of narcotic and psychedelic drugs. Recognizing that the use of tobacco products constitutes a health hazard, we are opposed to promotional advertising of such products and to subsidization of tobacco growing. We insist that caution must be taken in dealing with mental health cases, lest there be unjust and prejudiced incarcerations. We deplore those programs of mass medication which violate the rights of individuals. We insist on the right of everyone to a pure water supply and to an unpolluted atmosphere, and hold that each of our states must insure these.

We pledge enforcement of existing laws regulating these health concerns, the enactment of additional needed legislation and cooperation with state efforts to deal with the problems.

## Service, Not Spoils

The Prohibition Party first sponsored our civil service system. On the other hand, the dominant political parties are positively committed to the "spoils" system and, when in office, have prostituted governmental power to serve their own selfish party interests instead of the whole people. This has led to excessive expenditures, higher taxes and, in some situations, to an unfortunate alliance of crime with politics. We pledge ourselves to an honest, efficient and economical administration.

## The Alcohol Problem

Beverage alcohol must today be recognized as the chief cause of poverty, broken homes, juvenile delinquency, vice, crime, political corruption, wasted manpower and highway accidents. By the most conservative estimates, more than 6,000,000 alcoholics and 6,000,000 problem drinkers are currently victims of alcohol.

No greater mistake has ever been made by the American people and their government than the Repeal of Prohibition. Contrary to the promises made by the advocates of repeal, bootlegging has increased to the point where the liquor industry itself claims that one-third of all alcohol consumed today in America is illicit; drinking among our young people has reached epidemic proportions; liquor taxes pay only a small fraction of the traffic's cost to the taxpayers and the "open saloon" which was to be "banished forever" is back in a newer form and more numerous than ever.

The liquor traffic is linked with and supports a nationwide network of gambling, vice and crime. It also dominates both major political parties and, thru them, much of the governmental and political life of our nation. As long as the two dominant parties are largely controlled by the liquor traffic, just so long will they be unable to make moral principles prevail.

The Prohibition Party alone offers a program to deal with this greatest of social ills. We pledge ourselves to a program of publicity, education, legislation and administration, leading to the elimination of beverage alcohol industry. We will repeal all laws which legalize the liquor traffic and enact and rigorously enforce new laws which prohibit the manufacture, distribution and sale of alcoholic beverages.

We urge all Americans who favor sobriety and righteousness to join with us in electing an administration pledged to the above program.

## Republican Platform 1968

PREAMBLE, PURPOSES AND PLEDGES

Twice before, our Party gave the people of America leadership at a time of crisis—leadership which won us peace in place of war, unity in place of discord, compassion in place of bitterness.

A century ago, Abraham Lincoln gave that leadership. From it came one nation, consecrated to liberty and justice for all.

Fifteen years ago, Dwight D. Eisenhower gave that leadership. It brought the end of a war, eight years of peace, enhanced respect in the world, orderly progress at home, and trust of our people in their leaders and in themselves.

Today, we are in turmoil.

Tens of thousands of young men have died or been wounded in Vietnam.

Many young people are losing faith in our society.

Our inner cities have become centers of despair.

Millions of Americans are caught in the cycle of poverty—poor education, unemployment or serious under-employment, and the inability to afford decent housing.

Inflation has eroded confidence in the dollar at home and abroad. It has severely cut into the incomes of all families, the jobless, the farmers, the retired and those living on fixed incomes and pensions.

Today's Americans are uncertain about the future, and frustrated about the recent past.

America urgently needs new leadership—leadership courageous and understanding—leadership that will recapture control of events, mastering them rather than permitting them to master us, thus restoring our confidence in ourselves and in our future.

Our need is new leadership which will develop imaginative new approaches assuring full opportunity to all our citizens—leadership which will face and resolve the basic problems of our country.

Our Convention in 1968 can spark a "Republican Resurgence" under men and women willing to face the realities of the world in which we live.

We must urgently dedicate our efforts toward restoration of peace both at home and abroad.

We must bring about a national commitment to rebuild our urban and rural slum areas.

We must enable family farm enterprise to participate fully in the nation's prosperity.

We must bring about quality education for all.

We must assure every individual an opportunity for satisfying and rewarding employment.

We must attack the root causes of poverty and eradicate racism, hatred and violence.

We must give all citizens the opportunity to influence and shape the events of our time.

We must give increasing attention to the views of the young and recognize their key role in our present as well as the future.

We must mobilize the resources, talents and energy of public and private sectors to reach these goals, utilizing the unique strength and initiative of state and local governments.

We must re-establish fiscal responsibility and put an end to increases in the cost of living.

We must reaffirm our commitment to Lincoln's challenge of one hundred six years ago. To Congress he wrote: "The dogmas of the quiet past are inadequate to the stormy present. The occasion is piled high with difficulty and we must rise with the occasion. As our case is new, so we must think anew and act anew. We must disenthrall ourselves and then we shall save our country."

In this, our stormy present, let us rededicate ourselves to Lincoln's thesis. Let the people know our commitment to provide the dynamic leadership which they rightly expect of this Party—the Party not of empty promises, but of performance—the Party not of wastefulness, but of responsibility—the Party not of war, but the Party whose Administrations have been characterized by peace—the Republican Party.

To these ends, we solemnly pledge to every American that we shall think anew and act anew.

DOMESTIC POLICY

A peaceful, reunified America, with opportunity and orderly progress for all—these are our overriding domestic goals.

Clearly we must think anew about the relationship of man and his government, of man and his fellow-man. We must act anew to enlarge the opportunity and autonomy of the individual and the range of his choice.

Republican leadership welcomes challenge.

We eagerly anticipate new achievement.

A new, vital partnership of government at all levels will be a prime Republican objective. We will broaden the base of decision-making. We will create a new mix of private responsibility and public participation in the solution of social problems.

There is so much which urgently needs to be done.

In many areas poverty and its attendant ills afflict large numbers of Americans. Distrust and fear plague us all. Our inner cities teem with poor, crowded in slums. Many rural areas are run down and barren of challenge or opportunity. Minorities among us—particularly the black community, the Mexican-American, the American Indian—suffer disproportionately.

Americans critically need—and are eager for—new and dynamic leadership. We offer that leadership—a leadership to eradicate bitterness and discrimination—responsible, compassionate leadership that will keep its word—leadership every citizen can count on to move this nation forward again, confident, reunited, and sure of purpose.

*Crisis of the Cities*

For today and tomorrow, there must be—and we pledge—a vigorous effort, nation-wide, to transform the blighted areas of cities into centers of opportunity and progress, culture and talent.

For tomorrow, new cities must be developed—and smaller cities with room to grow, expanded—to house and serve another 100 million Americans by the turn of the century.

The need is critical. Millions of our people are suffering cruelly from expanding metropolitan blight—congestion, crime, polluted air and water, poor housing, inadequate educational, economic and recreational opportunities. This continuing decay of urban centers—the deepening misery and limited opportunity of citizens living there—is intolerable in America. We promise effective, sustainable action enlisting new energies by the private sector and by governments at all levels. We pledge:

Presidential leadership which will buttress state and local government;

Vigorous federal support to innovative state programs, using new policy techniques such as urban development corporations, to help rebuild our cities;

Energetic, positive leadership to enforce statutory and constitutional protections to eliminate discrimination;

Concern for the unique problems of citizens long disadvantaged in our total society by race, color, national origin, creed, or sex;

A greater involvement of vast private enterprise resources in the improvement of urban life, induced by tax and other incentives;

New technological and administrative approaches through flexible federal programs enabling and encouraging communities to solve their own problems;

A complete overhaul and restructuring of the competing and overlapping jumble of federal programs to enable state and local governments to focus on priority objectives.

These principles as urgently apply to rural poverty and decay. There must be a marked improvement of economic and educational opportunities to relieve widespread distress. Success with urban problems in fact requires acceleration of rural development in order to stem the flow of people from the countryside to the city.

Air and water pollution, already acute in many areas, require vigorous state and federal action, regional planning, and maximum cooperation among neighboring cities, counties and states. We will encourage this planning and cooperation and also spur industrial participation by means of economic incentives.

Skyrocketing building costs and interest rates have crippled home building and threaten a housing crisis in the nation, endangering the prospect of a decent home and a suitable living environment for every family. We will vigorously implement the Republican-conceived homeownership program for lower income families and also the Republican-sponsored rent certificate program. Economic incentives will be developed to attract private industry and capital to the low-cost housing market. By reducing interest rates through responsible fiscal and monetary policy we will lower the costs of homeownership, and new technologies and programs will be developed to stimulate low-cost methods of housing rehabilitation. Local communities will be encouraged to adopt uniform, modern building codes, research in cost-cutting technology through private enterprise will be accelerated, and innovative state and local programs will be supported. We will also stimulate the investment of "sweat equity" by home owners.

Our metropolitan transportation systems—the lifelines of our cities—have become tangled webs of congestion which not only create vast citizen inconvenience, discontent and economic inefficiency, but also tend to barricade inner city people against job opportunities in suburban areas. We will encourage priority attention by private enterprise and all levels of government to sound planning and the rapid development of improved mass transportation systems. Additionally, in the location of federal buildings and installations and the awarding of federal contracts,

account will be taken of such factors as traffic congestion, housing, and the effect on community development.

Americans are acutely aware that none of these objectives can be achieved unless order through law and justice is maintained in our cities. Fire and looting, causing millions of dollars of property damage, have brought great suffering to home owners and small businessmen, particularly in black communities least able to absorb catastrophic losses. The Republican Party strongly advocates measures to alleviate and remove the frustrations that contribute to riots. We simultaneously support decisive action to quell civil disorder, relying primarily on state and local governments to deal with these conditions.

America has adequate peaceful and lawful means for achieving even fundamental social change if the people wish it. We will not tolerate violence!

*Crime*

Lawlessness is crumbling the foundations of American society.

Republicans believe that respect for the law is the cornerstone of a free and well-ordered society. We pledge vigorous and even-handed administration of justice and enforcement of the law. We must re-establish the principle that men are accountable for what they do, that criminals are responsible for their crimes, that while the youth's environment may help to explain the man's crime, it does not excuse that crime.

We call on public officials at the federal, state and local levels to enforce our laws with firmness and fairness. We recognize that respect for law and order flows naturally from a just society; while demanding protection of the public peace and safety, we pledge a relentless attack on economic and social injustice in every form.

The present Administration has:

Ignored the danger signals of our rising crime rates until very recently and even now has proposed only narrow measures hopelessly inadequate to the need;

Failed to implement most of the recommendations of the President's own Crime Commission;

Opposed legislative measures that would assist law enforcement officials in bringing law-breakers to justice;

Refused to sanction the use of either the court-supervised wiretapping authority to combat organized crime or the revised rules of evidence, both made available by Congress;

Failed to deal effectively with threats to the nation's internal security by not prosecuting identified subversives.

By contrast, Republican leadership in Congress has:

Provided funds for programs administered by state and local governments to control juvenile delinquency and crime;

Created a National Institute of Law Enforcement and Criminal Justice to conduct crime research and facilitate the expansion of police training programs;

Secured enactment of laws enabling law enforcement officials to obtain and use evidence needed to prosecute criminals, while at the same time protecting the rights and privacy of all citizens;

Secured new laws aimed at "loan-sharking," the intimidation of witnesses, and obstruction of investigations;

Established disability as well as survivorship benefits for local police officers wounded or killed in pursuit of federal lawbreakers.

For the future, we pledge an all-out, federal-state-local crusade against crime, including:

Leadership by an Attorney General who will restore stature and respect to that office;

Continued support of legislation to strengthen state and local law enforcement and preserve the primacy of state responsibility in this area;

Full support of the F.B.I. and all law enforcement agencies of the federal government;

Improved federal cooperation with state and local law enforcement agencies;

Better coordination of the federal law enforcement, crime control, and criminal justice systems;

A vigorous nation-wide drive against trafficking in narcotics and dangerous drugs, including special emphasis on the first steps toward addiction—the use of marijuana and such drugs as LSD;

Total commitment to a federal program to deter, apprehend, prosecute, convict and punish the overlords of organized crime in America, including full implementation of the Congressional mandate that court-supervised wiretapping and

electronic surveillance tools be used against the mobsters and racketeers;

Increased public protection against racketeer infiltration into legitimate business;

Increased research into the causes and prevention of crime, juvenile delinquency, and drug addiction;

Creation of a Federal Corrections Service to consolidate the fragmented and overlapping federal efforts and to assist state and local corrections systems;

A new approach to the problem of chronic offenders, including adequate staffing of the corrections system and improvement of rehabilitative techniques;

Modernization of the federal judicial system to promote swift, sure justice;

Enactment of legislation to control indiscriminate availability of firearms, safeguarding the right of responsible citizens to collect, own and use firearms for legitimate purposes, retaining primary responsibility at the state level, with such federal laws as necessary to better enable the states to meet their responsibilities.

*Youth*

More than any other nation, America reflects the strength and creative energy of youth. In every productive enterprise, the vigor, imagination and skills of our young people have contributed immeasurably to progress.

Our youth today are endowed with greater knowledge and maturity than any such generation of the past. Their political restlessness reflects their urgent hope to achieve a meaningful participation in public affairs commensurate with their contributions as responsible citizens.

In recognition of the abilities of these younger citizens, their desire to participate, and their service in the nation's defense, we believe that lower age groups should be accorded the right to vote. We believe that states which have not yet acted should reevaluate their positions with respect to 18-year-old voting, and that each such state should decide this matter for itself. We urge the states to act now.

For greater equity we will further revise Selective Service policies and reduce the number of years during which a young man can be considered for the draft, thereby providing some certainty to those liable for military service. When military manpower needs can be appreciably reduced, we will place the Selective Service System on standby and substitute a voluntary force obtained through adequate pay and career incentives.

We encourage responsible young men and women to join actively in the political process to help shape the future of the nation. We invite them to join our Republican effort to assure the new direction and the new leadership which this nation so urgently needs and rightfully expects.

*Education*

The birthplace of American opportunity has been in the classrooms of our schools and colleges. From early childhood through the college years, American schools must offer programs of education sufficiently flexible to meet the needs of all Americans—the advantaged, the average, the disadvantaged and the handicapped alike. To help our educators meet this need we will establish a National Commission to Study the Quality and Relevance of American Education.

To treat the special problems of children from impoverished families, we advocate expanded, better programs for pre-school children. We will encourage state, local or private programs of teacher training. The development and increased use of better teaching methods and modern instruction techniques such as educational television and voluntary bilingual education will continue to have our support.

To help assure excellence and equality of educational opportunity, we will urge the states to present plans for federal assistance which would include state distribution of such aid to non-public school children and include non-public school representatives in the planning process. Where state conditions prevent use of funds for non-public school children, a public agency should be designated to administer federal funds.

Greater vocational education in high school and post-high school years is required for a new technological and service-oriented economy. Young people need expansion of post-high school technical institutes to enable them to acquire satisfactory skills for meaningful employment. For youths unable to obtain such training, we propose an industry youth program, coupled with a flexible approach to minimum wage laws for young entry-level workers during their training periods.

The rapidly mounting enrollments and costs of colleges and universities deprive many qualified young people of the opportunity to obtain a quality college education. To help colleges and universities provide this opportunity, we favor grant and loan programs for expansion of their facilities. We will also support a flexible student aid program of grants, loans and work opportunities, provided by federal and state governments and private organizations. We continue to favor tax credits for those burdened with the costs of higher education, and also tax deductions to encourage savings for this purpose. No young American should be denied a quality education because he cannot afford it or find work to meet its costs.

HUMAN DEVELOPMENT

The inability of the poor to cope meaningfully with their environment is compounded by problems which blunt opportunity—inadequate income, inferior education, inadequate health care, slum housing, limited job opportunities, discrimination, and crime.

Full opportunity requires a coordinated attack on the total problem through community human development programs. Federal revenue sharing would help provide the resources to develop such coordinated programs.

*Jobs*

The nation must look to an expanding free enterprise system to provide jobs. Republican policies and programs will encourage this expansion.

To qualify for jobs with permanence and promise, many disadvantaged citizens need special assistance and job training. We will enact the Republican-proposed Human Investment Act, offering tax credits to employers, to encourage such training and upgrading.

A complete overhaul of the nation's job programs is urgent. There are some 70 federally funded job training programs, with some cities having as many as 30 operating side by side. Some of these programs are ineffective and should be eliminated. We will simplify the federal effort and also encourage states and localities to establish single-headed manpower systems, to correlate all such federal activities and gear them to local conditions and needs. Local business advisory boards will assist in the design of such programs to fit training to employment needs. To help the unemployed find work we will also inaugurate a national Job Opportunity Data Bank to report the number, nature and location of unfilled jobs and to match the individuals with the jobs.

*The Poor*

Welfare and poverty programs will be drastically revised to liberate the poor from the debilitating dependence which erodes self-respect and discourages family unity and responsibility. We will modify the rigid welfare requirements that stifle work motivation and support locally operated children's day-care centers to free the parents to accept work.

Burdensome administrative procedures will be simplified, and existing programs will be revised so that they will encourage and protect strong family units.

This nation must not blink the harsh fact—or the special demands it places upon us—that the incidence of poverty is consistently greater among Negroes, Mexican-Americans, Indians and other minority groupings than in the population generally.

An essential element of economic betterment is the opportunity for self-determination—to develop or acquire and manage one's own business enterprise. This opportunity is bleak for most residents of impoverished areas. We endorse the concept of state and community development corporations. These will provide capital, technical assistance and insurance for the establishment and renewal of businesses in depressed urban and rural areas. We favor efforts to enable residents of such areas to become owners and managers of businesses and, through such agencies as a Domestic Development Bank, to exercise economic leadership in their communities.

Additionally, we support action by states, with federal re-insurance, to help provide insurance coverage for homes and small businesses against damage and fire caused by riots.

We favor maximum reliance on community leaders utilizing the regular channels of government to provide needed public services. One approach is the Republican-sponsored Community Service Corps which would augment cooperation and communication between community residents and the police.

In programs for the socially and economically disadvantaged we favor participation by representatives of those to be served. The failure so to encourage creative and responsible participation from among the poor has been the greatest among the host of failures of the War on Poverty.

Recent studies indicate that many Americans suffer from malnutrition despite six separate federal food distribution programs. Here again, fragmentation of federal effort hinders accomplishment. We pledge a unified federal food distribution program, as well as active cooperation with the states and innovative private enterprise, to help provide the hungry poor sufficient food for a balanced diet.

A new Republican Administration will strive for fairness for all consumers, including additional information and protection programs as necessary, state and local consumer education, vigorous enforcement of the numerous protection laws already enacted, and active encouragement of the many consumer-protection initiatives and organizations of private enterprise.

*Health*

The inflation produced by the Johnson-Humphrey Administration has struck hardest in the area of health care. Hospital costs are rising 16 percent a year—four times the national average of price increases.

We pledge to encourage the broadening of private health insurance plans, many of which cover hospital care only, and to review the operation of government hospital care programs in order to encourage more patients to utilize non-hospital facilities. Expansion of the number of doctors, nurses, and supporting staff to relieve shortages and spread the availability of health care services will have our support. We will foster the construction of additional hospitals and encourage regional hospital and health planning for the maximum development of facilities for medical and nursing care. We will also press for enactment of Republican-sponsored programs for financing of hospital modernization. New diagnostic methods and also preventive care to assure early detection of physical impairments, thus fostering good health and avoiding illnesses requiring hospitalization, will have our support.

Additionally, we will work with states and local communities to help assure improved services to the mentally ill within a community setting and will intensify research to develop better treatment methods. We will encourage extension of private health insurance to cover mental illness.

While believing no American should be denied adequate medical treatment, we will be diligent in protecting the traditional patient-doctor relationship and the integrity of the medical practitioner.

We are especially concerned with the difficult circumstances of thousands of handicapped citizens who daily encounter architectural barriers which they are physically unable to surmount. We will support programs to reduce and where possible to eliminate such barriers in the construction of federal buildings.

## The Elderly

Elderly Americans desire and deserve independence, dignity, and the opportunity for continued useful participation. We will strengthen the Social Security system and provide automatic cost of living adjustments under Social Security and the Railroad Retirement Act. An increase in earnings permitted to Social Security recipients without loss of benefits, provision for post-age 65 contributions to Social Security with deferment of benefits, and an increase in benefits to widows will also be provided. The age for universal Social Security coverage will be gradually reduced from 72 to 65 and the former 100 percent income tax deduction will be restored for medical and drug expenses for people over 65. Additionally, we will take steps to help improve and extend private pension plans.

## Veterans

The Republican Party pledges vigorous efforts to assure jobs for returning Vietnam war veterans, as well as other assistance to enable them and their families to establish living conditions befitting their brave service. We pledge a rehabilitation allowance for paraplegics to afford them the means to live outside a hospital environment. Adequate medical and hospital care will be maintained for all veterans with service-connected disabilities and veterans in need, and timely revisions of compensation programs will be enacted for service-connected death and disability to help assure an adequate standard of living for all disabled veterans and their survivors. We will see that every veteran is accorded the right to be interred in a national cemetery as near as possible to his home, and we pledge to maintain all veterans' programs in an independent Veterans Administration.

## Indian Affairs

The plight of American Indians and Eskimos is a national disgrace. Contradictory government policies have led to intolerable deprivation for these citizens. We dedicate ourselves to the promotion of policies responsive to their needs and desires and will seek the full participation of these people and their leaders in the formulation of such policies.

Inequality of jobs, of education, of housing and of health blight their lives today. We believe the Indian and Eskimo must have an equal opportunity to participate fully in American society. Moreover, the uniqueness and beauty of these native cultures must be recognized and allowed to flourish.

## THE INDIVIDUAL AND GOVERNMENT

In recent years an increasingly impersonal national government has tended to submerge the individual. An entrenched, burgeoning bureaucracy has increasingly usurped powers, unauthorized by Congress. Decentralization of power, as well as strict Congressional oversight of administrative and regulatory agency compliance with the letter and spirit of the law, are urgently needed to preserve personal liberty, improve efficiency, and provide a swifter response to human problems.

Many states and localities are eager to revitalize their own administrative machinery, procedures, and personnel practices. Moreover, there is growing inter-state cooperation in such fields as education, elimination of air and water pollution, utilization of airports, highways and mass transportation. We pledge full federal cooperation with these efforts, including revision of the system of providing federal funds and reestablishment of the authority of state governments in coordinating and administering the federal programs. Additionally, we propose the sharing of federal revenues with state governments. We are particularly determined to revise the grant-in-aid system and substitute bloc grants wherever possible. It is also important that state and local governments retain the historic right to raise funds by issuing tax-exempt securities.

The strengthening of citizen influence on government requires a number of improvements in political areas. For instance, we propose to reform the electoral college system, establish a nation-wide, uniform voting period for Presidential elections, and recommend that the states remove unreasonable requirements, residence and otherwise, for voting in Presidential elections. We specifically favor representation in Congress for the District of Columbia. We will work to establish a system of self-government for the District of Columbia which will take into account the interests of the private citizens thereof, and those of the federal government.

We will support the efforts of the Puerto Rican people to achieve statehood when they freely request such status by a general election, and we share the hopes and aspirations of the people of the Virgin Islands who will be closely consulted on proposed gubernatorial appointments.

We favor a new Election Reform Act that will apply clear, reasonable restraints to political spending and fund-raising, whether by business, labor or individuals, ensure timely publication of the financial facts in campaigns, and provide a tax deduction for small contributions.

We will prevent the solicitation of federal workers for political contributions and assure comparability of federal salaries with private enterprise pay. The increasing government intrusion into the privacy of its employees and of citizens in general is intolerable. All such snooping, meddling, and pressure by the federal government on its employees and other citizens will be stopped and such employees, whether or not union members, will be provided a prompt and fair method of settling their grievances. Further, we pledge to protect federal employees in the exercise of their right freely and without fear of penalty or reprisal to form, join or assist any employee organization or to refrain from any such activities.

Congress itself must be reorganized and modernized in order to function efficiently as a co-equal branch of government. Democrats in control of Congress have opposed Republican efforts for Congressional reform and killed legislation embodying the recommendations of a special bipartisan committee. We will again press for enactment of this measure.

We are particularly concerned over the huge and mounting postal deficit and the evidence, recently stressed by the President's Commission on Postal Organization, of costly and inefficient practices in the postal establishment. We pledge full consideration of the Commission's recommendations for improvements in the nation's postal service. We believe the Post Office Department must attract and retain the best qualified and most capable employees and offer them improved opportunities for advancement and better working conditions and incentives. We favor extension of the merit principle to postmasters and rural carriers.

Public confidence in an independent judiciary is absolutely essential to the maintenance of law and order. We advocate application of the highest standards in making appointments to the courts, and we pledge a determined effort to rebuild and enhance public respect for the Supreme Court and all other courts in the United States.

## A Healthy Economy

The dynamism of our economy is produced by millions of individuals who have the incentive to participate in decision-making that advances themselves and society as a whole. Government can reinforce these incentives, but its overinvolvement in individual decisions distorts the system and intrudes inefficiency and waste.

Under the Johnson-Humphrey Administration we have had economic mismanagement of the highest order. Inflation robs our pay checks at a present rate of 4½ percent per year. In the past three years the real purchasing power of the average wage and salary worker has actually declined. Crippling interest rates, some the highest in a century, prevent millions of Americans from buying homes and small businessmen, farmers and other citizens from obtaining the loans they need. Americans must work longer today than ever before to pay their taxes.

New Republican leadership can and will restore fiscal integrity and sound monetary policies, encourage sustained economic vitality, and avoid such economic distortions as wage and price controls. We favor strengthened Congressional control over federal expenditures by scheduled Congressional reviews of, or reasonable time limits on, unobligated appropriations. By responsibly applying federal expenditure controls to priority needs, we can in time live both within our means and up to our aspirations. Such funds as become available with the termination of the Vietnam war and upon recovery from its impact on our national defense will be applied in a balanced way to critical domestic needs and to reduce the heavy tax burden. Our objective is not an endless expansion of federal programs and expenditures financed by heavier taxation. The imperative need for tax reform and simplification will have our priority attention. We will also improve the management of the national debt, reduce its heavy interest burden, and seek amendment of the law to make reasonable price stability an explicit objective of government policy.

The Executive Branch needs urgently to be made a more efficient and economical instrument of public policy. Low priority activities must be eliminated and conflicting missions and functions simplified. We pledge to establish a new Efficiency Commission to root out the unnecessary and overlapping, as well as a Presidential Office of Executive Management to assure a vigorous follow-through.

A new Republican Administration will undertake an intensive program to aid small business, including economic incentives and technical assistance, with increased emphasis in rural and urban poverty areas.

In addition to vigorous enforcement of the antitrust statutes, we pledge a thorough analysis of the structure and operation of these laws at home and abroad in the light of changes in the economy, in order to update our antitrust policy and enable it to serve us well in the future.

We are determined to eliminate and prevent improper federal competition with private enterprise.

*Labor*

Organized labor has contributed greatly to the economic strength of our country and the well-being of its members. The Republican Party vigorously endorses its key role in our national life.

We support an equitable minimum wage for American workers—one providing fair wages without unduly increasing unemployment among those on the lowest rung of the economic ladder—and will improve the Fair Labor Standards Act, with its important protections for employees.

The forty-hour week adopted 30 years ago needs re-examination to determine whether or not a shorter work week, without loss of wages, would produce more jobs, increase productivity and stabilize prices.

We strongly believe that the protection of individual liberty is the cornerstone of sound labor policy. Today, basic rights of some workers, guaranteed by law, are inadequately guarded against abuse. We will assure these rights through vigorous enforcement of present laws, including the Taft-Hartley Act and the Landrum-Griffin Act, and the addition of new protections where needed. We will be vigilant to prevent any administrative agency entrusted with labor-law enforcement from defying the letter and spirit of these laws.

Healthy private enterprise demands responsibility—by government, management and labor—to avoid the imposition of excessive costs or prices and to share with the consumer the benefits of increased productivity. It also demands responsibility in free collective bargaining, not only by labor and management, but also by those in government concerned with these sensitive relationships.

We will bar government-coerced strike settlements that cynically disregard the public interest and accelerate inflation. We will again reduce government intervention in labor-management disputes to a minimum, keep government participation in channels defined by the Congress, and prevent back-door intervention in the administration of labor laws.

Repeated Administration promises to recommend legislation dealing with crippling economic strikes have never been honored. Instead, settlements forced or influenced by government and overriding the interests of the parties and the public have shattered the Administration's own wage and price guidelines and contributed to inflation.

Effective methods for dealing with labor disputes involving the national interest must be developed. Permanent, long-range solutions of the problems of national emergency disputes, public employee strikes and crippling work stoppages are imperative. These solutions cannot be wisely formulated in the heat of emergency. We pledge an intensive effort to develop practical, acceptable solutions that conform fully to the public interest.

*Transportation*

Healthy economic growth demands a balanced, competitive transportation system in which each mode of transportation—train, truck, barge, bus and aircraft—is efficiently utilized. The Administration's failure to evolve a coordinated transportation policy now results in outrageous delays at major airports and in glacial progress in developing high-speed train transportation linking our major population centers.

The nation's air transport system performs excellently, but under increasingly adverse conditions. Airways and airport congestion has become acute. New and additional equipment, modern facilities including the use of computers, and additional personnel must be provided without further delay. We pledge expert evaluation of these matters in developing a national air transportation system.

We will make the Department of Transportation the agency Congress intended it to be—effective in promoting coordination and preserving competition among carriers. We promise equitable treatment of all modes of transportation in order to assure the public better service, greater safety, and the most modern facilities. We will also explore a trust fund approach to transportation, similar to the fund developed for the Eisenhower interstate highway system, and perhaps in this way speed the development of modern mass transportation systems and additional airports.

RESOURCES AND SCIENCE

*Agriculture*

During seven and a half years of Democrat Administrations and Democrat Congresses the farmer has been the forgotten man in our nation's economy. The cost-price squeeze has steadily worsened, driving more than four and a half million people from the farms, many to already congested urban areas. Over eight hundred thousand individual farm units have gone out of existence.

During the eight years of the Eisenhower Administration, the farm parity ratio averaged 85. Under Democratic rule, the parity ratio has consistently been under 80 and averaged only 74 for all of 1967. It has now fallen to 73. Actions by the Administration, in line with its apparent cheap food policy, have held down prices received by farmers. Government payments to farmers, from taxes paid by consumers, have far from offset this loss.

Inflationary policies of the Administration and its Congress have contributed greatly to increased costs of production. Using 1958 as a base year with an index of 100, prices paid by farmers in 1967 had risen to a weighted index of 117, whereas the prices they received were at a weighted index of only 104. From the 1958 index of 100, interest was up to 259, taxes 178, labor costs 146, and farm machinery 130.

The cost-price squeeze has been accompanied by a dangerous increase in farm debt—up nearly $24 billion in the last seven years. In 1967 alone, net debt per farm increased $1,337 while net income per farm went down $605. While net farm equity has increased, it is due mainly to inflated land values. Without adequate net income to pay off indebtedness, the farm owner has no choice but to liquidate some of his equity or go out of business. Farm tenants are even worse off, since they have no comparable investment for inflation to increase in value as their indebtedness increases.

The Republican Party is committed to the concept that a sound agricultural economy is imperative to the national interest. Prosperity, opportunity, abundance, and efficiency in agriculture benefit every American. To promote the development of American agriculture, we pledge:

Farm policies and programs which will enable producers to receive fair prices in relation to the prices they must pay for other products;

Sympathetic consideration of proposals to encourage farmers, especially small producers, to develop their bargaining position;

Sound economic policies which will brake inflation and reduce the high interest rates;

A truly two-way export-import policy which

protects American agriculture from unfair foreign competition while increasing our overseas commodity dollar sales to the rapidly expanding world population;

Reorganization of the management of the Commodity Credit Corporation's inventory operations so that the Corporation will no longer compete with the marketings of farmers;

Improved programs for distribution of food and milk to schools and low-income citizens;

A strengthened program to export our food and farm technology in keeping with the Republican-initiated Food for Peace program;

Assistance to farm cooperatives including rural electric and telephone cooperatives, consistent with prudent development of our nation's resources and rural needs;

Greater emphasis on research for industrial uses of agricultural products, new markets, and new methods for cost-cutting in production and marketing techniques;

Revitalization of rural America through programs emphasizing vocational training, economic incentives for industrial development, and the development of human resources;

Improvement of credit programs to help finance the heavy capital needs of modern farming, recognizing the severe credit problems of young farm families seeking to enter into successful farming;

A more direct voice for the American farmer in shaping his own destiny.

*Natural Resources*

In the tradition of Theodore Roosevelt, the Republican Party promises sound conservation and development of natural resources in cooperative government and private programs.

An expanding population and increasing material wealth require new public concern for the quality of our environment. Our nation must pursue its activities in harmony with the environment. As we develop our natural resources we must be mindful of our priceless heritage of natural beauty.

A national minerals and fuels policy is essential to maintain production needed for our nation's economy and security. Present economic incentives, including depletion allowances, to encourage the discovery and development of vital minerals and fuels must be continued. We must

recognize the increasing demand for minerals and fuels by our economy, help ensure an economically stable industry, maintain a favorable balance of trade and balance of payments, and encourage research to promote the wise use of these resources.

Federal laws applicable to public lands and related resources will be updated and a public land-use policy formulated. We will manage such lands to ensure their multiple use as economic resources and recreational areas. Additionally, we will work in cooperation with cities and states in acquiring and developing green space—convenient outdoor recreation and conservation areas. We support the creation of additional national parks, wilderness areas, monuments and outdoor recreation areas at appropriate sites, as well as their continuing improvement, to make them of maximum utility and enjoyment to the public.

Improved forestry practices, including protection and improvement of watershed lands, will have our vigorous support. We will also improve water resource information, including an acceleration of river basin commission inventory studies. The reclaiming of land by irrigation and the development of flood control programs will have high priority in these studies. We will support additional multi-purpose water projects for reclamation, flood control, and recreation based on accurate cost-benefit estimates.

We also support efforts to increase our total fresh water supply by further research in weather modification, and in better methods of desalinization of salt and brackish waters.

The United States has dropped to sixth among the fishing nations of the world. We pledge a reversal of present policies and the adoption of a progressive national fisheries policy, which will make it possible for the first time to utilize fully the vast ocean reservoir of protein. We pledge a more energetic control of pollution, encouragement of an increase in fishery resources, and will also press for international agreements assuring multi-national conservation.

We pledge a far more vigorous and systematic program to expand knowledge about the unexplored storehouses of the sea and polar regions. We must undertake a comprehensive polar plan and an oceanographic program to develop these abundant resources for the continued strength of the United States and the betterment of all mankind.

*Science*

In science and technology the nation must maintain leadership against increasingly challenging competition from abroad. Crucial to this leadership is growth in the supply of gifted, skilled scientists and engineers. Government encouragement in this critical area should be stable and related to a more rational and selective scheme of priorities.

Vigorous effort must be directed toward increasing the application of science and technology, including the social sciences, to the solution of such pressing human problems as housing, transportation, education, environmental pollution, law enforcement, and job training. We support a strong program of research in the sciences, with protection for the independence and integrity of participating individuals and institutions. An increase in the number of centers of scientific creativity and excellence, geographically dispersed, and active cooperation with other nations in meaningful scientific undertakings will also have our support.

We regret that the Administration's budgetary mismanagement has forced sharp reductions in the space program. The Republican Party shares the sense of urgency manifested by the scientific community concerning the exploration of outer space. We recognize that the peaceful applications of space probes in communications, health, weather, and technological advances have been beneficial to every citizen. We regard the ability to launch and deploy advanced spacecraft as a military necessity. We deplore the failure of the Johnson-Humphrey Administration to emphasize the military uses of space for America's defense.

FOREIGN POLICY

Our nation urgently needs a foreign policy that realistically leads toward peace. This policy can come only from resolute, new leadership—a leadership that can and will think anew and act anew—a leadership not bound by mistakes of the past.

Our best hope for enduring peace lies in comprehensive international cooperation. We will consult with nations that share our purposes. We will press for their greater participation in

man's common concerns and encourage regional approaches to defense, economic development, and peaceful adjustment of disputes.

We will seek to develop law among nations and strengthen agencies to effectuate that law and cooperatively solve common problems. We will assist the United Nations to become the keystone of such agencies, and its members will be pressed to honor all charter obligations, including specifically its financial provisions. Worldwide resort to the International Court of Justice as a final arbiter of legal disputes among nations will have our vigorous encouragement, subject to limitations imposed by the U.S. Senate in accepting the Court's jurisdiction.

The world abounds with problems susceptible of cooperative solution—poverty, hunger, denial of human rights, economic development, scientific and technological backwardness. The worldwide population explosion in particular, with its attendant grave problems, looms as a menace to all mankind and will have our priority attention. In all such areas we pledge to expand and strengthen international cooperation.

A more selective use of our economic strength has become imperative. We believe foreign aid is a necessary ingredient in the betterment of less developed countries. Our aid, however, must be positioned realistically in our national priorities. Only those nations which urgently require America's help and clearly evince a desire to help themselves will receive such assistance as can be diverted from our pressing needs. In providing aid, more emphasis will be given to technical assistance. We will encourage multilateral agencies so that other nations will help share the burden. The administration of all aid programs will be revised and improved to prevent waste, inefficiency and corruption. We will vigorously encourage maximum participation by private enterprise.

No longer will foreign aid activities range free of our foreign policy. Nations hostile to this country will receive no assistance from the United States. We will not provide aid of any kind to countries which aid and abet the war efforts of North Vietnam.

Only when Communist nations prove by actual deeds that they genuinely seek world peace and will live in harmony with the rest of the world, will we support expansion of East-West trade.

We will strictly administer the Export Control Act, taking special care to deny export licenses for strategic goods.

In the development and execution of the nation's foreign policy, our career Foreign Service officers play a critical role. We strongly support the Foreign Service and will strengthen it by improving its efficiency and administration and providing adequate allowances for its personnel.

The principles of the 1965 Immigration Act —non-discrimination against national origins, reunification of families, and selective support for the American labor market—have our unreserved backing. We will refine this new law to make our immigration policy still more equitable and non-discriminatory.

The Republican Party abhors the activities of those who have violated passport regulations contrary to the best interests of our nation and also the present policy of re-issuing passports to such violators. We pledge to tighten passport administration so as to bar such violators from passport privileges.

The balance of payments crisis must be ended, and the international position of the dollar strengthened. We propose to do this, not by peremptory efforts to limit American travel abroad or by self-defeating restraints on overseas investments, but by restraint in Federal spending and realistic monetary policies, by adjusting overseas commitments, by stimulating exports, by encouraging more foreign travel to the United States and, as specific conditions require, by extending tax treatment to our own exports and imports comparable to such treatment applied by foreign countries. Ending inflation is the first step toward solving the payments crisis.

It remains the policy of the Republican Party to work toward freer trade among all nations of the free world. But artificial obstacles to such trade are a serious concern. We promise hardheaded bargaining to lower the non-tariff barriers against American exports and to develop a code of fair competition, including international fair labor standards, between the United States and its principal trading partners.

A sudden influx of imports can endanger many industries. These problems, differing in each industry, must be considered case by case. Our guideline will be fairness for both producers and workers, without foreclosing imports.

Thousands of jobs have been lost to foreign producers because of discriminatory and unfair trade practices.

The State Department must give closest attention to the development of agreements with exporting nations to bring about fair competition. Imports should not be permitted to capture excessive portions of the American market but should, through international agreements, be able to participate in the growth of consumption.

Should such efforts fail, specific countermeasures will have to be applied until fair competition is re-established. Tax reforms will also be required to preserve the competitiveness of American goods.

The basis for determining the value of imports and exports must be modified to reflect true dollar value.

Not the least important aspect of this problem is the relative obsolescence of machinery in this country. An equitable tax write-off is necessary to strengthen our industrial competitiveness in the world.

We also favor the broadening of governmental assistance to industries, producers and workers seriously affected by imports—assistance denied by the Johnson-Humphrey Administration's excessively stringent application of the Trade Expansion Act of 1962.

Ties of history and geography link us closely to Latin America. Closer economic and cultural cooperation of the United States and the Latin American countries is imperative in a broad attack on the chronic problems of poverty, inadequate economic growth and consequent poor education throughout the hemisphere. We will encourage in Latin America the progress of economic integration to improve opportunity for industrialization and economic diversification.

The principles of the Monroe Doctrine, affirmed at Caracas 14 years ago by all the independent nations of this hemisphere, have been discarded by Democrat Administrations. We hold that they should be reaffirmed and should guide the collective policy of the Americas. Nor have we forgotten in this context, the Cuban people who still cruelly suffer under Communist tyranny.

In cooperation with other nations, we will encourage the less developed nations of Asia and Africa peacefully to improve their standards of living, working with stronger regional organizations where indicated and desired.

In the tinderbox of the Middle East, we will pursue a stable peace through recognition by all nations of each other's right to assured boundaries, freedom of navigation through international waters, and independent existence free from the threat of aggression. We will seek an end to the arms race through international agreement and the stationing of peace-keeping forces of the United Nations in areas of severe tension, as we encourage peace-table talks among adversaries.

Nevertheless, the Soviets persist in building an imbalance of military forces in this region. The fact of a growing menace to Israel is undeniable. Her forces must be kept at a commensurate strength both for her protection and to help keep the peace of the area. The United States, therefore, will provide countervailing help to Israel, such as supersonic fighters, as necessary for these purposes. To replace the ancient rivalries of this region with new hope and opportunity, we vigorously support a well-conceived plan of regional development, including the bold nuclear desalinization and irrigation proposal of former President Eisenhower.

Our relations with Western Europe, so critical to our own progress and security, have been needlessly and dangerously impaired. They must be restored, and NATO revitalized and strengthened. We continue to pursue the goal of a Germany reunified in freedom.

The peoples of the captive nations of Eastern Europe will one day regain their freedom and independence. We will strive to speed this day by encouraging the greater political freedom actively sought by several of these nations. On occasions when a liberalization of trade in non-strategic goods with the captive nations can have this effect, it will have our support.

We do not intend to conduct foreign policy in such manner as to make the United States a world policeman. However, we will not condone aggression, or so-called "wars of national liberation," or naïvely discount the continuing threats of Moscow and Peking. Nor can we fail to condemn the Soviet Union for its continuing anti-Semitic actions, its efforts to eradicate all religions, and its oppression of minorities generally. Improved relations with Communist nations can come only when they cease to endanger other states by force or threat. Under existing conditions, we cannot favor recognition of Communist China or its admission to the United Nations.

We encourage international limitations of armaments, provided all major powers are proportionately restrained and trustworthy guarantees are provided against violations.

## VIETNAM

The Administration's Vietnam policy has failed —militarily, politically, diplomatically, and with relation to our own people.

We condemn the Administration's breach of faith with the American people respecting our heavy involvement in Vietnam. Every citizen bitterly recalls the Democrat campaign oratory of 1964: "We are not about to send American boys 9-10,000 miles away from home to do what Asian boys ought to be doing for themselves." The Administration's failure to honor its own words has led millions of Americans to question its credibility.

The entire nation has been profoundly concerned by hastily extemporized, undeclared land wars which embroil massive U.S. armed forces thousands of miles from our shores. It is time to realize that not every international conflict is susceptible of solution by American ground forces.

Militarily, the Administration's piecemeal commitment of men and material has wasted our massive military superiority and frittered away our options. The result has been a prolonged war of attrition. Throughout this period the Administration has been slow in training and equipping South Vietnamese units both for fighting the war and for defending their country after the war is over.

Politically, the Administration has failed to recognize the entirely novel aspects of this war. The overemphasis on its old-style, conventional aspects has blinded the Administration to the fact that the issue is not control of territory but the security and loyalty of the population. The enemy's primary emphasis has been to disrupt orderly government.

The Administration has paid inadequate attention to the political framework on which a successful outcome ultimately depends. Not only has the Administration failed to encourage assumption of responsibility by the Vietnamese, but their sense of responsibility has been in fact under-mined by our approach to pacification. An added factor has been a lack of security for the civilian population.

At home, the Administration has failed to share with the people the full implication of our challenge and of our commitments.

To resolve our Vietnam dilemma, America ob-viously requires new leadership—one capable of thinking and acting anew, not one hostage to the many mistakes of the past. The Republican Party offers such leadership.

We pledge to adopt a strategy relevant to the real problems of the war, concentrating on the security of the population, on developing a greater sense of nation-hood, and on strengthen-ing the local forces. It will be a strategy per-mitting a progressive de-Americanization of the war, both military and civilian.

We will see to it that our gallant American servicemen are fully supported with the highest quality equipment, and will avoid actions that unnecessarily jeopardize their lives.

We will pursue a course that will enable and induce the South Vietnamese to assume increas-ing responsibility.

The war has been conducted without a co-herent program for peace.

We pledge a program for peace in Vietnam—neither peace at any price nor a camouflaged surrender of legitimate United States or allied interests—but a positive program that will offer a fair and equitable settlement to all, based on the principle of self-determination, our national interests and the cause of long-range world peace.

We will sincerely and vigorously pursue peace negotiations as long as they offer any reasonable prospect for a just peace. We pledge to develop a clear and purposeful negotiating position.

We will return to one of the cardinal princi-ples of the last Republican Administration: that American interests are best served by cooperative multilateral action with our allies rather than by unilateral U.S. action.

Our pride in the nation's armed forces in Southeast Asia and elsewhere in the world is beyond expression.

In all our history none have fought more bravely or more devotedly than our sons in this unwanted war in Vietnam.

They deserve—and they and their loved ones

have—our total support, our encouragement, and our prayers.

NATIONAL DEFENSE

Grave errors, many now irretrievable, have characterized the direction of our nation's de-fense.

A singular notion—that salvation for America lies in standing still—has pervaded the entire effort. Not retention of American superiority but parity with the Soviet Union has been made the controlling doctrine in many critical areas. We have frittered away superior military capabilities, enabling the Soviets to narrow their defense gap, in some areas to outstrip us, and to move to cancel our lead entirely by the early Seventies. In a host of areas, advanced military research and development have been inhibited and stag-nated by inexpert, cost-oriented administrators imbued with a euphoric concept of Soviet de-signs. A strange Administration preference for such second-best weaponry as the costly Navy F111-B(TFX) has deprived our armed forces of more advanced weapons systems. Improvements in our submarines have been long delayed as the Soviets have proceeded apace with their own. Our anti-submarine warfare capabilities have been left seriously inadequate, new fighter planes held up, and new strategic weaponry left on the draw-ing boards.

This mismanagement has dangerously weak-ened the ability of the United States to meet future crises with great power and decisiveness. All the world was respectful of America's deci-sive strategic advantage over the Soviets achieved during the Eisenhower Administration. This su-periority proved its worth in the Cuban missile crisis six years ago. But now we have had an augury of things to come—a shameful, humiliat-ing episode, the seizure of the USS *Pueblo* and its crew, with devastating injury to America's prestige everywhere in the world.

We pledge to include the following in a com-prehensive program to restore the pre-eminence of U.S. military strength:

Improve our deterrent capability through an ocean strategy which extends the Polaris-Poseidon concept and accelerates submarine technology;

Redirect and stimulate military strength to en-courage major innovations rather than merely respond belatedly to Communist advances;

Strengthen intelligence gathering and evaluation by the various military services;

Use the defense dollar more effectively through simplification of the cumbersome, overcentralized administration of the Defense Department, expanded competitive bidding on defense contracts, and improved safeguards against excessive profits;

Reinvigorate the nation's most important security planning organization—the National Security Council—to prevent future haphazard diplomatic and military ventures, integrate the nation's foreign and military policies and programs, and enable our nation once again to anticipate and prevent crises rather than hastily contriving counter-measures after they arise.

Our merchant marine, too, has been allowed to deteriorate. Now there are grave doubts that it is capable of adequate response of emergency security needs.

The United States has drifted from first place to sixth place in the world in the size of its merchant fleet. By contrast, the Russian fleet has been rapidly expanding and will attain a dominant position by 1970. Deliveries of new ships are now eight to one in Russia's favor.

For reasons of security, as well as of economics, the decline of our merchant marine must be reversed. We therefore pledge a vigorous and realistic ship replacement program to meet the changing pattern of our foreign commerce. We will also expand industry-government maritime research and development, emphasizing nuclear propulsion, and simplify and revise construction and operating subsidy procedures.

Finally, we pledge to assemble the nation's best diplomatic, military and scientific minds for an exhaustive reassessment of America's worldwide commitments and military preparedness. We are determined to assure our nation of the strength required in future years to deter war and to prevail should it occur.

CONCLUSION

We believe that the principles and programs we have here presented will find acceptance with the American people. We believe they will command the victory.

There are points of emphasis which we deem important.

The accent is on freedom. Our Party historically has been the Party of freedom. We are the only barricade against those who, through excessive government power, would overwhelm and destroy man's liberty. If liberty fails, all else is dross.

Beyond freedom we emphasize trust and credibility. We have pledged only what we honestly believe we can perform. In a world where broken promises become a way of life, we submit that a nation progresses not on promises broken but on pledges kept.

We have also accented the moral nature of the crisis which confronts us. At the core of that crisis is the life, the liberty, and the happiness of man. If life can be taken with impunity, if liberty is subtly leeched away, if the pursuit of happiness becomes empty and futile, then indeed are the moral foundations in danger.

We have placed high store on our basic theme. The dogmas of the quiet past simply will not do for the restless present. The case is new. We must most urgently think anew and act anew. This is an era of rapid, indeed violent change. Clearly we must disenthrall ourselves. Only then can we save this great Republic.

We rededicate ourselves to this Republic—this one nation, under God, indivisible, with liberty and justice for all.

## Socialist Labor Platform 1968

"There is in the land a certain restlessness, a questioning."

The words were uttered by President Johnson in his January 17, 1968, State of the Union Message. They understated the case.

The American people in 1968 are assailed by foreboding and bitterness, frustration and fear, bewilderment and doubt. It is not the Socialist Labor Party alone that makes this severe assessment. Late in 1967, the National Committee for an Effective Congress issued a report in which it declared:

"At all levels of American life, people share similar fears, insecurities and gnawing doubts to such an intense degree that the country may in fact be suffering from a kind of national nervous breakdown."

Why? The Socialist Labor Party declares that when a sickness of this scope and intensity grips a nation it signifies that something very extraordinary is taking place, something far greater in a historical sense than division and dissent over a criminal and unconstitutional war, greater even than the crisis in race relations with its dire prospect of urban insurrection and, worse, of genocide.

The Socialist Labor Party declares that what this mortal national—really universal—sickness signifies is a vague and undefined, but mounting distrust in the ability of society *as presently organized* to cope with the problems that have arisen under it.

It is a serious error to imagine, as most people do, that revolutions occur when the mass of the people are starving and otherwise suffering intense deprivation. On the contrary, experience shows that revolutions occur when expectations of a better, more secure and more happy life are rising—and when these expectations are prevented from being fulfilled by outmoded laws and institutions. "Evils which are patiently endured when they seem inevitable," wrote de Tocqueville, "become intolerable when once the idea of escape from them is suggested."

Material justifications for rising expectations abound today on every hand. Since World War II industrial and scientific advances have been phenomenal. Output of the nation's industries is now more than twice as great as it was in 1950. In the past 10 years it has swollen an incredible 60 percent.

FAILURE OF REFORMS

Why, then, in the face of such material progress, do massive poverty and insecurity persist? What explains the dismal failure of President Johnson's "Great Society" reforms and the "war on poverty" on which billions of dollars have been spent without even beginning to solve a single problem?

The conspicuous failure of reforms, which raised the hopes of many so high when enacted, is not the least contributing reason for the despair, frustration and doubt that pervade this nation.

The Socialist Labor Party declares and proves that the maladies afflicting our society—maladies ranging from the monetary inflation that erodes the living standards of all workers, combined with fierce capitalist resistance to increase wages to offset it, to the frightening surge of crime

and violence, from deadly pollution of the natural environment to a crisis in race relations—have, not many causes, but *one* cause. This one cause is a social system—capitalism—that is outmoded, destructively competitive and profit-motivated. The Socialist Labor Party warns that if we keep this outmoded form of society, in which wealth is produced for the private profit of a few, not for the welfare and benefit of the people, catastrophic consequences, of which today's fears are a portent, are sure to follow.

SOCIALIST ALTERNATIVE

The alternative to the rapidly disintegrating capitalist world is a world organized on a sane foundation of social ownership and democratic administration of the industries and services, and production to satisfy human needs instead of for sale and private profit. The alternative to contradiction-ridden capitalism is a Socialist world of cooperation and human brotherhood.

In this hour of deadly peril when the whole world seems to be trembling on the very brink of chaos and cataclysmic disaster, the Socialist Labor Party appeals to all workers of all races, and to socially minded people generally, to reflect on the logic and downright common sense of a fundamental Socialist reconstruction of society.

Once society—which means all of us, collectively—gains control of the nation's productive facilities, once social production is planned and decisions respecting production are determined by human needs and human desires, poverty will be speedily eliminated. The nation's immensely productive resources will be mobilized, not to wage criminal and brutalizing wars, not to enable a small class of capitalist parasites to accumulate mountains of wealth, but constructively to replace slum areas with parks and habitations fit for humans to live in, to purify our polluted rivers, lakes and air—in short, to repossess America from the vandal capitalist class and make of it the heaven on earth it can be and ought to be.

In our Socialist world, democracy will be a vibrant, meaningful reality, not the mask for economic despotism that it is today. There will be no such ridiculous thing as a political government based, as today, on wholly arbitrary and artificial geographical demarcations. (Some of our state boundaries were determined by a king's grant two and a half centuries ago; they are meaningless in the industrial age!) To administer social production in the interests of the people, we need an *industrial democracy*, a government based on industrial constituencies.

In Socialist society there will be neither masters nor slaves. We will vote where we work, electing our representatives to administrative and planning bodies on an ascending scale. But note this: The people whom we elect to administrative posts will have the privilege to serve, never the power to rule. For the same rank and file that elects them will have the power to recall and replace them at will.

ADMINISTRATION OF THINGS

The democratically elected administrators and planners of Socialism will concern themselves with such practical things as what and how much to produce to insure an uninterrupted flow of the good things of life in abundance; the number of working hours required in the various industries; the erection of plants of production and educational, health and recreational facilities; the development of new technology; the planning and rebuilding of cities; the conservation of resources and the restoration of the natural environment and its preservation for all time.

All that stands in the way of this heaven on earth, a world in which all may enjoy good housing, abundant and nourishing food, the finest clothing, and the best of cultural, educational and recreational advantages, is the outmoded capitalist system.

This is no exaggeration. Nor merely a beautiful dream. It is based on the solid foundation of material facts. Automation, the supreme triumph of technology, has brought this heaven on earth within our reach. Yet, privately owned, as are all productive instruments under capitalism, automation is a blessing only to the capitalist owners; for workers it is a curse, a job-killer, which adds terrifying dimensions to worker insecurity.

THE BASIC SOCIAL QUESTION

Thus the question we face comes down to this: *"When the machine displaces man and does most of the work, who will own the machines and receive the rich dividends?"* (Supreme Court Justice William O. Douglas.)

The United States Constitution, in effect, legalizes revolution. The right to alter or abolish the social system and form of government is implicit in Article V, the Constitution's amendment clause. The Socialist Labor Party proposes to the American workers—and by "workers" we mean all who perform useful labor, teachers, technicians, stenographers and musicians, as well as machinists, assembly-line workers, longshoremen and miners—that we use our huge majorities at the polls to outlaw capitalist ownership and to make the means of social production the property of all the people collectively.

The Socialist Labor Party proposes further that we workers consolidate our economic forces on the industrial field in one integral Socialist Industrial Union to back up the Socialist ballot with an irresistible and invincible power capable of taking and holding the industries, locking out the outvoted capitalist class, and continuing social production without interruption.

THE LINE BETWEEN NONSENSE AND COMMON SENSE

Thomas Carlyle is credited with saying: "We must some day, at last and forever, cross the line between nonsense and common sense. And on that day we shall pass from class paternalism . . . to human brotherhood . . . ; from political government to industrial administration; from competition in individualism to individuality in cooperation; from war and despotism, in any form, to peace and liberty."

We *must* cross that line some day—why not now? Repudiate the Republican and Democratic parties, the political Siamese twins of capitalism —and reject also the self-styled "radicals," the so-called New Left and "liberals" whose platforms consist of measures to reform and patch up the poverty-breeding capitalist system, which is past reforming and patching. Study the Socialist Labor Party's Socialist Industrial Union program. Support the Socialist Labor Party's entire ticket at the polls. Unite with us to save humanity from catastrophe—and to set an example in free nonpolitical self-government for all mankind, in affluence and enduring peace.

## Socialist Workers Platform 1968

The bipartisan policies of the Democrats and Republicans are leading the people of the United States toward disaster.

Despite negotiations the war in Vietnam continues to escalate—more bombing, more troops, more death and destruction for the Vietnamese and more American casualties. And further escalation increases the danger of a nuclear war, a war which would leave the world's cities—our own included—heaps of radioactive rubble.

While U.S. troops are in Vietnam attempting to crush a popular revolution, police, national guard and army units are used to viciously smash the uprisings of black people in our own cities.

In spite of big promises and small concessions, black people remain subject to discrimination and oppression in housing, in jobs, in education and every other area of economic, political and social life. Police brutality, slumlord rent-hogs and price-gouging merchants are daily facts of life for Afro-Americans. Unemployment and low wages hit black people the hardest.

Tens of millions of Americans, black and white, live in poverty. One third of the nation lives below the "poverty line," by admission of the government itself. These Americans have not shared in the "prosperity" based on war production and exploitation of the colonial world.

The workers as a whole are feeling the squeeze of the war economy. Rising taxes and inflated prices have cut into pay checks, actually lowering real wages since the escalation of the war in Vietnam. And while they wallow in super profits, the corporations do everything they can to keep wages down and encroach upon union control over working conditions.

The bosses turn more and more to the government for aid in their crusade against the workers, and the Democrats and Republicans have proven more than willing servants of their class. The move by Congress forcing compulsory slave-labor arbitration on the railroad workers is only the latest in a long list of anti-labor laws and actions by the government.

Democratic rights, too, are being eroded. The response of the government—federal, state and local—to the black revolt has been the harassment and hounding of the most authoritative spokesmen of the movement for black power. This is creating the atmosphere in which all dissenting views will be liable to witchhunt attack.

Moral and cultural values are twisted and mangled in this war-breeding, racist system. The big lie has become standard operating procedure in everything from advertising swindles to White House ballyhoo on Vietnam.

The basic policies pursued by the Democratic and Republican politicians are not the accidental results of arbitrary decisions. They flow from the needs of the capitalist system and the outlook of the ruling capitalist class.

The Vietnam war is a prime example. It is now crystal clear that the U.S. ruling class is not fighting in Vietnam for "freedom" or "democracy." Their war aim is to prevent the workers and peasants of Vietnam from taking control of their own country. The Democrats and Republicans are sending our young men to die in Vietnam as part of a reckless global strategy of preserving and extending the capitalist system and capitalist profits.

Racism is also part and parcel of American capitalist society. Racism serves to keep white workers from realizing that their interests lie with the black masses, and not with the white capitalist rulers. Racism is a source of profit for the ruling class, providing a ready-made pool of cheap and available labor. Racism is utilized in the U.S. imperialist drive to subjugate and enslave the colored people around the world, as in Vietnam.

War, racism, poverty, the attack on labor, the erosion of the Bill of Rights—all these are bitter fruits of the capitalist system or of the measures taken by the capitalist rulers to uphold their system and increase their profits.

To fight against these evils, it is necessary to expose their roots in the system which produced them. We have to uproot this vicious system and fight for a new and better one.

That's why the Socialist Workers Party stands for a complete break with every form of capitalist politics. When black people, and workers as a whole, cease supporting the capitalist Democratic and Republican parties and organize parties of their own, a gigantic step forward will have been taken in the struggle against the system.

In 1968, a clear-cut opposition and radical alternative to the war-making and racist Democrats and Republicans will be presented by the SWP candidates for President and Vice President, Fred Halstead and Paul Boutelle.

Halstead and Boutelle are campaigning for the following program:

Stop the war in Vietnam—bring our men home now! Support the right of GIs to discuss the war and freely express their opposition to it. Abolish the draft—no draftees for Washington's imperialist war machine. Organize a national referendum to give the people the right to vote to withdraw all U.S. troops from Vietnam.

Hands off Cuba and China. Support the struggles of the Asian, Latin American, African and Arab peoples for national independence and social liberation.

Support the right of self-determination of all oppressed national minorities (Afro-Americans, Puerto Ricans, Mexican-Americans, Indians, etc.) inside the U.S.

Support the black people's fight for freedom, justice, and equality through black power. Black people have the unconditional right to control their own communities. The black communities should have control over their schools, and city, state and federal funds should be made available to them in whatever amount needed to overcome years of deprivation in education.

Appropriate what funds are necessary to provide jobs for every unemployed Afro-American, with preferential hiring and upgrading to equalize opportunities in apprenticeship programs, skilled trades, and higher paying technical and supervisory occupations.

In place of price-gouging merchants and landlords preying on the black community, black nonprofit cooperative shops and housing projects should be set up with federal financial aid. Price committees elected by the community should police prices.

It is the right of Afro-Americans to keep arms and organize themselves for self-defense from all attacks.

Keep the troops and racist cops out of the black community, and replace them with deputized, elected representatives of the community. As an immediate step, organize genuine review boards, elected by the black community, to control the cops.

For an independent black political party to organize and lead the struggle for black power on all fronts and by any means necessary.

Support labor's fight against inflation and government control. No freeze on wages. For union escalator clauses to offset rises in the cost of living. The trade unions should take the lead in setting up general committees of consumers to regulate prices.

Repeal all anti-labor laws. Defense of the unconditional right to strike. Complete union independence from government control and interference. Rank and file control over all union affairs.

A reduced work week with no cut in pay, and unemployment compensation at the union wage scale for all jobless persons 18 and over, whether or not they have been previously employed.

Equal rights in the union and on the job for black workers and for members of other minorities, and full union support to the Afro-American struggle for equality.

For an independent labor party based on the trade unions, to defend the rights of all working people against the parties of the bosses, and to fight for a workers government.

For a crash program of public housing and other public works. Take the billions spent on war and use them to build decent, low-rent homes for the working millions who need them, and to build schools and hospitals instead of bombs.

Support the demands of America's youth.

The right to vote at 18.

Free public education through the university level, with adequate pay for all students who need it. Student participation in all university decisions and functioning.

Support to young people's rejection of the sterile cultural values of our decaying capitalist order.

For a planned, democratic socialist America. Nationalize the major corporations and banks under the control of democratically elected workers committees. Plan the economy democratically for the benefit of all instead of for the profit of the few.

A socialist America will be an America of peace and prosperity, without poverty or slums or unemployment, and without wars like that in Vietnam. It will put an end to racism and, for the first time after over 400 years of oppression, guarantee unconditionally, the right of self-determination for the black Americans. It will signal an unparalleled growth in culture, freedom and in the development of the individual.

# CAMPAIGN OF 1972

In 1972, a harmonious Republican convention in Miami Beach renominated President Richard Nixon and Vice-President Spiro Agnew. The convention was carefully managed, decorous, and brief. In contrast, the Democratic convention, operating under new rules developed as the result of the controversial convention in Chicago in 1968, produced eighty-two credentials challenges of delegations and fascinating parliamentary maneuvers. On the third day, after opposition to him had virtually evaporated, Senator George McGovern of South Dakota was nominated for president on the first ballot over five competitors. He chose Senator Thomas F. Eagleton of Missouri as his running mate. Ten days later, Eagleton withdrew from the ticket and the Democratic National Committee ratified the candidate's new choice, R. Sargent Shriver of Maryland, the former director of the Peace Corps and the Office of Economic Opportunity in the Kennedy and Johnson administrations. The platform adopted by the Democrats in 1972 was the longest and possibly the most specific on issues ever proposed by a major party.

Representative John G. Schmitz of California was the American Party presidential candidate and Thomas J. Anderson of Tennessee the vice-presidential candidate. Dr. Benjamin Spock, the well-known author of a book about child care, ran for president on the People's Party ticket with Julius Hobson of the District of Columbia. Other minor parties and their candidates included Louis Fisher of Illinois and Genevieve Gunderson of Minnesota for the Socialist Workers Party; Linda Jenness of Georgia and Andrew Pulley of Illinois for the Socialist Labor Party; E. Harold Munn and Marchall Uncapher for the Prohibition Party; Gus Hall of New York and Jarvis Tyner for the Communist Party; and John Hospers of California and Theodora Nathan of Oregon for the Libertarian Party.

In a stunning victory in November, the Republicans received 47,170,179 votes—60.69 percent of the total vote—the largest number of popular votes ever polled by a political party in America. The Democratic Party garnered 29,171,791 votes—37.53 percent of those cast. The American Independent Party obtained 1,090,673 votes, and Benjamin Spock, for the People's Party, attracted 78,751 votes. Other totals included 65,290 votes for the Socialist Workers, 53,811 for the Socialist Labor Party, 25,343 for the Communists, and 12,818 for the Prohibition Party. A relatively small party, the Libertarian Party, received 3,671 votes. In the electoral vote, President Nixon carried every state except Massachusetts; he also lost the District of Columbia. His total reported to the Congress was 520 votes compared to 17 for Senator McGovern. One Republican elector from Virginia voted for John Hospers, the candidate of the Libertarian Party.

The platforms of the major and principal minor parties are presented in this volume; there were thirty-five minor presidential candidates who received a total of 28,592 votes scattered in individual states. For reasons stated in the preface, the statements of principles or platforms of these candidates have not been recorded here.

---

## American Platform 1972

### PREAMBLE

The American Party of the United States of America gratefully acknowledges the Lord God as the Creator, Preserver, and Ruler of the Universe and of the Nation, hereby appeals to Him for aid, comfort, and continuing guidance in its efforts to preserve this nation as a government of the people, by the people, and for the people in this time of peril.

The American Party speaks for the majority of Americans, the hard-working, productive tax-paying citizens who constitute the strength of America.

No other party today speaks for the average American or expresses his concepts, hopes, and goals.

The average man today does not think of himself in ideological terms, such as liberal and conservative. Rather, the average man thinks in terms of the basic problems which confront him. He is concerned with the opportunity for gainful employment, educational opportunity for his children, the safety of his wife and child on the streets of his community, an equity in taxation which makes him neither the victim of those who by refusing to work have no income to tax, or the multi-millionaires who use tax loopholes to avoid the payment of any taxes. He is concerned about the never-ending use of his sons for gunfodder in futile international involvements.

The platform of the American Party is a response to his desires, a voice which speaks for him as no other political party in America today so speaks.

No nation can survive if it fails to meet the problems which concern the average citizen. The American Party confronts these problems with the conviction that the little people of America are right and will be heard in a free Nation committed to Government of, by, and for the people. The people will ultimately have their way.

To these, the great American people, we offer this platform.

II. DOMESTIC POLICY

*Local Government*

The average man in America today believes in local, voter controlled institutions of government.

The American Party is totally committed to the governmental framework embodied in the Constitution of the United States with its emphasis on a maximum of individual freedom and local autonomy. We are unalterably opposed to Federal domination of local institutions, particularly our public schools.

*Individual Rights*

The American Party speaks for individual freedom; the right of each citizen to the ownership of property and the control of his own property, the right to engage in business or participate in his labor union without governmental interference.

We shall steadfastly oppose Federal legislation permitting the Federal bureaucracy to tell a business man who he must hire or fire, tamper with Union seniority lists and apprenticeship programs or invade the individual's right of privacy.

We call for the elimination of government competition with free and competitive institutions.

*Federal Judiciary*

The greatest obstacle to the achievement by the average man of his goals and desires for America is the unrepresentative, unresponsive, dictatorial, federal judiciary.

The American Party would end judicial usurpation of the constitutional process by requiring federal judges at the district court level to be directly elected by the people, by requiring federal judges at the appellate level, including Supreme Court Justices, to be reconfirmed in their appointments every four years, and by limiting the appellate jurisdiction of the federal courts in state constitutional cases.

*Protection from Crime and Violence*

The law-abiding citizen of the United States has a right to be protected from crime, violence and lawlessness.

The American Party pledges full support to local law enforcement in their crusade to control crime; reforms in our judicial system to provide a speedy and just determination in criminal cases; and retention of the historic constitutional right of each state and the federal government, to impose capital punishment for aggravated criminal offenses.

We support maximum penalties for the crime of skyjacking and political assassinations.

We support local control and financing of our local police forces and will oppose all attempts to establish federal control over them.

*Drug Abuse*

The American Party asserts that drugs are a serious problem in our nation, particularly among our youth, threatening the physical and mental health and even the life of users and leading to many crimes, accidents and other misfortunes.

We oppose legalization of marijuana. We favor strong local and state laws making it a criminal offense with a mandatory jail sentence for anyone convicted of selling or supplying drugs, excepting for prescribed medical purposes.

The ultimate source of most hard drugs in the United States is the poppy fields of Red China. We deplore President Nixon's failure to take any meaningful action to stop the flow of hard drugs from Red China to the United States and pledge our full support to stop this assault on our American youth.

## Respect for Life

A companion to the rise of crime in America has been the growing lack of respect for life and the institutions of home, marriage and family.

The American Party recognizes that the first and most important role of government at any level is the protection of the right to life. The American Party opposes all attempts to liberalize any anti-abortion laws which laws, by their very nature, protect the lives of those innocents least able to defend themselves.

We are opposed to euthanasia, the so-called "Mercy killing" of the aged, ailing or infirm, by the administration of drugs or the withholding of medication essential to the patient's comfort or possible recovery.

We fully support laws providing criminal penalties for the unsolicited presentation or exhibition of obscenity, including any public display of homosexuality.

## Gun Control

The American Party supports the right of all citizens to be fully protected in their homes, persons and property.

The Constitution of the United States affords to every citizen the right to keep and bear arms.

The lawless always acquire weapons and the result of disarming our citizens, coupled with judicial emasculation of local police protection, would be to leave the average citizen without protection from the lawless. We support a mandatory jail sentence for anyone using a firearm in the commission of a felony.

The American Party opposes laws which would deny the right of our citizens to own firearms.

## Welfare

The American Party is sensitive to the needs of America's aged, blind and disabled citizens and fully supports state and local programs to enable these citizens to live in dignity and economic security.

We are unalterably opposed to tax supported subsidies to able bodied persons who refuse to work, engage in welfare fraud, or utilize their reproductive capacities for the purpose of securing even larger welfare payments.

We support all necessary statutory and administrative amendments necessary to achieve the complete elimination of rampant fraud in public assistance programs.

We oppose all federal funding in public assistance programs.

## Social Security

The American Party fully appreciates the rightful aspiration of the aged to live in dignity and economic security.

The aged have been the principal victims of an irresponsible government fostered inflation. We support legislation to require the Federal government to protect Social Security Funds as a special trust, using those funds solely for the purpose of providing benefits to the beneficiaries. We support the removal of the earnings limitation of 62 and over in order that they may earn any amount of additional income.

We support the right of those entering the labor market to elect to participate in approved private retirement plans as an alternative to the Federal Social Security Program. Current studies establish that, at present rates, the same funds paid into social security over the average worker's productive life would produce, if paid into a private investment trust fund, a principal sum sufficient to provide the worker a retirement income at least several times larger than present social security benefits.

## Health Care

The average man today is threatened in his economic security by the high cost of medical care. We believe that the advantages of our scientific achievements in the medical field should be available to every citizen, through the free enterprise system.

We support cooperative efforts between private insurance carriers and private charitable institutions to provide low-cost medical insurance for the average citizen. We oppose any form of government controlled insurance.

We fully support the freedom of the citizen to choose his own physician.

We are particularly sensitive to the special needs of the handicapped and support state administered programs which offer these citizens the educational and employment opportunities to lead productive lives.

## Inflation

The average family in America is today the victim of government created inflation which robs the working man of the advantage achieved by high wage standards.

Government created the problem of inflation by deficit spending and Government must be curbed in such further activity.

The American Party supports all steps necessary to halt the inflationary spiral, including putting the Federal Government on a pay-as-you-go basis and restoring a sound monetary standard by permitting the individual citizen to own and exchange gold, and the American Party advocates the abolition of the Federal Reserve System (a private corporation), and together with such abolition, the American Party advocates a return to the gold standard.

We object strongly to the policy of present and past administrations in blaming either the working man or the business man for the problem of inflation.

The imposition of wage and price controls, ostensibly established to curb inflation, is a fraud upon every citizen of America. We call for the removal of such fraud upon every citizen of America. We call for the removal of such fraudulent wage and price controls.

## Taxation

Through ever-increasing tax rates the average man in America carries the full burden of the cost of a reckless and wasteful Federal government. The able-bodied who refuse to work produce no income, pay no taxes, and draw lavish welfare subsidies. The ultra-rich acquire vast sums, but use tax loopholes and tax-exempt foundations to evade the payment of taxes.

The American Party supports immediate tax relief for the lower and middle-income citizens of America, a closing of the tax loopholes for the ultra-rich, and taxation of the presently exempt foundations unless their purposes are narrowly limited to charitable pursuits.

We believe that the American Party should encourage the full consideration of a constitutional amendment reflecting long-standing and never refuted studies establishing that if the federal government is restricted to its constitutional functions, the present income, estate and gift tax programs can be eliminated at a proven profit of approximately 20% to the average American wage earner.

## Employment

The creation of job opportunities for our citizens is an essential requirement of today's economy.

The American Party would eliminate governmental red tape and restrictions which discourage the development and expansion of business enterprises which create job opportunities.

This is in the tradition of a free America which, without government restriction, has created the greatest abundance the world has ever known.

## Consumer Protection

The American Party supports reasonable programs to provide protection for consumers and wage earners against hazards to their health and safety.

Believing in free competitive enterprise, we are unrelenting in our opposition to government maintained monopolies which stifle competition. Where these monopolies exist, they must be strictly regulated to protect the public from unfair and arbitrary rate increases.

We are opposed to the use by those monopolies, such as the telephone company, of its consumer derived revenues for political purposes for the direct or indirect influencing of elections.

## Agriculture

The American Party supports honest value to the farmer for the crop he produces.

We support the phased complete withdrawal of government controls, restrictions, and subsidies from agriculture within a period of three to five years, as we withdraw similar subsidies from other areas of American economic life.

To protect the American farmer from unjust

foreign competition, we protest foreign imports from slave nations.

## Labor

The American Party fully supports the advances made by the working people of America. We shall continue to support the right of workers to organize, bargain collectively, and control the internal affairs of their union organizations without Federal government interference. We oppose compulsory federally enforced arbitration on local unions.

The American Party recognizes that all retirement and pension programs are a deferred part of every workers' wage or salary. As such, all participation in retirement and pension programs should remain the property of every participating employee regardless of wherever he may be employed. We strongly support legislation, union agreements, or professional organization efforts to guarantee that interest. Every working man, union or non-union, waged or salaried, should be allowed to take his pension benefits with him to wherever he might be employed, from his first job to his last.

We support the right of rank and file union members to control the destiny of their own local unions through democratic processes.

There is no "acceptable" level of unemployment as is implied by the current philosophies of the Democrat and Republican Parties. The unalterable position of the American Party is that there is opportunity for full employment through the free enterprise system.

## Education

The American Party fully supports the concept of quality education for every American child. We believe that education is a local responsibility and we are unalterably committed to the preservation of the neighborhood school without Federal control or interference. We believe that the educational dollar should be spent for improved classroom instruction, not for unproductive busing of pupils for purposes of social experimentation or racial balance. We strongly reaffirm our opposition to such busing and to the transfer of teachers for such purposes.

We also support all necessary legislation to encourage the development of systems of private education including tax setoffs for parents who choose to place their children in private schools.

We support the concept of voluntary non-denominational prayer in the public schools. We would protect the right of an individual not to participate, but do not believe the minority has the right to bar participation by the majority in desired religious exercises. We will resist any and all attempts by governmental agencies such as H.E.W. and the National Institute On Mental Health, et al, to use our educational systems to experiment with, or capture the minds and lives of our children through such programs as "National Child Advocacy System," sex-education, sensitivity training, and drug experimentation.

We favor placing our schools under the jurisdiction of parents and their local school boards, and school financing by state and local taxation.

## Natural Resources and Protection of the Environment

The American Party is deeply concerned with the protection of our environment and the conservation of our natural resources.

We support all reasonable efforts to solve the problems of air and water pollution, and America's other environmental maladies.

We do not believe that the solution to pollution can be found in destroying the private capital investment system, but rather by urging the enforcement of the common and statutory laws affecting these matters by the states and local enforcement agencies, and by the inventive genius of a free people in a competitive economic system.

## Elections

The development of the American Party is dependent upon an opportunity to fully participate in the election process in the several states. We shall work for the elimination of discriminatory state laws which make it difficult or impossible for new parties to participate in the election process. We shall support judicial or legislative action wherever necessary to achieve this objective, including legislation enabling the name "American Party" to be used in every state.

We support full disclosure of campaign contributions and expenditures.

The American Party welcomes America's young voters and invites them to participate in the only political party which offers real solutions to the problems encountered by young Americans. We encourage our newly enfranchised young voters to play an active part in the leadership and development of the American Party.

### Secrecy in Government

The American Party believes that government must be conducted in the full light of public scrutiny. Secrecy is the tool of dictatorship, not of government of, by and for the people. We pledge our full support to all necessary legislation to assure full disclosure to the people of the activities of their government, excepting for matters clearly in the interests of national security.

### Regional Government

The American Party is unalterably opposed to the creation of regional government entities which exercise tax and police powers without direct responsibility to the voters and the taxpayers which such agencies are alleged to serve. Too often, the objective of those seeking to create such regional bodies is the destruction or usurpation of the authority of local or state governments.

In connection with necessary vigilance on the subject of regional government, we encourage a re-examination of the concept of zoning laws, which frequently are a thinly veiled transfer of power from private property owners to local collectivist planners.

### Internal Subversion

The American Party expresses its undying opposition to the criminal Communist conspiracy and, in that regard, urges the enforcement of the Constitution and laws of the United States.

### Women's Liberation

Although "Equal Rights" for women may seem a desirable objective, in practice it means great loss—not gain. This deceit is planned to "liberate" women from their families, homes and property, and as in Communist countries, they would share hard labor alongside men. Women of the American Party say "NO" to this insidious socialistic plan to destroy the home, make women slaves of the government, and their children wards of the state. We urge the people to notify their state legislators to resist adoption of the so-called "Equal Rights Amendment" commonly known as "Women's Lib."

### Public Housing

We oppose public, subsidized and scatter site housing in any neighborhood or community unless first approved by a majority of the voters in the precinct and in the municipality concerned.

### III. Foreign Policy

### National Sovereignty

The United States is a free and sovereign republic which desires to live in friendship with all free nations, without interfering in their internal affairs, and without permitting their interference in ours. We are, therefore, unalterably opposed to entangling alliances, via treaties or any other form of commitment, which compromise our national sovereignty. To this end, we shall:
—Steadfastly oppose American participation in any form of world government organization;
—Call upon the President and Congress to terminate United States membership in the United Nations and its subsidiary organizations; and
—Propose that the Constitution be amended to prohibit the United States Government from entering any treaty or other agreement which makes any commitment of American military forces or tax money, compromises the sovereignty of the United States, or accomplishes a purpose properly the subject of domestic law.

### Pacts and Agreements

Since World War II, the United States has increasingly played the undesirable role of an international policeman. Through our involvements abroad, our country is being changed from a republic to a world empire in which our freedoms are being sacrificed on an altar of international involvement. The United States is now committed by treaty to defend 42 foreign nations in all parts of the world, and by agreements other than treaties to defend at least 19 more. Therefore, we:
—Call upon the President and the Congress to immediately commence a systematic withdrawal from any such treaties and agreements, unless such withdrawal would threaten the immediate national security of the United States; and
—Reaffirm our support of the Monroe Doctrine under which the United States has clearly stated its perpetual interest in the independence from foreign domination of the several

republics of the Western Hemisphere, so that all expansionist powers will be forewarned of our commitment to the freedom of the Western Hemisphere from foreign domination.

## Vietnam

The Executive Branch of our government, with the tacit approval of Congress, has involved us in an unconstitutional war in Vietnam which is contrary to the best interest of this nation. Through unbelievable mismanagement, or conscious design, the war has been prolonged, any goal of traditional military victory abandoned, and the enemy has been given privileged sanctuaries while over 50,000 American boys have been slaughtered on the battlefield.

Despite the fact that our nation became involved illegally in the Indo-China war there are, none the less, hundreds of valiant American servicemen now languishing in the prison camps of North Vietnam. America owes a duty and responsibility to these brave men and their families to force the Communist government of North Vietnam to release these American prisoners of war. America must not turn its back upon these brave men and abandon them to living deaths in Communist captivity, as has been the case with so many other American nationals held prisoner by Communist Russia and Red China.

The American Party further demands that never again shall U.S. troops be employed on any foreign field of battle without a declaration of war by Congress as required by the U.S. Constitution; that Congress refuse to fund unconstitutional, undeclared wars pursuant to Presidential whim or international obligations under which American sovereignty has been transferred to multinational agencies; and that such statutes be adopted as may be required to achieve these objectives. We further recognize that most of the wars to which America has been a party throughout our history as a nation, not excepting Vietnam, have resulted from the machinations of international finance in their centuries old drive toward world government. Let us never again help them build the traps with which they would ensnare us.

We are unalterably opposed to any American aid to *North* Vietnam upon termination of our participation in Southeast Asian hostilities.

We oppose unequivocally any amnesty for military deserters and draft dodgers.

## Relations with Communist Nations

The American Party is deeply concerned by the President's recent accord with Communist China during the very hour when American boys are being killed by the Communist enemy in Vietnam. Instead of consorting with Communist governments, we believe that the United States should terminate all trade with, and aid to, Communist countries. It has been estimated that the entirety of the Communist empire would collapse within six months if absolutely without aid and trade from the free world. It is in this fashion that the freedom-loving patriots of the Communist empire, including Nationalist China, Vietnam, Laos, and Cambodia, will regain their freedom. We should provide moral encouragement to the peoples of captive nations whose homelands are presently oppressed by the Communist tyranny. We specifically urge the United States to reiterate its friendship for Nationalist China. We are unalterably opposed to any recognition of the Castro Communist government in Cuba. In addition, we pledge the repudiation of the Kennedy-Khrushchev Pact which guarantees the communist enslavement of the Cuban people. We pledge the enforcement of the Monroe Doctrine which keeps foreign powers out of the Western Hemisphere, including the stationing of Soviet soldiers, sailors and airmen in Cuba and Chile.

We pledge not to interfere with Cuban exiles in their legitimate goals and aims of freeing their country from Communist tyranny.

We pledge to release all Cuban exiles held in United States jails for past activities connected with the liberation of their homeland.

## Middle East

The American Party is unalterably opposed to American involvement in the Middle East conflict between Israel and Arab States. The United States has no interest in the Middle East which justifies the sacrifice of our sons on a desert battlefield nor is our country properly cast as a merchant of death in the Middle East arms race.

At a time when all of our attention should be focused on termination of our involvement in the Indo-China war, it is shocking to find both the Republican administration and the Democratic presidential candidate openly thrusting us toward war on another foreign battlefield. We are not prepared to endorse an exchange of the slaughter of our sons in the jungle for the slaughter of our sons on the desert.

We therefore propose that:

—America declare its neutrality in the Middle East; and

—Repudiate any commitment expressed or implied to send U.S. troops to participate in the Middle East conflict.

### South Africa and Rhodesia

As it is not the prerogative of foreign nations to determine the internal policies of the United States, so it is not our prerogative to dictate the internal policies of foreign countries. We should, therefore, declare our friendship with all nations who genuinely desire friendship with us. Consequently, we:

—Call upon our government to cease its acts of hostility toward South Africa and Rhodesia, and, indeed, all other non-Communist countries who have by word and deed demonstrated their friendship for the United States;

—Commend the Congress for its action in ending American participation in U.N. sanctions against Rhodesia as they apply to chromite and certain other strategic minerals; and

—Pledge to end the present administration's anti-Rhodesian sanctions policy and extend to Rhodesia the full diplomatic recognition to which that nation is clearly entitled.

### Foreign Aid

Since World War II, the United States has been engaged in the greatest international giveaway program ever conceived by man, and is now spending over $32,000,000,000 a year to aid foreign nations. These expenditures have won us no friends and constitute a major drain on the resources of our taxpayers. Therefore, we demand that:

—No further funds be appropriated for any kind of foreign aid programs;

—United States participation in international lending institutions, such as the World Bank and the International Monetary Fund, be ended;

—All government subsidies and investment guarantees to encourage U.S. businesses to invest in foreign lands be immediately terminated; and

—All debts owed to the United States by foreign countries from previous wars be collected, by confiscation of property, if necessary.

### Tariffs and Trade

The American Party urges that:

—Congress take all necessary action to protect American workers, farmers, and businesses threatened by slave labor foreign competition;

—The United States cease participation in international tariff cutting organizations such as the General Agreement on Tariffs and Trade (GATT);

—The United States Government establish a firm policy that U.S. businesses investing abroad do so at their own risk and that there is no obligation by our Government to protect those investments with the lives of our sons, or the taxes of our citizens.

It is believed that the libertarian ideal of totally tariff free international trade is not realistic at this time in world history.

We support restoration of America's place as a major sea power with a far ranging merchant fleet.

### Immigration

Liberalization of American immigration laws is upsetting the labor balance in our country, and having an adverse effect on our economy. The mass importation of peoples with low standards of living threatens the wage structure of the American working man and, frequently, the political subversion of our American institutions. Therefore, we recommend that:

—United States immigration laws be re-written to limit immigration to modest quotas of immigrants from European and Western hemisphere countries and other people who share our general cultural traditions and background;

—All other immigration be prohibited except in hardship cases or other special circumstances; and that

—All immigrants be carefully screened to guarantee the loyalty to the United States of all persons entering this country.

### State Department

The State Department for almost 40 years has been actively engaged in the promotion of internationalism contrary to the best interests of the United States. Therefore, we recommend that:

—All necessary legislative and administrative action be taken to assure that every person serving in the State Department adheres to the objectives set forth in this platform; all persons found to be security risks be summarily discharged, defining sexual deviates and subversives as "security risks per se";

—Expenditures by the Department be reduced sufficiently to limit its activities to the purposes embodied in this platform;

—All non-conforming functions, such as the Peace Corps, USIA, etc., be eliminated; and that

—Our Government be prohibited from conducting secret negotiations or entering into secret treaties or agreements in any way binding on the United States.

In addition we recognize the Council on Foreign Relations as the principal organization controlling our State Department, and indeed, the general foreign policy of the United States, in the Council's drive to make America a part of a one-world socialist government.

We pledge full exposure of this conspiratorial apparatus.

### Defense Policies

The defense of the United States is a primary responsibility of the Federal Government.

The American Party supports all necessary measures to provide full protection of the United States from any threat.

We recognize that it is impossible to restore fiscal responsibility to Government without a complete reappraisal of defense expenditures. We insist that all so called defense programs not directly related to the protection of our national security be eliminated; that every item of expenditure be carefully reviewed to eliminate waste, fraud, theft, inefficiency and excess profits from all defense contracts and military expenditures.

We are opposed to compulsory military training but support a well trained and highly organized volunteer state home militia. Since World War II, the domestic prosperity of the United States has been built upon a hot and cold war economy. In this context, war has become an integral part of the domestic economic policy of both the Democrat and Republican administrations. Therefore we urge that:

—The United States Government take immediate steps to encourage the reorientation of the economy to provide domestic prosperity without the artificial and inflationary stimulus of war and threats of war;

—The United States Government continue to recognize the contribution of our servicemen to the national welfare by the extension of appropriate benefits to all veterans;

—In any war in which our country engages, sufficient taxes be imposed to take the profit out of war, and to equalize the sacrifices of those at home with those called upon to fight on the battlefield abroad.

### Disarmament

The principle of universal disarmament is a desirable goal. It can be achieved, however, only if all nations conform equally to disarmament agreements. There is no current evidence of a sincere desire by major world powers to disarm. Therefore, we recommend that:

—Public Law 87-297, otherwise known as the Arms Control and Disarmament Act be repealed;

—No further disarmament treaties be adopted in the absence of full evidence of good faith by all concerned powers, including the right of inspection and true equality of arms reductions;

—No disarmament treaty be adopted involving the implied or expressed obligation of the United States to go to war to enforce arms limitations, or to protect foreign nations jeopardized by powers violating disarmament agreements; and that

—No disarmament treaty be adopted granting to the United Nations the power to establish an international police force to enforce the provision of such treaty.

### World Government by the Back Door

Just as we are opposed to World Government by direct action, so we are opposed to World Government by the back door by bestowal of statehood on remote and sparsely populated insular territories. The present American territories should, upon qualification, be granted Commonwealth status—not statehood.

### Fishing Rights

The American Party hereby records its opposition to the unlawful commercial invasion of its maritime seas by foreign governments which, in violation of heretofore recognized international law and custom, seize our fishing ships, destroy our gear, lobster pots and nets. This invasion of American rights cannot be tolerated, and a redefinition of the limits of our maritime waters should be established to secure American rights in our commercial fishing waters.

## Communist Platform 1972

PREAMBLE

The United States of America is a deeply troubled nation—more troubled than ever before. Corruption and deceit are rampant. For solutions, the old-line politicians offer more deceit, false promises, bigotry and fear. While a heinous, immoral war is being waged and the profits of giant corporate interests soar, the quality of life for the overwhelming majority of America's people is steadily deteriorating. Unemployment mounts, our cities decay, drug addiction has reached epidemic proportions, and the very air we breathe is dangerously polluted.

The United States is not threatened from abroad. Yet, since the end of World War II, more than a trillion dollars has been spent on armaments and the military establishment. Almost $120 billion has been used for militarism and the war is Indochina. The total expenditure will exceed $350 billion. The Vietnamese did not invade our country: U.S. military forces invaded theirs. Tax money for tanks, planes, missiles; money for death and destruction is readily available. Why is there no money for urgently needed homes, schools and hospitals or mass transit?

The Nixon mis-administration has instituted a wage freeze. Demands for increased productivity are accompanied by increased pressure on the workers to work harder and faster in order to get the country out of a disastrous economic slump. It is the workers who are being blamed for the miserable failure of the Nixon economic policies. These policies will not create more jobs. They will put more workers out of work, thereby deepening the crises. The Nixon mis-administration speaks of price controls, but prices (and profits) continue to rise. Only wages are frozen: how convenient for business! The great wealth of this country, produced by generations of workers, has been usurped by giant corporations. This is the root cause of our social decay.

The history of U.S. capitalism is one of shameful oppression of minority peoples. Vicious racism is instigated and perpetuated by the capitalist ruling class in order to divide the people one from another. This racism serves to increase capitalist profits by preventing the unification of the people, thereby keeping them vulnerable to exploitation. In fostering racism, the capitalist ruling class seeks to obscure and divert attention from the fact that it alone is the real enemy of the people.

To reap even greater profits, the giant corporations invest their surplus capital abroad. These multinational corporations spread their tentacles throughout the world, oppressing, robbing, and exploiting people everywhere. As a result of the use and exploitation of overseas labor, millions of American workers are laid off.

Even as the ruling class robs foreign lands and hurls bombs and napalm on peoples fighting for their national liberation in Indochina, so does it also seek to destroy hard-won constitutional liberties and the living standards of the people at home—particularly of those fighting for peace, liberation of minority peoples, and the needs of labor. We have seen increased repression and police state measures, more frequent frameups (as in the Angela Davis and Berrigan cases), and a variety of measures designed to cancel the Bill of Rights and the rights of labor to organize and strike. There is a grave danger of a military-racist-fascist type of state, under which the survival of even limited capitalist democracy is threatened.

Both major parties represent big business. There is no real distinction between the Republican Nixon Administration and one under a Democratic president. Both serve as the voice and agent of the huge corporate monopolies that are the real rulers of this country.

A revolutionary change in the social system is the only real answer to the crises that confront our people. Capitalism has proved itself unable to provide the well-being, freedom, peace and security which are the "inalienable rights" of every human being. Only Socialism, wherein the working people own and control the country's wealth can achieve those humanistic ends. Only a united people, first of all the working class, convinced in the course of mass struggle, can achieve Socialism, the one real answer to the fundamental need for true democracy.

The platform of the Communist Party is geared to win what must be fought for today and in the immediate years ahead. In this election campaign, the Communist Party calls upon the people to unite their ranks and to organize a powerful movement that will challenge the might of the monopoly corporations and ultimately win power for the people. Toward this end, we urge the unity of all anti-racist, anti-fascist, and pro-labor forces in the country: unite to defeat the most reactionary, pro-war, racist, and anti-labor candidates.

We call for the largest possible vote for Gus Hall and Jarvis Tyner, the Communist Party presidential and vice-presidential candidates. This will be the most meaningful and forceful electoral protest against the reactionary policies and rule of monopoly capitalism. This will be the most affirmative and effective vote for peace, jobs, freedom and socialism. Only a determined people, united in struggle, can win a society that truly provides for their needs. The following platform points the way.

AN END TO WAR, MILITARISM, AND IMPERIALIST INTRIGUE

End the war in Indochina by a complete, unconditional withdrawal of all men, arms and supplies. Dismantle all military bases. End all support to the corrupt Thieu regime. The people of Indochina must have the right to determine their own form of government and social system without outside interference. Reparations must be paid to the peoples of Vietnam for the massive destruction caused by U.S. aggression. Establish peaceful relations with the Democratic Republic of Vietnam.

End all military expenditures and padlock the Pentagon. Shut down all foreign U.S. military bases.

End all economic, military and political intrigue against Chile. End all military and economic intervention against democratic people's movements in Latin America, Asia, Africa and Europe, particularly in Angola, Rhodesia, South Africa and Greece. Recognize the sovereign right of all nations to regain ownership of foreign properties on their soil. Provide interest-free loans and credits for upbuilding underdeveloped countries without strings attached.

Recognize and establish full diplomatic and trade relations with People's Republic of China, Cuba, the German Democratic Republic, the Democratic People's Republic of Korea, Albania, and the People's Republic of Bangla Desh. End

all barriers to full trade relations with all socialist countries.

Immediate unconditional independence for Puerto Rico.

End all complicity with British imperialism in its suppression of the Irish freedom struggle.

End the alliance of U.S. imperialism and Israeli expansionism and aggression against the peoples of the Arab countries and Africa. Total Israeli withdrawal from all occupied Arab lands in accord with the November, 1967 U.N. resolution as a prerequisite to a political settlement. Guarantee the rights of the Palestinian peoples and the continued existence of Israel.

AN END TO POVERTY; RAISING OF LIVING STANDARDS; DEFENSE OF LABOR'S RIGHT TO ORGANIZE AND STRIKE

End all government intervention against labor in contract negotiations. End the wage freeze. Abolish the Pay Board.

End all restrictions on the right to strike and defeat all attempts at compulsory arbitration. Repeal the Taft-Hartley, Landrum-Griffin and the so-called state "right to work" laws. Outlaw strikebreaking.

Outlaw all discrimination in employment or union membership based on race, color, age, sex, religion, or political beliefs. Black, Puerto Rican, Chicano, Indian and Asian workers, women and youth must have full equality within all unions at all levels.

Provide decent jobs or adequate income for all families and persons. Raise welfare benefits to provide decent living standards (at this time, $6,500 per family of four). Raise Social Security to adequate income levels and provide full retirement benefits at age 55.

Establish uniform and universal unemployment compensation for full period of unemployment at full take-home pay wages. Provide unemployment compensation for all strikers and for first-time job seekers.

Increase minimum wages to $5 an hour for all workers in all states and occupations, including agriculture, and regardless of age, sex or race. Reduce, by Federal law, the work week to 30 hours at 40 hours pay, with time-and-a-half after 30 hours and double pay after 40 hours.

Launch a massive public housing construction program of millions of low-rent quality housing units annually to end slums; hiring without discrimination to give first jobs to those unemployed in the community at union pay and conditions. Build urban and inter-urban mass transit systems to provide free transportation.

Establish a national health care program providing to every man, woman and child the best medical, dental, hospital and other health care as a public service free of charge. Prosecute the profiteers and pushers of drugs—not the victims. Rehabilitate the drug addicts.

Develop a people's farm program. Use government subsidies to protect small family farms by guaranteeing adequate income, thus encouraging production and reducing prices to the consumer. Support the organization of agricultural workers into unions.

Prohibit employers from introducing new machinery or other devices that speed up workers, create unemployment, and endanger health and safety of workers. Introduction of new machines must have prior consent of union committee on the job. Strengthen existing accident and safety laws and enforcement procedures. Guarantee fair compensation to victims of industrial accidents.

Nationalize major industries, plants, and factories under democratic controls. This shall be done wherever necessary to protect the jobs of workers, their safety, health and union conditions and to provide essential services to meet the needs of the people. Monopoly corporations, major stockholders and financial overlords who have profited from government subsidies, tax swindles and the exploitation of workers shall not be further compensated. The needs of the workers and the people shall be the only guidelines in nationalization with a committee of representatives from workers, and people's organizations to formulate proposals for immediate nationalization of certain industries and to plan for further steps.

AN END TO RACISM, FREEDOM FOR BLACK, CHICANO, PUERTO RICAN, ASIAN AND INDIAN PEOPLES

Full equality for all, regardless of race, nationality, religion or sex, in employment, housing, education, culture, and in all aspects of economic, political and social life. Rebalance the scale of hundreds of years of slavery and repression by massive compensatory measures.

Spend $120 billion per year—equal to current spending for war and related purposes—for the needs of the poor, the Black people and other oppressed nationalities and the impoverished white workers. Priority spending for housing, education, transportation, health care, child care, and other services to the oppressed peoples.

Make racism, anti-Semitism, or any form of racial, national or religious bigotry, a federal crime. Racists and religious bigots should be removed from all positions of authority in the armed forces, in the educational system, and in all public services. Declare as felonies all racist propaganda and actions, punishable by severe terms of imprisonment as well as by fines. Officials responsible for enforcement of anti-racist laws shall be removed from office, and made liable to criminal action, if they fail to enforce these laws.

The rights of all racial and national minorities must be respected. Political subdivisions should be restructured to give oppressed minorities maximum rights to local self-government and to fullest representation on all levels. The people living in ghettos and barrios shall have the right to control the schools, police, welfare bodies and all other institutions of their communities. Institute proportional representation on all governmental bodies and school boards and end all political gerrymandering. Remove all language barriers and protect voters from racist harassment at the polls and registration places.

The centuries-old Indian and Mexican treaties must be honored to guarantee the rights of Indian and Chicano peoples to their lands (including restoration of lands and natural resources taken from them), culture, language and other features of life.

End the brutality, terror, and repression directed against the Black, Chicano, Puerto Rican, Asian and Indian peoples and their militant leaders. Police must live in the communities they serve. Police departments must be under strict community control. Support the right of Black and other oppressed peoples to armed self-defense to protect themselves from racist violence.

Demand freedom for Angela Davis and all imprisoned victims of racism. Black, Chicano, Puerto Rican and other minority peoples accused of crime must be charged and tried by juries of their peers. Where language is a barrier, all court proceedings shall be conducted in both English and the mother tongue of the defendant.

End racism in the armed forces. Halt harassment and persecution of minority servicemen. Prosecute officers guilty of racist practices.

## Taxing the Rich—Taxing the Monopolies

Institute a sharply graduated tax on corporation profits and on assessed valuation of all corporation properties. End all tax give-aways to big business for depreciation and depletion allowances. Corporation advertising, executive expense allowances and other devices shall no longer be deductible. Close all tax loop-holes with stiff penalties for violations. Open all corporation books to public inspection to overcome tax evasion.

Abolish all income taxes on family earnings of $15,000 a year or less. Abolish property taxes on homes assessed at $25,000 or less. Establish sharply graduated personal income taxes on incomes above $15,000.

End tax exemption for trust funds and private foundations. End tax exemptions to institutions making profit on slum housing or income from investments. Update and enforce inheritance tax laws.

Return the bulk of federal tax money to the communities to be distributed according to the people's needs and population size and with guarantees against racial, religious, political, or ethnic discrimination.

## Extension of Democracy; An End to Police-State Methods

Curb the excessive powers of the presidency. End the illegal Presidential use of war-making powers.

Abolish the FBI and end political frame-ups, eavesdropping and wiretapping. Abolish the Subversive Activities Control Board, the House and Senate Internal Security Committees, and repeal all repressive laws.

End police brutality. Disarm all police. Forbid use of police, National Guard or the army to suppress labor and people's struggles. Repeal all stop and frisk, preventive detention and political conspiracy laws.

Remove all restrictive election laws aimed against minority and new parties. Remove all bars to the right of the Communist Party to ballot status in all states. End discrimination against Communists in employment, education and political life.

End the system of congressional seniority which perpetuates racist and reactionary control over congressional committees.

Demand a judicial and penal system that is not biased against working people and oppressed nationalities. The government must pay all court costs in trial cases, including the cost of the defense. The defense shall be entitled to its own choice of legal counsel. Persons charged with a crime shall be given release on bail in accord with their ability to pay or on personal word pending trial. All persons imprisoned today shall have their cases reviewed by Citizens Courts composed of their peers. Prisoners shall have the right to organize and all other rights under the Constitution and its Bill of Rights.

Free Angela Davis, the Harrisburg 7 and all other political prisoners. Remove all charges against draft resisters and military deserters.

Democratize the armed forces. All servicemen shall have the right to free speech, press, and assembly and to belong to organizations of their own choosing, including servicemen's unions. Servicemen under charges shall be tried only by a jury of their peers, not by military brass. Servicemen shall have the right to prefer charges against superior officers and to remove them from rank.

## A National Youth Act—Administered by Youth for the Needs of Youth

End the militarization of the youth. Bring all military forces home from all parts of the world. End the draft. Reduce domestic armed forces to minimum peace time needs. Provide civilian jobs at union conditions and wages for all vets and G.I.'s. Provide job-training and skilled-work opportunities.

Provide jobs for all youth who need them, at union pay and conditions. Create a massive job-training program to meet the full economic and social needs of the youth. Give special attention and priority to the Black, Puerto Rican, Chicano and Indian youth who are victims of racism. Provide full unemployment compensation to first job seekers from day of job application to day of employment.

Make available free public quality education from grade school through the university and graduate schools. Provide government subsidies to meet living expenses of students in college and higher education. Offer special programs, including open enrollment, to guarantee full opportunity for working class, Black and other minority youth. Achieve total integration of the schools through busing, redistricting, and school site selection and any other means necessary. Eliminate military and corporate controls and influence from the education process. Establish meaningful student-faculty participation in all administrative bodies. Establish a National Student Bill of Rights to be formulated and adopted by student referendum.

Organize a massive, peace-oriented cultural, recreational, athletic and health project for youth with young people having decisive positions in all policy-making bodies. Finance such a project with Federal funds now used for military forces and facilities of the Pentagon. Convert the Pentagon's properties to peaceful uses. Launch international, cultural and student exchanges, athletic events and conferences to strengthen international understanding and relationships. Organize similar domestic and national events to develop the struggle against racism.

Strengthen youth participation in all levels of political life, including election to public office at the age of 18 and insure full exercise of their right to vote.

WOMEN'S EQUALITY AND WORKING CLASS UNITY

Pass a Labor Bill of Rights for Women that would guarantee the rights of working class women on the job and would be inclusive of all workers where applicable. Such a bill would include the following: End discrimination against women on the job. End all wage differentials on the basis of sex. Guarantee equal pay for equal work. End the practice of giving the lowest paid and menial jobs to Black, Puerto Rican and Chicano women. Establish a system of skilled job training and upgrading of all women workers. Prosecute the employer who discriminates by use of separate male and female seniority lists and other devices.

Guarantee full enforcement of laws protecting the health and safety of women workers, particularly in those areas where women's biological and reproductive capacities are endangered. Provide maternity leaves at full pay for six months and abortion leaves on a similar basis. Both types of leave to be in addition to regular sick leave.

Pass a comprehensive Child Development Act. Guarantee equality for all women by freeing them of the major responsibility for child care and education and placing it on society as a whole. Provide nation-wide, 24 hour child care facilities on or near work places and in the communities. Such facilities shall be financed by the employers but controlled by the trade unions and the workers whose children attend these centers. Guarantee access to child care facilities to all women, regardless of age, or whether they are full-time housewives or employed outside the home.

Abolish the degrading, inhuman features of the present welfare system and the Nixon starvation-and-forced-labor program. Support the guaranteed family income program of the National Welfare Rights Organization for $6,500 per year, decent living standard for a family of four.

Guarantee full participation by women in all levels of political organization. Ensure active participation and leadership of women on all levels of government: local, state and federal, administrative and judicial.

## Democratic Platform 1972

NEW DIRECTIONS: 1972–76

Skepticism and cynicism are widespread in America. The people are *skeptical* of platforms filled with political platitudes—of promises made by opportunistic politicians.

The people are *cynical* about the idea that a rosy future is just around the corner.

And is it any wonder that the people are skeptical and cynical of the whole political process?

Our traditions, our history, our Constitution, our laws, all say that America belongs to its people.

But the people no longer believe it.

They feel that the government is run for the privileged few rather than for the many—and they are right.

No political party, no President, no government can by itself restore a lost sense of faith. No Administration can provide solutions to all our problems. What we can do is to recognize the doubts of Americans, to speak to those doubts, and to act to begin turning those doubts into hopes.

As Democrats, we know that we share responsibility for that loss of confidence. But we also know, as Democrats, that at decisive moments of choice in our past, our party has offered leadership that has tapped the best within our country.

Our party—standing by its ideals of domestic progress and enlightened internationalism—has served America well. We have nominated or elected men of the high calibre of Woodrow Wilson, Franklin Delano Roosevelt, Harry S. Truman, Adlai E. Stevenson, John Fitzgerald Kennedy, Lyndon Baines Johnson—and in the last election Hubert Humphrey and Edmund S. Muskie. In that proud tradition we are now prepared to move forward.

We know that our nation cannot tolerate any longer a government that shows no regard for the people's basic needs and no respect for our right to the truth from those who lead us.

What do the people want?

They want three things:

They want a personal life that makes us all feel that life is worth living;

They want a social environment whose institutions promote the good of all; and

They want a physical environment whose resources are used for the good of all.

They want an opportunity to achieve their aspirations and their dreams for themselves and their children.

We believe in the rights of citizens to achieve to the limit of their talents and energies. We are determined to remove barriers that limit citizens because they are black, brown, young or women; because they never had the chance to gain an education; because there was no possibility of being anything but what they were.

We believe in hard work as a fair measure of our own willingness to achieve. We are determined that millions should not stand idle while work demands to be done. We are determined that the dole should not become a permanent way of life for any. And we are determined that government no longer tax the product of hard work more rigorously than it taxes inherited wealth, or money that is gained simply by having money in the first place.

We believe that the law must apply equally to all, and that it must be an instrument of justice. We are determined that the citizen must be protected in his home and on his streets. We are determined also that the ordinary citizen should not be imprisoned for a crime before we know whether he is guilty or not while those with the right friends and the right connections can break the law without ever facing the consequences of their actions.

We believe that war is a waste of human life. We are determined to end forthwith a war which has cost 50,000 American lives, $150 billion of our resources, that has divided us from each other,

drained our national will and inflicted incalculable damage to countless people. We will end that war by a simple plan that need not be kept secret: The immediate total withdrawal of all Americans from Southeast Asia.

We believe in the right of an individual to speak, think, read, write, worship, and live free of official intrusion. We are determined that our government must no longer tap the phones of law-abiding citizens nor spy on those who have broken no law. We are determined that never again shall government seek to censor the newspapers and television. We are determined that the government shall no longer mock the supreme law of the land, while it stands helpless in the face of crime which makes our neighborhoods and communities less and less safe.

Perhaps most fundamentally, we believe that government is the servant, not the master, of the people. We are determined that government should not mean a force so huge, so impersonal, that the complaint of an ordinary citizen goes unheard.

That is not the kind of government America was created to build. Our ancestors did not fight a revolution and sacrifice their lives against tyrants from abroad to leave us a government that does not know how to listen to its own people.

The Democratic Party is proud of its past; but we are honest enough to admit that we are part of the past and share in its mistakes. We want in 1972 to begin the long and difficult task of reviewing existing programs, revising them to make them work and finding new techniques to serve the public need. We want to speak for, and with, the citizens of our country. Our pledge is to be truthful to the people and to ourselves, to tell you when we succeed, but also when we fail or when we are not sure. In 1976, when this nation celebrates its 200th anniversary, we want to tell you simply that we have done our best to give the government to those who formed it—the people of America.

Every election is a choice: In 1972, Americans must decide whether they want their country back again.

## II. Jobs, Prices and Taxes

"I went to school here and I had some training for truck driver school and I go to different places and put in applications for truck driving but they say, 'We can't hire you without the experience.'

Now, I don't have the experience. I don't get the experience without the job first. I have four kids, you know, and I'm on unemployment. And when my unemployment runs out, I'll probably be on relief, like a lot of other people. But, being that I have so many kids, relief is just not going to be enough money. I'm looking for maybe the next year or two, if I don't get a job, they'll probably find me down at the county jail, because I have to do something."—Robert Coleman, Pittsburgh Hearing, June 2, 1972.

The Nixon Administration has deliberately driven people out of work in a heartless and ineffective effort to deal with inflation. Ending the Nixon policy of creating unemployment is the first task of the Democratic Party.

The Nixon "game plan" called for *more* unemployment. Tens of millions of families have suffered joblessness or work cutbacks in the last four years in the name of fighting inflation . . . and for nothing.

Prices rose faster in early 1972 than at any time from 1960 to 1968.

Today there are 5.5 million unemployed. The nation will have suffered $175 billion in lost production during the Nixon Administration by election day. Twenty per cent of our people have suffered a period without a job each year in the last three.

Business has lost more in profits than it has gained from this Administration's business-oriented tax cuts.

In pockets of cities, up to 40 per cent of our young people are jobless.

Farmers have seen the lowest parity ratios since the Great Depression.

For the first time in 30 years, there is substantial unemployment among aerospace technicians, teachers and other white-collar workers.

The economic projections have been manipulated for public relations purposes.

The current Nixon game plan includes a control structure which keeps workers' wages down while executive salaries soar, discourages productivity and distributes income away from those who need it and has produced no significant dent in inflation, as prices for food, clothes, rent and basic necessities soar.

These losses were unnecessary. They are the price of a Republican Administration which has no consistent economic philosophy, no adequate regard for the human costs of its economic decisions and no vision of what a full employment economy could mean for all Americans.

*Jobs, Income and Dignity*

Full employment—a guaranteed job for all—is the primary economic objective of the Democratic Party. The Democratic Party is committed to a job for every American who seeks work. Only through full employment can we reduce the burden on working people. We are determined to make economic security a matter of right. This means a job with decent pay and good working conditions for everyone willing and able to work and an adequate income for those unable to work. It means abolition of the present welfare system.

To assure jobs and economic security for all, the next Democratic Administration should support:

A full employment economy, making full use of fiscal and monetary policy to stimulate employment;

Tax reform directed toward equitable distribution of income and wealth and fair sharing of the cost of government;

Full enforcement of all equal employment opportunity laws, including federal contract compliance and federally-regulated industries and giving the Equal Employment Opportunity Commission adequate staff and resources and power to issue cease and desist orders promptly;

Vastly increased efforts to open education at all levels and in all fields to minorities, women and other under-represented groups;

An effective nation-wide job placement system to enhance worker mobility;

Opposition to arbitrarily high standards for entry to jobs;

Overhaul of current manpower programs to assure training—without sex, race or language discrimination—for jobs that really exist with continuous skill improvement and the chance for advancement;

Economic development programs to ensure the growth of communities and industry in lagging parts of the nation and the economy;

Use of federal depository funds to reward banks and other financial institutions which invest in socially productive endeavors;

Improved adjustment assistance and job creation for workers and employers hurt by foreign competition, reconversion of defense-oriented companies, rapid technological change and environmental protection activities;

Closing tax loopholes that encourage the export of American jobs by American-controlled multinational corporations;

Assurance that the needs of society are considered when a decision to close or move an industrial plant is to be made and that income loss to workers and revenue loss to communities does not occur when plants are closed;

Assurance that, whatever else is done in the income security area, the social security system provides a decent income for the elderly, the blind and the disabled and their dependents, with escalators so that benefits keep pace with rising prices and living standards;

Reform of social security and government employment security programs to remove all forms of discrimination by sex; and

Adequate federal income assistance for those who do not benefit sufficiently from the above measures.

The last is not least, but it is last for good reason. The present welfare system has failed because it has been required to make up for too many other failures. Millions of Americans are forced into public assistance because public policy too often creates no other choice.

The heart of a program of economic security based on earned income must be creating jobs and training people to fill them. Millions of jobs —real jobs, not make-work—need to be provided. Public service employment must be greatly expanded in order to make the government the employer of last resort and guarantee a job for all. Large sections of our cities resemble bombed-out Europe after World War II. Children in Appalachia cannot go to school when the dirt road is a sea of mud. Homes, schools and clinics, roads and mass transit systems need to be built.

Cleaning up our air and water will take skills and people in large numbers. In the school, the police department, the welfare agency or the recreation program, there are new careers to be developed to help ensure that social services reach the people for whom they are intended.

It may cost more, at least initially, to create decent jobs than to perpetuate the hand-out system of present welfare. But the return—in new public facilities and services, in the dignity of bringing a paycheck home and in the taxes that will come back in—far outweigh the cost of the investment.

The next Democratic Administration must end the present welfare system and replace it with an income security program which places cash assistance in an appropriate context with all of the measures outlined above, adding up to an earned income approach to ensure each family an income substantially more than the poverty level ensuring standards of decency and health, as officially defined in the area. Federal income assistance will supplement the income of working poor people and assure an adequate income for those unable to work. With full employment and simpler, fair administration, total costs will go down, and with federal financing the burden on local and state budgets will be eased. The program will protect current benefit goals during the transitional period.

The system of income protection which replaces welfare must be a part of the full employment policy which assures every American a job at a fair wage under conditions which make use of his ability and provide an opportunity for advancement.

H.R. 1, and its various amendments, is not humane and does not meet the social and economic objectives that we believe in, and it should be defeated. It perpetuates the coercion of forced work requirements.

*Economic Management*

Every American family knows how its grocery bill has gone up under Nixon. Every American family has felt the bite of higher and higher prices for food and housing and clothing. The Administration attempts to stop price rises have been dismal failures—for which the working people have paid in lost jobs, missed raises and higher prices.

This nation achieved its economic greatness under a system of free enterprise, coupled with human effort and ingenuity, and thus it must remain. This will be the attitude and objective of the Party.

There must be an end to inflation and the ever-increasing cost of living. This is of vital concern to the laborer, the housewife, the farmer and the small businessman, as well as the millions of

Americans dependent upon their weekly or monthly income for sustenance. It wrecks the retirement plans and lives of our elderly who must survive on pensions or savings gauged by the standards of another day.

Through greater efficiency in the operation of the machinery of government, so badly plagued with duplication, overlapping and excesses in programs, we will ensure that bureaucracy will cease to exist solely for bureaucracy's own sake. The institutions and functions of government will be judged by their efficiency of operation and their contribution to the lives and welfare of our citizens.

A first priority of a Democratic Administration must be eliminating the unfair, bureaucratic Nixon wage and price controls.

When price rises threaten to or do get out of control—as they are now—strong, fair action must be taken to protect family income and savings. The theme of that action should be swift, tough measures to break the wage-price spiral and restore the economy. In that kind of economic emergency, America's working people will support a truly fair stabilization program which affects profits, investment earnings, executive salaries and prices, as well as wages. The Nixon controls do not meet that standard. They have forced the American worker, who suffers most from inflation, to pay the price of trying to end it.

In addition to stabilizing the economy, we propose:

To develop automatic instruments protecting the livelihood of Americans who depend on fixed incomes, such as savings bonds with purchasing power guarantees and cost-of-living escalators in government social security and income support payments;

To create a system of "recession insurance" for states and localities to replace lost local revenues with federal funds in economic downturns, thereby avoiding reduction in public employment or public services;

To establish longer-term budget and fiscal planning; and

To create new mechanisms to stop unwarranted price increases in concentrated industries.

## Toward Economic Justice

The Democratic Party deplores the increasing concentration of economic power in fewer and fewer hands. Five per cent of the American people control 90 per cent of our productive national wealth. Less than one per cent of all manufacturers have 88 per cent of the profits. Less than two per cent of the population now owns approximately 80 per cent of the nation's personally-held corporate stock, 90 per cent of the personally-held corporate bonds and nearly 100 per cent of the personally-held municipal bonds. The rest of the population—including all working men and women—pay too much for essential products and services because of national policy and market distortions.

The Democratic Administration should pledge itself to combat factors which tend to concentrate wealth and stimulate higher prices.

To this end, the federal government should:

Develop programs to spread economic growth among the workers, farmers and businessmen;

Help make parts of the economy more efficient —such as medical care—where wasteful and inefficient practices now increase prices;

Step up anti-trust action to help competition, with particular regard to laws and enforcement curbing conglomerate mergers which swallow up efficient small business and feed the power of corporate giants;

Strengthen the anti-trust laws so that the divestiture remedy will be used vigorously to break up large conglomerates found to violate the anti-trust laws;

Abolish the oil import quota that raises prices for consumers;

Deconcentrate shared monopolies such as auto, steel and tire industries which administer prices, create unemployment through restricted output and stifle technological innovation;

Assure the right of the citizen to recover costs and attorneys fees in all successful suits including class actions involving Constitutionally-guaranteed rights, or rights secured by federal statutes;

Adjust rate-making and regulatory activities, with particular attention to regulations which increase prices for food, transportation and other necessities;

Remove artificial constraints in the job market by better job manpower training and strictly enforcing equal employment opportunity;

Stiffen the civil and criminal statutes to make corporate officers responsible for their actions; and

Establish a temporary national economic commission to study federal chartering of large multinational and international corporations, concentrated ownership and control in the nation's economy.

## Tax Reform

The last ten years have seen a massive shift in the tax burden from the rich to the working people of America. This is due to cuts in federal income taxes simultaneous with big increases in taxes which bear heavily on lower incomes—state and local sales and property taxes and the payroll tax. The federal tax system is still grossly unfair and over-complicated. The wealthy and corporations get special tax favors; major reform of the nation's tax structure is required to achieve a more equitable distribution of income and to raise the funds needed by government. The American people neither should nor will accept anything less from the next Administration.

The Nixon Administration, which fought serious reform in 1969, has no program, only promises, for tax reform. Its clumsy administrative favoring of the well-off has meant quick action on corporate tax giveaways like accelerated depreciation, while over-withholding from workers' paychecks goes on and on while the Administration tries to decide what to do.

In recent years, the federal tax system has moved precipitously in the wrong direction. Corporate taxes have dropped from 30 per cent of federal revenues in 1954 to 16 per cent in 1973, but payroll taxes for Social Security—regressive because the burden falls more heavily on the worker than on the wealthy—have gone from ten per cent to 29 per cent over the same period. If legislation now pending in Congress passes, payroll taxes will have increased over 500 per cent between 1960 and 1970—from $144 to $755—for the average wage earner. Most people earning under $10,000 now pay more in regressive payroll tax than in income tax.

Now the Nixon Administration—which gave corporations the largest tax cut in American history—is considering a hidden national sales tax (Value Added Tax) which would further shift the burden to the average wage earner and raise prices of virtually everything ordinary people buy. It is cruel and unnecessary to pretend to relieve one bad tax, the property tax, by a new tax which is just as bad. We oppose this price-raising unfair tax in any form.

*Federal income tax.* The Democratic Party believes that all unfair corporate and individual tax preferences should be removed. The tax law is clogged with complicated provisions and special interests, such as percentage oil depletion and other favors for the oil industry, special rates and rules for capital gains, fast depreciation unrelated to useful life, easy-to-abuse "expense-account" deductions and the ineffective minimum tax. These hidden expenditures in the federal budget are nothing more than billions of "tax welfare" aid for the wealthy, the privileged and the corporations.

*We, therefore, endorse as a minimum step the Mills-Mansfield Tax Policy Review Act of 1972,* which would repeal virtually all tax preferences in the existing law over the period 1974–1976, as a means of compelling a systematic review of their value to the nation. We acknowledge that the original reasons for some of these tax preferences may remain valid, but believe that none should escape close scrutiny and full public exposure. The most unjustified of the tax loopholes should, however, be closed immediately, without waiting for a review of the whole system.

After the implementation of the minimum provisions of the Mills-Mansfield Act, the Democratic Party, to combat the economically-depressing effect of a regressive income tax scheme, proposes further revision of the tax law to ensure economic equality of opportunity to ordinary Americans.

We hold that the federal tax structure should reflect the following principles:

*The cost of government must be distributed more fairly among income classes.* We reaffirm the long-established principle of progressive taxation —allocating the burden according to ability to pay —which is all but a dead letter in the present tax code.

*The cost of government must be distributed fairly among citizens in similar economic circumstances:*

*Direct expenditures by the federal government which can be budgeted are better than tax preferences as the means for achieving public objectives.* The lost income of those tax preferences which are deemed desirable should be stated in the annual budget.

When relief for hardship is provided through federal tax policy, as for blindness, old age or poverty, benefits should be provided equally by credit rather than deductions which favor recipients with more income, with special provisions for those whose credits would exceed the tax they owe.

Provisions which discriminate against working women and single people should be corrected. In addition to greater fairness and efficiency, these principles would mean a major redistribution of personal tax burdens and permit considerable simplification of the tax code and tax forms.

*Social security tax.* The Democratic Party commits itself to make the Social Security tax progressive by raising substantially the ceiling on earned income. To permit needed increases in Social Security benefits, we will use general revenues as necessary to supplement payroll tax receipts. In this way, we will support continued movement toward general revenue financing for social security.

*Property tax.* Greater fairness in taxation at the federal level will have little meaning for the vast majority of American households if the burden of inequitable local taxation is not reduced. To reduce the local property tax for all American families, we support equalization of school spending and substantial increases in the federal share of education costs and general revenue sharing.

New forms of federal financial assistance to states and localities should be made contingent upon property tax reforms, including equal treatment and full publication of assessment ratios.

Tax policy should not provide incentives that encourage overinvestment in developed countries by American business, and mechanisms should be instituted to limit undesirable capital exports that exploit labor abroad and damage the American worker at home.

### Labor-Management Relations

Free private collective bargaining between management and independent labor unions has been, and must remain, the cornerstone of our free enterprise system. America achieved its greatness through the combined energy and efforts of the working men and women of this country. Retention of its greatness rests in their hands. Through their great trade union organizations, these men and women have exerted tremendous influence on the economic and social life of the nation and have attained a standard of living known to no other nation. The concern of the Party is that the gains which labor struggled so long to obtain not be lost to them, whether through inaction or subservience to illogical Republican domestic policies.

We pledge continued support for our system of free collective bargaining and denounce any attempt to substitute compulsory arbitration for it. We, therefore, oppose the Nixon Administration's effort to impose arbitration in transportation disputes through its last-offer-selection bill.

The National Labor Relations Act should be updated to ensure:

Extension of protection to employees of non-profit institutions;

Remedies which adequately reflect the losses caused by violations of the Act;

Repeal of section 14(b), which allows states to legislate the open shop and remove the ban on common-sites picketing; and

Effective opportunities for unions, as well as employers, to communicate with employees, without coercion by either side or by anyone acting on their behalf.

The Railway Labor Act should be updated to ensure:

That strikes on a single carrier or group of carriers cannot be transformed into nation-wide strikes or lockouts;

Incentives for bargaining which would enable both management and labor to resolve their differences without referring to government intervention; and

Partial operation of struck railroads to ensure continued movement of essential commodities.

*New legislation* is needed to ensure:

Collective bargaining rights for government employees;

Universal coverage and longer duration of the Unemployment Insurance and Workmen's Compensation programs and to establish minimum federal standards, including the establishment of equitable wage-loss ratios in those programs, including a built-in escalator clause that fairly reflects increases in average wage rates; and

That workers covered under private pension plans actually receive the personal and other fringe benefits to which their services for their employer entitle them. This requires that the fixed right to benefits starts early in employment, that reserves move with the worker from job to job and that re-insurance protection be given pension plans.

### Labor Standards

American workers are entitled to job safety at a living wage. Most of the basic protections needed have been recognized in legislation already enacted by Congress.

The Fair Labor Standards Act should be updated, however, to:

Move to a minimum wage of $2.50 per hour, which allows a wage earner to earn more than a poverty level income for 40 hours a week, with no subminimums for special groups or age differentials;

Expand coverage to include the 16 million workers not presently covered, including domestic workers, service workers, agricultural employees and employees of governmental and nonprofit agencies; and

Set overtime premiums which give an incentive to hire new employees rather than to use regular employees for extended periods of overtime.

The Longshoremen and Harbor Workers' Compensation Act should be updated to provide adequate protection for injured workers and federal standards for workmen's compensation should be set by Congress.

The Equal Pay Act of 1963 should be extended to be fully effective, and to cover professional, executive and administrative workers.

Maternity benefits should be made available to all working women. Temporary disability benefits should cover pregnancy, childbirth, miscarriage and recovery.

## Occupational Health and Safety

Each year over 14,000 American workers are killed on their jobs, and nine million injured. Unknown millions more are exposed to long-term danger and disease from exposure to dangerous substances. Federal and state laws are supposed to protect workers; but these laws are not being enforced. This Administration has hired only a handful of inspectors and proposes to turn enforcement over to the same state bureaucracies that have proven inadequate in the past. Where violations are detected, only token penalties have been assessed.

We pledge to fully and rigorously enforce the laws which protect the safety and health of workers on their jobs and to extend those laws to all jobs, regardless of number of employees. This must include standards that truly protect against all health hazards, adequate federal enforcement machinery backed up by rigorous penalties and an opportunity for workers themselves to participate

in the laws' enforcement by sharing responsibility for plant inspection.

We endorse federal research and development of effective approaches to combat the dehumanizing debilitating effects of monotonous work.

## Farm Labor

The Sixties and Seventies have seen the struggle for unionization by the poorest of the poor in our country—America's migrant farm workers.

Under the leadership of Cesar Chavez, the United Farm Workers have accomplished in the non-violent tradition what was thought impossible only a short time ago. Through hard work and much sacrifice, they are the one group that is successfully organizing farm workers.

Their movement has caught the imagination of millions of Americans who have not eaten grapes so that agribusiness employers will recognize their workers as equals and sit down with them in meaningful collective bargaining.

We now call upon all friends and supporters of this movement to refrain from buying or eating non-union lettuce.

Furthermore, we support the farm workers' movement and the use of boycotts as a non-violent and potent weapon for gaining collective bargaining recognition and contracts for agricultural workers. We oppose the Nixon Administration's effort to enjoin the use of the boycott.

We also affirm the right of farm workers to organize free of repressive anti-labor legislation, both state and federal.

## III. RIGHTS, POWER AND SOCIAL JUSTICE

"We're just asking, and we don't ask for much. Just to give us opportunity to live as human beings as other people have lived."—Dorothy Bolden, Atlanta Hearing, June 9, 1972.

"All your platform has to say is that the rights, opportunities and political power of citizenship will be extended to the lowest level, to neighborhoods and individuals. If your party can live up to that simple pledge, my faith will be restored." —Bobby Westbrooks, St. Louis Hearing, June 17, 1972.

"We therefore urge the Democratic Party to adopt the principle that America has a responsibility to offer every American family the best in health care, whenever they need it, regardless of income or any other factor. We must devise a system which will assure that . . . every American receives comprehensive health services from the day he is born to the day he dies, with an emphasis on preventive care to keep him healthy."—Joint Statement of Senator Edward M. Kennedy and Representative Wilbur Mills, St. Louis Hearing, June 17, 1972.

The Democratic Party commits itself to be responsive to the millions of hard working, lower- and middle-income Americans who are traditionally courted by politicians at election time, get bilked at tax-paying time, and are too often forgotten the balance of the time.

This is an era of great change. The world is fast moving into a future for which the past has not prepared us well; a future where to survive, to find answers to the problems which threaten us as a people, we must create qualitatively new solutions. We can no longer rely on old systems of thought, the results of which were partially successful programs that were heralded as important social reforms in the past. It is time *now* to rethink and reorder the institutions of this country so that everyone—women, blacks, Spanish-speaking, Puerto Ricans, Indians, the young and the old—can participate in the decision-making process inherent in the democratic heritage to which we aspire. We must restructure the social, political and economic relationships throughout the entire society in order to ensure the equitable distribution of wealth and power.

The Democratic Party in 1972 is committed to resuming the march toward equality; to enforcing the laws supporting court decisions and enacting new legal rights as necessary, to assuring every American true opportunity, to bringing about a more equal distribution of power, income and wealth and equal and uniform enforcement in all states and territories of civil rights statutes and acts.

In the 1970's, this commitment requires the fulfillment—through laws and policies, through appropriations and directives; through leadership and exhortation—of a wide variety of rights:

The right to full participation in government and the political process;

The rights of free speech and free political expression, of freedom from official intimidation, harassment and invasion of privacy, as guaranteed by the letter and the spirit of the Constitution;

The right to a decent job and an adequate income, with dignity;

The right to quality, accessibility and sufficient quantity in tax-supported services and amenities—including educational opportunity, health care, housing and transportation;

The right to quality, safety and the lowest possible cost on goods and services purchased in the market place;

The right to be different, to maintain a cultural or ethnic heritage or lifestyle, without being forced into a compelled homogeneity;

The rights of people who lack rights: Children, the mentally retarded, mentally ill and prisoners, to name some; and

The right to legal services, both civil and criminal, necessary to enforce secured rights.

*Free Expression and Privacy*

The new Democratic Administration should bring an end to the pattern of political persecution and investigation, the use of high office as a pulpit for unfair attack and intimidation and the blatant efforts to control the poor and to keep them from acquiring additional economic security or political power.

The epidemic of wiretapping and electronic surveillance engaged in by the Nixon Administration and the use of grand juries for purposes of political intimidation must be ended. The rule of law and the supremacy of the Constitution, as these concepts have traditionally been understood, must be restored.

We strongly object to secret computer data banks on individuals. Citizens should have access to their own files that are maintained by private commercial firms and the right to insert corrective material. Except in limited cases, the same should apply to government files. Collection and maintenance by federal agencies of dossiers on law-abiding citizens, because of their political views and statements, must be stopped, and files which never should have been opened should be destroyed. We firmly reject the idea of a National Computer Data Bank.

The Nixon policy of intimidation of the media and Administration efforts to use government power to block access to media by dissenters must end, if free speech is to be preserved. A Democratic Administration must be an open one, with the fullest possible disclosure of information, with an end to abuses of security classifications and executive privilege, and with regular top-level press conferences.

## The Right to Be Different

The new Democratic Administration can help lead America to celebrate the magnificence of the diversity within its population, the racial, national, linguistic and religious groups which have contributed so much to the vitality and richness of our national life. As things are, official policy too often forces people into a mold of artificial homogeneity.

Recognition and support of the cultural identity and pride of black people are generations overdue. The American Indians, the Spanish-speaking, the Asian Americans—the cultural and linguistic heritage of these groups is too often ignored in schools and communities. So, too, are the backgrounds, traditions and contributions of white national, ethnic, religious and regional communities ignored. All official discrimination on the basis of sex, age, race, language, political belief, religion, region or national origin must end. No American should be subject to discrimination in employment or restriction in business because of ethnic background or religious practice. Americans should be free to make their own choice of lifestyles and private habits without being subject to discrimination or prosecution. We believe official policy can encourage diversity while continuing to place full emphasis on equal opportunity and integration.

We urge full funding of the Ethnic Studies bill to provide funds for development of curriculum to preserve America's ethnic mosaic.

## Rights of Children

One measure of a nation's greatness is the care it manifests for all of its children. The Nixon Administration has demonstrated a callous attitude toward children repeatedly through veto and administrative decisions. We, therefore, call for a reordering of priorities at all levels of American society so that children, our most precious resource, and families come first.

To that end, we call for:

The federal government to fund comprehensive development child care programs that will be family centered, locally controlled and universally available. These programs should provide for active participation of all family members in the development and implementation of the program. Health, social service and early childhood education should be part of these programs, as well as a variety of options most appropriate to their needs. Child care is a supplement, not a substitute, for the family;

The establishment of a strong child advocacy program, financed by the federal government and other sources, with full ethnic, cultural, racial and sexual representation;

First priority for the needs of children, as we move toward a National Health Insurance Program;

The first step should be immediate implementation of the federal law passed in the 1967 Social Security Amendments providing for "early and periodic screening, diagnosis and treatment" of children's health problems;

Legislation and administrative decisions to drastically reduce childhood injuries—prenatal, traffic, poisoning, burns, malnutrition, rat bites and to provide health and safety education.

Full funding of legislation designed to meet the needs of children with special needs: The retarded, the physically and mentally handicapped, and those whose environment produces abuse and neglect and directs the child to anti-social conduct;

Reaffirmation of the rights of bilingual, handicapped or slow-learning children to education in the public schools, instead of being wrongly classified as retarded or uneducable and dismissed;

Revision of the juvenile court system; dependency and neglect cases must be removed from the corrections system, and clear distinctions must be drawn between petty childhood offenses and the more serious crimes;

Allocation of funds to the states to provide counsel to children in juvenile proceedings, legal or administrative; and

Creation by Congress of permanent standing committees on Children and Youth.

## Rights of Women

Women historically have been denied a full voice in the evolution of the political and social institutions of this country and are therefore allied with all under-represented groups in a common desire to form a more humane and compassionate society. The Democratic Party pledges the following:

A priority effort to ratify the Equal Rights Amendment;

Elimination of discrimination against women in public accommodations and public facilities, public education and in all federally-assisted programs and federally-contracted employment:

Extension of the jurisdiction of the Civil Rights Commission to include denial of civil rights on the basis of sex;

Full enforcement of all federal statutes and executive laws barring job discrimination on the basis of sex, giving the Equal Employment Opportunities Commission adequate staff and resources and power to issue cease-and-desist orders promptly;

Elimination of discriminatory features of criminal laws and administration;

Increased efforts to open educational opportunities at all levels, eliminating discrimination against women in access to education, tenure, promotion and salary;

Guarantee that all training programs are made more equitable, both in terms of the numbers of women involved and the job opportunities provided; jobs must be available on the basis of skill, not sex;

Availability of maternity benefits to all working women; temporary disability benefits should cover pregnancy, childbirth, miscarriage and recovery;

Elimination of all tax inequities that affect women and children, such as higher taxes for single women;

Amendment of the Social Security Act to provide equitable retirement benefits for families with working wives, widows, women heads of households and their children;

Amendment of the Internal Revenue Code to permit working families to deduct from gross income as a business expense, housekeeping and child care costs;

Equality for women on credit, mortgage, insurance, property, rental and financial contracts;

Extension of the Equal Pay Act to all workers, with amendment to read "equal pay for comparable work;"

Appointment of women to positions of top responsibility in all branches of the federal government to achieve an equitable ratio of women and men. Such positions include Cabinet members, agency and division heads and Supreme Court Justices; inclusion of women advisors in equitable ratios on all government studies, commissions and hearings; and

Laws authorizing federal grants on a matching basis for financing State Commissions of the Status of Women.

### Rights of Youth

In order to ensure, maintain and secure the proper role and functions of youth in American government, politics and society, the Democratic Party will endeavor to:

Lower the age of legal majority and consent to 18;

Actively encourage and assist in the election of youth to federal, state and local offices;

Develop special programs for employment of youth, utilizing governmental resources to guarantee development, training and job placement; and

Secure the electoral reforms called for under "People and the Government."

### Rights of Poor People

Poor people, like all Americans, should be represented at all levels of the Democratic Party in reasonable proportion of their numbers in the general population. Affirmative action must be taken to ensure their representation at every level. The Democratic Party guidelines guaranteeing proportional representation to "previously discriminated against groups" (enumerated as "women, young people and minorities") must be extended to specifically include poor people.

Political parties, candidates and government institutions at all levels must be committed to working with and supporting poor people's organizations and ending the tokenism and co-optation that has characterized past dealings.

Welfare rights organizations must be recognized as representative of welfare recipients and be given access to regulations, policies and decision-making processes, as well as being allowed to represent clients at all governmental levels.

The federal government must protect the right of tenants to organize tenant organizations and negotiate collective bargaining agreements with private landlords and encourage the participation of the tenants in the management and control of all subsidized housing.

### Rights of American Indians

We support rights of American Indians to full rights of citizenship. The federal government should commit all necessary funds to improve the lives of Indians, with no division between reservation and non-reservation Indians. We strongly oppose the policy of termination, and we urge the government to provide unequivocal advocacy for the protection of the remaining Indian land and water resources. All land rights due American Indians, and Americans of Spanish and Mexican descent, on the basis of treaties with the federal government will be protected by the federal government. In addition we support allocation of Federal surplus lands to American Indians on a first priority basis.

American Indians should be given the right to receive bilingual medical services from hospitals and physicians of their choice.

## Rights of the Physically Disabled

The physically disabled have the right to pursue meaningful employment and education, outside a hospital environment, free from unnecessary discrimination, living in adequate housing, with access to public mass transportation and regular medical care. Equal opportunity employment practices should be used by the government in considering their application for federal jobs and equal access to education from pre-school to the college level guaranteed. The physically disabled like all disadvantaged peoples, should be represented in any group making decisions affecting their lives.

## Rights of the Mentally Retarded

The mentally retarded must be given employment and educational opportunities that promote their dignity as individuals and ensure their civil rights. Educational treatment facilities must guarantee that these rights always will be recognized and protected. In addition, to assure these citizens a more meaningful life, emphasis must be placed on programs of treatment that respect their right to life in a non-institutional environment.

## Rights of the Elderly

Growing old in America for too many means neglect, sickness, despair and, all too often, poverty. We have failed to discharge the basic obligation of a civilized people—to respect and assure the security of our senior citizens. The Democratic Party pledges, as a final step to economic security for all, to end poverty—as measured by official standards—among the retired, the blind and the disabled. Our general program of economic and social justice will benefit the elderly

directly. In addition, a Democratic Administration should:

Increase social security to bring benefits in line with changes on the national standard of living;

Provide automatic adjustments to assure that benefits keep pace with inflation;

Support legislation which allows beneficiaries to earn more income, without reduction of social security payments;

Protect individual's pension rights by pension re-insurance and early vesting;

Lower retirement eligibility age to 60 in all government pension programs;

Expand housing assistance for the elderly;

Encourage development of local programs by which senior citizens can serve their community in providing education, recreation, counseling and other services to the rest of the population;

Establish federal standards and inspection of nursing homes and full federal support for qualified nursing homes;

Take the needs of the elderly and the handicapped into account in all federal programs, including construction of federal buildings, housing and transportation planning;

Pending a full national health security system, expand Medicare by supplementing trust funds with general revenues in order to provide a complete range of care and services; eliminate the Nixon Administration cutbacks in Medicare and Medicaid; eliminate the part B premium under Medicare and include under Medicare and Medicaid the costs of eyeglasses, dentures, hearing aids, and all prescription drugs and establish uniform national standards for Medicaid to bring to an end the present situation which makes it worse to be poor in one state than in another.

The Democratic Party pledges itself to adopt rules to give those over 60 years old representation on all Party committees and agencies as nearly as possible in proportion to their percentage in the total population.

## Rights of Veterans

It is time that the nation did far more to recognize the service of our 28 million living veterans and to serve them in return. The veterans of Vietnam must get special attention, for no end of the war is truly honorable which does not provide these men the opportunities to meet their needs.

The Democratic Party is committed to extending and improving the benefits available to American veterans and society, to ending the neglect shown by the Nixon Administration to these problems and to the human needs of our ex-servicemen.

*Medical care.*—The federal government must guarantee quality medical care to ex-servicemen, and to all disabled veterans, expanding and improving Veterans Administration facilities and manpower and preserving the independence and integrity of the VA hospital program. Staff-patient ratios in these hospitals should be made comparable to ratios in community hospitals. Meanwhile, there should be an increase in the VA's ability to deliver out-patient care and home health services, wherever possible treating veterans as part of a family unit.

We support future coordination of health care for veterans with the national health care insurance program, with no reduction in scale or quality of existing veterans care and with recognition of the special health needs of veterans.

The VA separate personnel system should be expanded to take in all types of health personnel, and especially physician's assistants; and VA hospitals should be used to develop medical schools and area health education centers.

The VA should also assume responsibility for the care of wives and children of veterans who are either permanently disabled or who have died from service-connected causes. Distinction should no longer be made between veterans who have seen "wartime," as opposed to "peacetime," service.

*Education.*—Educational benefits should be provided for Vietnam-era veterans under the GI Bill at levels comparable to those of the original Bill after World War II, supplemented by special veteran's education loans. The VA should greatly expand and improve programs for poor or educationally disadvantaged veterans. In addition, there should be a program under which servicemen and women can receive high school, college or job training while on active duty. GI Bill trainees should be used more extensively to reach out to other veterans who would otherwise miss these educational opportunities.

*Drug addiction.*—The Veterans Administration should provide either directly or through community facilities, a comprehensive, individually tailored treatment and rehabilitation program for all drug- and alcohol-addicted veterans, on a voluntary and confidential basis, and regardless of the nature of their discharge or the way in which they acquired their condition.

*Unemployment.*—There should be an increase in unemployment compensation provided to veterans, and much greater emphasis on the Veterans Employment Service of the Department of Labor, expanding its activities in every state. There should be a greatly enlarged effort by the federal government to employ Vietnam-era veterans and other veterans with service-connected disabilities. In addition, veterans' preferences in hiring should be written into every federal contract or subcontract and for public service employment.

### Rights of Servicemen and Servicewomen

Military discipline must be maintained, but unjustifiable restriction on the Constitutional rights of members of the armed services must cease.

We support means to ensure the protection of GI rights to express political opinion and engage in off-base political activity.

We should explore new procedures for providing review of discharges other than honorable, in cases involving political activity.

We oppose deferential advancement, punishment assignment or any other treatment on the basis of race, and support affirmative action to end discrimination.

We support rights of women in the armed forces to be free from unfair discrimination.

We support an amendment of the Uniform Code of Military Justice to provide for fair and uniform sentencing procedures.

### Rights of Consumers

Consumers need to be assured of a renewed commitment to basic rights and freedoms. They must have the mechanisms available to allow self-protection against the abuses that the Kennedy and Johnson programs were designed to eliminate. We propose a new consumer program:

*In the Executive Branch.* The executive branch must use its power to expand consumer information and protection:

Ensure that every policy-making level of government concerned with economic or procurement decisions should have a consumer input either through a consumer advisory committee or through consumer members on policy advisory committees;

Support the development of an independent

consumer agency providing a focal point on consumer matters with the right to intervene on behalf of the consumer before all agencies and regulatory bodies; and

Expand all economic policy-making mechanisms to include an assessment of social as well as economic indicators of human well-being.

*In the Legislative Branch.*—We support legislation which will expand the ability of consumers to defend themselves:

Ensure an extensive campaign to get food, drugs and all other consumer products to carry complete informative labeling about safety, quality and cost. Such labeling is the first step in ensuring the economic and physical health of the consumer. In the food area, it should include nutritional unit pricing, full ingredients by percentage, grade, quality and drained weight information. For drugs, it should include safety, quality, price and operation data, either on the label or in an enclosed manual;

Support a national program to encourage the development of consumer cooperatives, patterned after the rural electric cooperatives in areas where they might help eliminate inflation and restore consumer rights; and

Support federal initiatives and federal standards to reform automobile insurance and assure coverage on a first-party, no-fault basis.

*In the Judicial Branch.*—The Courts should become an effective forum to hear well-founded consumer grievances.

Consumer class action: Consumers should be given access to the federal courts in a way that allows them to initiate group action against fraudulent, deceitful, or misleading or dangerous business practices.

Small Claims Court: A national program should be undertaken to improve the workings of small claims courts and spread their use so that consumers injured in economically small, though individually significant amounts (e.g. $500), can bring their complaints to the attention of a court and collect their damages without self-defeating legal fees.

## The Quality and Quantity of Social Service

The new Democratic Administration can begin a fundamental re-examination of all federal domestic social programs and the patterns of service delivery they support. Simply advocating the expenditure of more funds is not enough, although

funds are needed, for billions already have been poured into federal government programs—programs like urban renewal, current welfare and aid to education, with meager results. The control, structure and effectiveness of every institution and government grant system must be fully examined and these institutions must be made accountable to those they are supposed to serve.

We will, therefore, pursue the development of new rights of two kinds: Rights to the service itself and rights to participate in the delivery process.

## Health Care

Good health is the least this society should promise its citizens. The state of health services in this country indicates the failure of government to respond to this fundamental need. Costs skyrocket while the availability of services for all but the rich steadily declines.

We endorse the principle that good health is a right of all Americans.

America has a responsibility to offer to every American family the best in health care whenever they need it, regardless of income or where they live or any other factor.

To achieve this goal the next Democratic Administration should:

Establish a system of universal National Health Insurance which covers all Americans with a comprehensive set of benefits including preventive medicine, mental and emotional disorders, and complete protection against catastrophic costs, and in which the rule of free choice for both provider and consumer is protected. The program should be federally-financed and federally-administered. Every American must know he can afford the cost of health care whether given in a hospital or a doctor's office;

Incorporate in the National Health Insurance System incentives and controls to curb inflation in health care costs and to assure efficient delivery of all services;

Continue and evaluate Health Maintenance Organizations;

Set up incentives to bring health service personnel back to inner-cities and rural areas;

Continue to expand community health centers and availability of early screening diagnosis and treatment;

Provide federal funds to train added health

manpower including doctors, nurses, technicians and para-medical workers;

Secure greater consumer participation and control over health care institutions;

Expand federal support for medical research including research in heart disease, hypertension, stroke, cancer, sickle cell anemia, occupational and childhood diseases which threaten millions and in preventive health care;

Eventual replacement of all federal programs of health care by a comprehensive National Health Insurance System;

Take legal and other action to curb soaring prices for vital drugs using anti-trust laws as applicable and amending patent laws to end price-raising abuses, and require generic-name labeling of equal-effective drugs; and

Expand federal research and support for drug abuse treatment and education, especially development of non-addictive treatment methods.

### Family Planning

Family planning services, including the education, comprehensive medical and social services necessary to permit individuals freely to determine and achieve the number and spacing of their children, should be available to all, regardless of sex, age, marital status, economic group or ethnic origin, and should be administered in a non-coercive and non-discriminatory manner.

### Puerto Rico

The Democratic Party respects and supports the frequently-expressed desire of the people of Puerto Rico to freely associate in permanent union with the United States, as an autonomous commonwealth. We are committed to Puerto Rico's right to enjoy full self-determination and a relationship that can evolve in ways that will most benefit both parties.

To this end, we support equal treatment for Puerto Rico in the distribution of all federal grants-in-aid, amendment of federal laws that restrict aid to Puerto Rico; and we pledge no further restrictions in future laws. Only in this way can the people of Puerto Rico come to participate more fully in the many areas of social progress made possible by Democratic efforts, on behalf of all the people.

Finally, the Democratic Party pledges to end all Naval shelling and bombardment of the tiny, inhabited island of Culebra and its neighboring keys, not later than June 1, 1975. With this action, and others, we will demonstrate the concern of the Democratic Party to develop and maintain a productive relationship between the Commonwealth and the United States.

### Virgin Islands, Guam, American Samoa and the Trust Territories of the Pacific

We pledge to include all of these areas in federal grant-in-aid programs on a full and equitable basis.

We praise the Democratic Congress for providing a non-voting delegate to the House of Representatives from Guam and the Virgin Islands and urge that these elected delegates be accorded the full vote in the committees to which they are assigned.

We support the right of American Samoans to elect their Governor, and will consider methods by which American citizens residing in American territories can participate in Presidential elections.

### IV. CITIES, COMMUNITIES, COUNTIES AND THE ENVIRONMENT

"When the Democratic Platform is written and acted on in Miami, let it be a blueprint for the life and survival of our cities and our people."

—Mayor Kenneth A. Gibson
U.S. Conference of Mayors
New Orleans
June 19, 1972

### Introduction

Always the vital center of our civilization, the American city since World War II has been suffering growing pains, caused partly by the change of the core city into a metropolitan city and partly by the movement of people from towns and rural areas into the cities.

The burgeoning of the suburbs—thrust outward with too little concern for social, economic and environmental consequences—has both broadened the city's limits and deepened human and neighborhood needs.

The Nixon Administration has failed to meet most of these needs. It has met the problem of urban decay with tired, decaying "solutions" that are unworthy of the name. It could act to revitalize our urban areas; instead, we see only rising crime, fear and flight, racial and economic polarization, loss of confidence and depletion of community resources.

This Administration has ignored the cities and suburbs, permitting taxes to rise and services to decline; housing to deteriorate faster than it can be replaced, and morale to suffer. It actually has impounded funds appropriated by a Democratic Congress to help cities in crisis.

The Administration has ignored the needs of city and suburban residents for public services, for property tax relief and for the planning and coordination that alone can assure that housing, jobs, schools and transportation are built and maintained in suitable locations and in needed numbers and quality.

Meanwhile, the Nixon Administration has forgotten small-town America, too, refusing to provide facilities that would make it an attractive alternative to city living.

This has become the American crisis of the 1970's. Today, our highest national priority is clear and precise: To deal effectively—and *now* with the massive, complex and urgent needs of our cities, suburbs and towns.

The federal government cannot solve all the problems of these communities. Too often, federal bureaucracy has failed to deliver the services and keep the promises that are made. But only the federal government can be the catalyst to focus attention and resources on the needs of every neighborhood in America.

Under the Nixon Administration, piecemeal measures, poorly funded and haphazardly applied, have proved almost totally inadequate. Words have not halted the decline of neighborhoods. Words have not relieved the plight of tenants in poorly managed, shoddy housing. Our scarce urban dollars have been wasted, and even the Republican Secretary of Housing and Urban Development has admitted it.

The Democratic Party pledges to stop the rot in our cities, suburbs and towns, and stop it now. We pledge commitment, coordination, planning and funds:

Commitment to make our communities places where we are proud to raise our children;

Coordination and planning to help all levels of government achieve the same goals, to ensure that physical facilities meet human needs and to ensure that land—a scarce resource—is used in ways that meet the needs of the entire nation; and

Funds to reduce the burden of the inequitable property tax and to help local government meet legitimate and growing demands for public facilities and services.

The nation's urban areas must and can be habitable. They are not only centers of commerce and trade, but also repositories of history and culture, expressing the richness and variety of their region and of the larger society. They are worthy of the best American can offer. They are America.

*Partnership among Governments*

The federal government must assist local communities to plan for their orderly growth and development, to improve conditions and opportunities for all their citizens and to build the public facilities they need.

Effective planning must be done on a regional basis. New means of planning are needed that are practical and realistic, but that go beyond the limits of jurisdictional lines. If local government is to be responsive to citizen needs, public services and programs must efficiently be coordinated and evolved through comprehensive regional planning and decision-making. Government activities should take account of the future as well as the present.

In aiding the reform of state and local government, federal authority must insist that local decisions take into account the views and needs of all citizens, white and black, haves and have-nots, young and old, Spanish and other non-English-speaking, urban, suburban and rural.

Americans ask more and more of their local governments, but the regressive property tax structure makes it impossible for cities and counties to deliver. The Democratic Party is committed to ensure that state and local governments have the funds and the capacity to achieve community service and development goals—goals that are nationally recognized. To this end:

We fully support general revenue sharing and the principle that the federal income tax should be used to raise more revenues for local use;

We pledge adequate federal funds to halt property tax increases and to begin to roll them back. Turning over federal funds to local governments will permit salaries of underpaid state and local government employees to climb to acceptable levels; and it will reduce tax pressures on the aged, the poor, Spanish and other non-English-speaking Americans and young couples starting out in life;

We further commit ourselves to reorganize categorical grant programs. They should be consolidated, expanded and simplified. Funding should be adequate, dependable, sustained, long-term and related to state and local fiscal timetables and priorities. There should be full funding of all programs, without the impounding of funds by the Executive Branch to thwart the will of Congress. And there should be performance standards governing the distribution of all federal funds to state and local governments; and

We support efforts to eliminate gaps and costly overlaps in services delivered by different levels of government.

## Urban Growth Policy

The Nixon Administration has neither developed an effective urban growth policy designed to meet critical problems, nor concerned itself with the needed re-creation of the quality of life in our cities, large and small. Instead, it has severely over-administered and underfunded existing federal aid programs. Through word and deed, the Administration has widened the gulf between city and suburb, between core and fringe, between haves and have-nots.

The nation's urban growth policies are seen most clearly in the legitimate complaints of suburban householders over rising taxes and center-city families over houses that are falling apart and services that are often non-existent. And it is here, in the center city, that the failure of Nixon Administration policies is most clear to all who live there.

The Democratic Party pledges:

A national urban growth policy to promote a balance of population among cities, suburbs, small towns and rural areas, while providing social and economic opportunities for everyone. America needs a logical urban growth policy, instead of today's inadvertent, chaotic and haphazard one that doesn't work. An urban growth policy that truly deals with our tax and mortgage insurance and highway policies will require the use of federal policies as leverage on private investment;

A policy on housing—including low- and middle-income housing—that will concentrate effort in areas where there are jobs, transportation, schools, health care and commercial facilities. Problems of over-growth are not caused so much by land

scarcity, as by the wrong distribution of people and the inadequate servicing of their needs; and

A policy to experiment with alternative strategies to reserve land for future development—land banks—and a policy to recoup publicly created land values for public benefit.

## The Cities

Many of the worst problems in America are centered in our cities. Countless problems contribute to their plight: decay in housing, the drain of welfare, crime and violence, racism, failing schools, joblessness and poor mass transit, lack of planning for land use and services.

The Democratic Party pledges itself to change the disastrous policies of the Nixon Administration toward the cities and to reverse the steady process of decay and dissolution. We will renew the battle begun under the Kennedy and Johnson Administrations to improve the quality of life in our cities. In addition to pledging the resources critically needed, we commit ourselves to these actions:

Help localities to develop their own solutions to their most pressing problems—the federal government should not stifle or usurp local initiative;

Carry out programs developed elsewhere in this Platform to assure every American decent shelter, freedom from hunger, good health care, the opportunity to work, adequate income and a decent education;

Provide sufficient management and planning funds for cities, to let them increase staff capacity and improve means of allocating resources;

Distribute funds according to standards that will provide center cities with enough resources to revitalize old neighborhoods and build new ones, to expand and improve community services and to help local governments better to plan and deliver these services; and

Create and fund a housing strategy that will recognize that housing is neighborhood and community as well as shelter—a strategy that will serve all the nation's urban areas and all the American people.

## Housing and Community Development

The 1949 Housing Act pledged "a decent home and suitable living environment for every American family." Twenty-three years later, this goal is still far away. Under this Administration, there simply has been no progress in meeting our housing needs, despite the Democratic Housing Act of 1968. We must build 2.6 million homes a year, including two-thirds of a million units of federally-subsidized low- and middle-income housing. These targets are not being met. And the lack of housing is particularly critical for people with low and middle incomes.

In the cities, widespread deterioration and abandonment are destroying once sound homes and apartments, and often entire neighborhoods, faster than new homes are built.

Federal housing policy creates walled compounds of poor, elderly and ethnic minorities, isolating them in the center city.

These harmful policies include the Administration's approach to urban renewal, discrimination against the center city by the Federal Housing Administration, highway policies that destroy neighborhoods and create ghettoes and other practices that work against housing for low- and middle-income families.

Millions of lower—and middle-class Americans—each year the income level is higher—are priced out of housing because of sharply rising costs.

Under Republican leadership, the Federal Housing Administration (FHA) has become the biggest slumlord in the country. Some unsophisticated home buyers have purchased homes with FHA mortgage insurance or subsidies. These consumers, relying on FHA appraisals to protect them, often have been exploited by dishonest real estate speculators. Unable to repair or maintain these houses, the buyers often have no choice but to abandon them. As a result, the FHA will acquire a quarter million of these abandoned houses at a cost to the taxpayers of billions of dollars.

Under the Republican Administration, the emphasis has been on housing subsidies for the people who build and sell houses rather than for those people who need and live in them. In many cases, the only decent shelter provided is a tax shelter.

To correct this inequity the Democratic Party pledges:

To overhaul completely the FHA to make it a consumer-oriented agency;

To use the full faith and credit of the Treasury to provide direct; low-interest loans to finance the construction and purchase of decent housing for the American people; and

To insist on building practices, inspection standards and management that will assure quality housing.

The next Administration must build and conserve housing that not only meets the basic need for shelter, but also provides a wider choice of quality housing and living environments. To meet this challenge, the Democratic Party commits itself to a housing approach that:

Prevents the decay and abandonment of homes and neighborhoods. Major rehabilitation programs to conserve and rehabilitate housing are needed. Consumers should be aided in purchasing homes, and low-income housing foreclosed by the FHA should be provided to poor families at minimal cost as an urban land grant. These houses should be rehabilitated and lived in, not left to rot;

Provides federal funds for preservation of existing neighborhoods. Local communities should decide whether they want renewal or preservation. Choosing preservation should not mean steady deterioration and inadequate facilities;

Provides for improved housing quality for all families through strict enforcement of housing quality standards and full compliance with state and local health and safety laws;

Provides effective incentives to reduce housing costs—to the benefit of poor and middle-income families alike—through effective use of unused, undeveloped land, reform of building practices and the use of new building techniques, including factory-made and modular construction;

Assures that residents have a strong voice in determining the destiny of their own neighborhoods;

Promotes free choice in housing—the right of all families, regardless of race, color, religion or income, to choose among a wide range of homes and neighborhoods in urban, suburban and rural areas—through the greater use of grants to individuals for housing, the development of new communities offering diversified housing and neighborhood options and the enforcement of fair housing laws; and

Assures fair and equitable relationships between landlords and tenants.

*New Towns*

New towns meet the direct housing and community needs of only a small part of our populations. To do more, new towns must be developed in concert with massive efforts to revitalize central cities and enhance the quality of life in still growing suburban areas.

The Democratic Party pledges:

To strengthen the administration of the New Towns program; to reduce onerous review requirements that delay the start of New Towns and thus thwart Congressional mandates; to release already appropriated monies and provide new planning and development funds needed to assure the quality of life in New Towns; and

To assure coordination between development of New Towns and renewed efforts to improve the quality of life in established urban and suburban areas. We also promise to use effectively the development of New Towns to increase housing choices for people now living in central and suburban areas.

## Transportation

Urban problems cannot be separated from transportation problems. Whether tying communities together, connecting one community to another or linking our cities and towns to rural areas, good transportation is essential to the social and economic life of any community. It joins workers to jobs; makes commercial activity both possible and profitable and provides the means for expanding personal horizons and promoting community cultural life.

Today, however, the automobile is the principal form of transportation in urban areas. The private automobile has made a major contribution to economic growth and prosperity in this century. But now we must have better balanced transportation —more of it public. Today, 15 times as much federal aid goes to highways as to mass transit; tomorrow this must change. At the same time, it is important to preserve and improve transportation in America's rural areas, to end the crisis in rural mobility.

The Democratic Party pledges:

To create a single Transportation Trust Fund, to replace the Highway Trust Fund, with such additional funds as necessary to meet our transportation crisis substantially from federal resources. This fund will allocate monies for capital projects on a regional basis, permitting each region to determine its own needs under guidelines that will ensure a balanced transportation system and adequate funding of mass transit facilities.

Moreover, we will:

Assist local transit systems to meet their capital operating needs;

End the deterioration of rail and rural transportation and promote a flexible rural transportation system based on local, state and regional needs;

Take steps to meet the particular transportation problems of the elderly, the handicapped and others with special needs; and

Assist development of airport terminals, facilities and access to them, with due regard to impact on environment and community.

## Environment, Technology and Resources

Every American has the right to live, work and play in a clean, safe and healthy environment. We have the obligation to ourselves and to our children. It is not enough simply to prevent further environmental deterioration and the despoilation of our natural endowment. Rather, we must improve the quality of the world in which we and they will live.

The Nixon Administration's record on the environment is one of big promises and small actions.

Inadequate enforcement, uncertain requirements, reduced funding and a lack of manpower have undercut the effort commenced by a Democratic Administration to clean up the environment.

We must recognize the costs all Americans pay for the environmental destruction with which we all live: Poorer health, lessened recreational opportunities, higher maintenance costs, lower land productivity and diminished beauty in our surroundings. Only then can we proceed wisely, yet vigorously, with a program of environmental protection which recognizes that, although environmental protection will not be cheap, it is worth a far greater price, in effort and money, than we have spent thus far.

Such a program must include adequate federal funding for waste management, recycling and disposal and for purification and conservation of air and water resources.

The next Administration must reconcile any conflicts among the goals of cleaner air and water, inexpensive power and industrial development and jobs in specific places. These difficulties do exist—to deny them would be deceptive and irresponsible. At the same time, we know they can be resolved by an Administration with energy, intelligence and commitment—qualities notably absent from the current Administration's handling of the problem.

We urge additional financial support to the United States Forest Service for planning and management consistent with the environmental ideal stated in this Platform.

*Choosing the Right Methods of Environmental Protection*

The problem we face is to choose the most efficient, effective and equitable techniques for solving each new environmental problem. We cannot afford to waste resources while doing the job, any more than we can afford to leave the job undone.

We must enforce the strict emission requirements on all pollution sources set under the 1970 Clean Air Act.

We must support the establishment of a policy of no harmful discharge into our waters by 1985.

We must have adequate staffing and funding of all regulatory and enforcement agencies and departments to implement laws, programs and regulations protecting the environment, vigorous prosecution of violators and a Justice Department committed to enforcement of environmental law.

We must fully support laws to assure citizens' standing in federal environmental court suits.

Strict interstate environmental standards must be formulated and enforced to prevent pollution from high-density population areas being dumped into low-density population areas for the purpose of evasion of strict pollution enforcement.

The National Environmental Policy Act should be broadened to include major private as well as public projects, and a genuine commitment must be made to making the Act work.

Our environment is most threatened when the natural balance of an area's ecology is drastically altered for the sole purpose of profits. Such practices as "clear cut" logging, strip mining, the indiscriminate destruction of whole species, creation of select ocean crops at the expense of other species and the unregulated use of persistent pesticides cannot be justified when they threaten our ability to maintain a stable environment.

Where appropriate, taxes need to be levied on pollution, to provide industry with an incentive to clean up.

We also need to develop new public agencies that can act to abate pollution—act on a scale commensurate with the size of the problem and the technology of pollution control.

Expanded federal funding is required to assist local governments with both the capital and operating expenses of water pollution control and solid waste management.

*Jobs and the Environment*

The United States should not be condemned to the choice between the development of resources and economic security *or* preservation of those resources.

A decent job for every American is a goal that need not, and must not, be sacrificed to our commitment to a clean environment. Far from slowing economic growth, spending for environmental protection can create new job opportunities for many Americans. Nevertheless, some older and less efficient plants might find themselves in a worse competitive position due to environmental protection requirements. Closely monitored adjustment assistance should be made available to those plants willing to modernize and institute environmental protection measures.

*Science and Technology*

For years, the United States was the world's undisputed leader in science and technology. Now that leadership is being challenged, in part because of the success of efforts in other countries, and in part because of the Nixon Administration's neglect of our basic human and material resources in this field.

As Democrats, we understand the enormous investment made by the nation in educating and training hundreds of thousands of highly skilled Americans in science and technology. Many of these people are now unemployed, as aerospace and defense programs are slowly cut back and as the Administration's economic policies deprive these Americans, as well as others, of their livelihood.

So far, however, the Nixon Administration has paid scant attention to these problems. By contrast, the Democratic Party seeks both to increase efforts by the federal government and to stimulate research in private industry.

In addition, the Democratic Party is committed to increasing the overall level of scientific research in the United States, which has been allowed to fall under the Nixon Administration. And we are eager to take management methods and techniques devised for the space and defense programs, as well as our technical resources, and apply them to the city, the environment, education, energy, transportation, health care and other urgent domestic needs. We propose also to work out a more effective relationship between government and industry in this area, to stimulate the latter to a greater research and development effort, thus helping buoy up the economy and create more jobs.

Finally, we will promote the search for new approaches in science and technology, so that the benefits of progress may be had without further endangering the environment—indeed, so that the environment may be better preserved. We must create a systematic way to decide which new technologies will contribute to the nation's development, and which will cause more problems than they solve. We are committed to a role for government in helping to bring the growth of technology into a harmonious relationship with our lives.

## Energy Resources

The earth's natural resources, once in abundant and seemingly unlimited supply, can no longer be taken for granted. In particular, the United States is facing major changes in the pattern of energy supply that will force us to reassess traditional policies. By 1980, we may well have to depend on imports from the Eastern Hemisphere for as much as 30 to 50 per cent of our oil supplies. At the same time, new forms of energy supply—such as nuclear, solar or geothermal power—lag far behind in research and development.

In view of these concerns, it is shocking that the Nixon Administration still steadfastly refuses to develop a national energy policy.

The Democratic Party would remedy that glaring oversight. To begin with, we should:

Promote greater research and development, both by government and by private industry, of unconventional energy sources, such as solar power, geothermal power, energy from water and a variety of nuclear power possibilities to design clean breeder fission and fusion techniques. Public funding in this area needs to be expanded, while retaining the principle of public administration of public funds;

Re-examine our traditional view of national security requirements in energy to reconcile them with our need for long-term abundant supplies of clean energy at reasonable cost;

Expand research on coal technology to minimize pollution, while making it possible to expand the efficiency of coal in meeting our energy needs;

Establish a national power plant siting procedure to examine and protect environmental values;

Reconcile the demand for energy with the demand to protect the environment;

Redistribute the cost of power among consumers, so that all, especially the poor, may be guaranteed adequate power at reasonable costs;

Develop a national power grid to improve the reliability and efficiency of our electricity system;

End the practice of allowing promotional utility advertising as an expense when rates are set; and

Find new techniques to encourage the conservation of energy. We must also require full disclosure of the energy needs of consumer products and home heating to enable consumers to make informed decisions on their use of energy.

## The Oceans

As with the supply of energy, no longer can we take for granted the precious resources we derive from the oceans. Here, too, we need comprehensive national and international policies to use and protect the vast potential contained in the sea. In particular we must:

Agree with other nations on stopping pollution of the seas, if they are not one day to become one large sewer, or be filled with dangerous poisons that will deprive us of vital food resources;

Agree with other nations on the conservation of food resources in the seas and promote the use of management techniques that will end the decline of the world's fish catch on the continental shelf through international cooperation for fishing gear regulations and species quota and preserve endangered species;

Agree on an international accord for the seas, so resources can be shared equitably among the world's nations. We must be prepared to act constructively at next year's Conference on the Law of the Seas;

Begin to reconcile competing interests in the future of the seas, including our national security objectives, to protect ocean resources in cooperation with other nations; and

Support strongly the protection of ocean mammals (seal, whale, walrus) from indiscriminate destruction by both foreign and tuna fishing industries, but specifically exempting those native Americans whose subsistence depends completely on their total use of the ocean's resources.

Ninety percent of all salt water fish species live on our continental shelves, where plant life is plentiful. For this reason, we support monitoring and strict enforcement of all safety regulations on all offshore drilling equipment and on environmentally-safe construction of all tankers transporting oil.

*Public Lands*

For generations, Americans have been concerned with preserving the natural treasures of our country: Our lakes and rivers, our forests and mountains. Enlightened Americans of the past decided that the federal government should take a major role in protecting these treasures, on behalf of everyone. Today, however, neglect on the part of the Nixon Administration is threatening this most valued heritage—and that of our children. Never before in modern history have our public lands been so neglected and the responsible agencies so starved of funds.

The Democratic Party is concerned about preserving our public lands, and promoting policies of land management in keeping with the broad public interest. In particular, it is imperative to restore lost funds for land, park and forest management. It is imperative that decisions about the future use of our public lands be opened up to all the people for widespread public debate and discussion. Only through such an open process can we set ground rules that appropriately limit the influence of special interests and allow for cohesive guidelines for national land-use planning.

We are particularly aware of the potential conflicts among the use of land, rivers, lakes and the seashore for economic development, large-scale recreation and for preservation as unspoiled wilderness. We recognize that there are competing goals, and shall develop means for resolving these conflicts in a way that reflects the federal government's particular responsibilities as custodian for the public. We need more National Seashores and expansion of the National Park system. Major steps must be taken to follow up on Congressional commitment to scenic riverways.

Recreation areas must be made available to people where they live. This includes the extension of our national wilderness preserves to include de facto wilderness areas and their preservation free of commercialization. In this way, we will help to preserve and improve the quality of life for millions of our people.

With regard to the development of the vast natural resources on our public lands, we pledge a renewed commitment to proceed in the interests of all our citizens.

V. EDUCATION

"The American people want overwhelmingly to give to our children and adults equitable educational opportunities of the highest possible quality, *not* predicated on race, *not* predicated on past social accomplishment or wealth, except in a compensatory way to those who have been deprived in the past."—Governor Jimmy Carter, Atlanta Hearing, June 9, 1972.

Our schools are failing our children. Never, more than now, have we needed the schools to play their traditional role—to create a sense of national unity and to reconcile ethnic, religious and racial conflicts. Yet the Nixon Administration—by ignoring the plight of the nation's schools, by twice vetoing funds for education—has contributed to this failure.

America in the 1970's requires something the world has never seen: Masses of educated people —educated to feel and to act, as well as to think. The children who enter school next fall still will be in the labor force in the year 2030; we cannot even imagine what American society will be like then, let alone what specific jobs they may hold. For them, education must be done by teaching them how to learn, how to apply man's wisdom to new problems as they arise and how to recognize new problems as they arise. Education must prepare students not just to earn a living but to live a life—a creative, humane and sensitive life.

*School Finance*

Achieving educational excellence requires adequate financial support. But today local property taxes—which do not keep pace with inflation—can no longer support educational needs. Continued reliance on this revenue source imposes needless hardship on the American family without supplying the means for good schools. At the same time, the Nixon recession has sapped the resources of state government, and the Administration's insensitivity to school children has meant inadequate federal expenditures in education.

The next Democratic Administration should:

Support equalization in spending among school districts. We support Court decisions holding unconstitutional the disparities in school expenditures produced by dependence on local property taxes. We pledge equality of spending as a way to improve schools and to assure equality of access to good education for all children;

Increase federal financial aid for elementary and secondary education to enhance achievement of quality education anywhere, and by fully funding the programs passed by the Congress and by fully funding ESEA Title I;

Step up efforts to meet the special needs and costs of educationally disadvantaged children handicapped by poverty, disability or non-English-speaking family background;

Channel financial aid by a Constitutional formula to children in non-public schools;

Support suburban-urban cooperation in education to share resources and expenses;

Develop and implement the retraining of displaced black and other minority teachers affected by desegregation; and

Continue with full federal funding the breakfast and lunch programs for all children and the development of other programs to combat hunger.

### Early Childhood Education

Our youngest children are most ignored by national policy and most harshly treated by the Nixon Administration. President Nixon's cruel, irresponsible veto of the Comprehensive Child Development Act of 1971 indicates dramatically the real values of the present Administration.

That legislation struck down by President Nixon remains the best program to bring support to family units threatened by economic and social pressures; to eliminate educational handicaps which leave disadvantaged children unable to compete in school; to prevent early childhood disease before it results in adult disability; to interrupt the painful, destructive cycle of welfare dependence, and, most important, to allow all children happy lives as children and the opportunity to develop their full potential.

We support legislation for positive and preventive approaches to early childhood education.

These approaches should be designed to help eliminate educational handicaps before they require remedial treatment. A Democratic President will support and sign a program for universal comprehensive child development.

We should give reality to the right of mentally retarded children to adequate health care and educational opportunities through such measures as including necessary care under national health insurance and federal aid to assure an opportunity for education for all retarded persons.

### Equal Access to Quality Education

The Supreme Court of the United States in Brown v Board of Education established the Constitutional principle that states may not discriminate between school children on the basis of their race and that separate but equal has no place in our public education system. Eighteen years later the provision of integration is not a reality.

We support the goal of desegregation as a means to achieve equal access to quality education for all our children. There are many ways to desegregate schools: School attendance lines may be redrawn; schools may be paired; larger physical facilities may be built to serve larger, more diverse enrollments; magnet schools or educational parks may be used. Transportation of students is another tool to accomplish desegregation. It must continue to be available according to Supreme Court decisions to eliminate legally imposed segregation and improve the quality of education for all children.

### Bilingual Education

Ten per cent of school children in the United States speak a language other than English in their homes and communities. The largest of the linguistic and cultural groups—Spanish-speaking and American Indians—are also among the poorest people in the United States. Increasing evidence indicates an almost total failure of public education to educate these children.

The drop-out rates of Spanish-speaking and Indian children are the worst of any children in the country. The injury is compounded when such children are placed in special "compensatory" programs or programs for the "dumb" or the "retarded" on the basis of tests and evaluations conducted in English.

The passage of the Bilingual Education Act

of 1967 began a commitment by the nation to do something about the injustices committed against the bilingual child. But for 1972–73, Congress appropriated $35 million—enough to serve only two per cent of the children who need help.

The next Democratic Administration should:

Increase federal support for bilingual, bicultural educational programs, pre-school through secondary school, including funding of bilingual Adult Basic Education;

Ensure sufficient teacher training and curriculum development for such schools;

Implement an affirmative action program to train and to hire bilingual-bicultural Spanish-speaking persons at all levels in the educational system;

Provide inventories for state and local districts to initiate bilingual-bicultural education programs;

Require testing of bilingual-bicultural children in their own languages; and

Prohibit discrimination against bilingual-bicultural children in school.

## Career Education

Academic accomplishment is not the only way to financial success, job satisfaction or rewarding life in America. Many young Americans think that college is the only viable route when for some a vocational-technical career offers as much promise of a full life. Moreover, the country desperately needs skilled workers, technicians, men and women who understand and can handle the tools and equipment that mean growth and jobs. By 1975 the need for skilled craftsmen will increase 18 per cent while the need for college-trained persons will remain stable.

Young people should be permitted to make a career choice consistent with their interests, aptitudes and aspirations. We must create an atmosphere where the dignity of work is respected, where diversity of talent and taste is encouraged and where continuing opportunity exists to keep pace with change and gives a saleable skill.

To aid this, the next Democratic Administration can:

Give vocational-technical education the same priority in funds and emphasis previously given academic education;

Support full appropriations for the recently-passed Occupational Education Act;

Strengthen the career counseling programs in elementary, secondary and post-secondary education so that young people are made aware of all of the opportunities open to them and provide special kinds of vocational-technical education and experience to meet specific area needs;

Develop and promote a climate conducive to free, rational choice by young people, dispelling the current prejudices that influence career decisions for most young people almost from birth;

Establish a lifetime system of continuing education to enhance career mobility, both vertically and laterally, so that the career choice made at 18 or 20 years of age does not have to be the only or the final choice; and

Grant equal representation to minorities and women in vocational-technical education.

## Higher Education

We support universal access to opportunities to post-secondary education. The American education system has always been an important path toward social and economic advancement. Federal education policy should ensure that our colleges and universities continue as an open system. It must also stimulate the creative development and expansion of higher education to meet the new social, economic and environmental problems confronting society. To achieve the goals of equal opportunity in education, to meet the growing financial crisis in higher education and to stimulate reform of educational techniques, the next Democratic Administration should:

Support guaranteed access for all students to loan funds with long-term repayment based on future earnings. Not only the poor, but families with moderate incomes must be provided relief from the cost of a college and professional education;

Grant supplements and contingent loans to institutions, based on enrollment of federally-aided students;

Provide research funds to stimulate a partnership between post-secondary, secondary and primary education, in an effort to find new patterns for learning and to provide training and retraining of teachers, especially in urban areas;

Develop broad opportunities for lifelong learning including encouragement for post-secondary education throughout adult years and permit "stopping-off" during higher education;

Develop affirmative programs in universities

and colleges for recruitment of minorities and women for administrative and teaching positions and as students; and

Create incentives for non-traditional education which recognize the contribution of experience to an individual's educational status.

### Arts and Humanities

Support for the arts and humanities is one of the benchmarks of a civilized society. Yet, the continued existence of many of America's great symphonies, theatres and museums, our film institutes, dance companies and other art forms, is now threatened by rising costs, and the public contribution, far less than in most advanced industrial societies, is a fraction of the need.

We should expand support of the arts and humanities by direct grants through the National Foundation for the Arts and Humanities, whose policy should be to stimulate the widest variety of artistic and scholarly expression.

We should support long-range financing for public broadcasting, insulated from political pressures. We deplore the Nixon Administration's crude efforts to starve and muzzle public broadcasting, which has become a vital supplement to commercial television.

### VI. Crime, Law and Justice

"I think we can reduce crime. Society has no more important challenge because crime is human conduct and more than any other activity of people it reflects the moral character of a nation." —Ramsey Clark, Washington Hearing, June 23, 1972.

We advocate and seek a society and a government in which there is an attitude of respect for the law and for those who seek its enforcement and an insistence on the part of our citizens that the judiciary be ever mindful of their primary duty and function of punishing the guilty and protecting the innocent. We will insist on prompt, fair and equal treatment for all persons before the bar of justice.

The problem of crime in America is real, immediate and fundamental; its costs to the nation are staggering; nearly three-quarters of a million victims of violent crime in one year alone; more than 15,000 murders, billions of dollars of property loss.

The indirect, intangible costs are even more ominous. A frightened nation is not a free nation. Its citizens are prisoners, suspicious of the people they meet, restricted in when they go out and when they return, threatened even in their own homes. Unless government at all levels can restore a sense of confidence and security to its people, there is the ever-present danger that alarm will turn to panic, triggering short-cut remedies that jeopardize hard-won liberties.

When law enforcement breaks down, not only the victims of street violence suffer; the worker's health and safety is imperiled by unsafe, illegal conditions on the job; the society is defenseless against fraud and pollution; most tragically of all, parents and communities are ravaged by traffic in dangerous drugs.

The Nixon Administration campaigned on a pledge to reduce crime—to strengthen the "peace forces" against the "criminal forces." Despite claims to the contrary, that pledge has been broken:

Violent crime has increased by one-third, to the highest levels in our history;

Fueled by the immense profits of narcotics traffic, organized crime has thrust its corruption farther and farther, into law enforcement agencies and the halls of justice;

The Department of Justice has become the handmaiden of the White House political apparatus, offering favors to those special interests which buy their "law" in Washington.

The Justice Department has failed to enforce laws protecting key legal rights, such as the Voting Rights Act of 1965;

Nixon and Mitchell use federal crime control funds for political purposes, squandering $1.5 billion.

To reverse this course, through equal enforcement of the law, and to rebuild justice the Democratic Party believes:

The impact of crime in America cuts across racial, geographic and economic lines;

Hard-line rhetoric, pandering to emotion, is both futile and destructive;

We can protect all people without undermining fundamental liberties by ceasing to use "law and order" as justification for repression and political persecution, and by ceasing to use stop-gap measures as preventive detention, "no-knock" entry, surveillance, promiscuous and unauthorized use of wire taps, harassment, and secret dossiers; and

The problems of crime and drug abuse cannot be isolated from the social and economic conditions that give rise to them.

## Preventing Crime

Effective law enforcement requires tough planning and action. This Administration has given us nothing but tough words. Together with unequal law enforcement by police, prosecutors and judges, the result is a "turnstile" system of injustice, where most of those who commit crime are not arrested, most of those arrested are not prosecuted, and many of those prosecuted are not convicted. Under this Administration, the conviction rate for federal prosecutions has declined to one-half its former level. Tens of thousands of offenders simply never appear in court and are heard from again only when they commit another crime. This system does not deter crime. It invites it. It will be changed only when all levels of government act to return firmness and fairness to every part of the criminal justice system.

Fear of crime, and firm action against it, is not racism. Indeed the greatest victims of crime today—whether of business fraud or of the narcotics plague—are the people of the ghetto, black and brown. Fear now stalks their streets far more than it does the suburbs.

So that Americans can again live without fear of each other the Democratic Party believes:

There must be equally stringent law enforcement for rich and poor, corporate and individual offenders;

Citizens must be actively involved with the police in a joint effort;

Police forces must be upgraded, and recruiting of highly qualified and motivated policemen must be made easier through federally-assisted pay commensurate with the difficulty and importance of their job, and improved training with comprehensive scholarship and financial support for anyone who is serving or will contract to serve for an appropriate period of police service;

The complex job of policing requires a sensitivity to the changing social demands of the communities in which police operate;

We must provide the police with increased technological facilities and support more efficient use of police resources, both human and material;

When a person is arrested, both justice and

effective deterrence of crime require that he be speedily tried, convicted or acquitted, and if convicted, promptly sentenced. To this end we support financial assistance to local courts, prosecutors, and independent defense counsel for expansion, streamlining, and upgrading, with trial in 60 days as the goal;

To train local and state police officers, a Police Academy on a par with the other service academies should be established as well as an Academy of Judicial Administration;

We will provide every assistance to our law enforcement agencies at federal and local levels in the training of personnel and the improvement of techniques and will encourage mutual cooperation between each in its own sphere of responsibility;

We will support needed legislation and action to seek out and bring to justice the criminal organization of national scope operating in our country;

We will provide leadership and action in a national effort against the usage of drugs and drug addiction, attacking this problem at every level and every source in a full scale campaign to drive this evil from our society. We recognize drug addiction as a health problem and pledge that emphasis will be put on rehabilitation of addicts;

We will provide increased emphasis in the area of juvenile delinquency and juvenile offenses in order to deter and rehabilitate young offenders;

There must be laws to control the improper use of hand guns. Four years ago a candidate for the presidency was slain by a handgun. Two months ago, another candidate for that office was gravely wounded. Three out of four police officers killed in the line of duty are slain with hand guns. Effective legislation must include a ban on sale of hand guns known as Saturday night specials which are unsuitable for sporting purposes;

A comprehensive fully-funded program is needed to improve juvenile justice, to ensure minimum standards, to expand research into rehabilitation techniques, including alternatives to reform schools and coordinate existing programs for treating juvenile delinquency; and

The block-grant system of the Law Enforcement Assistance Administration which has produced ineffectiveness, waste and corruption should be eliminated. Funds should go directly to operating agencies that are committed to change and improvement in local law enforcement, including agencies concerned with research, rehabilitation, training and treatment.

## Narcotic Drugs

Drug addiction and alcoholism are health problems. Drugs prey on children, destroy lives and communities, force crimes to satisfy addicts, corrupt police and government and finance the expansion of organized crime. A massive national effort, equal to the scale and complexity of the problem, is essential.

The next Democratic Administration should support:

A massive law enforcement effort, supported by increased funds and personnel, against the suppliers and distributors of heroin and other dangerous drugs, with increased penalties for major narcotics traffickers;

Full use of all existing resources to halt the illegal entry of narcotics into the United States, including suspension of economic and military assistance to any country that fails to take appropriate steps to prevent narcotic drugs produced or processed in that country from entering the United States illegally, and increases in customs personnel fighting smuggling of hard drugs;

An all-out investigative and prosecutory effort against corruption in government and law enforcement. Where corruption exists it is a major factor in permitting criminal activity, especially large-scale narcotic distribution, to flourish. It also destroys respect for the law in all who are conscious of its operation. We are determined that our children—whether in the ghetto or in a suburban high school—shall no longer be able to see a pusher protected from prosecution, openly plying his trade;

Strict regulation and vigorous enforcement of existing quotas regulating production and distribution of dangerous drugs, including amphetamines and barbiturates, to prevent diversion into illegal markets, with legislation for strong *criminal* penalties against drug manufacturers engaging in illegal overproduction, distribution and importation;

Expanded research into dangerous drugs and their abuse, focusing especially on heroin addiction among the young and development of effective, non-addictive heroin treatment methods;

Concentration of law enforcement efforts on major suppliers and distributors, with most individual users diverted into treatment before prosecution;

Immediate placement in medical or psychiatric treatment, available to any individual drug abuser without fear of disclosure or harassment. Work opportunities should be provided for addicts in treatment by supported work and other programs; and

Drug education in schools based on fact, not scare tactics to teach young people the dangers of different drugs, and full treatment opportunities for youthful drug abusers. Hard drug trafficking in schools must be met with the strongest possible law enforcement.

## Organized and Professional Crime

We are determined to exert the maximum power and authority of the federal government to protect the many victims who cannot help themselves against great criminal combinations.

Against the organized criminal syndicates, we pledge an expanded federal enforcement effort; one not restricted to criminals of any particular ethnic group, but which recognizes that organized crime in the United States cuts across all boundaries of race, national origin and class.

Against white-collar crime, we pledge to enforce the maximum penalties provided by law. Justice cannot survive when, as too often is the case, a boy who steals a television set is sentenced to a long jail term, while a stock manipulator who steals millions is only commanded to sin no more.

At least where life or personal injury are at stake, we pledge to seek expanded criminal penalties for the violation of federal laws. Employers who violate the worker safety and health laws, or manufacturers who knowingly sell unsafe products or drugs profit from death and injury as knowingly as the common mugger. They deserve equally severe punishment.

## Rehabilitation of Offenders

Few institutions in America are as uniformly condemned and as consistently ignored as our existing prison system. Many prisons that are supposed to rehabilitate and separate, in fact train their inmates for nothing but brutality and a life of further crime. Only when public understanding recognizes that our existing "corrections" system *contributes* to escalating crime, will we get the massive effort necessary for fundamental restructuring.

Therefore, the Democratic Party commits itself to:

Restoration, after release, of rights to obtain drivers licenses and to public and private employment, and, after completion of sentence and conditions of parole, restoration of civil rights to vote and hold public office;

Revision of sentencing procedures and greater use of community-based rehabilitation facilities, especially for juveniles;

Recognition of the constitutional and human rights of prisoners; realistic therapeutic, vocational, wage-earning, education, alcoholism and drug treatment programs;

Making correctional personnel an integral part of the rehabilitative process;

Emergency, educational and work-release furlough programs as an available technique, support for "self-help" programs; and

Restoration of civil rights to ex-convicts after completion of their sentences, including the right to vote, to hold public office, to obtain drivers' licenses and to public and private employment.

### The Quality of Justice

Justice is not merely effective law enforcement —though that is an essential part of it. Justice, rather, expresses the moral character of a nation and its commitment to the rule of law, to equality of all people before the law.

The Democratic Party believes that nothing must abridge the faith of the American citizens in their system of law and justice.

We believe that the quality of justice will be enhanced by:

Equal treatment for all citizens in the court without fear or favor—corporations as well as individual offenders;

Swift trials for accused persons;

Equitable pre-trial release systems and the elimination of plea bargaining abuses;

Ending subversion of the legal system for political gain in court appointments, in antitrust cases and in administration of law enforcement programs;

Administering the laws and funding enacted by the Congress;

Respecting and abiding by Constitutional protections of due process; and

Abolishing capital punishment, recognized as an ineffective deterrent to crime, unequally applied and cruel and excessive punishment.

### VII. Farming and Rural Life

"A blight hangs over the land caused by misguided farm policies."—Tony Dechant, Sioux City hearing, June 16, 1972.

For many decades, American agriculture has been the envy of the world; and American farmers and American ranchers have made possible a level of nutrition and abundance for our people that is unrivaled in history, while feeding millions of people abroad.

The basis for this success—and its promise for the future—lies with the family-type farm. It can and must be preserved, in the best interests of all Americans and the nation's welfare.

Today, as dwindling income forces thousands of family farmers into bankruptcy each year, the family-type farm is threatened with extinction. American farming is passing to corporate control.

These trends will benefit few of our people, while hurting many. The dominance of American food production by the large corporation would destroy individual enterprise and links that millions of our people have with the land; and it would lead to higher prices and higher food costs for everyone.

Major efforts must be made to prevent this disaster for the fabric of rural life, for the American farmer, rancher, farm worker and for the consumer and other rural people throughout our nation;

Farm income must be improved to enable farmers, ranchers and farm workers to produce a steady and dependable supply of food and fiber products in return for full parity; and

We must recognize and fulfill the social contract that exists between the family-farm producers of food and the non-farm consumer.

The Democratic Party understands these urgent needs; the Nixon Administration does not and has failed the American farmer. Its record today is consistent with the Republican record of the past: Low prices, farm surpluses that depress the market and callous disregard for the people in rural America.

This Administration has sold out agriculture to interests bent on eliminating family-type farmers and bent on delivering agriculture to conglomerates, agribusiness giants and rich investors seeking to avoid taxes.

Its policies have driven farm income as low as 67 per cent of parity, unequalled since the Depression. Between 50,000 and 75,000 farm families are driven off the land each year. Hundreds of thousands of demoralized people are being forced into overcrowded cities, emptying the countryside and bankrupting small business in rural towns and cities.

The Nixon Administration tries to hide its failures by misleading the people, juggling the parity formula to make prices look higher, distorting reports to make corporate farming look insignificant and trying to break up the U.S. Department of Agriculture and still the farmer's voice.

The Democratic Party will reverse these disastrous policies, and begin to recreate a rural society of widespread family farming, individual opportunity and private and cooperative enterprises, where honest work will bring a decent income.

We repudiate the Administration's set-aside program, which pushes up the cost of farm programs while building huge surpluses that depress prices.

We repudiate the Report of the USDA Young Executives Committee which would eliminate the family-type farm by ending price support, loan and purchasing programs on all farm commodities and which would put farm people on the welfare rolls.

We repudiate a Presidential commission report recommending that future federal investment in many small towns and cities should make their decline merely more bearable rather than reverse it.

In place of these negative and harmful policies, the Democratic Party pledges itself to take positive and decisive action:

We will replace the 1970 Farm Act, when it expires next year, with a permanent law to provide fair prices to family-type farm and ranch operators. This law will include loans and payments to farmers and effective supply management to raise family farm income to 100 percent of parity, based on the 1910–14 ratios:

We will resist a price ceiling on agriculture products until farm prices reach 110 per cent of parity, based on the 1910–14 ratios, and we will conduct a consumer education program to inform all Americans of the relationship between the prices of raw commodities and retail prices;

We will end farm program benefits to farm units larger than family-size; and

We will work for production adjustment that will assure adequate food and fiber for all our people, including low-income families and individuals whose purchasing power is supplemented with food stamps and that can provide enough commodities for export and for the Food for Peace Program.

*Exporting Our Abundance*

For many years, farm exports have made a major contribution to our balances of trade and payments. But this benefit for the entire nation must not be purchased with depressed prices for the producer.

The Democratic Party will ensure that:

Prices for commodities sent abroad as exports or aid return the cost of production plus a profit for the American farmer;

We will negotiate international commodity agreements to include prices that guarantee prices to producers based on cost of production plus a reasonable profit;

We will require U.S. corporations producing commodities outside the country for consumption here to pay duties high enough to prevent unfair competition for domestic producers;

We will assure that the same rigid standards for inspection of domestic dairy products and meat will be applied to imports; and

We will create a strategic reserve of storable commodities, insulated from the market, rotated regularly to maintain quality and stored to the extent possible on farms.

*Strengthening the Family Farm*

These policies and actions will not be enough on their own to strengthen the family farm. The Democratic Party also recognizes that farmers and ranchers must be able to gain economic strength in the marketplace by organizing and bargaining collectively for the sale of their products. And they need to be free of unfair competition from monopoly and other restrictive corporate practices. We therefore pledge:

To remove all obstacles to farm bargaining for the sale of products;

To extend authority for marketing orders to all farm commodities including those used for processing;

To prohibit farming, or the gaining of monopolistic control of production, on the part of corporations whose resources and income derive primarily from non-farm sources;

To investigate violations and enforce anti-trust laws in corporation-agriculture-agribusiness interlocks;

To prohibit corporations and individuals from setting up tax shelters or otherwise engaging in agriculture primarily for the purpose of tax avoidance or tax loss;

To encourage and support the use of cooperatives and membership associations in all areas of the country, which we pledge to protect from interference, punitive taxation or other hindrances; and

To assist small rural cooperatives to promote projects in housing, health, social services, marketing, farming, employment and transportation for rural areas with such things as technical assistance and credit.

## Guaranteeing Farm People a Voice

None of these policies can begin to work unless farmers, ranchers, farm workers and other rural people have full rights of participation in our democratic institutions of government. The Democratic Party is committed to seeing that family-type farmers and ranchers will be heard and that they will have ample opportunity to help shape policies affecting agriculture and rural America. To this end:

We support the appointment of a farmer or rancher as Secretary of Agriculture;

We oppose all efforts to abolish or dismantle the U.S. Department of Agriculture;

We will require that decisions relating to dams and other public land-use projects in rural areas involving federal funds be considered at well-publicized public hearings. Government is not now giving adequate protection to individual rights in condemnation procedures. It must set new and better procedures and requirements to assure individual rights;

We supported the United Farm Workers in their non-violent efforts to gain collective bargaining recognition and contracts. We also support unemployment insurance compensation benefits, workman's compensation benefits and delivery of health services for farm workers; and

We support the removal of sugar workers from the custody of the U.S. Department of Agriculture.

## Revitalizing Rural America

Sound rural development must start with improved farm income, which also promotes the prosperity of the small businesses that serve all rural people. But there must be other efforts, as well, to ensure equity for farm and rural people in the American economy. The Democratic Party pledges:

To support the rural cooperative electrification and telephone programs and to implement rural transportation programs as explained in the section Cities, Communities, Counties and the Environment of this Platform. We will extend the agricultural exemption in the Motor Carriers Act to products and supplies and ensure rural areas an equitable share of Highway Trust Funds;

To apply general revenue sharing in ways that will permit state and local taxation of family farm lands on the basis of value for farm use rather than value for land speculation;

To guarantee equal treatment of rural and urban areas in the provision of federal funds for schools, poverty programs, health facilities, housing, highways, air services, pollution control, senior citizen programs and employment opportunities and manpower and training programs;

To provide loans to aid young farm families and small businesses to get established in rural areas; and

To ensure agricultural research toward an examination of the social and economic consequences of technology.

The prime goal of land grant colleges and research should be to help family farms and rural people.

## VIII. FOREIGN POLICY

"The Administration is continuing a war—continuing the killing of Americans and Vietnamese —when our national security is not at stake.

"It is our duty as the opposition party to point out the Administration's errors and to offer a responsible alternative."—W. Averell Harriman, New York Hearing, June 22, 1972.

Strength in defense and wisdom in foreign affairs are essential to prosperity and tranquility. In the modern world, there can be no isolationism in reality or policy. But the measure of our nation's rank in the world must be our success in achieving a just and peaceful society at home.

For the Nixon Administration, foreign policy results have fallen short of the attention and the slogans:

After four years of "Vietnamization," the war in Southeast Asia continues and Nixon's plan is still a secret;

Vital foreign policy decisions are made without consultation with Congress or our allies; and

Executive secrecy runs wild with unparalleled efforts to intimidate the media and suppress those who seek to put a different view before the American people.

The next Democratic Administration should:

End American participation in the war in Southeast Asia;

Re-establish control over military activities and reduce military spending, where consistent with national security;

Defend America's real interests and maintain our alliances, neither playing world policeman nor abandoning old and good friends;

Not neglect America's relations with small third-world nations in placing reliance in great power relationships;

Return to Congress, and to the people, a meaningful role in decisions on peace and war; and

Make information public, except where real national defense interests are involved.

### Vietnam

Nothing better describes the need for a new American foreign policy than the fact that now, as for the past seven years, it begins with the war in Vietnam.

The task now is still to end the war, not to decide who is to blame for it. The Democratic Party must share the responsibility for this tragic war. But, elected with a secret plan to end this war, Nixon's plan is still secret, and we—and the Vietnamese—have had four more years of fighting and death.

It is true that our involvement on the ground has been reduced. Troops are coming home. But the war has been extended in Laos and Cambodia; the bombing of North Vietnam has been expanded to levels of destruction undreamed of four years ago; North Vietnam has been blockaded; the number of refugees increases each day, and the Secretary of Defense warns us of still further escalation.

All this has accomplished nothing except to prolong the war.

The hollowness of "Vietnamization"—a delusive

slogan seeming to offer cheap victory—has been exposed by the recent offensive. The Saigon Government, despite massive U.S. support, is still not viable. It is militarily ineffective, politically corrupt and economically near collapse. Yet it is for this regime that Americans still die, and American prisoners still rot in Indo-China camps.

The plight of these American prisoners justly arouses the concern of all Americans. We must insist that any resolution of the war include the return of all prisoners held by North Vietnam and other adversary forces and the fullest possible accounting for the missing. With increasing lack of credibility, the Nixon Administration has sought to use the prisoners of war as an excuse for its policies. It has refused to make the simple offer of a definite and final end to U.S. participation in the war, in conjunction with return of all U.S. prisoners.

The majority of the Democratic Senators have called for full U.S. withdrawal by October 1, 1972. We support that position. If the war is not ended before the next Democratic Administration takes office, we pledge, as the first order of business, an immediate and complete withdrawal of all U.S. forces in Indo-China. All U.S. military action in Southeast Asia will cease. After the end of U.S. direct combat participation, military aid to the Saigon Government, and elsewhere in Indo-China, will be terminated.

The U.S. will no longer seek to determine the political future of the nations of Indo-China. The issue is not whether we will depose the present South Vietnamese Government, rather when we will cease insisting that it must be the core of any political settlement. We will do what we can to foster an agreement on an acceptable political solution—but we recognize that there are sharp limits to our ability to influence this process, and to the importance of the outcome to our interest.

Disengagement from this terrible war will not be a "defeat" for America. It will not imply any weakness in America's will or ability to protect its vital interests from attack. On the contrary, disengagement will enable us to heal domestic diversions and to end the distortion of our international priorities which the war has caused.

A Democratic Administration will act to ease the hard transitions which will come with the end of this war. We pledge to offer to the people of Vietnam humanitarian assistance to help them repair the ravages of 30 years of war to the economy and to the people of that devastated land.

To our own people, we pledge a true effort to extend the hand of reconciliation and assistance to those most affected by the war.

To those who have served in this war, we pledge a full G.I. Bill of Rights, with benefits sufficient to pay for an education of the veteran's choice, job training programs and the guarantee of employment and the best medical care this country can provide, including a full program of rehabilitation for those who have returned addicted to dangerous drugs. To those who for reasons of conscience refused to serve in this war and were prosecuted or sought refuge abroad, we state our firm intention to declare an amnesty, on an appropriate basis, when the fighting has ceased and our troops and prisoners of war have returned.

*Military Policy*

We propose a program of national defense which is both prudent and responsible, which will retain the confidence of our allies and which will be a deterrent to potential aggressors.

Military strength remains an essential element of a responsible international policy. America must have the strength required for effective deterrence.

But military defense cannot be treated in isolation from other vital national concerns. Spending for military purposes is greater by far than federal spending for education, housing, environmental protection, unemployment insurance or welfare. Unneeded dollars for the military at once add to the tax burden and pre-empt funds from programs of direct and immediate benefit to our people. Moreover, too much that is now spent on defense not only adds nothing to our strength but makes us less secure by stimulating other countries to respond.

Under the Nixon stewardship of our defense policy, lack of sound management controls over defense projects threatens to price us out of an adequate defense. The reaction of the Defense Department to exposure of cost overruns has been to strike back at the critics instead of acting to stop the waste.

Needless projects continue and grow, despite evidence of waste, military ineffectiveness and even affirmative danger to real security. The "development" budget starts pressures for larger procurement budgets in a few years. Morale and

military effectiveness deteriorate as drugs, desertion and racial hatreds plague the armed forces, especially in Vietnam.

The Democratic Party pledges itself to maintain adequate military forces for deterrence and effective support of our international position. But we will also insist on the firm control of specific costs and projects that are essential to ensure that each defense dollar makes a real contribution to national security. Specifically, a Democratic Administration should:

Plan military budgets on the basis of our present needs and commitments, not past practices or force levels;

Stress simplicity and effectiveness in new weapons and stop goldplating and duplication which threatens to spawn a new succession of costly military white elephants; avoid commitment to new weapons unless and until it becomes clear that they are needed;

Reject calls to use the SALT agreement as an excuse for wasteful and dangerous acceleration of our military spending;

Reduce overseas bases and forces; and

Rebuild the morale and military tradition of our armed forces through creative programs to combat drug abuse, racial tensions and eroded pride in service. We will support reforms of the conditions of military life to restore military service as an attractive career for men and women from all segments of our society.

By these reforms and this new approach to budgeting, coupled with a prompt end to U.S. involvement in the war in Indo-China, the military budget can be reduced substantially with no weakening of our national security. Indeed a leaner, better-run system will mean added strength, efficiency and morale for our military forces.

Workers and industries now dependent on defense spending should not be made to pay the price of altering our priorities. Therefore, we pledge reconversion policies and government resources to assure jobs and new industrial opportunities for all those adversely affected by curtailed defense spending.

*Draft*

We urge abolition of the draft.

*Disarmament and Arms Control*

The Democratic Party stands for keeping America strong; we reject the concept of unilateral reductions below levels needed for adequate military defense. But effective international arms control and disarmament do not threaten American security; they enhance it.

The last Democratic Administration took the lead in pressing for U.S.-Soviet agreement on strategic arms limitation. The recent SALT agreement is an important and useful first step.

The SALT agreement should be quickly ratified and taken as a starting point for new agreements. It must not be used as an excuse for new "bargaining chip" military programs or the new round of the arms race.

The next Democratic Administration should:

Carry on negotiations to expand the initial SALT agreement to other areas, especially to seek limits to the qualitative arms race and to begin reducing force levels on each side;

Seek a comprehensive ban on all nuclear testing, verified, as SALT will be, by national means;

Press for wide adherence to the Non-Proliferation Treaty, signed in 1968, and for extension of the concept of nuclear-free regions;

Seek ratification of the Protocol on Chemical Warfare without reservations;

In concert with our allies, pursue with the U.S.S.R. mutual force reductions in Europe; and

Widen the range of arms control discussions to include new subjects, such as mutual budget cuts, control of arms transfer to developing countries, restrictions on naval force deployments and other measures to limit conventional forces.

## U.S. and the World Community

A new foreign policy must be adequate for a rapidly changing world. We welcome the opportunity this brings for improved relations with the U.S.S.R. and China. But we value even more America's relations with our friends and allies in the Hemisphere, in Western Europe, Japan and other industrialized countries, Israel and the Middle East, and in the developing nations of Asia and Africa. With them, our relations must be conducted on a basis of mutual trust and consultation, seeking to strengthen our ties and to resolve differences on a basis of mutual advantage. Throughout the world, the focus of our policy should be a commitment to peace, self-determination, development, liberty and international cooperation, without distortion in favor of military points of view.

*Europe.*—Europe's increasing economic and political strength and the growing cooperation and self-confidence of its people have made the Atlantic Alliance a partnership of equals. If we face the challenge of this new relationship, our historic partnership can endure.

The next Democratic Administration should:

Reduce U.S. troop levels in Europe in close consultation with our allies, as part of a program to adjust NATO to changed conditions. What is essential in our relations with the other NATO nations is not a particular troop level, but our continued commitment to collective defense;

Pledge to work in greater cooperation with the European economic communities to ensure that integration in Europe does not serve as a formula for discrimination against American goods and enterprises;

Cease American support for the repressive Greek military government; and

Make the voice of the United States heard in Northern Ireland against violence and terror and against the discrimination, repression and deprivation which brought about that awful civil strife.

We welcome every improvement in relations between the United States and the Soviet Union and every step taken toward reaching vital agreements on trade and other subjects. However, in our pursuit of improved relations, America cannot afford to be blind to the continued existence of serious differences between us. In particular, the United States should, by diplomatic contacts, seek to mobilize world opinion to express concern at the denial to the oppressed peoples of Eastern Europe and the minorities of the Soviet Union, including the Soviet Jews, of the right to practice their religion and culture and to leave their respective countries.

*Middle East.*—The United States must be unequivocally committed to support of Israel's right to exist within secure and defensible boundaries. Progress toward a negotiated political settlement in the Middle East will permit Israel and her Arab neighbors to live at peace with each other, and to turn their energies to internal development. It will also free the world from the threat of the explosion of Mid-East tensions into world war. In working toward a settlement, our continuing pledge to the security and freedom of Israel must be both clear and consistent.

The next Democratic Administration should:

Make and carry out a firm, long-term public

commitment to provide Israel with aircraft and other military equipment in the quantity and sophistication she needs to preserve her deterrent strength in the face of Soviet arsenaling of Arab threats of renewed war;

Seek to bring the parties into direct negotiations toward a permanent political solution based on the necessity of agreement on secure and defensible national boundaries;

Maintain a political commitment and a military force in Europe and at sea in the Mediterranean ample to deter the Soviet Union from putting unbearable pressure on Israel.

Recognize and support the established status of Jerusalem as the capital of Israel, with free access to all its holy places provided to all faiths. As a symbol of this stand, the U.S. Embassy should be moved from Tel Aviv to Jerusalem; and

Recognize the responsibility of the world community for a just solution to the problems of the Arab and Jewish refugees.

*Africa.*—The central feature of African politics today is the struggle against racism and colonialism in Southern Africa. There should be no mistake about which side we are on. We stand for full political, civil and economic rights for black and other nonwhite peoples in Southern Africa. We are against white-minority rule. We should not underwrite a return to the interventionism of the past. But we can end United States complicity with such governments.

The focus of America's concern with Africa must be on economic and social development. Economic aid to Africa, without political conditions, should be expanded, and African states assured an adequate share of the aid dollar. Military aid and aid given for military purposes should be sharply reduced.

All military aid to Portugal should be stopped and the Nixon $435 million deal for unneeded Azores bases should be canceled.

U.N. sanctions against the illegal racist regime in Southern Rhodesia should be supported vigorously, especially as they apply to chrome imports.

The U.S. should give full support to U.N. assertion of its control over Namibia (South West Africa), in accordance with the World Court's ruling.

The U.S. should make clear its opposition to the radical totalitarianism of South Africa. The U.S. government should act firmly to press U.S. businesses in South Africa to take measures for the fullest possible justice for their black employees. Blacks should be assigned at all levels to U.S. offices in South Africa, and throughout Africa. The South African sugar quota should be withdrawn.

No U.S. company or its subsidiary should be given U.S. tax credit for taxes paid to white-minority-ruled countries of Africa.

*Japan.*—Our relations with Japan have been severely strained by a series of "Nixon shocks." We must restore our friendship with Japan, the leading industrial nation of Asia and a growing world power. There are genuine issues between us and Japan in the economic area, but accommodation of trade problems will be greatly eased by an end to the Nixon Administration's calculated insensitivity to Japan and her interests, marked by repeated failures to afford advance warnings, much consultation over sudden shifts in U.S. diplomatic and economic policy that affect Japan.

*India, Pakistan and Bangla Desh.*—A Democratic Administration should work to restore the damage done to America's friendship with India as a result of the Administration's folly in "tilting" in favor of Pakistan and against Bangla Desh. The alienation by the Nixon Administration of India, the world's largest democracy, and the continued suspension of economic aid to India have seriously damaged the status of the United States in Asia. We pledge generous support for the essential work of reconstruction and reconciliation in Bangla Desh. At the same time, we will maintain friendship and developmental assistance to the "new" Pakistan which has emerged from these sad events.

*China.*—The beginnings of a new U.S.-China relationship are welcome and important. However, so far, little of substance has changed, and the exaggerated secrecy and rhetoric of the Nixon Administration have produced unnecessary complications in our relationship with our allies and friends in Asia and with the U.S.S.R.

What is needed now is serious negotiation on trade, travel exchanges and progress on more basic issues. The U.S. should take the steps necessary to establish regular diplomatic relations with China.

*Other Asian Countries.*—The future of Asia will be determined by its people, not by the United States. We should support accommodation and cooperation among all Asian countries and continue to assist in economic development.

*Canada.*—A Democratic Administration should restore close U.S.-Canadian cooperation and communication, respecting Canada's nationhood and pride. In settling economic issues, we should not compromise our interests; but seek mutually advantageous and equitable solutions. In areas such as environmental protection and social policies, the Americans and Canadians share common problems and we must act together.

*Latin America.*—The Good Neighbor policy of Franklin Roosevelt and the Alliance for Progress of John Kennedy set still-living goals—insulation from external political conflicts, mutual non-interference in internal affairs, and support for political liberty, social justice and economic progress. The Nixon Administration has lost sight of these goals, and the result is hostility and suspicion of the U.S. unmatched in generations.

The next Democratic Administration should:

Re-establish an inter-American alliance of equal sovereign nations working cooperatively for development;

Sharply reduce military assistance throughout the area;

Strive to deepen the exchange of people and ideas within the Hemisphere;

Take account of the special claims of democratically-elected governments on our resources and sympathy;

Pursue a policy of non-intervention by military means in domestic affairs of Latin American nations;

Recognize that, while Cuba must not be permitted to become a foreign military base, after 13 years of boycott, crisis and hostility, the time has come to re-examine our relations with Cuba and to seek a way to resolve this cold war confrontation on mutually acceptable terms; and

Re-establish a U.S.-Mexico border commission, with Mexican-American representatives, to develop a comprehensive program to desalinate and eradicate pollution of the Colorado River and other waterways flowing into Mexico, and conduct substantial programs to raise the economic level on both sides of the border. This should remove the economic reasons which contribute to illegal immigration and discourage run-away industries. In addition, language requirements for citizenship should be removed.

*The United Nations.* The U.N. cannot solve all the great political problems of our time, but in an increasingly interdependent world, a world body is essential and its potential must be increasingly relied upon.

The next Democratic Administration should:

Re-establish the U.N. as a key forum for international activity, and assign representatives with the highest qualification for diplomacy;

Give strong executive branch leadership for U.S. acceptance of its obligations for U.N. financing, while renegotiating arrangement for sharing U.N. costs;

Abide by the binding U.N. Security Council decision on Rhodesia sanctions, and support U.N. peace-keeping efforts;

Work for development of enforceable world law as a basis for peace, and endorse repeal of the Connally Reservation on U.S. acceptance of World Court jurisdiction; and

Work to involve the U.N. increasingly on the complex technical and social problems such as pollution, health, communication, technology and population policy, which are worldwide in scope and demand a worldwide approach, and help provide the means for these U.N. efforts and for U.N. economic development functions.

*International Economic Policy*

In a prosperous economy, foreign trade has benefits for virtually everyone. For the consumer, it means lower prices and a wider choice of goods. For the worker and the businessman, it means new jobs and new markets. For nations, it means greater efficiency and growth.

But in a weak economy—with over five million men and women out of work—foreign imports bring hardships to many Americans. The automobile or electrical worker, the electronics technician, the small businessman—for them, and millions of others, foreign competition coinciding with a slack economy has spelled financial distress. Our national commitment to liberal trade policies takes its toll when times are bad, but yields its benefits when the economy is fully employed.

The Democratic Party proposes no retreat from this commitment. Our international economic policy should have these goals: To expand jobs and business opportunities in this country and to establish two-way trade relations with other nations. To do this, we support the following policies:

End the high-unemployment policy of the Nixon Administration. When a job is available for everyone who wants to work, imports will no longer be a threat. Full employment is a realistic goal, it is a goal which has been attained under Democratic Administrations, and it is a goal we intend to achieve again;

Adopt broad programs to ease dislocations and relieve the hardship of workers injured by foreign competition;

Seek higher labor standards in the advanced nations where productivity far outstrips wage rates, thus providing unfair competition to American workers and seek to limit harmful flows of American capital which exploit both foreign and American workers;

Adhere to liberal trade policies, but we should oppose actions and policies which harm American workers through unfair exploitation of labor abroad and the encouragement of American capital to run after very low wage opportunities for quick profits that will damage the economy of the United States and further weaken the dollar;

Negotiate orderly and reciprocal reductions of trade barriers to American products. Foreign nations with access to our markets should no longer be permitted to fence us out of theirs;

Support reform of the international monetary system. Increased international reserves, provision for large margins in foreign exchange fluctuations and strengthened institutions for the coordination of national economic policies can free our government and others to achieve full employment;

Support efforts to promote exports of American farm products; and

Develop ground rules for pollution controls with our industrialized trading partners so that no country gains competitive advantage at the expense of the environment.

## Developing Nations

Poverty at home or abroad is part of a common problem. Great and growing income gaps among nations are no more tenable than such gaps among groups in our own country. We should remain committed to U.S. support for economic and social development of countries in need. Old ways of providing aid must be revised—to reduce U.S. involvement in administration; to encourage other nations to contribute jointly with us. But funding must be adequate to help poor countries achieve accelerated rates of growth.

Specifically, the next Democratic Administration should support:

Provision of more assistance through international organizations, along with measures to strengthen the development agencies of the U.N.;

A curtailment of military aid;

Improved access to the markets of industrial nations for the products of the developing countries;

A greater role in international monetary affairs for poor countries; in particular distributing the new Special Drawing Rights in support of the poor countries; and

A fair share for poor countries in the resources of the seabeds.

## The Methods and Structures of U.S. Foreign and Military Policy

The needed fundamental reordering of U.S. foreign and military policy calls for changes in the structure of decision-making, as well as in particular policies. This means:

Greater sharing with Congress of real decisions on issues of war and peace, and providing Congress with the information and resources needed for a more responsible role;

More honest information policies, beginning with a fundamental reform of the document classification system and including regular press conferences by the President, his cabinet and senior advisors;

Ending the present drastic overbalance in favor of military opinion by redefining the range of agencies and points of view with a proper claim to be heard on foreign and military policies;

Subjecting the military budget to effective civilian control and supervision;

Establishing effective executive control and legislative oversight of the intelligence agencies;

Ending political domination of USIA's reporting and Peace Corps dedication and, in general, making it clear that the White House understands the crucial distinction between dissent and disloyalty; and

Urging the appointment of minority Americans to top positions of ambassadors and diplomats, to let the world know that America is a multi-racial nation and proud of it.

## IX. THE PEOPLE AND THE GOVERNMENT

"Our people are dispirited because there seems to be no way by which they can call to office a government which will cut the ties to the past, meeting the challenge of leadership and begin a new era of bold action.

"Bold action by innovative government—responsive to the people's needs and desires—is essential to the achievement of our national hopes." —Leonard Woodcock, President, United Auto Workers, New York Hearing, June 22, 1972.

Representative democracy fails when citizens cannot know:

When public officials ignore or work against the principles of due process;

How their public officials conduct the public's business;

Whether public officials have personal financial stakes in the very matters they are legislating, administering or enforcing; and

What special interest pressures are being exerted on public officials by lobbyists.

Today, it is imperative that the Democratic Party again take the lead in reforming those practices that limit the responsiveness of government and remove it from the control of the people.

### Seniority

The seniority system is one of the principal reasons that party platforms—and parties themselves—have lost meaning and importance in our political life. Seniority has weakened Congress as an effective and responsive institution in a changing society. It has crippled effective Congressional leadership and made it impossible to present and enact a coherent legislative program. It has permitted the power of the Democratic majority to be misused and abused. It has stifled initiative and wasted the talents of many members by making length of service the *only* criterion for selection to the vital positions of Congressional power and leadership.

We, therefore, call on the Democratic Members of the Congress to use the powers inherent in their House and Senate caucuses to implement the policies and programs of the National Democratic Party. It is specifically not intended that Democratic members be directed how to vote on issues on the floor. But, in order that they be responsive to broad party policies and programs, we nonetheless call upon Members of Congress to:

Choose committee chairmen as provided in existing caucus rules and procedures, but by separate open ballot; chair-people should be chosen who will carry out party policies and programs which come within the jurisdiction of their committees;

Assure that Democratic programs and policies receive full and fair consideration and are brought to a vote in each house;

Discipline committee members, including chairpeople, who refuse to comply with caucus instructions regarding the reporting of legislation from their committees; and

Withhold any seniority benefits from a Member of Congress who fails to overtly identify with the Democratic organization in his state which is recognized by the National Democratic Party.

### Secrecy

Public business should be transacted publicly, except when national security might be jeopardized.

To combat secrecy in government, we call on the Democratic Members of Congress and state legislatures to:

Enact "open meetings" legislation, barring the practice of conducting the public business behind closed doors. This should include so-called mark-up sessions by legislative committees, but should allow for exceptions involving national security and invasions of privacy. To the extent possible, the same principle should apply to the Executive Branch;

Assure that all committee and floor votes are taken in open session, recorded individually for each legislator; record caucus votes, and make all of these available to the public;

Urge reservation of executive privilege for the President alone;

Urge that the judgment in the U.S. Senate in a contested election case be rendered in open Senate session;

Immediately strengthen the Federal Freedom of Information Act. Congress should improve its oversight of Executive secrecy by requiring federal agencies to report annually on every refusal to grant information requested under the Act. Citizens should have full recourse to the courts to deal with violation or circumvention of the Act. It should be amended to allow courts to review the reasonableness of a claim of executive privilege; and

Administer the security system so as to limit the number of officials who can make a document secret, and provide for frequent declassification of documents. Congress should be given the means to obtain documents necessary to fulfill its responsibilities.

We also call on the Democratic Members of

the House of Representatives to take action through their caucus to end the "closed rule," which is used to prevent amendments and votes on vital tax matters and other important issues, and we call on the Democratic Members of the Senate to liberalize the cloture rule, which is used to prevent votes in that body, so that after full and extensive debate majority rule can prevail.

## Administrative Agencies

There is, among more and more citizens, a growing revolt against large, remote and impersonal government agencies that are not responsive to human needs. We pledge to build a representative process into the Executive Branch, so that individuals affected by agency programs can be involved in formulating, implementing and revising them. This requires a basic restructuring of procedures—public hearings before guidelines and regulations are handed down, the processing of citizen complaints, the granting of citizen standing and the recovery of litigation fees for those who win suits against the government.

We recommend these specific changes in the rule making and adjudication process of the federal government:

There should be no non-written communication between an agency and outside parties about pending decisions. All written communications should promptly be made a part of the public record;

All communications between government employees and outside parties about possible future action should be made a part of the public record;

All government employees involved in rule-making and adjudication should be subject to conflict of interest laws;

The Justice Department should make available to the public any consent decree 90 days prior to its submission to court, to allow any interested party to comment on it to the Court; and

The Justice Department should report to Congress each year, to explain its action on major suits.

In addition, we must more effectively protect consumer rights before the government. The consumer must be made an integral part of any relationship between government and institutions (public or private) at every level of proceedings whether formal or informal.

A Democratic Administration would instruct all federal agencies to identify American Indians, Asian Americans and Spanish-speaking Americans in separate categories in all statistical data that note racial or ethnic heritage. Only in this way can these Americans be assured their rights under federal programs.

Finally, in appropriate geographical areas, agencies of the federal government should be equipped to conduct business in such a fashion that Spanish-speaking citizens should not be hampered by language difficulties.

## Conflict of Interest

The public interest must not be sacrificed to personal gain. Therefore, we call for legislation requiring full disclosure of the financial interests of Members of Congress and their staffs and high officials of the Executive Branch and independent agencies. Disclosure should include business directorships held and associations with individuals or firms lobbying or doing business with the government.

Further, Congress should forbid its members to engage in the practice of law or to retain association with a law firm while in office. Legislators serving on a committee whose jurisdiction includes matters in which they have a financial interest should divest themselves of the interest or resign from the committee.

## Campaign Finance

A total overhaul of the present system of financing elections is a national necessity. Candidates should not be dependent on large contributors who seek preferential treatment. We call for Congressional action to provide for public financing of more election costs by 1974. We recommend a statutory ceiling on political gifts at a reasonable limit. Publicly owned communications facilities such as television, radio and the postal service should be made available, but on a limited basis, to candidates for federal office.

## Regulation of Lobbyists

We also call upon Congress to enact rigorous lobbying disclosure legislation, to replace the present shockingly ineffective law. There should be full disclosure of all organized lobbying—including names of lobbyists, identity of the source of funds, total receipts and expenditures, the nature of the lobbying operation and specific target issues or bills. Reports should be filed at least quarterly, with criminal penalties for late filing. Lobbying regulations should cover attempts to influence both legislative and Executive Branch decisions. The legislation should specifically cover lobbying appeals in subscription publications.

As a safeguard, we urge the availability of subpoena and cease-and-desist powers to enforce these conflict of interest, campaign financing and lobby disclosure laws. We also affirm the citizens' right to seek enforcement through the courts, should public officials fail in enforcement.

*Taking Part in the Political Process*

The Presidential primary system today is an unacceptable patchwork. The Democratic Party supports federal laws that will embody the following principles:

Protect the opportunity for less-known candidates to build support;

Establish uniform ground rules;

Reduce the cost of primary campaigns;

Promote maximum voter turnout;

Ensure that issues are clarified;

Foster the selection of nominees with broad popular support to assure the continued viability of the two party system;

Ensure every citizen the ability to take part in the Presidential nomination process; and

Equalize the ability of people from all income levels to participate in the political decision-making processes of the Democratic Party, by providing financial assistance through party funds for delegates, alternates and standing committee members to state and national conventions.

We also call for full and uniform enforcement of the Voting Rights Act of 1965. But further steps are needed to end all barriers to participation in the political process:

Universal voter registration by post card;

Bilingual means of registration and voting;

Bilingual voter education programs;

Liberalized absentee voting;

Lower minimum age requirements for service in the Senate and House of Representatives;

Minimum residency requirements of 30 days for all elections, including primaries;

Student voting where they attend schools;

Study and review of the Hatch Act, to see what can be done to encourage good citizenship and reasonable participation by government employees;

Full home rule for the District of Columbia, including an elected mayor-city council government, broad legislative power, control over appointments, automatic federal payment and voting representation in both Houses of Congress;

No discriminatory districting;

We favor a Constitutional change to abolish the Electoral College and to give every voter a direct and equal voice in Presidential elections. The amendment should provide for a run-off election, if no candidate received more than 40 percent of the popular vote;

Early ratification of the equal rights amendment to the Constitution;

Appointment of women to positions of top responsibilities in all branches of the federal government, to achieve an equitable ratio of women and men;

Inclusion of women advisors in equitable ratios on all government studies, commissions and hearings; and

Laws authorizing federal grants on a matching basis for financing state commissions of the status of women.

These changes in themselves will not solve the problems of government for all time. As our society changes, so must the ways we use to make government more responsive to the people. Our challenge, today, as always, is to ensure that politics and institutions belong in spirit and in practice to all the people of our nation. In 1972, Americans are deciding that they want their country back again.

## Libertarian Platform 1972

STATEMENT OF PRINCIPLES

We, the members of the Libertarian Party, challenge the cult of the omnipotent state, and defend the rights of the individual.

We hold that each individual has the right to exercise sole dominion over his own life, and has the right to live his life in whatever manner he chooses, so long as he does not forcibly interfere with the equal right of others to live their lives in whatever manner they choose.

Governments throughout history have regularly operated on the opposite principle, that the State has the right to dispose of the lives of individuals and the fruits of their labor. Even within the United States, all political parties other than our own grant to government the right to regulate the life of the individual and seize the fruits of his labor without his consent.

We, on the contrary, deny the right of any government to do these things, and hold that the sole function of government is the protection of the rights of each individual: namely (1) the right to life—and accordingly we support laws prohibiting the initiation of physical force against others; (2) the right to liberty of speech and action—and accordingly we oppose all attempts by government to abridge the freedom of speech and press, as well as government censorship in any form; and (3) the right to property—and accordingly we oppose all government interference with private property, such as confiscation, nationalization, and eminent domain, and support laws which prohibit robbery, trespass, fraud and misrepresentation.

Since government has only one legitimate function, the protection of individual rights, we oppose all interference by government in the areas of voluntary and contractual relations among individuals. Men should not be forced to sacrifice their lives and property for the benefit of others. They should be left free by government to deal with one another as free traders on a free market; and the resultant economic system, the only one compatible with the protection of man's rights, is laissez-faire capitalism.

## INDIVIDUAL RIGHTS AND CIVIL ORDER

The protection of individual rights is the only proper purpose of government. No conflict exists between civil order and individual rights. Both concepts are based on the same fundamental principle: that no individual, group, or government may initiate force against any other individual, group, or government. Government is instituted to protect individual rights. Government is constitutionally limited so as to prevent the infringement of individual rights by the government itself.

### 1. Crime

We hold that no action which does not infringe the rights of others can properly be termed a crime. We favor the repeal of all laws creating "crimes without victims" now incorporated in Federal, state and local laws—such as laws on voluntary sexual relations, drug use, gambling, and at-tempted suicide. We support impartial and consistent enforcement of laws designed to protect the individual rights—regardless of the motivation for which these laws may be violated.

### 2. Due Process for Criminally Accused

Until such time as a person is proved guilty of a crime, that person should be accorded all possible respect for his individual rights. We are thus opposed to reduction of present safeguards for the rights of the criminally accused. Specifically, we are opposed to preventive detention, so-called "no-knock laws" and all other similar measures which threaten existing rights. We further pledge to do all possible to give life to the Sixth Amendment's guarantee of a speedy trial, and shall work for appropriate legislation to this end. We support full restitution for all loss suffered by persons arrested, indicted, imprisoned, tried, or otherwise injured in the course of criminal proceedings against them which do not result in their conviction. We look ultimately to the voluntary funding of this restitution.

### 3. Freedom of Speech and The Press

We pledge to oppose all forms of censorship, whatever the medium involved. Recent events have demonstrated that the already precarious First Amendment rights of the broadcasting industry are becoming still more precarious. Regulation of broadcasting can no longer be tolerated. We shall support legislation to repeal the Federal Communication's Act, and to provide for private ownership of broadcasting rights, thus giving broadcasting First Amendment parity with other communications media. We support repeal of pornography laws.

### 4. Protection of Privacy

Electronic and other covert government surveillance of citizens should be restricted to activity which can be shown beforehand, under high, clearly defined standards of probable cause, to be criminal and to present immediate and grave danger to other citizens. The National Census and other government compilations of data on citizens should be conducted on a strictly voluntary basis.

### 5. The Right to Keep and Bear Arms

In recognition of the fact that the individual is his own last source of self-defense, the authors of the Constitution guaranteed, in the Second

Amendment, the right of the people to keep and bear arms. This reasoning remains valid today. We pledge to uphold that guarantee. We oppose compulsory arms registration.

### 6. Volunteer Army

We oppose the draft (Selective Service), believing that the use of force to require individuals to serve in the armed forces or anywhere else is a violation of their rights, and that a well-paid volunteer army is a more effective means of national defense than the involuntary servitude exemplified by the draft. We recommend a complete review and possible reform of the Uniform Code of Military Justice, to guarantee effective and equal protection of rights under the law to all members of the U.S. armed forces, and to promote thereby the morale, dignity, and sense of justice within the military which are indispensable to its efficient and effective operation. We further pledge to work for a declaration of unconditional amnesty for all who have been convicted of, or who now stand accused of, draft evasion and for all military deserters who were draftees.

### 7. Property Rights

We hold that property rights are individual rights and, as such, are entitled to the same respect and protection as all other individual rights. We further hold that the owner of property has the full right to control, use, dispose of, or in any manner enjoy his property without interference, until and unless the exercise of his control infringes the valid rights of others. We shall thus oppose restrictions upon the use of property which do not have as their sole end the protection of valid rights.

### 8. Unions and Collective Bargaining

We support the right of free men to voluntarily associate in, or to establish, labor unions. We support the concept that an employer may recognize a union as the collective bargaining agent of some or all of his employees. We oppose governmental interference in bargaining, such as compulsory arbitration or the obligation to bargain. We demand that the National Labor Relations Act be repealed. We recognize voluntary contracts between employers and labor unions as being legally and morally binding on the parties to such contracts.

### Trade and the Economy

Because each person has the right to offer his goods and services to others on the free market, and because government interference can only harm such free activity, we oppose all intervention by government into the area of economics. The only proper role of government in the economic realm is to protect property rights, adjudicate disputes and protect contracts, and provide a legal framework in which voluntary trade is protected. All efforts by government to redistribute wealth, or to control or manage trade, are improper in a free society.

### 1. Money

We favor the establishment of a sound money system. We thus support the private ownership of gold, and demand repeal of all legal tender laws.

### 2. The Economy

Government intervention in the economy imperils both the material prosperity and personal freedom of every American. We therefore support the following specific immediate reforms:
   (a) reduction of both taxes and government spending;
   (b) an end to deficit budgets;
   (c) a halt to inflationary monetary policies, and elimination, with all deliberate speed, of the Federal Reserve System;
   (d) the removal of all governmental impediments to free trade—including the repeal of the National Labor Relations Act, the Interstate Commerce Act, all antitrust laws and the abolition of the Department of Agriculture, as the most pressing and critical impediments;
   (e) and the repeal of all controls on wages, prices, rents, profits, production, and interest rates.

### 3. Subsidies

In order to achieve a free economy in which government victimizes no one for the benefit of anyone else, we oppose all government subsidies to business, labor, education, agriculture, science, the arts, or any other special interests. Those who have entered into these activities with promises of government subsidy will be forewarned by being given a cutoff date beyond which all government aid to their enterprise will be terminated. Relief or exemption from involuntary taxation shall not be considered a subsidy.

### 4. Tariffs and Quotas

Like subsidies, tariffs and quotas serve only to give special treatment to favored interests and to diminish the welfare of other citizens. We therefore support abolition of all tariffs and quotas as well as the Tariff Commission and the Customs Court.

### 5. Interim Reforms

In order to effect our long-range goals, we recommend, among others, the following interim measures: the adoption of the Liberty Amendment, and provision for greater use of the referendum for reducing or repealing taxes.

### 6. Long-Range Goals

Since we believe that every man is entitled to keep the fruits of his labor, we are opposed to all government activity which consists of the forcible collection of money or goods from citizens in violation of their individual rights. Specifically, we support the eventual repeal of all taxation. We support a system of voluntary fees for services rendered as a method for financing government in a free society.

### DOMESTIC ILLS

Government intervention in current problems, such as crime, pollution, defraud of consumers, health problems, overpopulation, decaying cities, and poverty, is properly limited to protection of individual rights. In those areas where individual rights or voluntary relations are not involved, we support an immediate reduction of government's present role, and ultimately, a total withdrawal of government intervention, together with the establishment of a legal framework in which private, voluntary solutions to these problems can be developed and implemented.

### 1. Pollution

We support the development of an objective system defining individual property rights to air and water. We hold that ambiguities in the area of these rights (e.g. concepts such as "public property") are a primary cause of our deteriorating environment. Whereas we maintain that no one has the right to violate the legitimate property rights of others by pollution, we shall strenu-

ously oppose all attempts to transform the defense of such rights into any restriction of the efforts of individuals to advance technology, to expand production, or to use their property peacefully.

### 2. Consumer Protection

We shall support strong and effective laws against fraud and misrepresentation. We shall oppose, however, that present and prospective so-called "consumer protection" legislation which infringes upon voluntary trade.

### 3. Overpopulation

We support an end to all subsidies for child-bearing built into our present laws, including all welfare plans and the provision of tax-supported services for children. We further support the repeal of all laws restricting voluntary birth control or voluntary termination of pregnancies during their first hundred days. We shall oppose all coercive measures to control population growth.

### 4. Education

We support the repeal of all compulsory education laws, and an end to government operation, regulation, and subsidy of schools. We call for an immediate end of compulsory busing.

### 5. Poverty and Unemployment

We support repeal of all laws which impede the ability of any person to find employment—including, but not limited to, minimum wage laws, so-called "protective" labor legislation for women and children, governmental restrictions on the establishment of private day-care centers, the National Labor Relations Act, and licensing requirements. We oppose all government welfare and relief projects and "aid to the poor" programs, inasmuch as they are not within the proper role of government, and do contribute to unemployment. All aid to the poor should come from private sources.

### FOREIGN POLICY

The principles which guide a legitimate government in its relationships with other governments are the same as those which guide relationships between individuals and governments. It must protect itself and its citizens against the initiation of force from other nations. While we recognize the existence of totalitarian governments, we do not recognize them as *legitimate* governments. We will grant them no moral sanction. We will not deal with them as if they were proper governments. To do so is to ignore the rights of their victims and rob those victims of the knowledge that we know they have been wronged.

ECONOMIC

### 1. Foreign Aid

We support an end to the Federal foreign aid program.

### 2. Ownerships in Unclaimed Property

We pledge to oppose recognition of claims by fiat, by nations or international bodies, of presently unclaimed property, such as the ocean floor and planetary bodies. We urge the development of objective standards for recognizing claims of ownership in such property.

### 3. Currency Exchange Rates

We pledge to oppose all governmental attempts to peg or regulate currency exchange rates. International trade can truly be free only when currency exchange rates reflect the free-market value of respective currencies.

MILITARY

### 1. Military Alliances

The United States should abandon its attempts to act as policeman for the world, and should enter into alliances only with countries whose continued free existence is vital to the protection of the freedom of all American citizens. Under such an alliance, the United States may offer the protection of its nuclear umbrella, but our allies would provide their own conventional defense capabilities. We should in particular disengage from any present alliances which include despotic governments.

### 2. Military Capability

We shall support the maintenance of a sufficient military establishment to defend the United States against aggression. We should have a sufficient nuclear capacity to convince any potential aggressor that it cannot hope to survive a first strike against the United States. But, as our foreign commitments are reduced, and as our allies assume their share of the burden of providing a

conventional war capability, we should be able to reduce the size of our conventional defense, and thus reduce the overall cost and size of our total defense establishment.

DIPLOMATIC

### 1. Diplomatic Recognition

The United States should establish a scheme of recognition consistent with the principles of a free society, the primary principle being that, while individuals everywhere in the world have unalienable rights, governments which enslave individuals have no legitimacy whatsoever.

### 2. Secession

We shall support recognition of the right to secede. Political units or areas which do secede should be recognized by the United States as independent political entities where: (1) secession is supported by a majority within the political unit, (2) the majority does not attempt suppression of the dissenting minority, and (3) the government of the new entity is at least as compatible with human freedom as that from which it seceded.

### 3. The United Nations

We support withdrawal of the United States from the United Nations. We further support a Constitutional Amendment designed to prohibit the United States from entering into any treaty under which it relinquishes any portion of its sovereignty.

## People's Platform 1972

PREAMBLE

Though a leader in the world in wealth and technology and possessed of vast resources sufficient to give—right now—an abundant life to all our people, our nation is in crisis. Our Black, Spanish-speaking and Indian citizens are victims of institutionalized discrimination and oppression. Our workers, small home owners, small business people and family farmers are squeezed by inflation and unequal taxation. Our women, gay people, young people and old people are still denied their full rights. In short, our institutions have become perverted, our natural resources have been raped and polluted because private profit for the few has been given priority over the fulfillment of the basic needs of the people. And, because of this profit motive which underlies all of our policies, we have become increasingly the object of fear and distrust among the people of the world.

We recognize that the fulfillment of the basic needs common to all of us is frustrated by the big-finance, big-corporation, big-military establishment which maintains its control through its servants in the Demo-publican Party and which constantly tightens its stranglehold over our foreign and domestic policies and our very lives. This hold can only be broken if we the people, in our neighborhoods, in our schools, in our workplace, begin to organize our power to take back control of the institutions which affect the nature of our lives and the future of our nation.

Since we believe that the present political parties of the United States neither represent or reflect the political, economic and social hopes of a large segment of people in this country, we shall unite into a new party for positive change which will ensure a creative future of our people.

This new party, born out of the experience in struggle of the growing peoples' movement will be called the People's Party. Now in its formative period, the party seeks to unite all people in the various aspects of the people's movement—red, yellow, black, brown and white, regardless of age and sexual persuasion—into one mass party on the left. We shall organize, not merely for political electoral activity, but for the on-going struggle for the radical changes needed to assure the beneficial and creative rather than destructive use of our tremendous resources—natural, technological and human.

We advocate a complete program of action which will ensure for all people the full measure of political, social and economic justice which has been our nation's promise unfulfilled for two centuries. We must establish for ourselves a position of honor and harmony with all of humanity.
(The following platform was written and adopted by the over 200 delegates who attended the July 27–30, 1972 National Convention of the People's Party in St. Louis. The same convention nominated Dr. Benjamin Spock and Julius Hobson to be the party's Presidential and Vice-Presidential candidates.)

## AGEISM

Ageism is an attitude institutionalized in our society which discriminates against individuals solely on the basis of age. Under the present system, young people and senior citizens are denied their basic rights and opportunities and often are treated more like property than like human beings. The People's Party believes that peoples' rights and potentials should never be determined on the basis of one's age. Therefore, we support the following demands:
For Young People—

1) The right to vote and the right to hold electoral office, beginning at whatever age an individual decides to accept those responsibilities.

2) The right to be independent of one's parents if one so desires.

3) The full rights and responsibilities of citizenship.

4) The right to control those institutions that control their lives. Especially we support the right of young people to have an equal say with parents, teachers and administrators in their education.

5) The right to equal treatment under the law in the courts of the land. Young people must be treated with respect rather than as property.

6) The right to determine their own life style as full citizens.
For Senior Citizens—

1) The right to work productively, if they so desire. An end to mandatory retirement.

2) The right to guaranteed annual income, providing supplementary income, if necessary.

3) The right to make decisions about how one will spend the remaining years of one's life without interference from doting children or the law.

4) The right to control those institutions which control their lives.

5) The right to decent housing, without the burden of property tax, and the right to good transportation, without the burden of high costs.

## CULTURE AND THE ARTS

A Department of Culture and the Arts is as relevant to our society as is a Department of Agriculture. In peace or at war, in prosperity or depression, all the arts must be a part of the fabric of our society. All people should have the opportunity to participate in art, especially in light of the increasing leisure time for such activities. Our music, dance, poetry, fiction, visual and plastic arts, horticulture, craft, drama—all reflect, interpret or shape our political and social system. Our artists interpret and give form to the spirit of our society. The society, in turn, draws its moral and ethical sustenance from the expressions of its artists and inventors.

The United States, far from leading the world in the arts that are essential to the survival and well-being of the spirit of the people, lags far behind many other countries. This neglect is visible in the unrelieved barrenness of most public buildings, a significant factor contributing to the psychic breakdown in many of our urban and suburban areas. Israel, though living under the siege mentality perpetuated by its ruling class, manages to spend $1.35 per capita per year for the arts, Canada $1.40, Sweden and Austria $2.00 and Holland $3.69. The United States, the richest country in the world, spends only seven cents per capita.

Another factor contributing to the low state of our arts is the notion of professionalism as defined by the ruling economic powers which maintain strict control over our culture and continually create an elitist division between the paid and unpaid, producers and consumers.

The People's Party, therefore, proposes that:

1) We begin to recognize the achievements of our creative artists, as well as to stress the importance of art as an area of activity for all people and to encourage them by providing opportunities for their meaningful contributions to the society.

2) We establish a Department of Culture and the Arts, headed by a secretary at the cabinet level, which would be responsible for the creation of vastly increased opportunities for artists to do work without competition, censorship or discrimination in subject matter.

3) The department should encourage and fund local culture groups in all the arts.

4) The department commission works commemorating people-designated occasions.

5) The department provide a clearing house of artists available to offer skills to communities.

We want to de-professionalize the arts in order to encourage the creative potential in every individual, to stimulate creativity in everyday life by eliminating traditions and restraints placed so artificially upon the arts, to get away from com-

mercialism in art and to "bring art into the streets." Our long-range goal is to make America beautiful once again and to provide a visually healthy environment for present and future generations.

## ECOLOGY AND ENVIRONMENT

Life on earth is a delicate and complex interaction among all living things and the materials of the earth. Technology, by reordering these natural relationships, interferes with the life-supporting processes of the earth. A small technology, one which is carefully controlled, can draw upon the environment while preserving the balance of natural systems which support life, including human life. Our technology, however, is neither small or controlled; it has grown to the point of affecting vital processes over the entire planet. We have seized the immediate benefits of technology without accepting the responsibility for maintaining a well-balanced ecosystem favorable to human life. This now poses the serious and imminent threat that the ecological system will break down, triggering catastrophes of human suffering and social collapse.

The issue is one of such importance that we must begin now to change the attitude of our society toward the question of consumption. Great consumption is negative; it results in the gross exploitation of nature and lack of regard for the land and human life. Produce less, consume less and there will be less demand, less production. Education of the public is our immediate concern.

The United States has to a great extent created and controlled modern technology; it also bears a responsibility for the misuse of this technology, from air pollution to depletion of non-renewable resources. It is incumbent upon the United States, therefore, to take the lead in regulating technology and assuring the ecological balance upon which we depend. This most difficult and urgent job will require immediate and forceful action, including a change in our value system, a shift from exploitative goals and considerable rearrangement of our social structures (e.g., government agencies) and our daily lives (e.g., transportation).

The People's Party believes that technology can serve without destroying precious human life-support systems; that, if controlled and harmonized with nature's uncompromising demands, it can well be expected to transform the conditions of human life with an increasing quality; that, without intelligent management, it may well destroy human life.

The following steps, as a minimum, must be taken to achieve favorable balances in ecological relationships:

1) Control over natural resources must shift from profit-centered organizations to community-centered motivation. Policy decisions must place community well-being above the profits of corporations. Quality of life must be redefined and based on the right of all living things to eat, breathe and live in health with the assurance that they are not being poisoned. We must maximize human potential to the fullest.

2) New national policies must eliminate the widespread misuse of our resources. Renewable resources (plant and animal life, rivers, atmosphere, etc.) must be conserved and guarded from misuse. Non-renewable resources (mineral, fuel, etc.) must be extracted without destroying or upsetting the natural ecological balance in the area and must be used under strict controls reflecting the real needs of the community. We demand the immediate abolition of strip-mining and the reclamation of all stripped lands. This reclamation must be paid for by the corporations which through their greed have "eaten up" the land.

3) A center for Ecological Research and Action must be established and charged with the three-fold task of:

a. Researching areas, such as solar energy; air, water, noise and land pollution; subsoil, mineral and water rights; collecting data on pollution-related health, deaths and illnesses.

b. Utilizing computer simulation techniques of decision analysis, such as now used in war, business management and other complex systems guidance and control processes. Thus, it will be possible to analyze trends in the earth's ecosystem and to prescribe sensible and appropriate remedial action.

c. Preparation and dissemination of the necessary materials to provide the people with continuing education in ecological matters. And development and implementation of the necessary technological bases for improving and maintaining the environment.

4) Our energy policy must change. Presently, it assumes that the need for more and more energy to run an enlarged and exploitive technology is inexhaustible. Such thinking lies behind many unsound decisions, like increasing our min-

ing and consumption of coal and oil, damming more rivers for electrical power and building nuclear reactors and other energy systems that may well prove to be unsafe. Instead, we must assume the need for sound ecological practices. This means adjusting fuel consumption, halting construction of fission reactors and other energy systems until satisfactory systems are developed in terms of safety; stopping dam construction where undesirable ecological damage would result and sponsoring research to find better means of generating and using power. It will be necessary to reorder our society to get along on the energy which serves real community needs instead of building excessive weaponry, lighting unnecessary neon signs and running over-powered cars. We can make do with far less energy and at the same time preserve a favorable ecological balance and achieve an increasingly better quality of living. We call for an urban rapid transit system to be constructed and operated free to riders in order to encourage the drastic reduction of automobile use. Community advisory committees should help plan the routes to avoid unnecessary disruption of communities.

5) Though we do not accept the contention that population growth is responsible for ecological imbalance, a program aimed at a reasonable quality of life must be undertaken, including steps to voluntary control of U.S. population growth and steps to aid and encourage other countries in this respect. To this end, we propose the following:

a. Community education programs on sex and reproduction.

b. Publicity about contraceptives devices and instruction in their use. Contraceptives should be available at no cost to those unable to afford them.

c. Funding should be made immediately available for research into safer and more efficient methods of birth control.

d. All laws prohibiting safe abortions on request should be eliminated. Abortions should be provided free to anyone requesting them, also sterilization. However, we wish to make clear that we condone no efforts to force a person into an abortion or a sterilization as a requirement for receiving welfare assistance.

e. Under U.N., not U.S., control, we should develop a system of population control as a model for all countries. The population growth analysis of world problems is a smokescreen used to blame human fertility for the disasters being created by a capitalist elite. Population is not the problem; but congestion (i.e., population density created in certain places by capitalistic policies) leads to ecological problems. Population control policies, such as "zero population growth," are invariably aimed at lower class and Third World Peoples. The unstated racist assumption behind population growth analysis is that the average white nuclear family is the model for growth stability.

If the emphasis is that population is a key problem leading to ecological disaster (i.e., Paul Ehrlich and company), then the logical conclusion is not voluntary birth control but involuntary control—again aimed at "the most irresponsibly fertile" sector (meaning the lower classes and the Third World, at home and abroad). The People's Party categorically denies this emphasis on population as the problem.

When a society develops in such a way that it satisfies the physical, social, economic and psycho-cultural needs of the populace, population growth invariably stabilizes itself. It is poverty and oppression, not sexuality, that are the environmental stimuli to population growth. Therefore, population growth must be dealt with not by genocidal control policies, but through the destruction of poverty and oppression.

6) We must restructure the economy to meet requirements for a balanced ecosystem:

a. Non-biodegradable, toxic or radioactive chemicals released into the environment must be kept within strict tolerance limits until such time as it is possible to limit or prohibit their release completely. This means an immediate crackdown on enforcement of such laws as the Clean Water Act of 1899. The crackdown should begin with the largest industries first, right down to the smallest.

b. All reusable materials must be recycled on a sound ecological and economical basis. All containers should be reusable or recyclable. In recycling, most companies will save money on not using and developing raw materials. Some of this money should be passed on to the people recycling (collecting, transporting, etc.) the material so that recycling efforts will not have

to rely solely on volunteer help and will, thus, encourage a more effective job. This will decrease waste and pollution and slow down our consumption of raw materials.

c. New products and drugs must satisfy improved health and safety standards before being cleared for sale. This places community safety before community profits. Also, steps must be taken to prevent the marketing and sale of products which are inadequately tested.

7) Government environmental agencies must serve the community:

a. The U.S. Atomic Energy Commission should be reconstructed as the U.S. Energy Commission. The responsibilities of such an agency would be to deal solely with the development and use of energy.

b. The development and enforcement of safety and ecological standards should be the responsibility of the Environmental Protection Agency.

c. All government construction (including the Army Corps of Engineers' projects) must receive community approval in the place projected for the construction.

d. Information gathered by government regulatory agencies must be made freely available to the public. The public must also have access to information on ecological and health consequences of any product and in decision-making with respect to policies of government agencies.

## ECONOMICS

Despite the fact that we have developed the productive capacity to put people on the moon, and despite the fact that the output per person hour of American workers has grown more than 7.5 per cent in the last five years, the economic condition of the American people is degenerating.

Our cities are in decay. Twenty-five per cent of our population lives below the poverty level. Unemployment is running rampant. For every person unemployed there are ten who are underemployed. Even those who are fully employed are forced to accept dehumanizing conditions on the job and inadequate wages because of the constant threat of unemployment. Our wages are under "voluntary" control while prices are spiraling.

Third World people and women especially suffer from political, social and economic oppression, and our Third World communities are forced to bear the brunt of an economic system in decline.

The ownership of our economy has fallen into a few hands (i.e., 1.7 per cent of the adult population owns more than 82 per cent of the publicly held shares in American corporations), which, in pursuit of personal profits, have resorted more and more to planned obsolescence and the production of useless goods. This wastes our resources, poisons our environment and produces a sense of frustration on the part of working people who can no longer take pride in their work.

Although the U.S. government has spent a trillion dollars on armaments since 1945, the nation is more insecure than ever as a result of the proliferation of nuclear weapons and the threat of nuclear destruction.

By defending and encouraging growing investments abroad by U.S. corporations (which grew by $32.4 billion in 1970), the U.S. ruling elite is responsible for the impoverishment of other peoples, turning the people of the Third World against the U.S. We have been drawn by that same lying elite into foreign wars which support dictatorships and oligarchies which represent only a tiny percentage of the world's population.

The People's Party sees the mounting problems and the growing personal alienation that afflicts our country as a manifestation of the conflicts of interests between the people and the power and profit interests of the handful who control our entire economy.

Long Range Program:

We, therefore, put forward as our long range program the transformation of the economic system to let people control the institutions that affect their lives. The decision-making power for the nature and amount of things produced must pass from the owners of the large corporations to the workers and the communities affected by their production. And, the economy must be organized to improve the standard of living and the quality of human life to the highest level technologically possible. Wealth and production must be redistributed and adverse conditions that have been produced abroad by American corporate capitalism must be alleviated. The economy must be not only just humane, but also must conform to the ecological constraints dictated by the biological and physical order of this planet. To this end we propose the following long range program:

1) The major economy of this country should become the property of the people collectively, exercising their ownership through democratic institutions with adequate safeguards for local autonomy, the exact details of said institutions should be determined by a new constitutional convention.

2) Corporations should be reconstituted as public trusts with their day to day operations controlled by the worker, with governing bodies composed of workers and representatives responsible to the people.

3) Public funds should subsidize companies to produce goods needed by the community, yet which need external financial support, such as public transportation, medical services, education, non-commercial television, radio and newspapers, local housing, etc.

4) Welfare programs for the rich in the form of federal crop subsidies for wealthy farmers and special tax breaks for the big corporations must be eliminated, along with the present dehumanizing welfare system with its racist and piecemeal approach. All persons must have a reasonable base income. A maximum annual personal wealth should also be established to protect against excessive concentrations of wealth.

5) We must reorder our priorities to provide an adequate supply of all the necessities of life— health care, shelter, food, clothing and education —should be immediately made available to all. The cost should come out of the commonwealth of the people (represented by an appropriate tax system) which represents the wealth of the people held in common as the people's heritage.

6) Concerning the federal tax system:

All taxes should be levied in a simple and direct manner, understandable to all, and without manipulation, special privileges, or fraud.

The federal and state taxes shall no longer be taken involuntarily out of pay checks.

The establishment of a minimum income ($6,500 per year for a family of four) and a maximum wealth ($50,000 per year) and a steeply progressive income and wealth tax should apply in order to help break down the existing concentration of economic power. Property and inheritance should be assessed as wealth. These should be the only forms of taxes by all levels of government.

To equitably meet the social needs of all the people, tax revenues should be distributed to the different levels of the community on a per capita basis.

7) On the subject of large-scale coordination of a populist economic system, we propose that there should be a people's national planning and review board, directly elected by and subject to recall by the people, which would provide broad economic parameters within which regional and local development would take place, using an efficient and responsible allocation of resources, consistent with ecological balance.

Emergency Program:

The people must be mobilized immediately to head off the developing crisis and to fight for immediate aims under the present system. Only in this way can we defeat the enemies of the people and develop the institutions and attitudes necessary for popular control. Therefore, we seek to mobilize people around the following emergency program:

1) An end to the wage freeze; replacement of the phony price freeze by energetic government action combined with a general offensive of labor and consumers to roll back the inflated prices fixed by the multi-national corporations and to raise the wages of labor to a level that can support a standard of living worthy of a nation that can put people on the moon.

2) Tax reform to lift the burden of taxation from the backs of the poor and people of ordinary means and to increase the taxation of the super-rich and the greedy corporations. In particular, we oppose the sales taxes. And we uphold such proposals as:

a. Plugging the tax loopholes by which the super-rich escape taxation (i.e., tax incentives for U.S. companies investing overseas).

b. A progressive tax on wealth.

c. An excess profits tax.

d. As a transitional step to a one-tax system, tax relief up to $30,000 real value on owner's first residence. A proportionate tax reduction for renters should also be developed.

e. Abolish tax allowances such as the oil depletion allowance.

f. Abolish capital gains taxes and tax capital gains as income.

3) A federal job administration should assure a socially useful job at decent pay to every inhabitant of our country who wishes to work. This can be achieved through federal spending on the scale of total war, spending directed instead for a co-ordinated program of inexpensive housing, mass transportation, health facilities, pollution control, etc.

4) An end to further investment abroad by U.S. corporations (over 17 per cent of whose investments last year were in foreign countries). A tax on income of existing U.S. corporations located in other countries and a tax, at the highest income rate, on all income received by U.S. residents from foreign investments. These private investments not only exploit the workers of other countries, but aggravate international tensions and bring unemployment and economic hardship to workers at home as well. We support, also, the concept that private investments in other countries are the investor's own risk and should be controlled by the people in those countries. We also encourage maximum trade between this country and other countries on an equitable basis.

5) Decent payment and treatment for those who cannot work or cannot find work must be achieved. In particular:

a. We support the National Welfare Rights Organization's proposal for a $6,500 guaranteed annual income for a family of four.

b. Welfare should be paid directly through the federal government.

c. We oppose forced labor at welfare wages.

d. We support the strengthening and increasing of unemployment insurance coverage.

6) There should be a 30-hour work week for a minimum of 40 hours worth of pay.

7) Transferable, vested retirement rights should be funded by corporations.

8) There should be free mass transportation, child care centers and medical care.

9) The people should participate in making up the federal budget and full publicity concerning that budget should be made available.

10) We support unconditionally all presently existing alternative economic survival programs.

To eradicate the U.S. empire, we demand the nationalization by the people of the means of production, distribution and communication. Specifically, we propose that this nationalization begin with the largest U.S. corporation and continue until people's control is a reality.

We serve warning on the wealthy handful who control our economy that if this very minimal program to head off the present crisis is answered by sabotage and non-cooperation by great corporations, we will not hesitate to give this the rebuff it deserves by encouraging the seizure of property of the corporations by the people.

EDUCATION

The public schools of the United States serve the interests of the ruling class of the nation, the governing class of the rich and the powerful. Our schools perpetuate the myth of an open, free society. In practice, however, the schools are instruments of class, sexual and racial oppression. They also teach misconceptions of the role of the United States in the world. They oppress the working class by reinforcing class differences through elaborate and subtle tracking systems. This system offers the students limited choices in their learning experiences. Each student's choices are determined by that student's race, class and sex. The schools oppress racial minorities by supressing and distorting the true heritage of these students as well as by outright discrimination. They oppress men and women by teaching narrow and sexist role models. And they, like our other social institutions, turn those oppressed by the system against each other. In whatever direction the tracks lead students, there is an attempt to mold them into passive, obedient, interchangeable consumers and workers. The process ignores the individual differences and needs and stifles joyful and creative growth. To create an authentic and relevant education we must reverse this process so that it moves toward educational self-determination for young people. Education should inspire people to *be* more, rather than to have more. A new era in education geared to the above goal will profoundly change the character of our country.

Compulsory Education—

Compulsory education is the strength of the stranglehold of the traditional school over the student, stifling creativity, independent thinking and even learning itself. Compulsory education must be abolished. At the same time, young people must be protected from exploitation and guaranteed their right to an education. Public school must be "disestablished" as the state of education for American youth because the power of law is being used to force young people into institutions whose major purpose is social manipulation. This step must be taken if we wish to establish a fundamental dynamic for change in education soon enough to meet the real needs of young people currently in school. Young people must have the right to work and the right to receive money for the work of obtaining an education.

Community Control—

Schools should be subject to community control. Only general school policies affecting the school system as a whole should be set by state or local school boards. Individual schools should be directed by a board of students, parents and staff (one third for each segment), democratically elected by their peers. Teacher qualifications, hiring and firing should be determined by the individual boards. The administration should serve to coordinate the policies of the student-teacher-parent board. Major decisions should be made by these interest groups and the power of administrators should be limited to making recommendations. The board must guarantee the rights reiterated throughout this platform.

If quality education is to be achieved in this country, students, teachers, parents and administrators need to communicate more about the educational process. Each group must have power over the aspects of the process which are relevant to it. The schools should be more fully integrated into the communities and should make facilities available for the use of the groups in the community.

Statement on Bussing—

The People's Party supports bussing to achieve quality education and racial balance. But we recognize bussing as merely a temporary measure, contingent upon equal financing in the school. Our greatest problem with bussing is that it is opposed to the concept of community control. Therefore, we propose that programs of bussing be approved by the affected communities, both black and white. In cases where bussing is approved, we support pairing of districts and bussing of people to the community control board meetings.

Student Rights—

The People's Party supports the following Bill of Rights for Students:

1) An education which meets individual needs and allows a person to grow at her or his own pace. This must be the highest priority. Young people must be free from adult controls so they can adapt in authentic and viable ways to a

rapidly changing reality and through this adaptive process build a civilization that will be more humane.

2) Democratically elected student courts and trials by peers, not administrative hearings. Discipline should not be punitive; rather, it should be viewed in terms of a solution to a problem. If both the jury and the student feel the problem is no longer solvable by them, the case should be referred to the bipartite board—50 per cent students, 50 per cent teachers.

3) Student and parent presence at all hearing procedures, if the student so desires.

4) Student's right to counsel of her or his own choice.

5) An end to corporal punishment.

6) The right to privacy, including a no access or no search policy for individual lockers, as well as an adamant prohibition of electronic surveillance equipment. We call for prohibition of medical tests used as a tool of oppression by school authorities; no test may be performed without the consent of the student and her or his legal guardian.

7) Recognition as equal members of society and protection of students' dignity as individuals.

8) Immunity from prosecution for violation of rules that either the elected bipartite board or an elected student board has not passed or made public.

9) The right to due process of law, to freedom of assembly, to form and join political organizations and unions and the concomitant right to strike. Students must also have a right to free access to information on all aspects of a question. Leafletting on school grounds should never be prohibited.

10) The right of all cultural and ethnic minorities to have their heritage included in the curriculum in an accurate and dignified fashion, including if necessary bilingual and non-standard education as determined by the community.

11) Education should be a universal right, in other words available to those who have been traditionally excluded from public schools due to mental retardation and other handicaps.

12) Students of all grades should have access to all books and materials in the library as well as access to other educational resources (e.g., advanced educational software and electronic hardware resource centers).

The People's Party recognizes that no public school system can be considered independent of the social forces that act upon it. Even if a single school system decided to eliminate all formal tracking, the entrance policies of universities and the hiring policies of industries would impose an informal system of tracking on the schools. Nevertheless, the People's Party must insist that the schools actively resist tracking and keep educational options open to all from kindergarten through life-long education. The specific instruments of tracking, such as grades, advanced classes, achievement and standardized tests, teacher recommendations, etc., must be dropped since they serve only to reproduce class distinctions and raise fallacious notions of "ability" and "failure" which deprive students of the right to explore their own potentials.

The classroom itself should be directed through a lateral transaction of experiences shared by teachers and students reciprocally and not by the administration or school board. We can tolerate no censorship of any form at any level. Opportunities to hear all sides of an issue must be constantly available.

We encourage experimental and innovative teaching methods and expansion of curricula to include any material in which students indicate interest. For example, by developing total environmental and educational communities, students and teachers could explore novel models of theoretical cultures, which could be experienced for an understanding of human and non-human possibilities.

Certification and the Rights of Teachers and Other School Workers—

Teachers and other school workers should be treated as individuals and their individual rights should be respected, especially by school administrators. Teachers, like any other employees, have the inherent right to strike. Teachers should be considered for tenure, but firings for cause should remain within the jurisdiction of the community-controlled board. The board should also be able to require in-service training for teachers regarding issues and concerns deemed important.

Though teachers are important to the educational process, present certification requirements exclude many competent teachers and do not in any way guarantee the quality of those who are certified. A prime concern for the community-controlled board should be to actively seek out teachers who represent a broad spectrum of racial and ethnic backgrounds. Community-controlled boards should be allowed to hire teachers they feel are best qualified to teach.

All school employees have guaranteed to them through the Bill of Rights the right to privacy, to due process, to freedom of assembly, to form and join political organizations and unions, and to strike.

Financing—

1) All levels and aspects of education (books, supplies, resources, transportation, etc.) should be provided free.

2) The People's Party supports an end to non-commercial property taxes and flat rate taxes for financing education. The People's Party proposes financing public education by means of a steeply graduated personal income tax. We call for a vigorous campaign to change the Constitution to allow for such a tax.

3) The People's Party supports a tax on business profits. Provisions should be made to prevent any businesses from passing that tax on to the consumer or to the worker.

4) The People's Party also favors the equalization of school support on a nation-wide basis.

5) As an additional alternative and supplement, the People's Party believes support should be given to alternative educational institutions, though we oppose any schools run for private profit. We feel that these "free schools" should be helped either through a voucher plan or equalizing funds from the government. All non-research and developmental educational funds from the municipal, state and federal levels should be allocated yearly on a per capita basis, for educational use in the form of educational certificates. The individual student should be allowed to spend the certificates at any school he or she chooses, for self-directed study or for apprenticeship.

6) We call for the elimination of all state accreditation requirements at all levels of education.

7) All students shall be automatically registered to vote.

University Community—

Universities should not be involved in any way in military research or military education. This is especially so if such research or education has as its specific intention or result the degradation of human life. It is time to exert all energies toward improving the quality of life and not toward improving methods of death and destruction. Universities should devote an ever-increasing part of their capabilities to the communities in which they are located. Universities should be open to all seeking to enter them.

FARMER LIBERATION

Our farmers need to be liberated from the cost-price squeeze resulting from the scuttling of the parity formula that makes farmers the main shock absorber of an inflation-ridden economy.

Farmers need to be liberated also from the bi-partisan crunch they have been put into by being used to help meet the U.S. balance of payments. They are told that grain prices must be kept low in order to "compete in the world market." Yet the government as the chief grain exporter in the world sets the world market price and sets it low deliberately at $1.05 per bushel for corn, while the price in Europe is over twice that high.

Actually, there is no real "world market" as such, since every surplus grain producing country has been running a subsidized international discount house. The significant thing about the U.S. practice is that the U.S. farmer, not the government, is paying the subsidy in sub-parity prices.

The European Common Market comes nearest to being a "world market" for corn as it buys the largest volume. The extent to which the U.S. farmers are deceived and robbed is indicated by comparing the price supports here and in the Common Market. The national price support figure on corn in the U.S. is $1.05 per bushel. In the Common Market countries it is $2.45 per bushel now and will be $2.82 next year. Yet farmers are told such low price supports are needed here in order to compete with the very much higher figure abroad.

There is no single thing on which the people have been so misled, deceived and brainwashed as on the farm issue. There is no other matter on which so much misinformation, half truths and outright lies have been peddled to confuse voters as on the farm problem and its possible solutions.

There was perhaps one exception to that for a time—the long cold war and the hot wars in Southeast Asia. But, at long last people have become enlightened even on that question.

But the farm story still remains to be told. It is part of the mission of the People's Party to expose the falsifications about the farm problem and to substitute facts for fiction.

Some of the major points that need to be cleared up are:

1) What the farm problem is and what it is not. It is simply a very extended period of sub-parity prices—not a matter of too many farmers and unmanageable surpluses as the anti-farm propagandists would have us believe.

2) Farm legislation. We must have national planning for national goals, for the farm problem is a national problem. The nonsense that all farm programs, especially price supports, have been failures and very costly needs to be replaced with known facts. The earlier programs did work, including 90 per cent of parity price supports. Earlier programs that gave farmers parity cost but a fraction of what the recent programs have cost.

3) The government must be held to its commitment of parity to the farmers. This is not at all an impossible goal. Farmers averaged parity during the Roosevelt years and it was not because of three-and-a-half years of war. If war and military spending were good for farm prices, then corn should be getting $3.00 per bushel now.

4) The question of who is subsidizing whom needs to be cleared up. Leon K. Keyserling published his findings over ten years ago before the farm prices got down to the really low levels of recent years. He said that farmers had been short-changed seven billion dollars over the previous ten-year period. Recently, with farm prices lower, the estimate is ten billion dollars per year that farmers have been subsidizing consumers with cheap food. So the farmers get robbed of ten billion dollars per year, and when the thief—the federal government—gives back two billion in payments, it has the gall to accuse the farmers of an undeserved subsidy. In fact, the federal government has been subsidizing the big food corporations which are forcing up food prices for the consumer.

5) A "market oriented" agriculture is what the aim of the government is now. We hold that sound national policy requires an abundance of food and reserves for emergencies. But in a surplus situation the support price becomes the market price, with the rate being $1.05 per bushel that acts as a ceiling as well as a floor. Given the fact of abundance, a market-oriented agriculture and fair farm prices are incompatible. In fact, a market oriented system is an abomination without a single hope of redemption. If farm price relief is to be made contingent on scarcity, then the farm cause is indeed hopeless.

What Must Be Done—

Short Range Program:

1) Set price supports on storable grains at the maximum rate now permitted, 90 per cent of parity. This should apply immediately to crops.

2) Stop all sales of storable grains at less than parity prices.

3) Stop all sales of Commodity Credit Corp. bins. They will be needed in the near future.

4) Announce that it is the general policy to achieve the equivalent of parity prices for all farm program participants for the next four years and that the "social contract" made by the government commitment to parity will be honored.

5) Assure agricultural workers full rights under the Wagner Act. The People's Party supports the concept of the secondary boycott and the United Farm Workers Organizing Committee (UFWOC) lettuce boycott.

6) Farm workers must be included under the federal wage law.

7) In keeping with the concept of abundance, there shall no longer be payments for not growing food in order to raise prices on farm produced goods. Surplus food shall be used to subsidize hungry areas of the world and shall be held in reserve for emergencies. In other words, if farm production is based on supply and demand, farmers will be forced to produce just enough or not quite enough in order to get the prices they so deserve.

Long Range Program:

There should be instituted a land reform program or land use, residency requirement, the primary criteria for the right to land ownership. The policy must take into consideration conservation practices to conserve the soil for future generations and must also emphasize ecological advantages that family-type farming has over the large farming conglomerates.

With family-type farming and a small herd of cattle, hogs or poultry, and often some of each, the animal wastes are returned to the fields and plowed under to enrich the soil. Big conglomerates have operations where thousands of livestock are fed in one concentrated area and the wastes pollute streams, rivers and even the air.

Animal and grain producing agriculture are being separated. With the present cheap grain policy of the government, the grain farmers are subsidizing the big feeding operations by providing them with cheap corn—at about 40 per cent of parity.

Such a program of family-type farms will vary in size and types of farming and differing farming regions; but acreage limitations and residency requirements will not only assure a wider distribution of ownership and control of productive property, but it will halt the forced farm-to-city migration that merely compounds the problems of the cities while solving no farm problems whatever. In some areas, a back to the land program could well be called for as well as cooperative farms if desired.

But the most important step is a reversal of the low farm policy of the last 20 years, especially with respect to grains and a turnabout to carry out the commitment of the parity prices made in the first Agricultural Adjustment Act of 1933. A repudiation of the low price policy of recent years—about 40 per cent of parity for corn—is most imperative, not only for U.S. farmers but for farmers of the world. For in manipulating prices to as low a level as possible, the U.S. government exploits not only its own farmers but also the farmers of the world; for the U.S. farm production is the main supplier of the various markets and to a certain extent it sets the world price. In fact, some government officials have boasted of setting the world market price for corn.

This policy then constitutes a vicious form of neo-colonialism; and since U.S. farm production is the biggest contributor to the U.S. balance of payments, it is also a contributor to imperialist designs throughout the world; the farmers, therefore, are unwillingly helping to undergird U.S. militarism and to sustain such atrocities as the Vietnam War.

## FOREIGN POLICY

Foreign policy is the way a nation relates to other nations. In our world, nations are interdependent. The United States has built a worldwide empire. U.S.-based companies hold $125 billion in assets abroad. Our highly industrialized economy depends on materials imported from other countries (oil from Venezuela, tin from Malaya and Bolivia, etc.) and on the use of cheap labor in countries like Taiwan and Korea. U.S. corporations have chosen to exploit the weakness and poverty of these people rather than to pay for better conditions and higher wages for American workers. Our government gives economic aid to poor nations on the condition that they buy U.S.

products and participate in the system which exploits their people. This is called neo-colonialism.

U.S. enterprises abroad help to maintain wealth in a few hands, while the masses are forced to struggle against overwhelming odds. The Central Intelligence Agency (CIA) and the Agency for International Development (AID) deliberately interfere in the international affairs of other nations, stunting their national development and supporting an elite at the expense of the people.

U.S. military forces protect our assets abroad. This has necessitated maintenance of 2,000 military bases abroad (not including Vietnam) and the allocation of much of the national budget to the burgeoning military system. It provides weapons supporting many unpopular governments (Greece, Pakistan, etc.) and fighting two major wars in Korea and Southeast Asia. On numerous occasions, liberation movements have tried to regain popular control from a corrupt regime and have been defeated with the assistance of the U.S. The actual defense of the U.S., as opposed to maintain an empire, would require only a small, home-based army under the direct control of the people.

Global problems such as ecological imbalance, over-population and the spread of nuclear weapons threaten human survival. To cope with these, we must first transform our foreign policy to affirm our basic humaneness and the need for planetary survival through unity. We cannot continue to provide weapons and support for governments that oppress their own people. We must create a new trans-nationalism in which we unite with these around the world who also seek to change oppressive institutions and values.

To this end, the People's Party proposes that:
1) United States foreign policy must respect the right of self-determination of all peoples of the world.

a. U.S. and U.S.-supported troops must be withdrawn from Southeast Asia immediately and unilaterally. All aggressive military and economic intervention must cease.

b. U.S. troops and equipment must be withdrawn from foreign countries and military alliances must cease.

c. Military aid must cease.

d. The U.S. should recognize all governments—whether capitalist, communist or socialist—that draw support from broad masses of their people and do not engage in repression. There should be an end to trade with all governments that do not receive the support of their people.

e. All subversive intelligence and neo-colonial agencies, including the CIA and AID must be abolished.

Ultimately, we must recognize that the survival of all people depends on an end to nationalism and militarism on the part of all countries. The U.S. armed forces must be abolished, and only the Coast Guard and local militia should be retained.

2) Foreign policy should represent the best interests of the American people, not of the American corporations. Our real interests are in human unity and sharing. America, holding a disproportionate share of the world's wealth, must now redefine its aid policies and practices in order to:

a. Provide meaningful assistance to Third World people.

b. Guarantee supervision of all aid, not unilaterally, but through international organizations which truly serve the people of the world, not their own selfish interests.

3) U.S. foreign policy must be changed to reflect two-way cultural exchanges for mutual enrichment.

4) The present U.S. space program has distorted domestic priorities and misdirected the public into viewing space as an arena for jingoistic pride, thus contributing to a neglect of world-wide needs.

a. The present space program must be halted.

b. We must establish an international program of space research, directed at advancing the development of medicine and other world-wide needs. This includes such things as communications and weather forecasting.

c. The fruits of all space research must be shared toward an end of enlarging benefits for all mankind.

5) We propose that the U.S. announce policies to settle all international disputes it has through binding decisions of a World Court when it is the desire of the conflicting states to use that means. This is the first step toward setting up a binding world law for all nations.

6) We propose that further development of and additions to our nuclear strength cease. Furthermore, we urge an international convention of all nations to discuss a means of world-wide nuclear weapons abolition.

7) We call for the freedom of all territories not within the continental United States (i.e., Guam and Puerto Rico).

GOVERNANCE

People function within society both as individuals and as communities. A community comes into being when cultural, social, economic or environmental circumstances create a natural common bond among a group of people.

Governance is how a community makes decisions. When the power to make decisions rests with a group of individuals who are isolated from the needs and ideas of the people, social structures become tools for exploiting the people instead of serving their common interests.

Our social ills have provoked a growing sense of alienation and frustration among many Americans. Some people lapse into apathy, some turn to bombs and guns, some drop out to create new life styles and others withdraw into drugs. Politically, people have voted "no confidence" in the present system by withdrawing their participation in it. Of all adults eligible to vote in the United States, only some 69 per cent usually register to vote. Of these, only 80 per cent or fewer vote in national elections. Turnout for local election runs as low as 20 per cent.

A growing number of Americans feel powerless to influence government. Political institutions that claim to respond to the peoples' will respond instead to the demands of paid lobbyists and big-money interests that help them get elected by buying election through use of the mass media. This powerlessness constitutes a crisis in governance in our country.

If government is to respond to the needs of the people, institutions will have to undergo radical changes to return power of government back to the people. This means decentralizing the power structure, encouraging participation by all the people and bringing decision-making back to a level at which the public has access to it. Decentralization of power makes good the right of people to control the institutions that deal with their social policy, collective interests and general well-being. In all such proposals we must recognize the interrelationships among individual liberty, community control and social planning, and find imaginative ways to deal with these relationships.

Several changes must be made in this area:

1) Bipartisan gerrymandering of anachronistic legislative districts must be ended. Reapportionment of districts should be radically reformed to make meaningful the "one man, one vote" Supreme Court principle. Mandatory guidelines for districting, such as communities of interest, ecological factors, social planning considerations, etc., should be established.

2) Public institutions that serve a community (police, welfare agencies, educational agencies, etc.) should be controlled by that community. Community boards should be established to oversee their operation, including the hiring and firing of personnel.

3) The government should fund independent groups to develop new technical systems of communication between the people and their political institutions. These could include new methods of voting or public opinion polling, new uses of the media in politics, or the use of computer technology to make socio-political information available to the people. We should consider the eventual establishment of a participatory democracy using phone-computer technology to enable each citizen to vote on key issues and policies.

4) The government should encourage the formation of community groups charged with conveying the community's opinions to those in power. These groups should develop methods to measure popular opinion (by referenda, for example), to bring these opinions into the open, and to carry them through into action.

5) Voting procedures should be made fair and simple. Elections should be by direct vote, including direct primaries that are binding on the parties. The electoral college should be abolished. Residency requirements, except for the need to register before an election, should also be eliminated.

6) A Fair Campaign Practices Code should be enacted, including the principle that every political campaign be ensured a basic minimum funding from public monies and be mandatorily limited to a ceiling on expenditures.

7) In order for the people to exercise power, the control of non-governmental institutions such as corporations and the media must change.

Short Range Proposals:

1) The establishment of counter-institutions run by the community to fill community needs that are not fillable by present public institutions.

2) Massive voter registration drives among 18 to 21-year-olds and among members of disenfranchised communities, especially minority communities. Felons and inmates of mental institutions must have the right to vote.

3) The use of initiative, referendum and recall procedures, as provided for in the Constitution, to limit the abuses of corporate and political power under which we presently suffer.

4) We support the demands of the Washington, D.C. Statehood Party for the District to become a state in its own right. We also support the American Indian Nations' struggle to regain their sovereignty and have their treaties with the U.S. honored.

The People's Party feels that no individual can be coerced in any way that conflicts with his/her will. All conscription of men or women for military or military-related duty should be abolished. We call for establishment of a Department of Peace and Priorities with the principal goals of advising the American people, the Congress and the President on the best means of rechanneling funds to life-sustaining activities. This Department could also advise on actual and perceived threats to peace and could serve to mediate such threats. What cannot be resolved in this manner should be referred to the World Court. This Department should be separate from the executive branch and should be headed by a secretary elected by the American people for four-year terms in non-presidential general elections. We are committed to the radical reconstruction of local, state and national government to allow us to take control of our collective lives.

## HEALTH

Health care is a right, not a privilege. A high standard of health care must be made equally available to everyone. An effective attack on the problems of health care is impossible without a simultaneous and comprehensive attack on all social and economic conditions which breed poverty and illness. Unless education and living conditions improve at the same time, any improvement in health care will be minimal and temporary. We must translate our present vast health knowledge into effective health care. The allocation of resources for guaranteeing and promoting health and the prevention and treatment of disease should have high priority. It is the right of every community to participate in the planning and governing of its health care program.

Our existing system of health services has utterly failed its responsibility to the people:

1) The medical profession has absolute power over the patient; the community has no control over the delivery of services.

2) The AMA represents the reactionary force maintaining the present intolerable state of health care.

3) Health conditions among the poor and the minorities in the U.S. are statistically no better than those in underdeveloped countries. There are serious diseases which are almost limited in this country to the disadvantaged population groups. This is a form of institutionalized racism and reflects the basic injustice of the system.

4) The medical schools have also perpetrated poor health care. The emphasis of medical education should give priority to the delivery of health care.

5) The number of health professionals is inadequate. We must begin to provide greater numbers and more appropriately trained persons.

6) Too many people make exorbitant profit from the sickness of others. This injustice must stop.

A society which maintains economic and political power in the hands of a few cannot end these frustrations. The People's Party, therefore, supports all efforts by the people to challenge and attain power over those institutions of medicine which affect or oppress them. In essence, we believe in free quality physical, mental and preventive medical care for all our people.

## Labor

Working people constitute the great majority in the United States. Realistically, there could be no wealth without the labor of workers. Yet workers are being forced to absorb the economic consequences of an inflation created by the decisions of business and government bosses, decisions which are based on price fixing, excessive profits and the wasteful production of materials for continuing the exploitation of Third World countries such as those in Southeast Asia.

We therefore support the following:

1) Rejection of wage controls as a solution to inflation. We would support an independent move by workers to oppose the Nixon economics, using any means necessary up to and including a general strike. Recovery from inflation will come not from helping business increase profits, but by channeling money directly back to the consumer/worker through price controls, increased pay and tax rebates.

2) We believe workers have the right to fight to liberate themselves from the grip of nonrepresentative leadership. Workers at even the lowest organizational level must have a democratic say in hiring practices, hours, working conditions, training, retraining and organizing production.

3) The People's Party encourages a rank and file labor movement that would guarantee everyone the right to productive work and make the present apprentice program available to all potential workers. The apprentice program should be under the full control of the union locals.

4) Retraining at no loss of pay for workers whose jobs are phased out and for workers whose jobs are eliminated, full benefits until new jobs can be found for them. Retraining should also be under union control.

5) No discrimination against either of the sexes, ethnic minorities, homosexuals or former convicts in employment and promotions.

6) No restrictions on the right to strike and organize secondary boycotts. Public employees should have the right to bargain collectively and to strike.

7) We support rank and file demands for a 30 hour work week, perhaps in the form of three ten-hour workdays, with no reduction in pay—in other words, 30 hours with 40 hours of pay. This would provide the added benefit of developing full employment.

8) We feel that workers should be provided with a guaranteed insured pension free from corporate control with automatic standard of living increases to allow workers freedom from a specific job or place of work.

9) We wholeheartedly support the current movement of rank and file workers to organize caucuses within the presently unrepresentative unions. Further, we support the unionization of all American workers to protect themselves from the greed of the management and owners.

10) We support the right of the rank and file to organize into and to democratically control unions.

Management has made consumers believe that the worker and his union are to blame for inflation, for lack of jobs, for the decline in the quality of American goods, for all the ills of our economy. It's called blaming the victim for the crime. And this division is false and misleading. For the most part, workers and consumers are the same people, with the same hopes and desires. It is unnatural that workers and consumers should be pitted against each other. It's like a snake biting its own tail rather than defending itself from something afflicting it—in this case the affliction is the power structure. Consumers and workers should come together to determine their needs, establish priorities and develop movements in their communities for full employment and ecological balance. This means taking control of the means of production in the community and working closely with other communities.

LAW AND JUSTICE

Laws provide a system for the resolution of conflicts between individuals. We believe it is not the function of the legal system to either preserve or defend the government of the community or to regulate personal behavior or the individual.

When certain people and institutions have greater access to the legal resources of a society than the masses of people or when the few have greater influence over the decision-making (particularly through the selection of judges), the inequities of the society are legitimized, exacerbated and prolonged; conflicts are not resolved; and freedom is not shared by all.

If a legal system in any way violates these precepts, it is oppressive of the individual. We feel that the following steps must be taken immediately to erase these inequities in the American judicial system:

1) Law enforcement must come from and be controlled by the people in a specific community. A number of plans for community control have been developed. Obviously, the plan must fit the community's needs. The main element of such plans is that the local police force be appointed and reviewed by an elected board of community members. We also believe, with the Constitution, that citizens have the right to bear arms. Over and over we have seen that when people lay down their arms, they lose the power for which they have struggled.

2) Most access to legal institutions is through lawyers. Lawyers come from a specific segment of society, rarely from the poor minorities. Legal education must be made available financially and scholastically as well; and it must be available to anyone who wishes to pursue such a course of study. Lawyers from varied segments of society are more likely to represent the interests of the specific segment from which they come. Furthermore, legal education must provide para-professionals to increase the availability of legal services.

3) People must have access to lawyers. In many respects the working class has least access to lawyers, being ineligible for poverty lawyers and too poor to pay the price for private lawyers. Legal aid and public defender programs must be funded generously and without political strings attached so that people without sufficient funds can have access to legal remedies and protection. In addition, we advocate legal insurance programs that allow groups, such as unions, student bodies, etc., and individuals to hire lawyers on a salary basis and to insure themselves against the high cost of attorneys.

4) Minors must be ensured of all protections as outlined in the Constitution.

5) Individuals must be liable for breaking the law through their business practices. Fines on corporations must not be allowed to be deducted from taxes as a "cost of doing business" expense. The legal and financial responsibility for a corporation's illegalities should be borne by the person who is guilty of handling the illegality.

6) All judges should be elected, even when vacancies occur during a term of office. Community courts should be set up where disputes between citizens can be settled by citizens' judges. This would effectively remove some of the burden from present courts and give a wider range of legal knowledge to a greater number of people.

The parameters of acceptable behavior are set by criminal law. Criminal law is, by nature, repressive. It sets limits beyond which one should not go. While it is necessary to repress some destructive behavior, the extent of repression in our present society and the manner of dealing with unacceptable behavior is cruel and unusual. The majority of laws today are based on protection of the power structure's property. And the resulting repression today affects great proportions of society; and the so-called prison solution is counterproductive and merely trains criminals rather than rehabilitating them. We, therefore, call for these additional changes:

1) Both community members and police will deal with each other as human beings if they are both made answerable to the community for their actions. Law enforcement must come from and be controlled by the people.

2) Society must not legislate individual morality. We propose, therefore, the abolition of crimes without victims. The defendant also has the right to present his/her own defense with free legal advice and further, should have the choice of his/her own defense.

3) We propose the elimination of preventive detention and no-knock legislation, domestic spying, undercover agents, wiretapping, and other such unconstitutional methods of law enforcement.

4) Grand juries have become tools of government prosecutors, rather than the objective investigative bodies they are in theory. We would return the grand jury to its intended function; that is, a jury of peers determining whether a case against an individual is sufficient to warrant a trial. Witnesses before a grand jury must be protected by Constitutional guarantees. Prosecutors who introduce false, misleading, or illegally gathered evidence to a grand jury are guilty of a serious criminal offense against the accused and should be treated before the law as such.

5) Trial juries must include true representation by one's peers. Services should be made available to jurors (e.g., child care) to ensure that all can serve.

6) Most criminal defendants should be released on their own personal recognizance without having to post bail. If bail is required, it must relate to the person's ability to pay. Speedy trial must be given specific statutory recognition, and this right must be personally waived only by the defendant.

7) The present penal system should be abolished. We call for the establishment of community-controlled re-education centers, adequate for comfortable human living, where the emphasis is directed at training which will enable the inmates to function as individuals in society. These centers should be staffed by psychiatrists, psychologists, sociologists, instructors, and vocational counselors, rather than prison guards and wardens. Vocational and academic educational opportunities should be available to the inmates. The staff of each center should have authority to

release a person in their care when, in their opinion, the person is ready for release. This would mean that judges would no longer be able to establish minimum sentences.

8) We support the United Prisoners' Union and its demand for a Bill of Rights for prisoners, parolees, probationers and ex-convicts, including payment at union wages (no less than minimum wage) for work, an end to abuse of the indeterminate sentences, access to law books, the right to receive, send and possess any letters and publications and the abolition of capital punishment.

9) We support 24-hour communication programs between the inmates of correctional institutions and the outside community via the news media and other methods of communication in order that the abuses of inmates will stop and will receive immediate attention if it does happen.

10) We propose the following changes in the approach to drug users:

a. Abolition of laws dealing with the criminality of use, sale and possession of psychoactive drugs.

b. Creation of public clinics to educate and treat drug users and provide them with such (psycho-active) drugs at a nominal cost upon demand. There should be no charge to the indigent.

c. All such services will be performed by qualified educational and medical personnel.

It is to be understood that the People's Party takes no moral stand in favor of the use of psychoactive drugs. We realize that current trends in drug usage are a direct result of social forces which make chemical intoxication seem appealing in contrast to the tension of "normal" social interaction. The community's solution to any resulting insanity must be solved with the highest regard for human dignity. Drug addiction is recognized as a personal, not a criminal, problem. Therefore, we call for the decriminalization of all drug use. This means that there should be no arrests or convictions for use, though individuals must be held responsible for their behavior while using drugs.

11) We support the immediate abolition of laws making the possession, sale or use of marijuana a crime.

12) The People's Party demands that the U.S. government make reparations to foreign and domestic peoples who have been the victims of military, economic and other oppression.

13) We support the repatriation of all people

who have been imprisoned or who have fled the country because of their opposition to the Vietnam war.

14) The Universal Code of Military Justice must be abolished, and military personnel must be subject to civilian codes of law.

RACISM

Racism is the concept or ideology that holds that one race or group of people is superior to another. In the U.S., this has taken the form of white people feeling and acting superior to non-white people. The People's Party totally rejects this concept.

The Native Americans, depicted as inferior and savage, were subjected to genocide and in the course of expansion, their lands, culture, heritage, and pride as a race were lost.

Black people were brought in chains from their African homeland, robbed of their culture and language and forced into chattel slavery for nearly two centuries. This bloody past has left an all-encompassing and codified system which perpetuates the concept of racial superiority.

Spaniards, who previously conquered the Native Americans and blended with them to form the people of Mexico, were conquered in turn in a war of annexation in which a major part of Mexico was taken from them by the U.S. They were thereby forced into the U.S. and were also treated as an inferior and conquered people.

The waves of foreign born that came to the U.S. in succeeding generations were looked upon as a source of cheap labor, were victims of greed, and were subjected to the indignities of ghetto life.

The foreign born white population has generally been assimilated into the broad scheme of American life, but the non-whites today continue to be the racist victims of a special oppression.

Thus, the racial question manifests itself in the separation of people by physical characteristics. This separation is maintained by those in power through a policy of divide and conquer among the people, by institutionalizing racism, which reveals itself in patterns of discrimination, segregation, increased police repression, population control programs (genocide), and the denial of dignity. The result is the psychological destruction of the self, the sociological destruction of the individual family, and the destruction of the culture.

The fight against racism is essentially the fight for full social, political, and economic equality. The fight for equality cannot be tokenism, but a massive onslaught against the whole concept of racism whenever and wherever it manifests itself.

White Americans must now resurrect, respect, fulfill, and honor the principles and articles of the Declaration of Independence and the Constitution and their solemn treaties with all nations and especially those with Native Americans.

The fight for equality is a class struggle as well as a radical one. Because the majority of the non-white peoples are members of the working class, the capitalist class employs the strategy of pitting the white workers against the non-white workers in order to increase profits. The white workers generally comply, and these racist actions are rewarded by token economic and social privileges granted to them by the capitalist class.

The fight for equality is also a national issue in that it is a struggle by the non-white peoples to maintain their existence and identities as peoples and nations. Recognizing this as a national issue means that we affirm and reaffirm to the non-white peoples their right of self-determination.

We realize that the future direction of the quest for self-determination will depend upon the past and present conditions and struggles of the various non-white peoples.

We know that this question can best be solved with a complete change of the economic and political systems, but until that change is made we are concerned with the fight for equality *now*.

Therefore, we support and will participate in movements for:

1) Elimination of institutionalized racism (discrimination) against non-white people in the choice of jobs, education, and housing.

2) Immediate release from prison of all political prisoners, those jailed because of their opposition as Third World people against the oppression of a racist system.

3) Democratic representation of Third World people in all institutions and processes that affect people's lives, including ethnic reapportionment of all electoral districts.

4) Community control of police. The People's Party upholds the principle of a Third World individual's or a group's right to defend itself with any means against unprovoked and unjustified police attacks.

5) Community control of all educational and social institutions and processes. We oppose regionalism where the purpose is to dilute the power or strength of minority groups, such as city planning.

6) Realization of the demands, aspirations, and visions of the Native Americans, African-Americans, and Chicanos in their liberation struggle:

a. Enforcement of treaties for their benefit.

b. Protection of traditional lands.

c. National autonomy (i.e., Independent Hopi Nation, Northern New Mexico Alianza Movement, Republic of New Africa). Bicultural urban areas which would have separate city status for bi-national and bilingual government and schools.

d. Autonomous nations would be independent of U.S. laws; yet they would retain the right to vote in state and U.S. elections.

e. We support the traditional right of Chicanos to move freely across the U.S. border.

7) The People's Party supports the following anti-racism bill:

a. 1) No federal troops shall be sent to ghettos to suppress demonstrations or rebellions against racist treatment.

2) Any local, state, or federal policeman or other local, state, or federal government official who murders any person, especially a Black, Latin, Asian, or Native American person, shall be deemed to have committed a federal offense punishable by life imprisonment.

3) Any local, state, or federal policeman or other local, state, or federal government official who assaults any person, especially minority persons, except in provable self-defense, shall be deemed to have committed a federal offense punishable by not less than ten years imprisonment, depending upon the severity of the offense.

4) Anyone on trial for any offense shall have his or her choice of a lawyer, particularly Third World people.

b. 1) Rescind the Talmadge Amendment, which would force people on welfare, especially Third World people, to work at less than minimum wages.

2) There shall be a guaranteed annual income of $6500 for a family of four, available to anyone with no legal exceptions. This would be important for Third World people who are often kept deliberately below the poverty level.

3) Children shall not be taken forcibly from mothers and fathers on welfare, a procedure now being recommended for many Third World people by welfare bureaucrats.

c. 1) Repeal the racist immigration codes.

2) People born in other countries and residing in the U.S. shall not be deported or harassed. This is often done to Third World noncitizens in the U.S.

d. No college or university, public or private school, which employs officials who commit acts of racism against students, faculty or other employees, or which uses texts that propagate the view that Black or other minority people are culturally or genetically inferior shall receive any federal aid.

e. 1) Medical researchers who experiment on minors, especially Third World minors, shall be deemed to have committed a federal offense punishable by not less than ten years imprisonment and with a maximum of life imprisonment.

2) Medical researchers who experiment on any people, especially Third World people, without their full consent, shall be deemed to have committed a federal offense punishable by not less than ten years imprisonment and with a maximum of life imprisonment.

3) Anyone who practices forced sterilization or lobotomies on people, especially Third World people, shall be deemed to have committed a federal offense punishable by life imprisonment.

4) Captive populations such as prisoners, particularly Asian, African, Hispanic, and Native Americans, shall never be experimented on or medically abused. Anyone who commits this crime shall be deemed to have committed a federal offense punishable by not less than ten years imprisonment depending on the severity of the offense.

8) The People's Party recognizes the special repression coming down on Black people in the South, and it pledges its full support of those fighting that oppression.

9) We demand that the Small Business Administration help to solve the special problems of Black business people due to generations of discrimination. This agency should give special consideration to Black business people in granting

loans and shall not use these loans as a partisan tool.

10) All government agencies providing emergency services in hurricanes, floods, earthquakes and other disasters shall alert and advise all qualified recipients of their right to aid. Members of minority groups shall not be intimidated or denied assistance because of their minority status.

## SEXISM

Sexism means ascribing, or withholding, certain rights, opportunities, attitudes, and potentials to individuals on the basis of their sex. To eliminate this form of discrimination, both sexes must be liberated from stereotyped men-women role-playing and provided with equal opportunities in work and life-style. This will mean changing our laws, social organization, and beliefs about homosexuality and about male and female competence.

The traditional value system places the woman in the home, supported by her husband. Today, however, women make up 37 per cent of all workers and are the sole parent in 10 per cent of the families in the nation. Yet the structure of our society continues to reflect the traditional system and holds women to the lowest economic positions, while denying them fair representation in decision-making structures.

Of all male workers, 48 per cent hold jobs as proprietors, managers, professionals, or craftsmen; only 20 per cent of all women workers are so employed. Only one engineer, three lawyers, and seven doctors out of one hundred are women. At the other end of the scale, however, women swell the ranks of clerical, sales, service, and household workers. Over 64 per cent of all women workers hold this type of job, as opposed to 20 per cent of all the male workers. The highest economic positions in the country exclude women almost totally; a recent survey of the 60 largest corporations in California showed that, of the 1,009 directors, only six were women and, of these, only two were unrelated to other directors. At all levels of full-time employment, women receive approximately $3,000 less per year than their male counterparts.

Women also lack representation in the governing bodies that control the society. The U.S. Senate includes one woman senator out of a hundred. Of the 435 members of the House of Representatives, 12 are women. There are no woman governors, and of the 50 largest U.S. cities, only two have women mayors. Thus, while women constitute 51 per cent of the population, they have been selectively excluded from the higher levels of decision-making, and relegated unfairly to the lowest positions in the society.

The word "gay" refers to types of non-heterosexual expression, including that of female and male homosexuals, bisexuals, transsexuals, and transvestites. The People's Party recognizes and affirms that the goals and aims of Gay Liberation are an essential part of the general struggle against oppression. The state has no right to regulate the sex lives of its citizens either directly through punitive legislation or indirectly through selective employment practices.

Women's liberation is people liberation. The exploitation of women by our present legal, social and economic system is accompanied by a corresponding exploitation of men. Economically, women are discriminated against in hiring and paying practices. Men are economically unable to choose home and child care as their employment. Both situations are unfair. Socially, women are expected to be dependent upon and subservient to men, who, in turn, are expected to be independent and aggressive. Both expectations are narrow and unrealistic. Legally, women are considered the property of their husbands and men are responsible for their support. This is unfair to both because it keeps the women from a fulfilling life and men tied down with unjust responsibilities. We must do away with all legal, social and economic discrimination of men and women, straights and gays.

The People's Party therefore proposes that:

1) Legal discrimination against women must be eliminated. Specifically:

a. The U.S. Congress should pass and the states should ratify an Equal Rights amendment to the Constitution giving women specific guarantees of equal rights under the law.

b. Certain states maintain discriminatory laws concerning women, regarding jury service, property rights, use of birth name, alimony, rights to make binding contracts, severity of punishment for crimes, identification as heads of households, and sexual relations. We oppose these laws.

c. Protective legislation, initially written to

lessen hardships on female workers, now serves to justify sex discrimination. These laws must be eliminated or extended to cover all workers.

d. Vice laws must be rewritten to end the prosecution of prostitutes (male and female) and the regulation of sexual behavior between consenting individuals over the age of 13.

e. Federal and state legislation must ensure the right of women to be educated equally with men. All discrimination and segregation by sex, written or unwritten, must be eliminated at all levels of education, including college, graduate and professional school, loans and fellowships, and federal and state training programs such as Job Corps, and on-the-job training.

f. The "man in the household" welfare laws that preclude child support payment if a man lives in the house must be abolished.

g. Women in prisons should obtain work furloughs and conjugal visits to the same extent that men prisoners do. The understaffing of female prisons must be corrected.

h. Although the People's Party is opposed to the U.S. military draft, it is the right of women in the military to be trained, promoted and assigned on an equal basis with men. We do not ask that women be drafted. On the contrary, we consider the drafting of men an oppression rather than a privilege denied women.

i. Laws discriminating against unmarried persons, such as higher tax rates, unequal treatment by welfare departments, Social Security benefits, refusal to allow single people to adopt children, etc., must be abolished, whether applied to persons living singly or cohabiting.

j. The government has no business interfering in the private relationships of individuals. All laws relating to marriage and divorce must be abolished. Provisions must be made for equal rights for children and full protection under laws which would assure sufficient food, clothing, shelter and medical care, etc.

2) We must rearrange our social organization to give women an equal position in society. And there can be no equality as long as women do not receive, as a right, financial aid from the government to help them solve their special problems in an economic system organized to meet the needs of men. A federal stipend for women in pregnancy, in childbirth and in the care and education of their children is the minimum economic basis

which would move them toward winning their freedom.

a. Society should not control women's reproductive functions. We must abolish laws that limit access to birth control information and devices, or that govern abortions. The government should support birth control and abortion clinics staffed by qualified personnel. We oppose forced abortions and sterilizations.

b. We oppose forced maternity leave. Women should be paid maternity leave as a form of social security and/or employee benefit or accumulated sick leave. Legislation must protect the right of women to return to their jobs within a reasonable time after childbirth without loss of seniority or other accrued benefits.

c. The responsibility of caring for children should not rest entirely on women, but should be assumed by both parents and/or by the wider society. The standard work day should vary in length, with workers choosing the amount of time spent at work and the amount spent with the family. This would let both parents contribute to the care of their children. Fully-equipped 24-hour child care centers for children pre-school through adolescence should be provided as a public service. On-the-job child care facilities should be provided for nursing mothers. Methods of financing would include:

—government-financed child care centers for all public employees and civil servants located at places of work;

—government-financed neighborhood child care centers situated throughout the community;

—company-financed, parent-controlled child care centers located at the place of work;

—initiation of a government agency to take action in enforcing the above.

All of the above should be adopted to assure equal rights and full protection to men and women alike.

3) Homosexuals, both male and female, suffer from discrimination in employment, education, government, the military, and the society at large. The fundamental right of consenting individuals to engage in sexual practices of their own choosing must be recognized. The state has no right to regulate the sexual behavior of consenting citizens.

a. We must eliminate all laws that limit the right of self-determination of all people in the free expression of their true sexual natures. This includes laws that legislate sexual behavior in the private lives of any consenting individuals, as well as all educational, occupational, governmental, military and social legislation that discriminates against gays.

b. We must abolish all laws, institutions and practices of the government, both federal and state, that discriminate against persons because of actions expressive of their sexual natures.

c. Rights guaranteed by the Declaration of Independence and the Constitution, including the Bill of Rights, should not be denied or abridged because of sexual preference.

d. All "sex education" schooling should accord the same validity to homosexual and other forms of expression as to heterosexual forms.

e. We oppose laws which discriminate against the parental rights of gays.

f. There must be immediate release, restoration to full participation in society, and full reparation to all persons incarcerated in prisons and in mental institutions on charges of non-victim sexual crimes.

4) Widespread beliefs about female competence and decision-making ability have inhibited women from full participation in the society. Stereotypes of "real man" and "real woman" must be systematically eliminated.

a. The media—radio, television and newspapers—cater to these beliefs, facilitating further discrimination against women. We must eliminate the stereotyped, negative portrayal of women often depicted in advertisements. Stereotypes that portray men as aggressive and dominant and women as passive and supportive should be balanced in the public media by occasionally showing human beings as they really are.

b. Education does not expose female children to the full range of available occupations, but mostly teaches them about "female" occupations. Male children also fail to receive information about traditionally "female" occupations, such as child care and homemaking. All children should receive information and training and guidance for all types of occupations, without regard to sex.

c. Legislation must eliminate references in school textbooks to male supremacy, unique male competencies, and female ineptness. Textbooks must present the full range of occupations as occupied by both men and women workers, including portraying men occupied at domestic tasks. History texts should include women's history and gay history.

d. Institutions such as churches, the medical and psychiatric professions, schools, and the media perpetuate beliefs about appropriate sex role behaviors and practices which are oppressive. These beliefs must be eliminated.

Women must become inculturated. In many cases they have accepted as normal their status as second class citizens in a male-dominated society. As a result of the oppression with which they are forced to deal from birth, if women were to achieve their rightful place as equals in a society today, there would still be many who would self-impose oppression because of the process of inculturation. Some women will find it difficult to cope when they have spent their lives learning to play out a pre-determined role in society. Thus, the People's Party supports all consciousness-raising alternatives and supports the institution of many new alternatives.

## Prohibition Platform 1972

PREAMBLE

We, the representatives of the Prohibition Party, assembled in National Convention at Wichita, Kansas, June 24 and 25, 1971, recognizing Almighty God as the source of all just government, and with faith in the teachings of the Lord Jesus Christ, do solemnly promise that, if our party is chosen to administer the affairs of the nation, we will, with earnest dedication to the principles of righteousness, seek to serve the needs and to preserve the rights, the prerogatives, and the basic freedoms of the people of the United States of America. For the realization of these ends we propose the following program of government:

CONSTITUTIONAL GOVERNMENT

We affirm our sincere loyalty to the Constitution of the United States, and express our deep confidence in that document as the basic law of the land. We will resist all attempts to violate it, whether by legislation, by means of evasion, or through judicial interpretation. We believe in the Declaration of Independence and in the Preamble and Bill of Rights of our Constitution. We declare ourselves in hearty support of our system of representative government, with its plan of checks and balances, and express our firm intent to serve the people of our nation with a constructive, forward looking program of good government, dedicated to the general welfare.

## Communism—Totalitarianism

Recognizing that Communism is aggressively and unalterably opposed to our Constitutional government, we declare our opposition to it both as a way of life and as a governmental system. We believe that the program of Communism, with its intent to infiltrate and to overthrow our present form of government, must be pitilessly exposed. We challenge all loyal citizens to become fully aware of this menace to civilization, to exert every effort to defeat the Marxist program and to help preserve our American way of life.

We also declare ourselves opposed to any other form of totalitarian philosophy or form of government. We endorse the efforts of those agencies which have been honestly and earnestly exposing subversive activities and groups.

## Governmental Economy and Taxation

We view with alarm the extravagance and wasteful spending which have invaded government at all levels, demanding an ever increasing tax load upon our people. The constant increase in taxation, requiring approximately one third of the total income of our citizens to pay the expenses of government, is approaching the point of confiscation, leading to economic chaos. We believe that good government does not attempt to do for people what they can do for themselves. With proper economy, governmental costs can be lowered, the tax load lightened, and the public debt can be reduced. We promise to devote ourselves to such an end, even though it involves either the reorganization or abolition of certain departments, bureaus, and vested interests.

## The Federal Budget

Good government and a sound economy require a balanced budget. The inflationary effects and the disturbing influences of unbalanced budgets must be eliminated. We cannot, with impunity, continue to increase the mortgage on our future and the interest load of the present. As the level of taxation is already excessive, there must be either a decided reduction in governmental services and federal spending or a substantial improvement in efficiency, with consequent elimination of waste in both personnel and materials. Actually, both areas need careful exploration with a view not only to maintaining a balanced budget, but also to reduction of the national debt.

## Money and Finance

A sound financial program and dependable monetary policy are fundamental to a stable economy. Our Constitution gives to Congress the power to "coin money" and to "regulate the value thereof." We believe that Congress, working with the executive branch of government, should take immediate steps to establish a financial program that will block inflationary trends, insure a sound currency, stabilize price levels, and provide for systematic retirement of the national debt. We urge that careful consideration be given to a constructive program of monetary policy involving a favorable balance of payments in international exchange, believing that such a step would help stabilize our economy, would promote confidence in our monetary system and would underwrite a continuing program of sound finance and expanding industrial progress.

## The Income Tax

A federal income tax was first proposed by the Prohibition Party in 1896. However, the graduated tax and confiscatory rates of the present day were not contemplated. We question the exemption from taxation of certain types of bonds issued by government bodies. We seriously doubt the wisdom of the present system of taxation and demand a thorough review of the basic fiscal policies of our government.

## Revenue Sharing

Recognizing that local and state governments are having real difficulty in meeting their basic financial needs, we advocate a division of the revenue received from the federal income tax, with appropriate amounts of the tax collected in each state being distributed to each of the state governments before becoming the property of the federal government.

## INFLATION

For a period of years our people have been confronted with the problem of increasing prices and lowered purchasing power. There is both a need and a desire for appropriate stability in this area. We propose that immediate steps be developed to stabilize wages and prices, to secure more efficient production, and to maintain a proper relationship between the rates of growth of our monetary supply and of the gross national product.

## ENVIRONMENTAL AWARENESS

An awareness of the various problems related to the area of ecology is essential. We believe that all men have a right to a wholesome environment. Accordingly, government must establish standards and enforce a program which will insure a satisfactory stewardship of land, water and air throughout the nation. In particular, we insist on the right of everyone to a pure water supply and to an unpolluted atmosphere. We urge increased emphasis on tertiary treatment of sewage, on the development of fission type reactors and, as soon as technologically feasible, atomic fusion as a substitute for fossil fuels in electric power generation, and on the substitution of relatively non-polluting sources of power in motor vehicles.

## FOREIGN AFFAIRS

It has been charged that our government lacks a consistent, positive foreign policy. This is an area which involves both complex and baffling problems. There are no easy solutions.

We pledge ourselves to search for peaceful solutions to the problems of international relations and to deal with conflicts among nations by seeking to react creatively and constructively to the underlying causes of international tension and frustration before they explode into hostilities, and to strive for world peace and order based upon the teachings of the Prince of Peace.

We insist that no foreign government has an inherent right to financial aid at the expense of American taxpayers. In fact such aid does not usually purchase friendship. Often it seems to generate exactly the opposite. In order to maintain our national solvency and to sustain our ability to meet genuine need, great caution is essential. Most aid should be in the form of repayable loans

which will enable the beneficiaries to maintain their dignity and self respect. Direct aid should be limited to disaster relief and to under-developed countries of good will. It must be honestly used for internal development and must be denied to corrupt governments and to aggressor nations.

## A FREE ECONOMY

We are strongly opposed to burdensome restraints on our free enterprise system, to detailed regulation of our economic life and to federal interference with individual initiative. We believe that free enterprise is threatened in three ways: (1) by excessive governmental regulation, (2) by growth of public or private monopoly, and (3) by unethical practices of unscrupulous groups.

It will be the policy of our administration to encourage independent, non-monopolistic business enterprises which serve genuine consumer needs and are operated with a sense of responsibility to the public. We will take necessary steps to prevent the evils both of monopoly and of excessive regulation by government, and to protect adequately the consuming public from irresponsible or deceptive practices contrary to the general welfare.

We propose that our government withdraw, with reasonable promptness, from the fields of business activity and sell to private industry, at proper investment prices, those business enterprises now owned and operated by the federal government.

## LABOR AND INDUSTRY

In the area of labor and industrial relations we believe that the public welfare must be given paramount consideration. Both management and labor must be held responsible for their economic and their social behavior. Neither should be permitted to dominate at the expense of the other or of the common good. Rather, the antitrust laws must be applied equally to all monopolies, whether of business or of labor. Whenever the public welfare is seriously endangered because of disputes affecting quasi-public businesses and utilities we favor the compulsory arbitration of labor-management disputes, particularly in the area of public transportation. We would, in contrast to preceding administrations, enforce stringently the laws forbidding strikes by federal government employees.

## EMPLOYEE–EMPLOYER RIGHTS

Every individual has certain basic and fundamental rights. A person's right to join or not to join a labor union without affecting his employment and his right to work for an employer willing to hire him must be protected. Likewise, employees and employers must be free to bargain and to contract as they wish. Violence or coercion, whether on the part of management or of labor, should be prohibited.

## STATES RIGHTS

Our founding fathers recognized the importance of both individual and states rights, and determined to preserve them by making the Bill of Rights an integral part of our Constitution. During recent years there has been an increasing tendency toward an undesirable concentration of power and authority in the federal government.

To deal with overcentralization we urge more vigorous action by the state and local governments for the protection of the rights and the promotion of the welfare of their people, greater resort to the solution of local community problems through the voluntary action of existing or new civic and other non-governmental associations, where this is feasible, and the increasing pursuit by private business concerns of policies which promote the public interest.

We pledge ourselves to action that will preserve all legitimate rights and will maintain among the several states their constitutional place in our system of government.

## HUMAN RIGHTS

All American citizens, regardless of race, sex, religion, or national origin are entitled to equality of treatment under the provisions of our constitutions and under the laws of our land. No person or group of persons should be subjected to ostracism, humiliation, or embarrassment because of color or national background. We deplore the use of violent, anarchistic, or arbitrary pressure tactics, from whatever source, as a means of seeking to resolve tensions and divergences of opinion among our citizens.

We are opposed to those proposals which would destroy our neighborhood school systems through a program of artificial integration or convey special privileges to any minority group.

## PUBLIC MORALITY

Moral and spiritual considerations must be primary factors in determining both state and national policies. We deplore the gross neglect of such matters by the dominant political parties, culminating in the shocking revelations of crime and of political and economic corruption which have characterized recent years. We charge these parties with basic responsibility for the rapid decline in moral standards which followed the repeal of the Eighteenth Amendment. We believe that the program of nullification of law through non-enforcement which led to repeal contributed greatly to the disintegration of public morals, to a general deterioration of standards, and to a lowering of values among our people.

We pledge ourselves to break the unholy alliance which has made these things possible. We propose to strengthen and to enforce laws against gambling, narcotics, and commercialized vice, to emphasize the basic importance of spiritual and moral values to the development and growth of an enduring nation, and to maintain the integrity of our democracy by careful enforcement of law and loyal support of our Constitution.

It is our judgment that the emphasis in certain quarters upon civil disobedience represents a most unfortunate and a most distressing development of our era.

## NATIONAL PREPAREDNESS

Believing that "eternal vigilance is the price of liberty" we declare for a sound program of national military preparedness. While praying for peace we cannot place our freedom in peril by ignoring potential threats to our nation.

However, we believe that the present program of compulsory peacetime military training does not represent a genuine safeguard to world peace. We, rather, believe it is to be contrary, in principle, to our American way of life. This system places an unnecessary burden upon our peacetime economy, threatens us with possible military dictatorship, and often permits and promotes the moral and spiritual deterioration of our youth.

We urge that our peacetime defense be entrusted to professionally trained volunteers.

## NATIONAL SOVEREIGNTY

We declare our belief in national sovereignty

and oppose surrender of this sovereignty to any international group.

## CIVIL SERVICE

The Prohibition Party first sponsored our civil service system. On the other hand, the dominant political parties are positively committed to the "spoils" system and, when in office, have prostituted governmental power to serve their own selfish party interests instead of the whole people. This has led to excessive expenditures, higher taxes and, in some situations, to an unfortunate alliance of crime with politics. We pledge ourselves to an honest, efficient, and economical administration. Veteran preference in civil service must be limited as to time, and favoritism toward certain institutions in government appointments must be curbed.

## TIME STANDARDIZATION

We take exception to the twice yearly changes of our time. We believe that these changes add to our lives unnecessary confusion and avoidable frustration and are costly and unjust to those who need standardized time. We advocate the stabilization of our timekeeping by establishing Daylight Savings Time year round.

## THE NEWS MEDIA

We believe in the importance of freedom of the press and of other news media. There must be no suppression of this freedom when properly exercised. On the other hand, we deplore the role of the media in sensationalizing a growing moral permissiveness. We believe that this creates the impression that the media are acting as approving and applauding onlookers. We deplore the decline of investigative reporting, and demand that the media once again become responsible informants of the public.

## WELFARE

The present welfare programs of our state and national governments are a disgraceful shambles. As presently administered in many areas the chief outcome is to create a dependent economic and social sub-stratum. All too many welfare officials and employees seem determined to help increase the number on our welfare rolls at a rate many times that of our general population increase.

The Prohibition Party, which has always pioneered in social reform, insists that the handicapped, the aged, the chronically ill and those families without a breadwinner or one who is capable of working should be helped. The tragedy is that many who are truly deserving today are receiving insufficient aid. A large proportion of our welfare dollars is being siphoned off by those who are capable of working.

If the mushrooming welfare costs are not reduced and those undeserving of assistance are not removed from the welfare rolls, a taxpayers' revolt may one day kill the entire welfare program. The Prohibition Party believes that a complete overhaul of our welfare system is needed.

We specifically reject the concept of a guaranteed annual income. Such a concept will accelerate rather than retard the growth of the number of people on welfare rolls and will tend to destroy initiative among those whose earnings would be only slightly above such a guaranteed minimum income.

## RELIGIOUS LIBERTY

We believe in religious liberty. Freedom of the individual to worship, to fellowship, with others of similar faith, to evangelize, to educate, and to establish religious institutions, must be preserved. When religious liberty is lost, political liberty will perish with it. We deplore ever increasing efforts to restrict freedom of religious broadcasting and the establishment of new churches. We caution the Internal Revenue Service against using the power to control tax exemptions to discriminate against evangelical Christianity.

We believe, also, that our government should take a firm positive position against religious intolerance and persecution anywhere in the world.

## MARRIAGE AND DIVORCE

Ordained of God, the home is a sacred institution. Its sanctity must be protected and preserved. We favor the enactment of uniform marriage and divorce laws in the various states as an aid to building strong and enduring homes throughout our nation.

## SOCIAL SECURITY

We endorse the general principle of an actuarially sound social security insurance program which includes all employed groups. We question the recent trend toward a welfare emphasis. We condemn the maladministration of its provisions for political ends; we pledge ourselves to correct these evils, particularly, the denial of benefits to persons who have earned them and who are qualified for them, but who choose to continue in productive service.

## BALLOT LAW REFORM

True democracy requires that the needs and interests of minority groups be given fair, honest, and appropriate consideration. Instead, in many of our states, ballot laws have been enacted which are designed to make a two party system into a bipartisan political monopoly, keeping minor parties off the ballot. We demand passage of laws which protect independent voters and which guarantee to minority groups access to the ballot and the fundamental right of free political expression.

## CHURCH AND STATE

We affirm our continuing loyalty to the constitutional principle of separation of Church and State. We will expose, and resist vigorously, any attempt from whatever source to weaken or subvert this fundamental principle.

We declare our belief that the Bible is not a sectarian book, but is a volume of universal appeal and application which is woven into our history, our laws, and our culture. We deplore any interpretation which would limit its use in any area of our national life.

In the area of government, we endorse encouragement of nonprofit educational and religious institutions on a tax exempt basis, but we declare strong opposition to all efforts, direct or indirect, to secure appropriations of public money for private religious or sectarian purposes. We are opposed, however, to tax exemption on income received by religious organizations engaged in competition with commercial business enterprises, except for specific religious services, such as church publishing houses.

## EDUCATION

It is altogether appropriate that our federal government should be interested in and concerned about matters pertaining to all areas of educational growth and development. However, under the Tenth Amendment, public education is clearly to be under the control of the states. We are opposed to direct federal aid to education, believing that each state should both support and control its own educational program.

## AGRICULTURE

The production and distribution of agricultural products is of vital importance to the economy of any people. We believe that those engaged in agricultural pursuits, like other American citizens, should be free from authoritarian control and coercion. Hence we declare ourselves opposed to regimentation of farms and farmers and urge a sensible and orderly return to a free market program.

## PUBLIC HEALTH

The health of our people is a matter of fundamental importance. We are deeply concerned with this matter in its many aspects. We are disturbed by the increasing use of narcotic and psychedelic drugs. Recognizing that the use of tobacco products constitutes a health hazard, we are opposed to promotional advertising of such products and to subsidization of tobacco growing. We insist that caution must be taken in dealing with mental health cases, lest there be unjust and prejudiced incarcerations. We deplore those programs of mass medication which violate the rights of individuals. We pledge enforcement of existing laws regulating these health concerns, the enactment of additional needed legislation, and cooperation with state efforts to deal with the problems.

## THE ALCOHOL PROBLEM

Beverage alcohol must today be recognized as the chief cause of poverty, broken homes, juvenile delinquency, vice, crime, political corruption, wasted manpower and highway accidents. By the most conservative estimates, more than 8,000,000 alcoholics and 8,000,000 problem drinkers are currently victims of alcohol.

No greater mistake has ever been made by the American people and their government than the Repeal of Prohibition. Contrary to the promises made by the advocates of repeal, bootlegging has increased to the point where the liquor industry itself claims that one-third of all alcohol consumed today in America is illicit; drinking among our young people has reached epidemic proportions; liquor taxes pay only a small fraction of the traffic's cost to the taxpayers and the "open saloon" which was to be "banished forever" is back in a newer form and more numerous than ever.

The liquor traffic is linked with and supports a nationwide network of gambling, vice and crime. It also dominates both major political parties and, through them, much of the governmental and political life of our nation. As long as the two dominant parties are largely controlled by the liquor traffic, just so long will they be unable to make moral principles prevail.

The Prohibition Party alone offers a program to deal with this greatest of social ills. We pledge ourselves to a program of publicity, education, legislation and administration, leading to the elimination of beverage alcohol industry. We will repeal all laws which legalize the liquor traffic and enact and rigorously enforce new laws which prohibit the manufacture, distribution and sale of alcoholic beverages.

We urge all Americans who favor sobriety and righteousness to join with us in electing an administration pledged to the above program.

## Republican Platform 1972

PREAMBLE

This year our Republican Party has greater reason than ever before for pride in its stewardship.

When our accomplishments are weighed—when our opponents' philosophy, programs and candidates are assessed—we believe the American people will rally eagerly to the leadership which since January 1969 has brought them a better life in a better land in a safer world.

This political contest of 1972 is a singular one. No Americans before have had a clearer option. The choice is between going forward from dramatic achievements to predictable new achievements, or turning back toward a nightmarish time in which the torch of free America was virtually snuffed out in a storm of violence and protest.

It is so easy to forget how frightful it was.

There was Vietnam—so bloody, so costly, so bitterly divisive—a war in which more than a half-million of America's sons had been committed to

battle—a war, it seemed, neither to be won nor lost, but only to be endlessly fought—a war emotionally so tormenting as almost to obliterate America's other worldly concerns.

And yet, as our eyes were fixed on the carnage in Asia, in Europe our alliance had weakened. The Western will was dividing and ebbing. The isolation of the People's Republic of China with one-fourth of the world's population, went endlessly on.

At home our horrified people watched our cities burn, crime burgeon, campuses dissolve into chaos. A mishmash of social experimentalism, producing such fiscal extravaganzas as the abortive war on poverty, combined with war pressures to drive up taxes and balloon the cost of living. Working men and women found their living standards fixed or falling, the victim of inflation. Nationwide, welfare skyrocketed out of control.

The history of our country may record other crises more costly in material goods, but none so demoralizing to the American people. To millions of Americans it seemed we had lost our way.

So it was when our Republican Party came to power.

Now, four years later, a new leadership with new policies and new programs has restored reason and order and hope. No longer buffeted by internal violence and division, we are on course in calmer seas with a sure, steady hand at the helm. A new spirit, buoyant and confident, is on the rise in our land, nourished by the changes we have made. In the past four years:

We have turned toward concord among all Americans;

We have turned toward reason and order;

We have turned toward government responding sensitively to the people's hopes and needs;

We have turned toward innovative solutions to the nation's most pressing problems;

We have turned toward new paths for social progress—from welfare rolls to payrolls; from wanton pollution to vigorous environmental protection;

We have moved far toward peace: withdrawal of our fighting men from Vietnam, constructive new relationships with the Soviet Union and the People's Republic of China, the nuclear arms race checked, the Mid-East crisis dampened, our alliances revitalized.

So once again the foreign policy of the United States is on a realistic footing, promising us a nation secure in a full generation of peace, promising the end of conscription, promising a further allocation of resources to domestic needs.

It is a saga of exhilarating progress.

We have come far in so short a time. Yet, much remains to be done.

Discontents, frustrations and concerns still stir in the minds and hearts of many of our people, especially the young. As long as America falls short of being truly peaceful, truly prosperous, truly secure, truly just for all, her task is not done.

Our encouragement is in the fact that things as they are, are far better than things that recently were. Our resolve is that things to come can be, and will be, better still.

Looking to tomorrow, to President Nixon's second term and on into the third century of this Republic, we of the Republican Party see a quarter-billion Americans peaceful and prospering as never before, humane as never before, their nation strong and just as never before.

It is toward this bright tomorrow that we are determined to move, in concert with millions of discerning Democrats and concerned Independents who will not, and cannot, take part in the convulsive leftward lurch of the national Democratic Party.

The election of 1972 requires of the voters a momentous decision—one that will determine the kind of nation that is to be on its 200th birthday four years hence. In this year we must choose between strength and weakness for our country in the years to come. This year we must choose between negotiating and begging with adversary nations. This year we must choose between an expanding economy in which workers will prosper and a hand-out economy in which the idle live at ease. This year we must choose between running our own lives and letting others in a distant bureaucracy run them. This year we must choose between responsible fiscal policy and fiscal folly.

This year the choice is between moderate goals historically sought by both major parties and far-out goals of the far left. The contest is not between the two great parties Americans have known in previous years. For in this year 1972 the national Democratic Party has been seized by a radical clique which scorns our nation's past and would blight her future.

We invite our troubled friends of other political affiliations to join with us in a new coalition for progress. Together let us reject the New Left prescription for folly and build surely on the solid achievements of President Nixon's first term.

Four years ago we said, in Abraham Lincoln's words, that Americans must think anew and act anew. This we have done, under gifted leadership. The many advances already made, the shining prospects so clearly ahead, are presented in this Platform for 1972 and beyond.

May every American measure our deeds and words thoughtfully and objectively, and may our opponents' claims be equally appraised. Once this is done and judgment rendered on election day, we will confidently carry forward the task of doing for America what her people need and want and deserve.

## Toward a Full Generation of Peace

### Foreign Policy

When Richard Nixon became President, our country was still clinging to foreign policies fashioned for the era immediately following World War II. The world has changed dramatically in the 1960's, but our foreign policies had not.

America was hopelessly enmeshed in Vietnam. In all parts of the globe our alliances were frayed. With the principal Communist powers our relations showed little prospect of improvement. Trade and monetary problems were grave. Periodic crises had become the way of international economic life.

The nation's frustrations had fostered a dangerous spirit of isolationism among our people. America's influence in the world had waned.

In only four years we have fashioned foreign policies based on a new spirit of effective negotiation with our adversaries, and a new sense of real partnership with our allies. Clearly, the prospects for lasting peace are greater today than at any time since World War II.

### New Era of Diplomacy

Not all consequences of our new foreign policy are yet visible, precisely because one of its great purposes is to anticipate crises and avoid them rather than merely respond. Its full impact will be realized over many years, but already there are vivid manifestations of its success:

Before this Administration, a Presidential visit

to Peking would have been unthinkable. Yet our President has gone there to open a candid airing of differences so that they will not lead some day to war. All over the world tensions have eased as, after a generation of hostility, the strongest of nations and the most populous of nations have started discoursing again.

During the 1960's, Presidential visits to Moscow were twice arranged and twice cancelled. Now our President has conferred, in the Soviet Union, with Soviet leaders, and has hammered out agreements to make this world a much safer place. Our President's quest for peace has taken him to 20 other countries, including precedent-shattering visits to Rumania, Yugoslavia and Poland.

Around the globe America's alliances have been renewed and strengthened. A new spirit of partnership shows results in our NATO partners' expenditures for the common defense—up by some $2 billion in two years.

Historians may well regard these years as a golden age of American diplomacy. Never before has our country negotiated with so many nations on so wide a range of subjects—and never with greater success. In the last four years we have concluded agreements:

To limit nuclear weapons.

To ban nuclear weapons from the world's seabeds.

To reduce the risk of an accidental nuclear war.

To end the threat of biological and toxin warfare.

To terminate American responsibility for the administration of Okinawa.

To end the recurrent crises over Berlin.

To provide for U.S.-Soviet cooperation in health and space research.

To reduce the possibility of dangerous incidents at sea.

To improve emergency communications between the White House and the Kremlin.

To exercise restraint in situations threatening conflict.

To realign the world's currencies.

To reduce barriers to American exports.

To combat the international drug traffic.

To protect the international environment.

To expand cultural relations with peoples of Eastern Europe.

To settle boundary disputes with Mexico.

To restore the water quality of the Great Lakes in cooperation with Canada.

In Vietnam, too, our new policies have been dramatically effective.

In the 1960's, our nation was plunged into another major war—for the fourth time in this century, the third time in a single generation.

More than a half-million Americans were fighting in Vietnam in January 1969. Fatalities reached 562 in a single week. There was no plan for bringing Americans home; no hope for an end of the war.

In four years, we have marched toward peace and away from war. Our forces in Vietnam have been cut by 93 per cent. No longer do we have a single ground combat unit there. Casualties are down by 95 per cent. Our young draftees are no longer sent there without their consent.

Through it all, we have not abandoned an ally to aggression, not turned our back on their brave defense against brutal invasion, not consigned them to the bloodbath that would follow Communist conquest. By helping South Vietnam build a capability to withstand aggression, we have laid the foundation for a just peace and a durable peace in Southeast Asia.

From one sector of the globe to another, a sure and strong America, in partnership with other nations, has once again resumed her historic mission—the building of lasting peace.

*The Nixon Doctrine*

When President Nixon came into office, America's foremost problem was the bloody, costly, divisive involvement in Vietnam. But there was an even more profound task—to redefine the international role of the United States in light of new realities around the globe and new attitudes at home. Precisely and clearly, the President stated a new concept of a positive American role. This —the Nixon Doctrine—is monumentally important to every American and to all other people in the world.

The theme of this Doctrine is that America will remain fully involved in world affairs, and yet do this in ways that will elicit greater effort by other nations and the sustaining support of our people.

For decades, our nation's leaders regarded virtually every problem of local defense or economic development anyplace in the world as an exclusive American responsibility. The Nixon Doctrine recognizes that continuing defense and development are impossible unless the concerned nations shoulder the principal burden.

Yet, strong economic and military assistance programs remain essential. Without these, we are denied a middle course—the course between abruptly leaving allies to struggle alone against economic stagnation or aggression, or intervening massively ourselves. We cannot move from the overinvolvement of the Sixties to the selective involvement of the Seventies if we do not assist our friends to make the transition with us.

In the Nixon Doctrine, therefore, we define our interests and commitments realistically and clearly; we offer, not an abdication of leadership, but more rational and responsible leadership.

We pledge that, under Republican leadership, the United States will remain a leader in international affairs. We will continue to shape our involvement abroad to national objectives and realities in order to sustain a strong, effective American role in the world.

Over time we hope this role will eventually lead the peace-loving nations to undertake an exhaustive, coordinated analysis of the root causes of war and the most promising paths of peace, so that those causes may in time be removed and the prospects for enduring peace strengthened year by year.

*Peace in the 1970's*

We stand with our President for his strategy for Peace—a strategy of national strength, a new sense of international partnership, a willingness to negotiate international differences.

We will strengthen our relationships with our allies, recognizing them as full-fledged partners in securing the peace and promoting the common well-being.

With our adversaries, we will continue to negotiate in order to improve our security, reduce tension, and extend the realm of cooperation. Especially important is continued negotiation to maintain the momentum established by the Strategic Arms Limitation agreements to limit offensive and defensive nuclear weapons systems and further to reduce the danger of nuclear conflict. In addition, we will encourage increased trade for the benefit of our consumers, businessmen, workers, and farmers.

Along with NATO allies, we will seek agreement with the Warsaw Pact nations on a mutual and balanced reduction of military forces in Europe.

We will press for expansion of contacts with the people of Eastern Europe and the People's Republic of China, so long isolated from most of the world.

We will continue to seek a settlement of the Vietnam war which will permit the people of Southeast Asia to live in peace under political arrangements of their own choosing. We take specific note of the remaining major obstacle to settlement—Hanoi's demand that the United States overthrow the Saigon government and impose a Communist-dominated government on the South Vietnamese. We stand unequivocally at the side of the President in his effort to negotiate honorable terms, and in his refusal to accept terms which would dishonor this country.

We commend his refusal to perform this act of betrayal—and we most emphatically say the President of the United States should not go begging to Hanoi. We believe that the President's proposal to withdraw remaining American forces from Vietnam four months after an internationally supervised ceasefire has gone into effect throughout Indochina and all prisoners have been returned is as generous an offer as can be made by anyone—by anyone, that is, who is not bemused with surrender—by anyone who seeks, not a fleeting peace at whatever cost, but a real peace that will be both just and lasting.

We will keep faith with American prisoners of war held by the enemy, and we will keep faith, too, with their families here at home who have demonstrated remarkable courage and fortitude over long periods of uncertainty. We will never agree to leave the fate of our men unclear, dependent upon a cruel enemy's whim. On the contrary—we insist that, before all American forces are withdrawn from Vietnam, American prisoners must be returned and a full accounting made of the missing in action and of those who have died in enemy hands.

We pledge that upon repatriation our returned prisoners will be received in a manner befitting their valor and sacrifice.

We applaud the Administration's program to assure each returned prisoner the finest medical care, personal counseling, social services and career orientation. This around-the-clock personal service will ease their reintegration into American life.

North Vietnam's violation of the Geneva Convention in its treatment of our prisoners of war has called forth condemnation from leaders around the world—but not by our political opposition at home. We denounce the enemy's flagrant breach of international law and common decency. We will continue to demand full implementation of the rights of the prisoners.

If North Vietnam continues obdurately to reject peace by negotiation, we shall nevertheless achieve peace for our country through the successful program of Vietnamization, phasing out our involvement as our ally strengthens his defense against aggression.

In the Middle East, we initiated arrangements leading to a cease-fire which has prevailed for two years. We pledge every effort to transform the cease-fire into lasting peace.

Since World War II, our country has played the major role in the international effort to assist the developing countries of the world. Reform of our foreign assistance program, to induce a greater international sharing of the aid effort, is long overdue. The reforms proposed by the President have been approved only in part. We call for further reforms to make our aid more effective and protect the taxpayer's interests.

We stand for an equitable, non-discriminatory immigration policy, reaffirming our support of the principles of the 1965 Immigration Act—non-discrimination against national origins, reunification of families, and the selective admission of the specially talented. The immigration process must be just and orderly, and we will increase our efforts to halt the illegal entry of aliens into the United States.

We also pledge to strengthen the agencies of international cooperation. We will help multilateral organizations focus on international issues affecting the quality of life—for example the peaceful uses of nuclear energy and the protection of man's cultural heritage and freedom of communication, as well as drug abuse, pollution, overpopulation, exploitation of the oceans and seabeds, aircraft hijacking and international crime. We will seek to improve the performance of the United Nations, including more objective leadership. We support a more equitable sharing of the costs of international organizations and have serious concerns over the delinquency of many UN members in meeting their financial obligations.

Our country, which from its beginnings has proclaimed that all men are endowed with certain rights, cannot be indifferent to the denial of human rights anywhere in the world. We deplore oppression and persecution, the inevitable hallmarks of despotic systems of rule. We will continue to strive to bring them to an end, both to reestablish the right of self-determination and to encourage where and when possible the political freedom of subjugated peoples everywhere in the world.

We firmly support the right of all persons to emigrate from any country, and we have consistently upheld that doctrine. We are fully aware of and share the concern of many citizens for the plight of Soviet Jews with regard to their freedoms and emigration. This view, together with our commitment to the principles of the Universal Declaration of Human Rights of the United Nations, was made known to Soviet leaders during the President's discussions in Moscow.

### The Middle East

We support the right of Israel and its courageous people to survive and prosper in peace. We have sought a stable peace for the Middle East and helped to obtain a cease-fire which contained the tragic conflict. We will help in any way possible to bring Israel and the Arab states to the conference table, where they may negotiate a lasting peace. We will continue to act to prevent the development of a military imbalance which would imperil peace in the region and elsewhere by providing Israel with support essential for her security, including aircraft, training and modern and sophisticated military equipment, and also by helping friendly Arab governments and peoples, including support for their efforts to diminish their dependence on outside powers. We support programs of economic assistance to Israel pursued by President Nixon that have helped her achieve a nine-per cent annual economic growth rate. This and the special refugee assistance ordered by the President have also helped to provide resettlement for the thousands of immigrants seeking refuge in Israel.

We will maintain our technical forces in Europe and the Mediterranean area at adequate strength and high levels of efficiency. The irresponsible proposals of our political opposition to slash the defense forces of the United States—specifically, by cutting the strength of our fleet, by reducing our aircraft carriers from 16 to six and by unilateral withdrawals from Europe—would increase the threat of war in the Middle East and gravely menace Israel. We flatly reject these dangerous proposals.

With a settlement fair to all nations of the Middle East, there would be an opportunity for their peoples to look ahead to shared opportunities rather than backward to rancorous animosities. In a new environment of cooperation, Israel will be able to contribute much to economic renaissance in the Mid-East crossroads of the world.

### The Atlantic Community

We place high priority on the strengthening of the North Atlantic Alliance. One of the President's first initiatives was to visit Western European capitals to reinvigorate the NATO alliance and indicate its importance in U.S. foreign policy.

Right now, with plaintive cries of "come home America" echoing a new isolationism, the Republican Party states its firm belief that no nation can be an island or a fortress unto itself. Now, more than ever, there is need for interdependence among proven friends and old allies.

The North Atlantic Alliance remains the strongest most successful peacetime association ever formed among a group of free nations. The continued strengthening of the Alliance will remain an important element in the foreign policies of the second Nixon Administration.

### Japan

During the 1960's a number of economic and political issues developed in our country's relations with Japan, our major ally in Asia. To resolve these, President Nixon terminated our responsibility for the administration of Okinawa and initiated action to reduce our trade deficit with Japan. We are consulting closely to harmonize our two countries' separate efforts to normalize relations with Peking. In these ways we have shifted our vital alliance with Japan to a more sustainable basis for the long term, recognizing that the maintenance of United States-Japanese friendship advances the interests of both countries.

### The Soviet Union

Over many years our relations with the Soviet Nation have oscillated between superficial improvements and new crises. False hopes have been repeatedly followed by disillusioned confrontation. In the closing months of 1968, our relations with the Soviet Union deteriorated steadily, forcing the cancellation of a scheduled Presidential visit to Moscow and immobilizing projected negotiations on strategic arms limitation.

President Nixon immediately began the difficult task of building a new relationship—one based on a realistic acceptance of the profound differences in the values and systems of our two nations. He moved decisively on key issues—such as the Berlin problem and strategic arms limitation—so that progress in one area would add momentum to progress in other areas. The success of these efforts was demonstrated at the summit in Moscow. Agreements were reached on new areas of cooperation—public health, environmental control, space exploration and trade. The first historic agreements limiting strategic arms were signed last May 26 in Moscow, and the Soviet Union subscribed to a broad declaration of principles governing our relations.

We pledge to build upon these promising beginnings in reorienting relations between the world's strongest nuclear powers to establish a truly lasting peace.

### China

In the 1960's it seemed beyond possibility that the United States could dispel the ingrained hostility and confrontation with the China mainland. President Nixon's visit to the People's Republic of China was, therefore, an historic milestone in his effort to transform our era from one of confrontation to one of negotiation. While profound differences remain between the United States and China, at least a generation of hostility has been replaced by frank discussions. In February 1972 rules of international conduct were agreed upon which should make the Pacific region a more peaceful area now and in the future. Both the People's Republic and the United States affirmed the usefulness of promoting trade and cultural exchanges as ways of improving understanding between our two peoples.

All this is being done without affecting our mutual defense treaty or our continued diplomatic relations with our valued friend and ally on Taiwan, the Republic of China.

## Latin America

Our common long-range interests, as well as history and geography, give the relations among nations of the Western Hemisphere a special importance. We will foster a more mature partnership among the nations of this hemisphere, with a wider sharing of ideas and responsibility, a broader understanding of diversities, and firm commitment to the common pursuit of economic progress and social justice.

We believe the continuing campaign by Cuba to foment violence and support subversion in other countries makes it ineligible for readmission to the community of American states. We look forward to the day when changes in Cuba's policies will justify its re-entry into the American community—and to the day when the Cuban people achieve again their freedom and their true independence.

## Africa

Our ties with Africa are rooted in the heritage of many Americans and in our historic commitment to self-determination. We respect the hard-earned sovereignty of Africa's new states and will continue to do our utmost to make a meaningful contribution to their development. We have no illusions that the United States can single-handedly solve the seemingly intractable problems of apartheid and minority rule, but we can and will encourage non-violent, evolutionary change by supporting international efforts peacefully to resolve the problems of southern Africa and by maintaining our contacts with all races on the Continent.

## DEFENSE

We believe in keeping America strong.

In times past, both major parties shared that belief. Today this view is under attack by militants newly in control of the Democratic Party. To the alarm of free nations everywhere, the New Democratic Left now would undercut our defenses and have America retreat into virtual isolation, leaving us weak in a world still not free of aggression and threats of aggression. We categorically reject this slash-now, beg-later, approach to defense policy.

Only a strong America can safely negotiate with adversaries. Only a strong America can fashion partnerships for peace.

President Nixon has given the American people their best opportunity in this century to achieve lasting peace. The foundations are well laid. By adhering to a defense policy based on strength at home, partnership abroad and a willingness to negotiate everywhere, we hold that lasting peace is now achievable.

We will surely fail if we go crawling to the conference table. Military weakness is not the path to peace; it is invitation to war.

## A Modern, Well-Equipped Force

We believe that the first prerequisite of national security is a modern, well-equipped armed force.

From 1965 to 1969 the Vietnam war so absorbed the resources of the Defense Department that maintenance, modernization, and research and development fell into neglect. In the late 1960's the Soviet Union outspent the United States by billions of dollars for force modernization, facing the United States with the dangerous prospect that its forces would soon be qualitatively inferior. Our Reserve Forces and the National Guard had become a dumping ground for cast-off arms and equipment. The military posture of our country became seriously undermined.

To assure our strength and counter the mounting Soviet threat, President Nixon directed:

The most significant ship construction and modernization program since World War II;

The development of new types of tactical aircraft such as the F-155, a lightweight fighter, and a fighter plane for close support of ground troops;

Improvements in our strategic bomber force and development of the new B-1 strategic bomber;

Development of a new Trident submarine and undersea missile system;

Greatly increasing the capability of existing strategic missiles through multiple warheads;

Strengthening of strategic defenses, including initial deployment of an anti-ballistic missile system;

The largest research and development budget in history to insure continued technological superiority;

Equipping of the National Guard and Reserves with the most modern and sophisticated weapons;

Improved command and control communications systems.

We draw a sharp distinction between prudent reductions in defense spending and the meat-ax slashes with which some Americans are now beguiled by the political opposition. Specifically, we oppose plans to stop the Minuteman III and Poseidon programs, reduce the strategic bomber force by some 60 per cent, cancel the B-1 bomber, reduce aircraft carriers from 16 to 6, reduce tactical air wings by a third, and unilaterally reduce U.S. forces in Europe by half.

These slashes are worse than misguided; they are dangerous.

They would torpedo negotiations on arms and troop reductions, create a crisis of confidence with our allies, damage our own industrial and technological capacity, destabilize Europe and the Middle East, and directly endanger the nation's security.

### A New Partnership

The Nixon Doctrine has led to a new military strategy of realistic deterrence. Its essence is the sharing of the responsibilities and the burdens of defense. The strategy is based on the efficient utilization of the total force available—our own and our allies', and our civilian reserve elements as well as our regular forces.

For years our country shouldered the responsibility for the defense of other nations. There were fears that we were attempting to be the policeman of the world. Our country found it necessary to maintain a military force of 3.5 million persons, more than a million overseas at 2,270 installations.

A new partnership is emerging between the United States and other nations of the free world. Other countries are assuming a much greater responsibility for the common defense. Twice in the last two years our European allies have agreed to substantial increases in their support for NATO forces. In Asia we have been heartened by the efforts of the Koreans, Vietnamese, Thais, Nationalist Chinese, Australians, New Zealanders and others who have sought improvements in their own forces.

We have been able to reduce our military forces by more than one million men and women. We have cut by half the number deployed overseas, reduced overseas installations by more than 10 per cent, and sharply reduced the economic burden of defense spending from the Vietnam high. All this has been done by virtue of our new security posture, without impairing our own or our allies' security.

We pledge to press on toward a lasting peace. To that end we declare ourselves unalterably opposed to a unilateral slash of our military power, and we reject a whimpering "come back America" retreat into isolationism.

### An All-Volunteer Armed Force

We wholeheartedly support an all-volunteer armed force and are proud to our historic initiatives to bring it to pass.

Four years ago, the President pledged to work toward an early end of the draft. That promise has been kept. Today we approach a zero draft that will enlarge the personal freedom of millions of young Americans.

Prior to 1969, annual draft calls exceeded 300,000. The Selective Service System was inequitable in operation, and its rules caused prolonged uncertainty for young men awaiting call.

Since 1969, the Selective Service System has been thoroughly reorganized, and local draft boards are more representative than ever before. Today draftees are called by random selection of the youngest first, so that the maximum length of vulnerability is no longer seven years but one year only. Youth advisory committees are in operation all across the country.

Of critical importance, we are nearing the elimination of draft calls altogether. In every year since 1968, draft calls have been reduced. Monthly draft calls are now down to a few thousand, and no draftees are sent involuntarily to Vietnam. We expect to achieve our goal by July 1973. Then, for the first time in a quarter-century, we hope and expect that young Americans of all ages will be free from conscription.

Our political opponents have talked for years of their concern for young people. It is our Republican Administration that has taken the strong, effective action required to end the draft, with its many hardships and uncertainties for the youth of America.

### Improvements in Service Life

We believe that the men and women in the uniformed services deserve the gratitude and respect of all Americans and are entitled to better treatment than received in the past.

For years most servicemen have been underpaid, harassed with restrictions, and afforded few opportunities for self-development. Construction of military housing was allowed to fall badly behind.

Since 1968 improvements in service life have been many and major:

The largest pay raises in military history have been enacted. While increases have been in all grades, the largest have gone to new recruits whose base pay will have risen more than 300 per cent by the end of this year.

Construction of new housing for military personnel and their families has increased sixfold since January 1969.

Without sacrificing discipline, needlessly harsh, irksome and demeaning practices of the past have been abandoned.

An effective program against dangerous drugs has been initiated.

Educational and training opportunities have been expanded.

Major strides have been made toward wiping out the last vestiges of racial discrimination.

We regard these tasks as never completed, but we are well on the way and pledge ourselves to press forward assuring all men and women in the armed forces rewarding careers.

### Better Defense Management

In the 1960's, the Department of Defense became administratively top-heavy and inefficient. The acquisition of new weapons systems was handled with inadequate attention to cost or performance, and there was little recognition of the human dimensions of the Department. Morale was low.

Our improvements have been many and substantial. Healthy decentralization has taken place. The methods of acquiring new weapons systems have been reformed by such procedures as "fly before you buy," the use of prototypes and the elimination of frills. Service personnel and civilian employees are now treated as the most important asset of the Department.

We have sharply reduced defense spending. In 1968, 45 per cent of the Federal budget was spent for defense and 32 per cent for human resources. In the 1973 budget the proportions were reversed —45 per cent for human resources, 32 per cent for defense. The 1973 defense budget imposes the smallest economic burden on the country of any defense budget in more than 20 years, consuming only 6.4 per cent of the estimated Gross National Product.

### Arms Limitation

We believe in limiting arms—not unilaterally, but by mutual agreement and with adequate safeguards.

When the Nixon Administration began, the Soviet Union was rapidly building its strategic armaments, and any effort to negotiate limitations on such weapons seemed hopeless. The Soviet buildup threatened the efficacy of our strategic deterrent.

The Nixon years have achieved a great breakthrough in the long-term effort to curb major armaments by international agreement and given new momentum to arms limitations generally. Of greatest importance were agreements with the Soviet leaders to limit offensive and defensive nuclear weapons. The SALT accords established mutually agreed restraints between the United States and the Soviet Union and reduced tensions throughout the world.

With approval of the SALT agreements by the Congress, negotiations will be resumed to place further restrictions on nuclear weapons, and talks will begin on mutual, balanced force reductions in Europe.

We believe it is imperative that these negotiations go forward under President Nixon's continuing leadership. We pledge him our full support.

### For the Future

We will continue the sound military policies laid down by the President—policies which guard our interests but do not dissipate our resources in vain efforts to police the world. As stated by the President:

We will maintain a nuclear deterrent adequate to meet any threat to the security of the United States or of our allies.

We will help other nations develop the capability of defending themselves.

We will faithfully honor all of our treaty commitments.

We will act to defend our interests whenever and wherever they are threatened.

But where our vital interests or treaty commitments are not involved our role will be limited.

We are proud of the men and women who wear our country's uniform, especially of those who have borne the burden of fighting a difficult and unpopular war. Here and now we reject all proposals to grant amnesty to those who have broken the law by evading military service. We reject the claim that those who fled are more deserving, or obeyed a higher morality, than those next in line who served in their places.

In carrying out our defense policies, we pledge to maintain at all times the level of military strength required to deter conflict, to honor our commitments to our allies, and to protect our people and vital interests against all foreign threats. We will not let America become a second-class power, dependent for survival on the good will of adversaries.

We will continue to pursue arms control agreements—but we recognize that this can be successful only if we maintain sufficient strength and will fail if we allow ourselves to slip into inferiority.

## A NEW PROSPERITY

### Jobs, Inflation and the Economy

The goal of our Party is prosperity, widely shared, sustainable in peace.

We stand for full employment—a job for everyone willing and able to work in an economy freed of inflation, its vigor not dependent upon war or massive military spending.

Under the President's leadership our country is once again moving toward these peacetime goals. We have checked the inflation which had started to skyrocket when our Administration took office, making the difficult transition from inflation toward price stability and from war toward peace. We have brought about a rapid rise in both employment and in real income, and laid the basis for a continuing decline in the rate of unemployment.

All Americans painfully recall the grave economic troubles we faced in January 1969. The Federal budget in fiscal 1968 had a deficit of more than $25 billion even though the economy was operating at capacity. Predictably, consumer prices soared by an annual rate of 6.6 per cent in the first quarter of 1969. "Jawboning" of labor and business had utterly failed. The inevitable tax increase had come too late. The kaleidoscope of "Great Society" programs added to the inflationary fires. Our international competitive position slumped from a trade surplus of $7 billion in 1964

to $800 million in 1968. Foreign confidence in the value of the dollar plummeted.

### Strategies and Achievements

Our Administration took these problems head on, accepting the unpopular tasks of holding down the budget, extending the temporary tax surcharge, and checking inflation. We welcomed the challenge of reorienting the economy from war to peace, as the more than two and one-half million Americans serving the military or working in defense-related industries had to be assimilated into the peacetime work force.

At the same time, we kept the inflation fight and defense employment cuts from triggering a recession.

The struggle to restore the health of our nation's economy required a variety of measures. Most important, the Administration developed and applied sound economic and monetary policies which provided the fundamental thrust against inflation.

To supplement these basic policies, Inflation Alerts were published; a new National Commission on Productivity enlisted labor, business and public leaders against inflation and in raising real incomes through increased output per worker; proposed price increases in lumber, petroleum, steel and other commodities were modified. A new Construction Industry Stabilization Committee, with the cooperation of unions and management, braked the dangerously skyrocketing costs in the construction industry.

Positive results from these efforts were swift and substantial. The rate of inflation, more than 6 per cent in early 1969, declined to less than 4 per cent in early 1971.

Even so, the economic damage inflicted by past excesses had cut so deeply as to make a timely recovery impossible, forcing the temporary use of wage and price controls.

These controls were extraordinary measures, not needed in a healthy free economy, but needed temporarily to recapture lost stability.

Our mix of policies has worked. The nation's economic growth is once again strong and steady.

The rate of increase of consumer prices is now down to 2.7 per cent.

On the employment front, expenditures for manpower programs were increased from $2.3 billion to a planned $5.1 billion; new enrollees receiving training or employment under these programs were increased by more than half a million; computerized job banks were established in all cities; more than a million young people received jobs this summer through Federal programs, 50 per cent more than last year; engineers, scientists and technicians displaced by defense reductions were given assistance under the nation-wide Technology Mobilization and Reemployment program; 13 additional weeks of unemployment compensation were authorized; and a Special Revenue Sharing Program for Manpower was proposed to train more people for more jobs—a program still shelved by the opposition Congress.

Civilian employment increased at an annual rate of about 2.4 million from August 1971 to July 1972. Almost four and one-half million new civilian jobs have been added since President Nixon took office, and total employment is at its highest level in history.

The total productive output of this country increased at an annual rate of 9.4 per cent in the second quarter of 1972, the highest in many years.

Workers' real weekly take-home pay—the real value left after taxes and inflation—is increasing at an annual rate of 4.5 per cent, compared to less than one per cent from 1960 to 1970. For the first time in six years real spendable income is going up, while the rate of inflation has been cut in half.

Time lost from strikes is at the lowest level in many years.

The rate of unemployment has been reduced from 6.1 per cent to 5.5 per cent, lower than the average from 1961 through 1964 before the Vietnam buildup began, and is being steadily driven down.

In negotiation with other countries we have revalued the dollar relative to other currencies, helping to increase sales at home and abroad and increasing the number of jobs. We have initiated a reform of the international monetary and trading system and made clear our determination that this reform must lead to a strong United States position in the balance of trade and payments.

### The Road Ahead

We will continue to pursue sound economic policies that will eliminate inflation, further cut unemployment, raise real incomes, and strengthen our international economic position.

We will fight for responsible Federal budgets to help assure steady expansion of the economy without inflation.

We will support the independent Federal Reserve Board in a policy of non-inflationary monetary expansion.

We have already removed some temporary controls on wages and prices and will remove them all once the economic distortions spawned in the late 1960's are repaired. We are determined to return to an unfettered economy at the earliest possible moment.

We reaffirm our support for the basic principles of capitalism which underlie the private enterprise system of the United States. At a time when a small but dominant faction of the opposition Party is pressing for radical economic schemes which so often have failed around the world, we hold that nothing has done more to help the American people achieve their unmatched standard of living than the free-enterprise system.

It is our conviction that government of itself cannot produce the benefits to individuals that flow from our unique combination of labor, management and capital.

We will continue to promote steady expansion of the whole economy as the best route to a long-term solution of unemployment.

We will devote every effort to raising productivity, primarily to raise living standards but also to hold down costs and prices and to increase the ability of American producers and workers to compete in world markets.

In economic policy decisions, including tax revisions, we will emphasize incentives to work, innovate and invest; and research and development will have our full support.

We are determined to improve Federal manpower programs to reduce unemployment and increase productivity by providing better information on job openings and more relevant job training. Additionally, we reaffirm our commitment to removing barriers to a full life for the mentally and physically handicapped, especially the barriers to rewarding employment. We commit ourselves to the full educational opportunities and the humane care, treatment and rehabilitation services necessary for the handicapped to become fully integrated into the social and economic mainstream.

We will press on for greater competition in our economy. The energetic antitrust program of the past four years demonstrates our commitment to free competition as our basic policy. The Antitrust Division has moved decisively to invalidate those "conglomerate" mergers which stifle competition and discourage economic concentration. The 87 antitrust cases filed in fiscal year 1972 broke the previous one-year record of more than a decade ago, during another Republican Administration.

We will pursue the start we have made for reform of the international monetary and trading system, insisting on fair and equal treatment.

Since the 1930's it has been illegal for United States citizens to own gold. We believe it is time to reconsider that policy. The right of American citizens to buy, hold, or sell gold should be reestablished as soon as this is feasible. Review of the present policy should, of course, take account of our basic objective of achieving a strengthened world monetary system.

*Taxes and Government Spending*

We pledge to spread the tax burden equitably, to spend the Federal revenues prudently, to guard against waste in spending, to eliminate unnecessary programs, and to make sure that each dollar spent for essential government services buys a dollar's worth of value.

Federal deficit spending beyond the balance of the full employment budget is one sure way to refuel inflation, and the prime source of such spending is the United States Congress. Because of its present procedures and particularly because of its present political leadership, Congress is not handling Federal fiscal policies in a responsible manner. The Congress now permits its legislative committees—instead of its fiscal committees—to decide, independently of each other, how much should be devoted to individual programs. Total Federal spending is thus haphazard and uncontrolled. We pledge vigorous efforts to reform the Congressional budgeting process.

As an immediate first step, we believe the Nation needs a rigid spending ceiling on Federal outlays each fiscal year—a ceiling controlling both the executive branch and the Congress—as President Nixon strongly recommended when he submitted his fiscal 1973 budget. Should the total of all appropriations exceed the ceiling, some or all of them would be reduced by Executive action to bring the total within the ceiling.

Our tax system needs continual, timely reform. Early in this Administration we achieved the first comprehensive tax reform since 1954. The record

shows that as a result of the Tax Reform Act of 1969 and the Revenue Act of 1971:

9.5 million low-income Americans are removed from the Federal income tax rolls.

Persons in the lowest income tax bracket will pay 82 per cent less this year than they would have paid, had the 1969 and 1971 tax reforms not been enacted; those in the $10,000 to $15,000 income range will pay 13 per cent less, and those with incomes above $100,000 will pay about 7 per cent more.

This year the tax reduction for a family of four earning $7,500 a year will be $270.

In this fiscal year individual taxpayers will pay $22 billion less in Federal income taxes than they would have paid if the old tax rates and structures were still in force.

The tax disadvantage of single taxpayers is sharply reduced and we urge further changes to assure full equality.

Working parents can now deduct more of their costs for the care of their children during working hours.

The seven per cent automobile excise tax is repealed, saving the new-car buyer an average of $200 and creating more jobs in that part of the economy.

This is sound tax reform, the kind that more equitably spreads the tax burden and avoids incentive-destroying tax levels which would cripple the economy and put people out of work.

We reject the deceitful tax "reform" cynically represented as one that would soak the rich, but in fact one that would sharply raise the taxes of millions of families in middle-income brackets as well. We reject as well the lavish spending promised by the opposition Party which would more than double the present budget of the United States Government. This, too, would cause runaway inflation or force heavy increases in personal taxes.

Taxes and government spending are inseparable. Only if the taxpayers' money is prudently managed can taxes be kept at reasonable levels.

When our Administration took office, Federal spending had been mounting at an average annual rate of 17 per cent—a rate we have cut almost in half. We urge the Congress to serve all Americans by cooperating with the President in his efforts to curb increases in Federal spending—increases which will ordain more taxes or more inflation.

Since 1969 we have eliminated over $5 billion

of spending on unneeded domestic and defense programs. This large saving would have been larger still, had Congress passed the Federal Economy Act of 1970 which would have discontinued other programs. We pledge to continue our efforts to purge the Government of these wasteful activities.

Tax reform must continue. During the next session of Congress we pledge:

To pursue such policies as Revenue Sharing that will allow property tax relief;

Further tax reform to ensure that the tax burden is fairly shared;

A simplified tax system to make it easier for all of us to pay no more and no less than we rightly owe;

Prudent fiscal management, including the elimination of unnecessary or obsolete programs, to keep the tax burden to a minimum.

### International Economic Policy

In tandem with our foreign policy innovations, we have transformed our international economic policy into a dynamic instrument to advance the interests of farmers, workers, businessmen and consumers. These efforts are designed to make the products of American workers and farmers more competitive in the world. Within the last year we achieved the Smithsonian Agreements which revalued our currency, making our exports more competitive with those of our major trading partners, and we pledge continuing negotiations further to reform the international monetary system. We also established negotiations to expand foreign market access for products produced by United States workers, with further comprehensive negotiations committed for 1973.

As part of our effort to begin a new era of negotiations, we are expanding trade opportunities and the jobs related to them for American workers and businessmen. The President's Summit negotiations, for example, yielded an agreement for the Soviet purchase, over a three-year period, of a minimum of $750 million in United States grains —the largest long-term commercial trade purchase agreement ever made between two nations. This amounts to a 17-per cent increase in grain exports by United States farmers. A U.S.-Soviet Commercial Commission has been established, and negotiations are now underway as both countries seek a general expansion of trade.

As we create a more open world market for American exports, we are not unmindful of dangers to American workers and industries from severe and rapid dislocation by changing patterns of trade. We have several agreements to protect these workers and industries—for example, for steel, beef, textiles and shoes. These actions, highly important to key American industries, were taken in ways that avoided retaliation by our trading partners and the resultant loss of American jobs.

As part of this adjustment process, we pledge improvement of the assistance offered by government to facilitate readjustment on the part of workers, businessmen and affected communities.

In making the world trading system a fairer one, we have vigorously enforced anti-dumping and countervailing duty laws to make them meaningful deterrents to foreign producers who would compete unfairly.

The growth of multinational corporations poses both new problems and new opportunities in trade and investment areas. We pledge to ensure that international investment problems are dealt with fairly and effectively—including consideration of effects on jobs, expropriation and treatment of investors, as well as equitable principles of taxation.

At the same time that we seek a better environment for American exports, we must improve our productivity and competitiveness. We must have a strong domestic economy with increased investment in new plants and equipment and an advancing technology.

We pledge increased efforts to promote export opportunities, including coordination of tax policy and improved export financing techniques—designed to make America more competitive in exporting. Of critical importance will be new legislative proposals to equip American negotiators with the tools for constructing an open and fair world trading system.

We deplore the practice of locating plants in foreign countries solely to take advantage of low wage rates in order to produce goods primarily for sale in the United States. We will take action to discourage such unfair and disruptive practices that result in the loss of American jobs.

### Small Business

Small business, so vital to our economic system, is free enterprise in its purest sense. It holds forth opportunity to the individual, regardless of race or color, to fulfill the American dream. The seedbed of innovation and invention, it is the starting point of many of the country's large businesses, and today its roll in our increasingly technological economy is crucial. We pledge to sustain and expand that role.

We have translated this philosophy into many beneficial actions. Primarily through the Small Business Administration, we have delivered financial assistance to small business at a dramatically increasing rate. Today small business is receiving double the SBA funds it was receiving when our Administration took office. During the 1970–72 fiscal years the Agency loaned small business $3.3 billion—40 per cent of the total amount loaned in the entire 19-year history of the Small Business Administration.

Financial help to minorities has been more than tripled, and now more than 17 per cent of the SBA dollar goes to minority businesses. Procurement of Federal contracts for small business has surged above $12 billion.

In his first year in office, the President established a Task Force to discover ways in which the prospects of the small businessman could be improved.

The findings, reported to Congress, were followed by legislative proposals to give small business tax and interest advantages, to provide incentives for more participation on small business, to make venture capital and long-term credit easier to obtain, and to open the doors for disadvantaged minorities to go into business for themselves. Some of these measures have been signed into law. Others are still in the hands of the indifferent opposition in control of Congress.

The results of our efforts have been significant. Today small business is once again gaining ground. Incorporations are at a record level and the number of business failures is dropping. The current new growth of small businesses is about 100,000 units a year. For tomorrow, the challenges are many. We will:

Continue to fill the capital gap in the small business community by increasing SBA financing to upwards of $3 billion next year.

Provide more incentives for the private sector to join the SBA in direct action programs, such as lease guarantees, revolving lines of credit, and other sophisticated financial techniques, such as factoring and mortgage financing.

Increase SBA's Community Development program so that growth-minded communities can help themselves by building industrial parks and shopping centers.

Continue the rejuvenation of the Small Business Investment Company (SBIC) program, leading to greater availability of venture capital for new business enterprises.

See that a fair share of all Federal dollars spent on goods and services goes to small business.

Create established secondary financial markets for SBA loans, affording ready liquidity for financial institutions and opening up more financial resources to small firms.

Through tax incentives, encourage the start-up of more new businesses, and work for a tax system that more fairly applies to small business.

Establish special programs that will permit small firms to comply with consumer, environmental, and other new government regulations without undue financial burden.

## Improving the Quality of Life

### Health Care

Our goal is to enable every American to secure quality health care at reasonable cost. We pledge a balanced approach—one that takes into account the problems of providing sufficient medical personnel and facilities.

Last year President Nixon proposed one of the most all-inclusive health programs in our history. But the opposition Congress has dragged its feet and most of this program has yet to be enacted into law.

To increase the supply of medical services, we will continue to support programs to help our schools graduate more physicians, dentists, nurses, and allied health personnel, with special emphasis on family practitioners and others who deliver primary medical care.

We will also encourage the use of such allied personnel as doctors' assistants, foster new area health education centers, channel more services into geographic areas which now are medically deprived, and improve the availability of emergency medical care.

We note with pride that the President has already signed the most comprehensive health manpower legislation ever enacted.

To improve efficiency in providing health and medical care, we have developed and will continue to encourage a pluralistic approach to the delivery of quality health care, including innovative experiments such as health maintenance organizations. We also support efforts to develop ambulatory medical care services to reduce hospitalization and keep costs down.

To reduce the cost of health care, we stress our efforts to curb inflation in the economy; we will also expand the supply of medical services and encourage greater cost consciousness in hospitalization and medical care. In doing this we realize the importance of the doctor-patient relationship and the necessity of insuring that individuals have freedom of choice of health providers.

To assure access to basic medical care for all our people, we support a program financed by employers, employees and the Federal Government to provide comprehensive health insurance coverage, including insurance against the cost of long-term and catastrophic illnesses and accidents and renal failure which necessitates dialysis, at a cost which all Americans can afford. The National Health Insurance Partnership plan and the Family Health Insurance Plan proposed by the President meet these specifications. They would build on existing private health insurance systems, not destroy them.

We oppose nationalized compulsory health insurance. This approach would at least triple in taxes the amount the average citizen now pays for health and would deny families the right to choose the kind of care they prefer. Ultimately it would lower the overall quality of health care for all Americans.

We believe that the most effective way of improving health in the long run is by emphasis on preventive measures.

The serious physical fitness problem in our country requires urgent attention. The President recently reorganized the Council on Physical Fitness and Sports to increase the leadership of representatives of medicine, physical education, sports associations and school administrations. The Republican Party urges intensification of these efforts, particularly in the Nation's school systems, to encourage widespread participation in effective physical fitness programs.

We have initiated this Nation's first all-out assault against cancer. Led by the new National Cancer Institute, the drive to eliminate this cruel killer will involve Federal spending of nearly $430 million in fiscal year 1973, almost twice the funding of just two years ago.

We have also launched a major new attack on sickle cell anemia, a serious blood disorder afflicting many black Americans, and developed a comprehensive program to deal with the menace of lead-based paint poisoning, including the screening of approximately 1,500,000 Americans.

We support expanded medical research to find cures for the major diseases of the heart, blood vessels, lungs and kidneys—diseases which now account for over half the deaths in the United States.

We have significantly advanced efforts to combat mental retardation and established a national goal to cut its incidence in half by the year 2000.

We continue to support the concept of comprehensive community mental health centers. In this fiscal year $135 million—almost three times the 1970 level—will be devoted to the staffing of 422 community mental health centers serving a population of 56 million people. We have intensified research on methods of treating mental problems, increasing our outlays from $76 million in 1969 to approximately $96 million for 1973. We continue to urge extension of private health insurance to cover mental illness.

We have also improved consumer protection, health education and accident prevention programs. And in Moscow this year, President Nixon reached an agreement with the Soviet Union on health research which may yield substantial benefits in many fields in the years ahead.

*Education*

We take pride in our leadership these last four years in lifting both quality and equality in American education—from pre-school to graduate school —working toward higher standards than ever before.

Our two most pressing needs in the 1970's are the provision of quality education for all children, an equitable financing of steadily rising costs. We pledge our best efforts to deal effectively with both.

Months ago President Nixon sent Congress a two-part comprehensive proposal on school busing. The first is the Student Transportation Moratorium Act of 1972—legislation to halt immediately all further court-ordered busing and give Congress time to devise permanent new arrangements for assuring desegregated, quality education.

The details of such arrangements are spelled

out in a companion bill, the Equal Educational Opportunities Act. This measure would:

Provide $2.5 billion in Federal aid funds to help promote quality education while preserving neighborhood schools;

Accord equal educational opportunities to all children;

Include an educational bill of rights for Spanish-speaking people, American Indians, and others who face special language problems in schools;

Offer, for the first time, a real chance for good schooling for the hundreds of thousands of children who live in urban centers;

Assure that the people's elected representatives in Congress play their proper role in developing specific methods for protecting the rights guaranteed by the 14th amendment, rather than leaving this task to judges appointed for life.

We are committed to guaranteeing equality of educational opportunity and to completing the process of ending de jure school segregation.

At the same time, we are irrevocably opposed to busing for racial balance. Such busing fails its stated objective—improved learning opportunities —while it achieves results no one wants—division within communities and hostility between classes and races. We regard it as unnecessary, counterproductive and wrong.

We favor better education for all children, not more transportation for some children. We favor the neighborhood school concept. We favor the decisive actions the President has proposed to support these ends. If it is necessary to accomplish these purposes, we would favor consideration of an appropriate amendment to the Constitution.

In the field of school finance, we favor a coordinated effort among all levels of government to break the pattern of excessive reliance on local property taxes to pay educational costs.

Our nation's intellectual resources are remarkable for their strength and public availability. American intellectuals have at least two important historical roles of which we are deeply conscious. One is to inform the public, the other is to assist government by thoughtful criticism and consultation. We affirm our confidence in these functions and especially in the free play of ideas and discourse which they imply.

We cherish the nation's universities as centers of learning, as conservers of our culture, and as analysts of our society and its institutions. We will continue to strive to assure their economic well-being. The financial aid we have given and will continue to give in the form of funds for scholarships, research, building programs and new teaching methods must never be used as a device for imposing political controls on our schools.

We believe that universities should be centers of excellence—that they should recruit faculty on the basis of ability to teach and admit students on the basis of ability to learn. Yet, excellence can be too narrowly confined—abilities overlooked, and social conformity mistaken for educational preparation.

We pledge continued support of collegiate and university efforts to insure that no group in our society—racial, economic, sexual or regional—is denied access to the opportunities of higher education.

Our efforts to remedy ancient neglect of disadvantaged groups will continue in universities as well as in society at large, but we distinguish between such efforts and quotas. We believe the imposition of arbitrary quotas in the hiring of faculties or the enrollment of students has no place in our universities; we believe quotas strike at the excellence of the university.

We recognize that the public should have access to the most rational and most effective kinds of education. Vocational training should be available to both young and old. We emphasize the importance of continuing education, of trades and technologies, and of all the honorable vocations which provide the society with its basic necessities. Such training must complement our more traditional forms of education; it will relieve the pressures on our universities and help us adapt to the rapid pace of technological change. Perhaps most important, it will help to restore a public sense of importance to these essential jobs and trades.

Moreover, we believe our educational system should not instruct in a vacuum, unmindful that the students ultimately will engage in a career. Our institutions of learning, from earliest years to graduate schools, can perform a vital function by coupling an awareness of the world of work to the delivery of fundamental education. We believe this kind of career education, blended into our school curricula, can help to prevent the aimlessness and frustration now experienced by large numbers of young people who leave the education system unable to cope with today's complex society.

In recognizing the fundamental necessity for quality education of all children, including the exceptional child, we recommend research and assistance in programs directed to the problems of dyslectic and hyperkinetic children who represent an estimated ten per cent of the school population.

By every measure, our record in the field of education is exceptionally strong. The United States Office of Education is operating this year under its highest budget ever—$5.1 billion. Federal aid to elementary and secondary education has increased 60 per cent over the past four years. Federal aid for college students has more than tripled.

We are proud of these accomplishments. We pledge to carry them forward in a manner consistent with our conviction that the Federal Government should assist but never control the educational process. But we also believe that the output of results, not the input of dollars, is the best yardstick of effectiveness in education. When this Administration took office in 1969, it found American schools deficient at many points. Our reform initiatives have included:

An Office of Child Development to coordinate all Federal programs targeted on the first five years of life and to make the Head Start Program work better;

A Right to Read Program, aimed at massive gains in reading ability among Americans of all ages;

A Career Education curriculum which will help to prepare students for the world of work;

A National Institute of Education to be a center for research on the learning process; and

A proposed National Foundation for Higher Education.

We have also proposed grant and loan programs to support a national commitment that no qualified student should be barred from college by lack of money. The Education Amendment of 1972 embodied substantial portions of that proposal and marked the Nation's most far-reaching commitment to make higher education available to all.

Our non-public schools, both church-oriented and nonsectarian, have been our special concern. The President has emphasized the indispensable role these schools play in our educational system —from the standpoints of the large numbers of pupils they serve, the competition and diversity they help to maintain in American education, and the values they help to teach—and he has stated his determination to help halt the accelerating trend of nonpublic school closures.

We believe that means which are consistent with the Constitution can be devised for channeling public financial aid to support the education of all children in schools of their parents' choice, nonpublic as well as public. One way to provide such aid appears to be through the granting of income tax credits.

For the future, we also pledge Special Revenue Sharing for Education, continued work to develop and implement the Career Education concept, and continued efforts to establish a student financial aid system to bring together higher education within the reach of any qualified person.

*Welfare Reform*

The Nation's welfare system is a mess. It simply must be reformed.

This system, essentially unchanged since the 1930's has turned into a human and fiscal nightmare. It penalizes the poor. It provides discriminatory benefits. It kills any incentives its victims might have to work their way out of the morass.

Among its victims are the taxpayers. Since 1961 the Federal cost of welfare has skyrocketed over 10 times—from slightly over $1 billion then to more than $11 billion now. State and local costs add to this gigantic expenditure. And here are things we are paying for:

The present system drains work incentive from the employed poor, as they see welfare families making as much or more on the dole.

Its discriminatory benefits continue to ensnare the needy, aged, blind and disabled in a web of inefficient rules and economic contradictions.

It continues to break up poor families, since a father's presence makes his family ineligible for benefits in many States. Its dehumanizing lifestyle thus threatens to envelop yet another "welfare generation."

Its injustices and costs threaten to alienate taxpayer support for welfare programs of any kind.

Perhaps nowhere else is there a greater contrast in policy and philosophy than between the Administration's remedy for the welfare ills and the financial orgy proposed by our political opposition.

President Nixon proposed to change our welfare system "to provide each person with a means of escape from welfare into dignity." His goals were these:

A decent level of payment to genuinely needy welfare recipients regardless of where they live.

Incentives not to loaf, but to work.

Requiring all adults who apply for welfare to register for work and job training and to accept work or training. The only exceptions would be the aged, blind and disabled and mothers of pre-school children.

Expanding job training and child care facilities so that recipients can accept employment.

Temporary supplements to the incomes of the working poor to enable them to support their families while continuing to work.

Uniform Federal payment standards for all welfare recipients.

In companion actions, our efforts to improve the nutrition of poor people resulted in basic reforms in the Food Stamp Program. The number of recipients increased from some three million to 13 million, and now 8.4 million needy children participate in the School Lunch Program, almost three times the number that participated in 1968.

Now, nearly 10,000 nutrition aides work in low-income communities. In 1968 there were none.

Since 1969, we have increased the Federal support for family planning threefold. We will continue to support expanded family planning programs and will foster research in this area so that more parents will be better able to plan the number and spacing of their children should they wish to do so. Under no circumstances will we allow any of these programs to become compulsory or infringe upon the religious conviction or personal freedom of any individual.

We all feel compassion for those who through no fault of their own cannot adequately care for themselves. We all want to help these men, women and children achieve a decent standard of living and become self-supporting.

We continue to insist, however, that there are too many people on this country's welfare rolls who should not be there. With effective cooperation from the Congress, we pledge to stop these abuses.

We flatly oppose programs or policies which embrace the principle of a government-guaranteed income. We reject as unconscionable the idea that all citizens have the right to be supported by the government, regardless of their ability or desire to support themselves and their families.

We pledge to continue to push strongly for sound welfare reform until meaningful and helpful change is enacted into law by the Congress.

LAW ENFORCEMENT

We have solid evidence that our unrelenting war on crime is being won. The American people know that once again the thrust of justice in our society will be to protect the law-abiding citizenry against the criminal, rather than absolve the criminal of the consequences of his own desperate acts.

Serious crimes rose only one per cent during the first quarter of this year—down from six per cent last year and 13 per cent the year before. From 1960 to 1968 major crime went up 122 per cent.

The fact is, in the first quarter of 1972, 80 of our 155 largest cities had an actual decline in reported crime.

In our Nation's Capitol, our anti-crime programs have been fully implemented. Through such measures as increased police, street lighting, a Narcotics Treatment Administration, court reform and special prosecuting units for major offenders, we have steadily dropped the crime rate since November 1969. By the first quarter of this year, the serious crime rate was down to half its all-time high.

When our Administration took office, a mood of lawlessness was spreading rapidly, undermining the legal and moral foundations of our society. We moved at once to stop violence in America. We have:

Greatly increased Federal aid to State and local law enforcement agencies across the country, with more than $1.5 billion spent on 50,000 crime-fighting projects.

Augmented Justice Department funding four-fold and provided more marshals, more judges, more narcotics agents, more Assistant United States Attorneys in the field.

Raised the Law Enforcement Assistance Administration budget ten-fold, earmarking $575 million of the $850 million for 1973 to upgrade State and local police and courts through revenue sharing.

Added 600 new Special Agents to the FBI.

Raised Federal spending on juvenile delinquency from $15 million to more than $180 million and proposed legislation to launch a series of model youth services.

Appointed Attorneys General with a keen sense of the rights of both defendants and victims, and determination to enforce the laws.

Appointed judges whose respect for the rights of the accused is balanced by an appreciation of the legitimate needs of law enforcement.

Added to the Supreme Court distinguished lawyers of firm judicial temperament and fidelity to the Constitution.

Even more fundamentally, we have established a renewed climate of respect for law and law enforcement. Now those responsible for enforcing the law know they have the full backing of their Government.

We recognize that programs involving work release, study release and half-way houses have contributed substantially to the rehabilitation of offenders and we support these programs. We further support training programs for the staffs in our correctional institutions and will continue to see that minority group staff members are recruited to work in these institutions.

### The Fight against Organized Crime

To most of us, organized criminal activity seems remote and unreal—yet syndicates supply the narcotics pushed on our youth, corrupt local officials, terrify legitimate businesses and fence goods stolen from our homes. This Administration strongly supported the Organized Crime Control Act of 1970, and under our Strike Force concept we have combined Federal enforcement agencies to wage a concerted assault on organized crime. We have expanded the number of these strike forces and set a high priority for a new campaign against the syndicates.

Last year we obtained indictments against more than 2,600 members or associates of organized crime syndicates—more than triple the number indicted in 1968.

At last we have the lawless elements in our society on the run.

The Republican Party intends to keep them running.

### Rehabilitation of Offenders

We have given the rehabilitation of criminal offenders more constructive, top-level attention than

it has received at any time in our Nation's history. In November 1969, the President ordered a ten-year improvement program in prison facilities, correctional systems and rehabilitation methods and procedures.

We believe the correctional system not only should punish, but also should educate and rehabilitate. We are determined to press ahead with reform of the system to make it more effective against crime.

Almost a decade of inadequate Federal support of law enforcement has left deep scars in our society, but now a new mood pervades the country. Civil disorders and campus violence are no longer considered inevitable. Today, we see a new respect for law and order.

Our goal is justice—for everyone.

We pledge a tireless campaign against crime—to restore safety to our streets, and security to law-abiding citizens who have a right to enjoy their homes and communities free from fear.

We pledge to:

Continue our vigorous support of local police and law enforcement agancies, as well as Federal law enforcement agencies.

Seek comprehensive procedural and substantive reform of the Federal Criminal Code.

Accelerate the drive against organized crime.

Increase the funding of the Federal judiciary to help clear away the logjam in the courts which obstructs the administration of justice.

Push forward in prison reform and the rehabilitation of offenders.

Intensify efforts to prevent criminal access to all weapons, including special emphasis on cheap, readily-obtainable handguns, retaining primary responsibility at the State level, with such Federal law as necessary to enable the States to meet their responsibilities.

Safeguard the right of responsible citizens to collect, own and use firearms for legitimate purposes, including hunting, target shooting and self-defense. We will strongly support efforts of all law enforcement agencies to apprehend and prosecute to the limit of the law all those who use firearms in the commission of crimes.

### Drug Abuse

The permissiveness of the 1960's left no legacy more insidious than drug abuse. In that decade narcotics became widely available, most tragically among our young people. The use of drugs became endowed with a sheen of false glamour identified with social protest.

By the time our Nation awakened to this cancerous social ill, it found no major combat weapons available.

Soon after we took office, our research disclosed there were perhaps hundreds of thousands of heroin users in the United States. Their cravings multiplied violence and crime. We found many more were abusing other drugs, such as amphetamines and barbiturates. Marijuana had become commonplace. All this was spurred by criminals using modern methods of mass distribution against outnumbered authorities lacking adequate countermeasures.

We quickly launched a massive assault against drug abuse.

We intercepted the supply of dangerous drugs at points of entry and impeded their internal distribution. The budget for international narcotics control was raised from $5 million to over $50 million. Narcotics control coordinators were appointed in 59 United States embassies overseas to work directly with foreign governments in stopping drug traffic. We have narcotics action agreements with over 20 countries. Turkey has announced a total ban on opium production and, with our cooperation, France has seized major heroin laboratories and drugs.

To inhibit the distribution of heroin in our own country, we increased the law enforcement budget for drug control more than 10 times—from $20 million to $244 million.

We are disrupting major narcotics distribution in wholesale networks through the combined efforts of the Bureau of Narcotics and Dangerous Drugs, Customs operations at our borders, and a specially credited unit of over 400 Internal Revenue agents who conduct systematic tax investigations of targeted middle and upper echelon traffickers, smugglers, and financiers. Last January we established the Office of Drug Abuse Law Enforcement to disrupt street and mid-level heroin traffickers.

We established the "Heroin Hot Line"—a nationwide toll free phone number (800/368–5363) —to give the public a single number for reporting information on heroin pushers.

Last year we added 2,000 more Federal narcotics agents, and the Bureau of Narcotics and Dangerous Drugs has trained over 170,000 State and local personnel.

And we are getting results. This past year four times as much heroin was seized as in the year this Administration took office. Since 1969, the number of drug-related arrests has nearly doubled.

For drug abuse prevention and treatment we increased the budget from $46 million to over $485 million.

The demand for illicit drugs is being reduced through a massive effort directed by a newly created office in the White House. Federally funded drug treatment and rehabilitation programs were more than doubled last fiscal year, and Federal programs now have the capacity to treat more than 60,000 drug abusers a year.

To alert the public, particularly the youth, to the dangers of drugs, we established a National Clearinghouse for Drug Abuse Information in 1970 as well as a $3.5 million Drug Education and Training Program.

We realize that the problem of drug abuse cannot be quickly solved, but we have launched a massive effort where practically none existed before. Nor will we relax this campaign:

We pledge to seek further international agreements to restrict the production and movement of dangerous drugs.

We pledge to expand our programs of education, rehabilitation, training and treatment. We will do more than ever before to conduct research into the complex psychological regions of disappointment and alienation which have led many young people to turn desperately toward drugs.

We firmly oppose efforts to make drugs easily available. We equally oppose the legalization of marijuana. We intend to solve problems, not create bigger ones by legalizing drugs of unknown physical impact.

We pledge the most intensive law enforcement war ever waged. We are determined to drive the pushers of dangerous drugs from the streets, schools and neighborhoods of America.

### Agriculture and Rural Life

Our agriculture has become the economic marvel of the world. Our American farmers and ranchers have tripled per worker production in the last 20 years, while non-farm industries have increased theirs a little over half.

Yet when we took office three and a half years

ago, the farm community was being shockingly shortchanged for its remarkable achievements.

Inflation was driving up both the cost of farming and the cost of living—indeed, driving up all prices except the prices of products the farmers were taking to market. Overall farm income was down. Farm exports were low. Bureaucratic planting regulations were oppressive. All across the country family farms were failing.

Our moves to deal with these problems have been numerous and effective.

The rate of inflation has been curbed without forcing down prices for commodities, even as we have stepped up our drive against rising food costs in the cities.

Net farm income has soared to a record high of more than $18 billion. During these Republican years average net farm income has been over $2 billion a year higher than during the last two Administrations. For the same period average income per farm is up more than 40 percent.

And farm exports now stand at a record $8 billion, sharply up from the $5.7 billion when we took office.

Operating loans to help young farmers have reached the highest levels in history. Administration-backed legislation has given farmers much greater freedom to plant what they choose, and we have given assistance to cooperatives to strengthen the farmers' bargaining positions.

Rural development has been energetically carried forward, and small towns and rural areas have been helped to adjust and grow. The loan programs of the Farmers Home Administration for farm and rural people have been dramatically increased. Electric and telephone service in rural areas has been substantially expanded, a Rural Telephone Bank has been enacted, and the Farm Credit Administration has been streamlined. The total national investment in rural development has almost tripled. Heading the Department of Agriculture have been leaders who understand and forcefully speak out for the farming people of America.

Farmers are benefiting markedly from our successful efforts to expand exports—notably a $750 million sale of United States grains to the Soviet Union, with prospects of much more. Last year we negotiated a similar sale amounting to $135 million.

For the future, we pledge to intensify our efforts to:

Achieve a $10 billion annual export market by opening new foreign markets, while continuing to fight for fair treatment for American farm products in our traditional markets;

Follow sound economic policies to brake inflation and reduce interest rates;

Expand activities to assist farmers in bargaining for fair prices and reasonable terms in a rapidly changing marketing system;

Keep farm prices in the private sector, not subject to price controls;

Support family farms as the preferred method of organizing agricultural production, and protect them from the unfair competition of farming by tax-loss corporations and non-farm enterprises;

Reform Federal estate tax laws, which often force the precipitate sale of family farms to help pay the tax, in such ways as to help support the continuance of family farms as institutions of great importance to the American way of life;

Provide greater credit, technical assistance, soil and water conservation aid, environmental enhancement, economic stimulus and sympathetic leadership to America's rural areas and communities;

Concentrate research on new uses of agricultural products;

Continue assistance to farm cooperatives, including rural electric and telephone cooperatives, in their efforts to improve their members;

Develop land and water policy that takes account of the many uses to which these resources may be put;

Establish realistic environmental standards which safeguard wise resource use, while avoiding undue burdens on farmers;

Use forums of national leaders to create a better understanding by all citizens, those in the cities and suburbs as well as those in small towns, of the difficult problems confronting farm and ranch families in a modern agriculture.

We will not relax our efforts to increase net farm income, to narrow the spread between farm and non-farm income levels, and to pursue commodity programs that will enable farmers and ranchers to receive fair prices for what they produce.

## Community Development

For more than a quarter century the Federal Government has sought to assist in the conservation and rebuilding of our urban centers. Yet, after the spending of billions of dollars and the commitment of billions more to future years, we now know that many existing programs are unsuited to the complex problems of the 1970's. Programs cast in the mold of the "big government" philosophy of the 1930's are simply incapable of meeting the challenge of today.

Our Party stands, therefore, for major reform of Federal community development programs and the development of a new philosophy to cope with urban ills.

Republican urban strategy rejects throwing good money after bad money. Instead, through fundamental fiscal, management and program reforms, we have created a new Federal partnership through which State, county and municipal governments can best cope with specific problems such as education, crime, drug abuse, transportation, pollution and housing.

We believe the urban problems of today fall into these categories:

The fiscal crises of State, county and municipal governments;

The need for a better quality and greater availability of urban services;

The continual requirement of physical development;

The need for better locally designed, locally implemented, locally controlled solutions to the problems of individual urban areas.

In the last category—the importance of grass roots planning and participation—our Republican Party has made its most important contribution to solving urban problems.

We hold the government planners should be guided by the people through their locally elected representatives. We believe that real solutions require the full participation of the private sector.

To help ease the fiscal crises of State, county and municipal governments, we pledge increased Federal assistance—assistance we have more than doubled in the past four years. And, as stressed elsewhere in this Platform, we remain committed to General Revenue Sharing, which could reduce the oppressive property tax.

Our proposals for Special Revenue Sharing for Urban Development, transportation, manpower and law enforcement—all still bottled up by the opposition Congress—are designed to make our towns and cities places where Americans can once again live and work without physical or environmental hazard. Urban areas are already benefiting from major funding increases which we fought for in the Law Enforcement Assistance Administration programs and in our $10 billion mass transit program.

Urban areas are also benefiting from our new Legacy of Parks program, which is bringing recreation opportunities closer to where people live.

We are committed also to the physical development of urban areas. We have quadrupled subsidized housing starts for low and moderate income families since 1969, and effected substantial increases for construction of municipal waste treatment facilities.

We strongly oppose the use of housing or community development programs to impose arbitrary housing patterns on unwilling communities. Neither do we favor dispersing large numbers of people away from their homes and neighborhoods against their will. We do believe in providing communities, with their full consent, guidance and cooperation with the means and incentives to increase the quantity and quality of housing in conjunction with providing increased access to jobs for their low-income citizens.

We also pledge to carry forward our policy on encouraging the development of new towns in order to afford all Americans a wider range of residential choices. Additionally, our Special Revenue Sharing for Urban and Rural Community Development, together with General Revenue Sharing and nationwide welfare reform, are basic building blocks for a balanced policy of national growth, leading to better lives for all Americans, whether they dwell in cities, suburbs or rural areas.

Our Party recognizes counties as viable units of regional government with a major role in modernizing and restructuring local services, eliminating duplication and increasing local cooperation. We urge Federal and State governments, in implementing national goals and programs, to utilize the valuable resources of counties as area-wide, general-purpose governments.

## Housing

Our Republican Administration has made more and better housing available to more of our citizens than ever before.

We are building two-and-a-third million new homes a year—65 per cent more than the average in the eight years of the two previous Administrations. Progress has not been in numbers alone; housing quality has also risen to an all-time high—far above that of any other country.

We will maintain and increase this pattern of growth. We are determined to attain the goal of a decent home for every American.

Significant numbers of Americans still lack the means for decent housing, and in such cases—where special need exists—we will continue to apply public resources to help people acquire better apartments and homes.

We further pledge:

Continued housing production for low and moderate income families, which has sharply increased since President Nixon took office;

Improvement of housing subsidy programs and expansion of mortgage credit activities of Federal housing agencies as necessary to keep Americans the best-housed people in the world;

Continued development of technological and management innovations to lower housing costs—a program begun by Operation Breakthrough, which is assisting in the development of new methods for more economical production of low-cost, high-quality homes.

We urge prompt action by State, county and municipal governments to seek solutions to the serious problems caused by abandoned buildings in urban areas.

*Transportation*

When President Nixon took office a crisis in transportation was imminent, as indicated by declining mass transportation service, mounting highway deaths, congested urban streets, long delays at airports and airport terminals, deterioration of passenger train service, and a dwindling Merchant Marine. Within two years the President had proposed and signed into law:

A $10 billion, 12-year program—the Urban Mass Transportation Act of 1970—to infuse new life into mass transportation systems and help relieve urban congestion;

A major 10-year program involving $280 million annually for airport development projects as well as an additional $250 million annually to expand airways systems and facilities;

The Rail Passenger Service Act of 1970 to streamline and improve the Nation's passenger train service;

New research and development projects, including automatic people movers, improved Metroliner and Turbo-trains, quieter aircraft jet engines, air pollution reduction for mass transportation vehicles, and experimental safety automobiles. We strongly support these research and development initiatives of the Department of Transportation.

Four years ago we called attention to the decline of our Merchant Marine due to previous neglect and apathy. We promised a vigorous ship replacement program to meet the changing pattern of our foreign commerce. We also pledged to expand maritime research and development and the simplification and revision of construction and operating subsidy procedures.

By the enactment of the Merchant Marine Act of 1970, we have reversed the long decline of our Merchant Marine. We reaffirm our goals set forth in 1968 and anticipate the future development of a merchant fleet that will give us defensive mobility in time of emergency as well as economic strength in time of peace.

To reduce traffic and highway deaths, the National Highway Traffic Safety Administration has been reorganized and expanded, with dramatic results. In 1971, the number of traffic deaths per hundred million miles driven was the lowest in history.

To help restore decision-making to the people, we have proposed a new Single Urban Fund providing almost $2 billion a year by 1975 to State and metropolitan areas to assist local authorities in solving their own transportation problems in their own way.

Our proposal for Special Revenue Sharing for Transportation would also help governments close to the people meet local needs and provide greater freedom to achieve a proper balance among the Nation's major transportation modes.

To revitalize the surface freight transportation industry, we have recommended measures to modernize railway equipment and operations and to update regulatory practices. These measures, on which Congress still dawdles, would help curb inflation by saving the public billions of dollars a year in freight costs. Their enactment would also expand employment and improve our balance of trade.

The Nation's transportation needs are expected to double in the next 20 years. Our Party will continue to pursue policies and programs that will meet these needs and keep the country well ahead of rapidly changing transportation demands.

## Environment

In January 1969, we found the Federal Government woefully unprepared to deal with the rapidly advancing environmental crisis. Our response was swift and substantial.

First, new decision-making organizations were set in place—the first Council on Environmental Quality, the Environmental Protection Agency, the National Oceanic and Atmospheric Administration. We also proposed a new Department of Natural Resources, but Congress has failed to act. We also created a National Industrial Pollution Control Council to enlist the private sector more actively against environmental decay, and Presidential Federal Property Review Board was appointed to ferret out Federal property for transfer to local park and recreational uses.

Second, we gave top priority in the Federal Budget to environmental improvements. This fiscal year approximately $2.4 billion will be expended for major environmental programs—three times more than was being spent when President Nixon took office.

Third, sweeping environment messages were sent to Congress in 1970, 1971 and 1972 covering air quality, water quality, toxic waste substances, ocean dumping, noise, solid waste management, land use, parklands and many other environmental concerns. Almost all of these proposals still languish in the opposition Congress.

Although the President cannot move until and unless Congress passes laws in many of these areas, he nevertheless can act—and has acted—forcefully on many fronts:

He has directed the Federal Government to practice ecological leadership by using low-lead gasoline and recycled paper. He has cracked down on flagrant polluters, greatly increasing prosecutions and making the first use of Federal authority to shut down major industries during an air pollution crisis. The fragile and unique Everglades were saved from a jetport. Pesticide abuses were curtailed.

Strict new clean-air standards were set, and in many urban centers the air is improving. Regulations were issued to make one grade of lead-free and phosphorous-free gasoline available throughout the Nation by July 1, 1974, and a phased reduction was required in the lead content of regular and premium gasolines. Auto makers were required to design air pollution control systems to assure that vehicles comply with Federal emission standards throughout their usual life.

Additionally, the President launched the Legacy of Parks program to convert underutilized Federal properties to park and recreational use, with special emphasis on new parks in or near urban areas. More than 140 areas have already been made available to States, counties and municipalities for such use, including priceless stretches of ocean beach. Moreover, nearly two million acres of land have been purchased by Federal, State and local governments for recreation and for historical and natural preservation purposes.

A system of recreational trails for hiking, bicycling and horseback riding will help meet the pressing recreational needs of our increasingly urbanized society. Many State, county and municipal governments are developing bicycle, hiking, and horseback trails with our active assistance through various Federal programs. We pledge our continued commitment to seeking out practical ways for more and safer bicycling opportunities within our cities and metropolitan areas.

We have also provided effective leadership in international environmental activity. The President has negotiated the Great Lakes Water Quality Agreement with Canada and a Cooperative Agreement on Environmental Protection with the Soviet Union.

The United Nations Conference on the Human Environment in Stockholm adopted our government's initiatives for the creation of an international fund for the environment, a continuing United Nations agency for environmental problems, and the control of ocean dumping. Our President has led the effort for a ten-year moratorium on commercial whaling everywhere in the world.

We call upon the Congress to act promptly on the President's environmental proposals still stalled there—more than 20 in all. These include:

Legislation to control, and in some cases prohibit, the dumping of wastes into the oceans, estuaries and the Great Lakes;

A Federal Noise Control Act to reduce and regulate unwanted sound from aircraft, construction and transportation equipment;

Authority to control hundreds of chemical substances newly marketed each year;

Legislation to encourage the States to step up

to pressing decisions on how best to use land. Both environmentally critical areas such as wetlands and growth-inducing developments such as airports would have particular scrutiny;

A proposal to provide for early identification and protection of endangered wildlife species. This would, for the first time, make the taking of endangered species a Federal offense;

Establishment of recreational areas near metropolitan centers such as the Gateway National Recreational Area in New York and New Jersey and the Golden Gate National Recreation Area in and around San Francisco Bay.

The nostalgic notion of turning the clock back to a simpler time may be appealing but is neither practical nor desirable. We are not going to abandon the automobile, but we are going to have a clean-burning engine.

We are not going to give up electric lighting and modern industry, but we do expect cleanly-produced electric power to run them.

We are not going to be able to do without containers for our foods and materials, but we can improve them and make them reusable or biodegradable.

We pledge a workable balance between a growing economy and environmental protection. We will resolve the conflicts sensibly within that framework.

We commit ourselves to comprehensive pollution control laws, vigorous implementation of those laws and rigorous research into the technological problems of pollution control. The beginnings we have made in these first years of the 1970's are evidence of our determination to follow through.

We intend to leave the children of America a legacy of clean air, clean water, vast open spaces and easily accessible parks.

## Natural Resources and Energy

Wilderness areas, forests, fish and wildlife are precious natural resources. We have proposed 36 new wilderness areas, adding another 3.6 million acres to the National Wilderness Preservation System. We have made tough new proposals to protect endangered species of wildlife.

Public lands provide us with natural beauty, wilderness and great recreational opportunities as well as minerals, timber, food and fiber. We pledge to develop and manage these lands in a balanced way, both to protect the irreplaceable environment and to maximize the benefits of their use to our society. We will continue these conservation efforts in the years ahead.

We recognize and commend the humane societies and the animal welfare societies in their work to protect animals.

Water supplies are not a boundless resource. The Republican Party is committed to developing additional water supplies by desalinization, the discovery of new groundwater stocks, recycling and wiser and more efficient use of the waters we have.

We will continue the development of flood control, navigation improvement and reclamation projects based on valid cost-benefit estimates, including full consideration of environmental concerns.

No modern nation can thrive without meeting its energy needs, and our needs are vast and growing. Last year we proposed a broad range of actions to facilitate research and development for clean energy, provide energy resources on Federal lands, assure a timely supply of nuclear fuels, use energy more efficiently, balance environmental and energy needs and better organize Federal efforts.

The National Minerals Policy Act of 1970 encourages development of domestic resources by private enterprise. A program to tap our vast shale resources has been initiated consistent with the National Environmental Policy Act of 1969.

We need a Department of Natural Resources to continue to develop a national, integrated energy policy and to administer and implement that policy as the United States approaches the 21st Century. Energy sources so vitally important to the welfare of our Nation are becoming increasingly interchangeable. There is nothing inherently incompatible between an adequate energy supply and a healthy environment.

Indeed, vast quantities of energy are needed to do the work necessary to clean up our air and streams. Without sufficient supplies of power we will not be able to attain our goals of reducing unemployment and poverty and enhancing the American standard of living.

Responsible government must consider both the short-term and the long-term aspects of our energy supplies. Avoidance of brown-outs and power disruptions now and i⸱ 'he future call for sound policies supporting incentives that will encourage the exploration for, and development of, our fossil fuels. Such policies will buy us time to develop the sophisticated and complex technologies needed to utilize the exotic energy sources of the future.

National security and the importance of a favorable balance of trade and balance of payments dictate that we must not permit our Nation to become overly dependent on foreign sources of energy. Since more than half our Nation's domestic fossil resources now lie under Federal lands, high priority must be given to the governmental steps necessary to the development of these resources by private industry.

A liquid metal fast breeder reactor demonstration plant will be built with the financial support of the Atomic Energy Commission, the electric power industry and the Tennessee Valley Authority.

We will accelerate research on harnessing thermo-nuclear energy and continue to provide leadership in the production of energy from the sun and geothermal steam. We recognize the serious problem of assuring adequate electric generating capacity in the Nation, and pledge to meet this need without doing violence to our environment.

## Oceans

The oceans are a vast, largely untapped reservoir of resources, a source of food, minerals, recreation and pleasure, with great potential for economic development. For their maintenance we must:

Encourage the development of coastal zone management systems by the States, in cooperation with the Federal Government, to preserve the coastal environment while allowing for its prudent social and economic development;

Protect the oceans from pollution through the creation of binding domestic and international legal and institutional arrangements;

Foster arrangements to develop the untapped mineral resources of the seas in an equitable and environmentally sound manner;

Establish domestic and international institutions for the management of the ocean fisheries. Fishing in international waters, a way of life for many Americans, must be maintained without harassment on the high seas or unreasonable restrictions;

Protect and conserve marine mammals and other marine species to ensure their abundance and especially to protect species whose survival is endangered;

Maintain a national capability in ocean science and technology and, through the United Nations Conference on the Law of the Sea, work to codify an international legal framework for the peaceful conduct of ocean activities.

## Science and Technology

Basic and applied scientific research and development are indispensable to our national security, our international competitive position, and virtually every aspect of the domestic economy. We have initiated a new research-and-development strategy which emphasizes a public-private partnership in searching out new ideas and technologies to create new jobs, new internationally competitive industries and new solutions for complex domestic problems.

In support of this strategy we have increased Federal efforts in civilian research and development by 65 per cent—from $3.3 billion to $5.4 billion—and expanded research in drug abuse, law enforcement, health care, home building, motor vehicle safety, energy and child development as well as many other fields.

We will place special emphasis on these areas in which breakthroughs are urgently needed:

Abundant, clean energy sources;

Safe, fast and pollution-free transportation;

Improved emergency health care;

Reduction of loss of life, health and property in natural disasters;

Rehabilitation of alcoholics and addicts to dangerous drugs.

Additionally, we urge the fair and energetic enforcement of all fire-prevention laws and applaud the work of the National Commission on Fire Prevention and Control. We encourage accelerated research on methods of fire prevention and suppression, including studies on flammable fabrics, hazardous materials, fire equipment and training procedures.

The space program is yielding impressive dividends in earth-oriented applications of space technology—advances in medicine, industrial techniques and consumer products that would still be unknown had we not developed the technology to reach the moon. We will press ahead with the space shuttle program to replace today's expendable launch vehicles and provide low-cost access to space for a wide variety of missions, including those related to earth resources. We pledge to continue to extend our knowledge of the most distant frontiers in space.

We will also extend our exploration of the sea-bed and the sea. We will seek food for the hungry, power for future technologies, new medicines for the sick and new treatments of water for arid regions of the world.

The quantities of metals and minerals needed to maintain our economic health and living standards are so huge as to require the re-use of all recoverable commodities from solid waste materials. We pledge a vigorous program of research and development in order to seek out more economical methods to recover and recycle such commodities, including the processing of municipal solid wastes.

We pledge to extend the communications frontier, and to foster the development of orbiting satellite systems that will make possible wholly new, world-wide educational and entertainment programs.

We recognize that the productivity of our Nation's research and development efforts can be enhanced through cooperative international projects. The signing of the Moscow agreements for cooperation in space, environment, health and science and technology has opened a new era in international relations. A similar agreement between the United States and Polish Governments will permit expansion of programs such as the jointly-funded Copernicus Astronomical Center and Krakow Children's Hospital.

Finally, we pledge expanded efforts to aid unemployed scientists and engineers. We are determined to see that such on-going efforts as the Technology Mobilization and Reemployment Program are effective.

## The Individual and Government

Even though many urgently-needed Administration proposals have been long delayed or stopped by the opposition Congress, we have kept our 1968 promise to make government more accountable and more responsive to the citizen. One such proposal is General Revenue Sharing with State and local governments—a means of returning to the people powers which for 40 years have grown increasingly centralized in the remote Washington bureaucracy. Another is consolidation of scores of categorical grant programs into six Special Rev-

enue Sharing programs which would make available some $12 billion annually in broad policy fields for States and localities to apply in their own ways to their own needs. Yet another is our proposal to modernize the Executive Branch of the Federal Government by combining six Cabinet departments and several independent agencies into four new departments. So far, the opposition controlled Congress has blocked or ignored all of these proposals.

In addition, we have:

Improved domestic policy formulation and implementation by the new Domestic Council and Office of Management and Budget within the Executive Office of the President;

Established stronger liaison between the Federal Government and the States, counties and municipalities by a new Office of Intergovernmental Relations, headed by the Vice President;

Overhauled the fragmented and poorly coordinated Federal agencies concerned with drug abuse and the environment;

Utilized voluntary citizen effort through the formation of the ACTION agency in government and the National Center for Voluntary Action outside of government;

Proposed reorganization of the Federal regulatory agencies and appointed distinguished people to those agencies;

Assured more open government, ending abuse of document classification and providing fuller information to the public.

We pledge continuing reform and revitalization of government to assure a better response to individual needs.

We express deep concern for the flood victims of tropical Storm Agnes, the worst natural disaster in terms of property damage in our Nation's history. Past laws were totally inadequate to meet this crisis, and we commend the President's leadership in urgently recommending the newly-enacted $1.8 billion flood relief measure, greatly expanding and enlarging the present program. We pledge to reevaluate and enlarge the national flood disaster insurance program so that it will be adequate for future emergencies.

We will continue to press for the enactment of General and Special Revenue Sharing and to pursue further initiatives both to decentralize governmental activities and to transfer more such activities to the private sector.

We will continue to defend the citizen's right

to privacy in our increasingly interdependent society. We oppose computerized national data banks and all other "Big Brother" schemes which endanger individual rights.

We reaffirm our view that voluntary prayer should be freely permitted in public places—particularly, by school children while attending public schools—providing that such prayers are not prepared or prescribed by the state or any of its political subdivisions and that no person's participation is coerced, thus preserving the traditional separation of church and state.

We remain committed to a comprehensive program of human rights, social betterment and political participation for the people of the District of Columbia. We will build on our strong record in this area—a record which includes cutting the District of Columbia crime rate in half, aggressive support for a balanced transportation system in metropolitan Washington, initiation of a Bicentennial program and celebration in the national capital region, and support for the first Congressional Delegate in nearly a century. We support voting representation for the District of Columbia in the United States Congress and will work for a system of self-government for the city which takes fair account of the needs and interests of both the Federal Government and the citizens of the District of Columbia.

The Republican Party adheres to the principle of self-determination for Puerto Rico. We will welcome and support statehood for Puerto Rico if that status should be the free choice of its people in a referendum vote.

Additionally, we will pursue negotiations with the Congress of Micronesia on the future political status of the Trust Territories of the Pacific Islands to meet the mutual interests of both parties. We favor extending the right of electing the territorial Governor to the people of American Samoa, and will take complementary steps to increase local self-government in American Samoa. We vigorously support such action as is necessary to permit American citizens resident in Guam, Puerto Rico and the Virgin Islands to vote for President and Vice President in national elections. We support full voting rights in committees for the Delegates to Congress from Guam and the Virgin Islands.

In our territorial policy we seek a maximum degree of local self-sufficiency and self-government, while encouraging greater inclusion in Federal services and programs and greater participation in national decision-making.

### Volunteerism

In our free system, the people are not only the source of our social problems but also the main source of solutions Volunteerism, therefore, an indispensable national resource, is basic to our Republican philosophy. We applaud the Administration's efforts to encourage volunteerism by all Americans and commend the millions of volunteers who are working in communities and states across the country on myriad projects. We favor further implementation of voluntary action programs throughout the fifty States to assist public and private agencies in working to assure quality life for all human beings.

### Arts and Humanities

The United States is experiencing a cultural renaissance of inspiring dimension. Scores of millions of our people are now supporting and participating in the arts and humanities in quest of a richer life of the mind and the spirit. Our national culture, no longer the preserve of the elite, is becoming a people's heritage of importance to the whole world.

We believe, with the President, that "the Federal Government has a vital role as catalyst, innovator, and supporter of public and private efforts for cultural development."

We have supported a three-year extension of the National Foundation on the Arts and the Humanities, and increased the funding of its two endowments by more than four times the level of three years ago. The State Arts Councils, which operate in all 50 States and the five special jurisdictions, have also been strengthened.

The Arts Endowment has raised its support for the Nation's museums, orchestras, theatre, dance, opera companies and film centers and encouraged the creativity of individual artists and writers. In addition, the new Federal Expansion Arts Program has been sharply increased.

We have encouraged Federal agencies to use the arts in their programs, sponsored an annual Design Assembly for Federal administrators, requested the National Endowment for the Arts to recommend a program for upgrading the design of Federal buildings, and moved to set new standards of excellence in all design endeavors of the Federal Government.

Moreover, the National Endowment for the Humanities, now greatly enlarged, is fostering improved teaching and scholarship in history, literature, philosophy and ethics. The Endowment also supports programs to raise levels of scholarship and teaching in Afro-American, American Indian and Mexican-American studies, has broadened its fellowship programs to include junior college teachers, and stresses adult or continuing education, including educational television and film series. We have also expanded the funding of public broadcasting.

For the future, we pledge continuance of our vigorous support of the arts and humanities.

A BETTER FUTURE FOR ALL

*Children*

We believe, with the President, that the first five years of life are crucial to a child's development, and further, that every child should have the opportunity to reach his full potential as an individual.

We have, therefore, established the Office of Child Development, which has taken a comprehensive approach to the development of young children, combining programs dealing with their physical, social and educational needs and development.

We have undertaken a wide variety of demonstration programs to assure our children, particularly poor children, a good start in life—for example, the Parent and Child Center program for infant care, Home Start to strengthen the environment of the preschool child, and Health Start to explore new delivery systems of health care for young children.

We have redirected Head Start to perform valuable full-day child care and early education services, and more than 380,000 preschool children are now in the program. We have doubled funds for early childhood demonstration programs which will develop new tools and new teaching techniques to serve children who suffer from deafness, blindness and other handicaps.

So that no child will be denied the opportunity for a productive life because of inability to read effectively, we have established the Right to Read Program.

To add impetus to the entire educational effort,

our newly-created National Institute of Education ensures that broad research and experimentation will develop the best educational opportunities for all children. Additionally, we have taken steps to help ensure that children receive proper care while their parents are at work.

Moreover, as stated elsewhere in this Platform, we have broadened nutritional assistance to poor children by nearly tripling participation in the Food Stamp Program, more than doubling the number of needy children in the school lunch program, operating a summer feeding program for three million young people, increasing the breakfast program fivefold, and doubling Federal support for child nutritional programs. We are improving medical care for poor children through more vigorous treatment procedures under Medicaid and more effectively targeting maternal and child health services to low-income mothers. We will continue to seek out new means to reach and teach children in their crucial early years.

*Youth*

We believe that what our youth most want and need is not special treatment as a group apart, but just the opposite—the opportunity for full participation by exercising the rights and responsibilities of adults.

In 1970 the President approved legislation which gave the vote to more than 11 million 18-to-20 year olds. The 26th Amendment, which places this important new right in the Constitution, has our enthusiastic backing.

Our Administration has already made the draft a far less arbitrary factor in young men's lives. Now we near the point where we can end conscription altogether and achieve our goal of an all-volunteer armed force.

Our total war on drug abuse has had special benefits for youth, hardest hit by this menace. Last year we held the first White House Conference ever held by and for young people themselves. The Administration gave the Conference's more than 300 recommendations a searching review, and last spring the President returned a detailed response and action report to the conferees.

The anarchy which swept major campuses in the late 1960's penalized no one more severely than the young people themselves. The recent calm on campus is, we believe, in part the result of the President's leadership in winding down the war in Vietnam, reducing the draft, and taking a strong stand against lawlessness, but our view is that colleges themselves are responsible for maintaining a campus climate that will preserve academic freedom.

We have proposed legislation to ensure that no qualified student is denied a higher education by lack of funds, and have also moved to meet the often-overlooked concerns of the two-thirds of the college-age young not in school. We have developed a new job-oriented, career-education concept, expanded Federal manpower programs and provided a record number of summer job opportunities for young men and women.

To engage youthful idealism and energies more effectively, we have created the new ACTION volunteer service agency, bringing together the Peace Corps, VISTA, and other volunteer programs; and we encouraged the establishment of the independent National Center for Voluntary Action.

We stand for lowering the legal age of majority in all jurisdictions to 18; and we will seek to broaden the involvement of young people in every phase of the political process—as voters, party workers and leaders, candidates and elected officials, and participants in government at municipal, State and Federal levels.

We will continue to build on these solid achievements in keeping with our conviction that these young people should have the opportunity to participate fully in the affairs of our society.

### Equal Rights for Women

The Republican Party recognizes the great contributions women have made to our society as homemakers and mothers, as contributors to the community through volunteer work, and as members of the labor force in careers outside the home. We fully endorse the principle of equal rights, equal opportunities and equal responsibilities for women, and believe that progress in these areas is needed to achieve the full realization of the potentials of American women both in the home and outside the home.

We reaffirm the President's pledge earlier this year: "The Administration will . . . continue its strong efforts to open equal opportunities for women, recognizing clearly that women are often denied such opportunities today. While every woman may not want a career outside the home, every woman should have the freedom to choose whatever career she wishes—and an equal chance to pursue it."

This Administration has done more than any before it to help women of America achieve equality of opportunity.

Because of its efforts, more top-level and middle-management positions in the Federal Government are held by women than ever before. The President has appointed a woman as his special assistant in the White House, specifically charged with the recruitment of women for policy-making jobs in the United States Government. Women have also been named to high positions in the Civil Service Commission and the Department of Labor to ensure equal opportunities for employment and advancement at all levels of the Federal service.

In addition we have:

Significantly increased resources devoted to enforcement of the Fair Labor Standards Act, providing equal pay for equal work;

Required all firms doing business with the Government to have affirmative action plans for the hiring and promotion of women;

Requested Congress to expand the jurisdiction of the Commission on Civil Rights to cover sex discrimination;

Recommended and supported passage of Title IX of the Higher Education Act opposing discrimination against women in educational institutions;

Supported the Equal Employment Opportunity Act of 1972 giving the Equal Employment Opportunity Commission enforcement power in sex discrimination cases;

Continued our support of the Equal Rights Amendment to the Constitution, our Party being the first national party to back this Amendment.

Other factors beyond outright employer discrimination—the lack of child care facilities, for example—can limit job opportunities for women. For lower and middle income families, the President supported and signed into law a new tax provision which makes many child care expenses deductible for working parents. Part of the President's recent welfare reform proposal would provide comprehensive day care services so that women on welfare can work.

We believe the primary responsibility for a child's care and upbringing lies with the family. However, we recognize that for economic and many other reasons many parents require assistance in the care of their children.

To help meet this need, we favor the development of publicly or privately run, voluntary, comprehensive, quality day care services, locally controlled but federally assisted, with the requirement that the recipients of these services will pay their fair share of the costs according to their ability.

We oppose ill-considered proposals, incapable of being administered effectively, which would heavily engage the Federal Government in this area.

To continue progress for women's rights, we will work toward:

Ratification of the Equal Rights Amendment;

Appointment of women to highest level positions in the Federal Government, including the Cabinet and Supreme Court;

Equal pay for equal work;

Elimination of discrimination against women at all levels in Federal Government;

Elimination of discrimination against women in the criminal justice system, in sentencing, rehabilitation and prison facilities;

Increased opportunities for the part-time employment of women, and expanded training programs for women who want to reenter the labor force;

Elimination of economic discrimination against women in credit, mortgage, insurance, property, rental and finance contracts.

We pledge vigorous enforcement of all Federal statutes and executive orders barring job discrimination on the basis of sex.

We are proud of the contributions made by women to better government. We regard the active involvement of women at all levels of the political process, from precinct to national status, as of great importance to our country. The Republican Party welcomes and encourages their maximum participation.

*Older Americans*

We believe our Nation must develop a new awareness of the attitudes and needs of our older citizens. Elderly Americans are far too often forgotten Americans, relegated to lives of idleness and isolation by a society bemused with the concerns of other groups. We are distressed by the tendency of many Americans to ignore the heart-

break and hardship resulting from the generation gap which separates so many of our people from those who have reached the age of retirement. We deplore what is tantamount to cruel discrimination —age discrimination in employment, and the discrimination of neglect and indifference, perhaps the cruelest of all.

We commit ourselves to helping older Americans achieve greater self-reliance and greater opportunities for direct participation in the activities of our society. We believe that the later years should be, not isolated years, not years of dependency, but years of fulfillment and dignity. We believe our older people are not to be regarded as a burden but rather should be valuable participants in our society. We believe their judgment, their experience, and their talents are immensely valuable to our country.

Because we so believe, we are seeking and have sought in many ways to help older Americans— for example:

Federal programs of direct benefit to older Americans have increased more than $16 billion these past four years;

As part of·this, social security benefits are more than 50 per cent higher than they were four years ago, the largest increase in the history of social security;

Social security benefits have become inflation proof by making them rise automatically to match cost-of-living increases, a protection long advocated by the Republican Party;

We have upgraded nursing homes.

Expenditures under the Older Americans Act have gone up 800 per cent since President Nixon took office, with a strong emphasis on programs enabling older Americans to live dignified, independent lives in their own homes.

The valuable counsel of older people has been sought directly through the White House Conference on Aging. The President has appointed high-level advisers on the problems of the aging to his personal staff.

We have urged upon the opposition Congress— again, typically to no avail—numerous additional programs of benefit to the elderly. We will continue pressing for these new initiatives:

Increase the amount of money a person can earn without losing social security benefits;

Increase widow, widower, and delayed retirement benefits;

Improve the effectiveness of Medicare, including elimination of the monthly premium required under Part B of Medicare—the equivalent of more than a three per cent social security increase;

Strengthen private pension plans through tax deductions to encourage their expansion, improved vesting, and protection of the investments in these funds;

Reform our tax system so that persons 65 or over will receive increased tax-free income;

Encourage volunteer service activities for older Americans, such as the Retired Senior Volunteer Program and the Foster Grandparents Program;

Give special attention to bringing full government services within the reach of the elderly in rural areas who are often unable to share fully in their deserved benefits because of geographic inaccessibility;

Upgrade other Federal activities important to the elderly including programs for nutrition, housing and nursing homes, transportation, consumer protection, and elimination of age discrimination in government and private employment.

We encourage constructive efforts which will help older citizens to be better informed about existing programs and services designed to meet their needs, and we pledge to cut away excessive Federal redtape to make it easier for older Americans to receive the benefits to which they are entitled.

*Working Men and Women*

The skill, industry and productivity of American workers are the driving force of our free economy. The Nation's labor unions, comprised of millions of working people, have advanced the well-being not only of their members but also of our entire free-enterprise system. We of the Republican Party reaffirm our strong endorsement of Organized Labor's key role in our national life.

We salute the statesmanship of the labor union movement. Time and time again, at crucial moments, it has voiced its outspoken support for a firm and effective foreign policy and for keeping the Armed Forces of the United States modern and strong.

The American labor movement and the Republican Party have always worked against the spread of totalitarian forms of government. Together we can continue to preserve in America the best system of government ever devised for human happiness and fulfillment.

We are for the right of American workers and their families to enjoy and to retain to the greatest possible extent the rewards of their own labor.

We regard collective bargaining as the cornerstone of the Nation's labor relations policy. The government's role is not to encroach upon this process but rather to aid the differing parties to make collective bargaining more effective both for themselves and for the public. In furtherance of that concept, we will continue to develop procedures whereby the imagination, ingenuity and knowledge of labor and management can more effectively seek solutions for such problems as structural adjustment and productivity.

In the construction industry, for example, we will build on a new joint effort between government and all parts of the industry to solve such problems as seasonality and varying peaks of demand to ensure a stable growth in the number of skilled craftsmen.

We call upon management and labor to devote their best efforts to finding better ways to conduct labor-management relations so the good of all the people can be advanced without strikes or lockouts.

We will continue to search for realistic and fair solutions to emergency labor disputes, guided by two basic principles; first, that the health and safety of the people of the United States should always be paramount; and second, that collective bargaining should be kept as free as possible from government interference.

For mine health and safety, we have implemented the most comprehensive legislation in the Nation's history, resulting in a major reduction in mine-related accidents. We pledge continued advancement of the health and safety of workers.

We will continue to press for improved pension vesting and other statutory protections to assure that Americans will not lose their hard-earned retirement income.

We pledge further modernization of the Federal Civil Service System, including emphasis on executive development. We rededicate ourselves to promotion on merit, equal opportunity, and the setting of clear incentives for higher productivity. We will give continuing close attention to the evolving labor-management relationship in the Federal service.

We pledge realistic programs of education and training so that all Americans able to do so can make their own way, on their own ability, receiving an equal and fair chance to advance themselves. We flatly oppose the notion that the hardearned tax dollars of American workers should be used to support those who can work but choose not to, and who believe that the world owes them a living free from any responsibility or care.

We are proud of our many other solid achievements on behalf of America's working people—for example:

Nearly five million additional workers brought under the coverage of the unemployment insurance system, and eligibility deadlines twice extended;

Funding for more than 166,000 jobs under the Emergency Employment Act;

Expansion of vocational education and manpower training programs;

Use of the long-neglected Trade Expansion Act to help workers who lose their jobs because of imports. We strongly favor vigorous competition by American business in the world market but in ways that do not displace American jobs;

Negotiation of long-needed limitations on imports of man-made fibers, textiles and other products, thus protecting American jobs.

We share the desire of all Americans for continued prosperity in peacetime. We will work closely with labor and management toward our mutual goal of assuring a job for every man and woman seeking the dignity of work.

*Ending Discrimination*

From its beginning, our Party has led the way for equal rights and equal opportunity. This great tradition has been carried forward by the Nixon Administration.

Through our efforts de jure segregation is virtually ended. We pledge continuation of these efforts until no American schoolchild suffers educational deprivation because of the color of his skin or the language he speaks and all school children are receiving high quality education. In pursuit of this goal, we have proposed $2.5 billion of Federal aid to school districts to improve educational opportunities and build facilities for disadvantaged children. Further to assure minority progress, we have provided more support to predominantly black colleges than ever before—twice the amount being spent when President Nixon took office.

Additionally, we have strengthened Federal enforcement of equal opportunity laws. Spending for civil rights enforcement has been increased from $75 million to $602 million—concrete evidence of our commitment to equal justice for all. The President also supported and signed into law the Equal Employment Opportunity Act of 1972, which makes the Equal Employment Opportunity Commission a much more powerful body.

Working closely with leaders of construction unions, we have initiated 50 "home-town" plans which call for more than 35,000 additional minority hirings in the building trades during the next four years. We will continue to search out new employment opportunities for minorities in other fields as well. We believe such new jobs can and should be created without displacing those already at work. We will give special consideration to minority Americans who live and make their way in the rural regions of our Country—Americans too often bypassed in the advances of the general society.

We have made unprecedented progress in strengthening minority participation in American business. We created the Office of Minority Business Enterprise in March 1969 to coordinate the Federal programs assisting members of minority groups who seek to establish or expand businesses. We have more than tripled Federal loans, guarantees and grants to minority-owned businesses. More minority Americans are now in our Nation's economic mainstream than at any other time in our history, and we pledge every effort to expand these gains.

Minority businesses now receive 16 per cent of the Small Business Administration dollar—more than double the proportion in 1968. Many Minority Enterprise Small Business Investment Companies have been licensed since 1969 to provide venture capital for minority enterprises. More than $200 million is now available through this program, and we have requested additional funding.

In late 1970, we initiated a combined Government-private program to increase minority bank deposits. This year our goal of $100 million has been reached four times over.

We pledge to carry forward our efforts to place minority citizens in responsible positions—efforts we feel are already well under way. During the last four years the percentage of minority Federal employees has risen to a record high of almost 20 per cent and, perhaps more important, the quality of jobs for minority Americans has improved. We have recruited more minority citizens for top managerial posts in Civil Service than ever before. We will see that our progress in this area will continue and grow.

In 1970 President Nixon approved strong new amendments to the Voting Rights Act of 1965, and we pledge continued vigilance to ensure that the rights affirmed by this act are upheld.

The cultural diversity of America's heritage groups has always been a source of strength for our society and our Party. We reaffirm our commitment to the basic American values which have made this Nation the land of opportunity for these groups, originating from all sectors of the world, from Asia to Africa to Europe to Latin America. We will continue our Party's open-door policy and work to assure all minorities full opportunity for participation in the political process. We pledge vigorous support of the Bilingual Act and the Ethnic Studies Heritage Act.

### Spanish-Speaking Americans

In recognition of the significant contributions to our country by our proud and independent Spanish-speaking citizens, we have developed a comprehensive program to help achieve equal opportunity.

During the last four years Spanish-speaking Americans have achieved a greater role in national affairs. More than thirty have been appointed to high federal positions.

To provide the same learning opportunities enjoyed by other American children, we have increased bilingual education programs almost sixfold since 1969. We initiated a 16-point employment program to help Spanish-speaking workers, created the National Economic Development Association to promote Spanish-speaking business development and expanded economic development opportunities in Spanish-speaking communities.

We will work for the use of bilingual staffs in localities where this language capability is desirable for effective health care.

### Indians, Alaska Natives, and Hawaiians

President Nixon has evolved a totally new Indian policy which we fully support. The opposition Congress, by inaction on most of the President's proposals, has thwarted Indian rights and opportunities.

We commend the Department of the Interior for its stalwart defense of Indian land and water rights, and we urge the Congress to join in support of that effort. We further request Congress to permit Indian tribal governments to assume control over the programs of the Departments of Interior and Health, Education and Welfare in their homelands, to assure Indians a role in determining how funds can best be used for their children's schools, to expand Indian economic development opportunity, to triple the funds for Indian credit and create a new Assistant Secretary of the Interior for Indian and Territorial Affairs.

These reforms, all urged by the President, have been ignored by the Congress. We—with the Indian people—are impatiently waiting.

Knowing the Indians' love for their land and recognizing the many wrongs committed in years past, the President has restored Blue Lake in New Mexico to the Taos Pueblo and the Mt. Adams area in Washington to the Yakima Nation. We are seeking to protect Indian water rights in Pyramid Lake by bringing suit in the Supreme Court.

We are fully aware of the severe problems facing the Menominee Indians in seeking to have Federal recognition restored to their tribe and promise a complete and sympathetic examination of their pleas.

We have increased the Bureau of Indian Affairs' budget by 214 per cent, nearly doubled funds for Indian health, and are arranging with tribal leaders for the allocation of Bureau funds in accordance with priorities set by the tribal governments themselves.

We pledge continued attention to the needs of off-reservation Indians and have launched demonstration projects at Indian centers in nine major cities. We are determined that the first Americans will not be the forgotten Americans, and that their rights will be respected.

We will continue the policy of Indian preference in hiring and promotion and apply it to all levels, including management and supervisory positions in those agencies with programs affecting Indian peoples.

The standard of living of Indian Americans is still far below that of any of the peoples of the United States. This intolerable level of existence should be alleviated by the enactment of new legislation designed to further Indian self-determination without termination and to close this economic gap and raise the Indian standard of life to that of the rest of America. We favor the development of such legislation in the 93d Congress.

At the President's recommendation, the Congress voted an Alaska Native Claims Settlement which confirms the titles of the Eskimos, Indians and Aleuts to 40 million acres and compensates them with a generous cash settlement.

We will also preserve and continue to protect the Hawaiian Homes Commission Act which provides land already set aside for Hawaiians for homes and the opportunity to preserve their culture.

Our achievements for human dignity and opportunity are specific and real, not idle promises. They have brought tremendous progress to many thousands of minority citizens and made our society more just for all.

We will press on with our fight against social injustice and discrimination, building upon the achievements already made. Knowing that none of us can reap the fullest blessings of liberty until all of us can, we reaffirm our commitment to the upward struggle for universal freedom led by Abraham Lincoln a century ago.

## Consumers

The American consumer has a right to product safety; clearly specified qualities and values, honest descriptions and guarantees, fair credit procedures, and due recourse for fraud and deception. We are addressing these concerns forcefully, with executive action and legislative and legal initiatives.

The issues involved in this accelerating awareness on the part of consumers lie close to the heart of the dynamic American market: Good products at fair prices made it great; the same things will keep it great.

Enlightened business management is as interested in consumer protection and consumer education as are consumers themselves. In a marketplace as competitive and diverse as ours, a company's future depends on the reputation of its products. One safety error can wipe out an established firm overnight.

Unavoidably, the remoteness of business management from the retail counter tends to hamper consumers in resolving quality and performance questions. Technical innovations make it harder for the consumer to evaluate new products. Legal complexities often deny efficient remedies for deception or product failure.

To assist consumers and business, President Nixon established the first Office of Consumer Affairs in the White House and made its Director a member of his personal staff and of the Cost of Living Council. We have also proposed a Buyer's Bill of Rights, including:

Federal authority for the regulation of hazardous consumer products;

Requirement of full disclosure of the terms of warranties and guarantees in language all can understand.

We support the establishment of an independent Consumer Protection Agency to present the consumer's case in proceedings before Federal agencies and also a consumer product safety agency in the Department of Health, Education and Welfare. We oppose punitive proposals which are more anti-business than pro-consumer.

We pledge vigorous enforcement of all consumer protection laws and to foster more consumer education as a vital necessity in a marketplace ever increasing in variety and complexity.

## Veterans

We regard our Nation's veterans precisely as our President does:

"Americans have long known that those who defended the great values of our Nation in wartime are of great value to the Nation when the war is over. It is traditional that the American veteran has been helped by his Nation so that he can create his own 'peace story', a story of prosperity, independence and dignity.

"Veterans benefit programs have therefore become more than a recognition for services performed in the past; they have become an investment in the future of the veteran and of his country."

Under Republican leadership, far more for our veterans is being done than ever before:

G.I. Bill education benefits have been increased more than 35 per cent. Vietnam-era veterans have the highest assistance levels in history to help them pursue educational opportunities.

Major cost-of-living adjustments have been made in compensation and pension payments.

Medical services are the best in the history of the Veterans Administration and now include a strong new drug treatment and rehabilitation program.

Disability benefits have been increased.

G.I. home loan benefits have been expanded and improved.

The total Administration commitment is massive—$12.4 billion for this fiscal year. This is the largest Veterans Administration budget in history, and the third largest of all Federal agencies and departments.

We are giving the highest priority to the employment problems of Vietnam veterans. In 1971 we initiated a comprehensive program which recently placed more than one million Vietnam-era veterans in jobs, training and education programs.

For the future, we pledge:

Continuation of the Veterans Administration as a strong, independent agency;

Continuation of an independent system of Veterans Administration health care facilities to provide America's veterans with the best medical care available, including appropriate attention to the problems of the ex-serviceman afflicted with drug and alcohol problems;

Continuing attention to the needs of the Vietnam-era veteran, with special emphasis on employment opportunities, education and housing.

Continuation of our efforts to raise GI Bill education benefits to a level commensurate with post-World War II benefits in adjusted dollars;

Continued effort for a better coordinated national policy on cemeteries and burial benefits for veterans.

We will not fail our obligation to the Nation's 29 million veterans and will stand ever watchful of their needs and rights.

## CONCLUSION

The record is clear.

More than any President, Richard Nixon has achieved major changes in policy and direction in our government. He has restored faith—faith that our system will indeed reflect the will of the people —faith that there will be a new era of peace and human progress at home and around the world.

To be sure there is unfinished business on the agenda of our ever-restless Nation. We have great concern for those who have not participated more fully in the general prosperity. The twin evils of crime and drug abuse are still to be conquered. Peace in the world is not yet won.

But Republican leadership has restored stability and sanity to our land once again. We have vigorously attacked every major problem.

Once again our direction is peace; once again our determination is national strength; once again we are prospering; once again, on a host of fronts, we are making progress.

Now we look to tomorrow.

We pledge ourselves to go forward at an accelerated pace—with a determination and zeal unmatched before.

In four years we mark the 200th anniversary of the freest, most productive, most benevolent Nation of all human history. In four years we celebrate one of man's highest achievements—two hundred years as a constitutional republic founded on the noble concept that every person is a sovereign being, possessed of dignity and inalienable rights.

Almost two centuries ago, the Founding Fathers envisioned a Nation of free people, at peace with themselves and the world—each with equal opportunity to pursue happiness in his own way. Much of that dream has come true; much is still to be fulfilled.

We, the Republican Party, pledge ourselves to go forward, hand-in-hand with every citizen, to solve those problems that yet stand in the way of realizing that more perfect union, the dream of the Founding Fathers—a dream enhanced by the free and generous gift of people working together, not in shifting alliances of separated minorities, but in unison of spirit and purpose. We cannot favor, nor can we respect, the notion of group isolation in our United States of America. We must not divide and weaken ourselves by attitudes or policies which would segregate our citizens into separate racial, ethnic, economic, religious or social groups. It is the striving of all of us—our striving together as Americans—that will move our Nation continually onward to our Founders' dream.

Building on the foundations of peace in the world, and reason and prosperity at home, our Republican Party pledges a new era of progress for man—progress toward more freedom, toward greater protection of individual rights, toward more security from want and fear, toward greater fulfillment and happiness for all.

We pledge to the American people that the 200th anniversary of this Nation in 1976 will be more than a celebration of two centuries of unequaled success; we pledge it also to be the beginning of the third and greatest century for all of our countrymen and, we pray, for all people in the world.

## Socialist Labor Platform 1972

*During the three centuries since it emerged from the expiring feudal order, capitalism has profoundly transformed the world.*

*It has revolutionized the mode and scale of production.*

*It has revolutionized transportation and communication.*

*It has gathered the scattered continents into an interdependent global economy.*

*It has created the industrial means of abundance for all mankind.*

*But in accomplishing this tremendous historic task, capitalism has exacted a terrible price.*

*It has wantonly squandered the planet's natural wealth and polluted its lands, skies and waters.*

*It has repeatedly pitted nations against nations in devastating, decimating wars.*

*It has inexcusably perpetuated poverty and insecurity, thereby fomenting racial and ethnic strife.*

*It has engendered a social climate that breeds corruption, crime, drug abuse and mental illness.*

Social systems are mortal.

Like the human beings who compose them, they are born, mature, decline, and eventually die.

The history of capitalist society shows it is no exception. It too has moved from birth through maturity to decline, and is now approaching death.

Capitalism is dying because of a serious malfunction. This malfunction is not just a disorder of the system's old age. It first appeared in capitalism's lusty youth and has been revealing itself ever since through the periodic business crises that have punctuated capitalism's life.

In these crises, society has again and again faced an absurd catastrophe: an epidemic of "overproduction," with millions of workers deprived of their livelihoods because they were producing too much.

Not one of these catastrophes has ever resulted from an overproduction of society's needs. On the contrary, each time immense social wants were left unsatisfied as industry shut down.

Every business crisis has thus demonstrated anew that capitalist industry does not operate primarily to satisfy social wants. It produces to sell at a profit. And whenever more goods and services are being produced than can be profitably sold, capitalist industry naturally cuts back its operations.

### WHY CAPITALISM "OVERPRODUCES"

The recurrent crises have been inevitable because capitalism is basically geared to overproduce its market. The greatest part of that market consists of worker consumers. As producers, however, the workers are paid only a small part of the value of their products. That explains how capitalist profits are realized. But that also explains why the workers' purchasing power is nowhere near sufficient to absorb the full national output.

The ten-year-long crisis of the thirties marked the beginning of capitalism's end. It was the first in which drying up the oversupply of goods by holding down production failed to bring economic recovery. It was the first in which the capitalist State had to intervene and attempt a massive stimulation of demand.

The principal stimulant used was government deficit spending, the Keynesian prescription inspired by a frank recognition of capitalism's inherent malfunction. In the doses administered, the prescription proved to be inadequate.

Meanwhile, the struggle to win foreign markets for products that could not be sold at home embroiled the capitalist powers in an escalating commercial warfare which culminated in military conflict. Once World War II broke out, the problem of "overproduction" was temporarily overcome.

The problem remained dormant for a brief period after peace returned. As soon, though, as capitalist industry had satisfied the deferred demand of the war years, plus the orders arising from the rehabilitation of war-torn countries, "overproduction" reappeared. And again war stepped in to relieve it—the Korean War and the Cold War.

### STIMULANTS HAVE SIDE EFFECTS

Since then, the prolonged war in Vietnam and huge deficit spending in other directions have served to further postpone capitalism's final, total collapse. But these stimulants cannot go on doing so forever because they are having dangerous side effects that must ultimately ensure the system's collapse.

The most dangerous is inflation. Almost 40 years of government deficit spending has inordinately inflated the national money supply and thus depreciated the dollar to a fraction of its former value. As the dollar's value has fallen, prices have risen correspondingly, causing a serious erosion of domestic purchasing power.

Moreover, an acceleration of inflation in recent years pushed prices so high that American products found themselves being undersold by foreign products here at home as well as abroad. And to make bad enough worse, the long-standing international monetary arrangements based on the dollar were finally shattered by its steepening depreciation.

*So, capitalism is plainly damned if it feeds inflation . . . but equally damned if it doesn't.* For, when President Nixon opted in 1969 to cease deficit spending, his decision brought on a business slump. And despite the fact that he subsequently reversed himself and began outspending his predecessors, the downturn stubbornly refused to become an upturn. The only thing that headed upward again was inflation—and, consequently, prices.

### Emergency Economic Controls

By mid-1971, the situation had grown so grave that President Nixon, responding to capitalist forebodings of a complete breakdown, acted to halt inflation by imposing economic controls. Experience with Phases One and Two indicates that the controls are merely aggravating capitalism's basic plight because, while they are necessarily and conspicuously failing to curb inflation and prices, they are curbing wages and therefore making still smaller the part of the national output that the workers can buy.

A similar result is being produced by technology, which capitalism compulsively continues to revolutionize. Each improvement in the methods or tools of production that increases the workers' productivity also increases the already large difference between the value represented by their wages and that embodied in their products.

*Accordingly, the inherent malfunction that engulfed capitalism in a great crisis of "overproduction" at the outset of the thirties is unmistakably driving it towards a far greater one in the not distant future.* When that far greater crisis arrives, the enormously swollen public debt and recklessly depreciated currency with which the system has bought a longer lease on life will provide two big nails for its coffin. The vast industrial capacity built to meet the demands of war will provide a third.

### Workers Have Historic Task

And capitalism has prepared its gravediggers. They are the very workers whom the system has brought together and trained to carry on production. A total economic collapse is going to blast any remaining illusions workers may have that comfortable, secure lives are possible for them within capitalist society. They will be at last compelled to recognize that their well-being and aspirations require the construction of a new form of social organization.

Once the workers have reached a revolutionary frame of mind, they will quickly discover a number of important truths: They will discover that they are endowed with an irresistible power for social change by virtue of their industrial role. They will discover that capitalist industrialization has laid the foundation and erected the framework of a new society that can ensure their prosperity and security. They will discover that they have an inalienable right to reconstruct society and the possibility of democratically affirming this right via the ballot.

The workers will most certainly discover these truths because the Socialist Labor Party has for many, many years been exerting itself to make them known and will keep on so exerting itself throughout the approaching national campaign and in the days that follow.

Furthermore, when the revolutionary moment comes, the workers will have available a simple, workable program with which they can consummate the needed social reconstruction—the program of Socialist Industrial Unionism.

That program aims to unite the workers politically as well as industrially. Political unity is necessary because it will enable the worker majority to deliver a democratic mandate for social ownership of industry and production for social use. While industrial unity will supply the indispensable power with which to enforce and execute that mandate.

*Through their Socialist Industrial Unions, the workers themselves can take peaceful possession of the nation's economy in the name of all society. Then on the basis of their Industrial Unions, they can set up a democratic administration of production for the benefit of all society. This administration will be composed of representatives elected from the various industries by the workers voting in their respective industries. It will be an industrial self-government, an economic democracy, the highest, fullest freedom the human race has ever known.*

## Socialist Workers Platform 1972

The Democratic and Republican parties bear joint responsibility for the situation facing the people of the United States.

The Republican Nixon has carried on the military intervention in Indochina initiated by the Democrats Kennedy and Johnson. The White House continues to order murderous air raids on the people and countryside of Indochina. Despite Nixon's election promise to end the war, Vietnamese, Cambodians, Laotians, and Americans are still dying.

At home, continued war spending gives added impetus to the inflationary spiral. Working people are being forced to pay the astronomical costs of the war. While prices and taxes keep going up, wage controls imposed by the government prevent working people from gaining fair wage adjustments to offset the soaring cost of living. Skyrocketing prices make the continued high unemployment even more painful.

These economic hardships inflicted upon the American people result from the needs of the very wealthy—a tiny minority who run this country—to improve their competitive position on the world market. In line with this, the bosses are determined to hold real wages down and to squeeze more out of the workers by intensifying speedups and layoffs.

The Black community is confronted with savage police assaults and political frame-ups of activists such as Angela Davis, the Soledad Brothers, and others. Afro-Americans face racial discrimination in housing, education, job opportunities, and every other area of economic, social, and political life. Similar problems confront Chicanos, Puerto Ricans, Native Americans, and other oppressed nationalities.

Responsibility for the erosion of civil liberties in the United States lies squarely with the Republicans and Democrats. The twin parties of big business have failed to offer any meaningful programs to meet the needs of women; they have turned a deaf ear to the demands of American

youth; and they have refused to deal effectively with the ecological disaster that faces the country. Virtually an entire generation of young people feels increasingly alienated because of the sterility and decay marking the culture of American capitalism.

### THE CAPITALIST SYSTEM

The basic policies pursued by the Democrats and Republicans are not accidental, nor merely the results of decisions made by individual politicians. The policies of the capitalist parties flow from the needs of the capitalist system itself and from the outlook of the ruling capitalist class.

The Vietnam war is a prime example. The objectives of the U.S. government have nothing to do with "democracy" or "freedom" in Indochina. The war is part of a global strategy of counterrevolution designed to maintain world capitalism and to preserve the position of U.S. imperialism on an international scale.

This same policy has led to U.S. military interventions in the Dominican Republic, Cuba, the Congo, Korea, Lebanon, and many other countries—under both Democratic and Republican administrations. The capitalist politicians consider it part of the "game plan" to send young men to die all over the world to maintain and extend the capitalist system and capitalist profits.

Racism is also woven into the fabric of American capitalism. Racial oppression pays off in profits for the capitalist class, providing a pool of cheap labor to be drawn upon in periods of expansion. Racism is also used to justify imperialist domination of the colonial world by perpetuating the myth that it is "natural" for rich nations to exploit poor nations. Racism also serves to keep white workers from realizing that their interests lie with the Black and Brown masses, and not with the white capitalist rulers.

The imposition of wage controls shows once again how the capitalist government stands on the side of the rich and against the poor. Wage controls pare down the standard of living of the working people. They benefit only the bosses, who are already hauling in superprofits.

The government of the United States is not a neutral defender of the interests of the "public," as it claims to be. It is the instrument through which the profit-hungry capitalist class runs society in accordance with its own interests.

The passing differences that crop up among

politicians of the two capitalist parties reflect tactical differences over how best to maintain capitalist rule or factional squabbles over control of the pork barrel of government patronage. There is no fundamental difference between the Democrats and Republicans—they are both committed to preserving capitalist exploitation.

Regardless of how "sincere" or "honest" or even "militant" the politicians of the Democratic and Republican parties make themselves out to be, no real improvement in the conditions of working people can come about through supporting them. There is no "lesser evil" among the candidates of the capitalist parties.

Social progress has never been achieved except when masses of people have organized themselves and fought for it. That is how the capitalist system itself, along with all its evils, will be uprooted.

More and more people are coming to the conclusion that from the point of view of satisfying human needs, this system is totally irrational.

Millions of Americans, not to mention those in other countries, are underfed, while the government pays farmers not to produce. Why? Because producing abundant, inexpensive food isn't *profitable*.

In the richest of all countries, the crisis in housing in our cities has reached the proportions of a national disaster. Yet there is virtually no low-cost housing construction. Why? Because building low-cost housing is not *profitable*.

Today's technology makes possible substantial improvements in the quality of life for all Americans, yet this technological capacity is not used to make adequate medical care available to working people; it is not used in any effective way to stop pollution; it is not used to protect consumers against shoddy, worthless, or dangerous products. Why? Because none of this is as *profitable* as war spending or defrauding the consumer.

Billions of dollars are spent on instruments of mass destruction to be used in nuclear, chemical, and biological warfare; other billions are put into gadgets to be rocketed into outer space. Yet the government refuses with utmost callousness to make possible a decent life for millions of older citizens who live in poverty on paltry pensions or Social Security benefits. Funds are denied to schools, libraries, and hospitals. Child-care centers are not built. Why? Because under this system the private profit of the few comes first.

WHAT SOCIALISTS WANT

The Socialist Workers Party is campaigning in 1972 for the following program to meet the crisis facing the American people:

*Bring All the Troops Home Now! Stop the Bombing of Indochina!*

Nixon talks about "winding down the war" to confuse the majority of Americans into thinking that he is heeding their demand for peace. Yet the killing goes on and Nixon escalates the air war. Many politicians talk about "setting a date" for withdrawal—sometime in the future. But what the Vietnamese people want, and what the majority of Americans want, is the withdrawal of all U.S. troops and war matériel right now!

Abolish the draft! No more draftees for Washington's war machine. Support the right of GIs to freely express their views on any issues of concern to them, including racism in the military and the need to end the war in Indochina. Organize a national referendum to give the people the right to vote on whether to continue the war or end it at once. Unconditional amnesty for all those in jail or in exile who have been accused of evading the draft or deserting.

Dismantle all U.S. bases around the world. End all U.S. interference in the internal affairs of other countries.

Support the struggles of the Asian, Latin American, African, and Arab peoples for national independence and social liberation. Support national liberation struggles such as those in Ireland, Palestine, Bangladesh, Québec, and Puerto Rico.

*For a Program to Meet the Needs of Working People*

To fight the government's assault upon the rights and wages of the working people, the Socialist Workers Party calls for a united mobilization of the entire labor movement. We propose the convocation of a national conference of the labor movement, with delegates democratically elected by rank-and-file workers, to map out a campaign of struggle on all fronts against wage controls, inflation, and unemployment.

The Socialist Workers Party proposes the following program for an effective, united challenge to the government's antilabor policies:

Opposition to all wage controls.

End the war and war spending, the most important cause of inflation.

Cost-of living escalator clauses in all contracts to protect workers against inflation. Include cost-of-living increases in all pensions and social security payments, and in welfare and unemployment benefits.

Organize committees of the unions and consumer groups with the power to regulate prices.

To combat unemployment, shorten the workweek—with no reduction in pay—to whatever extent necessary to spread the available work to all those who need a job. As an immediate step, reduce the workweek to 30 hours.

Launch a crash program of public works to provide jobs for the unemployed.

Guaranteed unemployment compensation at union wages for all those out of work, whether or not they have worked before.

While the corporations rake in superprofits, they turn more and more to the government for aid in their crusade against the standard of living and democratic rights of working people. The right to strike is an unconditional right. Repeal all laws restricting the right to strike, and all laws undermining union independence from the government, such as the Taft-Hartley Act. For an end to "special" antistrike legislation, such as was threatened in the West Coast longshoremen's strike.

For rank-and-file control over all union affairs.

For equal rights in the unions and on the job for Black and Raza workers and for women, and for full union support to their struggles. Preferential hiring for women and for workers of the oppressed nationalities.

For an independent labor party based on the trade unions to defend the rights and standard of living of working people against the parties of the bosses, and to fight for a workers government.

### End the Burden on Low-Income Families

Today, one of every 10 U.S. families is living in poverty. Yet, while welfare rolls continue to rise, welfare spending is cut back.

To help alleviate the problems faced by working people and the unemployed, we propose:

Abolish all taxes on incomes under $10,000 a year. Confiscate all profits on war goods. A 100-per cent tax on incomes above $25,000 per year.

Roll back all rents on apartments to a maximum of 10 per cent of family income.

Free quality medical and dental care for all, through socialization of medicine.

For a food and drug administration controlled by workers and consumers, not the food and drug corporations.

For a nationally coordinated program to build safe, efficient, comfortable mass public transit systems. All mass transit to be free.

### For the Democratic Right of Black People to Control Their Own Communities

Slumlords and price-gouging merchants are a permanent part of life in the Black communities. Inequality of wages is being perpetuated by wage controls imposed by the Democrats and Republicans in office. Black youth continue to be drafted and killed in disproportionate numbers in the war in Indochina.

Black people should have control over schools, police, housing programs, hospitals, and other institutions in the Black community. Launch a crash program with federal, state, and city funds to build new housing, decent schools, and other projects in the Black communities to overcome years of deprivation and discrimination. The funds should be administered by the Black community.

Support busing in cases where Black people see that it can help obtain better education for their children. All decisions about busing should be made by the Black community.

Appropriate whatever funds are necessary to provide jobs for all Afro-Americans who need them, with preferential hiring and upgrading as needed to equalize opportunities.

It is the right of Afro-Americans to keep arms and organize themselves for self-defense against all attacks.

Black people are hampered in their struggle because they are denied equal political representation and lack political power. To fight effectively for control of the Black community and to help win the struggle for justice and equality, a mass Black political party is needed, a party independent of the Democrats and Republicans. The Gary, Ind., national Black political conference of nearly 8,000 Blacks showed the growing sentiment for Black political action and was an indication of the potential support such a party can have.

A mass Black political party, to be effective, would do much more than participate in elections.

Gearing its demands around actions, it would seek to mobilize all the forces of the Black people in the struggle to win Black community demands.

### Chicano Liberation

The massive Chicano Moratorium marches against the war have dramatized Chicano opposition to the slaughter in Indochina. Yet La Raza still suffers disproportionately from the draft and war casualties. Chicanos are denied the use of the Spanish language—in school, on the job, in the courtroom, and in prison. Discrimination in housing, education, and jobs confronts Chicanos at every turn.

Chicano and Mexican workers are continually harassed by U.S. government immigration agents. Attempts to organize agricultural workers are met with violence and other strikebreaking tactics by the growers.

The true history of the Chicano people is not taught, and racist stereotypes continue to appear in textbooks and advertising.

Chicanos have begun to organize themselves independently of the capitalist parties through La Raza Unida parties. The fight for Chicano control of the Chicano communities will be advanced by building these parties into mass parties on a national as well as a local scale.

### End the Oppression of Women

Laws restricting abortions deny women the right to choose whether to bear children. The Socialist Workers Party calls for repeal of all anti-abortion laws and removal of all restrictions on contraceptive information and devices. End forced sterilization.

For a massive government-funded program to develop safe and effective birth-control devices. Abortion and contraceptives to be free on demand.

Equal pay for equal work. For ratification of the Equal Rights Amendment, and enforcement of Title VII of the 1964 Civil Rights Act, which prohibits discrimination on the basis of sex. Protective legislation beneficial to women should be extended to cover men as well.

End discrimination against women in education. For open admissions to all institutions of higher learning.

For free, quality 24-hour child-care facilities, available to all children.

### Halt the Destruction of the Environment

The rape of the environment by the big corporations continues unchecked by government control. Legislation without teeth allows polluters to continue practices that threaten the entire continent with ruin.

For a 100 per cent tax on every cent in profits made by the polluters. All corporations to be compelled, under threat of confiscation, to install pollution-control equipment and to meet standards set and enforced by committees of workers and consumers.

### Support the Demands of America's Youth

Students and young working people face unique problems in this society. Students are told to "stay in school," but even college diplomas no longer guarantee a decent job. What is taught in school is increasingly irrelevant to today's problems and needs.

Cutbacks in funds for education and soaring college tuition costs keep many young people out of school. We call for free education through the university level, with government stipends for those students who need it. For guaranteed jobs when students leave school.

For *student-faculty* control of education. School facilities should be made available to the antiwar movement, the women's liberation movement, the labor movement, the oppressed nationalities, and others fighting for social progress.

Abolish all laws that discriminate against youth. Full constitutional rights for all students. For the right of young people to serve on juries, to register and vote where they go to school, and to run for public office.

### End Inhuman Treatment of Prisoners

Prisoners under capitalism are instruments of oppression against the most exploited sections of the population. They will have no place in a socialist society. As immediate steps toward establishing basic civil and human rights, we demand: An end to censorship and restrictions on mail, books, and newspapers. All labor to be paid at union wages. Humane treatment and conditions for all prisoners.

*For Democratic Election Laws*

The lack of equality under the law is shown by the fact that independent candidates and parties other than the Democrats and Republicans face a labyrinth of discriminatory and onerous election laws that make it difficult, often impossible, for any but the capitalist parties to get on the ballot. These laws have the intent and effect of legislating a permanent electoral monopoly for the capitalist parties.

*Full Civil and Human Rights for Gay People*

For an end to all laws that discriminate against homosexuals. For legislation and executive orders to prohibit harassment and discrimination against gay people.

*Protect and Extend Civil Liberties*

The government is resorting more and more to political trials of activists in its attempts to silence opposition to its policies and intimidate those who are fighting for social change. We are faced with increasing government use of police-state practices such as infiltration of agents-provocateurs, wiretaps, harassment of activists by FBI and U.S. Treasury agents, illegal surveillance of citizens, and continued use of the unconstitutional Attorney General's list of so-called "subversive" organizations.

*For Government Ownership of Industry*

Expropriate the major corporations and banks and operate them under the control of democratically elected workers committees. Plan the economy democratically for the benefit of all instead of for the profit of the few.

*For a Socialist America*

Bring to power a workers government, with full recognition of the right of self-determination to the oppressed nationalities, to reorganize America on a socialist basis.

*Support the Socialist Campaign*

Support the demonstrations of the antiwar movement. Support mass actions against the oppression of Blacks, Chicanos, and women.

For an independent labor party! For an independent Black party and an independent Chicano party!

The Socialist Workers Party campaign is the only national campaign in 1972 that presents this perspective of political action independent of capitalist politics.

The candidates of the Socialist Workers Party are dedicated to ending the capitalist system of war and inequality—a system that degrades human life, warps cultural values, and prevents the masses of people from controlling the institutions that affect their lives.

The Socialist Workers Party is fighting to build a society without war, poverty, or unemployment and to put an end to racism, sexism, and the exploitation of the working class. We want to open the way for the unparalleled growth in culture, freedom and development of every individual that will be possible when the vast resources available to us are used to serve human needs instead of *serving private profits.*

Such a society, a socialist society, is worth fighting to achieve. Join us!

Support the socialist campaign!

# CAMPAIGN OF 1976

In 1976, more than one hundred fifty persons filed with the Federal Elections Commission as potential presidential candidates. After a lengthy primary campaign, the number dwindled to two major- and twenty-five minor-party candidates.

In a closely contested Republican convention in Kansas City, incumbent President Gerald Ford of Michigan, who had become the chief executive after Spiro Agnew resigned as Vice-President and Richard Nixon resigned as President, was nominated over the former film actor and California governor, Ronald Reagan. Ford selected Senator Robert Dole of Kansas as his vice-presidential candidate.

The Democrats, meeting in New York City for the first time since 1924, nominated a former governor of Georgia, Jimmy Carter, for president on the first ballot. Carter had won a majority of the presidential primary elections he had entered, and many of his opponents withdrew before the first ballot was cast at the convention. Senator Walter Mondale of Minnesota was chosen as his running mate.

More than twenty-five minor parties were on the ballots in various states. Among the most prominent candidates was former Senator Eugene J. McCarthy of Minnesota, who ran as an independent candidate for the presidency with different vice-presidential candidates in respective states. The Libertarian Party nominated Roger MacBride of Virginia for president and David Bergland of California for vice-president. The American Independent Party, founded by Governor George Wallace in 1968 and represented by Representative John Schmitz on the American Party ticket in 1972, split into two factions in 1976. The American Party held its convention in Salt Lake City in June and nominated its chairman, Thomas Anderson of Tennessee, for president and Rufus Shakleford of Florida for the second spot on the ticket. Delegates from another faction, which called itself the American Independent Party, met in Chicago in August and selected a former governor of Georgia, Lester Maddox, as their presidential candidate and a former mayor of Madison, Wisconsin, William Dyke, as their vice-presidential candidate.

The People's Party, whose candidates ran fourth in 1972, nominated Margaret Wright of California for president at a party convention in St. Louis in 1975 and Dr. Benjamin Spock for the vice-presidency by a mail and phone poll of the delegates. Both Wright and Spock were reaffirmed as the party's final ticket at its 1976 national convention in San Francisco. Wright and Spock were also the candidates of the Peace and Freedom Party in California, the Human Rights Party in Michigan, and the Bicentennial Reality Party in Washington. The Socialist Workers ran Peter Camejo of Massachusetts and Willie Mae Reid of Illinois as their candidates. Jules Levin of New Jersey and Connie Blomen of Massachusetts constituted the Socialist Labor ticket, and the Communists again offered Gus Hall and Jarvis Tyner as their candidates. Benjamin C. Bubar of Maine and Earl F. Dodge of Michigan represented the Prohibition Party. A former mayor of Milwaukee, Frank P. Zeidler, and J. Quinn Brisben were the candidates of the Socialist Party. Lyndon LaRouche of New York ran for the presidency on the U.S. Labor Party ticket with Wayne Evans of Michigan.

In the November election, the Democrats edged the Republicans by polling 40,828,587 popular votes—50.1 percent of the total—to 39,147,613 —48 percent—for the Republicans. Eugene McCarthy attracted 751,728 votes. The Libertarian Party received 172,750 votes; the Maddox American Independent Party garnered 170,780 votes, and the Anderson American Party obtained 160,600. The Communist candidate received 59,115 votes; the Socialist Workers got 91,226; the People's Party polled 49,024 votes; the U.S. Labor Party drew 40,045; the Prohibition Party attracted 15,898 votes; and 9,590 votes were tabulated for the Socialist Labor Party candidate. The Socialist Party candidate, Frank Zeidler, reportedly received 6,022 votes. When the electoral votes were cast, Carter received 297 votes and 240 were counted for Ford. One Republican elector from the state of Washington cast his ballot for Ronald Reagan.

## American Platform 1976

PREAMBLE

Members of the American Party believe that the original Constitution of the United States and the Bill of Rights were prepared and adopted by men acting under the inspiration from Almighty God, that they are solemn compacts between the people of the states of this nation which all officers of government are under oath to obey, and that the eternal moral laws expressed therein must be adhered to or individual liberty will perish.

—from the Constitution of the American Party

The American Party offers the following platform in the sincere belief that these stands on the most important issues of the day are both right and necessary for peace, prosperity, justice and domestic tranquility.

DOMESTIC POLICY

*Agriculture*

A competitive free market is the best means of assuring a fair return to the farmer for the crops he produces. We therefore favor the phased termination of government production and price controls, subsidies, and government-owned reserves which depress farm prices. We favor the withdrawal of similar subsidies from other areas of economic life. While free two-way trade is essential for agricultural prosperity, we recognize the need for protection against foreign imports produced by slave labor or government subsidy.

*Business*

The federal government is notoriously inept at running a business. The Postal Service and Amtrak are two current flagrant examples. Both are inefficient and expensive. The history of government-run enterprises in all ages and nations makes it clear that no possible reforms or re-organizations can salvage such enterprises from insolvency and poor service. The solution is to divest the government of all commercial enterprises and turn them over to competitive free enterprise.

Since the government does not know how to run a business, it should not have the power to tell businessmen how to run theirs. Regulatory agencies such as the Interstate Commerce Com-

mission and the Occupational Safety and Health Administration intervene arbitrarily, unwisely, and despotically in the day-to-day conduct of most legitimate businesses. In so doing, they cost the citizens of this nation billions of dollars in taxes, higher prices, and the countless man hours required to fill out senseless forms. They should be abolished except in those few instances where they carry out the only constitutional function of government in relation to business affairs, which is to prevent fraud and enforce legitimate contracts.

We oppose the legislation of such things as conversion to the metric system. Those who find the metric system advantageous are free to adopt it but have no right to use government to force it at great cost and inconvenience on everyone else.

*Consumer Protection*

Government has the duty and the right to safeguard the people of America against fraud and the sale of dangerous products. In all cases, however, violators must be found guilty in a court of law, not an executive tribunal of an enforcing agency. Furthermore, agencies which monitor the safety of products and the honesty of claims made for them must limit their concerns narrowly to bona fide dangers and misrepresentations. They are not to expand the context of their responsibilities to such things as the unwarranted banning of ammunition as a "dangerous substance" or the specification of the size and shape of cereal boxes, etc. The American consumer is sufficiently market-wise to make his own choices and his right to do so is not by leave of any federal bureaucrat.

*Crime*

The primary concern of government at all levels should be the safety of the lives and property of law-abiding citizens, not the rights of criminals. Deterrence is the chief weapon against crime and the most effective deterrent is the certainty of apprehension, speedy conviction and fitting punishment. Fitting the punishment to the crime requires restoration of the death penalty for crimes of violence and for treason. It also rules out plea bargaining and demands greater uniformity of sentencing for convictions for the same crime. We support the autonomy of local law enforcement.

One of the weakest aspects of present penology

is an over-permissive parole system, which reduces sentences actually served to sometimes nominal terms. Paroles should be earned with difficulty. Felons should not receive special privileges, such as furloughs, due to the high incidence of crime committed by such furloughed prisoners. Prisoners in custody may expect humane treatment and nothing more.

## Child Care

Child care is not a legitimate function of the federal government but is an unwanted intrusion into the domestic affairs of American families. Working mothers should make their own arrangements for the care of their children during working hours.

Present state and local juvenile authorities have the authority and the responsibility to make certain that no children suffer neglect or maltreatment. Americans do not need federal child advocates to set acceptable standards of child-raising and tell parents how to bring up their children.

## Drug Abuse

America is suffering from a drug epidemic which must be brought under control by eliminating the source of supply. As with other criminals, pushers and suppliers must be deterred by certainty of apprehension, speedy trial, and stiff mandatory sentences.

Since the Communist Chinese regime is the source of roughly three-fourths of the world's illicit hard drugs, the United States should discontinue all diplomatic and commercial relations with Red China.

## Education

The present crisis in education must be solved in stages and at several levels. First, so that no parents need defy the law by refusing to send their children to schools of which they disapprove, compulsory attendance laws should be repealed. Second, the control of schools should be returned to the local system by Congressional limitation of the jurisdiction of federal courts and by an end to busing for racial balance. Third, the federal government should be eliminated entirely from interference in local schools by putting an end to federal aid with its inevitable guidelines.

We oppose any federal prohibition of voluntary non-denominational prayers in the public schools.

## Elections

The manner of conducting elections is the prerogative of the states according to the Constitution and this right is not to be usurped by federal government.

The appropriation of tax money to finance conventions and candidates is using money paid under compulsion to promote programs and persons to which and to whom many taxpayers are strongly opposed. Such use of public funds is therefore immoral and should be stopped at once.

## Energy Policy

The free enterprise system will automatically adjust to available energy resources and supply consumers in the optimum way if the producers of oil, gas and coal are not hamstrung by punitive or politically motivated price controls and taxes on the production and distribution of energy.

The development of nuclear and solar power as major energy sources of the future will also take place naturally and smoothly if such development is not stifled by bureaucratic regulation.

## Environmental Protection

The Environmental Protection Agency is an outstanding example of a tyrannical bureaucracy operating beyond the reach of popular control and should be abolished. Its automobile pollution and insecticide control programs have been costly blunders. Where governmental regulation is shown to be necessary, let each state assume its proper responsibility to pass whatever laws are required.

## Equal Rights Amendment

The proposed so-called Equal Rights Amendment will not assure women of rights they either do not have or cannot attain more simply and directly. It would, however, abolish privileges and immunities which most Americans believe should be accorded women, such as exemption from combat duty. Ratification of the Equal Rights Amendment should be opposed or repealed.

## Executive Orders

The Constitution specifies that only Congress may enact laws and that it may not delegate its legislative powers. Therefore, though the President may issue executive orders to administer the executive branch of government, neither the President nor any other officer may create laws by executive order. All such existing so-called laws should be declared void and further executive edicts forbidden. The alternative is tyranny.

## Federal Judiciary

Federal courts have for too long indulged in widespread judicial legislation which is a clear usurpation of power. They should be returned to their proper function of interpretation and adjudication by any or all of several means. The simplest is Congressional limitation of the powers of the Supreme Court and other federal courts, as provided in Article III, Section 2 of the Constitution.

## Gun Control

The right of citizens to keep and bear arms, whether for sporting purposes or personal defense, is guaranteed by the Second Amendment of the Bill of Rights and is not to be abridged. The purpose of government is not the control of law-abiding gun owners but the control of gun-wielding criminals. We therefore favor heavy mandatory state penalties for crimes committed with a gun. We oppose all laws existing and proposed for the registration of guns and ammunition.

## Health Care

Not only does the federal government have no Constitutional authority for general health care programs, but experience has already demonstrated that such programs are inefficient, slow, wasteful, and corruption-prone. Federal health care programs should be phased out while at the same time private medical insurance and hospitalization plans should be encouraged.

One of the many serious objections to government intrusion into health care is the unwarranted interference with the confidential doctor-patient relationship. Such interference is already being practiced by the federal Professional Services Review Organization, which should be abolished.

Another infringement of the doctor-patient relationship is the legal harassment of doctors and patients who employ bureaucratically prohibited treatments and medications which are admittedly not harmful and possibly beneficial. We favor freedom of choice in all health care.

By the same token, and as a part of such freedom, we oppose involuntary mass medication. Specifically, nothing may be added to public water supplies except chemicals intended for their purification.

With the grim examples of state-directed medical programs available to us in Canada and Europe, we oppose any similar trend toward socialized medicine in this country.

## Illegal Aliens

Illegal aliens should be identified and dealt with according to law.

## Inflation

Inflation is an insidious regressive tax for which only the government is to blame. The reckless deficit spending of the past four decades and the self-serving monetary manipulation of the Federal Reserve System have brought America to the brink of fiscal disaster. We must return to balanced federal budgets and fully redeemable currency in which a dollar is defined as a specific weight of gold for which "paper money" may be exchanged at any time. When this is done, the Federal Reserve System will be superfluous and should be abolished.

## Labor

The right of workers to form and join unions to promote their specific interests has in many instances been largely nullified by undemocratic and strong-arm methods resorted to by labor bosses. The law should give control of local unions to local members and guarantee the full exercise of that control.

Much of the power of union bosses derives from their control of politicians of both major parties through donations of labor, equipment and of money obtained from union dues and pension funds. Such activities are both immoral and illegal, and those guilty of giving and receiving such funds should be prosecuted just as certainly as corporations which break the laws concerning political campaign contributions.

Another source of labor bosses' muscle is their

self-serving power to coerce union membership and the payment of union dues even from workers who do not wish to join. Union dues and membership must be entirely voluntary. At the same time, unions must not be able to force employers to hire unnecessary workers.

Workers must be allowed the same freedom of access to their employer's case in collective bargaining discussions as to the union case.

Government workers hold their jobs as a privilege, not a right, and essential government services cannot be interrupted by strikes or threats of strikes by public employees. Collective bargaining for public employees must therefore be made illegal.

## Land Use

Land use laws are federal zoning laws or federally instigated state zoning laws. As such, they effectively confiscate or reduce the value of privately owned land without due process. We oppose such laws as tyrannical and oppressive and because they are an invitation to wholesale corruption. We also oppose compulsory federal flood control insurance and its built-in land use provisions.

## National Security

The United States must defend itself against espionage, sabotage, subversion and sedition or it will succumb to its foreign and domestic enemies. The full power of the federal government should be applied to the apprehension, conviction and punishment of persons guilty of these high crimes. We call for the re-establishment of and vigorous support for the House Internal Security Committee, the Senate Internal Security Subcommittee, and the Subversive Activities Control Board. All loyalty and security risks should be dismissed from government service.

Treason is defined by the Constitution and specified as a capital crime. We call for the enforcement of this provision of the Constitution.

## Open Housing

The sale of any property must be a voluntary transaction by both buyer and seller. The seller may not be coerced to sell to anyone for any reason and no private buyer may be subsidized with public money.

## Public Morality

Neither Congress nor the federal courts should infringe the rights of states and local government to enact laws restricting obscenity, pornography, and illicit sex acts, especially prostitution and homosexuality.

## Quotas

Qualifications for admissions, hirings or promotions within private organizations should only be by mutual agreement of the parties concerned. Tax-supported organizations should not determine admissions, hirings or promotions on the basis of race, religion or national origin, but on merit alone.

## Regional Government

Regional and metro government, to be run by appointed bureaucrats, is a device to impose direct federal control upon metropolitan areas and to bypass state and local sovereignty: backers of the scheme themselves admit it. As such it is a blow against local control of representative government and should be abolished. We believe that no appointed official should have authority equal to that of elected officials within the same jurisdiction.

## Revenue Sharing

Until the federal government gets out of debt, it has no revenue to share. Borrowing money to give to the states upon conditions set by the federal government is immoral and should be stopped at once. The states could raise their own revenues by taxes if the federal taxes were lower.

## Sanctity of Life

The duty to protect the life of each citizen is the paramount duty of any government. Though it may be superficially plausible that a pregnant woman should have complete control over her own body, neither she nor anyone else may extend that right of control to the body of the unborn child she carries. Government is obliged to protect the life of both child and mother and, if necessary, to protect the life of the child from the mother.

A life may be taken according to the law only

after conviction for a capital offense, or to save the mother's life.

## Social Security

Social Security is a bad bargain for those not already drawing benefits; future benefits will return only a small fraction of the amounts paid in and there is no guaranteed minimum, no cash value. Unless the entire system is soundly funded, it should be phased out. Much more advantageous insurance and retirement plans are offered by private programs.

As long as Social Security remains in force, all earnings limitations should be removed and all federal employees, including Congress and the President, should be required to participate.

## Taxes

Big government cannot exist without big taxes. We call for a limitation of government to its legitimate function of preventing violence and fraud and such as are enumerated in the Constitution, and for a simultaneous reduction of taxes. We would accomplish this by phasing out the Marxist progressive feature of the federal income tax by lowering the rates in the high-income brackets and eliminating exemptions by steps; everyone will then have an equal interest in keeping taxes minimal. To encourage people to save and invest, we would remove double taxation on dividends and phase out taxes on capital gains.

We call for an impartial, thoroughgoing investigation of the large tax-exempt foundations which have in effect served as questionable tax dodges for multimillionaires while fronting as charitable or educational organizations.

## Urban Renewal

Urban renewal uses the power of government to condemn private property for re-sale to new private owners and is therefore immoral. It has been an expensive failure and has resulted in the forcible displacement of millions of citizens from their homes, the destruction of hundreds of thousands of low-rent housing units. Its harmful effects have fallen most heavily on the poor and minorities. Urban renewal should be abolished.

## Unemployment

Persistent unemployment is caused by unrealistic minimum wage laws enforced by government, abuse in payment of unemployment compensation, and exorbitant wage rates imposed by some unions and exorbitant prices exacted by some monopolistic corporations. Unemployment may be made minimal by restoring freedom in the job market so that every potential worker will be free to compete for any job for which he is qualified.

## Welfare

Federal welfare programs are unconstitutional, needlessly expensive, and riddled with corruption. They should therefore be abolished, leaving such concerns to the several states, counties, municipalities and private charity.

## FOREIGN POLICY

## Communist Nations

All Communist dictatorships have achieved power by force, deception and bloodshed and survive in power through terrorist rule. They do not represent the people they have enslaved and are therefore illegitimate. The United States should withdraw diplomatic recognition of these regimes.

We favor a discontinuation of all trade and commerce with any countries which do not allow the emigration of any citizen who wishes to leave or prohibit his taking his possessions with him.

## Detente

Detente is a euphemism for appeasement and should be discontinued. It is not to the advantage of the United States or the free world to lessen the external and internal strains of Communist dictatorship. Exports of western technology to Communist dictatorships is arming our declared enemies and should be stopped.

## Foreign Aid

Foreign aid is an internal welfare scheme by the federal government. It is wasteful and more often than not retards the sound economic growth of the peoples supposed to be aided. It has so far cost Americans over $250 billion. Foreign aid must be stopped at once.

## Hemispheric Defense

Failure to assert and apply the Monroe Doctrine led to the establishment of the first Communist totalitarian state in the Western hemisphere. The Monroe Doctrine must be reasserted by giving every possible non-military form of assistance to Cubans seeking to restore a free government to Cuba.

### Imports

Buying goods from regimes which employ slave labor puts American workers at a disadvantage and makes slave labor profitable. Ban all imports from such countries.

### Middle East

The U.S. must pursue America's true interests in all parts of the world. In the Middle East this requires non-intervention and non-involvement. The U.S. must not orient its foreign policy primarily to conform to the interests of any foreign nation.

### Military Strength

International Communism is an implacable enemy which has declared and repeated its fixed purpose to destroy America and the free world. It is suicidal for this country to disarm. We must have a military establishment able to defend us against any combination of enemies.

### Offshore Resources

We must protect and enforce exclusive American claims to offshore oil, gas and mineral resources as well as fishing rights to a distance of 200 miles. Stern measures should be taken against Communist ships' harassment and destruction of American fishing in American waters.

### Panama Canal

The Panama Canal and the Canal Zone are American territory every bit as much as Florida, Alaska or the Louisiana Purchase. The Hay-Bunau-Varilla Treaty gives the United States full sovereignty over the Canal Zone in perpetuity. No President or Secretary of State may cede U.S. sovereignty or territory. We must make clear our intention not to yield or share any rights in the Panama Canal or Canal Zone.

### Secret Diplomacy

Ours is not a government of, by and for the people if we allow Presidents or Secretaries of State to bind us with secret treaties. We declare that no treaty or agreement should be honored unless it is made public and ratified by the U.S. Senate as required by the Constitution.

### State Department

For more than three decades the Department of State has been a scandal-ridden haven for known loyalty and security risks. Though presidential candidates have routinely promised to clean up the State Department, no effective action has yet been taken. The existing situation is intolerable, since it makes the effective functioning of patriotic members of the State Department not only most difficult, but also detrimental to their professional advancement and hazardous to their personal safety. Loyalty and security risks should be identified by a careful and thorough investigation and dismissed from government service.

### Treaty Law

Americans are not secure in their Constitutional rights if such rights can be superseded by provisions of any treaty. We therefore call for ratification of the Bricker Amendment which would assert the primacy of the U.S. Constitution.

### United Nations

During the more than thirty years the United Nations has been in existence, more people have lost their lives, homes, possessions and freedom than in any similar period in history. Totalitarian Communist regimes cast hundreds of vetoes in the UN Security Council to make the world safe for leftist dictatorships and they and their satellites control the UN's General Assembly while the American taxpayer foots the lion's share of the bill for keeping the UN going. The UN is a compact with tyrants and therefore cannot under any circumstances secure freedom, justice or peace. We should withdraw from the United Nations and every other organization which infringes the sovereignty of the United States.

### War

Our military involvements in both Vietnam and Korea were undeclared wars. We therefore would require that foreign military actions cannot be pursued more than 72 hours without a declaration of war by Congress. We denounce any no-win policy as treasonous. It is immoral to draft anyone to fight an undeclared war.

## American Independent Platform 1976

PREAMBLE

We the representatives of the national American Independent Party assembled together in the City of Chicago, on this 27th day of August in the year of our Lord 1976 in the BiCentennial of our Nation, recognize God as our Judge and the inspired Declaration of Independence and the Constitution of the United States as our political standard; and, recognizing that the twin political parties of our Republic have seriously departed from their own stated principles; We therefore declare our independence of those political organizations and hereby re-affirm our allegiance to American National Independence and the Constitutional Principles upon which this great Republic was established.

We believe in the Free Enterprise system and oppose Facism, Socialism, Communism, and all other forms of totalitarian government which deprive men of life, liberty, and property. We recognize the family as the essential and basic unit of a free civilization. We champion the rights and dignity of the individual and believe in less government, more individual responsibility and a better world under God.

The central issues of our day are: 1) The unconstitutional growth in size, control and reach of government in and over our daily lives, 2) The deliberate diminishment of our national sovereignty through entangling alliances with foreign nations and international organizations, 3) The attack on the family and the right to life via the murder of innocent unborn children by abortion, 4) The alienation of the average citizen from effective participation in the decision making process of government by the twin party political monopoly and 5) The decline of religion and morality in America. Consequently, we suffer from the loss of our individual and national liberties, crime, war, oppressive taxation, inflation, and despotic bureaucracy. The government structure must be brought under control now and reduced in size and scope by Constitutional remedies applied by

an aroused and informed citizenry, before the government destroys the very foundation of liberty upon which it rests.

Our Constitutional System is not at fault. We the people are at fault for failure to exercise our responsibilities as free citizens. We have consented to the yoke of the decadent political parties in control of our government and have elected and re-elected politicians who have sacrificed political and personal integrity and morality for personal gain and foreign ideologies. It is therefore fitting and proper in the BiCentennial to reapply the principles of Americanism in our individual and national lives and thus reverse the negative trends of the past half century, reduce governmental influence in our lives and return this nation to a responsible and free people.

No free nation can survive if it fails to meet the problems which concern the average citizen. The American Independent Party is dedicated and will be heard in a free Nation committed to government of, by and for the people. To the great people of America, we offer this platform as a binding contract.

BASIC PRINCIPLES

### Religious Faith

The government of the United States rests upon a Declaration of Independence in which the Creator is recognized as the source of all unalienable rights, and in which the appeal for the rectitude of national intentions is to the Supreme Judge of the World. Yet the government of the United States neither claims divine right nor imposes upon its citizens any specific religious doctrine. "In God We Trust" is a motto of the American people, whose consent is the criterion of the justice of their government.

The Federal government is precluded by the First Amendment from establishing exercise of religion. That all states have voluntarily avoided or repealed established religion does not mean that the people have rejected religion. It means, rather, that they recognize the relationship between God and those who believe in Him to be a matter in which freedom is of the essence, a matter with which the power of government should not interfere.

The constituencies of the American Independent Party 1976 Presidential Nominating Convenvention are at one with the authors and signers of the Declaration of Independence in "firm reliance on the protection of Divine Providence," and invoke the blessing of Almighty God on this collaborative effort to save and serve our country.

## NATIONAL LOYALTY

The American Independent Party 1976 Presidential Nominating Convention pledges full faith and loyalty to the United States of America and the sovereign people thereof. We believe with our forefathers of 1776 that "as free and independent States the former Colonies, united and liberated by their Declaration made good, have full power to levy war, conclude peace, contract alliances, establish commerce, and do all other acts and things which Independent States may of right do," and in renewal of the Spirit of '76 "we mutually pledge to each other our lives, our fortunes, and our sacred honor." In 1976 this is no idle ceremonial pledge, for the sovereignty of the American people is threatened as never before in two hundred years of history, and we are determined that the threat shall be repulsed by popular action.

## PERSONAL LIBERTY

Governments deriving their just powers from the consent of the governed tend to grow weary of depending upon such consent. Personnel employed as public servants seek to become public masters. A bureaucratic regime not checked becomes a police state of which the linchpin is physical and psychological terror. Today bureaucratic regulation has a stranglehold on personal liberty. Under pretext of protecting us against foreign enemies, natural hazards, and even ourselves, the leviathan state makes common cause with alien forces to insure our submission to bureaucratic control. The cancer of Big Government must be cut out before we are all overcome by taxation, regulation, giveaways, and sellouts.

## A NEW PARTY

### A New Party

The need for a political realignment in American politics has long been recognized by honest "conservatives" and "liberals" of good will. Ac-

cording to most polls, and verified by grass roots elections, more than 60% of the voting public is conservative. These conservatives comprise the majorities in both major political parties. However, these "conservative" majorities in both parties are continually out-maneuvered by the political bosses and the powerful financial interests that control both major political parties at the top. Consequently, numbers of disenchanted voters have increasingly registered as independents or refused to even go to the polls at election time. This trend has effectively disenfranchised many voters from further influence within the major parties and thus has enhanced the monopoly control of the political power brokers in control of our government. The majority has thus been artificially divided and conquered.

While political bosses have been thus solidifying their powerful grips on the party machinery, those parties have been losing the actual support of the independent American people. The Republican Party probably will never again be a decisive power. Its role in Congress has been permanently affixed as a minor and fading party. Our nation is very nearly now a one party nation—and that party controlled by political bosses, not by the people.

These disenfranchised independent Americans are the majority and we are uniting conservative democrats and republicans and independents, into a new majority party. A 1976 Presidential Nominating Convention attended by representatives of the American Independent Party, the American Independence Party and with the cooperation of the Committee for the New Majority, States Rights Democrats, Wallace Supporters, Conservative Republicans and Independent Voters, has provided a third line ballot position to the American people. This Convention thus exemplifies the tradition of united action by personally independent Americans and does now provide the American people with the leadership for the formation of a truly new and independent political party, a party concerned with representation of the average citizen. This American Independent Party is an idea whose time has come. We invite your participation in the formation of this new political party.

This new Party has been functioning in various states under different names, but with approximately the same principles, since 1968 or before.

INDIVIDUAL RIGHTS

The American Independent Party speaks for individual freedom; the right of each citizen to the ownership of property and the control of his own property, the right to engage in business or participate in his labor union without governmental interference.

We shall steadfastly oppose Federal legislation permitting the Federal bureaucracy to tell a business man whom he must hire or fire, tamper with union seniority lists and apprenticeship programs or invade the individual's right to privacy.

We call for the elimination of government competition with free competitive institutions.

The American Independent Party reaffirms the constitutional right of Americans to travel without governmental interference especially by automobile and strongly opposes unconstitutional federal restrictions and harassments such as the 55 mile per hour speed limit and compulsory, expensive and unwanted alleged "safety" devices such as "pollution" controls, safety belts, and airbags, and all federal policies which create gasoline shortages.

RIGHT TO BEAR ARMS

The American Independent Party supports the rights of all citizens to be fully protected in their homes, persons, and property.

The Second Amendment of the Constitution of the United States affords to every citizen the right to keep and bear arms, whether for sporting purposes or personal defense.

The lawless always acquire weapons and the result of disarming our citizens, coupled with judicial emasculation of local police protection, would be to leave the average citizen without protection from the lawless or from a tyrannical government. We support a mandatory prison sentence for anyone using a firearm in the commission of a felony.

The American Independent Party opposes any law which would in any manner interfere with the right of the citizens to keep and bear arms.

PROTECTION FROM CRIME AND VIOLENCE

The law-abiding citizen of the United States has a right to be protected from crime, violence and lawlessness.

The American Independent Party pledges full support to local law enforcement in its crusade to control crime; reforms in our judicial system to provide a speedy and just determinatiion in criminal cases; and retention of the historic constitutional right of each state, and the federal government, to impose capital punishment for aggravated criminal offenses.

We support maximum penalties for the crime of skyjacking and political assassinations.

LAW ENFORCEMENT

*Support of Local Police*

Local police forces are vital to the preservation of individual liberties and maintenance of law and order. Attempts are being made to establish a National Police Force and to place our local police under the control of the Federal Government, via Federal Aid, opening the way for dictatorship. We strongly support the return of powers usurped by the Federal Government to our communities and local police forces. We oppose the L.E.A.A. (Law Enforcemernt Assistance Administration) and seek its repeal.

DRUG ABUSE

The American Independent Party asserts that drugs are a serious problem in our nation, particularly among our youth, threatening the physical and mental health and even the life of users and leading to many crimes, accidents and other misfortunes.

We oppose legalization of marijuana. We favor strong local and state laws making it a criminal offense with a mandatory jail sentence for anyone convicted of selling or supplying drugs, excepting for prescribed medical purposes.

The ultimate source of most hard drugs in the United States is the poppy fields of Red China. We deplore the government's failure to take any meaningful action to stop the flow of hard drugs from Red China to the United States and pledge our full support to stop this assault on our American youth.

RIGHT TO LIFE

The American Independent Party believes ". . . that all men are created equal and are endowed by their Creator with certain unalienable rights; that among these are life, liberty and the pursuit of happiness. That to secure these rights governments are instituted among men. . . ."

We regret the Supreme Court decision of January 22, 1973, which withdrew government protection from the right to life. We will both join and support the efforts of those who seek enactment of a constitutional amendment which will specifically mandate every branch of government to protect this right for every human being at every stage of its development from fertilization to natural death.

## Protection of the Family

We believe that parents have the God-given responsibility to care for their children. We do not believe that the government has the right to appoint itself a partner in child raising and child care. Therefore, we oppose the basic premise of the Mondale sponsored child care act and all similar legislation.

## E.R.A.

The so-called "Equal Rights" Amendment will have the effect of nullifying present laws providing special protection for women in the social and economic fields.

It would disparage the position of the woman who chooses to be wife, mother and homemaker and would threaten the quality of the home environment so important to future generations of Americans.

American women traditionally have been free to do whatever befits their individual talents. While we strongly support equal pay for equal work, we believe that the solution to this problem already has been, or can be, accomplished by legislative action.

We oppose the ratification of the ERA by any more states and will support all state movements to rescind it.

American women do not need to be "liberated." Rights legalized can later be repealed, leaving the recipient in a worse condition than before. "Equal rights" bestowed by government would give government controls over women which would restrict their historic and God-given freedoms. If the ERA is adopted, women will have lost far more than they have gained.

## Morality versus Pornography

The American Independent Party fully supports laws providing maximum legal penalties for the criminal distribution, publication, or exhibition of obscenity, including any display of homosexuality. We further oppose the legalization of homosexuality. A nation that debases its moral codes is preparing the seal to its own death warrant.

## Education

The American Independent Party fully supports the concept of quality education for every American child. We believe that education is a local responsibility and we are unalterably committed to the preservatiion of the neighborhood school without Federal control or interference.

We also support all necessary legislation to encourage the development of systems of private education including tax set offs for parents who choose to place their children in private schools.

We support the concept of voluntary non-denominational prayer in the public schools. We would protect the right of an individual not to participate, but do not believe the minority has the right to bar participation by the majority in desired religious exercises. We will resist any and all attempts by governmental agencies such as H.E.W. and the National Institute on Mental Health, etc. to use our educational systems to experiment with, or capture the minds and lives of our children through such programs as "National Child Advocacy System," sex-education, sensitivity training and drug experimentation.

We favor placing our schools under the jurisdiction of parents and their local school boards and school financing by state and local taxation.

## Forced Busing

The American Independent Party strongly condemns the practice of forced busing. Such busing orders by the Federal Courts are clearly unconstitutional. The Supreme Court having ruled in error, the most appropriate way to correct forced busing is to adhere to Article III, Section 2, of the United States Constitution which states that the Congress shall have the power to remove the Supreme Court's jurisdiction in any matter whatsoever as set forth in the McDonald H.R. No. 12365.

## Elections

The development of the American Independent Party is dependent upon an opportunity to fully participate in the election process in the several states. We shall work for the elimination of discriminatory state laws which make it difficult or impossible for new parties to participate in the election process. We shall support judicial or legislative action wherever necessary to achieve this objective.

We support full disclosure of campaign contributions and expenditures.

The American Independent Party welcomes America's young voters and invites them to participate in the only political party which offers real solutions to the problems encountered by young Americans. We encourage our newly enfranchised young voters to play an active part in the leadership and development of the American Independent Party.

VOTING RIGHTS

The United States of America was formed by several sovereign States, which formed this Union based upon an equality of States. As such, any law which discriminates against certain States is repugnant to the concept of equality. Since the Voting Rights Act of 1965 discriminates against certain States, it should be amended so that all states are treated equally.

JUDICIAL TYRANNY

The late Alexander Bickel, Professor of Law at Yale University, in his book *The Supreme Court and the Idea of Progress,* speaking of the Warren Court, says that "centralized, unmitigatedly legalitarian government bears the seeds of tyranny." It might be added that when the seed comes to fruition the legalitarianism is dropped and the naked tyranny revealed. There is little or no pretense at taking the law or the Constitution seriously in many contemporary Supreme Court decisions, such as the abortion case, the school busing cases, or (most obviously) the school prayer decision, and the reapportionment decision. The following notes suggest the impudence with which the court flouts the plain intent of the Constitution. Reflect that no defense can be made that there are technical meanings in the Constitution which the layman cannot be expected to understand. A written Constitution which only a few experts can understand would be a fraud if it purported to be the basic law of a country in which government derives its just powers from the consent of the governed, for the people cannot give rational assent to that which they cannot understand. If only a few experts can understand the basic law of the land, then those few experts are *ipso facto* an oligarchy. Thus the Congress, which passes laws, and having sworn to "preserve, protect and defend the Constitution of the United States" asks the judges, who are appointed, to tell them what it is that they have sworn to uphold.

The abortion decision has the effect of depriving countless persons unborn (but conceived, and in biological and legal existence) of life without due process of law, in plain violation of the Fifth and Fourteenth Amendments.

The busing decision and the school desegregation decision on which it rests are both in violation of the Fourteenth Amendment as intended by those who drafted and ratified it, and if any law does not mean what its authors intended, it means nothing. (With which conclusion, ironically, the Supreme Court seems to agree.)

The decision forbidding prayer in the schools is a plain violation of the First Amendment, which it purports to enforce for the First Amendment guarantees the free exercise of religion, which the court in this case forbids.

The reapportionment decision, citing "one man, one vote" as a Constitutional principle, is the most flagrant of all these defiances of the Constitution, since the most basic feature of the United States Constitution is itself in direct conflict with "one man, one vote." We refer to the equal representation of states in the United States Senate. That Delaware and New York, Nevada and California, should have two Senators each is as precise a denial of "one man, one vote" as can be formulated. Yet Article V of the Constitution, which prescribes the process of amendment, provides that "no State, without its consent, shall be deprived of its equal suffrage in the Senate." This rejection of "one man, one vote," in other words, is the only thing in the Constitution which cannot be amended.

Besides the foregoing examples of the Supreme Court's evident contempt for the Constitution ("the Constitution is what the Supreme Court says it is" is the common way of expressing this contempt), there are examples of the contempt with which the Federal Judiciary treats law-abiding citizens, its tolerance of criminals, and its immense self-regard. Persons not charged with or even suspected of any crime may have their private financial records searched by the Internal Revenue Service, while criminals caught in the act must have their "Constitutional rights" scrupulously protected.

The height of judicial self-veneration was reached last February when a suit was filed, in which eighty-one Federal Judges have joined, to have their own pay automatically increased as inflation lowers the value of the dollar. Their plea is based on the provision of Article III of the Constitution that judges shall "receive for their services a compensation which shall not be diminished during their continuance in office." To construe the advance of inflation as a diminishing of compensation within the meaning of the Constitution is a specious approach which would no doubt be indignantly thrown out of any court where the beneficiary of, say, a life insurance policy might appear to demand twice the amount specified numerically in the policy, on the grounds that the value of the dollar had been cut in half since the policy was first taken out. Yet to consider the judges' case seriously while denying similar anti-inflation medicine to ordinary citizens is certainly to deny equal protection of the laws, besides condoning a display of avarice more disgusting than the infamous sex scandals of Washington.

If the Supreme Court and lower Federal courts are guilty of malfeasance—as innumerable thoughtful Americans have reluctantly come to believe—the Congress which has authority over the courts' jurisdiction, and has the power of impeachment—is guilty of nonfeasance. If members of the Supreme Court themselves violate their oath of office to uphold the Constitution and instead distort and pervert that basic law beyond all bounds of reason, then the President who enforces their illegal and criminal decisions is himself an accomplice in their crime. Note that the greatest crime of all against the Constitution is to say that the Constitution is what the Supreme Court says it is. That kind of an illogical monstrosity destroys utterly the basic American premise that we have a government of laws and not of men—in other words, that the Supreme Court is what the Constitution says it is.

To restrain the present mad course of judicial tyranny we must elect to Congress and the Presidency—and to state office as well—men who will regard their oath of office as a commitment to Almighty God, not to be interpreted by any Federal Judge as middleman.

We need a President who is capable of saying what Andrew Jackson reportedly said to the great Chief Justice of his day: "John Marshall has made his decision; now let him enforce it." Unjust judges cannot enforce their own decisions. A just President will not enforce unjust decisions, and a just Congress will not leave unjust judges untouched.

We independent Americans, committed to the cause of American independence, cannot yet directly deal with members of the judiciary, but we can deal with—vote for or against—candidates for the Presidency and for Congress, who do, on attaining office, have power to deal with the tenure and jurisdiction of the courts.

The American Independent Party would end judicial usurpation of the constitutional process by requiring federal judges at the district court level to be directly elected by the people, by requiring federal judges at the appellate level, including Supreme Court justices, to be reconfirmed in their appointments every four years, and by congressional action ending appellate jurisdiction of the federal courts in state constitutional cases.

COUNSEL OF CHOICE

We recognize the right of any citizen to speak for himself, or to have the counsel of his own choice in any transaction with government, without it being necessary for said counsel to be a member of any closed organization.

PUNISHMENT OF WRONGDOING BY GOVERNMENT OFFICIALS

It is the policy of this party to establish effective legislation for the prompt and adequate punishment of any government official who violates the rights of the citizens, and to provide for just indemnification to any citizen who has suffered losses and/or violation of rights by government officials.

JURIES

When our United States Constitution was written it was the recognized right of juries to decide both the facts and the law of a case. This was recognized as a proper power and a moral right of juries to protect citizens against tyrannical acts of wrongful prosecution by government. By a process of judicial usurpation, most jurors today are wrongfully sworn to uphold the law as the judge gives it rather than sworn to uphold the Constitution and the rights of the citizen. They thus become unwitting puppets to uphold unjust laws. The American Independent Party will bring legislation to restore the full rights of the juries, and to provide for effective punishment, including dismissal from office for judges who set themselves above the rights of the citizenry they are supposed to serve.

## Secrecy in Government

The American Independent Party believes that government must be conducted in the full light of public scrutiny. Secrecy is the tool of dictatorship, not of government of, by and for the people. We pledge our full support to all necessary legislation to assure full disclosure to the people of the activities of their government, excepting for matters clearly in the interests of national security.

This Convention urges a new investigation of the cover-up of the crimes of both Watergate and Dallas, to include as far as possible testimony of surviving members of the Warren Commission.

This Convention further urges re-examination of the great body of investigative material relating to the FBI and CIA, with particular attention to the possibility that our intelligence community has been infiltrated by the Soviet KGB (and its predecessors), and Soviet agents within the American government have incited and guided the investigations which have corrupted the intelligence function beyond the condition to which their own presence had already brought it.

## Internal Subversion

The American Independent Party expresses its undying opposition to the criminal Communist conspiracy and, in that regard, urges the enforcement of the Constitution and laws of the United States.

We call for a congressional investigation of the Council on Foreign Relations (CFR) and the Foreign Policy Association. We are concerned about the known security risks operating with immunity in the State Department.

## Regional Government

The American Independent Party is unalterably opposed to the creation of regional government, created by Executive Order, which exercises tax and police powers without direct responsibility to the voters and the taxpayers which such agencies are alleged to serve. Too often, the objective of those seeking to create such regional bodies is the destruction or usurpation of the authority of local or state governments.

In connection with necessary vigilance on the subject of regional government, we encourage a reexamination of the concept of zoning laws, which frequently are a thinly veiled transfer of power from private property owners to local collectivist planners.

Executive orders are used by the executive branch of legislation, creating a powerful fourth layer of government unanswerable to the Electorial Process. We call for restrictions of these orders to be used only for internal organization.

The regulatory agencies must be restrained from promoting any rules, regulations and guidelines upon the Citizens of the United States.

## States Rights

We fervently re-affirm our support of and belief in the 10th Amendment Constitutional provision that ". . . the powers not delegated to the United States by the Constitution, nor prohibited by it to the States, are reserved to the States respectively, or to the people. . . ."

## Federal Grants

We realize that any and all Federal aid to state programs has strings attached to force state compliance in many areas. We also realize that any money which goes through Federal channels, greatly shrinks before getting back to the state level. We believe that rather than being returned by the Federal Government to the states, it should be left with the people who earned it. The American Independent Party is unalterably opposed to the so-called Federal Revenue Sharing. If a state must tax for one of its' programs, it should at least receive 100% of its' citizens tax money.

## Water Rights

We believe that water rights are basic human

rights, best administered as needed at the local or state levels. It makes no sense for politicians and bureaucrats in Washington, D.C. to legislate a local situation, nor does the Constitution allow this federal usurpation of States' Rights.

### LAND USE

We feel that the Federal Government and its sub-agencies, such as the Bureau of Land Management, have no right to control land in our states other than for forts, magazines, arsenals, federal buildings, and dock yards, as provided for in the Constitutiion of the United States of America. We urge all necessary measures to insure immediate transfer of lands presently controlled by the Federal Government—but not as specified in the Constitution—back to the States. Until such time as the Federal powers vacate our lands, we endorse and support the Federal Mining Laws of 1872.

The American Independent Party is opposed to Federal Land Use legislation giving the Federal Government control over all private property, requiring States to submit under the threat of loss of their citizens' tax monies.

### NATURAL RESOURCES AND PROTECTION OF THE ENVIRONMENT

The American Independent Party is deeply concerned with the protection of our environment and the conservation of our natural resources.

We do not believe that the solution to pollution can be found in destroying the private capital investment system, but rather by urging the enforcement of the common and statutory laws affecting these matters by the States and local enforcement agencies, and by the inventive genius of a free people in a competitive economic system.

We propose that dams be built as approved by engineers to produce smog-free hydro-electric power as well as to provide flood control, water and irrigation systems, navigation and recreation.

We are opposed to restrictive safety laws which are above and beyond reasonable requirements for location, construction and operation of nuclear power plants. Safe nuclear power is available today.

### AGRICULTURE

The American Independent Party supports honest value to the farmer for the crop he produces.

We support the phased complete withdrawal of government controls, restrictions and subsidies from agriculture within a period of three to five years, as we withdraw similar subsidies from other areas of American economic life.

To protect the American farm and other producers from unjust foreign competition, we protest foreign imports from slave nations. We protest imports from nations which subsidize their exports.

### TARIFF AND TRADE

We support trade on the world market on a cash or equitable trade basis. Protective tariffs should be utilized to protect American farmers, merchants and labor from slave produced merchandise. We support a no-trade policy with any nation having a socialistic or communistic form of government, except when such trade would be in the best interest of the United States.

A strong merchant fleet is an essential element of our foreign trade policy and we therefore call for modernization and enlargement of the U.S. Merchant Fleet.

We urge that: The United States cease participation in internatiional tariff cutting organizations such as the General Agreement on Tariffs and Trade (GATT); and that: The United States eliminate tax advantages for American businesses moving abroad, and establish a firm policy that U.S. businesses investing abroad do so at their own risk and that there is no obligation by our Government to protect those investments with the lives of our sons, or the taxes of our citizens.

### FISHING RIGHTS AND OTHER SEA RESOURCES

The American Independent Party supports extension of territorial sovereignty of fishing rights and sea bed resources to the 200 mile limit and calls for strengthening the U. S. Coast Guard to the extent needed for adequate control and enforcement; providing armaments as necessary to insure survival in a potentially hostile environment.

Since the sea beds contain the world's greatest wealth in the form of food and minerals, and the waters of the oceans have always been open to all the peoples of the earth, the American Independent Party believes the oceans should be kept free beyond the 200 mile limits and not at any time put under control of the communist-dominated United Nations.

## EQUAL OPPORTUNITY

We support equal opportunity for all, without regard to race, creed, or color, based on ability; therefore, we oppose government, including court interference, imposed quotas, and reverse discrimination of any kind in jobs, both placement and promotion, education and housing and the like.

## EMPLOYMENT AND SMALL INDEPENDENT BUSINESSMAN

The creation of job opportunities for our citizens is an essential requirement of today's economy. We believe it can best be done under the free enterprise system and the small businessman (the largest employer in the USA) rather than through government sponsored programs.

The American Independent Party is opposed to the objectives of the Humphrey-Hawkins Bill and similar legislation which would substitute Federal Government makework projects in place of increased productivity by Free Enterprise.

The American Independent Party would eliminate governmental red tape and restrict the power of federal regulatory agencies in their demands for thousands of senseless forms.

This is the tradition of a free America which, without government restrictions has created the greatest abundance the world has ever known.

## LABOR

The American Independent Party fully supports the advances made by the working people of America. We shall continue to support the rights of workers to organize, bargain collectively, and control the internal affairs of their union organization.

We support the right of rank and file union members to control the destiny of their own local unions through democratic processes.

The unalterable position of the American Independent Party is that there is opportunity for full employment through the free enterprise system.

## IMMIGRATION

We support those measures as required by our Immigration Service to preclude illegal alien entry into our country and our territories and do support imprisonment for the alien convicted for a second entry violation. We are in sympathy with a limited entry for immigrants legitimately screened to assure their loyalty and openly welcome such individuals to become U. S. Citizens. In considering immigration policy, due consideration must be given to the interests of American workers in an already overcrowded job market.

## CONSUMER PROTECTION

The American Independent Party supports reasonable programs to provide protection for consumers and wage earners against hazards to their health and safety.

Believing in free competitive enterprise, we are unrelenting in our opposition to government maintained monopolies which stifle competition. Where the monopolies exist, they must be strictly regulated to protect the public from unfair and arbitrary rate increases.

We are opposed to the use by those monopolies, such as the telephone company, of its consumer derived revenues for political purposes for the direct or indirect influencing of elections.

## PRINCIPLES FOR A FISCAL POLICY

The Federal Government is a limited agency of the several states and its expenditures are limited to those purposes specifically delegated to it by the Constitution. Congress shall annually adopt a Federal budget for the following year and regulate expenditures and revenues so that no interest bearing debt is incurred, except in time of war declared by Congress.

## TAXATION

Through ever-increasing tax rates, the average taxpayer in America carries the full burden of the cost of a reckless and wasteful government, the ablebodied who refuse to work produce no income, pay no taxes, and frequently draw welfare subsidies from the producing citizens and the ultra-rich acquire vast sums, but use tax loopholes and tax-exempt foundations to evade the payment of taxes.

Inflation grows as the government goes farther into debt by spending beyond its income. Inflation becomes unlimited when the government increases its debt without limit. Inflation reduces the value of pensions, savings, social security, bonds, your personal insurance and your money. It is the "Dwindle Swindle" that affects all Americans.

The American Independent Party believes that the Federal government should be restricted to its constitutional functions, and that if this were done, it would be financially feasible to eliminate the federal personal graduated income tax, estate and gift taxes. Such a program, if adopted, would provide a profit of 20 percent to the average American wage earner. This proposal is contained in the Liberty Amendment, a proposed constitutional amendment, which has been introduced in Congress as House Joint Resolution 23, and the text of which follows:

Section 1. The Government of the United States shall not engage in any business, professional, commercial, financial or industrial enterprise except as specified in the Constitution.

Section 2. The constitution or laws of any State, or the laws of the United States shall not be subject to the terms of any foreign or domestic agreement which would abrogate this amendment.

Section 3. The activities of the United States Government which violate the intent and purpose of this amendment shall, within a period of three years from the date of the ratification of this amendment be liquidated and the properties and facilities affected shall be sold.

Section 4. Three years after the ratification of this amendment the sixteenth article of amendments to the Constitution of the United States shall stand repealed and thereafter Congress shall not levy taxes on personal incomes, estates, and/or gifts.

The American Independent Party supports immediate tax reduction for the lower- and middle-income citizens of America by closing of the tax loopholes for the ultra-rich, and by taxation of the presently tax-exempt foundations unless their purposes are narrowly limited to charitable pursuits.

## FEDERAL TELEPHONE TAX

The federal telephone tax is a nuisance and an unwarranted tax on speech. We call for its immediate repeal.

## MONETARY POLICY

The American Independent Party believes the inalienable rights of individuals to voluntarily exchange their services, goods and real property, using any items mutually agreed upon as their media of exchange, and to mine, own, use and trade precious metals, shall not be abridged by governments; nor shall governments declare anything legal tender except as provided by Article I, Section 8, Paragraph 5 of the United States Constitution.

## WELFARE

Public welfare is not and never has been a "Right."

The American Independent Party is sensitive to the needs of America's aged, blind, and disabled citizens and fully supports state and local programs to enable these citizens to live in dignity and economic security.

Government has removed from us both the opportunity and the incentive to be charitable and has removed from welfare recipients, the incentive to work.

We are unalterably opposed to tax-supported subsidies to able-bodied persons who refuse to work, who engage in welfare fraud or produce children simply for the purpose of securing ever-larger welfare payments. We support all necessary statutory and administrative amendments necessary to achieve the complete elimination of rampant fraud in public assistance programs.

## PUBLIC HOUSING

We oppose the concept of federally funded or subsidized public housing.

We hold that the solution to the problems of the slow down in the private housing industry is to lower the federally influenced high interest rates and to control inflation.

## HEALTH CARE

The average man today is threatened in his economic security by the high cost of health care. We believe that the advantages of our scientific achievements in the health field should be available to every citizen, through the free enterprise system.

We support the freedom of choice for an individual or group of individuals to advocate the distribution and voluntary use of any harmless health food or vitamin therapy which that individual or group of individuals feel is beneficial either psychologically or physically to the betterment of any American citizen.

We support cooperative effort between private insurance carriers and private charitable institutions to provide low cost health care insurance for the average citizen. We oppose any form of government controlled medicine.

We fully support the freedom of the citizen to choose his own healing practitioner.

Every citizen of the U.S. is entitled to seek health treatment of his choice and every health care practitioner in the U.S. is entitled to give his patient their mutually agreed upon treatment and should be restricted only if the treatment is conclusively proved harmful to the pateient.

We oppose compulsory mass medication in any form.

We are particularly sensitive to the special needs of the handicapped and we support private and state administered programs which offer these citizens the educational and employment opportunities to lead productive lives.

## Social Security

The American Independent Party fully appreciates the rightful aspirations of the aged to live in dignity and economic security. Government-caused inflation victimizes the aged.

We support requirements to protect social security funds as a special trust, to be used solely for the purpose of providing benefits to the beneficiaries.

We support the removal of the earnings limitation.

We support the right of those entering the labor market to elect to participate in private retirement plans as an alternative to the Social Security tax.

## Foreign Policy

We shall assert our determination to remain a free and sovereign nation. In consonance with this determination we shall pursue a course of diplomacy and trade that serves our national interest. The internal affairs of other nations are not of our concern and our internal affairs are concerns of this nation only. We shall immediately protest any transgression against this country, against our citizens and against our territories and possessions.

In 1976, the 200th Anniversary of the Independence of the United States, we are ever aware that the term "Captive Nations" is meaningless for many young Americans, and, unfortunately, to many older Americans.

We encourage the struggle for independent personal liberty and the resolve for national ethnic identity of over 160,000,000 individuals living under the yoke of communist Russian domination and tyranny, and encourage, support, and endorse an active role for the United States government in opposing—with every economic means available—continued community domination of freedom-minded peoples of the captive nations.

## National Sovereignty

The United States is a free and sovereign republic which desires to live in friendship with all free nations, without interfering in their internal affairs, and without permitting their interference in ours. We are, therefore, unalterably opposed to entangling alliances, via treaties or any other form of commitment, which compromise our national sovereignty. To this end, we shall:

> Steadfastly oppose American participation in any form of world government organization;
> Call upon the President and Congress to terminate United States membership in the United Nations and its subsidiary organizations; and
> Propose that the Constitution be amended to prohibit the United States Government from entering any treaty or other agreement which makes any commitment of American military forces or tax money, compromises the sovereignty of the United States, or accomplishes a purpose properly the subject of domestic law.

## Panama Canal

The American Independent Party emphatically endorses retention of our sovereignty over all present U.S. Possessions and Territories with special interest and concern for the Panama Canal.

## State Department

Too often and for too long, the national interests of our country and the personal interest of our citizens abroad have been placed secondary by policy and actions originating within the State Department bureaucracy.

The policy of detente is not in the interests of the American people and their security. Peaceful co-existence is surrender on the installment plan. The essence of the policy is the communist strategy of encirclement, demoralization and surrender, and in the few short years since its adoption, detente has been the cause of the swift crumbling of the sovereignty and defenses of the Free World.

We denounce the worldwide disruptive and divisive activities of Secretary of State Henry Kissinger and the entire concept of detente and the Helsinki agreement.

Our enemies are such that they can only understand, respect and be dealt with from a position of strength, not weakness. We would replace detente with a physically and morally pro-American policy.

It is considered imperative that all personnel now employed within the State Department immediately undergo an investigation to review their job competence and their loyalty to the United States. We call for an immediate restructuring of the Department and a redirection of the Department efforts towards total support of our national interest to the extent of being second to no one.

PACTS AND AGREEMENTS

Since World War II, the United States has increasingly played the undesirable role of an international policeman. Through our involvements abroad, our country is being changed from a republic to a world empire in which our freedoms are being sacrificed on an altar of international involvement. The United States is now committed by treaty to defend 42 foreign nations in all parts of the world, and by agreement other than treaties to defend at least 19 more.

Therefore we:

Call upon the President and the Congress to immediately commence a systematic withdrawal from any such treaties and agreements, unless such withdrawals would threaten the immediate national security of the United States; and

Reaffirm our support of the Monroe Doctrine under which the United States has clearly stated its perpetual interest in the independence from foreign domination of the several republics of the Western Hemisphere, so that all expansionistic powers will be forewarned of our commitment to the freedom of the Western Hemisphere from foreign domination.

NATIONALIST CHINA

As we oppose the spread of communism around the world, so we would repudiate the illegal government of Red China and insist that the U.S. strengthen trade ties to its anti-communist friends, including the Republic of China on Taiwan.

MIDDLE EAST

The American Independent Party is unalterably opposed to American involvement in the Middle East conflict between Israel and Arab States. The United States has no interest in the Middle East which justifies the sacrifice of our sons on a desert battlefield nor is our country properly cast as a merchant of death in the Middle East arms race.

We therefore propose that we:

Repudiate any commitment expressed or implied to send U.S. troops or military aid and equipment to participate in the Middle East conflict.

As it is not the prerogative of foreign nations to determine the internal policies of the United States, so it is not our prerogative to dictate the internal policies of foreign countries. We should, therefore, declare our friendship with all nations who genuinely desire friendship with us.

Consequently, we:

Call upon our government to cease its acts of hostility toward South Africa and Rhodesia, and, indeed, all other non-communist countries who have by word and deed demonstrated their friendship for the United States;

Commend the Congress for its action in ending American participation in UN sanctions against Rhodesia, particularly as they apply to the Byrd Amendment and as it applies to chromite and certain other strategic materials.

FOREIGN AID

Since World War II, the United States has been engaged in the greatest international giveaway program ever conceived by man, and is now in excess of $32,000,000,000 a year to aid foreign nations. These expenditures have won us no friends and constitute a major drain on the resources of our taxpayers.

Therefore, we demand that:

No further funds be appropriated for any kind of foreign aid programs;

United States participation in international lending institutions such as the World Bank and the International Monetary Fund, be ended;

All government subsidies and investment guarantees to encourage U. S. businesses to invest in foreign land be immediately terminated; and

All debts owed to the United States by foreign countries from previous wars be collected.

## NATIONAL DEFENSE

The American Independent Party believes a U.S. military posture second to none is the best guarantee for world peace and our only assurance of survival in a communist dominated world. Only those funds necessary will be expended for those armaments and manpower requirements to meet this goal. A continuous review of all expenditures will not only be expected but will be demanded from the Defense Department in order to eliminate waste and inefficiency in our military programs. The Defense Budget should reflect only those expenditures necessary for the National Defense, such hidden items as foreign aid should be removed.

We call for immediate abrogation of the Strategic Arms Limitation "SALT" agreement entered into with the Soviet Union.

We believe a vital component of our national defense rests with our Reserve Components and our National Guard State units. Recognizing the sacrifices and the dedication to duty of personnel within these units, we advocate equipment and training be provided to them on a par with the regular military programs.

We are opposed to blanket amnesty or pardon to draft dodgers who avoided the draft during the Vietnam War or to deserters.

We recommend that the United States Government continue to recognize the contribution of our servicemen to the national welfare by the extension of liberal benefits to all veterans.

## VETERANS

The American Independent Party commends all the American Veterans who served our Country honorably and the Veterans Organizations such as the V.F.W., American Legion, D.A.V., etc. who do such a good job of keeping alive a fervently patriotic spirit in the hearts of many Americans.

The Executive Branch of our government, with the tacit approval of Congress, in the past has involved us in an unconstitutional war in Vietnam which was contrary to the best interest of this nation.

While "no-win" wars encourage those who are called upon to serve in the armed services to resist the draft and to desert, blanket unconditional pardon or amnesty is not the answer. Such a program would only serve to encourage draft dodgers and deserters should the United States be forced into another war.

Hundreds of valiant American servicemen may now languish in the prison camps of Vietnam. America owes a duty and a responsibility to the brave men and their families to force the communist government of Vietnam to release any prisoners of war, and give a full and complete accounting of all Missing in Actions. America must not turn its back upon these brave men and abandon them to living deaths in communist captivity as has been the case with so many other American nationals held prisoner by communist Russia, Red China, and North Korea.

The American Independent Party further demands that never again shall U.S. troops be employed on any foreign field of battle without a declaration of war by Congress as required by the U.S. Constitution; that Congress refuse to fund unconstitutional, undeclared wars pursuant to Presidential whim or international obligations under which American sovereignty has been transferred to multi-national agencies; and that such statutes be adopted as may be required to achieve these objectives. We further recognize that most of the wars to which America has been a party throughout our history as a nation, not excepting Vietnam, have resulted from machinations of international finance in their centuries-old drive toward world government. Let us never again help them build the traps with which they would ensnare us.

We are unalterably opposed to any American aid to Vietnam.

The answer to the problem is not to involve the United States in a war unless there is the full known intention and effort to win the war and bring our fighting men home as soon as possible.

RECOMPUTATION OF MILITARY RETIREMENT PAY

By curbing government spending which is the main cause of inflation, we believe that benefits will accrue to all citizens and particularly to the elderly, retired and disabled. The American Independent Party does support a one-time recomputation for the military retirement pay to correct the inequity created by the Democratic controlled Congress.

*This Is Our Contract With You!*

## Communist Platform 1976

Nine-tenths of the U.S. people have no confidence in either the Republican President or the Democratic Congress. Why?

Because both major parties serve big business. They put profits before people.

They and their system are responsible for mass unemployment and inflation, with its sky-high prices, impossible rents for tenants and staggering interest rates for small homeowners and family farmers.

They add to their bloated profits by the wage freeze, speedup and attrition of workers. The real wages, the working conditions, safety and health of workers are scrapped—for more profit.

Now they're adopting a $120-billion military budget—highest in U.S. peace-time history—and are planning even higher ones for the coming years.

They use racism to divide the working people.

Who loses when Black, white, Chicano and Puerto Rican workers are pitted against each other for jobs? The working people lose.

They have ravaged our cities. They've slashed funds for the people's needs—homes, schools, hospitals, health care—at the same time they've handed out billions to Lockheed, Conrail (an amalgam of 17 railroads) and other corporate giants.

These same politicians feed at the Big Business trough. Gulf Oil, Exxon, Texaco—you name it—all have slipped millions to old party politicians in brazen violation of the laws against corrupt practices.

Now these same agents of big business demand "austerity" for the people. They say we're living too high on the hog. They want us all on short rations.

They peddle the notion that government spend-ing is the source of our problems. The real question is: Spending for what? Spending for the needs of the people—or spending for gold-plated guns for the Pentagon and give-aways to Lockheed and Conrail?

How do we meet this situation of crisis, of decline in living standards and quality of life?

The Communist Party candidates, Gus Hall for President and Jarvis Tyner for Vice President, have a fighting program to unite the working people, the family farmers—yes, the so-called plain people—in struggle to meet the needs of the day.

A FIGHTING PROGRAM

*1. Slash the Bloated Military Budget by 80%*

Use that wasted money for a different kind of war—a war on poverty and slums. Use it to rebuild our cities; for quality, low-rent housing; for low-interest loans to home-owners; for new schools, hospitals and mass transit.

*2. For Jobs—Cut the Work Week by Law to 30 Hours at 40 Hours' Pay*

Tax big business, not the working people, to finance jobs. Cut out the tax loopholes that permit the super-rich to get off tax-free. End all sales taxes and taxes on family incomes under $25,000.

*3. End All Cold War Policies*

To prevent a nuclear holocaust and to provide more jobs, strengthen detente and trade between our nation and the socialist world. End CIA-Pentagon intervention in other lands. Normalize relations with Cuba. Live up to the Paris treaty with Vietnam by paying reparations for reconstruction there.

*4. Independence for Puerto Rico*

End the sham of the so-called "commonwealth" status of Puerto Rico, which is actually a U.S. colony. Close all U.S. military bases on the island, and turn over all political and industrial authority to a government beholden only to the Puerto Rican people, not to U.S. big business and politicians.

*5. Outlaw Racism, Which Has Poisoned the Life of Our Nation*

Make racism a crime carrying prison penalties.

Outlaw the KKK, Nazi and other racist and anti-Semitic outfits. Strengthen existing civil rights laws and their enforcement in all aspects of life—employment, housing, education, health care and political representation.

### 6. Guarantee a Secure Future for Our Youth

End the scandalous situation where half the youth in the ghettos and barrios of our cities are jobless. Don't let the youth become an "excess baggage" generation. Restore and strengthen open admission and free tuition policies in the colleges. Pass a National Youth Act securing for youth the right to learn, work, live and hold public office. Guarantee job training and unemployment insurance for all youth, with or without previous job records.

### 7. End Discrimination and Establish Equality for Women in Social, Political and Economic Life

Guarantee equal pay for equal work by law. Pass affirmative action programs with teeth, including criminal penalties for discrimination against women.

### 8. Guarantee Justice to Our Senior Citizens

Step up the scale of social security payments with built-in cost-of-living escalators. Lift the permissible wage level for working senior citizens to $7,500 without loss of social security. Reduce the deductible on Medicare to zero. Free fare on all local interurban bus, rail and airlines.

### 9. Make the People's Health Care a No. 1 Priority

Pass a comprehensive National Health Act that will insure a program of preventive care and a full, free system of health and hospital facilities.

### 10. Abolish All Anti-democratic and Repressive Laws

Stop the disruption of people's organization by the FBI and CIA, and snooping on the people. Padlock the CIA and FBI. Abolish the anti-labor, anti-people's police "red squads." Repeal all anti-democratic election laws which restrict the ballot rights of minority parties and independents. Defeat the S.1 bill, loaded with danger to the people's constitutional rights.

UNITE AGAINST BIG BUSINESS

Gus Hall and Jarvis Tyner say frankly: we are for socialism. Capitalism has long ago outlived its usefulness. It is a rotten, dying system that breeds war, poverty and racism.

Whether you agree with our socialist ideals or not, we call on you to join in a giant fight against big business which dominates the economic and political life of our nation.

We want to help build a powerful anti-monopoly front of labor, small farmers, small business, professionals, and cultural workers which can turn our nation to a course of peace and progress.

We say: don't stay away from the elections. Get into the fight. Help place the Communist Party on the ballot and exercise your right to cast the vote with the most clout—a Communist vote.

*You wouldn't elect your boss as your shop steward. Why elect his stooge to public office?*

## Democratic Platform 1976

PREAMBLE

We meet to adopt a Democratic platform, and to nominate Democratic candidates for President and Vice President of the United States, almost 200 years from the day that our revolutionary founders declared this country's independence from the British crown.

The founder of the Democratic Party—Thomas Jefferson of Virginia—set forth the reasons for this separation and expressed the basic tenets of democratic government: *That all persons are created equal, that they are endowed by their creator with unalienable rights, that among these are Life, Liberty, and the Pursuit of Happiness—That to secure these rights, Governments are instituted among People, deriving their just powers from the consent of the governed.*

These truths may still be self-evident, but they have been tragically abused by our national government during the past eight years.

Two Republican Administrations have both misused and mismanaged the powers of national government, obstructing the pursuit of economic and social opportunity, causing needless hardship and despair among millions of our fellow citizens.

Two Republican Administrations have betrayed the people's trust and have created suspicion and distrust of government through illegal and unconstitutional actions.

We acknowledge that no political party, nor any President or Vice President, possesses answers to all of the problems that face us as a nation, but neither do we concede that every human problem is beyond our control. We recognize further that the present distrust of government cannot be transformed easily into confidence.

It is within our power to recapture, in the governing of this nation, the basic tenets of fairness, equality, opportunity and rule of law that motivated our revolutionary founders.

We do pledge a government that has as its guiding concern, the needs and aspirations of all the people, rather than the perquisites and special privilege of the few.

We do pledge a government that listens, that is truthful, and that is not afraid to admit its mistakes.

We do pledge a government that will be committed to a fairer distribution of wealth, income and power.

We do pledge a government in which the new Democratic President will work closely with the leaders of the Congress on a regular, systematic basis so that the people can see the results of unity.

We do pledge a government in which the Democratic members in both houses of Congress will seek a unity of purpose on the principles of the party.

Now, as we enter our 200th year as a nation, we as a party, with a sense of our obligations, pledge a reaffirmation of this nation's founding principles.

In this platform of the Democratic Party, we present a clear alternative to the failures of preceding administrations and a projection of the common future to which we aspire: a world at peace; a just society of equals; a society without violence; a society in consonance with its natural environment, affording freedom to the individual and the opportunity to develop to the fullest human potential.

## I. Full Employment, Price Stability and Balanced Growth

The Democratic Party's concern for human dignity and freedom has been directed at increasing the economic opportunities for all our citizens and reducing the economic deprivation and inequities that have stained the record of American democracy.

Today, millions of people are unemployed. Unemployment represents mental anxiety, fear of harassment over unpaid bills, idle hours, loss of self-esteem, strained family relationships, deprivation of children and youth, alcoholism, drug abuse and crime. A job is a key measure of a person's place in society—whether as a full-fledged participant or on the outside. Jobs are the solution to poverty, hunger and other basic needs of workers and their families. Jobs enable a person to translate legal rights of equality into reality.

Our industrial capacity is also wastefully underutilized. There are houses to build, urban centers to rebuild, roads and railroads to construct and repair, rivers to clean, and new sources of energy to develop. Something is wrong when there is work to be done, and the people who are willing to do it are without jobs. What we have lacked is leadership.

### Republican Mismanagement

During the past 25 years, the American economy has suffered five major recessions, all under Republican administrations. During the past eight years, we have had two costly recessions with continuing unprecedented peacetime inflation. "Stagflation" has become a new word in our language just as it has become a product of Republican economic policy. Never before have we had soaring inflation in the midst of a major recession.

Stagnation, waste and human suffering are the legacy left to the American people by Republican economic policies. During the past five years, U.S. economic growth has averaged only 1½ per cent per year compared with an historical average of about 4 per cent. Because of this shortfall, the nation has lost some $500-billion in the production of goods and services, and, if Republican rule continues, we can expect to lose another $600-$800-billion by 1980.

Ten million people are unemployed right now, and twenty to thirty million were jobless at some time in each of the last two years. For major groups in the labor force—minorities, women, youth, older workers, farm, factory and construction workers—unemployment has been, and remains, at depression levels.

The rising cost of food, clothing, housing, energy and health care has eroded the income of the average American family, and has pushed persons on fixed incomes to the brink of economic disaster. Since 1970, the annual rate of inflation has averaged more than 6 percent and is projected by the Ford administration to continue at an unprecedented peacetime rate of 6 to 7 per cent until 1978.

The depressed production and high unemployment rates of the Nixon-Ford administrations have produced federal deficits totaling $242 billion. Those who should be working and paying taxes are collecting unemployment compensation or other welfare payments in order to survive. For every one per cent increase in the unemployment rate—for every one million Americans out of work—we all pay $3 billion more in unemployment compensation and $2 billion in welfare and related costs, and lose $14 billion in taxes. In fiscal 1976, $76 billion was lost to the federal government through increased recession-related expenditures and lost revenues. In addition, state and local governments lost $27 billion in revenues. A return to full employment will eliminate such deficits. With prudent management of existing programs, full employment revenues will permit the financing of national Democratic initiatives.

For millions of Americans, the Republican Party has substituted welfare for work. Huge sums will be spent on food stamps and medical care for families of the unemployed. Social insurance costs are greatly increased. This year alone the federal government will spend nearly $20 billion on unemployment compensation. In contrast, spending on job development is only $2½ billion. The goal of the new Democratic administration will be to turn unemployment checks into pay checks.

## What Democrats Can Achieve

In contrast to the record of Republican mismanagement, the most recent eight years of Democratic leadership, under John F. Kennedy and Lyndon B. Johnson, produced economic growth that was virtually uninterrupted. The unemployment rate dropped from 6.7 per cent in 1961 to 3.6 per cent in 1968, and most segments of the population benefited. Inflation increased at an average annual rate of only 2 per cent, and the purchasing power of the average family steadily increased. In 1960, about 40 million people were living in poverty. Over the next eight years, 14½ million people moved out of poverty because of training opportunities, increased jobs and higher incomes. Since 1968, the number of persons living in poverty has remained virtually unchanged.

We have met the goals of full employment with stable prices in the past and can do it again. The Democratic Party is committed to the right of all adult Americans willing, able and seeking work to have opportunities for useful jobs at living wages. To make that commitment meaningful, we pledge ourselves to the support of legislation that will make every responsible effort to reduce adult unemployment to 3 per cent within 4 years.

## Modernizing Economic Policy

To meet our goals we must set annual targets for employment, production and price stability; the Federal Reserve must be made a full partner in national economic decisions and become responsive to the economic goals of Congress and the President; credit must be generally available at reasonable interest rates; tax, spending and credit policies must be carefully coordinated with our economic goals, and coordinated within the framework of national economic planning.

Of special importance is the need for national economic planning capability. This planning capability should provide roles for Congress and the Executive as equal partners in the process and provide for full participation by the private sector, and state and local government. Government must plan ahead just like any business, and this type of planning can be implemented without the creation of a new bureaucracy but rather through the well-defined use of existing bodies and techniques. If we do not plan, but continue to react to crisis after crisis, our economic performance will be further eroded.

## Full Employment Policies

Institutional reforms and the use of conventional tax, spending and credit policies must be accompanied by a broad range of carefully-targeted employment programs that will reduce unemployment in the private sector, and in regions, states and groups that have special employment problems.

The lack of formal coordination among federal, state and local governments is a major obstacle to full employment. The absence of economic policy coordination is particularly visible during times of high unemployment. Recessions reduce tax revenues, and increase unemployment-related expenditures for state and local governments. To maintain balanced budgets or reduce budget deficits these governments are forced to increase taxes and cut services—actions that directly undermine federal efforts to stimulate the economy.

Consistent and coherent economic policy requires federal anti-recession grant programs to state and local government, accompanied by public employment, public works projects and direct stimulus to the private sector. In each case, the programs should be phased in automatically when unemployment rises and phased out as it declines.

Even during periods of normal economic growth there are communities and regions of the country—particularly central cities and rural areas —that do not fully participate in national economic prosperity. The Democratic Party has supported national economic policies which have consciously sought to aid regions in the nation which have been afflicted with poverty, or newer regions which have needed resources for development. These policies were soundly conceived and have been successful. Today, we have different areas and regions in economic decline and once again face a problem of balanced economic growth. To restore balance, national economic policy should be designed to target federal resources in areas of greatest need. To make low interest loans to businesses and state and local governments for the purpose of encouraging private sector investment in chronically depressed areas, we endorse consideration of programs such as a domestic development bank or federally insured taxable state and local bonds with adequate funding, proper management and public disclosure.

Special problems faced by young people, especially minorities, entering the labor force persist regardless of the state of the economy. To meet the needs of youth, we should consolidate existing youth employment programs; improve training, apprenticeship, internship and job-counseling programs at the high school and college levels; and permit youth participation in public employment projects.

There are people who will be especially difficult to employ. Special means for training and locating jobs for these people in the private sector, and, to the extent required, in public employment, should be established. Every effort should be made to create jobs in the private sector. Clearly, useful public jobs are far superior to welfare and unemployment payments. The federal government has the responsibility to ensure that all Americans able, willing and seeking work are provided opportunities for useful jobs.

## Equal Employment Opportunity

We must be absolutely certain that no person is excluded from the fullest opportunity for economic and social participation in our society on the basis of sex, age, color, religion or national origin. Minority unemployment has historically been at least double the aggregate unemployment rate, with incomes at two-thirds the national average. Special emphasis must be placed on closing this gap.

Accordingly, we reaffirm this Party's commitment to full and vigorous enforcement of all equal opportunities laws and affirmative action. The principal agencies charged with anti-discrimination enforcement in jobs—the Equal Employment Opportunity Commission, the Department of Labor, and the Justice Department—are locked into such overlapping and uncoordinated strategies that a greatly improved government-wide system for the delivery of equal job and promotion opportunities must be developed and adequate funding committed to that end. New remedies to provide equal opportunities need exploration.

## Anti-Inflation Policies

The economic and social costs of inflation have been enormous. Inflation is a tax that erodes the income of our workers, distorts business investment decisions, and redistributes income in favor of the rich, Americans on fixed incomes, such as the elderly, are often pushed into poverty by this cruel tax.

The Ford administration and its economic advisors have been consistently wrong about the sources and cures of the inflation that has plagued our nation and our people. Fighting inflation by curtailing production and increasing unemployment has done nothing to restrain it. With the current high level of unemployment and low level of capacity utilization, we can increase production and employment without rekindling inflation.

A comprehensive anti-inflation policy must be established to assure relative price stability. Such a program should emphasize increased production and productivity and should take other measures to enhance the stability and flexibility of our economy.

The see-saw progress of our economy over the past eight years has disrupted economic growth. Much of the instability has been created by stop-and-go monetary policies. High interest rates and the recurring underutilization of our manufacturing plant and equipment have retarded new investment. The high cost of credit has stifled small business and virtually halted the housing industry. Unemployment in the construction industry has been raised to depression levels and home ownership has been priced beyond the reach of the majority of our people.

Stable economic growth with moderate interest rates will not only place downward pressure on prices through greater efficiency and productivity, but will reduce the prospects for future shortages of supply by increasing the production of essential goods and services and by providing a more predictable environment for business investment.

The government must also work to improve the ability of our economy to respond to change. Competition in the private sector, a re-examination, reform and consolidation of the existing regulatory structure, and promotion of a freer but fair system of international trade will aid in achieving that goal.

At times, direct government involvement in wage and price decisions may be required to ensure price stability. But we do not believe that such involvement requires a comprehensive system of mandatory controls at this time. It will require that business and labor must meet fair standards of wage and price change. A strong domestic council on price and wage stability should be established with particular attention to restraining price increases in those sectors of our economy where prices are "administered" and where price competition does not exist.

The federal government should hold public hearings, investigate and publish facts on price, profit, wage and interest rate increases that seriously threaten national price stability. Such investigations and proper planning can focus public opinion and awareness on the direction of price, profit, wage and interest rate decisions.

Finally, tax policy should be used if necessary to maintain the real income of workers as was done with the 1975 tax cut.

*Economic Justice*

The Democratic Party has a long history of opposition to the undue concentration of wealth and economic power. It is estimated that about three-quarters of the country's total wealth is owned by one-fifth of the people. The rest of our population struggles to make ends meet in the face of rising prices and taxes.

*Anti-trust enforcement.* The next Democratic administration will commit itself to move vigorously against anti-competitive concentration of power within the business sector. This can be accomplished in part by strengthening the anti-trust laws and insuring adequate commitment and resources for the enforcement of these laws. But we must go beyond this negative remedy to a positive policy for encouraging the development of small business, including the family farm.

*Small businesses.* A healthy and growing small business community is a prerequisite for increasing competition and a thriving national economy. While most people would accept this view, the federal government has in the past impeded the growth of small business.

To alleviate the unfavorable conditions for small business, we must make every effort to assure the availability of loans to small business, including direct government loans at reasonable interest rates particularly to those in greatest need, such as minority-owned businesses. For example, efforts should be made to strengthen minority business programs, and increase minority opportunities for business ownership. We support similar programs and opportunities for women. Federal contract and procurement opportunities in such areas as housing, transportation and energy should support efforts to increase the volume of minority and small business involvement. Regulatory agencies and the regulated small business must work together to see that federal regulations are met, without applying a stranglehold on the small firm or farm and with less paperwork and red tape.

*Tax reform.* Economic justice will also require a firm commitment to tax reform at all levels. In recent years there has been a shift in the tax burden from the rich to the working people of this country. The Internal Revenue Code offers massive tax welfare to the wealthiest income groups in the population and only higher taxes for the average citizen. In 1973, there were 622 people with adjusted income of $100,000 or more who still managed to pay no tax. Most families pay between 20 and 25 per cent of their income in taxes.

We have had endless talk about the need for tax reform and fairness in our federal tax system. It is now time for action.

We pledge the Democratic Party to a complete overhaul of the present tax system, which will review all special tax provisions to ensure that they are justified and distributed equitably among our citizens. A responsible Democratic tax reform program could save over $5-billion in the first year with larger savings in the future.

We will strengthen the internal revenue tax code so that high income citizens pay a reasonable tax on all economic income.

We will reduce the use of unjustified tax shelters in such areas as oil and gas, tax-loss farming, real estate, and movies.

We will eliminate unnecessary and ineffective tax provisions to business and substitute effective incentives to encourage small business and capital formation in all businesses. Our commitment to full employment and sustained purchasing power will also provide a strong incentive for capital formation.

We will end abuses in the tax treatment of income from foreign sources; such as special tax treatment and incentives for multinational corporations that drain jobs and capital from the American economy.

We will overhaul federal estate and gift taxes to provide an effective and equitable structure to promote tax justice and alleviate some of the legitimate problems faced by farmers, small business men and women and others who would otherwise be forced to liquidate assets in order to pay the tax.

We will seek and eliminate provisions that encourage uneconomic corporate mergers and acquisitions.

We will eliminate tax inequities that adversely affect individuals on the basis of sex or marital status.

We will curb expense account deductions.

And we will protect the rights of all taxpayers against oppressive procedures, harassment and invasions of privacy by the Internal Revenue Service.

At present, many federal government tax and expenditure programs have a profound but unintended and undesirable impact on jobs and on where people and business locate. Tax policies and other indirect subsidies have promoted deterioration of cities and regions. These policies should be reversed.

There are other areas of taxation where change is also needed. The Ford administration's unwise and unfair proposal to raise the regressive social security tax gives new urgency to the Democratic Party's goal of redistributing the burden of the social security tax by raising the wage base for earnings subject to the tax with effective exemptions and deductions to ease the impact on low income workers and two-earner families. Further revision in the Social Security program will be required so that women are treated as individuals.

The Democratic Party should make a reappraisal of the appropriate sources of federal revenues. The historical distribution of the tax burden between corporations and individuals, and among the various types of federal taxes, has changed dramatically in recent years. For example, the corporate tax share of federal revenue has declined from 30 per cent in 1954 to 14 per cent in 1975.

## Labor Standards and Rights

The purpose of fair labor standards legislation has been the maintenance of the minimum standards necessary for the health, efficiency and general well-being of workers. Recent inflation has eroded the real value of the current minimum wage. This rapid devaluation of basic income for working people makes a periodic review of the level of the minimum wage essential. Such a review should insure that the minimum wage rate at least keep pace with the increase in the cost of living.

Raising the pay standard for overtime work, additional hiring of part-time persons and flexible work schedules will increase the independence of workers and create additional job opportunities, especially for women. We also support the principle of equal pay for comparable work.

We are committed to full implementation and enforcement of the Equal Credit Opportunity Act.

Over a generation ago this nation established a labor policy whose purpose is to encourage the practice and procedure of collective bargaining and the right of workers to organize to obtain this goal. The Democratic Party is committed to extending the benefit of the policy to all workers and to removing the barriers to its administration. We support the right of public employees and agricultural workers to organize and bargain collectively. We urge the adoption of appropriate federal legislation to ensure this goal.

We will seek to amend the Fair Labor Standards Act to speed up redress of grievances of workers asserting their legal rights.

We will seek to enforce and, where necessary, to amend the National Labor Relations Act to eliminate delays and inequities and to provide for more effective remedies and administration.

We will support the full right of construction workers to picket a job site peacefully.

We will seek repeal of Section 14(b) of the Taft-Hartley Act which allows states to legislate the anti-union open shop.

We will maintain strong support for the process of voluntary arbitration, and we will enact minimum federal standards for workers compensation laws and for eligibility, benefit amounts, benefit duration and other essential features of the unemployment insurance program. Unemployment insurance should cover all wage and salary workers.

The Occupational Safety and Health Act of 1970 should cover all employees and be enforced as intended when the law was enacted. Early and periodic review of its provisions should be made to insure that they are reasonable and workable.

The Democratic Party will also seek to enact a comprehensive mine safety law, utilizing the most effective and independent enforcement by the federal government and support special legislation providing adequate compensation to coal miners and their dependents who have suffered disablement or death as a result of the black lung disease.

We believe these policies will put America back to work, bring balanced growth to our economy and give all Americans an opportunity to share in the expanding prosperity that will come from a new Democratic administration.

## II. GOVERNMENT REFORM AND BUSINESS ACCOUNTABILITY

The current Republican administration did not invent inept government, but it has saddled the country with ineffective government; captive government, subservient to the special pleading of private economic interests; insensitive government, trampling over the rights of average citizens; and remote government, secretive and unresponsive.

Democrats believe that the cure for these ills is not the abandonment of governmental responsibility for addressing national problems, but the restoration of legitimate popular control over the organs and activities of government.

There must be an ever-increasing accountability of government to the people. The Democratic Party is pledged to the fulfillment of four fundamental citizen rights of governance: the right to competent government; the right to responsive government; the right to integrity in government; the right to fair dealing by government.

### The Right to Competent Government

The Democratic Party is committed to the adoption of reforms such as zero-based budgeting, mandatory reorganization timetables, and sunset laws which do not jeopardize the implementation of basic human and political rights. These reforms are designed to terminate or merge existing agencies and programs, or to renew them, only after assuring elimination of duplication, overlap, and conflicting programs and authorities, and the matching of funding levels to public needs. In addition, we seek flexibility to reflect changing public needs, the use of alternatives to regulation and the elimination of special interest favoritism and bias.

To assure that government remains responsive to the people's elected representatives, the Democratic Party supports stepped-up congressional agency oversight and program evaluation, including full implementation of the congressional budget process; an expanded, more forceful role for the General Accounting Office in performing legislative audits for Congress; and restraint by the President in exercising executive privilege designed to withhold necessary information from Congress.

## The Right to Responsive Government

To begin to restore the shaken faith of Americans that the government in Washington is *their* government—responsive to their needs and desires, not the special interests of wealth, entrenched political influence, or bureaucratic self-interest—government decision-making must be opened up to citizen advocacy and participation.

Governmental decision-making behind closed doors is the natural enemy of the people. The Democratic Party is committed to openness throughout government: at regulatory commissions, advisory committee meetings and at hearings. Public calendars of scheduled meetings between regulators and the regulated, and freedom of information policies, should be designed to facilitate rather than frustrate citizen access to documents and information.

All persons and citizen groups must be given standing to challenge illegal or unconstitutional government action in court and to compel appropriate action. Where a court or an agency finds evidence of government malfeasance or neglect those who brought forward such evidence should be compensated for their reasonable expenses in doing so.

Democrats have long sought—against fierce Republican and big business opposition—the creation and maintenance of an independent consumer agency with the staff and power to intervene in regulatory matters on behalf of the consuming and using public. Many states have already demonstrated that such independent public or consumer advocates can win important victories for the public interest in proceedings before state regulatory agencies and courts.

This nation's Civil Service numbers countless strong and effective public servants. It was the resistance of earnest and steadfast federal workers that stemmed the Nixon-Ford efforts to undermine the integrity of the Civil Service. The reorganization of government which we envision will protect the job rights of civil servants and permit them to more effectively serve the public.

The Democratic Party is committed to the review and overhaul of Civil Service laws to assure:

insulation from political cronyism, accountability for nonfeasance as well as malfeasance, protection for the public servant who speaks out to identify corruption or failure, performance standards and incentives to reward efficiency and innovation and to assure nondiscrimination and affirmative action in the recruitment, hiring and promotion of civil service employees.

We support the revision of the Hatch Act so as to extend to federal workers the same political rights enjoyed by other Americans as a birthright, while still protecting the Civil Service from political abuse.

## The Right to Integrity in Government

The Democratic Party is pledged to the concept of full public disclosure by major public officials and urges appropriate legislation to effectuate this policy.

We support divestiture of all financial holdings which directly conflict with official responsibilities and the development of uniform standards, review procedures and sanctions to identify and eliminate potential conflicts of interest.

Tough, competent regulatory commissioners with proven commitment to the public interest are urgently needed.

We will seek restrictions on "revolving door" careerism—the shuttling back and forth of officials between jobs in regulatory or procurement agencies and in regulated industries and government contractors.

All diplomats, federal judges and other major officials should be selected on a basis of qualifications. At all levels of government services, we will recruit, appoint and promote women and minorities.

We support legislation to ensure that the activities of lobbyists be more thoroughly revealed both within the Congress and the Executive agencies.

The Democratic Party has led the fight to take the presidency off the auction block by championing the public financing of presidential elections. The public has responded with enthusiastic use of the $1 income tax checkoff. Similar steps must now be taken for congressional candidates. We call for legislative action to provide for partial public financing on a matching basis of the congressional elections, and the exploration of further reforms to insure the integrity of the electoral process.

## The Right to Fair Dealing by Government

A citizen has the right to expect fair treatment from government. Democrats are determined to find a means to make that right a reality.

An Office of Citizen Advocacy should be established as part of the executive branch, independent of any agency, with full access to agency records and with both the power and the responsibility to investigate complaints.

Freedom of information requirements must be interpreted in keeping with the right of the individual to be free from anonymous accusation or slander. Each citizen has the right to know and to review any information directly concerning him or her held by the government for any purpose whatsoever under the Freedom of Information Act and the Privacy Act of 1974, other than those exceptions set out in the Freedom of Information Act. Such information should be forthcoming promptly, without harassment and at a minimal cost to the citizen.

Appropriate remedies must be found for citizens who suffer hardship as the result of abuse of investigative or prosecutorial powers.

## Business Accountability

The Democratic Party believes that competition is preferable to regulation and that government has a responsibility to seek the removal of unreasonable restraints and barriers to competition, to restore and, where necessary, to stimulate the operation of market forces. Unnecessary regulation should be eliminated or revised, and the burden of excessive paperwork and red tape imposed on citizens and businesses should be removed.

The Democratic Party encourages innovation and efficiency in the private sector.

The Democratic Party also believes that strengthening consumer sovereignty—the ability of consumers to exercise free choice, to demand satisfaction, and to obtain direct redress of grievances—is similarly preferable to the present indirect government protection of consumers. However, government must not shirk its responsibility to impose and rigorously enforce regulation where necessary to ensure health, safety and fairness.

We reiterate our support for unflinching antitrust enforcement, and for the selection of an Attorney General free of political obligation and committed to rigorous antitrust prosecution.

We shall encourage consumer groups to establish and operate consumer cooperatives that will enable consumers to provide themselves marketplace alternatives and to provide a competitive spur to profit-oriented enterprises.

We support responsible cost savings in the delivery of professional services including the use of low-cost paraprofessionals, efficient group practice and federal standards for state no-fault insurance programs.

We reiterate our support for full funding of neighborhood legal services for the poor.

The Democratic Party is also committed to strengthening the knowledge and bargaining power of consumers through government-supported systems for developing objective product performance standards; advertising and labeling requirements for the disclosure of essential consumer information; and efficient and low-cost redress of consumer complaints including strengthened small claims courts, informal dispute settlement mechanisms, and consumer class actions.

The Democratic Party is committed to making the U.S. Postal Service function properly as an essential public service.

We reaffirm the historic Democratic commitment to assure the wholesomeness of consumer products such as food, chemicals, drugs and cosmetics, and the safety of automobiles, toys and appliances. Regulations demanding safe performance can be developed in a way that minimizes their own costs and actually stimulates product innovation beneficial to consumers.

## III. Government and Human Needs

The American people are demanding that their national government act more efficiently and effectively in those areas of urgent human needs such as welfare reform, health care and education.

However, beyond these strong national initiatives, state and local governments must be given an increased, permanent role in administering social programs. The federal government's role should be the constructive one of establishing standards and goals with increased state and local participation. There is a need for a new blueprint for the public sector, one which identifies and responds to national problems, and recognizes the proper point of administration for both new and existing programs. In shifting administrative responsibility, such programs must meet minimum federal standards.

Government must concentrate, not scatter, its resources. It should not divide our people by inadequate and demanding programs. The initiatives we propose do not require larger bureaucracy. They do require committed government.

The Democratic Party realizes that accomplishing our goals in the areas of human needs will require time and resources. Additional resources will become available as we implement our full-employment policies. Federal revenues also grow over time. After full-employment has been achieved, $20 billion of increased revenue will be generated by a fully operating economy each year. The program detailed in the areas of human needs cannot be accomplished immediately, but an orderly beginning can be made and the effort expanded as additional resources become available.

*Health Care*

In 1975, national health expenditures averaged $547 per person—an almost 40 per cent increase in four years. Inflation and recession have combined to erode the effectiveness of the Medicare and Medicaid programs.

An increasingly high proportion of health costs have been shifted back to the elderly. An increasing Republican emphasis on restricting eligibility and services is emasculating basic medical care for older citizens who cannot meet the rising costs of good health.

We need a comprehensive national health insurance system with universal and mandatory coverage. Such a national health insurance system should be financed by a combination of employer-employee shared payroll taxes and general tax revenues. Consideration should be given to developing a means of support for national health insurance that taxes all forms of economic income. We must achieve all that is practical while we strive for what is ideal, taking intelligent steps to make adequate health services a right for all our people. As resources permit, this system should not discriminate against the mentally ill.

Maximum personal interrelationships between patients and their physicians should be preserved. We should experiment with new forms of medical care delivery to mold a national health policy that will meet our needs in a fiscally responsible manner.

We must shift our emphasis in both private and public health care away from hospitalization and acute-care services to preventive medicine and the early detection of the major cripplers and killers of the American people. We further support increased federal aid to the government laboratories as well as private institutions to seek the cure to heart disease, cancer, sickle cell anemia, paralysis from spinal cord injury, drug addiction and other such afflictions.

National health insurance must also bring about a more responsive consumer-oriented system of health care delivery. Incentives must be used to increase the number of primary health care providers, and shift emphasis away from limited-application, technology-intensive programs. By reducing the barriers to primary preventive care, we can lower the need for costly hospitalization. Communities must be encouraged to avoid duplication of expensive technologies and meet the genuine needs of their populations. The development of community health centers must be resumed. We must develop new health careers, and promote a better distribution of health care professionals, including the more efficient use of paramedics. All levels of government should concern themselves with increasing the number of doctors and paramedical personnel in the field of primary health care.

A further need is the comprehensive treatment of mental illness, including the development of Community Mental Health Centers that provide comprehensive social services not only to alleviate, but to prevent mental stresses resulting from social isolation and economic dislocation. Of particular importance is improved access to the health care system by underserved population groups.

We must have national health insurance with strong built-in cost and quality controls. Rates for institutional care and physicians' services should be set in advance, prospectively. Alternative approaches to health care delivery, based on prepayment financing, should be encouraged and developed.

Americans are currently spending $133 billion for health care—8.3% of our Gross National Product. A return to full employment and the maintenance thereafter of stable economic growth will permit the orderly and progressive development of a comprehensive national health insurance program which is federally financed. Savings will result from the removal of inefficiency and waste in the current multiple public and private insurance programs and the structural integration of the delivery system to eliminate duplication and waste. The cost of such a program need not exceed the share of the GNP this nation currently expends on health care; but the resulting improvement of health service would represent a major improvement in the quality of life enjoyed by Americans at all economic levels.

## Welfare Reform

Fundamental welfare reform is necessary. The problems with our current chaotic and inequitable system of public assistance are notorious. Existing welfare programs encourage family instability. They have few meaningful work incentives. They do little or nothing for the working poor on substandard incomes. The patchwork of federal, state and local programs encourages unfair variations in benefit levels among the states, and benefits in many states are well below the standards for even lowest-income budgets.

Of the current programs, only Food Stamps give universal coverage to all Americans in financial need. Cash assistance, housing aid and health care subsidies divide recipients into arbitrary categories. People with real needs who do not fit existing categories are ignored altogether.

The current complexity of the welfare structure requires armies of bureaucrats at all levels of government. Food Stamps, Aid to Families with Dependent Children, and Medicaid are burdened by unbelievably complex regulations, statutes and court orders. Both the recipients of these benefits, and the citizen who pays for them, suffer as a result. The fact that our current system is administered and funded at different levels of government makes it difficult to take initiatives to improve the status of the poor.

We should move toward replacement of our existing inadequate and wasteful system with a simplified system of income maintenance, substantially financed by the federal government, which includes a requirement that those able to work be provided with appropriate available jobs or job training opportunities. Those persons who are physically able to work (other than mothers with

dependent children) should be required to accept appropriate available jobs or job training. This maintenance system should embody certain basic principles. First and most important, it should provide an income floor both for the working poor and the poor not in the labor market. It must treat stable and broken families equally. It must incorporate a simple schedule of work incentives that guarantees equitable levels of assistance to the working poor. This reform may require an initial additional investment, but it offers the prospect of stabilization of welfare costs over the long run, and the assurance that the objectives of this expenditure will be accomplished.

As an interim step, and as a means of providing immediate federal fiscal relief to state and local governments, local governments should no longer be required to bear the burden of welfare costs. Further, there should be a phased reduction in the states' share of welfare costs.

## Civil and Political Rights

To achieve a just and healthy society and enhance respect and trust in our institutions, we must insure that all citizens are treated equally before the law and given the opportunity, regardless of race, color, sex, religion, age, language or national origin, to participate fully in the economic, social and political processes and to vindicate their legal and constitutional rights.

In reaffirmation of this principle, an historic commitment of the Democratic Party, we pledge vigorous federal programs and policies of compensatory opportunity to remedy for many Americans the generations of injustice and deprivation; and full funding of programs to secure the implementation and enforcement of civil rights.

We seek ratification of the Equal Rights Amendment, to insure that sex discrimination in all its forms will be ended, implementation of Title IX, and elimination of discrimination against women in all federal programs.

We support the right of all Americans to vote for President no matter where they live; vigorous enforcement of voting rights legislation to assure the constitutional rights of minority and language-minority citizens; the passage of legislation providing for registration by mail in federal elections to erase existing barriers to voter participation; and full home rule for the District of Columbia, including authority over its budget and local revenues, elimination of federal restrictions in matters which are purely local and voting representation in the Congress, and the declaration of the birthday of the great civil rights leader, Martin Luther King, Jr., as a national holiday.

We pledge effective and vigorous action to protect citizens' privacy from bureaucratic technological intrusions, such as wiretapping and bugging without judicial scrutiny and supervision; and a full and complete pardon for those who are in legal or financial jeopardy because of their peaceful opposition to the Vietnam War, with deserters to be considered on a case-by-case basis.

We fully recognize the religious and ethical nature of the concerns which many Americans have on the subject of abortion. We feel, however, that it is undesirable to attempt to amend the U.S. Constitution to overturn the Supreme Court decision in this area.

The Democratic Party reaffirms and strengthens its legal and moral trust responsibilities to the American Indian. We believe it is honorable to obey and implement our treaty obligations to the first Americans. In discharging our duty, we shall exert all and necesssary assistance to afford the American Indians the protection of their land, their water and their civil rights.

Federal laws relating to American Indians and the functions and purposes of the Bureau of Indian Affairs should be reexamined.

We support a provision in the immigration laws to facilitate acquisition of citizenship by Resident Aliens.

We are committed to Puerto Rico's right to enjoy full self-determination and a relationship that can evolve in ways that will most benefit U.S. citizens in Puerto Rico. The Democratic Party respects and supports the present desire of the people of Puerto Rico to freely associate in permanent union with the United States, as an autonomous commonwealth or as a State.

*Education*

The goal of our educational policy is to provide our citizens with the knowledge and skills they need to live successfully. In pursuing this goal, we will seek adequate funding, implementation and enforcement of requirements in the education programs already approved by Congress.

We should strengthen federal support of existing programs that stress improvement of reading and math skills. Title I of the Elementary and Secondary Education Act must reach those it is intended to benefit to effectively increase these primary skills. "Break-throughs" in compensatory education require a concentration of resources on each individual child and a mix of home and school activities that is not possible with the underfunded Republican programs. Compensatory education is realistic only when there is a stable sequence of funding that allows proper planning and continuity of programs, an impossibility under Republican veto and impoundment politics.

We should also work to expand federal support in areas of educational need that have not yet been addressed sufficiently by the public schools—education of the handicapped, bilingual education and vocational education, and early childhood education. We propose federally financed, family centered developmental and educational child care programs—operated by the public schools or other local organizations, including both private and community—and that they be available to all who need and desire them. We support efforts to provide for the basic nutritional needs of students.

We recognize the right of all citizens to education, pursuant to Title VI of the Civil Rights Act of 1968, and the need in affected communities for bilingual and bicultural educational programs. We call for compliance with civil rights requirements in hiring and promotion in school systems.

For the disadvantaged child, equal opportunity requires concentrated spending. And for all children, we must guarantee that jurisdictions of differing financial capacity can spend equal amounts on education. These goals do not conflict but complement each other.

The principle that a child's education should depend on the property wealth of his or her school jurisdiction has been discredited in the last few years. With increased federal funds, it is possible to enhance educational opportunity by eliminating spending disparities within state borders. State-based equalizations, even state takeover of education costs, to relieve the overburdened property taxpayer and to avoid the inequities in the existing finance system, should be encouraged.

The essential purpose of school desegregation is to give all children the same educational opportunities. We will continue to support that goal. The Supreme Court decision of 1954 and the aftermath were based on the recognition that separate educational facilities are inherently unequal. It is clearly our responsibility as a party and as citizens to support the principles of our Constitution.

The Democratic Party pledges its concerted help through special consultation, matching funds, incentive grants and other mechanisms to communities which seek education, integrated both in terms of race and economic class, through equitable, reasonable and constitutional arrangements. Mandatory transportation of students beyond their neighborhoods for the purpose of desegregation remains a judicial tool of the last resort for the purpose of achieving school desegregation. The Democratic Party will be an active ally of those communities which seek to enhance the quality as well as the integration of educational opportunities. We encourage a variety of other measures, including the redrawing of attendance lines, pairing of schools, use of the "magnet school" concept, strong fair housing enforcement, and other techniques for the achievement of racial and economic integration.

The Party reaffirms its support of public school education. The Party also renews its commitment to the support of a constitutionally acceptable method of providing tax aid for the education of all pupils in non-segregated schools in order to insure parental freedom in choosing the best education for their children. Specifically, the Party will continue to advocate constitutionally permissible federal education legislation which provides for the equitable participation in federal programs of all low- and moderate-income pupils attending all the nation's schools.

The Party commits itself to support of adult education and training which will provide skills upgrading.

In higher education, our Party is strongly committed to extending postsecondary opportunities for students from low- and middle-income families, including older students and students who can attend only part-time. The Basic Educational Opportunity Grants should be funded at the full payment schedule, and campus-based programs of aid must be supported to provide a reasonable choice of institutions as well as access. With a co-ordinated and reliable system of grants, loans and work study, we can relieve the crisis in costs that could shut all but the affluent out of our colleges and universities.

The federal government and the states must develop strategies to support institutions of higher education from both public and private sources. The federal government should directly provide cost of education payments to all higher education institutions, including predominantly black colleges, to help cover per-student costs, which far exceed those covered by tuition and fees.

Finally, government must systematically support basic and applied research in the liberal arts, the sciences, education and the professions—without political interference or bureaucratic restraint. The federal investment in graduate education should be sustained and selectively increased to meet the need for highly trained individuals. Trainee-ships and fellowships should be provided to attract the most talented students, especially among minority groups and women.

Libraries should receive continuous guaranteed support and the presently impounded funds for nationwide library planning and development should be released immediately.

## Social Services

The Nixon-Ford administration would limit eligibility for federally-subsidized social services to the very poor. Social services can make significant changes in the lives of the non-poor, as well. The problems of alcoholism, drug abuse, mental retardation, child abuse or neglect, and mental illness arise at every income level, and quality daycare has become increasingly urgent for low- and middle-income families. Federal grants to the states should support a broad community-based program of social services to low- and middle-income families, to assure that these programs reach their intended populations.

The states are now being required to take over an increasing share of existing social service programs. In 1972, the ceiling for federal social service grants was frozen at $2.5 billion, and subsequent inflation of 28 per cent has reduced the effective federal aid to existing programs. While there must certainly be a ceiling on such grants, it should be raised to compensate for inflation and to encourage states and localities to expand social services to low- and moderate-income families.

## Disabled Citizens

We support greater recognition of the problems of the disabled and legislation assuring that all people with disabilities have reasonable access to all public accommodations and facilities. The

Democratic Party supports affirmative action goals for employment of the disabled.

## Older Citizens

The Democratic Party has always emphasized that adequate income and health care for senior citizens are basic federal government responsibilities. The recent failure of government to reduce unemployment and alleviate the impact of the rising costs of food, housing and energy have placed a heavy burden on those who live on fixed and limited incomes, especially the elderly. Our other platform proposals in these areas are designed to help achieve an adequate income level for the elderly.

We will not permit an erosion of social security benefits, and while our ultimate goal is a health security system ensuring comprehensive and quality care for all Americans, health costs paid by senior citizens under the present system must be reduced.

We believe that Medicare should be made available to Americans abroad who are eligible for Social Security.

Democrats strongly support employment programs and the liberalization of the allowable earnings limitation under Social Security for older Americans who wish to continue working and living as productive citizens. We will put an end to delay in implementation of nutrition programs for the elderly and give high priority to a transportation policy for senior citizens under the Older Americans Act. We pledge to enforce vigorously health and safety standards for nursing homes, and seek alternatives which allow senior citizens where possible to remain in their own homes.

## Veterans

America's veterans have been rhetorically praised by the Nixon-Ford administration at the same time that they have been denied adequate medical, educational, pension and employment benefits.

Vietnam veterans have borne the brunt of unemployment and economic mismanagement at home. As late as December 1975, the unemployment rate for Vietnam veterans was over 10 per cent. Younger Vietnam veterans (ages 20-24) have had unemployment rates almost twice the rate of similarly-aged non-veterans. Job training, placement, and information and counseling programs for veterans are inadequate.

The Veterans Administration health care program requires adequate funding and improved management and health care delivery in order to provide high quality service and effectively meet the changing needs of the patient population.

The next Democratic administration must act to rescue pensioner veterans below the poverty line. Thirty per cent of the veterans and 50 per cent of the widows receiving pensions have total incomes below the poverty line. Cost of living increases should be automatic in the veterans' pension and disability system.

Educational assistance should be expanded two years for those veterans already enrolled and drawing benefits in VA-approved educational and training programs.

## The Arts and Humanities

We recognize the essential role played by the arts and humanities in the development of America. Our nation cannot afford to be materially rich and spiritually poor. We endorse a strong role for the federal government in reinforcing the vitality and improving the economic strength of the nation's artists and arts institutions, while recognizing that artists must be absolutely free of any government control. We would support the growth and development of the National Endowments for the Arts and Humanities through adequate funding, the development of special anti-recession employment programs for artists, copyright reforms to protect the rights of authors, artists and performers, and revision of the tax laws that unfairly penalize artists. We further pledge our support for the concept and adequate financing of public broadcasting.

## IV STATES, COUNTIES AND CITIES

More than eight years ago, the Kerner Commission on Civil Disorders concluded that the disorders of the 1960s were caused by the deteriorating conditions of life in our urban centers—abject poverty, widespread unemployment, uninhabitable housing, declining services, rampant crime and disintegrating families. Many of these same problems plagued rural America as well. Little has been done by the Republican administrations to deal with the fundamental challenges to our society. This policy of neglect gives the lie to the current administration's rhetorical commitment to state and local governments.

By tolerating intolerable unemployment, by

vetoing programs for the poor, the old, and the ill, by abandoning the veterans and the young, and by withholding necessary funds for the decaying cities, the Nixon-Ford years have been years of retrogression in the nation's efforts to meet the needs of our cities. By abdicating responsibility for meeting these needs at the national level, the current administration has placed impossible burdens on fiscally hard-pressed state and local governments. In turn, local governments have been forced to rely excessively on the steadily diminishing and regressive property tax—which was originally designed to cover property related services and was never intended to support the services now required in many of our cities and towns.

Federal policies and programs have inadvertently exacerbated the urban crisis. Within the framework of a new partnership of federal, state and local governments, and the private sector, the Democratic Party is pledged to the development of America's first national urban policy. Central to the success of that policy are the Democratic Party's commitments to full employment, incentives for urban and rural economic development, welfare reform, adequate health care, equalization of education expenditures, energy conservation and environmental quality. If progress were made in these areas, much of the inappropriately placed fiscal burden would be removed, and local governments could better fulfill their appropriate responsibilities.

To assist further in relieving both the fiscal and service delivery problems of states and local governments, the Democratic Party reaffirms its support for general revenue sharing as a base for the fiscal health of all levels of government, acknowledging that the civil rights and citizens' participation provisions must be strengthened. We further believe that there must be an increase in the annual funding to compensate for the erosion of inflation. We believe the distribution formula should be adjusted to reflect better community and state needs, poverty levels, and tax effort.

Finally, to alleviate the financial burden placed on our cities by the combination of inflation and recession, the Democratic Party restates its support for an emergency anti-recession aid to states and cities particularly hard hit by recession.

*Housing and Community Development*

In the past eight Republican years, housing has become a necessity priced as a luxury. Housing prices have nearly doubled in the past six years and housing starts have dropped by almost one-quarter. The effect is that over three-fourths of American families cannot afford to buy an average-priced home. The basic national goal of providing decent housing and available shelter has been sacrificed to misguided tax, spending and credit policies which were supposed to achieve price stability but have failed to meet that goal. As a result, we do not have decent housing or price stability. The vision of the Housing Act of 1968, the result of three decades of enlightened Democratic housing policy, has been lost. The Democratic Party reasserts these goals, and pledges to achieve them.

The Democratic Party believes it is time for a housing and urban development policy which recognizes the needs and difficulties of both the buying and renting public and the housing industry. We support a revitalized housing program which will be able to meet the public's need for housing at reasonable cost and the industry's need for relief from years of stagnation and now-chronic unemployment.

We support direct federal subsidies and low interest loans to encourage the construction of low and moderate income housing. Such subsidies shall not result in unreasonable profit for builders, developers or credit institutions.

We support the expansion of the highly successful programs of direct federal subsidies to provide housing for the elderly.

We call for greatly increased emphasis on the rehabilitation of existing housing to rebuild our neighborhoods—a priority which is undercut by the current pattern of federal housing money which includes actual prohibitions to the use of funds for rehabilitation.

We encourage public and private commitments to the preservation and renovation of our country's historic landmarks so that they can continue as a vital part of our commercial and residential architectural heritage.

We will work to assure that credit institutions make greater effort to direct mortgage money into the financing of private housing.

We will take all necessary steps to prohibit the practice of red-lining by private financial institutions, the FHA, and the secondary mortgage market which have had the effect of depriving certain areas of the necessary mortgage funds which they need to upgrade themselves. We will further encourage an increase in loans and subsidies for housing and rehabilitation, especially in poverty stricken areas.

We support greater flexibility in the use of community development block grants at the local level.

The current Housing and Community Development Act should be reformed and restructured so that its allocation, monitoring, and citizen participation features better address the needs of local communities, major cities and underdeveloped rural areas.

The revitalization of our cities must proceed with an understanding that housing, jobs and related community facilities are all critical to a successful program. The Democratic Party will create the necessary incentives to insure that private and public jobs are available to meet the employment needs of these communities and pledges a more careful planning process for the location of the federal government's own employment-creating facilities.

The Democratic Party proposes a revitalization of the Federal Housing Administration as a potent institution to stabilize new construction and existing housing markets. To this end, the Agency's policies must be simplified, its operating practices and insurance rate structures modernized and the sense of public service which was the hallmark of the FHA for so many years must be restored. In addition, we propose automatic triggering of direct production subsidies and a steady flow of mortgage funds during periods when housing starts fall below acceptable levels.

Women, the elderly, single persons and minorities are still excluded from exercising their right to select shelter in the areas of their choice, and many "high-risk" communities are systematically denied access to the capital they require. The Democratic Party pledges itself to the aggressive enforcement of the Fair Housing Act; to the promotion and enforcement of equal opportunity in housing; and to the pursuit of new regulatory and incentive policies aimed at providing minority groups and women with equal access to mortgage credit.

In addition to direct attacks upon such known violations of the law, a comprehensive approach to these problems must include policies aimed at the underlying causes of unequal credit allocations. The Democratic Party pledges itself to ag-

gressive policies designed to assure lenders that their commitments will be backed by government resources, so that investment risks will be shared by the public and private sectors.

## The Special Needs of Older Cities

The Democratic Party recognizes that a number of major, older cities—including the nation's largest city—have been forced to undertake even greater social responsibilities, which have resulted in unprecedented fiscal crises. There is a national interest in helping such cities in their present travail, and a new Democratic President and the Congress shall undertake a massive effort to do so.

## Law Enforcement and Law Observance

The total crime bill in the United States has been estimated at $90 billion a year, almost as much as the cost of our national defense. But over and above the economic impact, the raging and unchecked growth of crime seriously impairs the confidence of many of our citizens in their ability to walk on safe streets, to live securely in peaceful and happy homes, and to work safely in their places of business. Fear mounts along with the crime rate. Homes are made into fortresses. In large sections of every major city, people are afraid to go out at night. Outside big cities, the crime rate is growing even faster, so that suburbs, small towns and rural areas are no longer secure havens.

Defaulting on their "law and order" promises, the Republicans in the last eight years have let the rising tide of crime soil the highest levels of government, allowed the crime rate to skyrocket and failed to reform the criminal justice system. Recognizing that law enforcement is essentially a local responsibility, we declare that control of crime is an urgent national priority and pledge the efforts of the Democratic Party to insure that the federal government act effectively to reverse these trends and to be an effective partner to the cities and states in a well-coordinated war on crime.

We must restore confidence in the criminal justice system by insuring that detection, conviction and punishment of lawbreakers is swift and sure; that the criminal justice system is just and efficient; that jobs, decent housing and educational opportunities provide a real alternative to crime to those who suffer enforced poverty and injustice.

We pledge equally vigorous prosecution and punishment for corporate crime, consumer fraud and deception; programs to combat child abuse and crimes against the elderly; criminal laws that reflect national needs; application of the law with a balanced and fair hand; a judiciary that renders equal justice for all; criminal sentences that provide punishment that actually punishes and rehabilitation that actually rehabilitates; and a correctional system emphasizing effective job training, educational and post-release programs. Only such measures will restore the faith of the citizens in our criminal justice system.

Toward these ends, we support a major reform of the criminal justice system, but we oppose any legislative effort to introduce repressive and anti-civil libertarian measures in the guise of reform of the criminal code.

The Law Enforcement Assistance Administration has not done its job adequately. Federal funding for crime-fighting must be wholly revamped to more efficiently assist local and state governments in strengthening their law enforcement and criminal justice systems, rather than spend money on the purchase of expensive equipment, much of it useless.

Citizen confidence in law enforcement can be enhanced through increased citizen participation, by informing citizens of police and prosecutor policies, assuring that police departments reflect a cross-section of the communities they serve, establishing neighborhood forums to settle simple disputes, restoring the grand jury to fair and vigorous independence, establishing adequate victim compensation programs, and reaffirming our respect for the individual's right to privacy.

Coordinated action is necessary to end the vicious cycle of drug addiction and crime. We must break up organized crime syndicates dealing in drugs, take necessary action to get drug pushers off the streets, provide drug users with effective rehabilitation programs, including medical assistance, ensure that all young people are aware of the costs of a life of drug dependency, and use worldwide efforts to stop international production and trafficking in illicit drugs.

A Democratic Congress in 1974 passed the Juvenile Justice and Delinquency Prevention Act to come to grips with the fact that juveniles account for almost half of the serious crimes in the United States, and to remedy the fact that federal programs thus far have not met the crisis of juvenile delinquency. We pledge funding and implementation of this Act, which has been ignored by the Republican Administration.

Handguns simplify and intensify violent crime. Ways must be found to curtail the availability of these weapons. The Democratic Party must provide the leadership for a coordinated federal and state effort to strengthen the presently inadequate controls over the manufacture, assembly, distribution and possession of handguns and to ban Saturday night specials.

Furthermore, since people and not guns commit crimes, we support mandatory sentencing for individuals convicted of committing a felony with a gun.

The Democratic Party, however, affirms the right of sportsmen to possess guns for purely hunting and target-shooting purposes.

The full implementation of these policies will not in themselves stop lawlessness. To insure professionally trained and equitably rewarded police forces, law enforcement officers must be properly recruited and trained, and provided with decent wages, working conditions, support staff, and federal death benefits for those killed in line of duty.

Effective police forces cannot operate without just and speedy court systems. We must reform bail and pre-trial detention procedures. We must assure speedy trials and ease court congestion by increasing the number of judges, prosecutors and public defenders. We must improve and streamline courthouse management procedures, require criminal justice records to be accurate and responsible, and establish fair and more uniform sentencing for crimes.

Courts should give priority to crimes which are serious enough to deserve imprisonment. Law enforcement should emphasize the prosecution of crimes against persons and property as a higher priority than victimless crimes. Current rape laws need to be amended to abolish archaic evidence rules that discriminate against rape victims.

We pledge that the Democratic Party will not tolerate abuses of governmental processes and unconstitutional action by the government itself. Recognizing the value of legitimate intelligence efforts to combat espionage and major crime, we call for new legislation to ensure that these efforts will no longer be used as an excuse for abuses such as bugging, wiretaps, mail opening and disruption aimed at lawful political and private activities.

The Attorney General in the next Democratic administration will be an independent, non-political official of the highest integrity. If lawlessness is found at any level, in any branch, immediate and decisive action will be taken to root it out. To that end, we will establish the machinery for appointing an independent Special Prosecutor whenever needed.

As a party, as a nation, we must commit ourselves to the elimination of injustice wherever it plagues our government, our people and our future.

## Transportation

An effective national transportation policy must be grounded in an understanding of all transportation systems and their consequences for costs, reliability, safety, environmental quality and energy savings. Without public transportation, the rights of all citizens to jobs and social services cannot be met.

To that end, we will work to expand substantially the discretion available to states and cities in the use of federal transportation money, for either operating expenses or capital programs on the modes of transportation which they choose. A greater share of Highway Trust Fund money should also be available on a flexible basis.

We will change further the current restrictive limits on the use of mass transit funds by urban and rural localities so that greater amounts can be used as operating subsidies; we emphatically oppose the Republican administration's efforts to reduce federal operating subsidies.

We are committed to dealing with the transportation needs of rural America by upgrading secondary roads and bridges and by completion of the original plan of 1956 for the interstate highway system where it benefits rural Americans. Among other benefits, these measures would help overcome the problems of getting products to market, and services to isolated persons in need.

We will take whatever action is necessary to reorganize and revitalize our nation's railroads.

We are also committed to the support of healthy trucking and bus, inland waterway and air transport systems.

A program of national rail and road rehabilitation and improved mass transit would not only mean better transportation for our people, but it would also put thousands of unemployed construction workers back to work and make them productive tax-paying citizens once again.

Further, it would move toward the Democratic Party's goal of assuring balanced transportation services for all areas of the nation—urban and rural. Such a policy is intended to reorganize both pressing urban needs and the sorry state of rural public transportation.

## Rural Development

The problems of rural America are closely linked to those of our cities. Rural poor and the rural elderly suffer under the same economic pressures and have at least as many social needs as their counterparts in the cities. The absence of rural jobs and rural vitality and the continuing demise of the family farm have promoted a migration to our cities which is beyond the capacity of the cities to absorb. Over 20 million Americans moved to urban areas between 1940 and 1960 alone. We pledge to develop programs to make the family farm economically healthy again so as to be attractive to young people.

To that end, the Democratic Party pledges to strengthen the economy and thereby create jobs in our great agricultural and rural areas by the full implementation and funding of the Rural Development Act of 1972 and by the adoption of an agricultural policy which recognizes that our capacity to produce food and fiber is one of our greatest assets.

While it is bad enough to be poor, or old, or alone in the city, it is worse in the country. We are therefore committed to overcome the problems of rural as well as urban isolation and poverty by insuring the existence of adequate health facilities, critically-needed community facilities such as water supply and sewage disposal systems, decent housing, adequate educational opportunity and needed transportation throughout rural America.

As discussed in the transportation section, we believe that transportation dollars should be available in a manner to permit their flexible use. In rural areas this means they could be used for such needs as secondary road improvement, taxi systems, buses, or other systems to overcome the problems of widely dispersed populations, to facilitate provisions of social services and to assure access of citizens to meet human needs.

Two thousand family farms are lost per week. To help assure that family farms stay in the family where they belong, we will push increases in relevant estate tax exemptions. This increased exemption, when coupled with programs to increase generally the vitality of rural America, should mean that the demise of the family farm can be reversed.

We will seek adequate levels of insured and guaranteed loans for electrification and telephone facilities.

Only such a coordinated program can make rural America again attractive and vigorous, as it needs to be if we are to deal with the challenges facing the nation as a whole.

### Administration of Federal Aid

Federal aid programs impose jurisdictional and administrative complications which substantially diminish the good accomplished by the federal expenditure of about $50 billion annually on state and local governments. An uncoordinated policy regarding eligibility requirements, audit guidelines, accounting procedures and the like comprise the over 800 categorical aid programs and threaten to bog down the more broadly conceived flexible block grant programs. The Democratic Party is committed to cutting through this chaos and simplifying the grant process for both recipient governments and program administrators.

The Democratic Party also reaffirms the role of state and general purpose local governments as the principal governments in the orderly administration of federal aid and revenue sharing programs.

## V. NATURAL RESOURCES AND ENVIRONMENTAL QUALITY

### Energy

Almost three years have passed since the oil embargo. Yet, by any measure, the nation's energy lifeline is in far greater peril today. America is running out of energy—natural gas, gasoline and oil.

The economy is already being stifled. The resulting threat of unemployment and diminished production is already present.

If America, as we know it, is to survive, we must move quickly to develop renewable sources of energy.

The Democratic Party will strive to replace the rapidly diminishing supply of petroleum and natural gas with solar, geothermal, wind, tide and other forms of energy, and we recommend that the federal government promptly expand whatever funds are required to develop new systems of energy.

We have grown increasingly dependent on imported oil. Domestic production, despite massive price increases, continues to decline. Energy stockpiles, while authorized, are yet to be created. We have no agreements with any producing nations for security of supply. Efforts to develop alternative energy sources have moved forward slowly. Production of our most available and plentiful alternative—coal—is not increasing. Energy conservation is still a slogan, instead of a program.

Republican energy policy has failed because it is based on illusions; the illusion of a free market in energy that does not exist, the illusion that ever-increasing energy prices will not harm the economy, and the illusion of an energy program based on unobtainable independence.

The time has come to deal with the realities of the energy crisis, not its illusions. The realities are that rising energy prices, falling domestic supply, increasing demand, and the threat to national security of growing imports, have not been contained by the private sector.

The Democratic energy platform begins with a recognition that the federal government has an important role to play in insuring the nation's energy future, and that it must be given the tools it needs to protect the economy and the nation's consumers from arbitrary and excessive energy price increases and help the nation embark on a massive domestic energy program focusing on conservation, coal conversion, exploration and development of new technologies to insure an adequate short-term and long-term supply of energy for the nation's needs. A nation advanced enough and wealthy enough to send a man to the moon must dedicate itself to developing alternate sources of energy.

*Energy pricing.* Enactment of the Energy Policy and Conservation Act of 1975 established oil ceiling prices at levels sufficient to maximize domestic production but still below OPEC equivalents. The act was a direct result of the Democratic Congress' commitment to the principle that beyond certain levels, increasing energy prices simply produce high-cost energy—without producing any additional energy supplies.

This oil-pricing lesson should also be applied to natural gas. Those not pressing to turn natural gas price regulation over to OPEC, while arguing the rhetoric of so-called deregulation, must not prevail. The pricing of new natural gas is in need of reform. We should narrow the gap between oil and natural gas prices with new natural gas ceiling prices that maximize production and investment while protecting the economy and the consumer. Any reforms in the pricing of new natural gas should not be at the cost of severe economic dislocations that would accelerate inflation and increase unemployment.

An examination must be made of advertising cost policies of utilities and the imposition of these costs on the consumer. Advertising costs used to influence public policy ought to be borne by stockholders of utility companies and not by the consumers.

*Domestic supply and demand.* The most promising neglected domestic option for helping balance our energy budget is energy conservation. But major investments in conservation are still not being made.

The Democratic Party will support legislation to establish national building performance standards on a regional basis designed to improve energy efficiency. We will provide new incentives for aiding individual homeowners, particularly average income families and the poor in undertaking conservation investments. We will support the reform of utility rate structures and regulatory rules to encourage conservation and ease the utility rate burden on residential users, farmers and other consumers who can least afford it; make more efficient use of electrical generating capacity; and we will aggressively pursue implementation of automobile efficiency standards and appliance labeling programs already established by Democratic initiative in the Energy Policy and Conservation Act.

Coal currently comprises 80 percent of the nation's energy resources, but produces only 16 per cent of the nation's energy. The Democratic Party believes that the United States' coal production can and must be increased without endangering the health and safety of miners, diminishing the land and water resources necessary for increased food production, and sacrificing the personal and property rights of farmers, ranchers and Indian tribes.

We must encourage the production of the high-est quality coal, closest to consumer markets, in order to insure that investments in energy production reinforce the economics of energy producing and consuming regions. Improved rail transportation systems will make coal available where it is actually needed, and will insure a rail transport network required for a healthy industrial and agricultural economy.

We support an active federal role in the research and development of clean burning and commercially competitive coal burning systems and technologies, and we encourage the conversion to coal of industrial users of natural gas and imported oil. Air quality standards that make possible the burning of coal without danger to the public health or degradation of the nation's clear air must be developed and implemented.

The Democratic Party wants to put an end to the economic depression, loss of life and environmental destruction that has long accompanied irresponsible coal development in Appalachia. Strip mining legislation designed to protect and restore the environment, while ending the uncertainty over the rules governing future coal mining, must be enacted.

The huge reserves of oil, gas and coal on federal territory, including the outer continental shelf, belong to all the people. The Republicans have pursued leasing policies which give the public treasury the least benefit and the energy industry the most benefit from these public resources. Consistent with environmentally sound practices, new leasing procedures must be adopted to correct these policies, as well as insure the timely development of existing leases.

Major federal initiatives, including major governmental participation in early high-risk development projects, are required if we are to harness renewable resources like solar, wind, geothermal, the oceans, and other new technologies such as fusion, fuel cells and the conversion of solid waste and starches into energy. The Ford Administration has failed to provide those initiatives, and, in the process, has denied American workers important new opportunities for employment in the building and servicing of emerging new energy industries.

U.S. dependence on nuclear power should be kept to the minimum necessary to meet our needs. We should apply stronger safety standards as we regulate its use. And we must be honest with our people concerning its problems and dangers as well as its benefits.

An increasing share of the nuclear research dollar must be invested in finding better solutions to the problems of nuclear waste disposal, reactor safety and nuclear safeguards—both domestically and internationally.

*Competition in the domestic petroleum industry.* Legislation must be enacted to insure energy administrators and legislators access to information they need for making the kind of informed decisions that future energy policy will require. We believe full disclosure of data on reserves, supplies and costs of production should be mandated by law.

It is increasingly clear that there is no free, competitive market for crude oil in the United States. Instead, through their control of the nation's oil pipelines, refineries and marketing, the major oil producers have the capability of controlling the field and often the downstream price of almost all oil.

When competition inadequate to insure free markets and maximum benefit to American consumers exists, we support effective restrictions on the right of major companies to own all phases of the oil industry.

We also support the legal prohibition against corporate ownership of competing types of energy, such as oil and coal. We believe such "horizontal" concentration of economic power to be dangerous both to the national interest and to the functioning of the competitve system.

*Improved energy planning.* Establishment of a more orderly system for setting energy goals and developing programs for reaching those goals should be undertaken. The current proliferation of energy jurisdictions among many executive agencies underscores the need for a more coordinated system. Such a system should be undertaken, and provide for centralization of overall energy planning in a specific executive agency and an assessment of the capital needs for all priority programs to increase production and conservation of energy.

*Mineral Resources.* As with energy resources, many essential mineral resources may soon be inadequate to meet our growing needs unless we plan more wisely than we have with respect to

energy. The Democratic Party pledges to undertake a long-range assessment of supply of our mineral reserves as well as the demand for them.

*Agriculture*

As a nation, we are blessed with rich resources of land, water and climate. When the supporting technology has been used to preserve and promote the family ownership and operation of farms and ranches, the people have been well served.

America's farm families have demonstrated their ability and eagerness to produce food in sufficient quantity to feed their fellow citizens and share with hungry people around the world as well. Yet this national asset has been neither prudently developed nor intelligently used.

The eight-year record of the Nixon-Ford administration is a record of lost opportunities, failure to meet the challenges of agricultural statesmanship, and favoritism to the special pleading of giant corporate agricultural interests.

Republican misrule in agriculture has caused wide fluctuations in prices to producers, inflated food prices to consumers, unconscionable profiteering on food by business, unscrupulous shipping practices by grain traders, and the mishandling of our abundance in export markets. Republican agricultural policy has spelled high food prices, unstable farm income, windfalls for commodity speculators and multinational corporations, and confrontations between farmer and consumer.

Foremost attention must be directed to the establishment of a national food and fiber policy which will be fair to both producer and consumer, and be based on the family farm agricultural system which has served the nation and the world so well for so long.

Maximum agricultural production will be the most effective means of achieving an adequate food and fiber supply and reasonable price stability to American consumers. Without parity income assurance to farmers, full production cannot be achieved in an uncertain economy. We must assure parity return to farmers based on costs of production plus a reasonable profit.

We must continue and intensify efforts to expand agriculture's long-term markets abroad, and at the same time we must prevent irresponsible and inflationary sales from the American granary to foreign purchasers. Aggressive but stable and consistent export policy must be our goal. The production of food and fiber in America must be used as part of a constructive foreign policy based on long-term benefits at home and abroad, but not at the expense of the farmers.

Producers shall be encouraged to produce at full capacity within the limits of good conservation practices, including the use of recycled materials, if possible and desirable, to restore natural soil fertility. Any surplus production needed to protect the people of the world from famine shall be stored on the farm in such a manner as to isolate it from the market place.

Excess production beyond the needs of the people for food shall be converted to industrial purposes.

Farmers as individual producers must deal constantly with organized suppliers and marketers, and compete with non-farm conglomerates. To assist them in bargaining for the tools of production, and to strengthen the institution of the family farm, the Democratic Party will: support the Capper-Volstead Act in its present form; curb the influence of non-farm conglomerates which, through the elimination of competition in the marketplace, pose a threat to farmers; support the farmer cooperatives and bargaining associations; scrutinize and remedy any illegal concentrations and price manipulations of farm equipment and supply industries; revitalize basic credit programs for farmers; provide adequate credit tailored to the needs of young farmers; assure access for farmers and rural residents to energy, transportation, electricity and telephone services; reinstate sound, locally administered soil conservation programs; eliminate tax shelter farming; and overhaul federal estate and gift taxes to alleviate some of the legal problems faced by farm families who would otherwise be forced to liquidate their assets to pay the tax.

Long overdue are programs of assistance to farm workers in housing, employment, health, social services and education.

To protect the health of our citizens the government shall insure that all agricultural imports must meet the same quality standards as those imposed on agricultural products produced in the United States and that only quality American agricultural products be exported.

*Fisheries.* America's fisheries must be protected and enhanced as a renewable resource through ecologically sound conservation practices and meaningful international agreements and compacts between individual states.

### Environmental Quality

The Democratic Party's strong commitment to environmental quality is based on its conviction that environmental protection is not simply an aesthetic goal, but is necessary to achieve a more just society. Cleaning up air and water supplies and controlling the proliferation of dangerous chemicals is a necessary part of a successful national health program. Protecting the worker from workplace hazards is a key element of our full employment program. Occupational disease and death must not be the price of a weekly wage.

The Democratic Party, through the Congress, has recognized the need for basic environmental scrutiny, and has authored a comprehensive program to achieve this objective. In eight years, the efforts to implement that program have been thwarted by an administration committed only to unfounded allegations that economic growth and environmental protection are incompatible.

Quite to the contrary, the Democratic Party believes that a concern for the environment need not and must not stand in the way of a much-needed policy of high economic growth.

Moreover, environmental protection creates jobs. Environmental legislation enacted since 1970 already has produced more than one million jobs, and we pledge to continue to work for additional laws to protect, restore and preserve the environment while providing still more jobs.

Today, permanently harmful chemicals are dispersed, and irrecoverable land is rendered worthless. If we are to avoid repeated environmental crises, we must now renew our efforts to restore both environmental quality and economic growth.

Those who would use the environment must assume the burden of demonstrating that it will not be abused. For too long this burden has been on government agencies, representing the public, to assess and hopefully correct the damage that has already been done.

Our irreplacable natural and aesthetic resources must be managed to ensure abundance for future generations. Strong land and ocean use planning is an essential element of such management. The artifacts of the desert, the national forests, the wilderness areas, the endangered species, the coastal beaches and barrier dunes and other precious resources are in danger. They cannot be restored. They must be protected.

Economic inequities created by subsidies for virgin materials to the disadvantage of recycled materials must be eliminated. Depletion allowances and unequal freight rates serve to discourage the growing numbers of businesses engaged in recycling efforts.

Environmental research and development within the public sector should be increased substantially. For the immediate future, we must learn how to correct the damage we have already done, but more importantly, we need research on how to build a society in which renewable and non-renewable resources are used wisely and efficiently.

Federal environmental anti-pollution requirement programs should be as uniform as possible to eliminate economic discrimination. A vigorous program with national minimum environmental standards fully implemented, recognizing basic regional differences, will ensure that states and workers are not penalized by pursuing environmental programs.

The technological community should be encouraged to produce better pollution-control equipment, and more importantly, to produce technology which produces less pollution.

VI. INTERNATIONAL RELATIONS

The next Democratic administration must and will initiate a new American foreign policy.

Eight years of Nixon-Ford diplomacy have left our nation isolated abroad and divided at home. Policies have been developed and applied secretly and arbitrarily by the executive department from the time of secret bombing in Cambodia to recent covert assistance in Angola. They have been policies that relied on ad hoc, unilateral maneuvering, and a balance-of-power diplomacy suited better to the last century than to this one. They have disdained traditional American principles which once earned the respect of other peoples while inspiring our own. Instead of efforts to foster freedom and justice in the world, the Republican administration has built a sorry record of disregard for human rights, manipulative interference in the internal affairs of other nations,

and, frequently, a greater concern for our relations with totalitarian adversaries than with our democratic allies. And its efforts to preserve, rather than reform, the international status quo betray a self-fulfilling pessimism that contradicts a traditional American belief in the possibility of human progress.

Defense policy and spending for military forces must be consistent with meeting the real security needs of the American people. We recognize that the security of our nation depends first and foremost on the internal strength of American society —economic, social and political. We also recognize that serious international threats to our security, such as shortages of food and raw materials, are not solely military in nature and cannot be met by military force or the threat of force. The Republican Administration has, through mismanagement and misguided policies, undermined the security of our nation by neglecting human needs at home while, for the first time in our nation's history, increasing military spending after a war. Billions of dollars have been diverted into wasteful, extravagant and, in some instances, destabilizing military programs. Our country can—and under a Democratic administration it will—work vigorously for the adoption of policies of full employment and economic growth which will enable us to meet both the justified domestic needs of our citizens and our needs for an adequate national defense.

A Democratic administration will work to create a foreign policy that does justice to the strength and decency of the American people through adherence to these fundamental principles and priorities:

We will act on the premise that candor in policy-making, with all its liabilities, is preferable to deceit. The Congress will be involved in the major international decisions of our government, and our foreign policies will be openly and consistently presented to the American people. For even if diplomatic tactics and national security information must sometimes remain secret, there can be no excuse for formulating and executing basic policy without public understanding and support.

Our policy must be based on our nation's commitment to the ideal of individual freedom and justice. Experience has taught us not to rely solely on military strength or economic power, as necessary as they are, in pursuit of our international objectives. We must rely too on the moral strength of our democratic values—the greatest inspiration to our friends and the attribute most feared by our enemies. We will ensure that human needs are not sacrificed to military spending, while maintaining the military forces we require for our security.

We will strengthen our ties to the other great democracies, working together to resolve common economic and social problems as well as to keep our defenses strong.

We will restore the Democratic tradition of friendship and support to Third World nations.

We must also seek areas of cooperation with our traditional adversaries. There is no other option, for human survival itself is at stake. But pursuit of detente will require maintenance of a strong American military deterrent, hard bargaining for our own interest, recognition of continuing competition, and a refusal to oversell the immediate benefits of such a policy to the American public.

We will reaffirm the fundamental American commitment to human rights across the globe. America must work for a release of all political prisoners—men and women who are in jail simply because they have opposed peacefully the policies of their governments or have aided others who have—in all countries. America must take a firm stand to support and implement existing U.S. law to bring about liberalization of emigration policy in countries which limit or prohibit free emigration. America must be resolute in its support of the right of workers to organize and of trade unions to act freely and independently, and in its support of freedom of the press. America must continue to stand as a bulwark in support of human liberty in all countries. A return to the politics of principle requires a reaffirmation of human freedom throughout the world.

### The Challenge of Interdependence

*The international economy.* Eight years of mismanagement of the American economy have contributed to global recession and inflation. The most important contribution a Democratic administration will make to the returning health of the world economy will be to restore the health of our own economy, with all that means to international economic stability and progress.

We are committed to trade policies that can benefit a full employment economy—through

creation of new jobs for American workers, new markets for American farmers and businesses, and lower prices and a wider choice of goods for American consumers. Orderly reductions in trade barriers should be negotiated on a reciprocal basis that does not allow other nations to deny us access to their markets while enjoying access to ours. These measures must be accompanied by improved programs to ease dislocations and to relieve the hardship of American workers affected by foreign competition.

The Democratic Party will also seek to promote higher labor standards in those nations where productivity far outstrips wage rates, harming American workers through unfair exploitation of foreign labor, and encouraging American capital to pursue low wage opportunities that damage our own economy and weaken the dollar.

We will exert leadership in international efforts to strengthen the world economic system. The Ford administration philosophy of reliance on the international "market economy" is insufficient in a world where some governments and multinational corporations are active in managing and influencing market forces.

We pledge constant efforts to keep world monetary systems functioning properly in order to provide a reasonably stable economic environment for business and to prevent the importation of inflation. We will support reform of the international monetary system to strengthen institutional means of coordinating national economic policies, especially with our European and Japanese allies, thus facilitating efforts by our government and others to achieve full employment.

The Democratic Party is committed to a strong and competitive merchant fleet, built in the United States and manned by American seamen, as an instrument of international relations and national security. In order to revitalize our merchant fleet, the party pledges itself to a higher level of coordination of maritime policy, reaffirmation of the objectives of the Merchant Marine Acts of 1936 and 1970, and the development of a national cargo policy which assures the U.S. fleet a fair participation in all U.S. trade.

A Democratic administration will vigorously pursue international negotiations to insure that the multinational activities of corporations, whether American or foreign, be made more responsible to the international community. We will give priority attention to the establishment of an international code of conduct for multinational corporations and host countries.

We will encourage multinational corporations—before they relocate production across international boundaries—to make sufficient advance arrangements for the workers whose jobs will be affected.

We will eliminate bribery and other corrupt practices.

We will prevent these corporations from interfering in the political systems of the countries in which they operate.

If such a code cannot be negotiated or proves to be unenforceable, our country should reserve the right to take unilateral action directed toward each of these problems, specifically including the outlawing of bribes and other improper payments to government officials of other nations.

In pursuit of open and fair international economic relationships, we will seek mechanisms, including legislation, to ensure that foreign governments cannot introduce third party boycotts or racial and religious discrimination into the conduct of American foreign commerce.

*Energy.* The United States must be a leader in promoting cooperation among the industrialized countries in developing alternative energy sources and reducing energy consumption, thus reducing our dependence on imports from the Middle East and restraining high energy prices. Under a Democratic Administration, the United States also will support international efforts to develop the vast energy potential of the developing countries.

We will also actively seek to limit the dangers inherent in the international development of atomic energy and in the proliferation of nuclear weapons. Steps to be given high priority will include: revitalization of the Nonproliferation Treaty, expansion of the International Atomic Energy Agency and other international safeguards and monitoring of national facilities, cooperation against potential terrorism involving nuclear weapons, agreement by suppliers not to transfer enrichment or reprocessing facilities, international assurance of supply of nuclear fuel only to countries cooperating with strict nonproliferation measures, subsidization of multinational nuclear facilities, and gradual conversion to international control of non-weapon fissionable material.

*The developing world.* We have a historic opportunity in the next decade to improve the extent and quality of cooperation between the rich and poor countries. The potential benefits to our nation of a policy of constructive cooperation with the developing world would be considerable: uninterrupted access at reasonable cost to raw materials and to basic commodities; lower rates of global inflation; improved world markets for our goods; and a more benign atmosphere for international negotiation in general. Above all, the prospects for the maintenance of peace will be vastly higher in a world in which fewer and fewer people suffer the pangs of hunger and the yoke of economic oppression.

We support efforts to stabilize and increase export earnings of developing countries through our participation in reasonable commodity arrangements. We support strengthening of global financing mechanisms and trade liberalization efforts. We will assist in promoting greater developing country capital markets.

Because our country provides food and fiber to all the world, the American farmer is heavily dependent on world markets. These markets must be developed in a way that prevents the wild gyrations of food prices and the periodic shortages that have been common under recent Republican Administrations. We pledge significant financial support to the International Fund for Agricultural Development; more effective food aid through further revision of the U.S. Food for Peace program; significant contributions to a multination world food reserve system, with appropriate safeguards for American farmers; and continuing efforts to promote American food exports.

The proliferation in arms, both conventional and nuclear, is a principal potential source of conflict in the developing as well as the industrialized world. The United States should limit significantly conventional arms sales and reduce military aid to developing countries, should include conventional arms transfers on the arms control agenda, and should regulate country-by-country justification for U.S. arms transfers, whether by sales or aid. Such sales or aid must be justified in terms of foreign policy benefits to the United States and not simply because of their economic value to American weapons producers.

A primary object of American aid, both military and economic, is first of all to enhance the condition of freedom in the world. The United States should not provide aid to any government—anywhere in the world—which uses secret police, detention without charges, and torture to enforce its powers. Exceptions to this policy should be rare, and the aid provided should be limited to that which is absolutely necessary. The United States should be open and unashamed in its exercise of diplomatic efforts to encourage the observance of human rights in countries which receive American aid.

Current world population growth is a threat to the long-range well-being of mankind. We pledge to support effective voluntary family planning around the world, as well as at home, and to recognize officially the link between social and economic development and the willingness of the individual to limit family size.

To be true to the traditional concern of Americans for the disadvantaged and the oppressed, our aid programs should focus on alleviating poverty and on support of the quest for human liberty and dignity. We will work to see that the United States does its fair share in international development assistance efforts, including participation in the fifth replenishment of the World Bank's International Development Association. We will implement a foreign assistance policy which emphasizes utilization of multilateral and regional development institutions, and one that includes a review of aid programs, country by country, to reinforce those projects whose financial benefits go to the people most in need and which are consistent with overall United States foreign policy goals.

*The world environment.* Decay of the environment knows no national boundary. A government committed to protect our environment knows no national boundary. A government committed to protect our environment at home must also seek international cooperation in defending the global environment.

Working through and supporting such organizations as the United Nations Environmental Program, we will join other governments in more effective efforts to preserve the quality and resources of the oceans; to preserve endangered species of fish and wildlife; to reverse the encroachment of the deserts, the erosion of the world's agricultural lands, and the accelerating destruction of its forests; to limit pollution of the atmosphere; and to control alterations of the global climate.

*Criminal justice rights of Americans abroad.* We will protect the rights and interests of Ameri-

cans charged with crimes or jailed in foreign countries by vigorously exerting all appropriate efforts to guarantee humane treatment and due process and to secure extradition to the United States where appropriate.

*International drug traffic.* We call for the use of diplomatic efforts to stop international production and trafficking in illicit drugs including the possible cut-off of foreign aid to noncooperating countries.

## Defense Policy

The size and structure of our military forces must be carefully related to the demands of our foreign policies in this new era. These should be based on a careful assessment of what will be needed in the long-run to deter our potential adversaries; to fight successfully, if necessary, conventional wars in areas in which our national security is threatened; and to reassure our allies and friends—notably in Western Europe, Japan and the Near East. To this end, our strategic nuclear forces must provide a strong and credible deterrent to nuclear attack and nuclear blackmail. Our conventional forces must be strong enough to deter aggression in areas whose security is vital to our own. In a manner consistent with these objectives, we should seek those disarmament and arms control agreements which will contribute to mutual reductions in both nuclear and conventional arms.

The hallmarks of the Nixon-Ford administration's defense policy, however, have been stagnation and vulnerability.

By its reluctance to make changes in those features of our armed forces which were designed to deal with the problems of the past, the Administration has not only squandered defense dollars, but also neglected making improvements which are needed to increase our forces' fighting effectiveness and their capability to deter future aggression.

By its undue emphasis on the overall size of the defense budget as the primary measure of both our national resolve and the proficiency of our armed forces, the administration has forgotten that we are seeking not to outspend, but to be able to deter and, if necessary, outfight our potential adversaries. While we must spend whatever is legitimately needed for defense, cutbacks on duplication and waste are both feasible and essential. Barring any major change in the international situation, with the proper management, with the proper kind of investment of defense dollars, and with the proper choice of military programs, we believe we can reduce present defense spending by about $5 billion to $7 billion. We must be tough-minded about the development of new weapons systems which add only marginal military value. The size of our defense budget should not be dictated by bureaucratic imperatives or the needs of defense contractors but by our assessment of international realities. In order to provide for a comprehensive review of the B-1 test and evaluation program, no decision regarding B-1 production should be made prior to February 1977.

The Pentagon has one of the federal government's most overgrown bureaucracies. The Department of Defense can be operated more effectively and efficiently and its budget reduced, without in any way compromising our defense posture. Our armed forces have many more admirals and generals today than during World War II, when our fighting force was much larger than now. We can reduce the ratio of officers to men and of support forces to combat troops.

Misdirected efforts such as the construction of pork-barrel projects under the jurisdiction of the Defense Department can be terminated. Exotic arms systems which serve no defense or foreign policy purpose should not be initiated.

By ignoring opportunities to use our advanced technology innovatively to obtain maximum effectiveness in weapons and minimize complexity and cost, the Republican administration has failed to reverse the trend toward increasingly intricate and expensive weapons systems. Thus, it has helped to put our forces—particularly the Navy—on the dangerous path of becoming both smaller in numbers and more vulnerable.

A new approach is needed. Our strategic nuclear forces should be structured to ensure their ability to survive nuclear attack, thereby assuring deterrence of nuclear war. Successful nuclear deterrence is the single most important task of our armed forces. We should, however, avoid becoming diverted into making expenditures which have only symbolic or prestige value or which themselves contribute to nuclear instability.

The United States Navy must remain the foremost fleet in the world. Our naval forces should be improved to stress survivability and our modern technology should be used in new ways to keep the essential sea lanes open. Concretely, we should put more stress on new sensors and armaments, and give priority to a navy consisting of a greater number of smaller and less vulnerable vessels.

Our land forces should be structured to fight effectively in support of our political and military commitments. To this end, modern, well-equipped and highly mobile land forces are more important than large numbers of sparsely-equipped infantry divisions.

Our tactical air forces should be designed to establish air superiority quickly in the event of hostilities, and to support our land and naval forces.

We can and will make significant economies in the overhead and support structure of our military forces.

The defense procurement system should be reformed to require, wherever possible and consistent with efforts to encourage full participation by small and minority businesses, advertised competitive bids and other improvements in procurement procedure so as to encourage full and fair competition among potential contractors and to cut the current waste in defense procurement. A more equitable formula should be considered for distribution of defense contracts and other federal procurement on a state or regional basis.

The United States and other nations share a common interest in reducing military expenditures and transferring the savings into activities which raise living standards. In order to smooth the path for such changes, the Executive Branch and the Congress should encourage long-range planning by defense-dependent communities and managements of defense firms and unions. This process should take place within the context of the Democratic Party's commitment to planned full employment.

Our civilian and military intelligence agencies should be structured to provide timely and accurate information and analysis of foreign affairs and military matters. Covert action must be used only in the most compelling cases where the national security of the U.S. is vitally involved; assassination must be prohibited. There should be full and thorough congressional oversight of our intelligence agencies. The constitutional rights of American citizens can and must be fully protected, and intelligence abuses corrected, without endangering the confidentiality of properly classified intelligence or compromising the fundamental intelligence mission.

*U.S.-U.S.S.R. relations.* The United States and the Soviet Union are the only powers who, by rivalry or miscalculation, could bring general nuclear war upon our civilization. A principal goal must be the continued reduction of tension with the U.S.S.R. This can, however, only be accomplished by fidelity to our principles and interests and through business-like negotiations about specific issues, not by the bad bargains, dramatic posturing, and the stress on general declarations that have characterized the Nixon-Ford administration's detente policy.

Soviet actions continue to pose severe threats to peace and stability in many parts of the world and to undermine support in the West for fruitful negotiations toward mutually beneficial agreements. The U.S.S.R. has undertaken a major military buildup over the last several years in its navy, in its strategic forces, and in its land forces stationed in Eastern Europe and Asia. It has sought one-sided advantages in negotiations, and has exerted political and military pressure in such areas as the Near East and Africa, not hesitating to dispatch to Angola its own advisors as well as the expeditionary forces of its clients.

The continued U.S.S.R. military dominance of many Eastern European countries remains a source of oppression for the peoples of those nations, an oppression we do not accept and to which we are morally opposed. Any attempt by the Soviet Union similarly to dominate other parts of Europe—such as Yugoslavia—would be an action posing a grave threat to peace. Eastern Europe will not truly be an area of stability until these countries regain their independence and become part of a large European framework.

Our task is to establish U.S.-U.S.S.R. relations on a stable basis, avoiding excesses of both hope and fear. Patience, a clear sense of our own priorities, and a willingness to negotiate specific firm agreements in areas of mutual interest can return balance to relations between the United States and the Soviet Union.

In the field of nuclear disarmament and arms control we should work toward: limitations on the international spread of fissionable materials and nuclear weapons; specific strategic arms limitation agreements which will increase the stability of the strategic balance and reduce the risk of nuclear war, emphasizing mutual reductions and limitations on future weapons deployment which most threaten the strategic balance because their characteristics indicate a potential first-strike use; a comprehensive ban on nuclear tests; mutual reduction with the Soviet Union and others, under assured safeguards, of our nuclear arsenals, leading ultimately to the elimination of such arsenals; mutual restrictions with the Soviet Union and others on sales or other transfers of arms to developing countries; and conventional arms agreements and mutual and balanced force reductions in Europe.

However, in the area of strategic arms limitation, the U.S. should accept only such agreements that would not overall limit the U.S. to levels of intercontinental strategic forces inferior to the limits provided for the Soviet Union.

In the long-run, further development of more extensive economic relations between the United States and the Soviet Union may bring significant benefit to both societies. The U.S.S.R. has sought, however, through unfair trade practices to dominate such strategic fields as merchant shipping. Rather than effectively resisting such efforts, the Nixon-Ford administration has looked favorably on such steps as subsidizing U.S.-U.S.S.R. trade by giving the Soviet Union concessionary credits, promoting trade increases because of a shortrun hope of using trade to modify political behavior, and even placing major United States energy investment in pawn to Soviet Union policy. Where bilateral trade agreements with the U.S.S.R. are to our economic advantage, we should pursue them, but our watch-words would be tough bargaining and concrete economic, political or other benefits for the United States. We should also press the Soviet Union to take a greater share of responsibility in multilateral solutions to such problems as creating adequate world grain reserves.

Our stance on the issue of human rights and political liberties in the Soviet Union is important to American self-respect and our moral standing in the world. We should continually remind the Soviet Union, by word and conduct, of its commitments in Helsinki to the free flow of people and ideas and of how offensive we and other free people find its violations of the Universal Declaration of Human Rights. As part of our programs of official, technical, trade, cultural and other exchanges with the U.S.S.R., we should press its leaders to open their society to a genuine interchange of people and ideas.

We must avoid assuming that the whole of American-Soviet relations is greater than the sum of its parts, that any agreement is superior to none, or that we can negotiate effectively as supplicants. We must realize that our firmness can help build respect for us and improve the long-run opportunities for mutually-beneficial concrete agreements. We must beware of the notion that Soviet-American relations are a seamless web in which concessions in one area will bring us benefits in others. By the same token, we must husband our resources to concentrate on what is most important to us. Detente must be military as well as political.

More fundamentally, we must recognize that the general character of our foreign policies will not be set by our direct relationship with the Soviet Union. Our allies and friends must come first. Nor can the pursuit of our interests elsewhere in the world be dominated by concern for Soviet views. For example, American policy toward China should continue to be based on a desire for a steady improvement and broadening of relations, whatever the tenor and direction of Chinese-Soviet relations.

Above all, we must be open, honest, mature and patient with ourselves and with our allies. We must recognize that, in the long-run, an effective policy toward the Soviet Union can only be grounded on honest discussion, and on a national and, to some extent, an international consensus. Our own institutions, especially the Congress, must be consulted and must help formulate our policy. The governments of our allies and friends must be made partners in our undertakings. Haste and secret bilateral executive arrangements in our dealings with the U.S.S.R. can only promote a mood of uncertainty and suspicion which undermines the public support essential to effective and stable international relations.

## America in the World Community

Many of the critical foreign policy issues we face require global approaches, but an effective international role for the United States also demands effective working with the special interests of specific foreign nations and regions. The touchstone of our policy must be our own interests, which in turn means that we should not seek or expect to control events everywhere. Indeed, intelligent pursuit of our objectives demands a realization that even where our interests are great and our involvement essential, we do not act alone, but in a world setting where others have interests and objectives as well.

We cannot give expression to our national values without continuing to play a strong role in the affairs of the United Nations and its agencies. Firm and positive advocacy of our positions is essential.

We should make a major effort at reforming and restructuring the U.N. systems. The intensity of interrelated problems is rapidly increasing, and it is likely that in the future, the issues of war and peace will be more a function of economic and social problems than of the military security problems that have dominated international relations since 1945.

The heat of debate at the General Assembly should not obscure the value of our supporting United Nations involvement in keeping the peace and in the increasingly complex technical and social problems—such as pollution, health, economic development and population growth—that challenge the world community. But we must let the world know that anti-American polemics are no substitute for sound policy and that the United Nations is weakened by harsh rhetoric from other countries or by blasphemous resolutions such as the one equating Zionism and racism.

A Democratic Administration should seek a fair and comprehensive Law-of-the-Sea Treaty that will balance the interests of the developed and less developed countries.

*Europe.* The nations of Western Europe, together with Japan, are among our closest allies. Except for our closest neighbors in this hemisphere, it is in these regions where our interests are most strongly linked with those of other nations. At the same time, the growing economic and political strength of Europe and Japan creates areas of conflict and tension in a relationship both sides must keep close and healthy.

On the great economic issues—trade, energy, employment, international finance, resources—we must work with the Europeans, the Japanese and other nations to serve our long-run mutual interests in stability and growth, and in the development of poorer nations.

The military security of Europe is fundamental to our own. To that end, NATO remains a vital commitment. We should retain in Europe a U.S. contribution to NATO forces so that they are sufficient to deter or defeat attack without premature resort to nuclear weapons. This does not exclude moderate reductions in manpower levels made possible by more efficiency, and it affirmatively requires a thorough reform and overhaul of NATO forces, plans and deployments. We encourage our European allies to increase their share of the contributions to NATO defense, both in terms of troops and hardware. By mutual agreement or through modernization, the thousands of tactical nuclear weapons in Europe should be reduced, saving money and manpower and increasing our own and international security.

Europe, like the rest of the world, faces substantial political change. We cannot control that process. However, we can publicly make known our preference for developments consistent with our interests and principles. In particular, we should encourage the most rapid possible growth of stable democratic institutions in Spain, and a continuation on the path of democracy of Portugal and Greece, opposing authoritarian takeover from either left or right. We can make clear our sense of the risks and dangers of Communist participation in Western European governments, while being equally clear that we will work on a broad range of non-military matters with any legally-constituted government that is prepared to do the same with us. We similarly must reaffirm our support for the continued growth and cohesion of the institutions of the European community.

The voice of the United States should be heard in Northern Ireland against violence and terror, against the discrimination, repression and deprivation which brought about that civil strife, and for the efforts of the parties toward a peaceful resolution of the future of Northern Ireland. Pertinent alliances such as NATO and international organizations such as the United Nations should be fully apprised of the interests of the United States with respect to the status of Ireland in the international community of nations.

We must do all that is possible, consistent with our interest in a strong NATO in Southern Europe and stability in the Eastern Mediterranean, to encourage a fair settlement of the Cyprus issue, which continues to extract human costs.

*Middle East.* We shall continue to seek a just and lasting peace in the Middle East. The cornerstone of our policy is a firm commitment to the independence and security of the State of Israel. This special relationship does not prejudice improved relations with other nations in the region. Real peace in the Middle East will permit Israel and her Arab neighbors to turn their energies to internal development, and will eliminate the threat of world conflict spreading from tensions there.

The Middle East conflict is complex, and a realistic, pragmatic approach is essential. Our policy must be based on firm adherence to these fundamental principles of Middle East policy:

We will continue our consistent support of Israel, including sufficient military and economic assistance to maintain Israel's deterrent strength in the region, and the maintenance of U.S. military forces in the Mediterranean adequate to deter military intervention by the Soviet Union.

We steadfastly oppose any move to isolate Israel in the international arena or suspend it from the United Nations or its constituent organizations.

We will avoid efforts to impose on the region an externally devised formula for settlement, and will provide support for initiatives toward settlement, based on direct face-to-face negotiation between the parties and normalization of relations and a full peace within secure and defensible boundaries.

We vigorously support the free passage of shipping in the Middle East—especially in the Suez Canal.

We recognize that the solution to the problems of Arab and Jewish refugees must be among the factors taken into account in the course of continued progress toward peace. Such problems cannot be solved, however, by recognition of terrorist groups which refuse to acknowledge their adversary's right to exist, or groups which have no legitimate claim to represent the people for whom they purport to be speaking.

We support initiation of government enforcement action to insure that stated U.S. policy—in opposition to boycotts against friendly countries—is fully and vigorously implemented.

We recognize and support the established status of Jerusalem as the capital of Israel, with free access to all its holy places provided to all faiths. As a symbol of this stand, the U.S. Embassy should be moved from Tel Aviv to Jerusalem.

*Asia.* We remain a Pacific power with important

stakes and objectives in the region, but the Vietnam War has taught us the folly of becoming militarily involved where our vital interests were not at stake.

Friendship and cooperation with Japan are the cornerstone of our Asian interests and policy. Our commitment to the security of Japan is central to our own, and it is an essential condition to a constructive, peaceful role for that nation in the future of Asia. In our economic dealings with Japan, we must make clear our insistence on mutuality of benefits and opportunities, while focusing on ways to expand our trade, avoiding economic shocks and resultant retaliation on either side. We must avoid the "shocks" to Japan which have resulted from Republican foreign policy.

We reaffirm our commitment to the security of the Republic of Korea, both in itself and as a key to the security of Japan. However, on a prudent and carefully planned basis, we can redeploy, and gradually phase out, the U.S. ground forces, and can withdraw the nuclear weapons now stationed in Korea without endangering that support, as long as our tactical air and naval forces in the region remain strong. Our continued resolve in the area should not be misunderstood. However, we deplore the denial of human rights in the Republic of Korea, just as we deplore the brutal and aggressive acts of the regime in North Korea.

We have learned, at a tragically high price, certain lessons regarding Southeast Asia. We should not seek to control the political future of that region. Rather, we should encourage and welcome peaceful relations with the nations of that area. In conjunction with the fullest possible accounting of our citizens still listed as missing in action, we should move toward normalized relations with Vietnam.

No foreign policy that reflects traditional American humanitarian concerns can be indifferent to the plight of the peoples of the Asian subcontinent.

The recent improvement in relations with China, which has received bipartisan support, is a welcome recognition that there are few areas in which our vital interests clash with those of China. Our relations with China should continue to develop on peaceful lines, including early movement toward normalizing diplomatic relations in the context of a peaceful resolution of the future of Taiwan.

*The Americas.* We recognize the fundamental importance of close relations and the easing of economic tension with our Canadian and Mexican neighbors.

In the last eight years, our relations with Latin America have deteriorated amid high-level indifference, increased military domination of Latin American governments, and revelations of extensive American interference in the internal politics of Chile and other nations. The principles of the Good Neighbor Policy and the Alliance for Progress, under which we are committed to working with the nations of the Americas as equals, remain valid today but seem to have been forgotten by the present administration.

The U.S. should adopt policies on trade, aid and investment that include commodity agreements and an appropriate system of trade preferences.

We must make clear our revulsion at the systematic violations of basic human rights that have occurred under some Latin American military regimes.

We pledge support for a new Panama Canal treaty, which insures the interests of the United States in that waterway, recognizes the principles already agreed upon, takes into account the interests of the Canal work force, and which will have wide hemispheric support.

Relations with Cuba can only be normalized if Cuba refrains from interference in the internal affairs of the United States, and releases all U.S. citizens currently detained in Cuban prisons and labor camps for political reasons. We can move towards such relations if Cuba abandons its provocative international actions and policies.

*Africa.* Eight years of indifference, accompanied by increasing cooperation with racist regimes, have left our influence and prestige in Africa at an historical low. We must adopt policies that recognize the intrinsic importance of Africa and its development to the United States, and the inevitability of majority rule on that continent.

The first task is to formulate a rational African policy in terms of enlightened U.S.-African priorities, not as a corollary of U.S.-Soviet policy. Angola demonstrated that we must have sound relations with Black Africa and disassociate our policies from those of South Africa to achieve the desired African response to Soviet expansionism in Africa. Our policy must foster high-level U.S.-Africa communications and establish a sound basis for dealing when crises arise.

The next Democratic administration will work aggressively to involve black Americans in foreign policy positions, at home and abroad, and in decisions affecting African interests.

To promote African economic development, the U.S. should undertake increased bilateral and multilateral assistance, continue congressional initiatives in food assistance and food production, with special aid to the Sahel and implementation of the Sahel Development Plan; and carry forward our commitment to negotiate with developing countries on key trade and economic issues such as commodity arrangements and trade preferences.

Our policy must be reformulated towards unequivocal and concrete support of majority rule in Southern Africa, recognizing that our true interests lie in peaceful progress toward a free South Africa for all South Africans, black and white. As part of our commitment to the development of a free and democratic South Africa, we should support the position of African nations in denying recognition to "homelands" given pseudoindependence by the South African government under its current policy of "separate development."

The Republican administration's relaxation of the arms embargo against South Africa must be ended, and the embargo tightened to prevent transfers of military significance, particularly of nuclear material. The U.S. government should not engage in any activity regarding Namibia that would recognize or support the illegal South African administration, including granting tax credits to U.S. companies doing business in Namibia and paying taxes to South Africa. Moreover, the U.S. government should deny tax advantages to all corporations doing business in South Africa and Rhodesia who support or participate in apartheid practices and policies.

The U.S. government should fully enforce the U.N.-ordered Rhodesia sanctions, seek universal compliance with such measures, and repeal the Byrd Amendment.

Efforts should be made to normalize relations with Angola.


## Libertarian Platform 1976

### INDIVIDUAL RIGHTS AND CIVIL ORDER

No conflict exists between civil order and individual rights. Both concepts are based on the same fundamental principle: that no individual, group, or government may initiate force against any other individual, group, or government.

### 1. Crime

A massive increase in violent crime threatens the lives, happiness, and belongings of Americans. At the same time, governmental violations of rights undermine the people's sense of justice with regard to crime. Impartial and consistent law enforcement protecting individual rights is the appropriate way to suppress crime.

### 2. Victimless Crime

We hold that only actions which infringe the rights of others can properly be termed crimes. We favor the repeal of all federal, state, and local laws creating "crimes" without victims. In particular, we advocate:

a. The repeal of all laws prohibiting the cultivation, sale, possession or use of drugs, and all medical prescription requirements for the purchase of drugs, vitamins, and similar substances.

b. The repeal of all laws regarding consensual sexual relations, including prostitution and solicitation, and the cessation of state oppression and harassment of homosexual men and women, that they, at last, be accorded their full rights as individuals.

c. The repeal of all laws regulating or prohibiting gambling.

d. The repeal of all laws interfering with the right to commit suicide as infringements of the ultimate right of an individual to his or her own life.

e. The use of executive pardon to free all those presently incarcerated for the commission of these "crimes."

### 3. Due Process for the Criminally Accused

Until such time as persons are proved guilty of crimes, they should be accorded full respect for their individual rights. We are thus opposed to reduction of present safeguards of the rights of the criminally accused.

Specifically, we are opposed to preventive detention, so-called "no-knock laws," and all other measures which threaten individual rights.

We advocate the repeal of all laws establishing

any category of crime applicable to minors for which adults would not be similarly answerable, and an end to the practice in many states of jailing children accused of no crime.

We support full restitution for all loss suffered by persons arrested, indicted, tried, imprisoned, or otherwise injured in the course of criminal proceedings against them which do not result in their conviction. Law enforcement agencies should be liable for this restitution unless malfeasance of the officials involved is proven, in which case they should be personally liable.

### 4. Justice for the Victim

The purpose of any system of courts is to provide justice. The present system of criminal law is based on punishment with little concern for the victim. We support restitution for the victim to the fullest degree possible at the expense of the criminal or the negligent wrongdoer.

We accordingly oppose all "no-fault" insurance laws which deprive the victim of the right to recover from the guilty in negligence cases.

### 5. Government and "Mental Health"

We oppose the involuntary commitment of any person to a mental institution. To incarcerate an individual not convicted of any crime, but merely asserted to be incompetent, is a violation of the individual's rights. We further advocate:

a. The repeal of all laws permitting involuntary psychiatric treatment of any persons, including children, and those incarcerated in prisons or mental institutions.

b. An immediate end to the spending of tax money for any program of psychiatric or psychological research or treatment.

c. An end to all involuntary treatments of prisoners in such areas as psycho-surgery, drug therapy, and aversion therapy.

d. An end of tax-supported "mental health" propaganda campaigns and community "mental health" centers and programs.

### 6. Freedom of Speech and the Press

We oppose all forms of government censorship, including anti-pornography laws, whatever the medium involved. Events have demonstrated that the already precarious First Amendment rights of the broadcast industry are becoming still more precarious. Regulation of broadcasting, including the "fairness doctrine" and "equal-time" provisions, can no longer be tolerated. We support legislation to repeal the Federal Communications Act, and to provide for private ownership of broadcasting rights, thus giving broadcasting First Amendment parity with other communications media. Government ownership or subsidy of broadcast band radio and television stations and networks—in particular, the tax funding of the Corporation for Public Broadcasting—must end. We oppose government restriction of the expansion of "pay TV" and cable broadcasting facilities.

### 7. Government Secrecy

We condemn the government's use of secret classifications to keep from the public information which it should have. We favor substituting a system in which no individual may be convicted for violating government secrecy classifications unless the government discharges its burden of proving that the publication:

a. Violated the right of privacy of those who have been coerced into revealing confidential or proprietary information to government agents, or

b. Disclosed defensive military plans so as to materially impair the capability to respond to invasion.

It should always be a defense to such prosecution that information divulged shows that the government has violated the law.

### 8. Freedom of Religion

We defend the rights of individuals to engage in any religious activities which do not violate the rights of others. In order to defend religious freedom, we advocate a strict separation of church and state. We oppose government actions which either aid or attack any religion. We oppose taxation of church property for the same reason that we oppose all taxation.

### 9. Protection of Privacy

The individual's privacy, property, and right to speak or not to speak should not be infringed by the government. The government should not use electronic or other means of covert surveillance of an individual's actions on private property without the consent of the owner or occupant. Correspondence, bank and other financial transactions and records, doctors' and lawyers' communications, employment records, and the like, should not be open to review by government without the consent of all parties involved in those actions. So long as the National Census and all federal, state, and other government agency compilations of data on an individual continue to exist they should be conducted only with the consent of the persons from whom the data are sought.

### 10. Internal Security and Civil Liberties

We call for the abolition of all federal secret police agencies. In particular, we seek the abolition of the Central Intelligence Agency and the Federal Bureau of Investigation, and we call for a return to the American tradition of local law enforcement. We support Congressional investigations of criminal activities of the CIA and of wrongdoing by other government agencies.

We support the abolition of the subpoena power as used by Congressional committees against individuals or firms. We hail the abolition of the House Internal Security Committee and call for the destruction of its files on private individuals and groups. We also call for the abolition of the Senate Subcommittee on Internal Security.

### 11. The Right to Keep and Bear Arms

Maintaining our belief in the inviolability of the right to keep and bear arms, we oppose all laws at any level of government requiring registration of, or restricting, the ownership, manufacture, or transfer or sale of firearms ammunition. We also oppose any government efforts to ban or restrict the use of tear gas, "mace," or other non-firearm protective devices.

We support the efforts of certain members of Congress to repeal the Federal Gun Control Act of 1968 and to prevent federal agencies from banning or regulating the ownership, manufacture, or transfer or sale of firearms or ammunition and urge passage of their bills for those purposes.

We favor the repeal of laws banning the concealment of weapons or prohibiting pocket weapons. We also oppose the banning of inexpensive handguns ("Saturday night specials").

### 12. Amnesty and the Military

We support the immediate and unconditional exoneration of all who have been accused or convicted of draft evasion, desertion from the military, and other acts of resistance to such transgressions as imperialistic wars and aggressive acts of the military. Members of the military should have the same right to quit their jobs as other persons, but will be liable for whatever consequences they contracted for when they enlisted. We call for the end of the Defense Department practice of discharging armed forces personnel for homosexual conduct when such conduct does not interfere with their assigned duties. We further call for retraction of all less-than-honorable discharges previously assigned for such reasons and deletion of such information from military personnel files. We oppose the draft (Selective Service), believing that the use of force to require individuals to serve in the armed forces or anywhere else is a violation of their rights. We recommend repeal of the Uniform Code of Military Justice and the recognition and equal protection of the rights of all members of the armed forces in order to promote thereby the morale, dignity, and sense of justice within the military.

### 13. Property Rights

There is no conflict between property rights and human rights. Indeed, property rights are the rights of humans with respect to property and, as such, are entitled to the same respect and protection as all other individual rights.

We further hold that the owners of property have the full right to control, use, dispose of, or in any manner enjoy their property without interference, until and unless the exercise of their control infringes the valid rights of others.

Where property, including land, has been taken from its rightful owners by government or private action in violation of individual rights, we favor restitution to the rightful owners.

### 14. Unions and Collective Bargaining

We support the right of free persons to voluntarily establish, or associate in, labor unions. An employer should have the right to recognize, or refuse to recognize, a union as the collective bargaining agent of some or all of his or her employees. Therefore we oppose "Right to Work" laws as they prohibit employers from making voluntary contracts with unions.

Unions should have the right to organize secondary boycotts if they so choose.

We oppose government interference in bargaining, such as compulsory arbitration or imposing an obligation to bargain.

We urge repeal of the National Labor Relations Act, which infringes upon individual rights by restricting voluntary labor negotiations.

### 15. Discrimination

No individual rights should be denied or abridged by the laws of the United States or any state or locality on account of sex, race, color, creed, age, national origin, or sexual preference. We condemn bigotry as irrational and repugnant.

Nonetheless, we oppose any governmental attempts to regulate private discrimination, including discrimination in employment, housing, and privately owned so-called "public" accommodations. The right to trade includes the right not to trade—for any reasons whatever.

### Trade and the Economy

Because each person has the right to offer goods and services to others on the free market, and because government interference can only harm such free activity, we oppose all intervention by government into the area of economics. The only proper role of existing governments in the economic realm is to protect property rights, adjudicate disputes, and provide a legal framework in which voluntary trade is protected. All efforts by government to redistribute wealth, or to control or manage trade, are improper in a free society.

### 1. Money

We call for the repeal of all legal tender laws and reaffirm the right to private ownership of, and contracts for, gold. We favor the abolition of government fiat money and compulsory governmental units of account. We favor the use of a free market commodity standard, such as gold coin denominated by units of weight.

### 2. The Economy

Government intervention in the economy imperils both the personal freedom and the material prosperity of every American. We therefore support the following specific immediate reforms:

a. Drastic reduction of both taxes and government spending;

b. An end to deficit budgets;

c. A halt to inflationary monetary policies, and elimination of the Federal Reserve System;

d. The removal of all governmental impediments to free trade—including the repeal of all transportation regulations, all "anti-trust" laws, such as the Robinson-Patman Act which restricts price discounts, and the abolition of farm subsidies, as the most pressing and critical impediments; and

e. The repeal of all control on wages, prices, rents, profits, production, and interest rates.

### 3. Subsidies

In order to achieve a free economy in which government victimizes no one for the benefit of anyone else, we oppose all government subsidies to business, labor, education, agriculture, science, broadcasting, the arts, and any other special interest. Relief or exemption from involuntary taxation should not be considered a subsidy. We oppose any resumption of the Reconstruction Finance Corporation, or any similar plan which would force the taxpayer to subsidize and sustain uneconomic business enterprises.

### 4. Tariffs and Quotas

Like subsidies, tariffs and quotas serve only to give special treatment to favored interests and to diminish the welfare of other individuals. These measures also reduce the scope of contacts and understanding among different peoples. We therefore support abolition of all tariffs and quotas as well as the Tariff Commission and the Customs Court.

### 5. Postal Service

We propose the abolition of the governmental Postal Service. The present system, in addition to being inefficient, encourages governmental surveillance of private correspondence. Pending abolition, we call for an end to the monopoly system and for allowing free private competition in all aspects of postal service.

### 6. Taxation

Since we believe that all persons are entitled to keep the fruits of their labor, we oppose all government activity which consists of the forcible collection of money or goods from individuals in violation of their individual rights. Specifically, we:

a. Recognize the right of any individual to challenge the payment of taxes on moral, legal, or constitutional grounds;

b. Oppose all personal and corporate income taxation, including capital gains taxes;

c. Support repeal of the Sixteenth Amendment, and oppose any increase in existing tax rates and the imposition of any new taxes;

d. Support the eventual repeal of all taxation; and

e. Support a declaration of unconditional amnesty for all those who have been convicted of, or who now stand accused of tax resistance.

We oppose as involuntary servitude any legal requirements forcing employers or business owners to serve as tax collectors for federal, state, or local tax agencies.

## 7. Energy

We oppose all government control of energy pricing, allocation, and production, such as that imposed by the Federal Power Commission, the Federal Energy Administration, state public utility commissions, and state pro-rationing agencies. Thus, we advocate decontrol of the prices of oil, petroleum products, and natural gas. We oppose all government subsidies for energy research, development, and operation. We favor repeal of the Price-Anderson Act through which the government limits liability for nuclear accidents. We favor privatization of the atomic energy industry.

We oppose all attempts to compel "national self-sufficiency" in oil or any other energy source, including any attempts to raise oil tariffs, revive oil import quotas, or to place a floor under world oil prices. We favor the creation of a free market in oil by repeal of all state pro-ration laws, which impose compulsory quotas reducing the production of oil. We call upon the government to turn over the public domain of land resources to private ownership, including the opening up of coal fields, the naval oil resources, offshore oil drilling, shale oil deposits, and geothermal sources.

## DOMESTIC ILLS

Current problems in such areas as crime, pollution, health care delivery, decaying cities, and poverty are not solved, but are primarily caused, by government. The welfare state, supposedly designed to aid the poor, is in reality a growing and parasitic burden on all productive people, and injures, rather than benefits, the poor themselves.

## 1. Pollution

We support the development of an objective system defining individual property rights to air and water. We hold that ambiguities in the area of these rights (e.g., the concept of "public property") are a primary cause of our deteriorating environment. Present legal principles which allow the violation of individual rights by polluters must be reversed. The laws of nuisance and negligence should be modified to cover damages done by air, water, and noise pollution. While we maintain that no one has the right to violate the legitimate property rights of others by polluting, we strenuously oppose all attempts to transform the defense of such rights into any restriction of the efforts of individuals to advance technology, to expand production, or to use their property peacefully. We therefore support the abolition of the Environmental Protection Agency.

## 2. Consumer Protection

We support strong and effective laws against fraud and misrepresentation. However, we oppose paternalistic regulations which dictate to consumers, impose prices, define standards for products, or otherwise restrict free choice. We oppose all so-called "consumer protection" legislation which infringes upon voluntary trade. We advocate the repeal of all laws banning or restricting the advertising of prices, products, or services. We specifically oppose laws requiring an individual to buy or use so-called "self-protection" equipment such as safety belts, air bags, or crash helmets. Likewise we advocate the immediate repeal of the federally imposed 55 mile-per-hour speed limit. We advocate the abolition of the Food and Drug Administration. We advocate an end to compulsory fluoridation of water supplies. We specifically oppose government regulation of the price, potency, or quantity able to be produced or purchased of drugs or other consumer goods. There should be no laws regarding what substances (nicotine, alcohol, hallucinogens, narcotics, vitamin supplements, or other "drugs") a person may ingest or otherwise use.

## 3. Education

We support the repeal of all compulsory education laws, and an end to government operation, regulation, and subsidy of schools and colleges. We call for an immediate end to compulsory busing.

As an interim measure to encourage the growth of private schools and variety in education, we support both a tax-credit system and a steady reduction of tax support for schools. We support the repeal of all taxes on the income or property of private schools, whether they are profit or nonprofit. We further support immediate relief from the burden of school taxes for those not responsible for the education of children.

## 4. Poverty and Unemployment

We support repeal of all laws which impede the ability of any person to find employment—including, but not limited to, minimum wage laws, so-called "protective" labor legislation for women and children, governmental restrictions on the establishment of private day-care centers, the National Labor Relations Act, and licensing requirements. We oppose all government welfare, relief projects, and "aid to the poor" programs. All aid for the poor should come from private sources.

## 5. Medical Care

We support the right of individuals to contract freely with practitioners of their choice, whether licensed by the government or not, for all medical services. We oppose any compulsory insurance or tax-supported plan to provide health services. We favor the abolition of Medicare and Medicaid programs. We further oppose governmental infringement on the doctor-patient relationship through regulatory agencies such as the Professional Standards Review Organization. We oppose any state or federal area planning boards whose stated purpose is to consolidate medical services or avoid their duplication. We oppose laws limiting the liability of doctors for negligence, and those regulating the supply of legal aid on a contingency fee basis. We oppose laws which invalidate settlements of malpractice suits through the use of private arbitration services. We also favor the deregulation of the medical insurance industry.

We call for the repeal of laws compelling individuals to submit to medical treatment, testing, or to the administration of drugs or other substances.

## 6. Land Use

The role of planning is properly the responsibility and right of the owners of the land. We therefore urge an end to governmental control of land use through such methods as urban renewal, zoning laws, building codes, eminent domain, regional planning, or purchasing of development rights with tax money, which not only violate property rights, but discriminate against minorities and tend to cause higher rents and housing shortages. We are further opposed to the use of tax funds for the acquisition or maintenance of land or other real property. We recognize the legitimacy of private, voluntary land use covenants.

## 7. Occupational Safety and Health Act (OSHA)

We call for the repeal of the Occupational Safety and Health Act. This law denies the right to liberty and property to both employer and employee, and it interferes in their private contractual relations. It denies to employers their property rights to immunity from search and seizure, due process of law, jury trial in a court of law, and confrontation of witness.

## 8. Social Security

We favor the repeal of the fraudulent, virtually bankrupt, and increasingly oppressive Social Security system. Pending that repeal, participation in Social Security should be made voluntary. Victims of the Social Security tax should have a claim against government property.

## 9. Civil Service

We call for the abolition of the Civil Service system, which entrenches a permanent and growing bureaucracy upon the land. We recognize that the Civil Service is inherently a system of concealed patronage. We therefore recommend return to the Jeffersonian principle of rotation in office.

## 10. Campaign Finance Laws

We urge the repeal of federal campaign finance laws, which repress the voluntary support of candidates and parties, compel taxpayers to subsidize political views they do not wish to support, and entrench the two major political parties. We also call for repeal of restrictive state laws that effectively prevent new parties and independent candidates from being on the ballot.

## FOREIGN POLICY

The principle of non-initiation of force should guide the relationships between governments. We should return to the historic libertarian tradition of avoiding entangling alliances, abstaining totally from foreign quarrels and imperialist adventures, and recognizing the right to unrestricted travel and immigration.

### Economic:

#### 1. Foreign Aid

We support the elimination of tax-supported military, economic, technical, and scientific aid to foreign governments. We further support abolition of the federal Export-Import Bank, which presently makes American taxpayers guarantors of loans to foreign governments.

We call for the repeal of all prohibitions on individuals or firms contributing or selling goods and services to any foreign country or organization.

#### 2. Law and the Sea

We oppose recognition of claims by fiat, by nations or international bodies, of ocean property such as: (1) transportation lanes, (2) oyster beds, (3) mineral rights, and (4) fishing rights. We urge the development of objective standards for recognizing claims of private ownership in such property.

#### 3. International Money

We favor the withdrawal of the United States from all international paper money and other inflationary credit schemes. We favor withdrawal from the World Bank and the International Monetary Fund.

### Military:

#### 1. Military Policy

We recognize the necessity for maintaining a sufficient military force to defend the United States against aggression. We should reduce the overall cost and size of our total governmental defense establishment.

We call for the withdrawal of all American troops from bases abroad.

We call for withdrawal from multilateral and bilateral commitments to military intervention (such as to NATO and to South Korea) and for abandonment of interventionist doctrines (such as the Monroe Doctrine).

Being opposed to the perils of both nuclear mass destruction and foreign aggression, we favor international negotiations toward nuclear disarmament provided all possible precautions are taken to effectively protect the lives and rights of the American people.

#### 2. Presidential War Powers

We call for reform of the Presidential War Powers Act to end the President's power to initiate military action, and for the abrogation of all Presidential declarations of "states of emergency." There must be no further secret commitments and unilateral acts of military intervention by the Executive Branch.

### Diplomatic:

#### 1. Negotiation

The important principle in foreign policy should be the elimination of intervention by the United States government in the affairs of other nations. We would negotiate with any foreign government without necessarily conceding moral legitimacy to that government. We favor a drastic reduction in cost and size of our total diplomatic establishment. In addition, we favor the repeal of the Logan Act, which prohibits private American citizens from engaging in diplomatic negotiations with foreign governments.

#### 2. The United Nations

We support immediate withdrawal of the United States from the United Nations. We also call for the United Nations to withdraw itself from the United States. We oppose any treaty that the United States may enter into or any existing treaty under which individual rights would be violated.

#### 3. The Middle East

We call upon the United States government to cease all interventions in the Middle East, including military and economic aid, guarantees, and diplomatic meddling, and to cease its prohibition of private foreign aid, both military and economic.

### 4. *Colonial Independence*

The United States should grant immediate independence to its colonial dependencies, including Samoa, Guam, Micronesia, the Virgin Islands, and Puerto Rico.

OMISSIONS

Our silence about any other particular government law, regulation, ordinance, directive, edict, control, regulatory agency, activity, or machination should not be construed to imply approval.

## People's Platform 1976

GENERAL PRINCIPLES

The People's Party is a national coalition of state and local organizations and individuals working together to build socialism. We struggle against the capitalist economic system, which puts power and wealth in the hands of a few. We work for a classless society. We work to abolish the employer-employee wage labor relationship. We work for production for people's needs rather than for private profit. At the same time, we struggle in our lives against oppressive power relationships: male domination, white skin privilege, privilege of adults over the young and elderly, and the privilege of heterosexuals over gay males and lesbians. To build this socialist system we recognize the long-term need for a united organization of all working class people. We seek cooperation, both for this organized class-wide unity and for ongoing struggles, with compatible groups and organizations. Elections can be used as a powerful educational and organizing tool, but are not an end in themselves. As a guide to the realization of these goals, the People's Party offers the following General Principles:

1. The building of working class people's power toward collective control of communities and workplaces (homes, shops, factories, offices, and schools).

2. Abolition of all rents, consumer debt, residental mortgages, and debts of governments to banks.

3. Redistribution of wealth and land.

4. An end to all discrimination and oppression based on race, sex, sexual preference, and age.

5. Full productive employment, not war-related, at prevailing union wages, for all.

6. The turning over of all properties of the U.S. multinational corporations in other countries to the workers and peasants of those countries; withdrawal from the more than 3,000 overseas U.S. military bases.

7. Abolition of the military establishment, the CIA, and all other known and secret agencies which exist to destroy peoples' struggles at home and abroad.

8. Honoring of all treaties with native tribes and peoples.

9. Self-determination for all peoples in the manner determined by them, including independence for Puerto Rico, Micronesia, and Guam, and statehood for the colony of Columbia (Washington, D.C.). Relinquishment of control of the Panama Canal Zone.

10. Respect for the right of self-defense for working people, including the right of people to defend themselves from rape and assault, and the constitutional right to keep and bear arms, so long as governments are armed.

11. Free, excellent quality health care, full educational opportunities, and quality housing for all.

12. Full production of healthful food—for people, not for profit.

13. Outlawing of the poisoning and pollution of the air, soil, water, and food. A stop to nuclear fission reactors; expansion of research on alternate energy sources—solar power now.

14. Unconditional amnesty for war objectors; freedom for all political prisoners; abolition of the present prison system.

15. Abolition of criminal penalties for drug use, prostitution, and other victimless crimes.

PREAMBLE

Though a leader in the world in wealth and technology and possessed of vast resources sufficient to give—right now—an abundant life to all our people, our country is in crisis. It is a crisis of confidence in the capitalist institutions, parties, and rulers who maintain the economic system that oppresses minorities, women, old people, and young people, in a patriarchal system that permeates every aspect of our daily lives. Why do we accept the manipulation, the institutionalized discrimination, the lack of control over our life energies? Our answer is that we do not.

We recognize that fulfillment of the basic needs common to all of us is frustrated by the big-finance, big-corporation, big-military establishment which maintains control through its servants in the capitalist two-party system and which constantly tightens its stranglehold over foreign and domestic policies and our very lives. This hold can be broken only if we the people, at home, in our neighborhoods, in our schools and other workplaces, begin to organize and take control of the institutions which affect our lives, our land, and the future of the country. It is up to us to make the changes that are necessary.

The People's Party is a socialist party representing the interests of the working class. This class includes the employed and unemployed, in unions and not organized, urban and rural, on welfare and denied welfare, women whose labor in the home is unpaid, retired and disabled, students and young people, prisoners and mental patients (prisoners in their own right), and enlisted people in the armed forces.

We seek a new form of society: a socialist democracy with the means of production owned, and all society managed, by a democratic government of all working people. Respecting individual rights of political, religious, and sexual freedom, it would manage all collective affairs from the workplace and neighborhood to the entire U.S. in a truly classless society. We endorse the basic principles of the workers of the Paris Commune of 1871 that all officials be elected, all be recallable at any time, and none receive more than a worker's wage for their public service. We reject the sick interpersonal dynamics around which Western relationships traditionally revolve—jealousy, possessiveness, and competition—the very qualities which the system of capitalism, with racism and patriarchy, counts on to divide the people.

We enter the capitalist electoral process only to bring this message to the American people. We cannot assume that the road to socialism will be easy—that the ruling capitalist class will peacefully surrender its power as the result of an election. The act of revolutionary transformation must involve some kind of forceful action. We balance and implement our general principles and platform with action programs, local and national,

and the awareness that collective self-defense will also be necessary to the changes we seek.

## Ageism

Under the present system, young people and older people are denied their basic rights and opportunities and often are treated more like property than human beings. Therefore, we support the following demands:

### For Young People

1) The rights of full citizenship, including the right to vote and hold electoral office beginning at whatever age an individual decides to accept those responsibilities.

2) The right to be independent of one's parents if one so desires. Young people must be allowed to have an alternative living facility of their choice, run by youths themselves.

3) The right to control the institutions that control their lives, especially the right of young people to control their education.

4) The right to all constitutional protections under the law, in a totally reformed legal and judicial system.

5) The right to work under conditions and with wages equal to adults and to be paid for going to school. Young people should be covered by any guaranteed annual income plan.

6) The right to determine their own life style as full citizens.

7) The right to choose their own sexual preference.

### For Older People

1) The right to continued, full, and productive employment, if they so desire.

2) The right to ample guaranteed annual income, fully adjusted to the cost of living or to special needs of the handicapped.

3) The right to make decisions about how and where one will spend one's life, without interference.

4) The right to especially convenient transportation.

5) The right to control the institutions which control their lives.

## Agriculture and Farm Labor

From Benson to Freeman to Butz, the two major capitalist parties have presided over the destruction of agriculture as a way of life and its replacement by repressive monopoly agri-business. Food should be not a weapon but a natural gift.

We recognize that, ultimately, the countryside and its natural beauty and productivity can be saved only through an alliance of farm workers, non-labor-hiring smallholders, new-style communal farmers, and artisans making decisions on a collective democratic basis.

The destiny of rural America must be seized from the destructive control of profit-motivated giant corporations.

We therefore demand the following programs:

*Short Range*

1) National/international planning for crop forecasting and needs.

2) Immediate rollback of food prices with corporate profits returned to the farmers.

3) A return to parity pricing.

4) Immediate unionization for all farm workers in unions of their own choice.

5) Support of U.F.W. organizing and boycott campaigns.

6) Application of federal wage laws to farm workers.

7) Priority given to free food distribution to hungry areas of the world.

8) Elimination of speculation in the commodities market.

9) Financial support for independent farmers' cooperatives.

10) Nationalization of key support industries (farm machinery, fertilizer, etc.).

11) Elimination of vertical integration of the food industry.

*Long Range*

1) Re-emphasis of agricultural research to benefit the consumer, the environment, and family farmers; investigation and establishment of organic pest control, crop diversification, recycling and composting of organic waste.

2) A shift of population migration from urban to rural areas.

3) De-emphasizing of meat production and consumption.

4) "Green belting" of all possible urban areas with farmer/worker/community land management.

5) A shift from wasteful, energy intensive, unemployment-causing farm technologies.

## ECOLOGY

Ecological deterioration is a worldwide phenomenon. Unrestricted technology has drastically altered the life-supporting processes of the earth. The Western world has to a great extent created and controlled modern technology and bears major responsibility for its misuse. The dialectics of selfish private profit have only accelerated this crisis.

The People's Party believes that controlled and harmonized technology can serve without destroying the ecological balance of the planet. In order to secure this balance with nature, we propose:

*Immediate*

1) Elimination of all chemicals which are not ecologically compatible with the environment:

   a) chlorinated fluoro-carbons (aerosol propellants),

   b) carcinogens such as vinyl chlorides and radioactive elements,

   c) non-biodegradables, and

   d) those which present bio-accumulative hazards, such as DDT.

2) Elimination of nuclear fission power.

3) Elimination of aluminum cans and no-deposit bottles and the requirement that all containers be re-usable.

4) Elimination of the Army Corps of Engineers.

5) A ban on killing endangered species (whales, seals, wolves, etc.).

6) Implementation of employment-creating clean air and water programs.

7) Implementation of the ecological disposal of sewage waste (composting, etc.).

8) Immediate implementation of drastic energy and natural resource conservation.

9) Elimination of the strip mining of coal and other minerals.

*Long Range*

1) Research and development of renewable energy sources.

2) Development of total recycling and conservation of all non-renewable resources.

3) Development of computer systems to assess present eco-damage and future effects.

4) The evolution of ecologically balanced transportation systems (mass transit, bicycles, etc.) toward the elimination of the internal combustion engine.

5) Recycling of urban wastes to the farms, thus eliminating the need for a chemical fertilizer industry.

6) Development of total environmental impact reports for all (old and new) technologies.

7) Development of population planning aimed at education and the elimination of poverty.

## Economics

The economic condition of the American people is degenerating. Our cities are in decay. Twenty-five percent of our population lives below the poverty level. Unemployment, underemployment, and mis-employment are rampant. Dehumanizing conditions on the job and inadequate wages are all too common. Spiraling prices are eroding our living standards.

Third World people and women especially suffer from political, social, and economic oppression. Third World communities are forced to bear the brunt of an economic system in decline.

Ownership of our economy has fallen into a few hands (1.7 percent of the adult population owns more than 82 percent of the publicly held shares in American corporations). Pursuit of personal profit is the dominating theme of the economy, and waste through the production of useless goods is one of the major results. Working people are demoralized. They can no longer take pride in their work.

The conflict is one of class, between those who work and those who own. We believe in production for use, not for profit. All people must be co-owners and co-managers of the economy by *right* —co-consumers and co-producers of society's goods and services. We must divide the required socially useful work among all, and develop the capabilities of everyone, recognizing that more capabilities mean less work required from each, and a better, richer life.

We want an economic system based not on the manipulation of scarcity but rather on the planned production of surplus with the goal of abundance for all—from each according to ability, to each according to need.

## Education

In a capitalistic society, the educational process is not neutral. Schools serve the interests of the ruling class. They perpetuate the myth of an open, free society. In practice, however, they are instruments of class, sexual, ageist, and racial oppression. They teach misconceptions of the role of the United States in the world. They oppress the working class by reinforcing class differences through tracking systems. They offer students limited choices that are determined by their race, class, age, and sex.

The schools teach unquestioning obedience, sexism, mistrustful competitiveness, and the supreme importance of possessions. Parent and community input is blocked. The educational process ignores individual differences, stifles creative growth, and attempts to mold students into passive consumers and workers.

We oppose all of the above because education should inspire people to self-realization—to *be* more, rather than to have more.

We support the following bill of rights for all students:

1) Community control of schools. We propose community boards of one-half students, one-fourth workers in the schools, and one-fourth parents and other community members.

2) Recognition of students as equal members of society, entitled to all constitutional and human rights.

3) Immunity from prosecution for violation of rules that have been passed by an elected student board.

4) Democratically elected student courts, with right to counsel.

5) An end to corporal punishment, to searches, and to obligatory medical tests.

6) The rights of students and teachers to freedom of assembly, to form and join political organizations and unions, and to strike.

7) The right of Third World people to establish and control programs concentrating on their history and culture.

8) An end to compulsory attendance/involuntary servitude, although all people should have the right to an education that meets their needs whenever they want.

9) An end to racism, sexism, and tracking in the schools.

10) The right to education of all those tradi-

tionally excluded from public schools, such as the physically handicapped and the mentally "retarded."

11) Positive information, made available to everyone in schools, on lesbianism and male homosexuality as both natural and healthy.

12) Funding of schools by a steeply graduated income tax.

## FOREIGN POLICY

U.S. foreign policy is a tool of the small group of capitalists who control the U.S. government and consists of war, threats of war, lies, intrigue, torture, assassination, subversion, and an ever-increasing expenditure of tax money on weapons of death, with a corresponding deterioration of social programs. Only a workers' socialist democracy can achieve world cooperation. Meanwhile, we call for:

1) Dismantling of the Defense Department, CIA, DIA, U.S. participation in Interpol, and all other agencies which exist to destroy the struggles of working people around the world, and termination of U.S. training of police agencies of other countries.

2) An end to all secrecy in the conduct of foreign affairs.

3) Freedom for all U.S. colonies and respect for all treaties with Native Americans.

4) Solidarity with the struggles of workers and peasants throughout the world for socialism and national liberation.

5) An end to U.S. interference in the affairs of other countries, including

   a) Termination of U.S. support for Zionism and recognition of the right of self-determination of the Palestinian people.

   b) An end to U.S. intrigue against the workers and the government of Portugal.

   c) An end to U.S. support for racist regimes in Southern Africa.

   d) An end to U.S. support of the facist regime of Chile.

   e) The return of the Panama Canal Zone to Panamanian sovereignty.

6) An end to all international sales or gifts of arms by U.S. corporations and the U.S. government.

7) Aid for the reconstruction of Indochina with no strings attached, under the obligations of the Paris Peace Accords of 1973.

## GOVERNANCE

Governments, in the final analysis, are set up for the preservation and regulation of social and economic systems. The government of the United States of America and its subsidiary state and local governments are owned by capitalists and operated for the profit of banks and corporations. Elected representatives, according to the myth of American Democracy, are supposed to represent the interests of all the people. But most "representatives" are only interested in aiding the concentration of corporate conglomerate power and the expansion and defense of the capitalist economic empire, and in acquiring more personal wealth.

The People's Party calls for an end to America's capitalist two-party phony democracy. In a real democracy, communities collectively control the institutions which affect them (police, schools, utilities, banks, etc.), which means individual control over one's own life.

Ultimately, we stand for the creation of an authentic, classless socialist democracy with elected and recallable working people's assemblies integrating workplaces industrially and communities regionally.

In the meantime, the People's Party will work for immediate reforms that will weaken corporate control over the political system, eliminate costly bureaucracy, and extend democratic rights. To this end, we propose:

1) Independence for Guam, Micronesia, Puerto Rico, and the Virgin Islands, and statehood for the Colony of Columbia (Washington, D.C.).

2) Establishment, on all levels of government, of procedures for referendum, initiatives, and the recall of all public officials (elected or appointed).

3) The enactment of strong campaign reform laws, designed to take big money out of election campaigns, with no discrimination against minor parties or independent candidates.

4) Payment to officials of no more than the average worker's wages.

5) The slashing of administrative budgets at all levels of government, without cutting social services.

6) The honoring of all treaties with Native American nations.

7) Abolition of the Selective Service system.

8) Retention and expansion of all civil rights and liberties.

9) Community control of the police.

10) Changing of appointed offices to elected offices.

11) Abolition of property taxes for residential property, to be replaced by a steeply graduated income tax.

12) The enactment of increased, direct, and proportional federal assistance to local communities. An end to federal and state red tape.

## HEALTH CARE

The profit system is a major cause of illness and also of the failure to prevent or cure it.

Industry pollutes the environment and degrades our foods. Competitiveness and insecurity wreck physical and emotional health. Industrial accidents kill 22,000 and disable two million yearly. Poverty deprives millions of adequate housing, recreation, diet, and serenity.

The emphasis of our profit-motivated health system is on treatment rather than on prevention.

Millions get little or no medical or dental care, and the disease and death rates among them are shamefully high, particularly among minority groups.

The pharmaceutical industry pushes the expensive drugs, sometimes without adequate testing. Herbal medicines and sound diet are ignored in medical practice and education.

The delivery of health services is in the control not of the consumers but of physicians, hospitals, and insurance organizations.

Health professionals are inadequate in numbers and poorly distributed.

The treatment of mental illness is too often only custodial and deprives the patients of their constitutional rights.

We will not have healthy, secure, and fulfilling lives until a socialist society enables us to control every aspect of our existence.

Until then, the People's Party demands a complete health insurance system with consumer control, the training of many more para-professionals as well as professionals, the scientific study of folk and herbal medicine, the provision of government funds for the establishment of free clinics by community groups, and the demystification of medicine through a broader and deeper public education concerning the body and its diseases.

## LABOR

Working people constitute the overwhelming majority in the United States. There can be no wealth without their labor.

"Organized" labor, however, is not the movement of *all* working people that it should be. The voice and militancy of the rank and file has been muted, left leadership purged or subverted, and the movement effectively diffused by the class-collaborationist policies of pro-establishment union leadership.

Nevertheless, unions remain the first line of defense of the working class. The pro-capitalist bureaucracy must be removed and unions (re-)organized along democratic, industry-wide lines in order to mobilize working people towards seizing control of the economy.

All people must become co-owners and co-managers of the economy—co-consumers and co-producers of society's goods and services, with the work required to sustain society divided equally among all.

In the present crisis, we must foster the organizing of the unorganized, the unemployed, the "nonemployed," and women who serve as unpaid labor in the home, and the re-organizing of the mis-organized, in order to enhance the strength of the entire working class. We support the right of everyone to organize and strike, a bill of rights in all workplaces, and the formation of workers' councils to democratize the new exclusive prerogatives of management. We endorse the struggles for full useful employment at union pay levels, for 40 hours' pay for a 30-hour week, for unlimited unemployment compensation at full pay levels, and for a moratorium on any further layoffs.

To the degree that all these demands cannot be realized, we urge that priority be given to the spreading of available work to include those workers who have already been laid off or are threatened with layoff.

## LAW & JUSTICE

The People's Party demands broad changes in the legal system. People's rights have been systematically violated by the courts and law enforcement agencies. We must institute community control of police and free legal representation for all people. We recognize that crime is a result of our capitalist society.

We must decriminalize all consensual sexual behavior, drug use, and all "victimless crimes."

We endorse the Prisoners' Bill of Rights and will work to institute community-controlled re-education centers as a replacement for the present penal system. We support restitution to the victims of crime and their families. Corporations must be held accountable for violations of the law and suitably punished. Prosecutors and law enforcement officials must also be punished for harassment of citizens or violation of their rights through grand jury proceedings, illegal gathering of evidence, or any other means. We demand freedom for all political prisoners.

We support full legal equality of all persons regardless of age, sex, sexual orientation, race, economic status, citizenship, and military status, including abolition of the Uniform Code of Military Justice. We favor total amnesty for all war resisters, imprisoned or otherwise.

## MEDIA

The People's Party recognizes the control of television, radio, movies, and printed media as an essential element of the control of society by the economic rulers of the capitalist system. Most working people depend on these media for information, entertainment, and ideas which influence their values and actions.

The private capitalist control of these sources is consciously used to distort and falsify news and manipulate people's values. Commercial advertising and selective and distorted news coverage reinforce stereotyped views of women, the old and the young, and minority people, as well as of working people as a class.

The lack of capital to establish a TV station, radio station, newspaper, or magazine effectively prevents poor and working people from being heard, except for token coverage to give the illusion of democracy.

Under the workers' socialist democracy toward which we struggle, the media will be open to democratic and cooperative use by the people. Only under a worker-owned and -controlled system will this access be realized and the immense *liberating* potential of the mass media become a reality.

For the present we demand access to the capitalist media by working class groups. Such groups must have substantial air time on radio and television and space in capitalist-owned newspapers and magazines as a right.

We also encourage the creation and growth of alternative newspapers, radio, and television by and for working people, so that we can communicate directly with each other on the problems that affect us all.

## RACISM

The People's Party totally rejects racism and its use by the capitalists to divide us. The national minority peoples in the U.S., oppressed for hundreds of years, are now in the forefront of the fight for democratic rights and socialism.

The People's Party supports the struggles of all Native Americans, Black people, Spanish-speaking people, Asian peoples, and all other oppressed nationalities to achieve equality and self-determination and to maintain their national identity, language, and culture.

The questions of national self-determination and racial equality are part of the class struggle. We denounce politicians who use flagrantly racist appeals to propagate division among the working people, as in Boston and other cities. We support community control of all educational and social services institutions. We support the democratic right of Blacks and other oppressed nationalities to quality education wherever they choose and by whatever means necessary.

We support busing wherever it is desired or necessary to defeat white racists. However, where Black and other oppressed nationalities oppose forced busing, we support their right to self-defense of their communities to insure self-determination.

We will act to end all forms of institutional racism as practiced by police, prisons, courts, banks, health-care institutions, welfare programs, and the government bureaucracy. We vehemently oppose the forced sterilization of Third World people and other programs of genocide. We support all Third World women in their struggle against their oppression as both women and Third World people.

The U.S. government must honor all treaties with Native American nations and peoples and must return land or make reparations for territory and labor stolen from minority peoples and native nations.

We pledge our support to the Wounded Knee warriors, Black freedom fighters in the South, and imprisoned comrades and struggling peoples everywhere.

We must unite all workers in the struggle to

put an end to all forms of racism and bring about a socialist society, which alone can insure the realization of true self-determination.

## SEXISM

Sexism is discrimination or oppression based on sex or sexual orientation. It is frequently manifested in aggressive behavior to intimidate other people. It is capitalistic exploitation that creates dehumanizing conditions; and it is sexism that puts females at the bottom in every category.

The People's Party objects to the restrictive sexual definitions of "feminine" and "masculine," which contain the underlying assumption that these qualities normally appear in females and males respectively. We must advocate positive individual and social actions that identify the People's Party with the struggles of the lesbian and male homosexual communities and will abolish all anti-gay mechanisms of identification, isolation, control, and oppression. All legislation concerning sexual orientation, transvestism, transsexualism, pornography, obscenity, soliciting, and prostitution must be abolished, except for those laws which protect people from being forced into such activities against their will. The People's Party is determined to create a society where forced prostitution does not exist. Individual, legal, economic, and property rights should be equally available to all persons regardless of sexual orientation, marital status, or living arrangement.

The People's Party opposes the use of any terminology that is sexually oppressive. In order for language to have a positive radical impact on destroying sexism, the People's Party recommends that masculine pronouns (him, his, etc.) be replaced by their female equivalents until such time as the society is no longer sexist, at which time neutral pronouns will be used.

The patriarchal nuclear family is one of the institutions in our society which directly oppresses all people. We put forth these general principles recognizing that it is the sexual oppression and exploitation of all people that allows for the continuation of capitalist society.

## ORGANIZATIONAL PRINCIPLES

The People's Party, meeting in Convention, August 25-31, 1975, sets the following as its Organizational Principles:

1. We are a socialist party, because in unity we believe that socialism is the answer to the decay and increasing barbarism of this society and that the working class, as opposed to the capitalist class, is the agent of revolutionary change, which can and will take power and run a new society on a collective democratic basis.

2. We define the working class as all those who must sell their labor power in order to survive, or who must survive in some other way not dependent on owning or managing capital. It includes employed and unemployed, those in unions and those not organized, on welfare and denied welfare, retired and disabled workers, working class students and young people, prisoners and "mental" prisoners, and armed forces enlisted people.

3. The purpose of our party is to help build a mass organization of the working class capable of taking power.

4. Our organizational structure must be united and democratic. By united we mean that all levels of the organization are accountable to the total organization. By democratic we mean that every member of the organization participates democratically both in making decisions and in carrying them out. Our leadership must be chosen democratically, so that it can be accountable to the organization as a whole. All of our party officers must be elected and recallable. Where feasible we try to distribute the tasks of leadership among many people in order to develop multiple leadership.

5. As socialists we specify clearly the form of worker's democracy toward which we work, and do not confuse it with a one-party state. The economic backwardness and necessity for post-revolutionary unity against powerful, armed imperialist powers, which gave a one-party form to such states, as they exist today, will be absent in the U.S. Production of commodities is socialized on a mass scale, and the working class is a huge and generally literate majority. Conditions for open, democratic socialism, based on workers' state power, are present.

6. Thus, we do not follow the theory or practice of any party, including those allegedly Marxist-Leninist, which practices elitism and sectarianism. We make it crystal clear to the rest of the working class that we do not aspire to be the Only Vanguard Party or to rule society after the revolution.

7. We seek practical working unity with all

working class groups and parties who share our goal. We believe that the institutions of democratic workers' government must be built by the organized effort of all class-conscious groups and workers on the principle of equal democratic participation by all working class people.

8. While rejecting self-righteous go-it-alone vanguardism, we also reject the theory and practice of "socialist" parties which rely only on elections as a strategy to achieve socialism. This perspective is reformist by definition. Such parties have historically and will in the future become accomplices in the capitalist system of political control. We use elections only as a tool and a tactic to organize toward a socialist democracy.

9. We participate in the trade union movement to defend the living and working conditions of workers. In our political organizing we also seek to win workers to the goal of a socialist democracy. In both of these tasks we must organize rank-and-file workers against the economic and political bosses, including pro-capitalist international and local union bureaucrats.

10. Within the party, in our party work, and in our personal lives we strive for relations of equality, mutual respect, and comradely consideration with our fellow workers of all races, sexes, and nationalities.

11. We support all struggles for equality and self-determination of minority nation workers.

12. We support all struggles for equality of women workers.

13. We support all struggles for equality of gay workers.

14. We do not align ourselves with any one existing so-called socialist country, but support each and every one of them against all imperialist wars, threats, and maneuvers.

15. We must develop a multi-national working class culture, in opposition to the manipulated mass culture and perverted values of capitalism.

16. We support all struggles to preserve the ecological life-cycle from profit-motivated destruction by capitalist bosses. In particular, we oppose the construction of nuclear fission reactors, especially breeder reactors.

17. We support the struggles of exploited and oppressed peoples around the world for socialist liberation from the grip of imperialism.

18. We work for immediate measures such as the preservation and extension of social services and other reforms necessary to the survival of working people.

## Prohibition Platform 1976

### PREAMBLE

We, the representatives of the Prohibition Party, assembled in National Convention at Denver, Colorado, June 26 and 27, 1975, recognizing Almighty God as the source of all just government and with faith in the teachings of the Lord Jesus Christ, do solemnly promise that, if our party is chosen to administer the affairs of the nation, we will, with earnest dedication to the principles of righteousness, seek to serve the needs and to preserve the rights, the prerogatives, and the basic freedoms of the people of the United States of America. For the realization of these ends we propose the following program of government:

### Constitutional Government

We affirm our loyalty to the Constitution of the United States, and express our confidence in that document as the basic law of the land. We will resist all attempts to violate it, whether by legislation, by means of evasion, or through judicial interpretation. We support our system of representative government with its plan of checks and balances. We support appropriate Constitutional changes to restrict the ever-expanding power of the federal judiciary as a non-elected legislative branch.

### Communism-Totalitarianism

Communism is aggressively and unalterably opposed to our Constitutional government and seeks to infiltrate and overthrow our present form of government by means of subversion and violence. We oppose Communism both as an economic program and a governmental system.

We also oppose all other totalitarian philosophies and forms of government.

### Government Economy and Taxation

America today faces mounting unemployment, run-away inflation and a tax system which takes nearly one-third of the earnings of our citizens to operate our government. We believe that unwise fiscal policies of our government are the chief cause of the serious economic plight in which our nation finds itself.

To combat inflation, lighten our tax load and insure fiscal responsibility we propose:

1. A sharp cut in government expenditures thru the elimination of waste and unwise programs;

2. A decrease in the tax-load particularly for middle-income taxpayers;

3. A Constitutional limit on the spending and taxing powers of Congress except in time of war declared by Congress in accordance with the Constitution;

4. Legislation which requires a balanced budget except in time of war declared by Congress;

5. Governmental withdrawal from competition with private enterprise and the sale of such government-owned businesses and properties. Proceeds from such sales should be applied to the reduction of the national debt;

6. A systematic reduction of the national debt, the interest on which now costs the American taxpayer many billions of dollars each year.

### Foreign Affairs

Our government has long lacked a consistent, positive foreign policy. We favor a foreign policy whose objectives are the preservation of American freedom and the encouragement of those governments and nations which grant a large measure of freedom to their citizens.

No foreign government has an inherent right to financial aid at the expense of American taxpayers. Any foreign aid should be granted only to nations friendly to the United States and whose governments are not corrupt nor aggressors against other nations. Most aid should be in the form of loans at current commercial rates of interest. Such loans will enable recipient nations to maintain their self-respect. No aid of any kind should go to nations which have reneged on past loan agreements.

The United States has no right to interfere in the internal affairs of other nations unless those nations are committing acts which are hostile to our nation.

### A Free Economy

We oppose burdensome restraints on our free enterprise system, detailed regulation of our economic life and federal interference with individual initiative. We believe that free enterprise is threatened by:

1. Excessive governmental regulation,

2. Growth of public or private monopoly and

3. Unethical practices of unscrupulous groups.

We will encourage independent, non-monopolistic business enterprises which serve genuine consumer needs and which operate with a sense of responsibility to the public. We will act to prevent both monopoly and excessive governmental regulation and to protect adequately the consuming public from irresponsible or deceptive business practices.

### Labor and Industry

Both management and labor must be held responsible for their economic behavior. Neither can be permitted to dominate at the expense of the other or of the common good. Anti-trust laws must be applied to all monopolies, whether of business or of labor. We will enforce stringently the laws forbidding strikes by federal government employees.

A person's right to work for an employer willing to hire him and his right to join or not join a labor union without affecting his employment must be protected. Employers and employees must be free to bargain and contract without governmental interference. Violence or coercion, by management or labor, must be prohibited.

### States Rights

Our Founding Fathers recognized the importance of both individual and states rights, and determined to preserve them by making the bill of rights an integral part of our Constitution. During recent years the Federal Government has usurped many of the states' Constitutional Rights. The states, which created the Federal Government, are now dominated by their creature.

We specifically reject any system of so-called "regional government" which would impose new units of government composed of non-elected officials between the states and the federal government and between the states and county and local governmental units. We pledge ourselves to action that will preserve, and where necessary restore, the legitimate Constitutional rights guaranteed to the several states.

## Individual Rights

All American citizens, regardless of race, sex, religion or national origin are entitled to equality of treatment under the provisions of our Constitution and under the laws of our land. We oppose the use of violent, anarchistic or arbitrary pressure tactics as a means of seeking to resolve tensions and divergencies of opinion among our citizens.

We oppose those proposals, including forced busing, which are seriously harming many public schools today, in the name of integration. We oppose all discriminatory measures such as quotas in employment or housing which discriminate against the majority as strongly as we oppose discriminatory measures against minority groups.

## Public Morality

We deplore the low level of public morality culminating in the shocking revelations of crime and of political and economic corruption which have characterized recent years.

We will break the unholy alliance which has made these things possible. We will strengthen and enforce laws against gambling, narcotics and commercialized vice, emphasize the basic importance of spiritual and moral values to the development and growth of an enduring nation, and maintain the integrity of our system of government by careful law enforcement and loyal support of our Constitution.

## Right to Life

The God-given Right to Life should not be arbitrarily denied by governmental action. The massive destruction of unborn infants authorized by a U.S. Supreme Court ruling and by some state abortion-on-demand laws is morally indefensible. We support a Constitutional Amendment to protect the unborn by prohibiting abortion except in those very rare cases where the life of the mother is seriously endangered.

We oppose any legislation which would allow, encourage or authorize the practice of euthanasia (so-called mercy killing). We hold that life is the gift of God and that it is the responsibility of government to protect life—not to abort or shorten it.

## Military Preparedness

Believing that eternal vigilance is the price of liberty we declare for a sound program of military preparedness. While praying for peace we cannot place our freedom in peril by ignoring potential threats to our nation. We will work hard to protect the taxpayer by eliminating the unnecessary waste and duplication in military programs.

We are gratified that, at last, our government has adopted the concept of a peacetime voluntary armed forces which was first advocated by the Prohibition Party.

## National Sovereignty

We declare our belief in national sovereignty and oppose surrender of this sovereignty to any international organization.

## Welfare

The Prohibition Party has always pioneered in social reform and we favor the rendering of help to the handicapped, the aged, the chronically ill and those families without a breadwinner. Today, however, so many undeserving persons are on our welfare rolls that rising welfare expenditures are becoming a crushing burden on taxpayers.

The undeserving must be removed from the rolls and emphasis must be placed on helping more welfare recipients become self-supporting or a taxpayers revolt may well result in the death of the entire welfare program.

We reject the idea of a guaranteed annual income. Such a program would further swell the welfare ranks and stifle initiative among those with incomes slightly above the welfare level.

The government practice of providing birth-control devices to minors without consent of their parents is one which encourages immorality and must be ended.

## Marriage and Divorce

Ordained by God, the home is a sacred institution which must be protected and preserved. We favor the enactment of uniform marriage and divorce laws by the several states as an aid to building strong and enduring homes.

## Church and State

We support the Constitutional Principle of Separation of Church and State and oppose any attempt to weaken or subvert this fundamental principle. We support tax exemption for non-profit religious institutions including church publishing houses but we favor full taxation of all income received by religious organizations from operations which compete with private tax-paying businesses. We oppose the appropriation of any public money for private religious or sectarian purposes.

The Founding Fathers recognized that God and His Word were vital to the success of any great nation. We believe, as they did, that the Bible is not a sectarian book but is a volume of universal appeal and application which is woven into our history, our laws and our culture. We reject any effort to prohibit its use or the reading of same in public schools or other public institutions.

### Religious Liberty

We believe in the freedom of the individual to worship, to fellowship with others of similar faith, to evangelize, to educate and to establish religious institutions as his conscience dictates. We oppose efforts to restrict freedom of religious broadcasting and the establishment of new churches. The Internal Revenue Service must be prohibited from using its power to control tax exemptions to discriminate against any religious body as it has done in the past. Our government should oppose religious persecution anywhere in the world and refuse to extend any aid to nations which practice persecution.

### Ballot Law Reform

In most states Republicans and Democrats have enacted election laws designed to either prevent other political parties from gaining access to the ballot or require them to spend all their meagre resources to do so. They fear competition which will give voters an alternative to their bankrupt policies.

We demand passage of state laws which will end this two-party monopoly of the electoral system and give to all legitimate political parties and to Independents their Constitutional rights. Such rights should not extend to those who are dedicated to the overthrow of our governmental system by means of force if necessary.

### Education

Under the Tenth Amendment, public education is clearly to be under the control of the states and the people. We therefore oppose all direct federal aid to education and to federal interference in education matters, whether such interference comes from the executive, legislative or judicial branches of the federal government. Each state should support and control its own educational program.

### Social Security

We endorse the principle of an actuarially sound Social Security program. The present system is NOT actuarially sound and is destructive of individual initiative and freedom. We propose to reform the system by:

1. Allowing workers the option of placing their payments and those of their employers into private insurance and retirement plans.

2. Establishing a sound actuarial basis for taxes and payments which will be fairer to taxpayers and recipients and will eliminate the need for ever-increasing tax-rates to sustain the system.

3. The removal of any penalty for those who continue to work after becoming eligible for Social Security retirement payments.

4. A built-in system for adjusting Social Security payments as inflation requires without making such increases a political consideration.

### Agriculture

The production and distribution of agricultural products is of vital importance to our economy. Those engaged in agricultural pursuits, like other American citizens, should be free from authoritarian control and coercion. Likewise, consumers should not be subjected to artificially contrived higher food prices. We therefore propose a sane and sensible return to a free market program with the elimination of all governmental controls and subsidies.

### Public Health

We favor the continuance of the legal bans against such harmful drugs as marijuana, LSD and heroin. Since tobacco has been identified as the prime cause of lung cancer and many other health problems, we oppose promotional advertising and government subsidies for tobacco products.

We support new laws to adequately protect citizens against unjust incarceration in mental institutions. We oppose those programs of mass medication which violate individual rights.

We favor strong governmental anti-pollution

programs since clean air and a pure water supply are benefits which should be available to all our citizens.

We oppose socialized medicine and urge an end to federal interference in the operation of hospitals, nursing homes and other medical care facilities.

## The Environment

The American people are entitled to an environment in which air, water and land are maintained in as clean a condition as is possible. To this end we propose careful study of the problems involved and the development of those measures which, on a realistic basis, will insure the preservation of an environment which is both safe and stimulating.

## The Alcohol Problem

Beverage alcohol is today the chief cause of poverty, broken homes, juvenile delinquency, vice, crime, political corruption, wasted manpower, and highway accidents. By conservative estimates more than 20,000,000 Americans are now alcoholics or problem drinkers.

Contrary to the promises made when Prohibition was repealed, bootlegging is today a growing business. The liquor traffic itself estimates that one-third of all alcoholic beverages consumed in America today is illegally produced and sold. An estimated 400,000 Americans die yearly because of highway deaths, homicides and health problems which can be traced directly to beverage alcohol.

The liquor traffic is linked with and supports a nationwide network of gambling, vice and crime. It also dominates the Republican and Democratic parties and, thru them, much of the governmental and political life of our nation. This is one of the major reasons for the inability of either party to operate on a morally sound basis.

The Prohibition Party alone offers a program to deal with this greatest of all social ills. We pledge ourselves to a program of publicity, education, legislation and administration, leading to the elimination of the liquor traffic. We will repeal all laws which legalize that traffic and rigorously enforce new laws which will prohibit the manufacture, distribution and sale of alcoholic beverages.

## Challenge

Voters who are concerned about the widespread corruption and erosion of our freedoms accompanied by a new low level of morality in government will NOT see a solution to those problems if they continue to give their support to the two parties which created those problems. The Prohibition Party, with a clean record of over one hundred years of service to America, invites the support of all who believe in the foregoing program of good government.

Our bi-centennial observance can mark a turning point in America's history if enough voters will support the one party dedicated to the basic principles upon which this nation was founded.

## Republican Platform 1976

PREAMBLE

To you, an American citizen:

You are about to read the 1976 Republican Platform. We hope you will also find time to read the Democrats' Platform. Compare. You will see basic differences in how the two parties propose to represent you.

"The Platform is the Party's contract with the people." This is what it says on the cover of the official printing of the Democrat Platform. So it should be. The Democrats' Platform repeats the same thing on every page: more government, more spending, more inflation. Compare. This Republican Platform says exactly the opposite—less government, less spending, less inflation. In other words, we want you to retain more of your own money, money that represents the worth of your labors, to use as you see fit for the necessities and conveniences of life.

No matter how many statements to the contrary that Mr. Carter makes, he is firmly attached to a contract with you to increase vastly the powers of government. Is bigger government in Washington really what you want?

Make no mistake: you cannot have bigger programs in Washington and less government by Washington. You must choose.

What is the cost of these added or expanded programs? The Democrats' Platform is deliberately vague. When they tell you, as they do time after time, that they will "expand federal support," you are left to guess the cost. The price tag of five major Democrat Platform promises could add as much as $100 billion to the annual cost of government. But the Democrats' Platform proposes over 60 new or expanded spending programs and the expansion or creation of some 22 Washington agencies, offices or bureaus. In fact, the total of all Democrat proposals can be as high as $200 billion a year. While this must be a rough estimate, it does give you a clue to the magnitude and direction of these commitments. The Democrats' Platform can increase federal spending by 50 percent. If a Democrat Congress passes the Democrat Platform and it is signed by a Democrat President, what happens then? The Democrats could raise your taxes by 50 percent to pay for the new programs. Or the Democrats could not raise taxes and the result would be a runaway inflation. Of course, contract or no contract, the Democrats may not honor their promises. Are you prepared to risk it?

In stark contrast to the Democrats' Platform, we offer you a responsive and moderate alternative based on these principles:

We believe that liberty can be measured by how much freedom you have to make your own decisions—even your own mistakes. Government must step in when your liberties impinge on your neighbor's. Government must protect your constitutional rights. Government must deal with other governments and protect you from aggressors. Government must assure equal opportunity. And government must be compassionate in caring for those citizens who are unable to care for themselves.

Our federal system of local-state-national government is designed to sort out on what level these actions should be taken. Those concerns of a national character—such as air and water pollution that do not respect state boundaries or the national transportation system or efforts to safeguard your civil liberties—must, of course, be handled on the national level.

As a general rule, however, we believe that government action should be taken first by the government that resides as close to you as possible. Governments tend to become less responsive to your needs the farther away they are from you. Thus, we prefer local and state government to national government, and decentralized national government wherever possible.

We also believe that you, often acting through voluntary organizations, should have the opportunity to solve many of the social problems of your community. This spirit of freely helping others is uniquely American and should be encouraged in every way by government.

Every dollar spent by government is a dollar earned by you. Government must always ask: Are your dollars being wisely spent? Can we afford it? Is it not better for the country to leave your dollars in your pocket?

Your elected officials, their appointees, and government workers are expected to perform their public acts with honesty, openness, diligence, and special integrity. At the heart of our system must be confidence that these people are always working for you.

We believe that your initiative and energy create jobs, our standard of living and the underlying economic strength of the country. Government must work for the goal of justice and the elimination of unfair practices, but no government has yet designed a more productive economic system or one which benefits as many people.

The beauty of our land is our legacy to our children. It must be protected by us so that they can pass it on intact to their children.

The United States must always stand for peace and liberty in the world and the rights of the individual. We must form sturdy partnerships with our allies for the preservation of freedom. We must be ever willing to negotiate differences, but equally mindful that there are American ideals that cannot be compromised. Given that there are other nations with potentially hostile designs, we recognize that we can reach our goals only while maintaining a superior national defense.

We support these principles because they are right, knowing full well that they will not be easy to achieve. Acting with restraint is most difficult when confronted by an opposition Congress that is determined to promise everything to everybody. And this is what the Democrat Congress has been doing. A document, such as this Platform, which refuses to knuckle under to special interest groups, will be accused of being "uncaring." Yet it is exactly because we do care about your basic freedom to manage your own life with a minimum of government interference, because we do care about encouraging permanent and meaningful jobs, because we do care about your getting paid in sound dollars, because we do care about resisting the use of your tax dollars for wasteful or unproven programs—it is for these reasons that we are proposing only actions that the nation can afford and are opposing excessive tinkering with an economic system that works better than any other in the world.

Our great American Republic was founded on the principle: "one nation under God, with liberty and justice for all." This bicentennial year marks the anniversary of the greatest secular experiment in history: That of seeking to determine that a people are truly capable of self-government. It was our "Declaration" which put the world and posterity on notice "that Men are . . . endowed by their Creator with certain unalienable Rights" and that those rights must not be taken from those to whom God has given them.

Recently, Peggy Pinder, a 23-year-old student from Grinnell, Iowa, who is a delegate to this convention, said that she joined our party "because Republicans understand the place of government in the people's lives better than the Democrats. Republicans try to find ways to take care of needs through the private sector first while it seems automatic for Democrats to take care of them through the governmental system."

The perception of Peggy Pinder governs this Platform. Aren't these the principles that you want your elected representatives to have?

JOBS AND INFLATION

We believe it is of paramount importance that the American people understand that the number one destroyer of jobs is inflation. We wish to stress that the number one cause of inflation is the government's expansion of the nation's supply of money and credit needed to pay for deficit spending. It is above all else deficit spending by the federal government which erodes the purchasing power of the dollar. Most Republicans in Congress seem to understand this fundamental cause-and-effect relationship and their support in sustaining over 40 Presidential vetoes in the past two years has prevented over $13 billion in federal spending. It is clear that most of the Democrats do not understand this vital principle, or, if they do, they simply don't care.

Inflation is the direct responsibility of a spendthrift Democrat-controlled Congress that has been unwilling to discipline itself to live within our means. The temptation to spend and deficit spend for political reasons has simply been too great for

most of our elected politicians to resist. Individuals, families, companies and most local and state governments must live within a budget. Why not Congress?

Republicans hope every American realizes that if we are permanently to eliminate high unemployment, it is essential to protect the integrity of our money. That means putting an end to deficit spending. The danger, sooner or later, is runaway inflation.

Wage and price controls are not the solution to inflation. They attempt to treat only the symptom —rising prices—not the cause. Historically, controls have always been a dismal failure, and in the end they create only shortages, black markets and higher prices. For these reasons the Republican Party strongly opposes any reimposition of such controls, on a standby basis or otherwise.

Unfortunately, the Democrat-controlled Congress now persists in attempting to obtain control over our nation's money creation policies by taking away the independence of the Federal Reserve Board. The same people who have so massively expanded government spending should not be allowed politically to dominate our monetary policy. The independence of the Federal Reserve System must be preserved.

Massive, federally-funded public employment programs, such as the Humphrey-Hawkins Bill currently embraced by the new National Platform of the Democrat Party will cost billions and can only be financed either through very large tax increases or through ever increasing levels of deficit spending. Although such government "make-work" programs usually provide a temporary stimulus to the economy, "quick-fix" solutions of this sort—like all narcotics—lead to addiction, larger and larger doses, and ultimately the destruction of far more jobs than they create. Sound job creation can only be accomplished in the private sector of the economy. Americans must not be fooled into accepting government as the employer of last resort.

Nor should we sit idly by while 2.5 million American jobs are threatened by imports of textile products. We encourage the renewal of the GATT Multifiber Arrangement and the signing of other necessary bilateral agreements to protect our domestic textile industry.

In order to be able to provide more jobs, businesses must be able to expand; yet in order to build and expand, they must be profitable and able to borrow funds (savings) that someone else has been willing to part with on a temporary basis. In the long run, inflation discourages thrift, encourages debt and destroys the incentive to save which is the mainspring of capital formation. When our government—through deficit spending and debasement of the currency—destroys the incentive to save and to invest, it destroys the very wellspring of American productivity. Obviously, when production falls, the number of jobs declines.

The American people are beginning to understand that no government can ever add real wealth (purchasing power) to an economy by simply turning on the printing presses or by creating credit out of thin air. All government can do is confiscate and redistribute wealth. No nation can spend its way into prosperity; a nation can only spend its way into bankruptcy.

## TAXES AND GOVERNMENT SPENDING

The Republican Party recognizes that tax policies and spending policies are inseparable. If government spending is not controlled, taxes will inevitably rise either directly or through inflation. By failing to tie spending directly to income, the Democrat-controlled Congress has not kept faith with the American people. Every American knows he cannot continually live beyond his means.

The Republican Party advocates a legislative policy to obtain a balanced federal budget and reduced tax rates. While the best tax reform is tax reduction, we recognize the need for structural tax adjustments to help the working men and women of our nation. To that end, we recommend tax credits for college tuition, postsecondary technical training and child care expenses incurred by working parents.

Over the past two decades of Democrat control of the Congress, our tax laws have become a nightmare of complexity and unfair tax preferences, virtually destroying the credibility of the system. Simplification should be a major goal of tax reform.

We support economic and tax policies to insure the necessary job-producing expansion of our economy. These include hastening capital recovery through new systems of accelerated depreciation, removing the tax burden on equity financing to encourage more capital investment, ending the unfair double taxation of dividends, and support-

ing proposals to enhance the ability of our working and other citizens to own "a piece of the action" through stock ownership. When balanced by expenditure reductions, the personal exemption should be raised to $1,000.

## AGRICULTURE AND RURAL DEVELOPMENT

The bounty of our farms is so plentiful that we may tend to forget what an amazing production achievement this really is. Each American farmer and rancher produces enough food to feed over 56 people—a three-fold increase in productivity in 20 years.

Rural America must be maintained as a rewarding place to live. To accomplish this, our rural areas are entitled to services comparable to their urban neighbors, such as water and sewer systems, improved electricity and telephone service, adequate transportation, available and adequate financial credit, and employment opportunities which will allow small farmers to supplement their incomes.

Farm exports have continued to expand under the policies of this Republican Administration—from a low of $6 billion in 1968, the last Democrat year, to $22 billion in 1975. These exports are not giveaway programs; most are earning dollars from the marketplaces of the world, establishing a favorable balance of trade and a higher standard of living for all. Through our farm exports we fight the problem of world hunger, especially with the humanitarian Food for Peace Program (Public Law 480) of the Eisenhower Administration and the Republican-controlled Congress of 1954.

Republican farm policy has permitted farmers to use their crop land fully. We are at last moving toward making effective use of our superb resources. Net farm income from 1972 through 1975 averaged $26 billion, more than double the average of the 1960's. Government should not dictate to the productive men and women who work the land. To assure this, we support the continuation of the central principles of the Agricultural Act of 1973, with adjustments of target prices and loan levels to reflect increased production costs.

We oppose government-controlled grain reserves, just as we oppose federal regulations that are unrealistic in farm practices, such as those imposed by the Occupational Safety and Health Administration (OSHA) and the Environmental Protection Agency (EPA).

We urge prompt action by Congress in amending the Grain Inspection Act to strengthen the present inspection system and restore its integrity.

We firmly believe that when the nation asks our farmers to go all out to produce as much as possible for world-wide markets, the government should guarantee them unfettered access to those markets. Our farmers should not be singled out by export controls. Also, when a foreign nation subsidizes its farm exports, our farmers deserve protection against such unfair practices. The federal government should assure that foreign imported commodities are equal in quality to our domestic commodities. Nations from whom we buy commodities should not be allowed to circumvent import restriction laws, such as the Meat Import Quota Act of 1964.

We recognize the importance of the multilateral trade negotiations now in progress and urge our representatives to obtain the most beneficial agreements for our farmers and the nation's economy.

In order to assure the consumers of America an uninterrupted source of food, it is necessary to pass labor relations legislation which is responsive to the welfare of workers and to the particular needs of food production. Such legislation should recognize the need to prevent work stoppages during the critical harvest periods.

We must help farmers protect themselves from drought, flood and other natural disasters through a system of all-risk crop insurance through Federal government reinsurance of private insurance companies combined with the existing disaster payment program.

As in 1972, we urge prompt passage of the Republican-sponsored legislation now pending in Congress which will increase the estate tax exemption to $200,000, allow valuation of farm property on a current use basis and provide for extension of the time of payment in the case of farms and small businesses. This overdue estate and gift tax legislation must be approved this year. We favor a liberalized marital deduction and oppose capital gains tax at death.

Innovations in agriculture need to be encouraged by expanding research programs including new pest and predator control measures, and utilization of crops as a new energy resource. If we expect our farmers to produce an abundant food supply, they must have all the energy they need to produce, market and process their crops and livestock.

We continue to support farmer cooperatives, including rural electric and telephone cooperatives, in their efforts to improve services to their members. We support the Capper-Volstead Act.

We believe that non-farm corporations and tax-loss farming should be prevented from unfairly competing against family farms, which we support as the preferred method of farm organization.

Since farmers are practicing conservationists, they should not be burdened with unrealistic environmental regulations. We are concerned about regulations issued by the Army Corps of Engineers that will regulate all "routine" agricultural and forestry activities on "all" our waters and wetland, and support legislation to exempt routine farming operations from these requirements. The adjudication of water rights should be a matter of state determination.

## SMALL BUSINESS

Small business, so vital to our economic system, is free enterprise in its purest sense. It holds forth opportunity to the individual, regardless of race or sex, to fulfill the American dream. Small businesses are the base of our economy and its main source of strength. Some 9.6 million small firms generate 55 percent of our private employment— or the livelihood of over 100 million Americans. Yet while small businesses have a unique place in our society, they also have unique problems that government must address. Therefore, we recommend that the Small Business Administration (SBA):

Assure adequate financing to those credit worthy firms that cannot now obtain funds through conventional channels;

Include the proper mix of loan programs to meet the needs of the many different types of firms that constitute the American small business community;

Serve as an aggressive advocate for small business and provide procurement, management and technological assistance.

For survival, small businesses must have relief from the overwhelming burden placed on them by many regulatory bodies. Paperwork proliferation has grown out of control, and small business is not equipped to deal with this aggravation.

The present tax structure does not allow small firms to generate enough capital to grow and create jobs. Estate taxes need liberalization to benefit the family business in the same manner as the family farm. Encouraging investment in small businesses through more equitable tax treatment remains the best and least expensive method of creating productive employment.

The Republican Party, recognizing that small and independent business is the backbone of the American competitive system, pledges itself to strengthen this vital institution.

## ANTITRUST

The Republican Party believes in and endorses the concept that the American economy is traditionally dependent upon fair competition in the marketplace. To assure fair competition, antitrust laws must treat all segments of the economy equally.

Vigorous and equitable enforcement of antitrust laws heightens competition and enables consumers to obtain the lowest possible price in the marketplace.

## BUREAUCRATIC OVERREGULATION

We believe that the extent of federal regulation and bureaucratic interference in the lives of the American people must be reduced. The programs and activities of the federal government should be required to meet strict tests of their usefulness and effectiveness.

In particular, we consider essential an analysis of the extensive growth of laws and regulations governing production processes and conditions and standards for consumer products, so as to determine whether the services and benefits the American people receive are worth the price they are paying for these services in higher taxes and consumer prices.

We are intensely aware of the need to protect our environment and provide safe working conditions in American industry, while at the same time preventing the loss of jobs and the closing of small businesses through unrealistic or over-rigorous government regulations. We support a balanced approach that considers the requirements of a growing economy and provides jobs for American workers.

The average businessman and employer is being overwhelmed by government-required paperwork. We support legislation to control and reduce the burden of federal paperwork, particularly that generated by the Internal Revenue Service and the Census Bureau.

## GOVERNMENT THAT WORKS

We believe that Americans are fed up with and frustrated by national government that makes great promises and fails to deliver. We are! We think that Democrat Congresses—in control for 40 out of the last 44 years—are the grand masters of this practice. We think that a national government grown so big that the left hand doesn't know what the right hand is doing has caused the condition we are in.

What we now have is a government organization that doesn't make any sense. It has not developed by design. It just grew—by whim, bureaucratic fighting, and the caving in of Democrat Congresses to special interest demands. So today we find that nine federal departments and twenty independent agencies are involved in education; seven departments and eight agencies in health; federal recreation areas are administered by six agencies in three departments; and so forth.

What we need is a top-to-bottom overhaul. Two high level presidential commissions under two Presidents—one a Democrat, one a Republican—have investigated and come up with the same answer: There must be functional realignment of government, instead of the current arrangement by subject areas or constituencies.

We want federal domestic departments to reflect the major purposes of government, such as natural resources, human resources, community development and economic affairs. Unfortunately, the Democrat Congress has refused to address this problem. Now we insist that attention must be paid.

Too often in the past, we have been content with organizational or procedural solutions to complex economic and social regulatory problems. We should no longer accept rhetoric as a substitute for concrete results. The President has proposed to Congress the Agenda for Government Reform Act, which would guarantee the systematic re-examination and reform of all federal regulatory activities within the next four years. This legislation requires Congress and the President to agree to undertake an exhaustive reassessment of the combined effects of all government regulations, and it requires them to adhere to a disciplined timetable to assure annual results. The American people deserve no less. Every agency of government must be made efficient, and every government regulation should be subjected to cost benefit analysis. The Occupational Safety and

Health Administration (OSHA) is a typical example of a well-intentioned regulatory effort which has imposed large costs but has not solved our problems.

The beauty of America's original concept of government was its diversity, the belief that different purposes are best served by governments at different levels. In our lifetime, however, Democrat Congresses have allowed this system to become warped and over-nationalized. As powers have flowed to Washington, the ability to attend to our problems has often dried up in our communities and states. This trend must be reversed. Local government is simply accountable to the people, and local people are perfectly capable of making decisions.

We reaffirm the long standing principle of the Republican Party that the best government is the one closest to the people. It is less costly, more accountable, and more responsive to the people's needs. Our confidence in the people of this nation was demonstrated by initiating the Revenue Sharing Program. To date, $30 billion of federal tax dollars have been returned to the states and localities. This program is administered with fewer than 100 people and a computer. Revenue Sharing is an effort to reverse the trend toward centralization. Revenue Sharing must continue without unwarranted federal strictures and regulations.

As a further step in this direction, the Republicans in Congress promoted the new concept of federal block grants to localities for much greater flexibility. Under block grants, federal funds can be tailored by the states and localities to the wishes of each community. There are now two block grant programs—in community development and employment training. Block grant programs should be extended to replace many existing categorical health, education, child nutrition and social services programs. The Democrat Congress stands guilty of failing to enact these vital reforms. Our ultimate goal is to restore taxing and spending to the local level.

The Republican Party has always believed that the proper role of government is to do only those things which individuals cannot do for themselves. We encourage individual initiative and oppose the trend of ever expanding government programs which is destroying the volunteer spirit in America. We firmly believe that community involvement is essential to the development of effective solutions to the problems confronting our country.

While we oppose a uniform national primary, we encourage the concept of regional presidential primaries, which would group those states which voluntarily agree to have presidential primaries in a geographic area on a common date.

We encourage full participation in our electoral process. We further recognize the sanctity and value of the ballot. In that regard, we oppose "federal post card registration." The possibilities of fraud are inherent in registration by mail. Such possibilities could not only cheapen our ballot, but in fact threaten the entire electoral process.

Control of the United States Congress by the Democrat Party for 40 of the past 44 years has resulted in a system dominated by powerful individuals and riddled with corruption. Recent events have demonstrated an unwillingness and inability by the Democrat Party to cleanse itself. Selective morality has been the order of the day. Positive Republican initiatives have languished in Democrat-controlled Congressional Committees while business as usual has continued in Washington. The American people demand and deserve reform of the United States Congress. We offer these proposals of far-reaching reform:

Repeal of legislation which permits automatic increases in the salaries of Members of Congress, congressional staffs, and official expense allowances. Public accountability demands that Members publicly vote on increases on the expenses of their office. Members' salary increases should not become effective until a new Congress is elected.

Elimination of proxy voting which allows Members to record votes in Committee without being present for the actual deliberations or vote on a measure.

Elimination of Democrat Caucus rules which allow a Party to bind its Members' votes on legislation. Each Member of Congress represents his constituency and must be free to vote in accordance with the dictates of his constituency and individual conscience.

A complete audit by the General Accounting Office of all congressional allowances and appropriate disciplinary measures for those who have violated the public trust.

Full public disclosure of financial interests by Members and divestiture of those interests which present conflicts of interest.

Changes in the House rules which would allow a House majority to require the House Ethics Committee to conduct an investigation into alleged misconduct by any Member of Congress if the Committee refuses to act on its own.

Quarterly publication of names, titles and salaries of all Congressional employees.

Improved lobby disclosure legislation so that the people will know how much money is being spent to influence public officials.

Citizens are demanding the end to the rapid and wasteful increase in the size of Washington government. All steps must be taken to insure that unnecessary federal agencies and programs are eliminated and that Congress carefully scrutinize the total budget of each agency. If it is determined that sunset laws and zerobased budgeting can accomplish these ends, then they will have our support. Washington programs must be made as cost-effective as those in the states and localities. Among the many serious complaints that we wish to register on behalf of the American people is the poor operation of the United States Postal Service.

We note the low respect the public has for Congress—a Democrat-controlled institution—and wonder how the Democrats can possibly honor their pledge to reform government when they have utterly failed to reform Congress.

## A Safe and Just Society

Every American has a right to be protected from criminals. Violence has no place in our land. A society that excuses crime will eventually fall victim to it. The American people have been subjected to an intolerable wave of violent crime.

The victim of a crime should be treated with compassion and justice. The attacker must be kept from harming others. Emphasis must be on protecting the innocent and punishing the guilty. Prevention of crime is its best deterrent and should be stressed.

Fighting crime is—and should be—primarily a local responsibility. We support the continuation of the federal help given through the Law Enforcement Assistance Administration (LEAA) to law enforcement officials in our states, counties and municipalities. Each state should have the power to decide whether it wishes to impose the death penalty for certain crimes. All localities are urged to tighten their bail practices and to review their sentencing and parole procedures.

The federal criminal code should include automatic and mandatory minimum sentences for persons committing offenses under federal jurisdiction that involve the use of a dangerous weapon; that involve exceptionally serious crimes, such as trafficking in hard drugs, kidnapping and aircraft hijacking; and that involve injuries committed by repeat offenders.

The work presently being done to tighten the antiobscenity provisions of the criminal code has our full support. Since the jurisdiction of the federal government in this field is limited to interstate commerce and the mails, we urge state and local governments to assume a major role in limiting the distribution and availability of obscene materials.

We support the right of citizens to keep and bear arms. We oppose federal registration of firearms. Mandatory sentences for crimes committed with a lethal weapon are the only effective solution to this problem.

Sure and swift justice demands additional judges, United States Attorneys and other court workers. The Democrat Congress has created no new federal judgeships since 1970; we deplore this example of playing politics with the justice system.

Drug abuse is not simply a health problem, but also a very real law enforcement concern and a problem of worldwide dimension. Controlling drug abuse calls for the ratification of the existing international treaty on synthetic drugs, increased emphasis on preventing the diversion of amphetamines and barbiturates into illegal markets, and intensive effort to keep drugs out of this country. Heroin continues to come across our borders. Drug enforcement agents and international cooperation must cut off this supply. We say: Treat the addicts, but, at the same time, remove the pushers from the street and give them mandatory sentences.

Juveniles now account for almost half the arrests for serious crimes—murder, rape, robbery and aggravated assault. The cost of school violence and vandalism is estimated at $600 million annually, about what is spent on textbooks. Primary responsibility for raising our children, instilling proper values and thus preventing juvenile delinquency lies with the family, not the government. Yet when families fail, local law enforcement authorities must respond. Law enforcement block grant funds can be used by states in correcting and preventing juvenile delinquency. The LEAA should promote additional research in this area.

The structure of the family must be strengthened. All enterprises have to be encouraged to find more jobs for young people. A youth differential must be included in the minimum wage law. Citizen action should let the television industry know that we want it to curb violence in programming because of its effect on our youth.

The criminal justice system must be more vigilant in preventing rape, eliminating discrimination against the victim and dealing with the offenders.

States should recognize that antiquated and overcrowded prisons are not conducive to rehabilitation. A high priority of prison reform should be to help the young first-time offender. There should be adequate separation of young adult offenders, more relevant prison industries, better counseling, community-based alternatives and more help in getting a job for the offender who has served his or her time.

Terrorism—both domestic and international—must be stopped. Not only must the strongest steps be taken in the United States, but collective action must come from all nations. Deterring every form of hijacking calls for sanctions against countries that aid terrorists. The world community should take appropriate action to deal with terrorist organizations. We applaud the daring rescue by Israel of innocent civilian hostages who were kidnapped by terrorists. While we regret that loss of life was involved, the courageous manner in which the hostages were freed speaks eloquently to our abhorrence of world bandits.

## The Right to Privacy

Liberty depends in great measure on the privacy that each American retains.

We are alarmed by Washington's growing collection of information. The number of federal data banks is now estimated at between 800 and 900 and more than 50 agencies are involved. We question the need for all these computers to be storing the records of our lives. Safeguards must protect us against this information being misused or disclosed. Major changes, for example, are needed to maintain the confidentiality of tax returns and Social Security records.

Recent Supreme Court decisions have held that an individual has no constitutional right to the privacy of records held in banks or other depository institutions and that they can be readily obtained by law enforcement agencies without a person's consent or knowledge. Law enforcement authorities must be able to pursue criminal violators, yet at the same time, there should be reasonable controls imposed to protect the privacy of law-abiding citizens. We support legislation, now pending, to assure this protection.

Too many government records, on the other hand, are unnecessarily classified. Congress and the Executive should devise a more reasonable system for classifying and handling government information.

The President's achievements in protecting privacy are unequalled by past administrations and must be built upon in the future. We particularly note changes in federal record-keeping systems, the appointment of the Commission on the CIA, the reorganization of the intelligence community and restriction of White House access to income tax returns.

## The American Family

Families must continue to be the foundation of our nation.

Families—not government programs—are the best way to make sure our children are properly nurtured, our elderly are cared for, our cultural and spiritual heritages are perpetuated, our laws are observed and our values are preserved.

If families fail in these vitally important tasks, there is little the government, no matter how well-intentioned, can do to remedy the results. Schools cannot educate children adequately if families are not supportive of the learning process. Law enforcement authorities are nearly helpless to curb juvenile delinquency without family cooperation in teaching young people respect for property and laws. Neither medicine nor school feeding programs can replace the family's ability to provide the basis for good health. Isolation from meaningful family contact makes it virtually impossible for the elderly to avoid loneliness or dependence. The values of hard work and responsibility start with the family.

As modern life brings changes in our society, it also puts stresses on families trying to adjust to new realities while maintaining cherished values. Economic uncertainty, unemployment, housing difficulties, women's and men's concerns with their changing and often conflicting roles, high divorce rates, threatened neighborhoods and schools, and public scandal all create a hostile atmosphere that erodes family structures and family values. Thus it is imperative that our government's programs, actions, officials and social welfare institutions never be allowed to jeopardize the family. We fear the government may be powerful enough to destroy our families; we know that it is not powerful enough to replace them.

Because of our concern for family values, we affirm our beliefs, stated elsewhere in this Platform, in many elements that will make our country a more hospitable environment for family life —neighborhood schools; educational systems that include and are responsive to parents' concerns; estate tax changes to establish more realistic exemptions which will minimize disruption of already bereaved families; a position on abortion that values human life; a welfare policy to encourage rather than discourage families to stay together and seek economic independence; a tax system that assists rather than penalizes families with elderly members, children in day care or children in college; economic and employment policies that stop the shrinkage of our dollars and stimulate the creation of jobs so that families can plan for their economic security.

EDUCATION

Our children deserve quality education.

We believe that segregated schools are morally wrong and unconstitutional. However, we oppose forced busing to achieve racial balances in our schools. We believe there are educational advantages for children in attending schools in their own neighborhoods and that the Democrat-controlled Congress has failed to enact legislation to protect this concept. The racial composition of many schools results from decisions by people about where they choose to live. If Congress continues to fail to act, we would favor consideration of an amendment to the Constitution forbidding the assignment of children to schools on the basis of race.

Our approach is to work to eradicate the root causes of segregated schools, such as housing discrimination and gerrymandered school districts. We must get on with the education of all our children.

Throughout our history, the education of our children has been a community responsibility. But now federal categorical grant programs pressure local school districts into substituting Washington-

dictated priorities for their own. Local school administrators and school boards are being turned into bookkeepers for the federal government. Red tape and restrictive regulations stifle imagination and creativity. We are deeply concerned about the decline in the performance of our schools and the decline in public confidence in them.

We favor consideration of tax credits for parents making elementary and secondary school tuition payments.

Local communities wishing to conduct nonsectarian prayers in their public schools should be able to do so. We favor a constitutional amendment to achieve this end.

We propose consolidating federal categorical grant programs into block grants and turning the money over to the states to use in accordance with their own needs and priorities and with minimum bureaucratic controls. A single program must preserve the funding that is directed at the needs of such special groups as the handicapped and the disadvantaged.

Responsibility for education, particularly on the elementary and secondary levels, belongs to local communities and parents. Intrusion by the federal government must be avoided. Bureaucratic control of schools by Washington has the potential for destruction of our educational system by taking more and more decisions away from parents and local school authorities. Financial dependence on the federal government inevitably leads to greater centralization of authority. We believe, therefore, that a study should be authorized concerning funding of elementary and secondary education, coupled with a study regarding return to the states of equivalent revenue to compensate for any loss in present levels of federal funding.

Unless steps are taken immediately, soaring prices will restrict a college education to the rich and those poor enough to qualify now for government aid. Federal higher education policy should continue to focus on financial aid for needy individuals, but because the financial ability to go to college is fast slipping out of the grasp of middle income families, more realistic eligibility guidelines for student aid are essential.

Government interference in the management of colleges and universities must be stopped. Federal support to assist in meeting the grave financial problems of higher education should be forthcoming, but such funds should never be used as devices for imposing added controls.

Diversity in education has great value. Public schools and non-public schools should share in education funds on a constitutionally acceptable basis. Private colleges and universities should be assisted to maintain healthy competition and to enrich diversity. The cost of expanding public campuses can be kept down if existing private institutions are helped to accommodate our student population.

We favor continued special federal support for vocational education.

## HEALTH

Every American should have access to quality health care at an affordable price.

The possibility of an extended illness in a family is a frightening prospect, but, if it does happen, a person should at least be protected from having it wipe out lifetime savings. Catastrophic expenses incurred from major illnesses and accidents affect only a small percentage of Americans each year, but for those people, the financial burden can be devastating. We support extension of catastrophic illness protection to all who cannot obtain it. We should utilize our private health insurance system to assure adequate protection for those who do not have it. Such an approach will eliminate the red tape and high bureaucratic costs inevitable in a comprehensive national program.

The Republican Party opposes compulsory national health insurance.

Americans should know that the Democrat Platform, which offers a government-operated and financed "comprehensive national health insurance system with universal and mandatory coverage," will increase federal government spending by more than $70 billion in its first full year. Such a plan could require a personal income tax increase of approximately 20 percent. We oppose this huge, new health insurance tax. Moreover, we do not believe that the federal government can administer effectively the Democrats' cradle-to-grave proposal.

The most effective, efficient and economical method to improve health care and extend its availability to all is to build on the present health delivery and insurance system, which covers nine out of every ten Americans.

A coordinated effort should be mounted immediately to contain the rapid increase in health care costs by all available means, such as development of healthier life styles through education, improved preventive care, better distribution of medical manpower, emphasis on out-of-hospital services and elimination of wasteful duplication of medical services.

We oppose excessive intrusions from Washington in the delivery of health care. We believe in preserving the privacy that should exist between a patient and a physician, particularly in regard to the confidentiality of medical records.

Federal health programs should be consolidated into a single grant to each state, where possible, thereby allowing much greater flexibility in setting local priorities. Our rural areas, for example, have different health care delivery needs than our cities. Federal laws and regulations should respect these differences and make it possible to respond differently to differing needs. Fraud in Medicare and Medicaid programs should be exposed and eliminated.

We need a comprehensive and equitable approach to the subject of mental health. Such a program should focus on the prevention, treatment and care of mental illness. It should cover all aspects of the interrelationships between emotional illness and other developmental disabilities that seek to remove us from the dark ages in these areas.

Alcoholism and drug abuse, growing problems in America today, should receive the utmost attention.

While we support valid medical and biological research efforts which can produce life-saving results, we oppose any research on live fetuses. We are also opposed to any legislation which sanctions ending the life of any patient.

## CHILD NUTRITION

Every child should have enough to eat. Good nutrition is a prerequisite of a healthy life. We must focus our resources on feeding needy children. The present school lunch programs provide a 20 percent subsidy to underwrite the meals of children from middle- and upper-income families.

The existing 15 child nutrition programs should be consolidated into one program, administered by the states, and concentrated on those children truly in need. Other federal programs should insure that low-income people will be able to purchase a nutritionally adequate food supply.

## Equal Rights and Ending Discrimination

Roadblocks must be removed that may prevent Americans from realizing their full potential in society. Unfair discrimination is a burden that intolerably weighs morally, economically and politically upon a free nation.

While working to eradicate discriminatory practices, every citizen should be encouraged to take pride in and foster the cultural heritage that has been passed on from previous generations. Almost every American traces ancestry from another country; this cultural diversity gives strength to our national heritage.

There must be vigorous enforcement of laws to assure equal treatment in job recruitment, hiring, promotion, pay, credit, mortgage access and housing. The way to end discrimination, however, is not by resurrecting the much discredited quota system and attempting to cloak it in an aura of new respectability. Rather, we must provide alternative means of assisting the victims of past discrimination to realize their full worth as American citizens.

Wiping out past discrimination requires continued emphasis on providing educational opportunities for minority citizens, increasing direct and guaranteed loans to minority business enterprises, and affording qualified minority persons equal opportunities for government positions at all levels.

### Women

Women, who comprise a numerical majority of the population, have been denied a just portion of our nation's rights and opportunities. We reaffirm our pledge to work to eliminate discrimination in all areas for reasons of race, color, national origin, age, creed or sex and to enforce vigorously laws guaranteeing women equal rights.

The Republican Party reaffirms its support for ratification of the Equal Rights Amendment. Our Party was the first national party to endorse the E.R.A. in 1940. We continue to believe its ratification is essential to insure equal rights for all Americans. In our 1972 Platform, the Republican Party recognized the great contributions women have made to society as homemakers and mothers, as contributors to the community through volunteer work, and as members of the labor force in careers. The Platform stated then, and repeats now, that the Republican Party "fully endorses the principle of equal rights, equal opportunities and equal responsibilities for women." The Equal Rights Amendment is the embodiment of this principle and therefore we support its swift ratification.

The question of abortion is one of the most difficult and controversial of our time. It is undoubtedly a moral and personal issue but it also involves complex questions relating to medical science and criminal justice. There are those in our Party who favor complete support for the Supreme Court decision which permits abortion on demand. There are others who share sincere convictions that the Supreme Court's decision must be changed by a constitutional amendment prohibiting all abortions. Others have yet to take a position, or they have assumed a stance somewhere in between polar positions.

We protest the Supreme Court's intrusion into the family structure through its denial of the parents' obligation and right to guide their minor children. The Republican Party favors a continuance of the public dialogue on abortion and supports the efforts of those who seek enactment of a constitutional amendment to restore protection of the right to life for unborn children.

The Social Security System, our federal tax laws, and unemployment and disability programs currently discriminate against women and often work against married couples as well. These inequities must be corrected. We recognize that special support must be given to the increasing number of women who have assumed responsibility as the heads of households while also being wage earners. Programs for job training, counseling and other services should be established to help them attain their dual role in society.

We reiterate the pledges elsewhere in this platform of support for child care assistance, part-time and flexible-time work that enables men and women to combine employment and family responsibilities, estate tax reform, small business assistance for women, rape prevention and elimination of discriminatory housing practices.

### Ethnic Americans

Ethnic Americans have enriched this nation with their hard work, self-reliance and respect for the rights and needs of others. Ethnic groups reaching our shores at various times have given our country its unique identity and strength among the nations of the world. We recognize and value the contributions of Ethnic Americans to our free and democratic society.

## Hispanic-Americans

When language is a cause for discrimination, there must be an intensive educational effort to enable Spanish-speaking students to become fully proficient in English while maintaining their own language and cultural heritage. Hispanic-Americans must not be treated as second-class citizens in schools, employment or any other aspect of life just because English is not their first language. Hispanic-Americans truly believe that individual integrity must be paramount; what they want most from government and politics is the opportunity to participate fully. The Republican Party has and always will offer this opportunity.

## Indians and Alaska Natives

We have a unique commitment to Native Americans; we pledge to continue to honor our trust relationship with them, and we reffirm our federal Indian policy of self-determination without termination. This means moving smoothly and quickly away from federal domination to effective participation and communication by Indians in the political process and in the planning, content and administration of federal programs. We shall pursue our joint effort with Indian leaders to assist in the orderly development of Indian and native-owned resources and to continue to attack the severe health, education and unemployment problems which exist among Indians and Alaska Natives.

## Puerto Rico, the District of Columbia and the Territories

The principle of self-determination also governs our positions on Puerto Rico and the District of Columbia as it has in past platforms. We again support statehood for Puerto Rico, if that is the people's choice in a referendum, with full recognition within the concept of a multicultural society of the citizens' right to retain their Spanish language and traditions; and support giving the District of Columbia voting representation in the United States Senate and House of Representatives and full home rule over those matters that are purely local.

We will continue to negotiate with the Con-

gress of Micronesia on the future political status of the Trust Territories of the Pacific Islands to meet the mutual interests of both parties. We support a plebiscite by the people of American Samoa on whether they wish to elect a territorial governor. We favor whatever action is necessary to permit American citizens resident in Guam, Puerto Rico and the Virgin Islands to vote for President and Vice President in national elections. With regard to Guam and the Virgin Islands, we urge an increased degree of self-sufficiency and support maximum broadening of self-government.

## Responsibilities

Finally, the most basic principle of all: Achievement and preservation of human rights in our society is based on the willing acceptance by millions of Americans of their responsibilities as free citizens. Instead of viewing government programs with ever increasing expectations, we must readily assume the obligations of wage-earners, taxpayers and supporters of our government and laws. This is often forgotten, and so it is appropriate to remind ourselves in this Platform that this is why our society works.

### HANDICAPPED CITIZENS

Handicapped persons must be admitted into the mainstream of our society.

Too often the handicapped population of the nation—over 30 million men, women and children —has been denied the rights taken for granted by other citizens. Time after time, the paths are closed to the handicapped in education, employment, transportation, health care, housing, recreation, insurance, polling booths and due process of law. National involvement is necessary to correct discrimination in these areas. Individual incentive alone cannot do it.

We pledge continued attention to the problems caused by barriers in architecture, communication, transportation and attitudes. In addition, we realize that to deny education and employment simply because of an existing disability runs counter to our accepted belief in the free enterprise system and forces the handicapped to be overly dependent on others. Similarly, the denial of equal access to credit and to acquisition of venture capital on the basis of a handicap or other disability conflicts with Republican philosophy. We advocate the elimination of needless barriers for all handicapped persons.

## WORKING AMERICANS

Free collective bargaining remains the best way to insure that American workers receive a fair price for their labors.

The special problems of collective bargaining in state and local government should be addressed at those levels. Washington should not impose its standards on local governments. While we oppose strikes by public employees, we recognize that states have the right to permit them if they choose.

Union membership as a condition of employment has been regulated by state law under Section 14(b) of the Taft-Hartley Act. This basic right should continue to be determined by the states. We oppose strikes by federal employees, the unionization of our military forces and the legalization of common-situs picketing.

Employees of the federal government should not engage in partisan politics. The Civil Service System must remain non-partisan and non-political. The Hatch Act now protects federal employees; we insist that it be uniformly administered.

Among the rights that are the entitlement of every American worker is the right to join a union —large, small or independent; the right to be protected against racial discrimination and misuse of dues; the right to union elections that are fair and democratic; and the right to be assured of ultimately receiving his or her promised pension benefits.

Safe and healthful working conditions are goals of utmost importance. We should expect the Occupational Safety and Health Administration to help employers, particularly in small businesses, comply with the law, and we will support legislation providing on-site consultation.

There should be considerable concern over the presence of several million illegal aliens in the country who fill jobs that otherwise would be available to American workers. We support increased efforts to deal more effectively with this problem and favor legislation prohibiting employers from knowingly hiring illegal aliens. The Democrat leaders in Congress have systematically killed every attempt to debate this legislation in recent years.

Increased part-time and flexible-hour work should be encouraged wherever feasible. In keeping with our belief in family life, we want to expand more opportunities for men and women to combine family responsibilities and employment.

## WELFARE REFORM

The work of all Americans contributes to the strength of our nation, and all who are able to contribute should be encouraged to do so.

In every society there will be some who cannot work, often through no fault of their own. The measure of a country's compassion is how it treats the least fortunate.

We appreciate the magnificent variety of private charitable institutions which have developed in the United States.

The Democrat-controlled Congress has produced a jumble of degrading, dehumanizing, wasteful, overlapping and inefficient programs failing to assist the needy poor. A systematic and complete overhaul of the welfare system should be initiated immediately.

The following goals should govern the reform of the welfare system:

1. Provide adequate living standards for the truly needy;

2. End welfare fraud and prevent it in the future with emphasis on removing ineligible recipients from the welfare rolls, tightening food stamp eligibility requirements, and ending aid to illegal aliens and the voluntarily unemployed;

3. Strengthen work requirements, particularly directed at the productive involvement of able-bodied persons in useful community work projects;

4. Provide educational and vocational incentives to allow recipients to become self-supporting;

5. Better coordinate federal efforts with local and state social welfare agencies and strengthen local and state administrative functions.

We oppose federalizing the welfare system; local levels of government are most aware of the needs of their communities. Consideration should be given to a range of options in financing the programs to assure that state and local responsibilities are met. We also oppose the guaranteed annual income concept or any programs that reduce the incentive to work.

Those features of the present law, particularly the food stamp program, that draw into assistance programs people who are capable of paying for their own needs should be corrected. The humanitarian purpose of such programs must not be corrupted by eligibility loopholes. Food stamp program reforms proposed by Republicans in Congress would accomplish the twin goals of directing resources to those most in need and streamlining administration.

We must never forget that unemployment compensation is insurance, not a welfare program. It should be redesigned to assure that working is always more beneficial than collecting unemployment benefits. The benefits should help most the hard-core unemployed. Major efforts must be encouraged through the private sector to speed up the process of finding jobs for those temporarily out of work.

## OLDER AMERICANS

Older Americans constitute one of our most valuable resources.

Families should be supported in trying to take care of their elderly. Too often government laws and policies contribute to the deterioration of family life. Our tax laws, for example, permit a contribution to a charitable institution that might care for an elderly parent, but offer little or no incentive to provide care in the home. If an elderly parent relinquishes certain assets and enters a nursing home, the parent may qualify for full Medicaid coverage, but if parents live with their children, any Supplemental Security income benefit for which they are eligible may be reduced. Incentives must be written into law to encourage families to care for their older members.

Along with loneliness and ill health, older Americans are deeply threatened by inflation. The costs of the basic necessities of life—food, shelter, clothing, health care—have risen so drastically as to reduce the ability of many older persons to subsist with any measure of dignity. In addition to our program for protecting against excessive costs of long-term illness, nothing will be as beneficial to the elderly as the effect of this Platform's proposals on curbing inflation.

The Social Security benefits are of inestimable importance to the well-being and financial peace-of-mind of most older Americans. We will not let the Social Security system fail. We will work to make the Social Security system actuarily sound. The Social Security program must not be turned into a welfare system, based on need rather than contributions. The cost to employers for Social Security contributions must not be raised to the point where they will be unable to afford contributions to employees' private pension programs. We will work for an increase in the earned income ceiling or its elimination so that, as people live longer, there will not be the present penalty on work. We will also seek to correct those provisions of the system that now discriminate against women and married couples.

Such programs as Foster Grandparents and Senior Companions, which provide income exempt from Social Security limitations, should be continued and extended to encourage senior citizens to continue to be active and involved in society. Appropriate domiciliary care programs should be developed to enable senior citizens to receive such care without losing other benefits to which they may be entitled.

We favor the abolitiion of arbitrary age levels for mandatory retirement.

The Medicare program must be improved to help control inflation in health care costs triggered by present regulations.

Other areas of concern to the elderly that need increased attention are home and outpatient care, adequate transportation, nutrition, day care and homemaker care as an alternative to costly institutional treatment.

A nation should be judged by its ability to help make all the years of life as productive and gainful as possible. This nation still has a job to do.

## VETERANS

The nation must never forget its appreciation and obligation to those who have served in the armed forces.

Because they bear the heaviest burdens of war, we owe special honor and compensation to disabled veterans and survivors of the war dead.

We are firmly committed to maintaining and improving our Veterans Administration hospital system.

Younger veterans, especially those who served in the Vietnam conflict, deserve education, job and housing loan benefits equivalent to those of World War II and the Korean conflict. Because of our deep and continuing concern for those still listed as Prisoners of War or Missing in Action in Vietnam, the Foreign Policy section of this Republican Platform calls for top priority actions.

And we must continue to provide for our veterans at their death a final resting place for their remains in a national cemetery and the costs of transportation thereto.

## A NATIONAL URBAN STRATEGY

The decay and decline of communities in this country is not just a physical and economic crisis, but is traceable to the decline of a real "sense of community" in our society. Community development cannot be achieved merely by throwing dollars and mortar at our community problems; what must be developed is a new sense of mutual concern and responsibility among all members of a community for its improvement.

We recognize the family, the neighborhood and the private volunteer sector to be the most basic and vital units within our communities and we recognize their central role in revitalizing our communities. We propose a strategy for urban revitalization that both treats our urban areas as social organisms and recognizes that the family is the basic building block in these organisms.

Effectively helping our cities now requires a coordinated National Urban Policy. The cornerstone of this policy must be to curb inflation. This policy must be based on the principle that the levels of government closest to the cities' problems are best able to respond. Thus federal and state assistance to cities and counties should give the greatest flexibility to those directly on the scene, the local elected officials. Such a policy should replace the welter of confusing and often conflicting federal categorical grant programs—the approach of the Democrat Congress—with block grant programs that allow cities and counties to set their own priorities.

Without an urban policy, the Democrat-controlled Congress has created a hodge-podge of programs which have all but destroyed our once vital cities. At the same time, urban crime rates have skyrocketed and the quality and promise of metropolitan education systems have plummeted. All this has happened during the years that the number of federal urban programs has increased almost tenfold: from 45 in 1946 to 435 in 1968; and expenditures have increased 3000 percent; from $1 billion to $30 billion.

The Republican programs of revenue sharing and block grants for community development and manpower have already helped our cities and counties immensely. We favor extension of revenue sharing and the orderly conversion of categorical grants into block grants. When federal assistance programs for general purpose local governments are administered through the states, there should be direct pass-through and effective roles for cities and counties in the planning, allocation and use of the funds.

Federal, state and local government resources combined are not enough to solve our urban problems. The private sector must be the major participant. Economic development is the best way to involve business and industry. Government support should emphasize capital formation and technical assistance for small and minority businesses.

We can bring about a new birth of freedom by following the example of those individuals, organizations and community leaders who have successfully solved specific undesirable conditions and problems through private efforts. Government officials should be aware of these successes in developing new approaches to public problems.

Financial institutions should be encouraged to participate in the financial requirements of urban development. Each institution should recognize its responsibility in promoting and maintaining economic growth and stability in the central cities.

Our urban policies should encourage families and businesses to improve their neighborhoods by means of participation in neighborhood self-help groups, improving and rehabilitating their homes and businesses, and investing in and managing local businesses. We support the revision of federal business assistance programs to encourage joint efforts by local merchants' associations.

We need a comprehensive approach to plan, develop and implement a variety of programs which take into account the many diverse needs of each neighborhood. The establishment of a National Neighborhood Policy will signal a commitment to the improvement of the quality of our life in our neighborhoods.

We call for an expansion of the President's Committee on Urban Development and Neighborhood Revitalization to include representatives of elected state and local officials and the private sector.

Taken together, the thrust of the proposals in this section and in such related areas as housing, transportation, safety and taxes should contribute significantly to making our cities again pleasant places to live. The Republican National Urban Strategy has been formed in the realization that when the bell tolls for the cities it tolls for all of America.

HOUSING

In the United States today we are the best housed nation in the history of world civilization. This accomplishment was achieved by a private enterprise system using free market concepts.

All of our citizens should be given the opportunity to live in decent, affordable housing.

We believe that we should continue to pursue the primary goal of expanding housing opportunities for all Americans and we should pursue the companion goal of reducing the degree of direct federal involvement in housing.

To most Americans the American dream is a home of their own. The time has come to face some hard realities, primarily that the greatest impediment to decent and affordable housing is inflation. It logically follows that one effective housing program would be simply to elect a Republican Congress which would balance the federal budget.

To meet the housing needs of this country there must be a continuous, stable and adequate flow of funds for the purpose of real estate mortgages at realistic interest rates.

To continue to encourage home ownership, which now encompasses 64 percent of our families, we support the deductibility of interest on home mortgages and property taxes.

We favor the concept of federal revenue sharing and block grants to reduce the excessive burden of the property tax in financial local government.

We are concerned with the excessive reliance of financing welfare and public school costs primarily by the property tax.

We support inflation-impact studies on governmental regulations, which are inflating housing costs.

Current economic problems and environmental concerns must be balanced in each community by a policy of "Sensible Growth."

We oppose discrimination in housing, whether by individuals or by institutional financing policies.

We urge continued incentives to support the development of low and moderate income housing in order to assure the availability of adequate shelter for the less fortunate.

Rehabilitation and preservation of existing housing stock should be given high priority in federal housing policy.

We urge the continuation of the self-help restoration of housing, such as urban homesteading, which is providing housing for low-income families.

TRANSPORTATION

The federal government has a special responsibility to foster those elements of our national transportation system that are essential to foreign and interstate commerce and national defense. In other transportation systems that primarily support local needs, the federal government's responsibility is to encourage the greatest possible decision-making and flexibility on the part of state and local governments to spend funds in ways that make the best sense for each community. Thus all levels of government have an important role in providing a balanced and coordinated transportation network.

In keeping with national transportation goals, the Railroad Revitalization and Regulatory Reform Act of 1976 has begun the task of removing regulatory constraints of the Interstate Commerce Commission on America's ailing railroads. Now we should carefully assess the need to remove many of the regulatory constraints imposed on the nation's airlines and motor carriers. Consumers pay too high a price for the artificial fare and rate structures imposed by federal regulations.

The great Interstate Highway System, initiated by President Eisenhower, has brought new freedom of travel to every American and must be completed and maintained. Our road network should always stress safety through better design as well as bridge maintenance and replacement.

We must also have a safe and efficient aviation system capable of responding to the air transportation needs of the future and of reducing exposure to aircraft noise. This includes airport development, navigational and safety facilities, and the design and adequate staffing of advanced air traffic control systems. In airplane use as in other modes of transportation, the impact on the physical environment must always be a basic consideration in federal decisions and such decisions should also include appraisals of impact on the economy. We deplore unfair treatment of United States airlines under foreign landing regulations.

Research must be continued to find safe, more fuel-efficient automobile engines and airplanes; safer, faster rail service; and more convenient, less expensive urban transportation. Tax policies should be considered which would stimulate the development and installation of new energy sources in transportation, such as railroad electrification.

The disorganization of a Democratic-controlled Congress frustrates the coordination of transportation policy. Currently there are more than 50 congressional subcommittees with independent jurisdiction in the transportation field. This hopelessly disjointed and disorganized approach must be reformed.

In keeping with the local goal setting in transportation, the Republican Party applauds the system under which state and local governments can divert funds from interstate highway mileage not essential to interstate commerce or national defense to other, more pressing community needs, such as urban mass transit.

We support the concept of a surface transportation block grant which would include the various highway and mass transit programs now in existence. This will provide local elected officials maximum flexibility in selecting and implementing the balanced transportation systems best suited to each locality. It will encompass both capital and operating subsidies for urban mass transit. It will eliminate red tape and over-regulation. We regret that the Democrat-controlled Congress has not adopted such reform.

## ENERGY

In 1973, Americans were shocked to discover that a plentiful supply of energy could no longer be assumed. Unfortunately, the Democrat majority in Congress still has not responded to this clear and urgent warning. The United States is now consuming more imported oil than it was three years ago and our dependence on foreign sources has continued to increase to the point where we now import more than 40% of our oil.

One fact should now be clear: We must reduce sharply our dependence on other nations for energy and strive to achieve energy independence at the earliest possible date. We cannot allow the economic destiny and international policy of the United States to be dictated by the sovereign powers that control major portions of the world's petroleum supplies.

Our approach toward energy self-sufficiency must involve both expansion of energy supply and improvement of energy efficiency. It must include elements that insure increased conservation at all levels of our society. It must also provide incentive for the exploration and development of domestic gas, oil, coal and uranium, and for expanded research and development in the use of solar, geothermal, co-generation, solid waste, wind, water, and other sources of energy.

We must use our non-renewable resources wisely while we develop alternative supplies for the future. Our standard of living is directly tied to a continued supply of energy resources. Without an adequate supply of energy, our entire economy will crumble.

Unwise government intervention in the marketplace has caused shortage of supply, unrealistic prices and increased dependence on foreign sources. We must immediately eliminate price controls on oil and newly-discovered natural gas in order to increase supply, and to provide the capital that is needed to finance further exploration and development of domestic hydrocarbon reserves.

Fair and realistic market prices will encourage sensible conservation efforts and establish priorities in the use of our resources, which over the long run will provide a secure supply at reasonable prices for all.

The nation's clear and present need is for vast amounts of new capital to finance exploration, discovery, refining, and delivery of currently usable forms of energy, including the use of coal as well as discovery and development of new sources. At this critical time, the Democrats have characteristically resorted to political demagoguery seeking short-term political gain at the expense of the long-term national interest. They object to the petroleum industry making any profit. The petroleum industry is an important segment of our economy and is entitled to reasonable profits to permit further exploration and development.

At the height of the energy crisis, the Republican Administration proposed a strong, balanced energy package directed at both expansion of supply and conservation of energy. The response from the Democrats in Congress was to inhibit expanded production through artificially set price and allocation controls, thereby preventing market forces from working to make energy expansion economically feasible.

Now, the Democrats proposed to dismember the American oil industry. We vigorously oppose such divestiture of oil companies—a move which would surely result in higher energy costs, inefficiency and undercapitalization of the industry.

Democrats have also proposed that the federal government compete with industry in energy development by creating a national oil company. We totally oppose this expensive, inefficient and wasteful intrusion into an area which is best handled by private enterprise.

The Democrats are playing politics with energy. If they are permitted to continue, we will pay a heavy price in lost energy and lost jobs during the decades ahead.

Immediate removal of counter-productive bureaucratic redtape will eliminate hindrances to the exploration and development of hydrocarbons and other energy resources. We will accelerate development of oil shale reserves, Alaskan petroleum and the leasing of the Outer Continental Shelf, always within the context of preserving the fullest possible protection for the environment. We will reduce complexity and delays involved in siting, licensing and the regulatory procedures affecting power generation facilities and refineries.

Coal, America's most abundant energy resource, is of inestimable value to the American people. It can provide the energy needed to bridge the gap between oil and gas and nuclear and other sources of energy. The uncertainties of governmental regulation regarding the mining, transportation and use of coal must be removed and a policy established which will assure that governmental restraints, other than proper environmental controls, do not prevent the use of coal. Mined lands must be returned to beneficial use.

Uranium offers the best intermediate solution to America's energy crisis. We support accelerated use of nuclear energy processes that have been proven safe. Government research on the use of nuclear energy will be expanded to include perfecting a long-term solution to the problems of nuclear waste.

Among alternative future energy sources, fusion, with its unique potential for supplying unlimited clean energy and the promise of new methods of natural resource recovery, warrants continued emphasis in our national energy research program, and we support measures to assure adequate capital investment in the development of new energy sources.

## ENVIRONMENT AND NATURAL RESOURCES

A clean and healthy natural environment is the rightful heritage of every American. In order to preserve this heritage, we will provide for proper development of resources, safeguards for clean air and water, and protection and enhancement of our recreation and scenic areas.

As our environmental sophistication grows, we must more clearly define the role of the federal government in environmental protection.

We believe that it is a national responsibility to support scientific and technological research and development to identify environmental problems and arrive at solutions.

We are in complete accord with the recent Supreme Court decision on air pollution that allows the level of government closest to the problem and the solution to establish and apply appropriate air quality standards.

We are proud of the progress that the current Republican Administration has made toward bringing pollution of water, land and air under control. We will meet the challenges that remain by stepping up efforts to perfect our understanding of pollutants and the means for reducing their effects. Moreover, as the nation develops new energy sources and technologies, we must insure that they meet safe environmental standards.

We renew our commitments to the development of additional water supplies by desalinization, and to more efficient use and re-use of waters currently available.

We are determined to preserve land use planning as a unique responsibility of state and local government.

We take particular pride in the expanded use of the National Park system in recent years, and will provide for continued improvement of the national parks and historic sites.

We support establishment of a presidential panel, including representatives of environmental groups, industry, the scientific community and the public to assist in the development of national priorities on environmental and energy issues. This panel will hear and consider alternative policy recommendations set forth by all of the interested groups, and then develop solutions that represent the overall public interest on environmental and energy matters.

One of this nation's greatest assets has been our abundant natural resources which have made possible our strong economic and strategic role in the world. We still have a wealth of resources, but they are not of infinite quantity. We must recognize that our material blessings stem from what we grow in the soil, take from the sea, or extract from the ground. We have a responsibility to future generations to conserve our non-renewable natural resources. Consistent with our needs, conservation should remain our national policy.

The vast land holdings of the federal government—approximately one-third of our nation's area —are the lands from which much of our future production of minerals must come. Public lands must be maintained for multiple use management where such uses are compatible. Public land areas should not be closed to exploration for minerals or for mining without an overriding national interest.

We believe Americans want their resources developed properly, their environment kept clean and their recreational and scenic areas kept intact. We support appropriate measures to achieve these goals.

We also believe that Americans are realistic and recognize that the emphasis on environmental concerns must be brought into balance with the needs for industrial and economic growth so that we can continue to provide jobs for an ever-growing work force.

The United States possesses the most productive softwood forests in the world, as well as extensive hardwood forests. Demands for housing, fuel, paper, chemicals and a multitude of other such needs require that these renewable resources be managed wisely on both public and private forest lands—not only to meet these needs, but also to provide for soil conservation, wildlife habitats and recreation.

Recognizing that timber is a uniquely renewable resource, we will use all scientifically sound means to maximize sustained yield, including clear-cutting and replanting where appropriate. We urge the Congress to strengthen the National Forest Service so that it can realize its potential in becoming an effective participant in the reforestation program.

We will support broader use of resource recovery and recycling processes through removal of economic disincentives caused by unnecessary government regulation.

One of the important issues at stake in the United Nations Law of the Sea Conference is access to the mineral resources in and beneath the sea. Technology, developed by United States industry, is at hand which can unlock resources of petroleum, manganese, nickel, cobalt, copper and other minerals. We will safeguard the national interest in development and use of these resources.

SCIENCE AND TECHNOLOGY

Every aspect of our domestic economy and well-being, our international competitive position, and national security is related to our past and present leadership in basic and applied research and the development of our technology. But there can be no complacency about our continued commitment to maintain this leadership position.

In the past, most of these accomplishments have been achieved through a unique partnership between government and industry. This must continue and be expanded in the future.

Because our society is so dependent upon the advancement of science and the development of technology, it is one of the areas where there must be central federal policy. We support a national science policy that will foster the public-private partnership to insure that we maintain our leadership role.

The national space program plays a pioneer role in exploring the mysteries of our universe and we support its expansion.

We recognize that only when our technology is fully distributed can it be assimilated and used to increase our productivity and our standard of living. We will continue to encourage young Americans to study science and engineering.

Finally, we support new initiatives to utilize better the recoverable commodities from solid waste materials. We can no longer afford the luxury of a throw-away world. Recycling offers environmental benefits, economic expansion, resource conservation and energy savings. We support a policy which will reward recycling and economic incentives which will encourage its expansion.

ARTS AND HUMANITIES

The arts and humanities offer an opportunity for every American to become a participant in activities that add fullness, expression, challenge and joy to our daily lives. We Republicans consider the preservation of the rich cultural heritages of our various ethnic groups as a priority goal.

During our bicentennial year we have celebrated our anniversary with cultural activities as varied and colorful as our cultural heritage. The Republican Party is proud of its record of support to the arts and humanities during the last eight years. We are committed to steadily increase our support through the National Endowments for the nation's museums, theaters, orchestras, dance, opera and film centers as well as for individual artists and writers.

This upward trend in funding for the National Arts and Humanities Endowments deserves to continue. But Washington's presence should never dominate; it must remain limited to supporting and stimulating the artistic and cultural lives of each community.

We favor continued federal assistance to public broadcasting which provides us with creative educational and cultural alternatives. We recognize that public broadcasting is supported mainly through private sector contributions and commend this policy as the best insurance against political interference.

In 1976, we have seen vivid evidence that America's history lives through the nation. We support the continued commemoration throughout the bicentennial era by all Americans of those significant events between 1776 and 1789 which contributed to the creation of this nation. We support the efforts of both the public and private sectors, working in partnership, for the historic sites and buildings.

We propose safeguarding the rights of performing artists in the copyright laws, providing tax relief to artists who contribute their own talents and art works for public enjoyment, and encouraging the use of one percent of the cost of government buildings for art works.

Much of the support of the arts and humanities comes from private philanthropy. This generosity should be encouraged by government policies that facilitate charitable donations.

## FISCAL RESPONSIBILITY

As Republicans, we are proud that in this Platform we have urged tax reductions rather than increased government spending. With firm restraint on federal spending this Platform pledges that its proposals for tax changes—reductions, structural adjustments, differentials, simplifications and job-producing incentives—can all be achieved within the balanced federal budgets we also demand as vital to the interests of all Americans. Without such spending restraint, we cannot responsibly cut back taxes. We reaffirm our determination that any net reduction of revenues must be offset by reduced government spending.

## FOREIGN POLICY, NATIONAL DEFENSE AND INTERNATIONAL ECONOMIC POLICY

### Prologue

The foreign policy of the United States defines the relationships we seek with the world as a whole, with friends and with adversaries. Our policy must be firmly rooted in principle and must clearly express our goals. Our principles cannot be subject to passing whim; they must be true, strong, consistent and enduring.

We pledge a realistic and principled foreign policy designed to meet the needs of the nation in the years ahead. The policies we pursue will require an informed consensus; the basis of that consensus will be the American people, whose most cherished desire is to live in freedom and peace, secure from war or threat of war.

The United States is a world power with worldwide interests and responsibilities. We pledge the continuation of efforts to revitalize our traditional alliances and to maintain close consultation with our friends. International cooperation and collaboration are required because we can achieve neither our own most important objectives nor even our own security in the type of "splendid isolation" which is urged upon us by so many strident voices. The regrettable emergence of neo-isolationism often expressed in Congress and elsewhere is detrimental, we believe, to a sound foreign policy.

The branches of government can and should work together as the necessary prerequisite for a sound foreign policy. We lament the reckless intrusion of one branch into the clear constitutional prerogative of another. Confronted by so many challenges and so many crises, the United States must again speak with one voice, united in spirit and in fact. We reject partisan and ideological quarrels across party lines and urge Democrats to join with us to lay the foundations of a true bipartisan spirit. Let us speak for this country with one voice, so that our policies will not be misunderstood by our allies or our potential adversaries.

Effective policy must rest on premises which are understood and shared, and must be defined in terms of priorities. As the world has changed in a dynamic fashion, so too have our priorities and goals, and so too have the methods of debating and discussing our objectives. When we assumed Executive office eight years ago, we found the national security and foreign policy machinery in shambles. Last-minute reactions to crises were the practice. The National Security Council, so effective under President Eisenhower, had fallen into disuse. As an important first step, the National Security Council machinery was streamlined to cope with the problems of the moment and long-range planning. This restored process allows once again the exhaustive consideration of all the options from which a President must choose. Far from stifling internal debate and dissent as had been the practice in the past. Republicant leadership now invites and stimulates evaluation of complex issues in an orderly decision-making process.

Republican leadership has also taken steps to report comprehensively its foreign policy and national security objectives. An annual "State of the World" message, designed to increase communication with the people and with Congress, has become a permanent part of Presidential practice.

A strong and effective program of global public diplomacy is a vital component of United States foreign policy. In an era of instant communications, the world is infinitely and forever smaller, and we must have the capacity to communicate to the world—to inform, to explain and to guard against accidental or willful distortion of United States polices.

Interdependence has become a fact of international life, linking our actions and policies with those of the world at large. The United States should reach out to other nations to enrich that interdependence. Republican leadership has demonstrated that recognition of the ties that bind us to our friends will serve our mutual interests in a creative fashion and will enhance the chances for world peace.

## Morality in foreign policy

The goal of Republican foreign policy is the achievement of liberty under law and a just and lasting peace in the world. The principles by which we act to achieve peace and to protect the interests of the United States must merit the restored confidence of our people.

We recognize and commend that great beacon of human courage and morality, Alexander Solzhenitsyn, for his compelling message that we must face the world with no illusions about the nature of tyranny. Ours will be a foreign policy that keeps this ever in mind.

Ours will be a foreign policy which recognizes that in international negotiations we must make no undue concessions; that in pursuing detente we must not grant unilateral favors with only the hope of getting future favors in return.

Agreements that are negotiated, such as the one signed in Helsinki, must not take from those who do not have freedom the hope of one day gaining it.

Finally, we are firmly committed to a foreign policy in which secret agreements, hidden from our people, will have no part.

Honestly, openly, and with firm conviction, we shall go forward as a united people to forge a lasting peace in the world based upon our deep belief in the rights of man, the rule of law and guidance by the hand of God.

## National defense

A superior national defense is the fundamental condition for a secure America and for peace and freedom for the world. Military strength is the path to peace. A sound foreign policy must be rooted in a superior defense capability, and both must be perceived as a deterrent to aggression and and supportive of our national interests.

The American people expect that their leaders will assure a national defense posture second to none. They know that planning for our national security must be a joint effort by the President and Congress. It cannot be the subject of partisan disputes. It should not be held hostage to domestic political adventurism.

A minimum guarantee to preserve freedom and insure against blackmail and threats, and in the face of growing Soviet military power, requires a period of sustained growth in our defense effort. In constant dollars, the present defense budget will no more than match the defense budget of 1964, the year before a Democrat Administration involved America so deeply in the Vietnam War. In 1975 Soviet defense programs exceeded ours in investment by 85 percent, and exceeded ours in operating costs by 25 percent, and exceeded ours in reach and development by 66 percent. The issue is whether our forces will be adequate to future challenges. We say they must be.

We must always achieve maximum value for each defense dollar spent. Along with the elimination of the draft and the creation, under a Republican President, of all-volunteer armed services, we have reduced the personnel requirements for support functions without affecting our basic posture. Today there are fewer Americans in the uniformed services than at any time since the fall of 1950. Substantial economies have been made in weapons procurement and we will continue to act in a prudent manner with our defense appropriations.

Our national defense effort will include the continuation of the major modernization program for our strategic missile and bomber forces, the development of a new intercontinental ballistic missile, a new missile launching submarine force and a modern bomber—the B-1—capable of penetrating the most sophisticated air defenses of the 1980's. These elements will comprise a deterrent of the first order.

We will increase our army to 16 divisions, reinforce our program of producing new tanks and other armored vehicles, and support the development of new, highly accurate precision weapons.

Our Navy, the guarantor of freedom of the seas, must have a major shipbuilding program, with an adequate balance between nuclear and non-nuclear ships. The composition of the fleet must be based on a realistic assessment of the threat we face, and must assure that no adversary will gain naval superiority.

An important modernization program for our tactical air forces is under way. We will require new fighters and interceptor aircraft for the Air Force, Navy and Marines. As a necessary component of our long-range strategy, we will produce and deploy the B–1 bomber in a timely manner, allowing us to retain air superiority.

Consistent with our total force policy, we will maintain strong reserve components.

Our investments in military research and development are of great importance to our future defense capabilities. We must not lose the vital momentum.

With increasing complexity of weapons, lead times for weapons systems are often as long as a decade, requiring careful planning and prudent financial decisions. An outstanding example of this process is the development and deployment of the cruise missile, which incorporates pinpoint precision by means of sophisticated guidance systems and is an exceptionally economical weapon to produce.

Security assistance programs are important to our allies and we will continue to strengthen their efforts at self-defense. The improvement of their capabilities can help to ensure that the world balance is not tipped against us and can also serve to lessen chances for direct U.S. involvement in remote conflicts.

As a vital component of our over-all national security posture, the United States must have the best intelligence system in the world. The effectiveness of the intelligence community must be restored, consonant with the reforms instituted by President Ford. We favor the creation of an independent oversight function by Congress and we will withstand partisan efforts to turn any part of our intelligence system into a political football. We will take every precaution to prevent the breakdown of security controls on sensitive intelligence information, endangering the lives of United States officials abroad, or affecting the ability of the President to act expeditiously whenever legitimate foreign policy and defense needs require it.

## NATO and Europe

Fundamental to a stable, secure world is the continuation of our traditional alliances. The North Atlantic Treaty Organization (NATO) now approaching the end of its third decade, remains healthy and vigorous.

The threat to our mutual security by a totalitarian power bent on expansion brought 15 nations together. The expression of our collective will to resist resulted in the creation and maintenance of a military deterrent which, while not without occasional strains, has served our vital interests well. Today that threat continues.

We have succeeded in extending our cooperation within NATO and have taken bold new steps in economic cooperation with our partners. Faced with a serious crisis in the energy field following the imposition of the oil boycott, we demonstrated that it was possible to coordinate our joint activities with the other NATO nations.

The economic strength of Western Europe has increased to the point where our NATO partners can now assume a larger share of the common defense; in response to our urging, our allies are demonstrating a greater willingness to do so. This is not the time to recommend a unilateral reduction of American military forces in Europe. We will, however, pursue the balanced reduction of forces in both Western and Eastern Europe, based on agreements which do not jeopardize the security of the Alliance. With our Alliance partners, we affirm that a strong NATO defense, based on a United States military presence, is vital to the defense of Western Europe.

Some of our NATO allies have experienced rapid and dynamic changes. We are encouraged by developments in the Iberian peninsula, where both Portugal and Spain now face more promising futures. Early consideration should be given to Spain's accession to NATO.

At the same time we would view with concern any political developments elsewhere in Europe which are destabilizing to NATO interests. We support the rights of all nations to choose their leaders. Democracy and freedom are best served by ensuring that those fundamental rights are preserved and extended for future generations to choose in freedom.

The difficult problem of Cyprus, which separates our friends in Greece and Turkey, should be addressed and resolved by those two countries. The eastern flank of NATO requires restored cooperation there and, eventually, friendly relations between the two countries.

Republican leadership has strengthened this nation's good relations with the European Economic Community (EEC) in an age of increasing competition and potential irritations. We will maintain and strengthen the excellent relations we have achieved with the EEC.

In the final analysis, the NATO Alliance will be as effective as our will and determination, as well as that of our allies, to support it. The function of collective security is to deter wars and, if necessary, to fight and win those wars not successfully deterred. Our vigilance is especially required during periods of prolonged relaxation of tensions with our adversaries because we cannot permit ourselves to accept words and promises as a sub-

stitute for deeds. We are determined that the NATO Alliance shall not be lulled into a false sense of security. It can and must respond vigorously when called upon to act.

### Asia and the Pacific

The United States has vital interests in the entire Pacific Basin and those interests lie foremost in Asian tranquility and stability.

The experience of ending direct American involvement in a difficult and costly war initiated during Democrat Administrations has taught us a great deal about how we ought to define our interests in this part of the world. The United States is indisputably a Pacific power. We have sought to express our interests in the area through strengthening existing friendly ties and creating new ones.

Japan will remain the main pillar of our Asian policy. We have helped to provide the framework, over the course of thirty years, for the development of the Japanese economy, which has risen to second place among free world nations. This nation, without natural resources, has maximized its greatest resource, the Japanese people, to achieve one of the world's most significant economic advances. We will continue our policy of close consultation and cooperation with this valued friend. We have succeeded in establishing an exceptional relationship with Japan. Our long-range goals of stability and economic cooperation are identical, forming the essential strength of a relationship which both countries seek actively to deepen.

With respect to the Republic of Korea, a nation with which we have had traditionally close ties and whose economy has grown rapidly in recent years, we shall continue our policy of military and economic assistance. United States troops will be maintained in Korea so long as there exists the possibility of renewed aggression from North Korea. Time has not dimmed our memories of the sudden assault against South Korea. We reaffirm our commitment of the United States to the territorial integrity and the sovereignty of the Republic of Korea. Simultaneously we encourage the governments of South Korea and North Korea to institute domestic policy initiatives leading to the extension of basic human rights.

When Republicans assumed executive office in 1969, we were confronted with a war in Vietnam involving more than 500,000 United States troops, and to which we had committed billions of dollars and our national honor and prestige. It was in the spirit of bipartisan support for Presidential foreign policy initiatives, inaugurated in the postwar era by Senator Arthur Vandenberg, that most Republicans supported the United States commitment to assist South Vietnam resist Communist-sponsored aggression. The human cost to us was great; more than 55,000 Americans died in that conflict, and more than 300,000 were wounded.

A policy of patient, persistent and principled negotiations extricated the United States from that ill-fated war with the expectation that peace would prevail. The refusal of the Democrat-controlled Congress to give support to Presidential requests for military aid to the beleaguered nations of South Vietnam, Cambodia and Laos, coupled with sustained military assaults by the Communists in gross violation of the Paris Peace Accords, brought about the collapse of those nations and the subjugation of their people to totalitarian rule.

We recognize that there is a wide divergence of opinion concerning Vietnam, but we pledge that American troops will never again be committed for the purpose of our own defense, or the defense of those to whom we are committed by treaty or other solemn agreements, without the clear purpose of achieving our stated diplomatic and military objectives.

We must achieve the return of all Americans who may be held in Southeast Asia, and a full accounting for those listed as Missing in Action. We strongly urge continued consultation between the President and the National League of Families of American Prisoners and Missing in Southeast Asia. This country owes at least this much to all of these courageous people who have anguished so long over this matter. To this end, and to underscore our top priority commitment to the families of these POWs and MIAs, we recommend, among other actions, the establishment of a presidential representative.

We condemn the inhumane and criminal retributions which have taken place in Cambodia, where mass executions and forced resettlements have been imposed on innocent civilians.

The important economic developments taking place in Singapore, Indonesia, Malaysia, the Philippines and other Asia countries, will lead to much improved living standards for the people there.

We reaffirm our friendship with these nations. Equally, our relationships with Australia and New Zealand are historic and important to us; they have never been better and provide a firm base on which to build.

### United States-Chinese relations

A development of significance for the future of Asia and for the world came to fruition in 1972 as our communications were restored with the People's Republic of China. This event has allowed us to initiate dialogue with the leaders of a quarter of the earth's population, and trade channels with the People's Republic have been opened, leading to benefits for each side.

The People's Republic of China can and will play an increasingly important role in world affairs. We shall seek to engage the People's Republic of China in an expanded network of contacts and trade. Such a process cannot realistically proceed at a forced or incautious pace; the measured but steady growth of our relations best serves our interests. We do not ignore the profound differences in our respective philosophies, governmental institutions, policies and views on individual liberty, and we are hopeful that basic human rights will be extended to the Chinese people. What is truly fundamental is that we have established regular working channels with the People's Republic of China and that this process can form an important contribution to world peace.

Our friendly relations with one great power should not be considered as a challenge to any other nation, large or small. The United States government, while engaged in a normalization of relations with the People's Republic of China, will continue to support the freedom and independence of our friend and ally, the Republic of China, and its 16 million people. The United States will fulfill and keep its commitments, such as the mutual defense treaty, with the Republic of China.

### The Americas

The relations of the United States with the Americas are of vital and immediate importance. How we conduct our affairs with our neighbors to the North and South will continue to be a priority.

In the recent past our attention has at times

been diverted to more distant parts of the world. There can be no sensible alternative to close relationships and understandings among the nations of the hemisphere.

It is true for a series of new departures in our relations with Canada. Canada is our most important trading partner, and we are hers. We, as Americans, feel a deep affinity for our Canadian friends, and we have much at stake in the development of closer relationships based on mutual understanding and complete equality.

To our neighbors in Mexico, Central America and South America, we also say that we wish the opportunity to expand our dialogue. The needs of our friends are great, but this must not serve as an obstacle for a concerted effort to work together more closely. The United States has taken steps to adjust tariffs so as to maximize access to our markets. We recognize that our neighbors place no value on complex and cumbersome aid schemes; they see self-help, modernization, and expanded trade as the main sources of economic progress. We will work with them to define specific steps that we can take to help them achieve greater economic strength, and to advance our mutual interests.

By continuing its policies of exporting subversion and violence, Cuba remains outside the Inter-American family of nations. We condemn attempts by the Cuban dictatorship to intervene in the affairs of other nations; and, as long as such conduct continues, it shall remain ineligible for admissions to the Organization of American States.

We shall continue to share the aspirations of the Cuban people to regain their liberty. We insist that decent and humane conditions be maintained in the treatment of political prisoners in the Cuban jails, and we will seek arrangements to allow international entities, such as the International Red Cross, to investigate and monitor the conditions in those jails.

The present Panama Canal Treaty provides that the United States has jurisdictional rights in the Canal Zone as "if it were the sovereign." The United States intends that the Panama Canal be preserved as an international waterway for the ships of all nations. This secure access is enhanced by a relationship which commands the respect of Americans and Panamanians and benefits the people of both countries. In any talks with Panama, however, the United States negotiators should in

no way *cede, dilute, forfeit, negotiate or transfer any rights, power, authority, jurisdiction, territory or property that are necessary for the protection and security of the United States and the entire Western Hemisphere.*

We reaffirm our faith in the ability of the Organization of American States, which remains a valuable means of inter-American consultation.

*The Middle East*

The preservation of peace and stability in the Middle East is a paramount concern. The efforts of two Republican Administrations, summoning diplomatic and political skills, have been directed toward reduction of tension and toward avoiding flashpoints which could serve as an excuse for yet another round of conflict between Israel and the Arab countries.

Our commitment to Israel is fundamental and enduring. We have honored and will continue to honor that commitment in every way—politically, economically and providing the military aid that Israel requires to remain strong enough to deter any potential aggression. Forty percent of all United States aid that Israel has received since its creation in 1948 has come in the last two fiscal years, as a result of Republican initiatives. Our policy must remain one of decisive support for the security and integrity of Israel.

An equally important component of our commitment to Israel lies in continuing our efforts to secure a just and durable peace for all nations in that complex region. Our efforts have succeeded, for the first time since the creation of the state of Israel, in moving toward a negotiated peace settlement which would serve the interests and the security of all nations in the Middle East. Peace in the Middle East now requires face-to-face direct negotiations between the states involved with the recognition of safe, secure and defensible borders for Israel.

At the same time, Republic Administrations have succeeded in reestablishing communications with the Arab countries, and have made extensive progress in our diplomatic and commercial relations with the more moderate Arab nations.

As a consequence of the Middle East conflict of 1973, the petroleum producing states imposed an embargo on the export of oil to most of the advanced industrial countries. We have succeeded in creating numerous cooperative mechanisms to protect ourselves, working in concert with our allies, against any future embargoes. The United States would view any attempt to reimpose an embargo as an essentially hostile act. We will oppose discriminatory practices, including boycotts of any type.

Because we have such fundamental interests in the Middle East, it will be our policy to continue our efforts to maintain the balance of power in the Mediterranean region. Our adversaries must recognize that we will not permit a weakening of our defenses or any attempt to disturb valued Alliance relationships in the Eastern Mediterranean.

We shall continue to support peace initiatives in the civil war in Lebanon; United States envoys engaged in precisely such an initiative were murdered, and we express our sorrow for their untimely deaths and for all other dedicated government employees who have been slain elsewhere while in service to their country. In Lebanon, we stand ready to provide food, medical and other humanitarian assistance.

## Africa

The United States has always supported the process of self-determination in Africa. Our friendship for the African countries is expressed in support for continued peaceful economic development, expansion of trade, humanitarian relief efforts and our belief that the entire continent should be free from outside military intervention. Millions of Americans recognize their historical and cultural ties with Africa and express their desire that United States policy toward Africa is a matter of great importance.

We support all forces which promote negotiated settlements and racial peace. We shall continue to deplore all violence and terrorism and to urge all concerned that the rights of tribal, ethnic and racial minorities be guaranteed through workable safeguards. Our policy is to strengthen the force of moderation recognizing that solutions to African problems will not come quickly. The peoples of Africa can coexist in security, work together in freedom and harmony, and strive together to secure their prosperity. We hope that the Organization of African Unity will be able to achieve mature and stable relationships within Africa and abroad.

The interests of peace and security in Africa are best served by the absence of arms and greater concentration on peaceful development. We reserve the right to maintain the balance by extending our support to nations facing a threat from Soviet-supplied states and from Soviet weapons.

## United States-Soviet relations

American foreign policy must be based upon a realistic assessment of the Communist challenge in the world. It is clear that the perimeters of freedom continue to shrink throughout the world in the face of the Communist challenge. Since 1917, totalitarian Communism has managed through brute force, not through the free electoral process, to bring an increasingly substantial portion of the world's land area and peoples under its domination. To illustrate, most recently South Vietnam, Cambodia, and Laos have fallen under the control of Communist dictatorships, and in that part of the world the Communist pressure mounts against Thailand, the Republic of China, and the Republic of Korea. In Africa, Communist Cuba forces, brazenly assisted by the Soviet Union, have recently imposed a Communist dictatorship upon the people of Angola. Other countries in Africa and throughout the world generally await similar fates. These are the realities of world power in our time. The United States is thoroughly justified in having based its foreign policy upon these realities.

Thirty years ago relations between the United States and the Soviet Union were in a phase of great difficulty, leading to the tensions of the Cold War era. Although there have been changes in this crucial superpower relationship, there remain fundamental and profound differences between us. Republican Presidents, while acknowledging the depth of the gulf which separates our free society from the Soviet society, have sought methodically to isolate and develop those areas of our relations which would serve to lessen tension and reduce the chance of unwanted conflict.

In a world beset by countless opportunities for discord and armed conflict, the relationship between the United States and the Soviet Union is critically important; on it rest the hopes of the world for peace. We offer a policy that maintains our fundamental strength and demonstrates our steadfast determination to prevent aggressive use of Soviet power.

The role of a responsible, participating Congress

in maintaining this diplomatic and military posture is critical to success. The United States must remain a loyal and dependable ally, and must be prepared to carry out commitments and to demonstrate a willingness to act. Resistance to open aggression, such as the Soviet-sponsored Cuban intervention in Angola, must not be allowed to become the subject of a partisan debate, nor can it be allowed to become an unchallenged and established pattern of international behavior, lest our credibility and deterrent strength be greatly diminished.

Soviet military power has grown rapidly in recent years, and while we shall prevent a military imbalance or a sudden shift in the global balance of power, we shall also diligently explore with the Soviet Union new ways to reduce tensions and to arrive at mutually beneficial and self-enforcing agreements in all fields of international activity. Important steps have been taken to limit strategic nuclear arms. The Vladivostok Agreement of November 1974 placed a ceiling on the strategic forces of both the United States and the Soviet Union. Further negotiations in arms control are continuing. We shall not agree for the sake of agreement; on the contrary, we will make sure that any agreements yield fundamental benefits to our national security.

As an example of hard-headed bargaining our success in concluding agreements limiting the size of peaceful nuclear explosions and nuclear weapons tests will, for the first time, permit the United States to conduct on-site inspections in the Soviet Union itself. This important step can now be measured in practical terms. All such agreements must stand the test of verification. An agreement that does not provide this safeguard is worse than no agreement at all.

We support the consolidation of joint efforts with our allies to verify that our policies regarding the transfer of technology to the Soviet Union and its allies are in concert and that consultation will be designed to preclude the sale of those technology-intensive products to the Soviet Union by the United States and our allies which will directly or indirectly jeopardize our national security.

Our trade in non-strategic areas creates jobs here at home, substantially improves our balance-of-payments position, and can contribute to an improved political climate in the world. The overseas sale of our agricultural products benefits American farmers and consumers. To guard against any sudden shift in domestic prices as the consequence of unannounced purchases, we have instituted strict reporting procedures and other treaty safeguards. We shall not permit concessional sales of agricultural products to the Soviet Union, nor shall we permit the Soviet Union or others to determine our agricultural export policies by irregular and unpredictable purchases.

The United States and the Soviet Union remain ideological competitors. We do not shrink from such a challenge; rather, we welcome the opportunity to demonstrate that our way of life is inherently preferable to regimentation and government-enforced orthodoxy. We shall expect the Soviet Union to implement the United Nations Declaration on Human Rights and the Helsinki Agreements, which guarantee conditions for the free interchange of information and the right to emigrate, including emigration of Soviet Jews, Christians, Moslems and others who wish to join relatives abroad. In this spirit we shall expect the immediate end of all forms of harassment, including imprisonment and military service, aimed at preventing such emigration. America must take a firm stand to bring about liberalization of emigration policy in countries which limit or prohibit free emigration. Governments which enjoy the confidence of their people need have no fear of cultural, intellectual or press freedom.

Our support for the people of Central and Eastern Europe to achieve self-determination will continue. Their ability to choose their future is of great importance to peace and stability. We favor increasing contacts between Eastern and Western Europe and support the increasing economic ties of all the countries of Europe. We strongly support the continuation of the Voice of America, Radio Free Europe and Radio Liberty with adequate appropriations. Strict reciprocity must govern our diplomatic relations with the Soviet Union. We express our concern for the safety of our diplomatic representatives in the Soviet Union, and we insist that practices such as microwave transmissions directed at the United States Embassy be terminated immediately.

Thus our relations with the Soviet Union will be guided by solid principles. We will maintain our strategic and conventional forces; we will oppose the development of Soviet power for unilateral advantages or political and territorial expansion; we will never tolerate a shift against us in the strategic balance; and we will remain firm in the face of pressure, while at the same time expressing our willingness to work on the basis of strict reciprocity toward new agreements which will help achieve peace and stability.

*International Cooperation*

Strong support for international cooperation in all fields has been a hallmark of United States international policy for many decades. Two Republican Administrations have strengthened agencies of international cooperation not only because of our humanitarian concern for others, but also because it serves United States interests to be a conscientious member of the world community.

The political character of the United Nations has become complex. With 144 sovereign members, the U.N. experiences problems associated with a large, sometimes cumbersome and diverse body. We seek to accommodate to these changes in the spirit of friendly concern, but when the United Nations becomes arrayed against the vital interests of any of its member states on ideological or other narrow grounds, the very principles of the organization are threatened. The United States does not wish to dictate to the U.N., yet we do have every right to expect and insist that scrupulous care be given to the rights of all members. Steamroller techniques for advancing discriminatory actions will be opposed. Actions such as the malicious attempt to depict Zionism as a form of racism are inconsistent with the objectives of the United Nations and are repugnant to the United States. The United States will continue to be a firm supporter and defender of any nation subjected to such outrageous assaults. We will not accept ideological abuses of the United States.

In the many areas of international cooperation which benefit the average American—elimination of terrorism, peacekeeping, non-proliferation of nuclear weapons, termination of the international drug trade, and orderly use of ocean resources—we pledge to build new international structures of cooperation. At the same time, we shall seek to insure that the cost of such new structures, as well as the cost of existing structures, is more equitably shared among participating nations. In the continued tradition of American concern for the quality of human life everywhere, we shall give vigorous support to the non-political work of the specialized agencies of the United Nations which deal with such areas as nutrition and disaster relief for the world's poor and disadvantaged.

The United States should withdraw promptly from the International Labor Organization if that body fails to stop its increasing politicization.

Eight years ago we pledged to eliminate waste and to make more business-like the administration of the United States foreign aid programs. We have endeavored to fulfill these pledges. Our foreign economic assistance programs are now being operated efficiently with emphasis on helping others to help themselves, on food production and rural development, on health programs and sound population planning assistance, and on development of human resources.

We have sought to encourage others, including the oil producing countries, to assume a larger share of the burden of assistance. We shall continue our efforts to secure adequate sources of financing for economic projects in emerging countries.

The world's oceans, with their vast resources, must become areas of extended cooperation. We favor a successful conclusion to the Law of the Sea Conference provided it will suitably protect legitimate national interests, freedom of the seas and responsible use of the seas. We are are determined to maintain the right of free and unmolested passage for ships of all nations on the high seas and in international waterways.

We favor an extension of the territorial sea from three to twelve miles, and we favor in principle the creation of a 200-mile economic zone in which coastal states would have exclusive rights to explore and develop natural resources.

We strongly condemn illegal corporate payments made at home and abroad. To eliminate illegal payments to foreign officials by American corporations, we support passage of President Ford's proposed legislation and the OECD Declaration on Investment setting forth reasonable guidelines for business conduct.

The growth of civilian nuclear technology, and the rising demand for nuclear power as an alternative to increasingly costly fossil fuel resources, combine to require our recognition of the potential dangers associated with such developments. All nations must work to assure that agreements and treaties currently governing nuclear technology and nuclear exports are carefully monitored. We shall work to devise new multilateral policies governing the export of sensitive nuclear technologies.

### International Economic Policy

The tumultuous events of the past several years in the world economy were an enormous challenge to our creativity and to our capacity for leadership. We have emerged from this difficult period in a new position in the world, and we have directed and guided a sound recovery.

To assure the permanence of our own prosperity, we must work with others, demonstrating our leadership and the vitality of our economy. Together with the industrial democracies, we must ensure steady, non-inflationary growth, based on expanded international cooperation.

The Republican Administration will cooperate fully in strengthening the international trade and monetary system, which provides the foundation for our prosperity and that of all nations. We shall bargain hard to remove barriers to an open economic system, and we shall oppose new restrictions to trade. We shall continue to represent vigorously our nation's economic interest in the trade negotiations taking place in Geneva, guard against protectionism, and insist that the principles of fair trade be scrupulously observed. When industries and jobs are adversely affected by foreign competition, adjustment assistance under the Trade Act of 1974 is made available. This Act must be under continuous review to ascertain that it reflects changing circumstances.

The Republican Party believes that cooperation in the energy field is indispensable to international stability. Most of the industrial democracies and the less-developed countries are increasingly dependent on imported oil, which causes them to be politically, economically and strategically vulnerable. Through the establishment of the International Energy Agency, steps have been taken to expand consumer cooperation. We shall also continue the dialogue with the oil producing countries.

We shall continue to work closely with the less-developed countries to promote their economic growth. Those countries will be encouraged to enter into mutually beneficial trade relationships with us that contribute to world peace. To achieve this, we must strengthen the confidence of the major industrial countries as they take part in discussions with less-developed countries. There is no reason for us to be defensive; our combined assets can be used in a coordinated strategy to make our influence effective. We will not yield to threats or confrontational politics.

While we shall support a global increase of investment in natural resources of all types, we shall also oppose the replacement of the free market mechanism by cartels, price-fixing arrangements or commodity agreements. We shall continue policies designed to assure free market consumers abroad that the United States will remain a dependable supplier of agricultural commodities.

### Conclusion

The American people can be proud of our nation's achievements in foreign policy over the past eight years.

We are at peace.

We are strong.

We re-emphasize the importance of our ties with the nations of the Americas.

Our relations with allies in the Atlantic community and with Japan have never been closer.

Significant progress has been made toward a just and durable settlement in the Middle East.

We have sought negotiation rather than confrontation with our adversaries, while maintaining our strategic deterrent.

The world economic recovery, led by the United States, is producing sustainable growth.

In this year of our nation's bicentennial, the American people have confidence in themselves and are optimistic about the future.

We, the Republican Party, proudly submit our record and our Platform to you.

## Socialist Platform 1976

### GENERAL PRINCIPLES

The people of the United States deserve better choices in public policy than those presented by the major parties. The parties presently in power and their non-socialist opposition are not offering methods that will help the people get out of the depression, meet the need for full employment, provide full legal rights for all people, protect public resources, or stop the drift toward war.

The American people should have an opportunity to choose democratic socialism. Socialism means the democratic control of the major means of production and distribution. We should not only have a meaningful choice when we elect public officials, but we should also have a meaningful influence in determining the conditions of our jobs, the prices we pay, the future of our neighborhoods, the way in which the surplus wealth of our society should be spent, and the directions in which that society should move.

We offer this program to help Americans develop a society in which each individual can achieve the maximum personal development in harmony with the rights and aspirations of others:

## Agriculture

The American farmer must not continue to labor, often as a serf, under the domination of the Board of Trade and the vertical monopolies of the agri-corporations. These institutions must be abolished to establish economic justice for farm families. Farm workers must have the right to unionize. We support cooperative farming.

## Communication

Neither socialism nor democracy is possible without adequate information and free discussion of all issues. It is not enough to oppose repression of communications media when they expose the worst excesses of government or of business. The media must be restructured to provide adequate communications to all publics, no matter how large or small; to provide free access to all points of view; and to provide alternatives to dependence on either corporate advertising or state subsidies. Such alternatives can include cooperative cable communication; equal access of parties to television time; encouragement of cooperatively owned and published periodicals or newspapers; public ownership of the telephone companies; and publicly controlled and democratically sponsored radio and television stations.

## Education

Every human being has the right to the fullest development of his/her potential to serve society and him/herself. Educational institutions should never be used as they often are, to reinforce the unjust discriminations of capitalist society, to pro-

vide detention camps for those young persons for whom no meaningful employment is provided, or to provide subsidized research and development for war and the perpetuation of injustice. Teachers and all school employees must be accorded the democratic right to strike. We favor expanded educational opportunities such as the educaid program and free and equal access for all individuals. The Socialist Party believes in integrated education in schools of excellence. We hold that where public transportation of pupils is required to achieve such ends, we encourage the use of such transportation.

## Foreign Affairs

Easing tensions among the major powers must be encouraged. The present waste of the people's wealth for armaments must end. Socialists, an international group to whom no human being is foreign, know that no conceivable balance of power can achieve permanent peace while glaring inequalities exist between developed and underdeveloped countries and while legitimate aspirations to self-determination, democracy, and economic justice are suppressed anywhere in the world.

## Human Rights

As Socialists, we believe in and work toward the fulfillment of human rights for all individuals and groups. For this fulfillment, civil rights and civil liberties must be defined not only in class and/or economic terms, but also in social, cultural, and psychological terms. We call for an equal emphasis and struggle toward a social, cultural, and psychological overhaul of society so that exploitation in areas other than the economic is also abolished. We are militant in support of the aspirations and needs of women, and the aspirations and needs of American ethnic, racial, social, and cultural groups.

## Constitutional Rights

We are appalled by the recent revelations of spying on private organizations, of burglaries, of the disruption of political and reform organizations by such agencies as the CIA, FBI, IRS, military intelligence agencies, and local police forces. These activities constitute a grave danger to constitutional rights and threaten to turn America into a police state. We call for abolition of the CIA and legislation to prevent the abuses committed by public agencies. Criminal activities of public agents must be punished.

## URBAN PROBLEMS

The private theft of publicly-created values has created an urban environment that is uncomfortable, dirty, dangerous, alienating, and inhumane. All people must have power to control the wealth that their labor has created and to build livable communities. The problems of cities are the concern of all.

## ENVIRONMENT

The greed and shortsightedness inherent in our present system have upset the balance of nature and put the future of our planet in danger. The natural forces of the earth belong to all of the people and their preservation is the responsibility of everyone. In the interest of the environment, as in all other things, private property must be subordinated to the public need.

## ENERGY AND TRANSPORTATION

Our society can no longer afford private ownership of energy production and distribution or the subversion of transportation policy for the profit of the automobile and oil industries and of the road contractors. Energy and transportation must be socially controlled as in any public utility. There must be a national plan of energy use and conservation, and public allocation of energy resources in the interest of all people. Emphasis must be placed on the development of public transportation.

## CORRUPTION

Continuing political scandals are not due to a few bad individuals but to a bad system. The ethics of Watergate are the ethics of every corporate boardroom in the capitalist world. No permanent political reform is possible until the power of giant wealth over politics is abolished.

## THE ECONOMY

Inflation, unfair taxes, rising unemployment, the declining quality of consumer goods, and the neglect of our society's real needs are symptoms of capitalism that affect us. Only social control of the production and distribution of goods will create the base for building a new society. Neither reactionary economists nor capitalist advocates of government spending pretend any longer even to have temporary solutions to the continuing decline in real wages and job opportunities. Social control of banking and credit has become an immediate pressing need.

## UNION DEMOCRACY

All labor unions should be controlled by their members with respect for individual and civil liberties. Union officials should be fairly and frequently elected, conventions should be controlled by the rank-and-file, union publications should be open to all members, and the rights and safety of members in opposition to the leadership should always be protected.

## HOUSING

We favor a large-scale program of public housing, and financial encouragement for cooperatives, and technological restructuring of the housing industry.

## INFLATION

The 100 billion dollar Pentagon budget is an insult to all earthly intelligence and is the godhead of inflation. Instead of a planned economy we have planned destruction. We refuse to vote a military budget, and would apply the savings toward domestic benefits.

## AMNESTY

Amnesty should be unconditional and universal for all war resisters.

## HEALTH

We demand a comprehensive national health policy which would make the benefits of modern medical technology and organization available to all while removing the burden from individuals and families.

## WORKERS' CONTROL

A goal of the Socialist Party is workers' control of all industry through democratic organization of the work-place, with workers making all the decisions now made by management. The Socialist Party proposes a society of free, continuing, and democratic participation through shop councils, and through councils for the management of each industry by workers and others most affected by it, including consumers. Spheres of life other than industry should also have popular control. These are the bases for democratic socialism, and can be achieved only through radical social change.

The Socialist Party supports moves toward democratic decision making whether in private or government enterprise, which genuinely limits management authority by institutionalizing power in the hands of working people and their democratic organizations. We favor, in general, an increase in the decision-making power of work groups.

We oppose totalitarianism in every form.

We believe that the eventual government of civilized people must be international, humanitarian, democratic, and libertarian, if our species is to survive its own future.

## Socialist Labor Platform 1976

What is socialism and how can it be established in the United States?

While Americans will be swamped in this bicentennial election year with an endless stream of empty debate "on the issues," the national candidates of the Socialist Labor Party will be putting this question before as many workers as possible. Even more importantly, they'll be answering it.

### BASIC CAUSES, BASIC SOLUTIONS

The program of socialism on which they'll run speaks to the needs and problems of the American people in a way no other political platform can. It ties all the many and varied problems confronting workers today, from economic crises to racism, from eroding democratic rights to environmental suicide, back to their common origins in the system of capitalism.

It bares the basic reason why a people increasingly dissatisfied with the oppression and deteriorating quality of life in the U.S. have not been able to gain the freedom and security they've sought

for decades. In a nation that prides itself on its democratic traditions, the obvious reality is that the great majority of people have no control over their lives and no way to insure even the basic necessities of life for themselves and their families. In every sphere of society, they confront the rule of a small class whose ideas and interests predominate.

The socialist program cuts through superficial excuses for this unequal status quo and gets to its roots. It shows that tinkering with the system as it is, or waiting for "better times," or relying on politicians, are only ways in which the class that owns and controls the U.S. keeps the majority from challenging its domination.

The platform of the SLP is neither a bundle of promises nor a package of slogans. It's a plan for mobilizing the working people of the nation into organizations that will enable them to resist and overturn the rule of the capitalist class, and to build a better society, more democratic, more open and more free than any that has ever existed.

### NECESSITY OF SOCIAL CHANGE

Anything short of such a revolutionary change is a formula for leaving control of society where it is, in ruling-class hands. And no matter how that control may be "modified," if the ruling power of society is left where it is now, this nation is headed for disaster.

The tremendous productive potential of the economy will continue to be used for private gain and corporate profit. It will be used, as it is today, to exploit workers on the job, to rape the environment for profit, and to amass mountains of wealth for the few. It will keep pitting worker against worker, race against race, and sex against sex, fighting over scraps while the capitalist class reaps the harvest of society's labor. A small ruling class will continue to shape the entire course of the nation.

If control of society remains where it is now, the government will remain an instrument for advancing the ends of a ruling minority against the rest. It will continue to serve capitalist interests at home and imperialist interests abroad. The repression and lies which have become regular orders of government business will grow more drastic and dangerous. The system will head toward ever-worsening crises, more conflicts and the inevitable threat of another world war.

To change this course the political and economic power of society must be transferred from the small ruling class to the working majority. In essence, this is what socialism is all about.

Socialism does not mean control by the state, or domination by a party, or the regulation of capitalist rule, or more reforms and bureaucracy. It means the transfer of power over all social institutions and operations to the rank-and-file workers themselves.

## A Revolutionary Program

How can this be done?

Such a revolutionary change can only come through the direct activity of the workers themselves. They must break with the illusion that they have to endure capitalism forever, or are powerless to change society. Through their conscious political and economic organization, they can not only overturn class-ruled society, but, in the same process, build a better one in its place.

Politically workers must draw together in a party that stands for their own collective interests. For too long workers have relied on capitalist politicians to speak for them. They must build their own political organization, to challenge the domination of the capitalist class and help all workers realize how socialism serves their needs, and how it can be won.

But a political party by itself is not enough. Socialism means more than a change in ideas, or a different set of political figures in government. It means that the masses of working people must build the new forms of socialist government.

These new socialist organizations of workers on the job are needed to mobilize labor's strength against capitalism on a militant, classconscious basis. They must unite all workers, skilled and unskilled, employed and unemployed. Workers in all jobs and industries must be united into a socialist labor movement to back up the workers' political organization, and ultimately take control of the economy in the name of society.

These same socialist unions would then form the building blocks of the new socialist government. Organized along the same lines as the economy itself, socialist industrial government would be geared to administering production for social needs and wants. The economy would be run on democratic socialist principles for use instead of profit.

## Socialist Society

In socialist society, there would be no political bureaucracy and no small class controlling the economy. All government representatives would be elected directly by rank-and-file workers on the job. They would receive no special privileges or power over those they represent, and would be subject to recall whenever a majority of those who elected them deemed it necessary.

On such a foundation a society could be built where all power in every social institution would rest with the rank and file. Outmoded, repressive political government would be superseded by a socialist industrial society, and for the first time the majority would have direct democratic control over their own affairs.

This is the revolutionary alternative the SLP campaign will be putting before the workers of the country. Find out more about it and join us in the effort.

## Socialist Workers Platform 1976

The United States is in a deepening crisis. We are in the midst of the worst depression since the 1930s. The quality of life for most people is going from bad to worse. And the present system offers us no hope for improvement.

There is no end to wars—one after another since the end of World War II. After Korea came Vietnam; now the Middle East is a powder keg. And Washington is looking for a way to help turn Portugal into the next Chile.

Huge stockpiles of hydrogen weapons are a constant reminder of the threat of nuclear war.

Pollution is destroying our environment—from the water we drink to the air we breathe.

Millions are unemployed, and layoffs throw more out of work every day. Breakdowns, shortages, and high prices—each week our real take-home pay is less. Suffering the most are those at the bottom of the ladder—Blacks, Chicanos, Puerto Ricans, women, and other doubly oppressed people.

Neither the Republican administration nor the Democratic Congress can offer a solution. They are only interested in shifting the responsibility and escaping the blame.

They try to pit white workers against Blacks in a struggle for jobs, housing, and education.

They blame all working people, claiming we eat too much and live too well. They say that inflation will slow down if we tighten our belts and stop demanding higher wages.

They blame people in other countries. They point to a "population explosion" in Asia, Africa, and Latin America—while the corporations they represent plunder the resources of these same countries.

They say the Arabs caused the energy crisis, as if skyrocketing profits of the U.S. oil monopolies weren't responsible.

The Democratic and Republican proposals are clear: don't struggle to defend your living standards; pay the costs of foreign wars; eat less and pay more; victimize foreign-born workers; use less electricity and gasoline; forget about health and safety, social services, and jobs.

This way of running the country can be stated in nine words: "What's good for big business is good for America."

The Rockefellers, DuPonts, Mellons, Morgans, and other super-rich families who rule America think they were born with rights and privileges that come before the welfare and security of the rest of us. For the sake of profits they think it is perfectly justifiable to lay off millions of workers, to destroy our environment, or to plunge the country into war.

They are a tiny minority trampling on the rights of the American people.

## DEFEND THE DEMOCRATIC RIGHTS OF THE MAJORITY

Nearly 200 years ago, when our country won its war of independence against British tyranny, the workers and small farmers waged a fight to add ten amendments to the Constitution—the Bill of Rights. These were intended to help guarantee "life, liberty, and the pursuit of happiness."

Among these rights are:

Freedom of speech, press, assembly, and religion

Right to a jury trial by one's peers

Right to bear arms

Protection from unreasonable search and seizure, excessive bail or fines, and cruel or unusual punishment.

A second revolution—the Civil War—resulted in additional amendments to the Constitution protecting the rights of the American people:

Outlawing of slavery

No deprivation of life, liberty, or property without due process of law

Right of all male citizens age 21 or over to vote, regardless of race or color.

More than fifty years ago women won the right to vote, and recently this was extended to all citizens over the age of 18.

These rights were won through struggle, and bitter battles have been required to preserve them against witch-hunters, racists, bigots, and anti-labor forces. Especially significant was the recent victory of Blacks in the South, who fought for nearly two decades to restore voting rights forcibly denied them since the defeat of Reconstruction in the 1870s.

Yet all these rights have never been fully implemented, nor are they extended to everyone. In reality, millions of Americans are being pushed into second-class status by the powerful few who rule this country. Their whole strategy is to divide working people by trying to create a class of pariahs—oppressed minorities, women, foreign-born workers of color, the unemployed—those that relatively better-off white workers view as "them" rather than "us."

The only way to counter the rulers' attempts to undermine working class solidarity is for all working people to support the struggles of oppressed minorities and women for equal opportunities.

Preferential hiring and upgrading are necessary to help achieve equality on the job. Employers must not be allowed to use layoffs to reduce the proportion of minority and women workers.

To gain equality, Blacks and other oppressed minorities must have the right to live in the neighborhoods of their choice. They must have the right to decide where to send their children to school, and to use busing if necessary to transport them to better, predominantly white schools.

Minorities who don't speak English as their first language must be provided with education, civil service exams, ballots, and voting instructions in their own language to help achieve equality.

The struggle of women for the right to safe, legal abortions and to get the Equal Rights Amendment adopted and implemented should be supported to help achieve equality in all spheres of life.

Watergate revealed a tiny bit of the illegal

spying, bugging, and harassment carried out by the government against unions, Black organizations, socialists, and other dissenters. Subsequent revelations have shown how the secret agencies coldly calculated to frame up people demanding their rights and then tried to sabotage their legal defense efforts—for example the American Indian Movement and the Attica defendants.

As the economic crisis deepens and big business tightens its squeeze on labor, the civil liberties of working people are threatened even more. Our rights to assembly, free speech, and individual privacy are being challenged.

Government interference infringes on the rights of unions to organize, bargain collectively, and strike. All laws that allow government interference in the unions or that bar public employees from striking should be repealed.

Democratic and human rights should be applied to prisoners, GIs, gays, foreign-born workers, and and young people. Repressive legislation must be abolished, along with all cruel and unusual punishment including the death penalty.

### A Bill of Rights for Working People

Not only is it necessary to fight back and reassert our rights, but we need to broaden these rights to protect working people against the threat of new wars, racist offensives, and attacks on our working conditions. We need a new bill of rights to meet the present needs of the majority, those who must work for a living.

The Socialist Workers Party proposes the following:

1. Right to a job
2. Right to an adequate income, protected against inflation
3. Right to free education
4. Right to free medical care
5. Right to a secure retirement
6. Right of oppressed national minorities to control their own affairs
7. Right to know the truth about and decide the political policies that affect our lives
8. Right to know the truth about and decide economic and social policies

### 1. Right to a Job

It is an elementary obligation of society to guarantee steady work for everyone. This can be done by the following measures:

An emergency public works program should be launched to provide jobs through construction of housing, mass transportation, hospitals, schools, child care facilities, parks, and other social necessities. Priority should be given to projects in the workers' neighborhoods, where they are most needed—especially in Black, Chicano, and Puerto Rican communities.

The huge sums necessary to pay for this program should come from eliminating the mammoth war budget and from a 100 percent tax on war profits. A moratorium should be declared on using our taxes to pay billions of dollars to bankers for interest on public debt.

Working hours should be reduced with no reduction in take-home pay in order to spread the available work and achieve full employment.

Unemployment compensation should be paid by the government at full union wages for as long as a person is unemployed.

In order to assure economic independence for women, government-financed free child care centers should be established. Maternity leaves with full pay should be provided. Women must also have the right to decide whether or not to give birth to children. This includes the right to abortion and contraception on demand as well as protection from forced sterilization.

And fellow workers who are not U.S. citizens, including those without immigration documents, are entitled to jobs and equal pay without fear of racist harassment or deportation.

### 2. Right to an Adequate Income Protected against Inflation

A guaranteed living wage is a basic human right. As a protection against inflation, wages must be free to rise. There must be no government wage controls.

To offset price gouging on food, rent, gas, electricity, and other basic necessities, wages must be protected with cost-of-living escalator clauses in union contracts, so that wages increase—promptly and fully—with each rise in living costs.

Escalator provisions should be pegged to the real rate of inflation as determined by committees set up by unions and consumer groups—not the Labor Department's Consumer Price Index which is based on a "market basket" that deliberately underestimates price increases.

All pension, Social Security benefits, unemployment and disability compensation, welfare and veterans' benefits should be raised to union wage scales and protected with cost-of-living escalator provisions.

Small working farmers, who are gouged by banks on one hand and squeezed by the food trusts on the other, should be allowed to make a decent living. They have a right to low-interest, long-term government loans.

*3. Right to Free Education*

*4. Right to Free Medical Care*

*5. Right to a Secure Retirement*

Education, health, and security should not be privileges of the rich. These are rights that should be guaranteed to everyone. They are the responsibility of society.

Tuition, books, and living expenses should be furnished to all who want to attend colleges and trade schools.

Everyone, from birth to old age, should be guaranteed free medical and dental care through a full program of socialized medicine.

All retired and disabled persons should receive government-financed benefits at full union wages.

Government-financed programs should be instituted not only to provide care for people who are ill, but for medical research and public education about health.

Adult education and cultural programs should be expanded to permit working people to develop themselves to the fullest extent possible.

*6. Right of Oppressed National Minorities to Control Their Own Affairs*

Blacks, Chicanos, Puerto Ricans, and other oppressed peoples have a right to control the schools, hospitals, child care centers, parks, and other institutions in their communities. They have a right to determine how federal and state funds will be used in their communities.

To end police brutality and lower the crime rate, the police should be removed from the ghettos and barrios. They should be replaced with a security force democratically selected and supervised by the people who live in these communities.

*7. Right to Know the Truth About and Decide Political Policies That Affect Our Lives*

Republican and Democratic administrations claim that their foreign policy decisions advance peace and democracy throughout the world. The Pentagon Papers, the CIA's intervention in Chile, and Nixon's secret promise to the Thieu regime to send U.S. troops and B-52s back into Vietnam show that this is not true. We have a right to know the full truth.

Let us see what the rulers really have in mind when they make decisions that affect our lives:

Publish all secret treaties and agreements Washington has made with other countries!

Open all police, CIA, FBI, and IRS files!

No secret diplomacy behind the backs of the American people!

Let the public know the truth about U.S. support for dictatorships all over the world, from South Africa to South Korea.

Take the war-making power away from the White House and Congress. Let the people vote in a referendum before the country is dragged into more wars. Let us have the right to say no to policies that can lead to nuclear holocaust and the end of humanity.

We have the right to say no to government stockpiling and testing of weapons that threaten our health and safety and endanger the ecology. We have a right to veto the stationing of U.S. forces throughout the world and support of puppet military dictators.

*8. Right to Know the Truth About and Decide Economic and Social Policies*

When the corporations claim they can't grant wage increases, and when they lay off workers, make them *open their books*.

Make the oil, food, and auto monopolies show their records to elected workers' committees so we can see their real profits, production statistics, technological possibilities, and secret dealings. Then we can see who is rigging prices, deliberately creating shortages, and hoarding reserves.

When employers close down plants, those plants should be *nationalized* and put under the control of these workers' committees. With access to all financial and technical information kept secret by the bosses, the workers' committees will be able to make the necessary decisions on retooling and reopening the plants to produce for the needs of society.

These workers' committees can expose the hundreds of business secrets that tie industry and agribusiness to the big banks, the transportation and retailing monopolies, government agencies, Democratic and Republic politicians, and judges.

Workers have the right to control their working conditions through their own democratically elected committees. They have the right to regulate the pace of work in the safest and least dehumanizing way.

Workers—for example, the miners—have a right to elect their own safety inspectors. Production must be shut down on the demand of the workers and at the expense of the boss whenever the safety of personnel is involved.

Workers have a right to halt industrial processes that contaminate the air and water and endanger the environment.

They have a right to veto arbitrary and discriminatory layoffs.

Workers also have a right to insist that things they produce will be safe and durable and that production will be for social needs rather than private profits.

When monopolies like the utilities, the postal service, the railroads, and the airlines cry bankruptcy, charge exorbitant rates, or refuse services to those who can't pay their rates, they should be nationalized and operated under the control of workers' committees.

In order to make sound decisions, the committees will have to cooperate with similar committees throughout their industry on a national scale and in other industries in their region, as well as with committees of consumers, housewives, and other affected groups.

To acquire the needed information and resources for economic planning, the entire banking system—in reality the accounting and credit system of the capitalist class—will have to be taken over, opened up to the workers' committees, and placed under their control.

Only in that way can the entire economy be democratically planned and organized so as to prevent the recurring breakdowns and chaos that result from the anarchy of production for private profit.

If the majority had known the truth about the oil industry and had the right to make the decisions about the country's energy needs, the energy crisis would have been prevented. The oil trusts deliberately cut back their refining capacity in order to create a shortage and drive up prices and profits. A national plan worked out and overseen by the workers themselves would not have allowed this to happen.

Such a national economic plan would divert the colossal sums now spent for military purposes to social needs. It would end the threat of worldwide famine and war.

However, this will only be possible if the government itself passes completely into the hands of the majority—the masses of working people.

FOR A WORKERS' GOVERNMENT

When the American colonists could no longer tolerate British rule and drew up their Declaration of Independence, they stated that "whenever any form of government becomes destructive of these ends [life, liberty, and the pursuit of happiness], it is the right of the people to alter or to abolish it, and to institute new government, laying its foundation on such principles, and organizing its powers in such form, as to them shall seem most likely to effect their safety and happiness."

Today, we are ruled by a new tyranny. Industrial and financial barons govern us by the rule of profits, denying the basic democratic and social rights we need for life, liberty, and the pursuit of happiness. This government of the few must be abolished and replaced by a workers' government that will represent the majority.

A workers' government will guarantee democracy and implement a new bill of rights for working people.

It will immediately recognize the right of Blacks and Chicanos to self-determination. It will immediately grant independence to Puerto Rico.

It will end all discrimination against foreign-born workers and extend them equal rights with all other workers.

It will adopt a policy of peace and friendship with peoples throughout the world and offer massive economic and technical assistance and food to other countries—with no strings attached. It will stop U.S. interference in the internal affairs of other countries and dismantle all U.S. military bases abroad. It will stop shedding the blood of America's youth in foreign adventures.

Instead of supporting oppressors and dictators, it will aid the struggles of the oppressed—Palestinians driven from their homeland by Israel; South African Blacks ruled by a white majority; South Koreans dominated by U.S.-backed generals, bankers, and landlords; Chileans repressed by the bloody military junta.

A workers' government in the United States would be a tremendous inspiration to people all over the world. With a knowledge that the mighty USA was not their enemy, oppressed people everywhere would rise up against their oppressors. The entire world would be changed for the better.

The working people of the Soviet Union would throw out their hated rulers and revive the democratic and humanitarian goals of the Russian Revolution. The hand of friendship would be extended between the Soviet and American peoples, and the threat of nuclear war would be eliminated. Socialist democracy would open up a new epoch for humanity.

#### How Can These Goals Be Achieved?

The majority can win its rights only by its own independent action. *Rallies* demanding jobs for all; *strikes* for higher wages and cost-of-living clauses; *demonstrations* against new war threats, against cutbacks in education and social services, and for the rights of women; a *boycott* of scab lettuce, grapes, and wine; *marches* against racist attacks on busing and school desegregation—these are examples of struggles now being waged.

But it doesn't make sense to strike, rally, demonstrate, boycott, or march against the deterioration of our rights and living standards on one day, and then vote for the two parties responsible for them on the next.

The colonists fighting British rule and the abolitionists fighting against slavery learned that they could have no faith in the goodwill of colonial governors or the slave-owners' parties.

They formed their own organizations, including committees of correspondence, continental congresses, and Black conventions.

Likewise today, working people cannot rely on the Democratic and Republican parties, which are financed and controlled by big business to defend its profits. We must break from them.

The Socialist Workers Party believes that the only way to effectively organize the power of American working people on the scale necessary to abolish the present government of big business, and initiate a workers' government, is through a mass socialist party. This will not be anything like the Democratic and Republican parties; it will be a fighting party that will help lead the struggles of working people and all the oppressed. This is what the Socialist Workers Party is campaigning

for and what it intends to become.

The first big step toward a working class break from the two parties of big business would be the formation of an independent *labor party* based on the power of the unions. Workers running as independent labor candidates on a local scale can help set an example and point the way to a nationwide party of labor. Such a party would organize union power into a new social movement to fight for the rights of *all* the oppressed. It would lead the way toward a mass socialist movement that can start building a new social system.

The Socialist Workers Party is campaigning for a new society—a socialist society—where industry and science will be put at the service of the vast majority; where wars, racism, sexual oppression, and all other forms of human degradation and exploitation will no longer exist. We believe that this is a realistic goal, and a necessary one if humanity is to survive.

Join us in this struggle.

### U.S. Labor Platform 1976

#### A New Kind of World Leadership for the USA

The United States of America is its people—the largest concentration of skilled workers, productive farmers, and scientists in any region of the world. Although most of our productive capacity has been slipping into obsolescence for most of the past 30 years, although our most productive factories are now being emptied by the depression, our agriculture is under financial attack, our transportation network collapsing, large food surpluses rotting in storage, our cities sinking into physical and social blight, and our shrinking ratio of scientists largely denied meaningful undertakings and facilities, nevertheless our people's *potential* for technological advancements of a rapidly expanding industrial capacity remains rightfully the awe of the rest of the earth.

At this moment we have entered into the collapse phase of the worst depression in all recorded history. Already, direct comparison of current monetary instabilities and rates of collapse with corresponding periods of the 1929–1933 Great Depression proves that the present capitalists' world depression is at least several times worse than that of the 1930s. When we look deeper, we discover that the rates of mass starvation and development of new diseases in the most depressed regions (such as the Indian subcontinent, Brazil, Great Britain) is rapidly producing the preconditions for an inevitable worldwide pandemic more devastating than the Black Death. Without massive, quick recovery from the present depression, the initial wave of worldwide killer plagues will hit all parts of the world by approximately 1980. Following that, viruses, bacteria, fungi, and insects will cannibalize the earth's biosphere, possibly rendering the human race itself virtually extinct within about 15 years or less from the present time.

Never before in recorded history has mankind faced so awful and urgent a decision as the people of these United States, in particular, must confront during the 1976 presidential election campaign period. Your choice will decide, in large part, whether or not you and your children survive into the 1980s, and whether there is any future human existence at all beyond a decade or so to come.

There is no objective reason that this present capitalists' world depression must continue even throughout 1976. With extremely practicable measures, the depression collapse-spiral can be halted (for North America, Western Europe, Japan) within approximately any thirty days—provided you, the majority of the people of the U.S., could force your elected representatives to promptly enact the legislative proposals which the Labor Party has already placed upon their desks.

Contrary to the myths of "limits to growth," a fraud created and circulated by the Rockefeller brothers and their lackeys, there are no objective "ecological" or other outer boundaries preventing an immediate and sustained rapid expansion of industralized development of the globe.

Technologically, mankind is already at the doorstep of an entire new technology known as Controlled Thermonuclear Reactions (CTR). Provided we are determined to bring that result about, by the middle of the 1980s we can see CTR plants proliferating around the world, providing energy resources sufficient for several millions of years at present rates of world energy consumption. The same CTR technology makes ordinary rock and sand economically practicable sources of minerals.

The only real "limits to growth" are the Rockefeller faction's policy of aggravated world misery, on the one hand, and a general gutless reluctance —to date—by the victims of Rockefeller's policies to take power out of the hands of that faction and its lackeys.

## Our Global Policies

Despite all the present misery and political obstacles, we can not only end the present capitalists' world depression, but break through into worldwide economic and social development on a scale generally believed unattainable up to this time. This success depends upon initial agreement among especially the U.S.A., the Comecon sector (Soviet bloc economies), and key forces of the Third World on three basic points of policy as elaborated in the International Development Bank (IDB) proposal.

1. A commitment to define the coming decade (1976–1985) as committed to the realization of operational CTR technology by the middle of the 1980s.

2. A ten-year commitment to accelerate the development of industrially advanced foci in both the developed and developing regions, to lay the basis for completing the transformation of the world to a generally advanced level in all principal parts during the 1985–1990 period.

3. A immediate priority emphasis on developing agricultural production to levels of not less than 3,500 calories and 250 grams of usable protein per day per capita low-cost consumption for a population in the order of 4 billion persons. This must be the general application of industrially produced means of agricultural production (tractors, implements, drainage and irrigation, desalinization, fertilizers, adequate inventories of alternate genetic strains of seed-stocks) to increase the per hectare output and decrease the labor per hectare for all existing agricultural areas currently in production. This raising of the level of agricultural output and productivity in all areas must be complemented by major development programs for three of the richest food-growing areas of the developing sector: the region of the Rio de la Plata in Latin America, the Sahel in Africa, and the Ganges-Brahmaputra region of the Indian subcontinent.

An agreement to these fundamental policies by the three major groups of political forces cited would ensure enthusiastic support of the same policies by the overwhelming majority of the earth's population.

More important, any effort to find a solution in alternative policies must fail. The reasons are absolutely scientific, not issues of taste or mere opinion.

First, the possibility of continued human existence depends upon accelerating the rate of useful energy consumption per capita in all forms of production and by households. Any program which attempts to stop the rate of increase of useful energy consumption or, worse, to reduce per capita energy throughputs, is pushing the human race in the direction of ecological holocaust and virtual extinction of our species. The party which does not propose massive commitments to the development of CTR technology is at best a gaggle of useless fools.

Second, the primary basis for human development and even human existence as such has been and will always remain the application of new technologies for increasing the amount of human nutrition per hectare and per hour of agricultural labor. By using industrial technology to reduce the percentage of all human productive activity required to meet the nutritional needs of the entire population, the social cost of food per capita is reduced. This makes possible the further development and expansion of industry (which in turn makes possible further developments of agriculture), the enlargement of the proportion of the population engaged in the development of science, and the increase in per capita leisure—leisure which enables a population to assimilate and further develop technological advances.

Finally, without a massive expansion of industrial development throughout the world, we could neither sustain the development of food production nor implement the transition to the new world of CTR technology.

That three-point global program for 1976–1985 is the foundation of the U.S. Labor Party's domestic 1976 electoral campaign. Our U.S. domestic program summarized in the Emergency Employment Act of 1976 (EEA), is designed to effect immediate recovery from the depression in the North American sector through mobilization of this region's productive potential to perform its proper role of leadership in the development of the world.

It would be childish to imagine that "purely domestic" solutions exist. Schactian measures such as the Humphrey-Hawkins bill and "Project Independence" are a combination of reckless incom-petence and nationalist-demagogic windbaggery. The U.S. sector *inescapably* depends upon the world market for approximately half its primary and related resources. To obtain these necessary resources the U.S. must export categories of capital goods and consumer commodities which are actually desired and needed by other countries. In large part, this export-import relationship is three-way; the U.S. must not only export to the Third World, but must pay for part of its Third World imports indirectly by exports to Western Europe, Japan, and the Comecon sector.

*Why the Depression?*

The immediate triggering cause of all depressions, including this one, is a massive build-up of the ratio of accumulated governmental, corporate and private debt in contrast to the current value of useful production. In order to understand the practicable measures for halting a depression, it is essential to begin with the ABCs of the debt-equity problem.

The continued existence of the human species over the past 50,000 years has depended upon the successful evolutionary development of those forms of society which were able to sustain the useful production and consumption of a "social surplus" in excess of the costs of simply maintaining existing extents of production. In economic theory since the Physiocrats, this margin of social surplus is sometimes termed an *absolute profit*, which is simply the margin of absolute increase in the amount of total useful wealth of a society resulting from production.

Immediately, this social surplus is the essential basis for even simple increases in the society's population. In the longer run, social surplus performs an even more essential task for continued human existence by providing the material basis for development of groups of persons performing the functions broadly classifiable as science and for the development of new essential categories of productive activity.

The successful development of capitalist society has been based on its approach to two essential aspects of the realization of social surplus. First, the aggregate profits of the capitalists are made possible by the existence of social surplus in the form of absolute profit. The continuation of those profits depends upon the capitalists' investment of a major part of the social surplus in expanded forms of production. Second, the possibility of sustaining the profitability and successful existence of the capitalist economy has depended upon the constant introduction of more advanced forms of technology.

The political freedoms which prosperous capitalist economies have enjoyed, relative to earlier non-capitalist modes of existence, is directly premised on the essential connection between the organic development of new political and technological conceptions within the population and the successful continuation of capitalist investment through innovation.

So far as these aspects of capitalist society are concerned—production of social surplus, technological development, fostering free scientific inquiry in the development and propagation of political and scientific conceptions, and so forth— there is not only no fault with the principles of capitalist development, but these same principles must be enhanced in future forms of society.

All the essential failures of capitalism in general are connected to three of its other features. Depressions and the political horrors—such as wars —which otherwise recurringly afflict the capitalist sector are all directly products of these three faults.

The principal common root of these problems is the effect of technological advancement upon the current value of capital stocks carried over from earlier periods. Since all successful technological development has the effect of making all production more efficient in terms of required labor-content, the effect of technological advances is to reduce the current real value of carried-over capital stocks. This devaluation of "dead capital" ought to represent no problem to the economy, but for the fact that the current value of those carried-forward stocks is a large part of the total investment owned by the capitalists.

As technology makes industry increasingly capital-intensive, the ratio of plant, machinery, equipment, and so forth to current production increases. As a result of this increasing capital-intensity, the more capitalism advances the more serious becomes the technologically caused devaluation of "dead capital" within the capitalists' investment portfolios. So, the successful advancement of capitalist economy through technological development causes a *tendency* for the rate of profit to decline on combined current and "dead" book-values of capitalists' total investments.

Actually, no such simple statistical tendency for

declining profits appears on the surface. Rather, the effect of credit-monetary expansion is to cause a combined general inflation and growth of debt ratios, which conceals the underlying problem up to the point of a new depression.

A brief further explanation is needed.

Foolish babblers, some of whom are highly respected college professors of economics, argue that capitalism has an inherent "buy-back" problem. Since the existence of profit means that the total price of output is greater than the price paid for used-up labor materials, and so forth, they emphasize that the money put into circulation as payments for wages, materials, and so forth, is obviously less than the amount of money needed to "buy back" the total production. Their reasoning is nonsensical.

The capitalist system "sells" the margin of production corresponding to profit by creating credit for the sale of that margin. Provided values are not inflated, and provided that the commodities for which credit is issued are invested as either wages or physical means of production, the resulting profitable production increase covers the debt and debt-service caused by the issuance of credit. Any individual who does not understand that point does not have the competence to meddle in economic affairs.

However, the capitalist credit-monetary system (or "market") does not plan and authorize expansion of the money-supply explicitly in that form. Instead, capitalist governments and financial institutions issue credit against the current market price structure. Since modern capitalist corporations, the dominant sector of the market, price their commodities on the basis of competitive rates of return on total book-value of combined current and dead-capital investments, any amount of credit sufficient to maintain "full employment" levels necessarily includes a built-in inflationary factor.

This margin of inflation is properly called either *relative surplus value* or *fictitious value*. This means that, in terms of the current ratios of social-reproductive efficiency applicable to real production, the margin of profit corresponding to relative surplus value or fictitious values does not represent real values of wage-commodities or capital goods which can be invested for profitable expansion of production in general. Consequently, this margin of fictitious value generates a kind of "buy-back problem" within financial markets as such. What follows is the accumulation of this margin of ultimately illiquid credit in the form of a growing permanent debt.

The growth of illiquid debt accumulations is aggravated by pure speculation (e.g., stock market, real estate, etc.), and also by the tendency of the debt to grow geometrically on account of debt-service ratios (interest, etc.).

This process leads to a new depression—such as the present one—in the following way. Since debt-turnover and debt-service payments ordinarily have first claim on income and loans in a capitalist economy, and since the mass of debt-service required is growing in comparison to the mass of realizable profit from current production, the creation of credit for circulation of the profitable margin of commodities must first absorb the demands of debt-turnover and debt-service over and above current production. This generates an accelerating tendency for monetary inflation in the prices of all commodities.

As the inflationary effects of credit-expansion become aggravated, the inflation itself causes rises in interest rates and also causes a decrease in the amount of investment-credit issued for development of production. Since production requires investments with a life in the range of three to ten years, the inflation-caused shift from long-term and intermediate-term investment loans into high-interest short-term loans merely feeds speculation at the expense of production, and the combined effects of higher interest rates and speculation result in a tendency for galloping inflation under conditions of stagnation or even significant decline in levels of productive employment.

Consequently—as history demonstrates—every major depression is immediately preceded by a succession of inflationary outbreaks.

As this process of deterioration of the monetary system continues, the point is reached at which the continuation of sufficient credit-expansion for maintaining existing levels of productive employment must cause an outbreak of hyperinflation (like that of 1919–1923 Germany). At that point, either the capitalists cut back credit expansion, causing the spiralling collapse which the layman associates with depression, or continued credit-expansion sets off a hyperinflation which absolutely destroys both productive levels and financial markets generally.

*At that point—the present situation—there is only one course of action which can effectively halt the depression: a massive moratorium on debt-service payments.* Under conditions such as the present, it is impossible to force credit expansion into useful production unless we cut off the major portion of debt-service payments demands.

The major problem caused by broad debt moratoria is the threatened collapse of the banking system whose assets are tied up with that debt. This danger is to be eliminated in two ways.

First, we must prevent the collapse of the banking system (as an administrative agency for the orderly circulation of credit and money) by nationalizing any essential banks threatened with collapse.

Second, we must issue government credits and grants in the order required to restore full production levels. At the present moment, the probable total amount of such special supplementary central government credits and grants must be between $200 and $250 billion annually.

The three points to be underscored from the EEA are the heart of the Labor Party's domestic recovery program for the U.S. sector.

1. A general debt moratorium for a period of not less than 18 months, covering carried-forward debts of agriculture, state and local governments, public authorities, key public utilities needing such assistance, production facilities essential to national production threatened with debt-caused liquidation, carried-forward real estate debt, and carried-forward personal indebtedness of unemployed persons.

2. An emergency nationalization mechanism for ensuring the integrity of functioning of the banking system as an administrative agency of credit and monetary circulation.

3. A series of government-credit-supported production-development programs amounting to an estimated $200–250 billions per year to mobilize full-scale production around a focus on priority needs of global and national economic development.

### Labor Party versus Wall Street

Given these basic facts, there is no mystery as to the cause of the vicious incompetence of the Rockefeller-Ford regime, or the foolish babbling of windbags like Senator Hubert Humphrey.

No anti-depression program can succeed unless it is based on major debt moratoria of approximately eighteen months duration. However, the Rockefeller and allied Atlanticist financier interests base their financial power principally upon the same massive debt-service claims for which payment must be suspended! Not only do the Rockefeller interests viciously resist all of the urgent efforts to institute debt moratoria, but worse, they propose programs to satisfy the demands of their cancerous debt holdings at the expense of the material preconditions of life of the majority of the world's population.

Contrary to widespread consoling illusions, Wall Street interests efficiently control the dominant forces of both the Republican and Democratic parties. Senator Henry Jackson (D.-Wash.), New York's Democratic Governor Hugh Carey, and Senator Hubert H. Humphrey (D.-Minn.) are as much Wall Street puppets as the pathetic President Ford or Senator Jake Javits (R.-N.Y.).

Worse, the majority of the top trade-union leadership and the bulk of the so-called liberal organizations in the U.S. are also Rockefeller-Harriman hirelings, openly or otherwise.

The Rockefellers' machine has effectively dominated the U.S. and NATO "national security" apparatus (which includes the CIA) throughout the post-war period. In turn, the leadership of the AFL-CIO has been an overt branch of the CIA throughout the world during the same period.

This has also been the role of the majority of top Social Democratic political and trade-union figures throughout Latin America, Western Europe, and so forth. A major portion of the "liberal" strata has been effectively mobilized around Rockefeller-controlled academic and other "intellectual figures" through the financier cabal's political control of major campuses and major national newspaper and radio-TV news media as psychological warfare facilities.

Although there are sometimes embittered secondary factional differences among these forces, those machines have been conditioned to fight out such merely secondary and tertiary issues within the limits of what the Rockefeller-dominated international cabal of economic and political forces will tolerate.

For these reasons, the top machinery of the Republican Party, the Democratic Party, and the major trade unions' top bureaucracies is constitutionally incapable of developing or tolerating effective anti-depression measures. Worse, the stronger the social pressures of mass unemployment become, the more vigorously the "liberal" wing of the bankers' camp will campaign for demagogic "full employment" reforms essentially modeled on those instituted by Adolf Hitler during the 1933–1936 period. The attempt to find band-aid reforms within terms acceptable to Wall Street interests leads directly and inevitably to nothing but fascism—as Woodcock and a number of other trade-union officials have already publicly demonstrated.

We do not discount the important positive contributions of secondary leaders within the Democratic and Republican parties. In the midst of all the morally imbecilic scoundrels who dominate those parties, there are also men and women who under conditions of crisis will act upon their conscience as members of the human species, courageously adhering to that despite criminal forms of harassment by Rockefeller's CIA, Law Enforcement Assistance Administration, FBI, and other hooligan forces. However, despite their individual courage and integrity, these persons cannot by themselves win a fight confined to the existing machine organizations of the Democratic and Republic parties. The effectiveness of those individuals depends upon the growth of a massive new workers' and farmers' political machine outside either of those two parties.

Consequently, in that sense there is no organized political force but the U.S. Labor Party presently capable of representing the fundamental interests of humanity in these United States.

The Labor Party's immediate source of political strength, the immediate basis for its present rapid growth as a national political force, is the absolute necessity for its existence. The worker, farmer, scientist has no other meaningful political alternative.

We represent the only force which competently understands the present world and national situation, the only force able to assemble the workers, farmers, and scientists of this nation around an effective program at this juncture.

*The Labor Party Campaign*

The program of the U.S. Labor Party is neither "pie-in-the-sky" nor a set of policies we are committed to carry out "if" and "when" we are elected. The form and essence of this presidential campaign throughout 1976 will be a struggle on many fronts to get as much of our program instituted—both here and abroad—as is conceivably possible long before the November 1976 elections.

For example:

*Debt Moratoria.* Debt moratoria for agriculture are already urgently needed during the Spring of 1975. Such moratoria, combined with the credits designated in the Labor Party's Emergency Employment Act, are needed now—not waiting until early 1977!—to prevent a broad collapse of sectors of agricultural production and to stabilize agricultural net incomes pending direct measures for effectively dealing with longer-term issues of agricultural prices.

Debt moratoria are urgently needed by state and local governments throughout the U.S. to prevent an immediate collapse of essential services. Typified by New York City's reported $1.7 billion debt-service obligation, the institution of debt moratoria now—not waiting until 1977!—means that states and municipalities could at least maintain urgent services out of existing revenue programs.

Federal legislative action to override the "remedies" clauses in the bonded debts of public authorities is urgently needed to ensure the success of debt moratoria in guaranteeing the maintenance of public transportation, health, and other essential programs affected.

The same point applies to our national transportation system. Debt claims against collapsing rail services must be effectively suspended, and credit issued for development of roadbed and equipment must not be drained away into the debt-claims sinkhole. This can not wait until 1977 —except at massive social cost to the nation.

*Agricultural development.* Without immediate action to fund agricultural production and to generate worldwide agricultural development, tens of millions of persons will die of starvation and its side effects during 1976, and the infrastructure of both U.S. and world agriculture will be seriously damaged for an extended period to come.

Either we fund tractor and related forms of urgently needed industrial output, or our opponents will employ unemployed workers at forced-labor incomes in "leaf-raking" and related fascist-welfarist labor-intensive wasteful "projects." The solution must not wait until early 1977.

SCIENCE POLICY

An effective "brute force" CTR development program requires that we confront a too-long-postponed need for a competent guiding social policy concerning broad fostering of the creative scientific development so visibly essential to the successful continuation of human existence.

The problems of comprehensive mastery of an efficiently confined plasma undergoing controlled thermonuclear fusion bring experimental inquiry to the boundaries of unresolved fundamental problems of mathematical physics in particular. Contrary to the commonplace mistaken view of the layman and undergraduate student, modern physics has in no sense produced a competent overview of the essential nature of the physical universe. Today's significant work in plasma physics research, in particular, represents very much a frontier on which working scientists and their theoretical-mathematical collaborators are compelled to confront afresh fundamental, unresolved problems which have plagued scientific knowledge for more than a century without real solutions.

*CTR in Particular*

The layman might mistakenly believe that the proper cheaper approach to CTR development would be to limit expenditures to development of several basic models of devices which appear to have proven their probable feasibility. We know that *in the long run* some form of magnetic confinement of a plasma will succeed: in part, our "brute force" effort must explore a large spectrum of known and yet-to-be proposed approaches to exploring that potentiality. We also know that we should be able to shortcut certain important problems by employing laser technology as an aid to effecting microexplosions in inertially confined "charges" within the tolerances of very small charges and billionths of a second. Finally, to some experts the fact that the "hydrogen bomb" has been proven experimentally hints at the feasibility of a controlled combined fusion-fission reaction—and the feasibility of safely disposing of the radioactive fission by-products. These and other apparent mainline approaches must be intensively explored, but none of them might be expected to succeed in due time unless such mainline experiments were broadly complemented by intensive research into the broadest related topics of both experimental work and accompanying fundamental mathematical-physical inquiries.

Our policy problem in this connection can be most simply described by emphasizing that each step forward in aid of ostensibly main-line development efforts intersects special problems which require experimental investigation in their own right. These problems must then be solved as a precondition to further progress of main-line investigations. The "practical" bureaucrat might respond to this by proposing that each such problem be funded for investigation "as it comes up" serially in the progress of main-line investigations. With such a bureaucrat's misguided "budgetary allocation" approach, *a successful result which ought to require only a few years might be postponed for decades.*

The Labor Party's policy is to launch a broad assault on all the main lines of problems affecting plasma physics knowledge, in particular, and to also push parallel investigations in numerous relevant specialist fields of applications typified by metallurgy. Using this approach, we ensure that most of the problems arising in the course of main-line experimental investigations will either have been solved or at least half-solved at the point that they appear as obstacles to further progress along the main lines. The relevant accomplishment effected in this way is that we shall not have solutions or semi-solutions to such problems being developed in parallel to main lines of investigation, but, equally important, we shall have available teams of specialists who have already developed competence to attack the special tasks reflected by each such developmental problem.

What the usually misinformed layman and government bureaucrat has obviously failed to understand so far is that the effective progress of science as such cannot be attained by small groups of "individual geniuses" working in isolation "under tight national security wraps." Historically, the progress of basic scientific accomplishment has depended upon a broad cooperative division of mental efforts among pioneering investigators. By contrast with that reality, the conceits of the misinformed layman and bureaucrat belong to the same category of foolishness as the pathetic attempt to adduce an economic theory from a Robinson Crusoe model of an island "economy" of one person. The advancement of industry and science over the past century and a half has been accompanied by an increase in the numbers of specialized inquiries each cooperatively essential to producing the completed joint product.

Limiting our attention for the moment to only that basic practical fact of scientific work, it should be apparent that the competent way to deliberately accomplish any major push forward in practicable forms of scientific knowledge is to push the entirety of scientific investigations forward in parallel, developing every fruitful line of new investigations which suggests even indirect relevance to the principal objectives being sought.

As we undertake this "brute force" CTR development effort, we must be efficiently aware of two classes of problems inherited from the past. The first involves the appropriate social circumstances for the world's community of scientists. The second involves the unresolved fundamental theoretical problems which now leer back at the physicist from the plasmas he investigates.

### The Sociology of Science

The theoretical and empirical study of the progress of European society since the last half of the 15th century demonstrates most emphatically that the continuation of human existence depends upon a secular tendency for increasing the proportion of the total population engaged in basic scientific discovery and occupied also in its introductory forms of practicable application to human practice in general.

From this standpoint, the reputation which science has gained for its achievements of the past half-century are misleading and overconfidently exaggerated. Although the specific accomplishments of recent decades' work are quite real and generally essential to human life on earth today, contemporary science is based on the working out of fundamental discoveries which were completed in essence by approximately the end of the 1920s. Although contemporary scientists frequently verge on areas of investigation in which qualitative breakthroughs in knowledge might potentially develop, there has been a combined lack of sufficient total commitment by society and an associated profound and deepening intellectual demoralization among most scientists themselves. The indispensable passionate intellectual commitment and material means of fundamental scientific progress have been generally aborted by the successive blows of the First World War, the Great Depression, and the widespread loss of intellectual integrity imposed upon the majority of scientists by the "national security" bureaucratization of the "Cold War" period.

The impressive progress that has been made in fact, despite those hideous circumstances, demonstrates the magnificent potentialities embodied in the fundamental contributions of Planck, Einstein, Minkowski, and their leading contemporaries.

## Historical Background For Policy

The summary history of scientific progress since the French Revolution ought to be common knowledge of working people today, as background for their adoption of appropriate policies of scientific development for today's needs.

The great achievements of the period from 1800 to approximately 1930 were principally the accomplishment of leading thinkers and investigators in industrially-developing Europe, a community of thinkers for which Germany increasingly represented the center of intellectual progress. The underlying and guiding central features of this century of achievement were the philosophical impact of the work of Immanuel Kant and G. W. F. Hegel upon leading mathematicians and others, and the practical impetus given thermodynamics by the development of powered machinery and uses of electricity.

The nature of the problems newly raised for scientific development by thermodynamics was first influentially exposed by Fourier. On closer investigation of Fourier's attempts to solve comprehensively the more advanced classes of mathematical problems which thermodynamics posed, it was recognized increasingly that the classical axiomatic systems of Newton, Euler, Lagrange, et al. were inadequate and might even have to be substantially overthrown.

The grandfather of the successful formal-mathematical attacks on this problem was the contradictory figure of the great German mathematician Gauss. Gauss' student and protege, Riemann, notably in parallel with Weierstrass and with subsequent fundamental contributions from Cantor, made possible the most essential features of modern mathematical rigor. The leading achievements of Planck, Einstein, Minkowski, and their European peers are principally the direct outgrowth of the Weierstrass-Riemann-Cantor "thermodynamical revolution" in the conception of theoretical functions representing physical processes.

With the close of the First World War, this massive flow of fundamental scientific progress was reduced to a relative trickle by the systematic destruction of the European scientific centers most vividly seen in Germany—to the point that during the 1930s only a small portion of the central European scientists displaced could be saved through the limited alternative appointments available in Great Britain, the U.S., and France. With the Great Depression, irreparable damage was done to the continuity of development of the community of scientific workers—from which disaster science in general has never fully recovered. More recently, especially during the latter portion of the 1960s, science has been in massive retreat, in North America and Western Europe, both financially and morally.

The growing preeminence of German science in the 19th century was neither genetic, linguistic, nor accidental in nature.

Germany had begun to enter the modern industrial world only after the Napoleonic wars. Consequently, its science confronted the task of rendering the preceding accomplishments of relatively advanced England and France into a systematic form suitable for the rapid cultural development of professional and industrial strata in Germany itself.

This was reflected in the qualitative superiority of German philosophy over both its French and especially its British peers. Germany, struggling to conceptualize scientific knowledge, created its leading philosophy (Kant, Hegel) on the basis of the most advanced practice. This is in contrast to the English and French, whose underlying philosophical outlook had been more or less shackled to the form it had developed at an earlier, cruder level of emerging cultural development.

Similarly, the development of German industry began at the level of the most advanced industrial technology of the nations from which it initially borrowed, such that the key industrial heartlands industries of Germany were soon more advanced on the average than those of Britain and France. This fact confronted German industry with a more advanced starting point for further technological developments. Therefore the progress of the relatively most advanced science was a more urgently practical question for German capitalists than for their British and French counterparts, who were hampered by the emphasis on the need to bring obsolescent capacities up to already established standards of modernity.

## The U.S. Case

The industrial development of the U.S.A. and Japan follow the German model more closely than the British or French. The enormous industrial complexes built through foreign investment in Czarist Russia are illustrations of the same principle. In the history of generally rising capitalist development, up through the First World War, the advanced capitalist nations which were the latest to undergo full development as world powers developed relatively more massive and more advanced forms of industry on the whole than those older capitalist nations mired in the heritage of by then obsolescent earlier developments.

The United States' development seems to violate the science aspect of the model shown by 19th century Germany. The U.S. broadly relied upon importing its intellectual culture, and evolved a predominantly Anglotropic eclectic porridge of various cultural elements, rather than developing—like Germany—an original intellectual culture of its own. Up to the present time, the U.S. has failed to become a cultural center of original *fundamental* contributions to human thought—a failure which the Labor Party campaign is directed in part to correcting.

The chief element of potential greatness in U.S. culture has been the half-conscious organic attitude sometimes known as the "frontier outlook." The essential dynamic of the U.S.A. from before its independent existence was the practice of combining the immigrants and culture of (especially) Europe, combining these constituents into a social force that mastered the U.S. frontier in waves of industrial progress following close upon agricultural pioneering settlements. The relative political freedom essential to this frontier orientation persisted (despite our characteristic American propensity for violence) until the gates of Ellis Island were slammed down in the early 1920s, and the upraised arm of the Statue of Liberty came to signal "Stop," rather than lighting the welcoming doorway.

Although the U.S. has heretofore produced no great centers of profound and original intellectual fruitfulness, in our nation's use of European culture the orientation toward progress along the physical frontiers was cross-infected with an increasingly predominant emphasis on technological progress, and fruitful reformist innovations in accompanying social-political forms.

Although the U.S. has historically failed to produce groups of great thinkers of world-historical importance, in the sense that England, France, and Germany have before us, the American belief in the idea of progress developed a vigorous, broadly based moral strength among our people on the basis of our eclectic skills in transforming European science into American technological innovations of large-scale applicability and practical excellence.

The worldwide crisis in science today can be usefully described as caused chiefly by the failure of the hegemonic U.S. to assume the main burdens of continued fundamental scientific progress at the point that the economic basis of European scientific leadership had collapsed. Nineteenth century American pragmatism is a vastly superior culture to modern British pragmatism. Traditional "frontier" U.S. pragmatism is the empiricism of solving problems through progressive change, as opposed to the comparative emphasis on tradition and obsolescence which has come to permeate the stagnating British culture. However, no profound scientific achievements can broadly flourish in a moral climate dominated by *any* form of pragmatism.

## The Strict Proof

The rigorous proof of this understanding of the sociology of scientific development is supplied by the elementary facts of economic science.

The social-reproductive ratio which characterizes capitalist progress, $S'/(C+V)$, is at bottom a ratio of man's total useful output of combined industrial, extractive, and agricultural production to those social categories of human activity which are essential to continuing and developing the productive forces through which human needs are satisfied.

These essential social constituents are properly reduced to four basic categories, as follows. The first cost, V, is the proportion of total output necessary for the consumption of the households which produce productive labor for industry, mining, agriculture. The second cost, C, is the amount that must be expended on improvements of nature, on plant machinery, equipment, materials and so forth to provide labor with the appropriate indispensable material preconditions for production. The third category, d, is represented by various administrative, scientific, engineering, and similar activities which must be sustained. The fourth, S, is the net social surplus, the margin of total output on which society depends for both its expansion and qualitative development. S′ and d combined are gross social surplus, S.

The precondition for the development (and continued existence) of society is that both ratios, S/(C+V) and (S-d)/(C+V), must increase. This increase is the result of technological advances in the form of human productive activity as such, advances which depend upon first, absolute increases in the per capita energy throughput per worker in production, and second, increases in the material standards of living and leisure rates of households, the basis for potential advances in the cognitive powers of the population, i.e., the population's mental potential for assimilating more advanced technologies.

In the normal form of successful capitalist development, the social effects of increases in those ratios are the following. First, the proportion of the total population engaged in agriculture is reduced, thus cutting the effective social cost of nutrition, and increasing the proportion of the population available for employment in manufacturing and mining. Second, the absolute product per capita of industrial and mining labor increases through *capital intensive* forms of technological advances, and increasing division of labor, such that the standard of living and leisure rates of labor potentially rise. Third, the required rate of technological development and per capita energy consumption increases exponentially with respect to simple increases in the ratio S/C+V.

The necessary increases in technological advances and per capita net useful energy consumption define the need for diverting increasing portions of the population from industrial labor into science and engineering. As the proportion of both agricultural and industrial labor required from the total population decreases, a growing proportion of that "freed labor-time" must be absorbed in the expansion of the population of such professionals as engineers.

It is the growth in the relative mass and intensity of the creative mental efforts of those scientists and other professionals which provides society with its essential increased effective rates of technological progress and, in the course of that, successive qualitative advances in scientific knowledge.

This means that the ratio of scientists and engineers to total numbers of productive workers and farmers must grow at a slowly accelerating rate if the pace of scientific progress is to be sufficient to satisfy mankind's growing requirement for technological advance. Once the history of science over the period 1815–1975 is considered from this standpoint, our point concerning the past half-century's decay of scientific development becomes indisputably clear.

It is equally relevant to competent policy that a successful fostering of scientific professional progress cannot subsist in a general climate in which the philosophical world-outlook of working people generally is qualitatively at variance with the philosophical world-outlook essential to scientific work. The basis for recruiting large numbers of new scientists from the households of workers, and for the ability of the general population to assimilate the practicable accomplishments of scientific work, is the sharing of a common scientific world-outlook among scientists, engineers, workers, and farmers. Science, to be socially effective, cannot be maintained as a kind of priest-caste qualitatively apart from the mass of workers and farmers in world-outlook. Science—and scientists—must be chiefly developed as a growing technological vanguard of the advancing scientific world-outlook becoming commonplace among educated workers and farmers in general.

## The Advancement of Science

Despite the qualitative leaps exemplified by the notion of general relativity, contemporary science is crippled by the continued influence of the fundamental (reductionist-axiomatic) fallacies embedded in the heritage of, notably, Newton, Euler, and Lagrange. Although the rudimentary form of a solution to this difficulty was developed during the 19th century, chiefly by Riemann and Cantor, and although a handful of leading thinkers have recommended appropriate approaches to solution, the success of mathematical physics in particular is cruelly limited by the persistence of that flaw.

For reasons which are obvious after the fact, the key to solving this continuing crisis in science was not and could not be discovered in mathematical physics as such. The various steps which have led toward a solution developed out of early 20th century progress in biology, owing more to the influence of Pasteur than Newton and Gauss. However, although the holistic study of the biosphere begun during the 1920s points in the proper direction, the crucial empirical evidence needed to isolate the exact solution could only be adduced—as has been the case—from the study of the evolutionary progress of human societies. We shall briefly describe the evidence in the course of this section.

This fact is no mere academic issue. The point to be made bears directly on defining the most effective approach to organizing of broad scientific efforts for the urgent "brute force" development of CTR technology.

Although the formal solution to this problem has not yet been developed into the terms of a comprehensive new set of statements of the coherent laws of the physical universe, we presently know with certainty enough about the subject to draw the line, so to speak, between the new physics of the future and the practical accomplishments which are within the reach of the physics of the present. At the same time, we are able to isolate those kinds of experimental and related problems of contemporary theoretical and experimental work whose exploration will bring us up to the approximate limits of progress defined by the boundary line.

From that standpoint, we know that a complete solution to the problems encountered in plasma physics will require our crossing that boundary line. (Einstein emphasized the same point in somewhat different terms toward the end of his life.) This we are able to determine in advance from the standpoint of the epistemological form of the experimental-theoretical problems encountered. There are certain classes of problems which present-day physics cannot systematically comprehend, because of the embedded axiomatic principles governing mathematical statements. Wherever nature manifests behavior contrary to the embedded axiomatic assumptions of prevailing mathematical physics, we know—with absolute certainty—that we have reached an aspect of the boundary line.

The basic strategic policy for scientific development is therefore to select those numerous areas of experimental investigation which pertain to the gaps in knowledge between present knowledge and the this-side of the boundary line. The ultimate consequence of such a broad-based attack must be to isolate several crucial experiments which can then be directly attacked, both theoretically and experimentally, as the means of entry into the physics of the future. In the course of

launching such an approach, emphasizing the problems of plasma physics, we shall meanwhile most efficiently secure the specific knowledge and technique necessary to accomplish any form of technological progress which is feasible this side of the boundary line.

This is precisely the concept for the "brute force" development of CTR technology. Although the embedded axiomatic assumptions physics has inherited as unresolved flaws from the 19th century preclude a comprehensive mastery of "microphysical" processes, by a full spectrum of research efforts in the direction of the boundary line we are certain that we can push past the last short barriers met in our present close proximity to successful net-energy production from successful experimental models of controlled fusion. For the very immediate future, we are not expecting a comprehensive solution to all the potentialities of CTR; we are concentrating on isolating those special cases of CTR application which are within the epistemological competence of existing classes of mathematical physical skills.

There is no guesswork in any of this argument. There is crucial empirical proof of all of this, proof which brings us much, much closer to the corresponding practical results than the decisive neutron-emission experiments of the 1930s brought the possibility of the fission bomb.

There are two general points to be made in support of this policy: first, a summary of the basis on which the unique proof of the underlying discovery was finally resolved; second, where the implications of that discovery intersect the systematic problems of modern physics.

With the emergence of the biosphere, life as a whole has always been fundamentally characterized by a "reproductive function" analogous to the $S'/(C+V)$ of social reproduction. Since human existence is a dominant aspect and outgrowth of that biosphere, the analogy is not merely heuristic.

The life-process of the biosphere is not the sum of the reproductive and predicated functions of its constituent species, but the reverse; the fundamental location of the existence of all life in particular is in the biosphere. It is the biosphere as a whole which determines the essential "thermodynamics" on which the available energy of the included species is determined.

The characteristic feature of the biosphere is the capture of energy (ultimately taken chiefly from the cumulative net throughput of solar energy to the earth), energy which is converted into biological material (biomass) through the mediation of inorganic material and biological waste-material. This is to emphasize that the characteristic of living processes is not matter as such, but energy.

Of the total energy captured by the biosphere as added biomass, one part is consumed in maintaining the inorganic preconditions of life, another is consumed in maintaining the biomass of existing species, and a third part, "free energy" or S', is the margin of expansion and development of the biosphere.

In any state of its evolution, the biosphere has the same conditioning, limiting characteristics as a human society. The composite mode of biological reproduction represented by the biosphere as a whole represents both a certain potential for capturing energy (the most essential limitation) and for reducing inorganic material into forms suitable for conversion into biomass. The very characteristic expansion invariant of biomass therefore impels the biosphere's growth toward the relatively finite limit of rates of energy capture and net resources as defined by its current mode of reproduction. Hence, without evolutionary transformation of the biosphere to higher forms as a whole (e.g., the "invention" of chlorophyll), the biosphere would be turned into a self-destroying auto-cannibalistic mass by means of the very "free energy" characteristics which define life.

Consequently, we arrive at definite general laws for the science of ecology by three steps of successive approximation. In the first approximation, we measure the effective transformation of captured energy into simple increases in the caloric value of the biomass as a whole. In the second approximation, we measure the increase in the "free energy" ratio for the biosphere. Third, since the biosphere overcomes the apparent resource limits of its existence by increased "reducing" potential, the achievement of a gradual increase in the simple "free energy" ratios demands an underlying, determining tendency corresponding approximately to exponential tendencies for increase in the free energy ratio.

In this approach, we rigorously determine that evolution is not something which happens to living processes; evolution is the invariant quality of biological processes. It is generally accepted that this evidence of the "free energy" directedness of all living processes demonstrates absolutely that

living processes are characterized by "negative entropy" (or *negentropy*), and thus belie the axiomatically introduced conceit ("God's clock") that the physical (or, "inorganic") universe as a whole is governed by laws whose characteristic feature is entropy.

Over especially the past 10,000 years of human development, we have the most conclusive empirical demonstration of the concrete expression of negentropy in living forms. Using even crude "thermodynamic" models to describe the necessary conditions and actual basis for continued human existence, we isolate the cause for the technological and other inventions which have increased man's power to increase the reproduction of his species, both numerically and in individual quantity, in the creative innovations originally produced by the cognitive processes of individual minds. The application of these ideas to generalized social practice determines an increase in the effective negentropy of human existence as a whole.

In effect, the form of development of the biosphere seen as biological evolution among all lower species is not only replicated and superseded by human creative thought, but the rate of negentropy of the biosphere realized by human creative processes is vastly greater than that resulting from ordinary species-evolution.

Either we account for this creative quality as something intruding from outside the universe, or we are compelled to conclude that the biological processes associated with creative cognitive synthesis of new conceptions are negentropic. From more extended rigorous consideration of this and directly related points, provided we reject the mysticism of an *elan vital*, we have shown from the combined evidence of human social development and the development of the biosphere that the "inorganic substrate" of the existence of life is itself governed by "hylozoic" universal laws whose fundamental premises are negentropy rather than entropy.

Turning back from this conclusion to rigorously examine the internal features of mathematical physics in terms of the actual history of their elaboration we have been able to show that every feature of physics which seems to justify an entropy interpretation of the universe results from the imposition of arbitrary and fallacious axiomatic assumptions upon the interpretation of experimental evidence.

This discovery should have been obvious to all educated scientists beforehand. Sir Isaac Newton, as well as Leibniz, plainly recognized the obvious metaphysics he had introduced to science by the effort to explain physical evidence in terms of the arbitrary introduction of "field-particle" metaphysics as the fundamental assumptions of his mathematical schema. Newton and Leibniz explicitly emphasized that the insertion of this arbitrary metaphysical assumption was the direct cause for the interpretation of the universe as entropic ("God's clock," a universe which God must periodically wind up again).

During the middle of the 19th century, Riemann laid the basis for further work eliminating such fallacious assumptions from physics, by developing a conception of the physical universe in which the "properties" of space and time were not arbitrary ("Euclidean") schemas existing outside actual physical processes. As Minkowski emphasized in his famous lecture on the implications of special relativity (pointing toward general relativity in this way), this was what the crucial physical evidence demanded. However, Weyl and other of Einstein's leading collaborators produced a vulgarized interpretation of Riemann by accommodating one aspect of Riemann's contributions to the embedded ("Euclidean") axiomatic fallacies of affine systems.

Such leading evidence concerning the major fallacies of present-day mathematical physics suffices to demonstrate conclusively that the notions of physical processes associated with the idea of universal entropy are not the result of empirical evidence but of arbitrary metaphysical fallacies superimposed upon the way scientists have been trained to think systematically, to design experimental investigations, and so forth.

Consequently, the unique empirical evidence conclusively adduced from life and human development provides the rigorous basis for knowing that our universe is fundamentally characterized by negentropy, not entropy. We know, in particular, that the insertion of the adduced notions of negentropy into the fuller development of the Riemann approach to physics represents the basis for a new physics, which must be deliberately achieved as a major goal of science as such during the remainder of this century. The kinds of phenomena which define the boundary lines between this new physics and the present entropy-oriented physics are also susceptible of distinct enumeration from the standpoint of this knowledge in itself.

Although our policy is directly relevant to the most effective and rapid achievement of CTR technology, even if CTR energy sources were already in use the nature of the tasks before mankind would demand exactly the approach to scientific development we have advanced.

In the course of human development, the time has ended when mankind could exist in forms of society (such as capitalism) which depend upon large margins of looting (primitive accumulation) of the biosphere as a whole. To ensure the successful advancement of the conditions of life, it is essential that we move quickly to assume conscious policies of maintenance and development of the total biosphere. Hence, unless our basic conceptions of science are coherent with the characteristic laws of the biosphere as a whole, science would cease to be a reliable agency, and for that reason our scientific policies for maintaining the earth as man's "hot-house" garden would fail.

The problem of food production points this up. In addition to the significant potential for increasing per hectare yields of agricultural production in the industrially advanced sector, there are three major regions of the developing sector (the Rio de la Plata, the Sahel, and the Ganges region) which have a natural potential for development and maintenance as a source of vastly increased food supplies—to the extent that there need be no food shortage for any conceivable rate of potential increase of the earth's population well into the next century. This represents, together with undepleted mineral resources, the last undeveloped margin of human survival within the limits of achievement of the old kinds of science. The continued successful existence of the human species beyond our age demands that we move quickly and deliberately into a new physics, a physics which is competent to comprehend the kinds of negentropic principles expressed both by living processes generally and by the creative processes of human cognition.

## DOMESTIC ECONOMIC POLICY

The depression-collapse of the U.S. economy confronts us with two opposite basic facts. In capitalist monetary terms, the U.S. is hopelessly bankrupt; no band-aid reforms, such as New Deal type measures, could effect even a noticeable dent in the crisis and its resulting human misery. Yet, despite decades in which decay and obsolescence have been the net features of our productive capacities, the U.S. population and its industrial and agricultural capacities represent the most powerful apparatus for creating useful wealth existing in any nation of the world. To solve the present crisis, we have but to free the second, healthy feature of our economy from the burden of the diseased first feature.

The following immediate emergency measures are essential. Without these measures no solution is possible.

1. An immediate emergency debt moratorium of not less than eighteen months duration on major categories of carried-forward debt, excepting tax payments due to Federal, state, and local governments.

2. Emergency nationalization of banks, pension funds, and insurance companies to prevent the collapse of essential administrative mechanisms for circulation of credit and money.

3. The creation of central government credits and grants for programs of emergency world agricultural development (tractors, fertilizers, and so forth), housing and related construction, transportation development, and energy development.

## Debt Moratoria

Debt moratoria should cover the following principal categories of carried-foward indebtedness: state, local, and municipal debt; public authority debt; debt of all essential transportation and power facilities, including privately-owned transportation and utility systems; agricultural debt; real estate debt; "consumer debt" of unemployed persons, and pension and disability payment recipients. It should also include categories of corporate debt of manufacturing and mining institutions participating as "prime contractors" or vendors to such contractors for programs conducted under Federal credit and grants.

This measure is primarily intended to prevent new credits and grants issued from being diverted out of financing of useful production of net tangible wealth into debt-service and debt-retirement payments. This measure is indispensable to prevent credit issued from becoming the source of hyperinflation, and to prevent debt demands from shrinking the net credit available for productive investment to the infinitesimal proportions of the present depression-spiral. Except for those funds directly spent for essential social services, including various social security payments, U.S. credit and grants policy must be: "not a nickel except for research, development, and for useful production of increased net tangible wealth."

Specific Federal legislation is urgently needed to suspend "remedies" clauses of extant debt agreements and to forestall creditors' "relief action" through the courts. In the area of municipal debt, for example, this action should free on the order of $20 billion of local revenues for maintenance of essential services, minimizing the required municipal relief actions from the Federal government.

## Nationalization

The institution of debt moratoria means a suspension of major portions of payments otherwise due to banks and other financial institutions. This consequence of the moratoria represents no competent objection to such action, since a chain-reaction collapse of financial institutions must occur even if moratoria were not instituted. Nonetheless, the institution of debt moratoria must be accompanied by complementary actions essential to maintaining the integrity of the banking system as an administrative instrument for the circulation of credit and currency.

All banking institutions must be nationalized "for the duration of the depression crisis" through the administrative instrumentality of the Federal Reserve System.

The principal amount of all deposits and amounts due the banks shall be accounted as if the nationalization had not occurred, except that accounting procedures shall suspend debiting and crediting of interest and related payments to all accounts except as explicitly excepted by Act of Congress, for the duration of the emergency.

All deposits except those of governmental agencies shall be frozen except as provided by administrative procedures specified by Act of Congress. A fixed maximum amount of prior balances on deposit within banks shall be allowed to be withdrawn by each individual as identified by personal social security number, and withdrawals from commercial account deposits shall be limited to payroll disbursements, materials, machinery, supplies, and equipment purchases, rent, and tax disbursements.

All new deposits made after a stipulated effective date shall be free of these restrictions.

## Social Security Supplements

To prevent debt moratoria from causing significant social dislocation, all payments of identified categories of unemployment, pension, disability, and medical disbursements assistance payments shall be consolidated under the Social Security Administration. By Act of Congress unemployment compensation payments shall be set at an acceptable minimum wage rate per week, and pensions paid to individuals for reasons of age or disability, as well as welfare payments, shall be identical amounts. The Social Security account shall be reimbursed for such payments through charges against the relevant insurance companies and other financial organizations which have a payment liability to individuals on this account.

All health care assistance is to be promptly nationalized under the Social Security Administration for the duration of the emergency. To avoid cumbersome administrative procedures, the following provisions are to be made for this program. Who shall receive medical care and what type and quality of care shall be determined solely by licensed representatives of the medical professions with the consent of their patients. Hospital, clinic, radiological, and laboratory services shall not be billed to the account of individual patients; instead, the operating maintenance costs of these institutions shall be directly subsidized by the Federal government as a Social Security item in the form of direct aid to appropriate local governments. Physicians' services shall be paid at established rates. Other medical and paramedical services and analogous forms of health services, including prescribed care for aged and disabled persons, shall be compensated at prevailing rates or through subsidized institutions under the same program.

The essential characteristic of the emergency features of the Social Security program is that its standards and procedures must be simple. Provided the sums paid for unemployment and other direct payments programs are set at minima consistent with maintaining a modern standard of living, the need for elaborate (and enormously costly) clerical administrative bureauracies is eliminated. The aggregate cost of a small percentage of individual abuses is far less than the maintenance of costly bureaucracies which degrade both the general population and the bureaucrat.

For example, physicians are not going to irresponsibly flood hospitals and other scarce treatment facilities with patients, or dispense medical services wildly simply because they are being trusted to conduct their profession with a minimum of "red tape" and supervision.

It must not be overlooked that the process which brings the Labor Party into the government is inseparable from an accompanying moral renaissance among the majority of those citizens who organize themselves to that end. The election of such a government signals the establishment of a qualitatively new moral climate throughout the majority of the nation, constituting a moral force which will more effectively foster honest practices among our citizens than the most massive amount of clerical and other police measures. That new moral climate will prevent the extent of abuses which occur under present massive auditing and control procedures, and will provide efficient circumstances for isolating and remedying the small margin of stubborn cases of demoralized individuals who practice abuses despite that climate.

## Grants and Credits

The development program consists of two main parts. The first category is represented by authorized programs in which the government is the ultimate consumer (and purchaser) for the entire program. The "brute force" effort to develop CTR technology is exemplary of this first category of outright grants. The second category includes programs in which the government may be the final purchaser of some part of the product, but in which the intended major portion of the product will be consumed as means of production or consumer purchases. The Emergency Employment Act typifies this category of combined governmental credits and grants.

In the first category, the enacted program takes the form of disbursements out of the public revenues to the U.S. Treasury. In the second category, the government places the credit of the United States in support of production in a manner analogous to a bank's issuance of construction loans to builders constructing properties for ultimate sale to a public or private purchaser.

In this second case, the government authorizes the Federal Reserve System to discount letters of credit for the purpose of financing specified production. This provides the basis for central banking system loans to provide machinery, equipment, materials, supplies, and payrolls for that production. The sale of the completed product creates bills of exchange which relieve the credit issued for production, and money payment for ultimate sale liquidates the credit used to discount the bills of exchange. So, the government credit created is recycled for the continuation of production, recycling the money issued against the initial letter of credit back into the banking system which originally issued it and can now issue it again.

The primary problem to be controlled is the risk of a high ratio of disbursements for non-productive clerical and social services in respect to the total value of production of tangible net useful wealth. If the percentile of the national labor force productively employed in production of tangible goods is sufficiently high, there is absolutely no danger. At the highest present levels of skilled wage rates, we can readily maintain these incomes for all productively employed workers and farmers in manufacturing, extraction, transportation, construction, and agriculture, and still generate a fabulous gross national social surplus, provided the ratio of the labor force employed as operatives in such industries is sufficiently high. The danger would occur only if one or a combination of three categories of income disbursements for non-productive activities were high: first, a high ratio of sales, clerical and other administrative (non-productive) employment in government and industry; second, a high ratio of persons on social security incomes (N.B., unemployment) to productive operatives; third, a combination of both. The same danger exists in such forms of "WPA" concealed unemployment as "leaf-raking" types of "relief 'public works' employment" or other imitations of New Deal foolishness, or if a high ratio of military goods production is used as an anti-unemployment tactic.

Government purchases from categories of production will include primarily three categories of purchases: housing and domestic urban redevelopment—for which rental income will be pro-

grammed; overhaul of the transportation system; foreign development aid exports. Although such governmental expenditures will tend to have the same inflationary effects in the short run as high ratios of non-productive members of the labor force, the benefits of urban development and transportation to the social productivity of the entire economy will totally absorb those costs over the intermediate term of emergency development programs. Provided that the ratio of productive employment is high, the outlays for foreign development aid can be readily absorbed as part of the social surplus produced and will represent no problem to the internal economy or the stability of the reorganized monetary system.

## FOREIGN POLICY

The U.S. foreign policy of the Labor Party government is determined entirely by total commitment to open diplomacy on behalf of our three-point global development program as outlined in the IDB proposal.

To the extent that any state or group of states enters into cooperation with the U.S. sector for 1. "brute force" development of CTR and related technology, 2. massive application of industrial technology for substantial increases in the output and social productivity of world agriculture, 3. accelerated development of the industrialized sector and developing-sector urban foci as a means for generating a sufficiently enlarged mass of social surplus to meet world needs for development by the end of the 1975–1985 decade, the relations between the U.S. sector and those states are totally subsumed by the agencies of economic and scientific cooperation mutually created for such a three-fold common purpose.

There are only two seeming exceptions which require explanation within the context of that foreign policy: first, the persistence of two political forms of government and economy, socialist and capitalist; second, the possible brief persistence, in a minority of cases, of states whose ruling regimes have not renounced military policy and military-police forms of domestic government, and who may also be hysterically antagonistic to our policy.

## Debt Moratorium

Although the initiators of the U.S. Labor Party are socialists, personally committed to the establishment of a workers and farmers government in this nation, barring the intervention of reactionary forces to destroy the integrity of the democratic electoral process we confidently rely upon the judgment of the U.S. population concerning this nation's transition from capitalism to socialism at some point in the early future.

This policy is exemplified by our immediate programmatic measures for debt moratoria. We are certain that expropriative repudiation of the bulk of major debt is the most appropriate measure. Yet, we also know that such repudiation implies and requires nationalization of our major industries, and therefore an end to the capitalist form of economy (although numerous smaller privately-owned firms would persist). The compromise tactic, the debt moratoria, permits us to provide the U.S. population with the most urgent benefits of an actual debt repudiation, and yet gives that population time to consider and democratically resolve the more fundamental issue of capitalism versus socialism.

Our foreign policy must honor that same popular decision process wherever it is being undertaken by the population of other states.

The persistence of capitalist political-economic forms does represent an obstacle to unlimited economic cooperation with socialist states. These obstacles are partially soluble. What is required is the establishment of special trading banks whose function is to discount at nominal interest rates the letters of credit and bills of exchange created on account of international trade and related forms of economic cooperation between capitalist and socialist states. Since the cooperation for global development around the three-point program will cover the major portion of international trade among capitalist, socialist, and developing states and regional associations of states, the deposit of gold reserves to such a bank by the governments of the participating nations (of those who hold such gold) will provide an adequate basis for general liquidity of this trade against short-term imbalances.

## U.S. Military Policy

The issue of military policy is not a formal but a practical question. In fact—in practice—a strategically decisive number of states will enthusiastically accept the foreign policy we have presented, notably the Comecon group and the majority of states of the Asian subcontinent, as well as a de-

cisive margin of African states. This ensures the immediate possibility of a drastic reduction of military establishments, limiting military responsibilities to those of containment of anachronistic tyrannies.

The handful of anachronistic armed tyrannies which might briefly persist beyond the inauguration of a U.S. Labor Party government cannot survive for long. With the election of a Labor Party government, the principal backing of such unhappy regimes will be eliminated, and the populations of those states will not long tolerate such regimes—which will have been morally and economically undermined almost decisively by the mere fact of a new U.S. foreign policy.

The principal policy concerning the immediate use of reduced military establishments will be their redirection as an emergency logistical and engineering resource—analogous to a local community's firefighting force—utilizing the facilities and organization for their most obvious constructive employments. As we eliminate the further need for even residual military-type duties, we should complete the reorganization of those forces entirely as an emergency large-scale engineering task-force for those types of emergencies which require rapid mobilization and deployment of such forces.

## Initial Institutional Forms of Cooperation

Although we do not propose that the U.S. sector shall *dictate* to other nations on this account, we strongly suggest the following initial steps for organizing international cooperation. These are recommended because they conform to the general objective interests of the parties, and represent the needed starting-point from which alternative arrangements could be evolved. We especially recommend these measures as a way of emphasizing the importance of the problems directly addressed.

The need for regional organizations composed of groups of states is established by the fact that modern technology requires so extensive a division of productive labor that no nation represents a sufficiently large population to provide within its own borders even a significant number of the basic industries required. Although the entire world is essentially interdependent with respect to the economical satisfaction of the internal needs of each and every nation, there are meaningful distinctions of degrees of preponderant present and future interdependence which merit more intimate collaboration among groups of nations.

For example, the U.S.A., Canada, and Mexico represent the kernel of one such grouping of nations. The degree of expansion of U.S. and Canadian industrial and agricultural capacities and outputs will require significantly more employable productive labor than is available from those nations' present populations, even considering full absorption of the presently unemployed, marginally employed and mis-employed persons available. Mexico includes up to thirty million persons from households whose employable members cannot immediately be efficiently assimilated into modern forms of employment in that nation itself.

Consequently, the obvious rational approach to this core aspect of the North American development task is to develop adequate housing and essential social services (especially education) to assimilate up to 25 million Mexican members of households, as family units, for employment in the U.S. and Canada. By committing ourselves to upgrading this Mexican labor from unskilled to semi-skilled and skilled labor, and the education of the resident children of those households as future skilled labor, technicians, professionals, and scientists, we shall both increase the output of the North American sector as a whole (greater than if Mexico were left to "independent" national self-development), and create bilingual Spanish-speaking cadres for the accelerated development of Latin America.

Meanwhile, while employing a large segment of the Mexican population as resident households of the U.S. and Canada, we can more readily develop Mexico itself. By the chain-reaction effects of this on the Caribbean generally, we accelerate the progress of that entire region.

This regional arrangement requires, of course, the concurrence of the Mexican and Canadian people, but when the benefits of the arrangement are weighed against the poorer results of alternative approaches, one has little reason to doubt that we shall easily negotiate some form of agreement along these lines.

The proposed regional cooperation among the U.S., Canada, and Mexico meshes directly with the obvious case for one or two regional groupings for South America. There are three major existing launching-points for general development of South America. The richest such region is the Rio de la Plata sector (southern Brazil, Uruguay, northern Argentina), which is one of three major natural opportunities of the entire developing sector. Agriculture (especially grain and beef) industrial potential, and riparian opportunities combine to provide the greatest immediate basis for a leap in the gross and per capita output of South America as a whole. The second region, the northern cap, exemplified by Venezuela and Colombia, possesses considerable natural opportunities in the form of petroleum, vast stocks of coal, other minerals, and agricultural opportunities. The third is the Pacific Andes Spine region.

The obvious mesh with a North American regional grouping is underlined by the matter of language. The Western Hemisphere requires four principal languages—English, Spanish, French, and Portuguese. The problems of education and associated cultural development, of adaptability of industrial and professional cadres to new assignments, and associated problems of technology mean that by making North American regions bilingual in combinations of English, Spanish and French, and South America bilingual in Spanish and Portuguese with some use of English there, we can efficiently shift bodies of cadres trained in one area to development occurring in another, and efficiently solve problems of textbooks, industrial education and instructions, professional collaboration, and so forth.

The problems confronted are slightly different as we turn our attention to the Old World, Eurasia, and Africa.

The first case is the Comecon sector plus Yugoslavia, and then the special case of China. Next, we have the industrially developed nations of Europe, plus the Iberian penninsula, the Italian Mezzogiorno, Greece and Turkey. In the Middle East and North Africa we face the developing Arab nations, which—as an area—represent principally mineral resources to be traded off against agricultural and industrial development. Abutting these Arab nations, we have Iran, which, except for its Arab Gulf oil reserves, is essentially a ravaged Central Asian nation. We then have the special case of industrially developed Japan, and next the two crucial developing regions of the Asian subcontinent and the African states overlapping and adjoining the Sahel.

Toward the south of the nations of the Sahel strip we have a region with some mineral resources, bordered by South Africa.

Since the production of an abundance of low-cost, balanced nutrition is the essential basis for all development, we efficiently analyze the Old World in terms of three central regions of agricultural development: first, the Eurasian grain belt extending from Western Europe across the Soviet Union deep into Siberia; second, the vast potential of the subcontinent, centered upon the northern riparian region flowing into the Bay of Bengal; and third, the Sahel.

We must immediately realize the large gains in output and agricultural productivity most immediately accessible through concerted application of industrial technology to the Eurasian grain and meat belt, where the most rapid increase is made possible by the easier assimilation of modern technology by existing farm populations.

We must immediately begin a general development of the agricultural potential of the subcontinent. We must stop the destruction of the Sahel and begin reversing current trends, to begin to realize the vast potential of this region.

The organization of the needed program begs for the following steps of regional cooperation.

The industrially developed nations of Western Europe must adopt policies for the Iberian Peninsula, the Mezzogiorno, Greece and Turkey, analogous to the proposed U.S. policies toward Mexico, while basing general industrial development on intense cooperation with the Comecon sector and Yugoslavia. At the other extremity of the Comecon bloc, close cooperation between the Soviet Union and Japan is necessary.

This northern tier of states must then, as groups, cooperate with the developing sector through agreements reached jointly with the Arab and oil-short states.

Two general groupings of developing states are recommended for this purpose. First, an Eastern region centered on the Bay of Bengal, reaching to the Indochina states, cooperating with the Arab Gulf states in joint cooperation with Western Europe, the Comecon and Japan. This will provide the basis for cooperation with China, the Philippines, and Indonesia and for direct cooperation with Australia and New Zealand. Second, a Sahel-centered region, a center of direct cooperation with the North African Arab states and the black nations to the south.

The nation of Japan, which faces a serious future food shortage, has a special role to perform in the self-interest of its population, in heavy

development assistance for the creation of a large export capacity in the Bay of Bengal region.

With this general arrangement, the massive output potential of the North American region can be directed to key large-scale aspects of the intra-regional development programs of the Eurasian-African and South American groupings.

As the inevitable transition to workers' governments occurs in Western Europe, the ensuing emergence of a more rational division of labor in the industrially developed Eurasian northern tier will become a single "internal economy" with far greater capacity and output than would be possible if the division of labor were kept in its relatively narrowed present emphasis upon national and regional forms. This northern tier will develop increasing interdependence in the development of its division of labor with the developing regions of Asia and Africa, just as the closeness of economic interdependence between North and South America will increase with development.

Meanwhile, the two major northern tiers will be approaching a future closer economic integration, converging upon the point, during the 1985–1990 period, when the term "developing sector" begins to lose further significance for identifying any region of the earth.

*Foreign Economic Policy*

No one should imagine that we are proposing to crank up North American output simply to "give it away" to the developing sector. Nonetheless, since numerous persons especially most professional economists, are ignorant of the ABCs of competent economic theory, we may expect that the mistaken charge will be made often enough. On that account, we are obliged to be painstakingly clear concerning the scientific principles underlying our development export policy.

There are two interconnected false arguments frequently made against effective forms of development aid. The more general of these two complaints is that these nations could not conceivably "repay" substantial amounts of aid. The narrower is the observation that since labor is so cheap in certain of these nations, mechanization of agriculture and so forth can frequently not be "economically justified." The solution to both misconceived problems is found by correctly defining what we should be "buying" with such assistance.

There are three essential determinants of the

social productivity of a population. The first and most essential is the cultural development of that population itself. Second, to realize the productive potential of a population we must provide the material preconditions of modern productive technology, machinery and so forth. Third, the required energy consumption per capita for production and household consumption generally tends to increase at a "geometric" rate relative to the manifest rate of productive growth.

To bring the so-called developing sector up to the level of social productivity we require for continued general development of our globe, we have to introduce these three essential elements of development. It would be unreasonable—and even downright silly— to propose that the amount of development aid pumped in during one or two years could produce a significant exportable surplus product from developing nations generally. However, if the development program is properly designed and on a sufficiently large scale, over a period of from ten to fifteen years we can quite practicably effect a giant leap in the social productivity of even the most poorly developed large sectors of the earth.

One cannot instantly bring the rural peasantry of the developing sector to the rates of potential social productivity of the U.S. However, by introducing selected types of technological assistance to agricultural development (mechanization, irrigation, drainage, fertilizers, and so forth) we can achieve large leaps in per hectare outputs without yet depending upon substantial advances in the educational level of the peasantry. The gains which can be effected in this way can rapidly end the food crisis in the developing sector, and also provide a margin of social surplus (relative to present consumption standards) through which to begin educating the school-age generation, provide wide-scale adult literacy, and introduce a modern hygienic standard of household life. This provides the "leverage" for supplementary measures, such that we can effect a qualitative advancement in the potential social-productivity of the population over a ten to fifteen year period.

The "pay-off" for the presently advanced sector will occur in a rather different and far more important way than critics of aid might expect. It is the ABC of scientific economic knowledge that the backwardness of any portion of an intercon-

nected network of production holds back the rate of development of every portion of that network. At the point that the developing sector begins to produce a social surplus at rates approximately comparable to those of the present advanced sector, the direct result will be an acceleration of the rate of development of the entire world. When the size of the present population of the developing sector is considered, it should be clear that every marginal rise in the social productivity of this sector has an enormous beneficial effect on the potential rate of development in every other sector of the world.

CRIMINAL JUSTICE AND CRIME CONTROL

The indispensable first step for drastically reducing crime in the U.S.A. is the disbandment of such irreparably corrupted criminal justice and related institutions as the Central Intelligence Agency, the Law Enforcement Assistance Administration, and the Federal Bureau of Investigation. Although there may be isolated exceptions to this general rule among the personnel associated with these agencies, persons who have been subjected to the immoral climate permeating these agencies have been inevitably conditioned to an outlook which a free society cannot tolerate in persons entrusted with duties related to criminal justice.

A few examples of the problem are sufficient.

For years heroin and other "hard" drugs have been delivered into our urban centers and other areas with a regularity approximating that of the postman's rounds. Since the majority of the sources of these imports are limited and well known, and the channels of distribution intrinsically vulnerable to detection and disruption, it would have been impossible for the hard drug traffic to flourish as it has without a combination of complicity and malfeasance by major law enforcement agencies such as the FBI. Instead of disrupting this criminal traffic the FBI, in particular, has been misallocating major portions of its resources to predominantly unlawful and unconstitutional offenses against our citizens and their civil liberties.

Federal criminal justice agencies have not only broadly participated in and instigated activities which are unlawful and unconstitutional, but have implicated themselves in the promotion of forms of "behavior modification" which border upon or actually represent the crime of "menticide," as that crime is defined under the title of "Crimes against Humanity" in the Nuremberg Code.

In general, these agencies have variously committed or condoned the misuse of criminal justice agencies as a virtual Gestapo, in violation of the civil liberties guaranteed by the U.S. Constitution.

Not only are the agents of such institutions morally unfit for positions of authority in our society, but as long as we tolerate such outlaw organizations in our criminal justice system, we contribute to a diseased moral climate and incur cynical contempt for any system of criminal justice among large portions of the population.

Although the election of a Labor Party government will directly and indirectly reduce substantially the principal causes for the present spread of actual crime, crime will continue to be a significant—if substantially decreased—problem of life. We require an effective national system of criminal justice and crime control to deal with this. The disbandment of the CIA, LEAA, and FBI must be accompanied by the creation of a new national law enforcement agency under a reorganized Department of Justice, as developed in the Labor Party's Law Enforcement Reform Act of 1976.

# Subject Index

## Key to Political Parties

| | | | |
|---|---|---|---|
| A | American (1972–1976) | PE | People's (1972–1976) |
| AI | American Independent (1968–1976) | R | Republican (1856–1976) |
| C | Workers (Communist) (1976) | S | Socialist (1904–1976) |
| D | Democratic (1840–1976) | SL | Socialist Labor (1892–1976) |
| LIB | Libertarian (1972–1976) | SW | Socialist Workers (1948–1976) |
| P | Prohibition (1872–1976) | USL | U.S. Labor (1976) |

Abortion, (P 1976) 963, (R 1976) 976

Accelerated Public Works Act of 1962, (D 1964) 656, 657

ACTION, (R 1972) 877, 880

AFL-CIO, (S 1960) 625

Africa, (D 1960) 578, (AI 1968) 714, (D 1972) 815, (R 1972) 857, (D 1976) 945–46, (R 1976) 991

Aged, programs for, (D 1960) 588, 590, (D 1964) 662, (R 1968) 754, (C 1976) 915

Agency for International Development, (D 1964) 652, (PE 1972) 835

Agricultural Conservation Program, (D 1964) 660

Agriculture, (D 1960) 585, (P 1960) 603, (R 1960) 610, 611, (S 1960) 630, (D 1964) 659, (P 1964) 676, (R 1964) 681, (AI 1968) 707, 708, (D 1968) 729, (P 1968) 747, (A 1972) 772, (LIB 1972) 822, (P 1972) 850, (R 1972) 870, (A 1976) 895, (AI 1976) 908, (D 1976) 935, (P 1976) 964, (S 1976) 995; and farm labor, (PE 1976) 954–55; and rural development, (R 1976) 968, (USL 1976) 1009

Agriculture, Department of, (R 1960) 611, (R 1964) 682, (LIB 1972) 822

Aid to depressed areas, (D 1960) 583, (D 1964) 657

Alaska and Hawaii, (R 1960) 614, (R 1972) 885

Alcohol, (P 1960) 604, (P 1964) 676, 677, (P 1968) 747, 748, (P 1972) 850, (P 1976) 965, (R 1976) 975

Aliens, illegal, (A 1976) 897

Alliance for Progress, (D 1964) 653, (AI 1968) 714, (D 1968) 727

American Indians, (D 1960) 597, (D 1964) 670, (SW 1976) 1000

Amnesty, (LIB 1976) 948, (S 1976) 996

Anti-inflation policies, (D 1976) 918

Anti-racism bill, (PE 1972) 842

Antitrust Division, Department of Justice, (D 1964) 660, (D 1976) 919, (R 1976) 970

Appalachian Redevelopment Commission, (D 1964) 658

Area redevelopment, (D 1964) 656, 657, (D 1968) 721

Armed force, all volunteer, (LIB 1972) 822, (R 1972) 858

Arms, right to bear, (LIB 1972) 859, (AI 1976) 903, (LIB 1976) 948

Arms control, (D 1960) 576, (D 1964) 650, (D 1968) 725, (R 1972) 859

Arts and humanities, (D 1960) 597, (D 1964) 670, (D 1972) 806, (R 1972) 878, (D 1976) 928, (R 1976) 984

Asia, (D 1976) 945, (R 1976) 988

Aswan Dam, (SW 1960) 637

Atlantic community, (D 1960) 579, 580, (R 1972) 856

Atomic energy, (D 1960) 576, 594, (SL 1960) 635, (D 1964) 667, (R 1972) 876

Attica defendants, (SW 1976) 1000

Balance of payments, (AI 1968) 713

Ballot reform, (P 1960) 603, (P 1964) 675, (P 1968) 747, (P 1972) 850, (P 1976) 964

Banks, nationalization of, (USL 1976) 1017

Basic Educational Opportunity Grants, (D 1976) 927

Bay of Pigs, (R 1964) 679, (SW 1964) 694

Berlin, (D 1960) 580, (R 1960) 605, (D 1964) 654, (R 1964) 679, (D 1968) 723

Berlin Wall, (R 1964) 688

Bilingual education, (D 1968) 734, (D 1972) 804

Black people, community rights, (SW 1972) 891

Blue Lake, N.M., (R 1972) 884

Brown v. Board of Education, (D 1972) 804

Budget, federal, (P 1960) 601, (P 1964) 673, (P 1968) 744, (P 1972) 846

Business, (A 1976) 895

Busing, (PE 1972) 831, (AI 1976) 904, (P 1976) 963, (R 1976) 974

Cambodia, (D 1972) 812

Campaign finance, (D 1972) 819, (LIB 1976) 951; public, (D 1976) 922

Canada, (D 1972) 816, (R 1976) 990

Capitalist system, (SW 1972) 889

Caracas Declaration of Solidarity, (R 1964) 688

Career education, (D 1972) 805, (R 1972) 867

Celler-Kefauver Anti-Merger Act, (D 1960) 587

CENTO, (R 1960) 606, (R 1964) 678, 688

Central Intelligence Agency, (SW 1964) 694, (PE 1972) 835

Chicano people, (C 1972) 780, (SW 1972) 892

Child Development, Office of, (R 1972) 867, 869

Child Safety Act, (D 1968) 722

Child welfare, (D 1960) 589, (R 1972) 879, (A 1976) 896, (R 1976) 975

China, (D 1960) 581, (R 1960) 605, (SL 1960) 636, (D 1964) 643, (D 1968) 724, 726, (D 1972) 815, (R 1972) 851, 856, (AI 1976) 912, (D 1976) 945, (R 1976) 989

Chinese refugee program, (D 1964) 652

Church and state, (P 1964) 675, (P 1968) 747, (P 1972) 850, (P 1976) 963

Cities, (R 1968) 749

Cities and suburbs, (D 1960) 592, 593, (D 1964) 648, 666, (AI 1968) 703, (D 1972) 796, 798

Civil defense, (D 1960) 575, 576, (D 1964) 642

Civil liberties, (D 1960) 597, (D 1964) 670, 671, (SW 1972) 893

Civil rights, (D 1960) 599, (R 1960) 618, (D 1964) 671, (P 1964) 674, (SW 1964) 696, (D 1976) 925; legislation, (D 1968) 720; employment pledges, (R 1960) 619; housing pledges, (R 1960) 619; voting pledges, (R 1960) 619

Civil Rights Acts of 1957 and 1960, (D 1960) 599, (S 1960) 629

Civil Rights Act of 1960, (R 1960) 619

Civil Rights Act of 1964, (D 1964) 644, 658, (R 1964) 683, (AI 1968) 701, (D 1968) 720, (SW 1972) 892

Civil Rights Acts of 1964 and 1968, (D 1968) 734, (D 1976) 926

Civil Rights Commission, (R 1960) 619

Civil Service, (D 1960) 594, 595, (P 1960) 603, 604, (P 1972) 849, (R 1972) 882, (D 1976) 922, (LIB 1976) 951

Cold war, (S 1960) 625

Collective bargaining, (D 1964) 658, (R 1972) 882

Colonial independence, (LIB 1976) 953

Commission on Equal Job Opportunity, (R 1960) 619

Commission on Technology, Automation, and Economic Progress, (D 1964) 659

Commodity Credit Corporation, (R 1960) 611, (R 1968) 758

Common Market, (D 1960) 580, (R 1960) 607

Communications, (D 1968) 732, (S 1976) 995

Communications Satellite Act, (D 1968) 732

Communism, (D 1960) 580, 581, (P 1960) 600, (R 1960) 620, (S 1960) 622, (D 1964) 642, 653, (P 1964) 672, (R 1964) 678, 687, (P 1968) 743, 744, (P 1972) 846, (P 1976) 961

Communist conspiracy, (A 1972) 774

Communist nations, relations with, (A 1972) 775, (A 1976) 899

Communist Party, (D 1964) 649

Community action programs, (D 1964) 657

Community development needs, (R 1972) 871

Community Health Services and Facilities Act of 1961, (D 1964) 661

Competitive system, Republican faith in the, (R 1964) 684

Comprehensive Child Development Act of 1971, (D 1972) 804

Conference of Punta Del Este, (D 1964) 653

Congress, (D 1972) 818, 819

Congressional inquisitions, (SW 1964) 695

Congressional procedures, (D 1960) 596, (D 1964) 668

Connally reservation, on World Court jurisdiction, (D 1972) 816

Conscription, (S 1960) 630

Consumer Affairs, Office of, (D 1968) 731, (R 1972) 885, (D 1976) 922

Consumer protection, (R 1960) 618, (D 1964) 668, (D 1968) 730, 731, (A 1972) 772, (LIB 1972) 823, (A 1976) 895, (AI 1976) 909, (LIB 1976) 950

Controlled thermonuclear reactions (CTR), (USL 1976) 1004

Copernicus Astronomical Center, (R 1972) 877

Corruption, (S 1976) 996

Cost of Living Council, (R 1972) 885

Council on Foreign Relations, (A 1972) 777

Crime, (AI 1968) 702, (R 1968) 750, (A 1972) 770, (D 1972) 806, 807, 808, (LIB 1972) 821, (A 1976) 895, (AI 1976) 903, (LIB 1976) 946, (USL 1976) 1023

Cuba, (D 1960) 580, (D 1964) 643, 654, (R 1964) 678, 688, (SW 1964) 693, 694, 697, (AI 1968) 714, (D 1968) 723, (A 1972) 775

Cuban missile crisis, (D 1964) 654

Cuban refugee program, (D 1964) 652

Culture and the arts, (PE 1972) 825

Currency exchange rates, (LIB 1972) 824

Cyprus, (R 1976) 988

Czechoslovakia, (D 1968) 723, 724

Davis-Bacon Act, (D 1960) 584, (SW 1960) 637

Death penalty, (SW 1960) 639

Debt moratorium, (USL 1976) 1007, 1019

Defense policies, (A 1972) 777, (R 1972) 857, 859, (A 1976) 899, (D 1976) 940, (R 1976) 986

Democracy, extension of, (C 1972) 781

Detente, (A 1976) 899

Developing nations, (D 1972) 817

Developing world, (D 1968) 726

Development loan fund, (D 1960) 579, (R 1960) 607

Diplomacy: agreements concluded, (R 1972) 853; secret, (A 1976) 900

Diplomatic recognition, (LIB 1972) 824

Disabled citizens, (D 1976) 927

Disability, (S 1960) 626

Disarmament, (S 1960) 623, (A 1972) 777, (D 1972) 813

Discrimination, (D 1964) 658, (R 1972) 883, (C 1976) 915, (LIB 1976) 949

District of Columbia, (D 1960) 596, (R 1960) 614, (D 1964) 648, (D 1968) 741, (R 1968) 755, (D 1972) 820, (R 1972) 878, (D 1976) 925

Dixiecrats, (SW 1964) 693

War, (A 1976) 900
War and militarism, end to, (C 1972) 779
War on poverty, *See* Poverty, war on
War policies, (C 1976) 914
War powers of the President, (LIB 1976)
Warsaw Pact nations, (R 1972) 854
Water conservation, (D 1964) 665
Water rights, (AI 1976) 907
Welfare, (A 1972) 771; legislation, (D 1964) 663;
   reform of, (R 1972) 867, (D 1976) 924, (R 1976)
   978
Welfare and Pension Plans Disclosure Act, (R 1960)
   610, (P 1972) 849, (A 1976) 899, (AI 1976) 910,
   (P 1976) 963
White House Conference on Aging, (R 1960) 616,
   (R 1972) 881
Wholesome Meat and Poultry Acts, (D 1968) 722
Wilderness Act of 1964, (D 1964) 647, (D 1968)
   722
Wilderness Preservation System, (R 1972) 875
Wildlife legislation, (D 1964) 666
Women, (R 1976) 976; oppression of, (SW 1972)

892. *See also* Rights of women
Women, President's Commission on the Status of,
   (D 1964) 664
Women's equality, (C 1972) 782
Women's liberation, (A 1972) 774
Workers' government, (SW 1976) 1002; task of, (SL
   1972) 888
Working class unity, (C 1972) 782
Working men and women, (R 1972) 882, (SW 1972)
   890
Work-study programs, (D 1964) 657
World Bank, (D 1968) 726, (LIB 1976) 952
World community, and the United States, (D 1972)
   814
World Food Program, (D 1964) 655
World government, opposition to, (A 1972) 777
World trade, (D 1960) 577

Youth, (R 1968) 751, 752; demands for, (PE 1976)
   954; demands of, (SW 1972) 892; programs for,
   (R 1972) 879. *See also* Rights of youth
Youth Conservation Corps, (D 1960) 590

# Index of Names

Trujillo, Rafael, (S 1960) 624, (SW 1960) 637
Truman, Harry S., (D 1972) 783
Tyner, Jarvis, 769, (C 1972) 779, 894, (C 1976) 914, 915

Uncapher, Marchall, 769

Vandenberg, Arthur, (R 1976) 989

Wallace, George C., 699, (AI 1968) 700, 894
Weiss, Myra Tanner, 574
Westbrooks, Bobby, (D 1972) 789
Wilson, Woodrow, (D 1972) 783

Woodcock, Leonard, (D 1972) 818
Wright, Margaret, 894

Zeidler, Frank P., 894